Object-Oriented Analysis and Design with Applications

Third Edition

The Addison-Wesley Object Technology Series

Grady Booch, Ivar Jacobson, and James Rumbaugh, Series Editors
For more information, check out the series web site at www.awprofessional.com/otseries.

The Component Software Series

Clemens Szyperski, Series Editor
For more information, check out the series web site at www.awprofessional.com/csseries.

Object-Oriented Analysis and Design with Applications

Third Edition

Grady Booch
Robert A. Maksimchuk
Michael W. Engle
Bobbi J. Young, Ph.D.
Jim Conallen
Kelli A. Houston

✛Addison-Wesley

Upper Saddle River, NJ • Boston • Indianapolis • San Francisco
New York • Toronto • Montreal • London • Munich • Paris • Madrid
Capetown • Sydney • Tokyo • Singapore • Mexico City

This Book Is Safari Enabled

The Safari® Enabled icon on the cover of your favorite technology book means the book is available through Safari Bookshelf. When you buy this book, you get free access to the online edition for 45 days.

Safari Bookshelf is an electronic reference library that lets you easily search thousands of technical books, find code samples, download chapters, and access technical information whenever and wherever you need it.

To gain 45-day Safari Enabled access to this book:

- Go to http://www.awprofessional.com/safarienabled
- Complete the brief registration form
- Enter the coupon code A7LL-9MZM-SGNL-UNMB-SJX7

If you have difficulty registering on Safari Bookshelf or accessing the online edition, please e-mail customer-service@safaribooksonline.com.

Visit us on the Web: www.awprofessional.com

Library of Congress Cataloging-in-Publication Data
Object-oriented analysis and design with applications / Grady Booch...[et al.]. — 3rd ed.
   p. cm.
  Rev. ed. of: Object-oriented analysis and design with applications / Grady Booch, 2nd ed.
  Includes bibliographical references and index.
  ISBN 0-201-89551-X (hardback : alk. paper)
 1. Object-oriented programming (Computer science) I. Booch, Grady. II. Booch, Grady. Object-oriented analysis and design with applications.

  QA76.64.B66 2007
  005.1'17—dc22   2007002589

ISBN 0-201-89551-X
Text printed in the United States on recycled paper at Courier in Westford, Massachusetts.
First printing, April 2007

To Jan
my friend, my lover, my wife

—Grady

Contents

Sidebars

Chapter 8

Chapter 9

Chapter 12

Preface

> Mankind, under the grace of God, hungers for spiritual peace, esthetic achievements, family security, justice, and liberty, none directly satisfied by industrial productivity. But productivity allows the sharing of the plentiful rather than fighting over scarcity; it provides time for spiritual, esthetic, and family matters. It allows society to delegate special skills to institutions of religion, justice, and the preservation of liberty.
>
> HARLAN MILLS
> *DPMA and Human Productivity*

As computer professionals, we strive to build systems that work and are useful; as software engineers, we are faced with the task of creating complex systems in the presence of constrained computing and human resources. Object-oriented (OO) technology has evolved as a means of managing the complexity inherent in many different kinds of systems. The object model has proven to be a very powerful and unifying concept.

Changes to the Second Edition

Since the publication of the second edition of *Object-Oriented Analysis and Design with Applications*, we have seen major technological advances. This list includes some highlights, among many others.

- High-bandwidth, wireless connectivity to the Internet is widely available.
- Nanotechnology has emerged and has started to provide valuable products.

- Our robots are cruising the surface of Mars.
- Computer-generated special effects have enabled the film industry to recreate any world imaginable with complete realism.
- Personal hovercraft are available.
- Mobile phones have become pervasive to the point of being disposable.
- We have mapped the human genome.
- Object-oriented technology has become well established in the mainstream of industrial-strength software development.

We have encountered the use of the object-oriented paradigm throughout the world. However, we still encounter many people who have not yet adopted the object paradigm of development. For both of these groups, this revision of this book holds much value.

For the person new to object-oriented analysis and design (OOAD), this book gives the following information:

- The conceptual underpinnings of and evolutionary perspective on object orientation
- Examples of how OOAD can be applied across the system development lifecycle
- An introduction to the standard notation used in system and software development, the Unified Modeling Language (UML 2.0)

For the experienced OOAD practitioner, the content herein provides value from a different perspective.

- UML 2.0 is still new to even experienced practitioners. Here you will see the key changes in the notation.
- More focus on modeling is provided, per feedback received about the previous edition.
- You can gain a great appreciation for "why things are the way they are" in the object-oriented world, from the Concepts section of the book. Many people may never have been exposed to this information on the evolution of the OO concepts themselves. Even if you have been, you may not have grasped its significance when you were first learning the OO paradigm.

There are four major differences between this edition and the previous publication.

1. UML 2.0 has been officially approved. Chapter 5, Notation, will introduce UML 2.0. To enhance the reader's understanding of this notation, we explicitly distinguish between its fundamental and advanced elements.

2. This edition introduces some new domains and contexts in the Applications chapters. For example, the application domains range broadly across various levels of abstraction from high-level systems architecture to the design details of a Web-based system.

3. When the previous edition was published, C++ was relatively new, as was the very concept of OO programming. Readers tell us that this emphasis is no longer a primary concern. There is an abundance of OO programming and technique books and training available, not to mention additional programming languages designed for OO development. Therefore, most of the coding discussions have been removed.

4. Finally, in response to requests received from readers, this edition focuses much more on the modeling aspects of OOAD. The Applications section will show you how to use the UML, with each chapter emphasizing one phase of the overall development lifecycle.

Goals

This book provides practical guidance on the analysis and design of object-oriented systems. Its specific goals are the following:

- To provide a sound understanding of the fundamental concepts and historical evolution of the object model
- To facilitate a mastery of the notation and process of object-oriented analysis and design
- To teach the realistic application of object-oriented analysis and design within a variety of problem domains

The concepts presented all stand on a solid theoretical foundation, but this is primarily a pragmatic book that addresses the practical needs and concerns of software engineering practitioners, from the architect to the software developer.

Audience

This book is written for the computer professional as well as for the student.

- For the practicing systems and software developer, we show you how to effectively use object-oriented technology to solve real problems.
- In your role as an analyst or architect, we offer you a path from requirements to implementation, using object-oriented analysis and design. We

develop your ability to distinguish "good" object-oriented architectures from "bad" ones and to trade off alternate designs when the perversity of the real world intrudes. Perhaps most important, we offer you fresh approaches to reasoning about complex systems.

■ For the program manager, we provide insight on topics such as allocation of resources of a team of developers, software quality, metrics, and management of the risks associated with complex software systems.

■ For the student, we provide the instruction necessary for you to begin acquiring several important skills in the science and art of developing complex systems.

This book is also suitable for use in undergraduate and graduate courses as well as in professional seminars and individual study. Because it deals primarily with a method of software development, it is most appropriate for courses in software engineering and as a supplement to courses involving specific object-oriented programming languages.

Structure

The book is divided into three major sections—Concepts, Method, and Applications—with considerable supplemental material woven throughout.

Concepts

Section I examines the inherent complexity of software and the ways in which complexity manifests itself. We present the object model as a means of helping us manage this complexity. In detail, we examine the fundamental elements of the object model such as: abstraction, encapsulation, modularity, and hierarchy. We address basic questions such as "What is a class?" and "What is an object?" Because the identification of meaningful classes and objects is the key task in object-oriented development, we spend considerable time studying the nature of classification. In particular, we examine approaches to classification in other disciplines, such as biology, linguistics, and psychology, and then apply these lessons to the problem of discovering classes and objects in software systems.

Method

Section II presents a method for the development of complex systems based on the object model. We first present a graphic notation (i.e., the UML) for object-oriented analysis and design, followed by a generic process framework. We also examine the pragmatics of object-oriented development—in particular, its place in the software development lifecycle and its implications for project management.

Applications

Section III offers a collection of five nontrivial examples encompassing a diverse selection of problem domains: system architecture, control systems, cryptanalysis, data acquisition, and Web development. We have chosen these particular problem domains because they are representative of the kinds of complex problems faced by the practicing software engineer. It is easy to show how certain principles apply to simple problems, but because our focus is on building useful systems for the real world, we are more interested in showing how the object model scales up to complex applications. The development of software systems is rarely amenable to cookbook approaches; therefore, we emphasize the incremental development of applications, guided by a number of sound principles and well-formed models.

Supplemental Material

A considerable amount of supplemental material is woven throughout the book. Most chapters have sidebars that provide information on related topics. We include an appendix on object-oriented programming languages that summarizes the features of a few common languages. We also provide a glossary of common terms and an extensive classified bibliography that lists references to source material on the object model.

A Note about Tools

Readers always ask about the tools used to create the diagrams in the book. Primarily, we have used two fine tools for the diagrams: IBM Rational Software Architect and Sparx Systems Enterprise Architect. Why not use just one? The reality of the marketplace is that no tool does everything. The longer you do OOAD, you will eventually find some atypical "corner case" that no tool supports. (In that case, you may have to resort to basic drawing tools to show what you want.) But don't let those rare instances stop you from using robust OOAD tools such as those we mentioned.

Using This Book

This book may be read from cover to cover or it may be used in less structured ways. If you are seeking a deep understanding of the underlying concepts of the object model or the motivation for the principles of object-oriented development, you should start with Chapter 1 and continue forward in order. If you are primarily interested in learning the details of the notation and process of object-oriented analysis and design, start with Chapters 5 and 6; Chapter 7 is especially useful to managers of projects using this method. If you are most interested in the practical application of object-oriented technology to specific problems, select any or all of Chapters 8 through 12.

Acknowledgments

This book is dedicated to my wife, Jan, for her loving support.

Through both the first and second editions, a number of individuals have shaped my ideas on object-oriented development. For their contributions, I especially thank Sam Adams, Mike Akroid, Glenn Andert, Sid Bailin, Kent Beck, Dave Bernstein, Danicl Bobrow, Dick Bolz, Dave Bulman, Kayvan Carun, Dave Collins, Damian Conway, Steve Cook, Jim Coplien, Brad Cox, Ward Cunningham, Tom DeMarco, Mike Devlin, Richard Gabriel, William Genemaras, Adele Goldberg, Ian Graham, Tony Hoare, Jon Hopkins, Michael Jackson, Ralph Johnson, James Kempf, Norm Kerth, Jordan Kreindler, Doug Lea, Phil Levy, Barbara Liskov, Cliff Longman, Jamcs MacFarlane, Masoud Milani, Harlan Mills, Robert Murray, Steve Neis, Gene Ouye, Dave Parnas, Bill Riddel, Mary Beth Rosson, Kenny Rubin, Jim Rumbaugh, Kurt Schmucker, Ed Seidewitz, Dan Shiffman, Dave Stevenson, Bjarne Stroustrup, Dave Thomas, Mike Vilot, Tony Wasserman, Peter Wegner, Iseult White, John Williams, Lloyd Williams, Niklaus Wirth, Mario Wolczko, and Ed Yourdon.

A good part of the pragmatics of this book derives from my involvement with complex software systems being developed around the world at companies such as Alcatel, Andersen Consulting, Apple, AT&T, Autotrol, Bell Northern Research, Boeing, Borland, Computer Sciences Corporation, Contel, Ericsson, Ferranti, General Electric, GTE, Holland Signaal, Hughes Aircraft Company, IBM, Lockheed, Martin Marietta, Motorola, NTT, Philips, Rockwell International, Shell Oil, Symantec, Taligent, and TRW. I have had the opportunity to interact with literally hundreds of professional software engineers and their managers, and I thank them all for their help in making this book relevant to real-world problems.

A special acknowledgment goes to Rational for its support of my work. Thanks also to Tony Hall, whose cartoons brighten what would otherwise be just another stuffy technical book. Finally, thanks to my three cats, Camy, Annie, and Shadow, who kept me company on many a late night of writing.

—Grady Booch

First I want to thank God, without whom none of this would be possible. I want to thank my family, who, once again, had to deal with those long hours of my absence while working on this project. Thanks to my parents, who gave me their strong work ethic. Thanks to Mary T. O'Brien, who started it all by offering me this opportunity, and thanks to Chris Guzikowski for helping drive this to completion. To my fellow writers, thank you for agreeing to join me on this journey and for all your hard work and contributions toward this project. Last, but absolutely not least, my heartfelt thanks to Grady for all his work those many years ago, creating one of the original, foundational books on object-oriented analysis and design.

—Bob Maksimchuk

I want to express my gratitude to my family for their love and support, which provide the foundation for all my endeavors. I wish to thank Grady for giving me the opportunity to contribute to the third edition of his classic book. Finally, I want to thank Bob Maksimchuk for guiding me in the process of becoming a writer.

—Mike Engle

I would like to dedicate my work to the memory of my mother, Jean Smith, who encouraged me to take on this project. I also want to express my love and appreciation to my family, Russell, Alyssa, and Logan, for their support and encouragement. Thank you, Bob Maksimchuk and Mike Engle, for giving me the opportunity to share in this endeavor.

—Bobbi J. Young

I would like to extend a very special thank you to my husband, Bob, and to my two children, Katherine and Ryan, whose love and support are my true inspiration.

—Kelli A. Houston

Thank you to our reviewers, especially Davyd Norris and Brian Lyons, and to the many other people at Addison-Wesley who worked on this book, especially to Chris Zahn, not only for his development work but also for providing continuity on this long project.

About the Authors

Grady Booch is recognized internationally for his innovative work on software architecture, software engineering, and modeling. He has been with IBM Rational as its Chief Scientist since Rational's founding in 1981. Grady was named an IBM Fellow in March 2003.

Grady is one of the original developers of the Unified Modeling Language (UML) and was also one of the original developers of several of Rational's products. Grady has served as architect and architectural mentor for numerous complex software-intensive projects around the world.

Grady is the author of six best-selling books, including the *UML Users Guide* and the seminal *Object-Oriented Analysis with Applications*. Grady has published several hundred technical articles on software engineering, including papers published in the early 1980s that originated the term and practice of object-oriented design. He has lectured and consulted worldwide.

Grady is a member of the Association for Computing Machinery (ACM), the Institute of Electrical and Electronics Engineers (IEEE), the American Association for the Advancement of Science (AAAS), and Computer Professionals for Social Responsibility (CPSR). He is an IBM Fellow, an ACM Fellow, a World Technology Network Fellow, and a Software Development Forum Visionary. Grady was a founding board member of the Agile Alliance, the Hillside Group, and the Worldwide Institute of Software Architects. He also serves on the advisory board of Northface University.

Grady received his bachelor of science from the United States Air Force Academy in 1977 and his master of science in electrical engineering from the University of California at Santa Barbara in 1979.

Grady lives with his wife and cats in Colorado. His interests include reading, traveling, singing, and playing the harp.

Robert A. Maksimchuk is a Research Director in the Unisys Chief Technology Office. He focuses on emerging modeling technologies to advance the strategic direction of the Unisys 3D-Visual Enterprise modeling framework. Bob brings an abundance of systems engineering, modeling, and object-oriented analysis and design expertise, in numerous industries, to this mission. He is the coauthor of the books *UML for Mere Mortals* and *UML for Database Design* and has also written various articles. He has traveled worldwide as a featured speaker in numerous technology forums and led workshops and seminars on UML and object-oriented development. Bob is a member of the Institute of Electrical and Electronics Engineers (IEEE) and the International Council on Systems Engineering (INCOSE).

Michael W. Engle is a Principal Engineer with the Lockheed Martin Corporation. He has over 26 years of technical and management experience across the complete system development lifecycle, from project initiation through operations and support. Using his background as a systems engineer, software engineer, and systems architect, Mike employs object-oriented techniques to develop innovative approaches to complex systems development.

Bobbi J. Young, Ph.D., is a Director of Research for the Unisys Chief Technology Office. She has many years of experience in the IT industry working with commercial companies and Department of Defense contractors. Dr. Young has been a consultant mentoring in program management, enterprise architecture, systems engineering, and object-oriented analysis and design. Throughout her career, she has focused on system lifecycle processes and methodologies, as well as enterprise architecture. Dr. Young holds degrees in biology, computer science, and artificial intelligence, and she earned a Ph.D. in management information systems. She is also a Commander (retired) in the United States Naval Reserves.

Jim Conallen is a software engineer in IBM Rational's Model Driven Development Strategy team, where he is actively involved in applying the Object Management Group's (OMG) Model Driven Architecture (MDA) initiative to IBM Rational's model tooling. Jim is also active in the area of asset-based development and the Reusable Asset Specification (RAS). Jim is a frequent conference speaker and article writer. His areas of expertise include Web application development.

He developed the Web Application Extension for UML (WAE), an extension to the UML that lets developers model Web-centric architectures with the UML at appropriate levels of abstraction and detail. This work served as the basis for IBM Rational Rose and Rational XDE Web Modeling functionality.

Jim has authored two editions of the book *Building Web Applications with UML*, the first focusing on Microsoft's Active Server Pages and the latest on J2EE technologies.

Jim's experiences are also drawn from his years prior to Rational, when he was an independent consultant, Peace Corps volunteer, and college instructor, and from his life as a father of three boys. Jim has undergraduate and graduate degrees from Widener University in computer and software engineering.

Kelli Houston is a Consulting IT Specialist at IBM Rational. She is the method architect for IBM's internal method authoring method and is part of the team responsible for integrating IBM's methods. In addition to her method architect role, Kelli also leads the Rational Method Composer (RMC) Special Interest Group (SIG) within IBM and provides consulting and mentoring services to customers and internal IBM consultants on the effective use of RMC.

Concepts

Sir Isaac Newton secretly admitted to some friends:
He understood how gravity behaved, but not how it worked!
LILY TOMLIN
The Search for Signs of Intelligent Life in the Universe

In the early days of object technology, many people were initially introduced to "OO" through programming languages. They discovered what
these new languages could do for them and tried to practically apply the
languages to solve real-world problems. As tlme passed, languages
improved, development techniques evolved, best practices emerged, and
formal object-oriented methodologies were created.

Today object-oriented development is a rich and powerful development
model. This section takes a step back to look at the underpinning theory
that supplies the foundation for all of the above and provides insight into
why things work the way they do in the object-oriented paradigm.

Chapter 1

Complexity

A physician, a civil engineer, and a computer scientist were arguing about what was the oldest profession in the world. The physician remarked, "Well, in the Bible, it says that God created Eve from a rib taken out of Adam. This clearly required surgery, and so I can rightly claim that mine is the oldest profession in the world." The civil engineer interrupted, and said, "But even earlier in the book of Genesis, it states that God created the order of the heavens and the earth from out of the chaos. This was the first and certainly the most spectacular application of civil engineering. Therefore, fair doctor, you are wrong: mine is the oldest profession in the world." The computer scientist leaned back in her chair, smiled, and then said confidently, "Ah, but who do you think created the chaos?"

✓ "The more complex the system, the more open it is to total breakdown" [5]. Rarely would a builder think about adding a new sub-basement to an existing 100-story building. Doing that would be very costly and would undoubtedly invite failure. Amazingly, users of software systems rarely think twice about asking for equivalent changes. Besides, they argue, it is only a simple matter of programming.

✓ Our failure to master the complexity of software results in projects that are late, over budget, and deficient in their stated requirements. We often call this condition the software crisis, but frankly, a malady that has carried on this long must be called normal. Sadly, this crisis translates into the squandering of human resources—a most precious commodity—as well as a considerable loss of opportunities. There are simply not enough good developers around to create all the new software that users need. Further-more, a significant number of the development personnel in any given organization must often be dedicated to the maintenance or preservation of geriatric software. Given the indirect as well as the direct contribution of software to the economic base of most industrialized countries, and considering the ways in which software can amplify the powers of the individual, it is unacceptable to allow this situation to continue.

1.1 The Structure of Complex Systems

How can we change this dismal picture? Since the underlying problem springs from the inherent complexity of software, our suggestion is to first study how complex systems in other disciplines are organized. Indeed, if we open our eyes to the world about us, we will observe successful systems of significant complexity. Some of these systems are the works of humanity, such as the Space Shuttle, the England/France tunnel, and large business organizations. Many even more complex systems appear in nature, such as the human circulatory system and the structure of a habanero pepper plant.

The Structure of a Personal Computer

A personal computer is a device of moderate complexity. Most are composed of the same major elements: a central processing unit (CPU), a monitor, a keyboard, and some sort of secondary storage device, usually either a CD or DVD drive and hard disk drive. We may take any one of these parts and further decompose it. For example, a CPU typically encompasses primary memory, an arithmetic/logic unit (ALU), and a bus to which peripheral devices are attached. Each of these parts may in turn be further decomposed: An ALU may be divided into registers and random control logic, which themselves are constructed from even more primitive elements, such as NAND gates, inverters, and so on.

Here we see the hierarchic nature of a complex system. A personal computer functions properly only because of the collaborative activity of each of its major parts. Together, these separate parts logically form a whole. Indeed, we can reason about how a computer works only because we can decompose it into parts that we can study separately. Thus, we may study the operation of a monitor independently of the operation of the hard disk drive. Similarly, we may study the ALU without regard for the primary memory subsystem.

Not only are complex systems hierarchic, but the levels of this hierarchy represent different levels of abstraction, each built upon the other, and each understandable by itself. At each level of abstraction, we find a collection of devices that collaborate to provide services to higher layers. We choose a given level of abstraction to suit our particular needs. For instance, if we were trying to track down a timing problem in the primary memory, we might properly look at the gate-level architecture of the computer, but this level of abstraction would be inappropriate if we were trying to find the source of a problem in a spreadsheet application.

The Structure of Plants and Animals

In botany, scientists seek to understand the similarities and differences among plants through a study of their morphology, that is, their form and structure. Plants are complex multicellular organisms, and from the cooperative activity of various plant organ systems arise such complex behaviors as photosynthesis and transpiration. *→ the passage of water through a plant from the roots to the vascular system to the atmosphere*

Plants consist of three major structures (roots, stems, and leaves). Each of these has a different, specific structure. For example, roots encompass branch roots, root hairs, the root apex, and the root cap. Similarly, a cross-section of a leaf reveals its epidermis, mesophyll, and vascular tissue. Each of these structures is further composed of a collection of cells, and inside each cell we find yet another level of complexity, encompassing such elements as chloroplasts, a nucleus, and so on. As with the structure of a computer, the parts of a plant form a hierarchy, and each level of this hierarchy embodies its own complexity.

All parts at the same level of abstraction interact in well-defined ways. For example, at the highest level of abstraction, roots are responsible for absorbing water and minerals from the soil. Roots interact with stems, which transport these raw materials up to the leaves. The leaves in turn use the water and minerals provided by the stems to produce food through photosynthesis.

There are always clear boundaries between the outside and the inside of a given level. For example, we can state that the parts of a leaf work together to provide the functionality of the leaf as a whole and yet have little or no direct interaction with the elementary parts of the roots. In simpler terms, there is a clear separation of concerns among the parts at different levels of abstraction.

In a computer, we find NAND gates used in the design of the CPU as well as in the hard disk drive. Likewise, a considerable amount of commonality cuts across all parts of the structural hierarchy of a plant. This is God's way of achieving an economy of expression. For example, cells serve as the basic building blocks in all structures of a plant; ultimately, the roots, stems, and leaves of a plant are all composed of cells. Yet, although each of these primitive elements is indeed a cell, there are many different kinds of cells. For example, there are cells with and without chloroplasts, cells with walls that are impervious to water and cells with walls that are permeable, and even living cells and dead cells.

In studying the morphology of a plant, we do not find individual parts that are each responsible for only one small step in a single larger process, such as photosynthesis. In fact, there are no centralized parts that directly coordinate the activities of lower-level ones. Instead, we find separate parts that act as independent agents, each of which exhibits some fairly complex behavior, and each of which contributes to many higher-level functions. Only through the mutual cooperation of meaningful collections of these agents do we see the higher-level functionality of a plant. The science of complexity calls this emergent behavior: The behavior of the whole is greater than the sum of its parts [6].

synergy

Turning briefly to the field of zoology, we note that multicellular animals exhibit a hierarchical structure similar to that of plants: Collections of cells form tissues, tissues work together as organs, clusters of organs define systems (such as the digestive system), and so on. We cannot help but again notice God's awesome economy of expression: The fundamental building block of all animal matter is the cell, just as the cell is the elementary structure of all plant life. Granted, there are differences between these two. For example, plant cells are enclosed by rigid cellulose walls, but animal cells are not. Notwithstanding these differences, however, both of these structures are undeniably cells. This is an example of commonality that crosses domains.

A number of mechanisms above the cellular level are also shared by plant and animal life. For example, both use some sort of vascular system to transport nutrients within the organism, and both exhibit differentiation by sex among members of the same species.

The Structure of Matter

The study of fields as diverse as astronomy and nuclear physics provides us with many other examples of incredibly complex systems. Spanning these two disciplines, we find yet another structural hierarchy. Astronomers study galaxies that are arranged in clusters. Stars, planets, and debris are the constituents of galaxies. Likewise, nuclear physicists are concerned with a structural hierarchy, but one on an entirely different scale. Atoms are made up of electrons, protons, and neutrons; electrons appear to be elementary particles, but protons, neutrons, and other particles are formed from more basic components called quarks.

Again we find that a great commonality in the form of shared mechanisms unifies this vast hierarchy. Specifically, there appear to be only four distinct kinds of forces at work in the universe: gravity, electromagnetic interaction, the strong force, and the weak force. Many laws of physics involving these elementary forces, such as the laws of conservation of energy and of momentum, apply to galaxies as well as quarks.

The Structure of Social Institutions

As a final example of complex systems, we turn to the structure of social institutions. Groups of people join together to accomplish tasks that cannot be done by individuals. Some organizations are transitory, and some endure beyond many lifetimes. As organizations grow larger, we see a distinct hierarchy emerge. Multinational corporations contain companies, which in turn are made up of divisions, which in turn contain branches, which in turn encompass local offices, and so on. If the organization endures, the boundaries among these parts may change, and over time, a new, more stable hierarchy may emerge.

The relationships among the various parts of a large organization are just like those found among the components of a computer, or a plant, or even a galaxy. Specifically, the degree of interaction among employees within an individual office is greater than that between employees of different offices. A mail clerk usually does not interact with the chief executive officer of a company but does interact frequently with other people in the mail room. Here, too, these different levels are unified by common mechanisms. The clerk and the executive are both paid by the same financial organization, and both share common facilities, such as the company's telephone system, to accomplish their tasks.

1.2 The Inherent Complexity of Software

A dying star on the verge of collapse, a child learning how to read, white blood cells rushing to attack a virus: These are but a few of the objects in the physical world that involve truly awesome complexity. Software may also involve elements of great complexity; however, the complexity we find here is of a fundamentally different kind. As Brooks points out, "Einstein argued that there must be simplified explanations of nature, because God is not capricious or arbitrary. No such faith comforts the software engineer. Much of the complexity that he must master is arbitrary complexity" [1].

Defining Software Complexity

We do realize that some software systems are not complex. These are the largely forgettable applications that are specified, constructed, maintained, and used by the same person, usually the amateur programmer or the professional developer working in isolation. This is not to say that all such systems are crude and inelegant, nor do we mean to belittle their creators. Such systems tend to have a very limited purpose and a very short life span. We can afford to throw them away and replace them with entirely new software rather than attempt to reuse them, repair them, or extend their functionality. Such applications are generally more tedious than difficult to develop; consequently, learning how to design them does not interest us.

Instead, we are much more interested in the challenges of developing what we will call industrial-strength software. Here we find applications that exhibit a very rich set of behaviors, as, for example, in reactive systems that drive or are driven by events in the physical world, and for which time and space are scarce resources; applications that maintain the integrity of hundreds of thousands of records of information while allowing concurrent updates and queries; and systems for the command and control of real-world entities, such as the routing of air or railway traffic. Software systems such as these tend to have a long life span, and over time, many users come to depend on their proper functioning. In the world of industrial-strength software, we also find frameworks that simplify the creation of domain-specific applications, and programs that mimic some aspect of human intelligence. Although such applications are generally products of research and development, they are no less complex, for they are the means and artifacts of incremental and exploratory development.

The distinguishing characteristic of industrial-strength software is that it is intensely difficult, if not impossible, for the individual developer to comprehend all the subtleties of its design. Stated in blunt terms, the complexity of such systems exceeds the human intellectual capacity. Alas, this complexity we speak of seems to be an essential property of all large software systems. By *essential* we mean that we may master this complexity, but we can never make it go away.

Why Software Is Inherently Complex

As Brooks suggests, "The complexity of software is an essential property, not an accidental one" [3]. We observe that this inherent complexity derives from four elements: the complexity of the problem domain, the difficulty of managing the development process, the flexibility possible through software, and the problems of characterizing the behavior of discrete systems.

The Complexity of the Problem Domain

The problems we try to solve in software often involve elements of inescapable complexity, in which we find a myriad of competing, perhaps even contradictory, requirements. Consider the requirements for the electronic system of a multi-engine aircraft, a cellular phone switching system, or an autonomous robot. The raw functionality of such systems is difficult enough to comprehend, but now add all of the (often implicit) nonfunctional requirements such as usability, performance, cost, survivability, and reliability. This unrestrained external complexity is what causes the arbitrary complexity about which Brooks writes.

This external complexity usually springs from the "communication gap" that exists between the users of a system and its developers: Users generally find it very hard to give precise expression to their needs in a form that developers can understand. In some cases, users may have only vague ideas of what they want in a software system. This is not so much the fault of either the users or the developers of a system; rather, it occurs because each group generally lacks expertise in the domain of the other. Users and developers have different perspectives on the nature of the problem and make different assumptions regarding the nature of the solution. Actually, even if users had perfect knowledge of their needs, we currently have few instruments for precisely capturing these requirements. The common way to express requirements is with large volumes of text, occasionally accompanied by a few drawings. Such documents are difficult to comprehend, are open to varying interpretations, and too often contain elements that are designs rather than essential requirements.

A further complication is that the requirements of a software system often change during its development, largely because the very existence of a software development project alters the rules of the problem. Seeing early products, such as design documents and prototypes, and then using a system once it is installed and operational are forcing functions that lead users to better understand and articulate their real needs. At the same time, this process helps developers master the problem domain, enabling them to ask better questions that illuminate the dark corners of a system's desired behavior.

The task of the software development team
is to engineer the illusion of simplicity.

Because a large software system is a capital investment, we cannot afford to scrap an existing system every time its requirements change. Planned or not, systems tend to evolve over time, a condition that is often incorrectly labeled software maintenance. To be more precise, it is *maintenance* when we correct errors; it is *evolution* when we respond to changing requirements; it is *preservation* when we continue to use extraordinary means to keep an ancient and decaying piece of software in operation. Unfortunately, reality suggests that an inordinate percentage of software development resources are spent on software preservation.

The Difficulty of Managing the Development Process

The fundamental task of the software development team is to engineer the illusion of simplicity—to shield users from this vast and often arbitrary external complexity. Certainly, size is no great virtue in a software system. We strive to write less code by inventing clever and powerful mechanisms that give us this illusion of simplicity, as well as by reusing frameworks of existing designs and code. However, the sheer volume of a system's requirements is sometimes inescapable and forces us either to write a large amount of new software or to reuse existing software in novel ways. Just a few decades ago, assembly language programs of only a few thousand lines of code stressed the limits of our software engineering abilities. Today, it is not unusual to find delivered systems whose size is measured in hundreds of thousands or even millions of lines of code (and all of that in a high-order programming language, as well). No one person can ever understand such a system completely. Even if we decompose our implementation in meaningful ways, we still end up with hundreds and sometimes thousands of separate modules. This amount of work demands that we use a team of developers, and ideally we use as small a team as possible. However, no matter what its size, there are always significant challenges associated with team development. Having more developers means more complex communication and hence more difficult coordination, particularly if the team is geographically dispersed, as is often the case. With a team of developers, the key management challenge is always to maintain a unity and integrity of design.

The Flexibility Possible through Software

A home-building company generally does not operate its own tree farm from which to harvest trees for lumber; it is highly unusual for a construction firm to build an onsite steel mill to forge custom girders for a new building. Yet in the software industry such practice is common. Software offers the ultimate flexibility, so it is possible for a developer to express almost any kind of abstraction. This flexibility turns out to be an incredibly seductive property, however, because it also forces the developer to craft virtually all the primitive building blocks on which these higher-level abstractions stand. While the construction industry has uniform building codes and standards for the quality of raw materials, few such standards exist in the software industry. As a result, software development remains a labor-intensive business.

P4 *The Problems of Characterizing the Behavior of Discrete Systems*

If we toss a ball into the air, we can reliably predict its path because we know that under normal conditions, certain laws of physics apply. We would be very surprised if just because we threw the ball a little harder, halfway through its flight it suddenly stopped and shot straight up into the air.[1] In a not-quite-debugged software simulation of this ball's motion, exactly that kind of behavior can easily occur.

Within a large application, there may be hundreds or even thousands of variables as well as more than one thread of control. The entire collection of these variables, their current values, and the current address and calling stack of each process within the system constitute the present state of the application. Because we execute our software on digital computers, we have a system with discrete states. By contrast, analog systems such as the motion of the tossed ball are continuous systems. Parnas suggests, "when we say that a system is described by a continuous function, we are saying that it can contain no hidden surprises. Small changes in inputs will always cause correspondingly small changes in outputs" [4]. On the other hand, discrete systems by their very nature have a finite number of possible states; in large systems, there is a combinatorial explosion that makes this number very large. We try to design our systems with a separation of concerns, so that the behavior in one part of a system has minimal impact on the behavior in another. However, the fact remains that the phase transitions among discrete states cannot be modeled by continuous functions. Each event external to a software system has the potential of placing that system in a new state, and furthermore, the mapping from state to state is not always deterministic. In the worst circumstances, an external event may corrupt the state of a system because its designers failed to take into account certain interactions among events. When a ship's propulsion

In this case describes a system whose time evolution can be predicted exactly

---

1. Actually, even simple continuous systems can exhibit very complex behavior because of the presence of chaos. Chaos introduces a randomness that makes it impossible to precisely predict the future state of a system. For example, given the initial state of two drops of water at the top of a stream, we cannot predict exactly where they will be relative to one another at the bottom of the stream. Chaos has been found in systems as diverse as the weather, chemical reactions, biological systems, and even computer networks. Fortunately, there appears to be underlying order in all chaotic systems, in the form of patterns called attractors.

system fails due to a mathematical overflow, which in turn was caused by someone entering bad data in a maintenance system (a real incident), we understand
the seriousness of this issue. There has been a dramatic rise in software-related
system failures in subway systems, automobiles, satellites, air traffic control systems, inventory systems, and so forth. In continuous systems this kind of behavior
would be unlikely, but in discrete systems all external events can affect any part of
the system's internal state. Certainly, this is the primary motivation for vigorous
testing of our systems, but for all except the most trivial systems, exhaustive testing is impossible. Since we have neither the mathematical tools nor the intellectual capacity to model the complete behavior of large discrete systems, we must
be content with acceptable levels of confidence regarding their correctness.

1.3 The Five Attributes of a Complex System

Considering the nature of this complexity, we conclude that there are five
attributes common to all complex systems.

Hierarchic Structure

Building on the work of Simon and Ando, Courtois suggests the following:

> Frequently, complexity takes the form of a hierarchy, whereby a complex system
> is composed of interrelated subsystems that have in turn their own subsystems,
> and so on, until some lowest level of elementary components is reached. [7]

Simon points out that "the fact that many complex systems have a nearly decomposable, hierarchic structure is a major facilitating factor enabling us to understand, describe, and even 'see' such systems and their parts" [8]. Indeed, it is
likely that we can understand only those systems that have a hierarchic structure.

It is important to realize that the architecture of a complex system is a function of
its components as well as the hierarchic relationships among these components.
"All systems have subsystems and all systems are parts of larger systems. . . . The
value added by a system must come from the relationships between the parts, not
from the parts per se" [9].

The architecture of a complex system is a function of its components as well as the hierarchic relationships among these components.

A2 Relative Primitives

Regarding the nature of the primitive components of a complex system, our experience suggests that:

> The choice of what components in a system are primitive is relatively arbitrary and is largely up to the discretion of the observer of the system.

What is primitive for one observer may be at a much higher level of abstraction for another.

A3 Separation of Concerns

Simon calls hierarchic systems *decomposable* because they can be divided into identifiable parts; he calls them *nearly decomposable* because their parts are not completely independent. This leads us to another attribute common to all complex systems:

> Intracomponent linkages are generally stronger than intercomponent linkages. This fact has the effect of separating the high-frequency dynamics of the components—involving the internal structure of the components—from the low-frequency dynamics—involving interaction among components. [10]

This difference between intra- and intercomponent interactions provides a clear *separation of concerns* among the various parts of a system, making it possible to study each part in relative isolation.

A4 Common Patterns

As we have discussed, many complex systems are implemented with an economy of expression. Simon thus notes that:

> Hierarchic systems are usually composed of only a few different kinds of sub-systems in various combinations and arrangements. [11]

In other words, complex systems have common patterns. These patterns may involve the reuse of small components, such as the cells found in both plants and animals, or of larger structures, such as vascular systems, also found in both plants and animals.

A5 Stable Intermediate Forms

Earlier, we noted that complex systems tend to evolve over time. Specifically, "complex systems will evolve from simple systems much more rapidly if there are stable intermediate forms than if there are not" [12]. In more dramatic terms:

> A complex system that works is invariably found to have evolved from a simple system that worked. . . . A complex system designed from scratch never works and cannot be patched up to make it work. You have to start over, beginning with a working simple system. [13]

As systems evolve, objects that were once considered complex become the primitive objects on which more complex systems are built. Furthermore, we can never craft these primitive objects correctly the first time: We must use them in context first and then improve them over time as we learn more about the real behavior of the system.

1.4 Organized and Disorganized Complexity

The discovery of common abstractions and mechanisms greatly facilitates our understanding of complex systems. For example, with just a few minutes of orientation, an experienced pilot can step into a multiengine jet aircraft he or she has never flown before and safely fly the vehicle. Having recognized the properties common to all such aircraft, such as the functioning of the rudder, ailerons, and throttle, the pilot primarily needs to learn what properties are unique to that particular aircraft. If the pilot already knows how to fly a given aircraft, it is far easier to learn how to fly a similar one.

The Canonical Form of a Complex System

approved

This example suggests that we have been using the term *hierarchy* in a rather loose fashion. Most interesting systems do not embody a single hierarchy; instead, we find that many different hierarchies are usually present within the same complex system. For example, an aircraft may be studied by decomposing it into its propulsion system, flight-control system, and so on. This decomposition represents a structural, or "part of" hierarchy.

Alternately, we can cut across the system in an entirely orthogonal way. For example, a turbofan engine is a specific kind of jet engine, and a Pratt and Whitney TF30 is a specific kind of turbofan engine. Stated another way, a jet engine represents a generalization of the properties common to every kind of jet engine; a turbofan engine is simply a specialized kind of jet engine, with properties that distinguish it, for example, from ramjet engines.

This second hierarchy represents an "is a" hierarchy. In our experience, we have found it essential to view a system from both perspectives, studying its "is a" hierarchy as well as its "part of" hierarchy. For reasons that will become clear in the next chapter, we call these hierarchies the *class structure* and the *object structure* of the system, respectively.[2]

For those of you who are familiar with object technology, let us be clear. In this case, where we are speaking of class structure and object structure, we are not referring to the classes and objects you create when coding your software. We are referring to classes and objects, at a higher level of abstraction, that make up complex systems, for example, a jet engine, an airframe, the various types of seats, an autopilot subsystem, and so forth. You will recall from the earlier discussion on the attributes of a complex system that whatever is considered primitive is relative to the observer.

In Figure 1–1 we see the two orthogonal hierarchies of the system: its class structure and its object structure. Each hierarchy is layered, with the more abstract

---

2. Complex software systems embody other kinds of hierarchies as well. Of particular importance is the module structure, which describes the relationships among the physical components of the system, and the process hierarchy, which describes the relationships among the system's dynamic components.

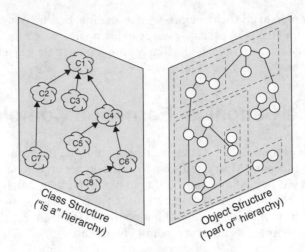

Figure 1–1 The Key Hierarchies of Complex Systems

classes and objects built on more primitive ones. What class or object is chosen as primitive is relative to the problem at hand. Looking inside any given level reveals yet another level of complexity. Especially among the parts of the object structure, there are close collaborations among objects at the same level of abstraction.

Combining the concept of the class and object structures together with the five attributes of a complex system (hierarchy, relative primitives [i.e., multiple levels of abstraction], separation of concerns, patterns, and stable intermediate forms), we find that virtually all complex systems take on the same (canonical) form, as we show in Figure 1–2. Collectively, we speak of the class and object structures of a system as its *architecture*.

Notice also that the class structure and the object structure are not completely independent; rather, each object in the object structure represents a specific instance of some class. (In Figure 1–2, note classes C3, C5, C7, and C8 and the number of the instances 03, 05, 07, and 08.) As the figure suggests, there are usually many more objects than classes of objects within a complex system. By showing the "part of" as well as the "is a" hierarchy, we explicitly expose the redundancy of the system under consideration. If we did not reveal a system's class structure, we would have to duplicate our knowledge about the properties of each individual part. With the inclusion of the class structure, we capture these common properties in one place.

Also from the same class structure, there are many different ways that these objects can be instantiated and organized. No one particular architecture can really be deemed "correct." This is what makes system architecture challenging— finding the balance between the many ways the components of a system can be structured, the five attributes of complex systems, and the needs of the system user.

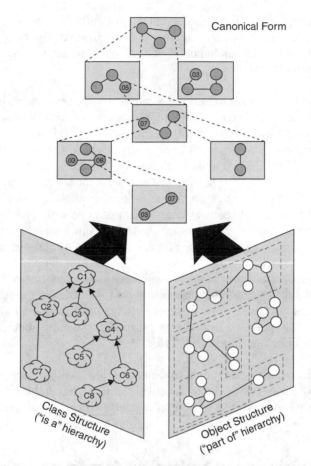

Figure 1–2 The Canonical Form of a Complex System

Our experience is that the most successful complex software systems are those whose designs explicitly encompass well-engineered class and object structures and embody the five attributes of complex systems described in the previous section. Lest the importance of this observation be missed, let us be even more direct: We very rarely encounter software systems that are delivered on time, that are within budget, and that meet their requirements, unless they are designed with these factors in mind.

The Limitations of the Human Capacity for Dealing with Complexity

If we know what the design of complex software systems should be like, then why do we still have serious problems in successfully developing them? This concept of the organized complexity of software (whose guiding principles we call the *object model*) is relatively new. However, there is yet another factor that dominates: the fundamental limitations of the human capacity for dealing with complexity.

As we first begin to analyze a complex software system, we find many parts that must interact in a multitude of intricate ways, with little perceptible commonality among either the parts or their interactions; this is an example of disorganized complexity. As we work to bring organization to this complexity through the process of design, we must think about many things at once. For example, in an air traffic control system, we must deal with the state of many different aircraft at once, involving such properties as their location, speed, and heading. Especially in the case of discrete systems, we must cope with a fairly large, intricate, and sometimes nondeterministic state space. Unfortunately, it is absolutely impossible for a single person to keep track of all of these details at once. Experiments by psychologists, such as those of Miller, suggest that the maximum number of chunks of information that an individual can simultaneously comprehend is on the order of seven, plus or minus two [14]. This channel capacity seems to be related to the capacity of short-term memory. Simon additionally notes that processing speed is a limiting factor: It takes the mind about five seconds to accept a new chunk of information [15].

We are thus faced with a fundamental dilemma. The complexity of the software systems we are asked to develop is increasing, yet there are basic limits on our ability to cope with this complexity. How then do we resolve this predicament?

1.5 Bringing Order to Chaos

Certainly, there will always be geniuses among us, people of extraordinary skill who can do the work of a handful of mere mortal developers, the software engineering equivalents of Frank Lloyd Wright or Leonardo da Vinci. These are the people whom we seek to deploy as our system architects: the ones who devise innovative idioms, mechanisms, and frameworks that others can use as the architectural foundations of other applications or systems. However, "The world is only sparsely populated with geniuses. There is no reason to believe that the software engineering community has an inordinately large proportion of them" [2]. Although there is a touch of genius in all of us, in the realm of industrial-strength software we cannot always rely on divine inspiration to carry us through. Therefore, we must consider more disciplined ways to master complexity.

The Role of Decomposition

"The technique of mastering complexity has been known since ancient times: divide et impera (divide and rule)" [16]. When designing a complex software system, it is essential to decompose it into smaller and smaller parts, each of which we may then refine independently. In this manner, we satisfy the very real constraint that exists on the channel capacity of human cognition: To understand any given level of a system, we need only comprehend a few parts (rather than all parts) at once. Indeed, as Parnas observes, intelligent decomposition directly addresses the inherent complexity of software by forcing a division of a system's state space [17].

step-by-step problem-solving

Algorithmic Decomposition

Most of us have been formally trained in the dogma of top-down structured design, and so we approach decomposition as a simple matter of algorithmic decomposition, wherein each module in the system denotes a major step in some overall process. Figure 1–3 is an example of one of the products of structured design, a structure chart that shows the relationships among various functional elements of the solution. This particular structure chart illustrates part of the design of a program that updates the content of a master file. It was automatically generated from a data flow diagram by an expert system tool that embodies the rules of structured design [18].

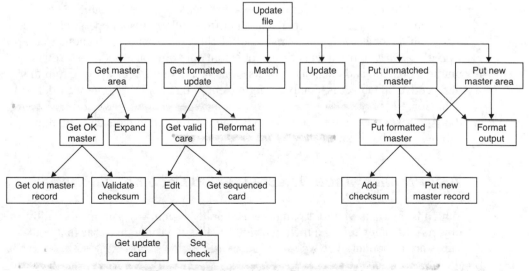

Figure 1–3 Algorithmic Decomposition

Object-Oriented Decomposition

We suggest that there is an alternate decomposition possible for the same problem. In Figure 1–4, we have decomposed the system according to the key abstractions in the problem domain. Rather than decomposing the problem into steps such as *Get formatted update* and *Add checksum*, we have identified objects such as *Master File* and *Checksum*, which derive directly from the vocabulary of the problem domain.

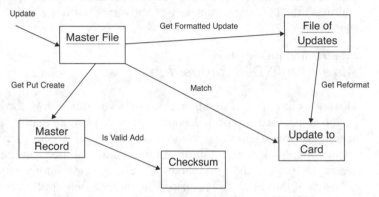

Figure 1–4 Object-Oriented Decomposition

Although both designs solve the same problem, they do so in quite different ways. In this second decomposition, we view the world as a set of autonomous agents that collaborate to perform some higher-level behavior. *Get Formatted Update* thus does not exist as an independent algorithm; rather, it is an operation associated with the object *File of Updates*. Calling this operation creates another object, *Update to Card*. In this manner, each object in our solution embodies its own unique behavior, and each one models some object in the real world. From this perspective, an object is simply a tangible entity that exhibits some well-defined behavior. Objects do things, and we ask them to perform what they do by sending them messages. Because our decomposition is based on objects and not algorithms, we call this an *object-oriented decomposition*.

Algorithmic versus Object-Oriented Decomposition

Which is the right way to decompose a complex system—by algorithms or by objects? Actually, this is a trick question because the right answer is that both views are important: The algorithmic view highlights the ordering of events, and the object-oriented view emphasizes the agents that either cause action or are the subjects on which these operations act.

Categories of Analysis and Design Methods

We find it useful to distinguish between the terms *method* and *methodology.* A method is a disciplined procedure for generating a set of models that describe various aspects of a software system under development, using some well-defined notation. A methodology is a collection of methods applied across the software development lifecycle and unified by process, practices, and some general, philosophical approach. Methods are important for several reasons. Foremost, they instill a discipline into the development of complex software systems. They define the products that serve as common vehicles for communication among the members of a development team. Additionally, methods define the milestones needed by management to measure progress and to manage risk.

Methods have evolved in response to the growing complexity of software systems. In the early days of computing, one simply did not write large programs because the capabilities of our machines were greatly limited. The dominant constraints in building systems were then largely due to hardware: Machines had small amounts of main memory, programs had to contend with considerable latency within secondary storage devices such as magnetic drums, and processors had cycle times measured in the hundreds of microseconds. In the 1960s and 1970s the economics of computing began to change dramatically as hardware costs plummeted and computer capabilities rose. As a result, it was more desirable and now finally economical to automate more and more applications of increasing complexity. High-order programming languages entered the scene as important tools. Such languages improved the productivity of the individual developer and of the development team as a whole, thus ironically pressuring us to create software systems of even greater complexity.

Many design methods were proposed during the 1960s and 1970s to address this growing complexity. The most influential of them was top-down structured design, also known as *composite design.* This method was directly influenced by the topology of traditional high-order programming languages, such as FORTRAN and COBOL. In these languages, the fundamental unit of decomposition is the subprogram, and the resulting program takes the shape of a tree in which subprograms perform their work by calling other subprograms. This is exactly the approach taken by top-down structured design: One applies algorithmic decomposition to break a large problem down into smaller steps.

Since the 1960s and 1970s, computers of vastly greater capabilities have evolved. The value of structured design has not changed, but as Stein observes, "Structured programming appears to fall apart when applications exceed 100,000 lines or so of code" [19]. Dozens of design methods have been proposed, many of them invented to deal with the perceived shortcomings of top-down structured design. The more interesting and successful design methods are cataloged by Peters [20], by Yau and Tsai [21], and in a comprehensive survey by Teledyne Brown Engineering [22]. Perhaps not surprisingly, many of these methods are largely variations on a similar theme. Indeed, as Sommerville suggests, most methods can be categorized as one of three kinds [23]:

- Top-down structured design
- Data-driven design
- Object-oriented design

Top-down structured design is exemplified by the work of Yourdon and Constantine [24], Myers [25], and Page-Jones [26]. The foundations of this method derive from the work of Wirth [27, 28] and Dahl, Dijkstra, and Hoare [29]; an important variation on structured design is found in the design method of Mills, Linger, and Hevner [30]. Each of these variations applies algorithmic decomposition. More software has probably been written using these design methods than with any other. Nevertheless, structured design does not address the issues of data abstraction and information hiding, nor does it provide an adequate means of dealing with concurrency. Structured design does not scale up well for extremely complex systems, and this method is largely inappropriate for use with object-based and object-oriented programming languages.

Data-driven design is best exemplified by the early work of Jackson [31, 32] and the methods of Orr [33]. In this method, mapping system inputs to outputs derives the structure of a software system. As with structured design, data-driven design has been successfully applied to a number of complex domains, particularly information management systems, which involve direct relationships between the inputs and outputs of the system but require little concern for time-critical events.

The underlying concept of object-oriented analysis is that one should model software systems as collections of cooperating objects, treating individual objects as instances of a class within a hierarchy of classes. Object-oriented analysis and design directly reflects the topology of high-order programming languages such as Smalltalk, Object Pascal, C++, the Common Lisp Object System (CLOS), Ada, Eiffel, Python, Visual C#, and Java.

However, the fact remains that we cannot construct a complex system in both ways simultaneously, for they are completely orthogonal views.[3] We must start

---

3. Langdon suggests that this orthogonality has been studied since ancient times. As he states, "C. H. Waddington has noted that the duality of views can be traced back to the ancient Greeks. A passive view was proposed by Democritus, who asserted that the world was composed of matter called atoms. Democritus' view places things at the center of focus. On the other hand, the classical spokesman for the active view is Heraclitus, who emphasized the notion of process" [34].

decomposing a system either by algorithms or by objects and then use the resulting structure as the framework for expressing the other perspective.

Our experience leads us to apply the object-oriented view first because this approach is better at helping us organize the inherent complexity of software systems, just as it helped us to describe the organized complexity of complex systems as diverse as computers, plants, galaxies, and large social institutions. As we will discuss further in Chapter 2, object-oriented decomposition has a number of highly significant advantages over algorithmic decomposition. Object-oriented decomposition yields smaller systems through the reuse of common mechanisms, thus providing an important economy of expression. Object-oriented systems are also more resilient to change and thus better able to evolve over time because their design is based on stable intermediate forms. Indeed, object-oriented decomposition greatly reduces the risk of building complex software systems because they are designed to evolve incrementally from smaller systems in which we already have confidence. Furthermore, object-oriented decomposition directly addresses the inherent complexity of software by helping us make intelligent decisions regarding the separation of concerns in a large state space.

The Applications section of this book demonstrates these benefits through several applications, drawn from a diverse set of problem domains. The sidebar in this chapter, Categories of Analysis and Design Methods, further compares and contrasts the object-oriented view with more traditional approaches to design.

The Role of Abstraction

Earlier, we referred to Miller's experiments, from which he concluded that an individual can comprehend only about seven, plus or minus two, chunks of information at one time. This number appears to be independent of information content. As Miller himself observes, "The span of absolute judgment and the span of immediate memory impose severe limitations on the amount of information that we are able to receive, process and remember. By organizing the stimulus input simultaneously into several dimensions and successively into a sequence of chunks, we manage to break . . . this informational bottleneck" [35]. In contemporary terms, we call this process *chunking* or *abstraction.*

As Wulf describes it, "We (humans) have developed an exceptionally powerful technique for dealing with complexity. We abstract from it. Unable to master the entirety of a complex object, we choose to ignore its inessential details, dealing instead with the generalized, idealized model of the object" [36]. For example, when studying how photosynthesis works in a plant, we can focus on the chemical reactions in certain cells in a leaf and ignore all other parts, such as the roots and stems. We are still constrained by the number of things that we can comprehend at one time, but through abstraction, we use chunks of information with increasingly greater semantic content. This is especially true if we take an object-oriented view of the world because objects, as abstractions of entities in the real world, represent a particularly dense and cohesive clustering of information. Chapter 2 examines the meaning of abstraction in much greater detail.

The Role of Hierarchy

Another way to increase the semantic content of individual chunks of information is by explicitly recognizing the class and object hierarchies within a complex software system. The object structure is important because it illustrates how different objects collaborate with one another through patterns of interaction that we call *mechanisms*. The class structure is equally important because it highlights common structure and behavior within a system. Thus, rather than study each individual photosynthesizing cell within a specific plant leaf, it is enough to study one such cell because we expect that all others will exhibit similar behavior. Although we treat each instance of a particular kind of object as distinct, we may assume that it shares the same behavior as all other instances of that same kind of object. By classifying objects into groups of related abstractions (e.g., kinds of plant cells versus animal cells), we come to explicitly distinguish the common and distinct properties of different objects, which further helps us to master their inherent complexity [37].

Identifying the hierarchies within a complex software system is often not easy because it requires the discovery of patterns among many objects, each of which may embody some tremendously complicated behavior. Once we have exposed these hierarchies, however, the structure of a complex system, and in turn our understanding of it, becomes vastly simplified. Chapter 3 considers in detail the nature of class and object hierarchies, and Chapter 4 describes techniques that facilitate our identification of these patterns.

1.6 On Designing Complex Systems

The practice of every engineering discipline—be it civil, mechanical, chemical, electrical, or software engineering—involves elements of both science and art. As Petroski eloquently states, "The conception of a design for a new structure can involve as much a leap of the imagination and as much a synthesis of experience and knowledge as any artist is required to bring to his canvas or paper. And once that design is articulated by the engineer as artist, it must be analyzed by the engineer as scientist in as rigorous an application of the scientific method as any scientist must make" [38]. Similarly, Dijkstra observes, "the programming challenge is a large-scale exercise in applied abstraction and thus requires the abilities of the formal mathematician blended with the attitude of the competent engineer" [39].

Engineering as a Science and an Art

The role of the engineer as artist is particularly challenging when the task is to design an entirely new system. Especially in the case of reactive systems and systems for command and control, we are frequently asked to write software for an entirely unique set of requirements, often to be executed on a configuration of target processors constructed specifically for this system. In other cases, such as the creation of frameworks, tools for research in artificial intelligence, or information management systems, we may have a well-defined, stable target environment, but our requirements may stress the software technology in one or more dimensions. For example, we may be asked to craft systems that are faster, have greater capacity, or have radically improved functionality. In all these situations, we try to use proven abstractions and mechanisms (the "stable intermediate forms," in Simon's words) as a foundation on which to build new complex systems. In the presence of a large library of reusable software components, the software engineer must assemble these parts in innovative ways to satisfy the stated and implicit requirements, just as the painter or the musician must push the limits of his or her medium.

The Meaning of Design

In every engineering discipline, design encompasses the disciplined approach we use to invent a solution for some problem, thus providing a path from requirements to implementation. In the context of software engineering, Mostow suggests that the purpose of design is to construct a system that:

- Satisfies a given (perhaps informal) functional specification
- Conforms to limitations of the target medium
- Meets implicit or explicit requirements on performance and resource usage
- Satisfies implicit or explicit design criteria on the form of the artifact
- Satisfies restrictions on the design process itself, such as its length or cost, or the tools available for doing the design [40]

As Stroustrup suggests, "the purpose of design is to create a clean and relatively simple internal structure, sometimes also called an architecture. . . . A design is the end product of the design process" [41]. Design involves balancing a set of competing requirements. The products of design are models that enable us to reason about our structures, make trade-offs when requirements conflict, and in general, provide a blueprint for implementation.

The Importance of Model Building

The building of models has a broad acceptance among all engineering disciplines, largely because model building appeals to the principles of decomposition, abstraction, and hierarchy [42]. Each model within a design describes a specific aspect of the system under consideration. As much as possible, we seek to build new models upon old models in which we already have confidence. Models give us the opportunity to fail under controlled conditions. We evaluate each model in both expected and unusual situations, and then we alter them when they fail to behave as we expect or desire.

We have found that in order to express all the subtleties of a complex system, we must use more than one kind of model. For example, when designing a personal computer, an electrical engineer must take into consideration the component-level view of the system as well as the physical layout of the circuit boards. This component view forms a logical picture of the design of the system, which helps the engineer to reason about the cooperative behavior of the components. The board layout represents the physical packaging of these components, constrained by the board size, available power, and the kinds of components that exist. From this view, the engineer can independently reason about factors such as heat dissipation and manufacturability. The board designer must also consider dynamic as well as static aspects of the system under construction. Thus, the electrical engineer uses diagrams showing the static connections among individual components, as well as timing diagrams that show the behavior of these components over time. The engineer can then employ tools such as oscilloscopes and digital analyzers to validate the correctness of both the static and dynamic models.

The Elements of Software Design Methodologies

Clearly, there is no magic, no "silver bullet" [43] that can unfailingly lead the software engineer down the path from requirements to the implementation of a complex software system. In fact, the design of complex software systems does not lend itself at all to cookbook approaches. Rather, as noted earlier in the fifth attribute of complex systems, the design of such systems involves an incremental and iterative process.

Still, sound design methods do bring some much-needed discipline to the development process. The software engineering community has evolved dozens of different design methodologics, which we can loosely classify into three categories (see the Categories of Analysis and Design Methods sidebar). Despite their differences, all of these have elements in common. Specifically, each includes the following:

- Notation   The language for expressing each model
- Process   The activities leading to the orderly construction of the system's models
- Tools   The artifacts that eliminate the tedium of model building and enforce rules about the models themselves, so that errors and inconsistencies can be exposed

A sound design method is based on a solid theoretical foundation yet offers degrees of freedom for artistic innovation.

The Models of Object-Oriented Development

Is there a "best" design method? No, there is no absolute answer to this question, which is actually just a veiled way of asking the earlier question: What is the best way to decompose a complex system? To reiterate, we have found great value in building models that are focused on the "things" we find in the problem space, forming what we refer to as an object-oriented decomposition.

Object-oriented analysis and design is the method that leads us to an object-oriented decomposition. By applying object-oriented design, we create software that is resilient to change and written with economy of expression. We achieve a greater level of confidence in the correctness of our software through an intelligent separation of its state space. Ultimately, we reduce the risks inherent in developing complex software systems.

In this chapter, we have made a case for using object-oriented analysis and design to master the complexity associated with developing software systems. Additionally, we have suggested a number of fundamental benefits to be derived from applying this method. Before we present the notation and process of object-oriented design, however, we must study the principles on which object-oriented development is founded, namely, abstraction, encapsulation, modularity, hierarchy, typing, concurrency, and persistence.

Summary

- Software is inherently complex; the complexity of software systems often exceeds the human intellectual capacity.

- The task of the software development team is to engineer the illusion of simplicity.
- Complexity often takes the form of a hierarchy; it is useful to model both the "is a" and the "part of" hierarchies of a complex system.
- Complex systems generally evolve from stable intermediate forms.
- There are fundamental limiting factors of human cognition; we can address these constraints through the use of decomposition, abstraction, and hierarchy.
- Complex systems can be viewed by focusing on either things or processes; there are compelling reasons for applying object-oriented decomposition, in which we view the world as a meaningful collection of objects that collaborate to achieve some higher-level behavior.
- Object-oriented analysis and design is the method that leads us to an object-oriented decomposition; object-oriented design uses a notation and process for constructing complex software systems and offers a rich set of models with which we may reason about different aspects of the system under consideration.

Chapter 2

The Object Model

Object-oriented technology is built on a sound engineering foundation, whose elements we collectively call the *object model of development* or simply the *object model*. The object model encompasses the principles of abstraction, encapsulation, modularity, hierarchy, typing, concurrency, and persistence. By themselves, none of these principles are new. What is important about the object model is that these elements are brought together in a synergistic way.

Let there be no doubt that object-oriented analysis and design is fundamentally different than traditional structured design approaches: It requires a different way of thinking about decomposition, and it produces software architectures that are largely outside the realm of the structured design culture.

2.1 The Evolution of the Object Model

Object-oriented development did not spontaneously generate itself from the ashes of the uncounted failed software projects that used earlier technologies. It is not a radical departure from earlier approaches. Indeed, it is founded in the best ideas from prior technologies. In this section we will examine the evolution of the tools of our profession to help us understand the foundation and emergence of object-oriented technology.

As we look back on the relatively brief yet colorful history of software engineering, we cannot help but notice two sweeping trends:

1. The shift in focus from programming-in-the-small to programming-in-the-large
2. The evolution of high-order programming languages

Most new industrial-strength software systems are larger and more complex than their predecessors were even just a few years ago. This growth in complexity has prompted a significant amount of useful applied research in software engineering, particularly with regard to decomposition, abstraction, and hierarchy. The development of more expressive programming languages has complemented these advances.

The Generations of Programming Languages

Wegner has classified some of the more popular high-order programming languages in generations arranged according to the language features they first introduced [2]. (By no means is this an exhaustive list of all programming languages.)

- First-generation languages (1954–1958)

FORTRAN I	Mathematical expressions
ALGOL 58	Mathematical expressions
Flowmatic	Mathematical expressions
IPL V	Mathematical expressions

- Second-generation languages (1959–1961)

FORTRAN II	Subroutines, separate compilation
ALGOL 60	Block structure, data types
COBOL	Data description, file handling
Lisp	List processing, pointers, garbage collection

- Third-generation languages (1962–1970)

PL/1	FORTRAN + ALGOL + COBOL
ALGOL 68	Rigorous successor to ALGOL 60
Pascal	Simple successor to ALGOL 60
Simula	Classes, data abstraction

- The generation gap (1970–1980)

  Many different languages were invented, but few endured. However, the following are worth noting:

C	Efficient; small executables
FORTRAN 77	ANSI standardization

Let's expand on Wegner's categories.

- Object-orientation boom (1980–1990, but few languages survive)

Smalltalk 80	Pure object-oriented language
C++	Derived from C and Simula
Ada83	Strong typing; heavy Pascal influence
Eiffel	Derived from Ada and Simula

- Emergence of frameworks (1990–today)

  Much language activity, revisions, and standardization have occurred, leading to programming frameworks.

Visual Basic	Eased development of the graphical user interface (GUI) for Windows applications
Java	Successor to Oak; designed for portability
Python	Object-oriented scripting language
J2EE	Java-based framework for enterprise computing
.NET	Microsoft's object-based framework
Visual C#	Java competitor for the Microsoft .NET Framework
Visual Basic .NET	Visual Basic for the Microsoft .NET Framework

In successive generations, the kind of abstraction mechanism each language supported changed. First-generation languages were used primarily for scientific and engineering applications, and the vocabulary of this problem domain was almost entirely mathematics. Languages such as FORTRAN I were thus developed to allow the programmer to write mathematical formulas, thereby freeing the programmer from some of the intricacies of assembly or machine language. This first generation of high-order programming languages therefore represented a step closer to the problem space and a step further away from the underlying machine.

Among second-generation languages, the emphasis was on algorithmic abstractions. By this time, machines were becoming more and more powerful, and the economics of the computer industry meant that more kinds of problems could be automated, especially for business applications. Now, the focus was largely on telling the machine what to do: read these personnel records first, sort them next, and then print this report. Again, this new generation of high-order programming languages moved us a step closer to the problem space and further away from the underlying machine.

By the late 1960s, especially with the advent of transistors and then integrated circuit technology, the cost of computer hardware had dropped dramatically, yet processing capacity had grown almost exponentially. Larger problems could now be solved, but these demanded the manipulation of more kinds of data. Thus, third-generation languages such as ALGOL 60 and, later, Pascal evolved with support for data abstraction. Now a programmer could describe the meaning of related kinds of data (their type) and let the programming language enforce these design decisions. This generation of high-order programming languages again moved our software a step closer to the problem domain and further away from the underlying machine.

The 1970s provided us with a frenzy of activity in programming language research, resulting in the creation of literally a couple of thousand different programming languages and dialects. To a large extent, the drive to write larger and larger programs highlighted the inadequacies of earlier languages; thus, many new language mechanisms were developed to address these limitations. Few of these languages survived (have you seen a recent textbook on the languages Fred, Chaos, or Tranquil?); however, many of the concepts that they introduced found their way into successors of earlier languages.

What is of the greatest interest to us is the class of languages we call *object-based* and *object-oriented*. Object-based and object-oriented programming languages best support the object-oriented decomposition of software. The number of these languages (and the number of "objectified" variants of existing languages) boomed in the 1980s and early 1990s. Since 1990 a few languages have emerged as mainstream OO languages with the backing of commercial programming tool vendors (e.g., Java, C++). The emergence of programming frameworks (e.g., J2EE, .NET), which provide a tremendous amount of support to the programmer by offering components and services that simplify the common and often mundane programming tasks, has greatly boosted productivity and demonstrated the elusive promise of component reuse.

The Topology of First- and Early Second-Generation Programming Languages

Let's consider the structure of each generation of programming languages. In Figure 2–1, we see the topology of most first- and early second-generation programming languages. By *topology*, we mean the basic physical building blocks of the language and how those parts can be connected. In this figure, we see that for languages such as FORTRAN and COBOL, the basic physical building block of all applications is the subprogram (or the paragraph, for those who speak COBOL).

Applications written in these languages exhibit a relatively flat physical structure, consisting only of global data and subprograms. The arrows in this figure indicate dependencies of the subprograms on various data. During design, one can logically separate different kinds of data from one another, but there is little in these languages that can enforce these design decisions. An error in one part of a program can have a devastating ripple effect across the rest of the system because the global data structures are exposed for all subprograms to see.

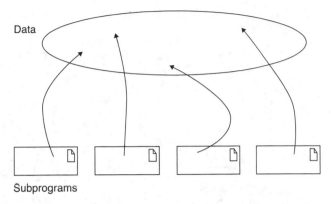

Data

Subprograms

Figure 2–1 The Topology of First- and Early Second-Generation
Programming Languages

When modifications are made to a large system, it is difficult to maintain the
integrity of the original design. Often, entropy sets in: After even a short period of
maintenance, a program written in one of these languages usually contains a tremendous amount of cross-coupling among subprograms, implied meanings of
data, and twisted flows of control, thus threatening the reliability of the entire system and certainly reducing the overall clarity of the solution.

The Topology of Late Second- and Early Third-Generation Programming Languages

By the mid-1960s, programs were finally being recognized as important intermediate points between the problem and the computer [3]. "The first software
abstraction, now called the 'procedural' abstraction, grew directly out of this
pragmatic view of software. . . . Subprograms were invented prior to 1950, but
were not fully appreciated as abstractions at the time. . . . Instead, they were originally seen as labor-saving devices. . . . Very quickly though, subprograms were
appreciated as a way to abstract program functions" [4].

The realization that subprograms could serve as an abstraction mechanism had
three important consequences. First, languages were invented that supported a
variety of parameter-passing mechanisms. Second, the foundations of structured
programming were laid, manifesting themselves in language support for the nesting of subprograms and the development of theories regarding control structures
and the scope and visibility of declarations. Third, structured design methods
emerged, offering guidance to designers trying to build large systems using subprograms as basic physical building blocks. Thus, it is not surprising, as Figure 2–2
shows, that the topology of late second- and early third-generation languages is
largely a variation on the theme of earlier generations. This topology addresses

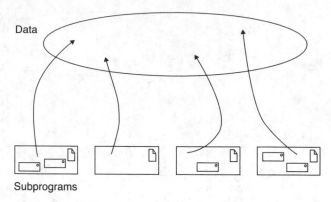

Data

Subprograms

Figure 2–2 The Topology of Late Second- and Early Third-Generation
Programming Languages

some of the inadequacies of earlier languages, namely, the need to have greater
control over algorithmic abstractions, but it still fails to address the problems of
programming-in-the-large and data design.

The Topology of Late Third-Generation Programming Languages

Starting with FORTRAN II, and appearing in most late third-generation program
languages, another important structuring mechanism evolved to address the growing issues of programming-in-the-large. Larger programming projects meant
larger development teams, and thus the need to develop different parts of the same
program independently. The answer to this need was the separately compiled
module, which in its early conception was little more than an arbitrary container
for data and subprograms, as Figure 2–3 shows. Modules were rarely recognized
as an important abstraction mechanism; in practice they were used simply to
group subprograms that were most likely to change together.

Most languages of this generation, while supporting some sort of modular structure, had few rules that required semantic consistency among module interfaces.
A developer writing a subprogram for one module might assume that it would be
called with three different parameters: a floating-point number, an array of ten
elements, and an integer representing a Boolean flag. In another module, a call to
this subprogram might incorrectly use actual parameters that violated these
assumptions: an integer, an array of five elements, and a negative number. Similarly, one module might use a block of common data that it assumed as its own,
and another module might violate these assumptions by directly manipulating this

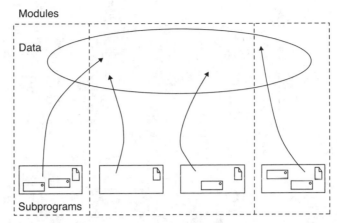

Modules

Data

Subprograms

Figure 2–3 The Topology of Late Third-Generation Programming Languages

data. Unfortunately, because most of these languages had dismal support for data abstraction and strong typing, such errors could be detected only during execution of the program.

The Topology of Object-Based and Object-Oriented Programming Languages

Data abstraction is important to mastering complexity. "The nature of abstractions that may be achieved through the use of procedures is well suited to the description of abstract operations, but is not particularly well suited to the description of abstract objects. This is a serious drawback, for in many applications, the complexity of the data objects to be manipulated contributes substantially to the overall complexity of the problem" [5]. This realization had two important consequences. First, data-driven design methods emerged, which provided a disciplined approach to the problems of doing data abstraction in algorithmically oriented languages. Second, theories regarding the concept of a type appeared, which eventually found their realization in languages such as Pascal.

The natural conclusion of these ideas first appeared in the language Simula and was improved upon, resulting in the development of several languages such as Smalltalk, Object Pascal, C++, Ada, Eiffel, and Java. For reasons that we will explain shortly, these languages are called object-based or object-oriented. Figure 2–4 illustrates the topology of such languages for small to moderate-sized applications.

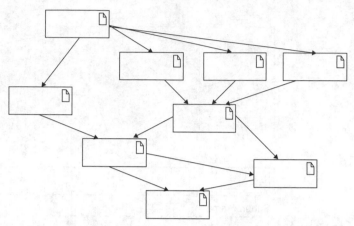

Figure 2–4 The Topology of Small to Moderate-Sized Applications Using Object-Based and Object-Oriented Programming Languages

The physical building block in such languages is the module, which represents a logical collection of classes and objects instead of subprograms, as in earlier languages. To state it another way, "If procedures and functions are verbs and pieces of data are nouns, a procedure-oriented program is organized around verbs while an object-oriented program is organized around nouns" [6]. For this reason, the physical structure of a small to moderate-sized object-oriented application appears as a graph, not as a tree, which is typical of algorithmically oriented languages. Additionally, there is little or no global data. Instead, data and operations are united in such a way that the fundamental logical building blocks of our systems are no longer algorithms, but instead are classes and objects.

By now we have progressed beyond programming-in-the-large and must cope with programming-in-the-colossal. For very complex systems, we find that classes, objects, and modules provide an essential yet insufficient means of abstraction. Fortunately, the object model scales up. In large systems, we find clusters of abstractions built in layers on top of one another. At any given level of abstraction, we find meaningful collections of objects that collaborate to achieve some higher-level behavior. If we look inside any given cluster to view its implementation, we unveil yet another set of cooperative abstractions. This is exactly the organization of complexity described in Chapter 1; this topology is shown in Figure 2–5.

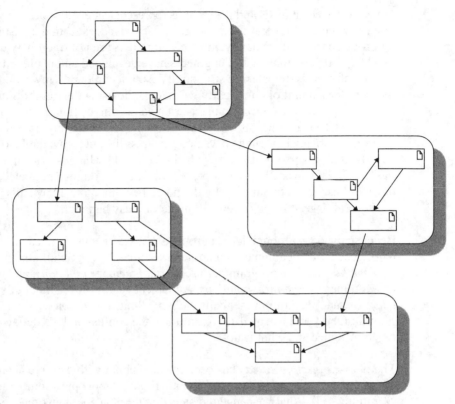

Figure 2–5 The Topology of Large Applications Using Object-Based and
Object-Oriented Programming Languages

2.2 Foundations of the Object Model

Structured design methods evolved to guide developers who were trying to build
complex systems using algorithms as their fundamental building blocks. Similarly, object-oriented design methods have evolved to help developers exploit the
expressive power of object-based and object-oriented programming languages,
using the class and object as basic building blocks.

Actually, the object model has been influenced by a number of factors, not just
object-oriented programming. Indeed, as further discussed in the sidebar, Foundations—The Object Model, the object model has proven to be a unifying concept
in computer science, applicable not just to programming languages but also to the
design of user interfaces, databases, and even computer architectures. The reason
for this widespread appeal is simply that an object orientation helps us to cope
with the complexity inherent in many different kinds of systems.

Object-oriented analysis and design thus represents an evolutionary development, not a revolutionary one; it does not break with advances from the past but builds on proven ones. Unfortunately, most programmers are not rigorously trained in OOAD. Certainly, many good engineers have developed and deployed countless useful software systems using structured design techniques. However, there are limits to the amount of complexity we can handle using only algorithmic decomposition; thus we must turn to object-oriented decomposition. Furthermore, if we try to use languages such as C++ and Java as if they were only traditional, algorithmically oriented languages, we not only miss the power available to us, but we usually end up worse off than if we had used an older language such as C or Pascal. Give a power drill to a carpenter who knows nothing about electricity, and he would use it as a hammer. He will end up bending quite a few nails and smashing several fingers, for a power drill makes a lousy hammer.

Because the object model derives from so many disparate sources, it has unfortunately been accompanied by a muddle of terminology. A Smalltalk programmer uses *methods*, a C++ programmer uses *virtual member functions*, and a CLOS programmer uses *generic functions*. An Object Pascal programmer talks of a *type coercion*; an Ada programmer calls the same thing a *type conversion*; a C# or Java programmer would use a *cast*. To minimize the confusion, let's define what is object-oriented and what is not.

The phrase *object-oriented* "has been bandied about with carefree abandon with much the same reverence accorded 'motherhood,' 'apple pie,' and 'structured programming'"[7]. What we can agree on is that the concept of an object is central to anything object-oriented. In the previous chapter, we informally defined an object as a tangible entity that exhibits some well-defined behavior. Stefik and Bobrow define objects as "entities that combine the properties of procedures and data since they perform computations and save local state" [8]. Defining objects as entities begs the question somewhat, but the basic concept here is that objects serve to unify the ideas of algorithmic and data abstraction. Jones further clarifies this term by noting that "in the object model, emphasis is placed on crisply characterizing the components of the physical or abstract system to be modeled by a programmed system. . . . Objects have a certain 'integrity' which should not—in fact, cannot—be violated. An object can only change state, behave, be manipulated, or stand in relation to other objects in ways appropriate to that object. Stated differently, there exist invariant properties that characterize an object and its behavior. An elevator, for example, is characterized by invariant properties including [that] it only travels up and down inside its shaft. . . . Any elevator simulation must incorporate these invariants, for they are integral to the notion of an elevator" [32].

Foundations—The Object Model

As Yonezawa and Tokoro point out, "The term 'object' emerged almost independently in various fields in computer science, almost simultaneously in the early 1970s, to refer to notions that were different in their appearance, yet mutually related. All of these notions were invented to manage the complexity of software systems in such a way that objects represented components of a modularly decomposed system or modular units of knowledge representation" [9]. Levy adds that the following events have contributed to the evolution of object-oriented concepts:

■ Advances in computer architecture, including capability systems and hardware support for operating systems concepts
■ Advances in programming languages, as demonstrated in Simula, Smalltalk, CLU, and Ada
■ Advances in programming methodology, including modularization and information hiding [10]

We would add to this list three more contributions to the foundation of the object model:

■ Advances in database models
■ Research in artificial intelligence
■ Advances in philosophy and cognitive science

The concept of an object had its beginnings in hardware over twenty years ago, starting with the invention of descriptor-based architectures and, later, capability-based architectures [11]. These architectures represented a break from the classical von Neumann architectures and came about through attempts to close the gap between the high-level abstractions of programming languages and the low-level abstractions of the machine itself [12]. According to its proponents, the advantages of such architectures are many: better error detection, improved execution efficiency, fewer instruction types, simpler compilation, and reduced storage requirements. Computers can also have an object-oriented architecture.

Closely related to developments in object-oriented architectures are object-oriented operating systems. Dijkstra's work with the THE multiprogramming system first introduced the concept of building systems as layered state machines [18]. Other pioneering object-oriented operating systems include the Plessey/System 250 (for the Plessey 250 multiprocessor), Hydra (for CMU's C.mmp), CALTSS (for the CDC 6400), CAP (for the Cambridge CAP computer), UCLA Secure UNIX (for the PDP 11/45 and 11/70), StarOS (for CMU's Cm*), Medusa (also for CMU's Cm*), and iMAX (for the Intel 432) [19].

Perhaps the most important contribution to the object model derives from the class of programming languages we call object-based and object-oriented. The fundamental ideas of classes and objects first appeared in the language Simula 67. The Flex system, followed by various dialects of Smalltalk, such as Smalltalk-72, -74, and -76, and finally the current version, Smalltalk-80, took Simula's object-oriented paradigm to its natural conclusion by making everything in the language an instance of a class. In the 1970s languages such as Alphard, CLU, Euclid, Gypsy, Mesa, and Modula were developed, which supported the then-emerging ideas of data abstraction. Language research led to the grafting of Simula and Smalltalk concepts onto traditional high-order programming languages. The unification of object-oriented concepts with C has lead to the languages C++ and Objective C. Then Java arrived to help programmers avoid common programming errors often seen when using C++. Adding object-oriented programming mechanisms to Pascal has led to the languages Object Pascal, Eiffel, and Ada. Additionally, many dialects of Lisp incorporate the object-oriented features of Simula and Smalltalk. Appendix A discusses some of these and other programming language developments in greater detail.

The first person to formally identify the importance of composing systems in layers of abstraction was Dijkstra. Parnas later introduced the idea of information hiding [20], and in the 1970s a number of researchers, most notably Liskov and Zilles [21], Guttag [22], and Shaw [23], pioneered the development of abstract data type mechanisms. Hoare contributed to these developments with his proposal for a theory of types and subclasses [24].

Although database technology has evolved somewhat independently of software engineering, it has also contributed to the object model [25], primarily through the ideas of the entity-relationship (ER) approach to data modeling [26]. In the ER model, first proposed by Chen [27], the world is modeled in terms of its entities, the attributes of these entities, and the relationships among these entities.

In the field of artificial intelligence, developments in knowledge representation have contributed to an understanding of object-oriented abstractions. In 1975, Minsky first proposed a theory of frames to represent real-world objects as perceived by image and natural language recognition systems [28]. Since then, frames have been used as the architectural foundation for a variety of intelligent systems.

Lastly, philosophy and cognitive science have contributed to the advancement of the object model. The idea that the world could be viewed in terms of either objects or processes was a Greek innovation, and in the seventeenth century, we find Descartes observing that humans naturally apply an object-oriented view of the world [29]. In the twentieth century, Rand expanded on these themes in her philosophy of objectivist epistemology [30]. More recently, Minsky has proposed a model of human intelligence in which he considers the mind to be organized as a society of otherwise mindless agents [31]. Minsky argues that only through the cooperative behavior of these agents do we find what we call *intelligence*.

Object-Oriented Programming

What, then, is object-oriented programming (OOP)? We define it as follows:

> Object-oriented programming is a method of implementation in which programs are organized as cooperative collections of objects, each of which represents an instance of some class, and whose classes are all members of a hierarchy of classes united via inheritance relationships.

There are three important parts to this definition: (1) Object-oriented programming uses objects, not algorithms, as its fundamental logical building blocks (the "part of" hierarchy we introduced in Chapter 1); (2) each object is an instance of some class; and (3) classes may be related to one another via inheritance relationships (the "is a" hierarchy we spoke of in Chapter 1). A program may appear to be object-oriented, but if any of these elements is missing, it is not an object-oriented program. Specifically, programming without inheritance is distinctly not object-oriented; that would merely be programming with abstract data types.

By this definition, some languages are object-oriented, and some are not. Stroustrup suggests that "if the term 'object-oriented language' means anything, it must mean a language that has mechanisms that support the object-oriented style of programming well. . . . A language supports a programming style well if it provides facilities that make it convenient to use that style. A language does not support a technique if it takes exceptional effort or skill to write such programs; in that case, the language merely enables programmers to use the techniques" [33]. From a theoretical perspective, one can fake object-oriented programming in non-object-oriented programming languages like Pascal and even COBOL or assembly language, but it is horribly ungainly to do so. Cardelli and Wegner thus say:

> [A] language is object-oriented if and only if it satisfies the following requirements:
> - It supports objects that are data abstractions with an interface of named operations and a hidden local state.
> - Objects have an associated type [class].
> - Types [classes] may inherit attributes from supertypes [superclasses]. [34]

For a language to support inheritance means that it is possible to express "is a" relationships among types, for example, a red rose is a kind of flower, and a flower is a kind of plant. If a language does not provide direct support for inheritance, then it is not object-oriented. Cardelli and Wegner distinguish such languages by calling them *object-based* rather than *object-oriented*. Under this definition, Smalltalk, Object Pascal, C++, Eiffel, CLOS, C#, and Java are all object-oriented, and Ada83 is object-based (support for object orientation was later added to Ada95). However, since objects and classes are elements of both kinds of languages, it is both possible and highly desirable for us to use object-oriented design methods for both object-based and object-oriented programming languages.

Object-Oriented Design

The emphasis in programming methods is primarily on the proper and effective use of particular language mechanisms. By contrast, design methods emphasize the proper and effective structuring of a complex system. What, then, is object-oriented design (OOD)? We suggest the following:

> Object-oriented design is a method of design encompassing the process of object-oriented decomposition and a notation for depicting both logical and physical as well as static and dynamic models of the system under design.

There are two important parts to this definition: object-oriented design (1) leads to an object-oriented decomposition and (2) uses different notations to express different models of the logical (class and object structure) and physical (module and process architecture) design of a system, in addition to the static and dynamic aspects of the system.

The support for object-oriented decomposition is what makes object-oriented design quite different from structured design: The former uses class and object abstractions to logically structure systems, and the latter uses algorithmic abstractions. We will use the term *object-oriented design* to refer to any method that leads to an object-oriented decomposition.

Object-Oriented Analysis

The object model has influenced even earlier phases of the software development lifecycle. Traditional structured analysis techniques, best typified by the work of DeMarco [35], Yourdon [36], and Gane and Sarson [37], with real-time extensions by Ward and Mellor [38] and by Hatley and Pirbhai [39], focus on the flow of data within a system. Object-oriented analysis (OOA) emphasizes the building of real-world models, using an object-oriented view of the world:

> Object-oriented analysis is a method of analysis that examines requirements from the perspective of the classes and objects found in the vocabulary of the problem domain.

How are OOA, OOD, and OOP related? Basically, the products of object-oriented analysis serve as the models from which we may start an object-oriented design;

the products of object-oriented design can then be used as blueprints for completely implementing a system using object-oriented programming methods.

2.3 Elements of the Object Model

Jenkins and Glasgow observe that "most programmers work in one language and use only one programming style. They program in a paradigm enforced by the language they use. Frequently, they have not been exposed to alternate ways of thinking about a problem, and hence have difficulty in seeing the advantage of choosing a style more appropriate to the problem at hand" [40]. Bobrow and Stefik define a programming style as "a way of organizing programs on the basis of some conceptual model of programming and an appropriate language to make programs written in the style clear" [41]. They further suggest that there are five main kinds of programming styles, listed here with the kinds of abstractions they employ:

1. Procedure-oriented   Algorithms
2. Object-oriented   Classes and objects
3. Logic-oriented   Goals, often expressed in a predicate calculus
4. Rule-oriented   If–then rules
5. Constraint-oriented   Invariant relationships

There is no single programming style that is best for all kinds of applications. For example, rule-oriented programming would be best suited for the design of a knowledge base, and procedure-oriented programming would be best for the design of computation-intense operations. From our experience, the object-oriented style is best suited to the broadest set of applications; indeed, this programming paradigm often serves as the architectural framework in which we employ other paradigms.

Each of these styles of programming is based on its own conceptual framework. Each requires a different mindset, a different way of thinking about the problem. For all things object-oriented, the conceptual framework is the object model. There are four major elements of this model:

1. Abstraction
2. Encapsulation
3. Modularity
4. Hierarchy

By *major*, we mean that a model without any one of these elements is not object-oriented.

There are three minor elements of the object model:

1. Typing
2. Concurrency
3. Persistence

By *minor*, we mean that each of these elements is a useful, but not essential, part of the object model.

Without this conceptual framework, you may be programming in a language such as Smalltalk, Object Pascal, C++, Eiffel, or Ada, but your design is going to smell like a FORTRAN, Pascal, or C application. You will have missed out on or otherwise abused the expressive power of the object-oriented language you are using for implementation. More importantly, you are not likely to have mastered the complexity of the problem at hand.

The Meaning of Abstraction

Abstraction is one of the fundamental ways that we as humans cope with complexity. Dahl, Dijkstra, and Hoare suggest that "abstraction arises from a recognition of similarities between certain objects, situations, or processes in the real world, and the decision to concentrate upon these similarities and to ignore for the time being the differences" [42]. Shaw defines an abstraction as "a simplified description, or specification, of a system that emphasizes some of the system's details or properties while suppressing others. A good abstraction is one that emphasizes details that are significant to the reader or user and suppresses details that are, at least for the moment, immaterial or diversionary" [43]. Berzins, Gray, and Naumann recommend that "a concept qualifies as an abstraction only if it can be described, understood, and analyzed independently of the mechanism that will eventually be used to realize it" [44]. Combining these different viewpoints, we define an abstraction as follows:

> An abstraction denotes the essential characteristics of an object that distinguish it from all other kinds of objects and thus provide crisply defined conceptual boundaries, relative to the perspective of the viewer.

An abstraction focuses on the outside view of an object and so serves to separate an object's essential behavior from its implementation. Abelson and Sussman call this behavior/implementation division an abstraction barrier [45] achieved by applying the *principle of least commitment*, through which the interface of an object provides its essential behavior, and nothing more [46]. We like to use an additional principle that we call the *principle of least astonishment*, through which an abstraction captures the entire behavior of some object, no more and no less, and offers no surprises or side effects that go beyond the scope of the abstraction.

Abstraction focuses on the essential characteristics of some object,
relative to the perspective of the viewer.

Deciding on the right set of abstractions for a given domain is the central problem
in object-oriented design. Because this topic is so important, the whole of Chapter 4
is devoted to it.

"There is a spectrum of abstraction, from objects which closely model problem
domain entities to objects which really have no reason for existence" [47]. From
the most to the least useful, these kinds of abstractions include the following:

■ Entity abstraction	An object that represents a useful model of a problem domain or solution domain entity
■ Action abstraction	An object that provides a generalized set of operations, all of which perform the same kind of function
■ Virtual machine abstraction	An object that groups operations that are all used by some superior level of control, or operations that all use some junior-level set of operations
■ Coincidental abstraction	An object that packages a set of operations that have no relation to each other

We strive to build entity abstractions because they directly parallel the vocabulary of a given problem domain.

A client is any object that uses the resources of another object (known as the server). We can characterize the behavior of an object by considering the services that it provides to other objects, as well as the operations that it may perform on other objects. This view forces us to concentrate on the outside view of an object and leads us to what Meyer calls the *contract model* of programming [48]: the outside view of each object defines a contract on which other objects may depend, and which in turn must be carried out by the inside view of the object itself (often in collaboration with other objects). This contract thus establishes all the assumptions a client object may make about the behavior of a server object. In other words, this contract encompasses the responsibilities of an object, namely, the behavior for which it is held accountable [49].

Individually, each operation that contributes to this contract has a unique signature comprising all of its formal arguments and return type. We call the entire set of operations that a client may perform on an object, together with the legal orderings in which they may be invoked, its *protocol*. A protocol denotes the ways in which an object may act and react and thus constitutes the entire static and dynamic outside view of the abstraction.

Central to the idea of an abstraction is the concept of invariance. An *invariant* is some Boolean (true or false) condition whose truth must be preserved. For each operation associated with an object, we may define *preconditions* (invariants assumed by the operation) as well as *postconditions* (invariants satisfied by the operation). Violating an invariant breaks the contract associated with an abstraction. If a precondition is violated, this means that a client has not satisfied its part of the bargain, and hence the server cannot proceed reliably. Similarly, if a postcondition is violated, this means that a server has not carried out its part of the contract, and so its clients can no longer trust the behavior of the server. An exception is an indication that some invariant has not been or cannot be satisfied. Certain languages permit objects to throw exceptions so as to abandon processing and alert some other object to the problem, which in turn may catch the exception and handle the problem.

As an aside, the terms *operation*, *method*, and *member function* evolved from three different programming cultures (Ada, Smalltalk, and C++, respectively). They all mean virtually the same thing, so we will use them interchangeably.

All abstractions have static as well as dynamic properties. For example, a file object takes up a certain amount of space on a particular memory device; it has a name, and it has contents. These are all static properties. The value of each of these properties is dynamic, relative to the lifetime of the object: A file object may grow or shrink in size, its name may change, its contents may change. In a procedure-oriented style of programming, the activity that changes the dynamic value of objects is the central part of all programs; things happen when subprograms are called and statements are executed. In a rule-oriented style of programming, things happen when new events cause rules to fire, which in turn may trigger other rules, and so on. In an object-oriented style of programming, things happen whenever we operate on an object (i.e., when we send a message to an object). Thus, invoking an operation on an object elicits some reaction from the object. What operations we can meaningfully perform on an object and how that object reacts constitute the entire behavior of the object.

Examples of Abstraction

Let's illustrate these concepts with some examples. We defer a complete treatment of how to find the right abstractions for a given problem to Chapter 4.

On a hydroponics farm, plants are grown in a nutrient solution, without sand, gravel, or other soils. Maintaining the proper greenhouse environment is a delicate job and depends on the kind of plant being grown and its age. One must control diverse factors such as temperature, humidity, light, pH, and nutrient concentrations. On a large farm, it is not unusual to have an automated system that constantly monitors and adjusts these elements. Simply stated, the purpose of an automated gardener is to efficiently carry out, with minimal human intervention, growing plans for the healthy production of multiple crops.

One of the key abstractions in this problem is that of a sensor. Actually, there are several different kinds of sensors. Anything that affects production must be measured, so we must have sensors for air and water temperature, humidity, light, pH, and nutrient concentrations, among other things. Viewed from the outside, a temperature sensor is simply an object that knows how to measure the temperature at some specific location. What is a temperature? It is some numeric value, within a limited range of values and with a certain precision, that represents degrees in the scale of Fahrenheit, Centigrade, or Kelvin, whichever is most appropriate for our problem. What is a location? It is some identifiable place on the farm at which we desire to measure the temperature; presumably, there are only a few such locations. What is important for a temperature sensor is not so much where it is located but the fact that it has a location and identity unique from all other temperature sensors. Now we are ready to ask: What are the responsibilities of a temperature sensor? Our design decision is that a sensor is responsible for knowing the temperature at a given location and reporting that temperature when asked. More concretely, what operations can a client perform on a temperature sensor? Our design decision is that a client can calibrate it, as well as ask what the current temperature is. (See Figure 2–6. Note that this representation is similar to the representation of a class in UML 2.0. You will learn the actual representation in Chapter 5.)

Abstraction: Temperature Sensor
Important Characteristics:
temperature location
Responsibilities:
report current temperature calibrate

Figure 2–6 Abstraction of a `Temperature Sensor`

The abstraction we have described thus far is passive; some client object must operate on an air `Temperature Sensor` object to determine its current temperature. However, there is another legitimate abstraction that may be more or less appropriate depending on the broader system design decisions we might make. Specifically, rather than the `Temperature Sensor` being passive, we might make it active, so that it is not acted on but rather acts on other objects whenever the temperature at its location changes a certain number of degrees from a given setpoint. This abstraction is almost the same as our first one, except that its responsibilities have changed slightly: A sensor is now responsible for reporting the current temperature when it changes, not just when asked. What new operations must this abstraction provide?

This abstraction is a bit more complicated than the first (see Figure 2–7). A client of this abstraction may invoke an operation to establish a critical range of temperatures. It is then the responsibility of the sensor to report whenever the temperature at its location drops below or rises above the given setpoint. When the function is invoked, the sensor provides its location and the current temperature, so that the client has sufficient information to respond to the condition.

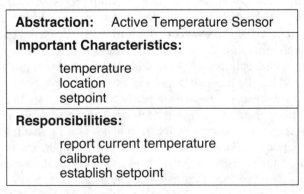

Abstraction: Active Temperature Sensor
Important Characteristics:
temperature location setpoint
Responsibilities:
report current temperature calibrate establish setpoint

Figure 2–7 Abstraction of an `Active Temperature Sensor`

How the `Active Temperature Sensor` carries out its responsibilities is a function of its inside view and is of no concern to outside clients. These then are the secrets of the class, which are implemented by the class's private parts together with the definition of its member functions.

Let's consider a different abstraction. For each crop, there must be a growing plan that describes how temperature, light, nutrients, and other conditions should change over time to maximize the harvest. A growing plan is a legitimate entity abstraction because it forms part of the vocabulary of the problem domain. Each crop has its own growing plan, but the growing plans for all crops take the same form.

A growing plan is responsible for keeping track of all interesting actions associated with growing a crop, correlated with the times at which those actions should take place. For example, on day 15 in the lifetime of a certain crop, our growing plan might be to maintain a temperature of 78°F for 16 hours, turn on the lights for 14 of these hours, and then drop the temperature to 65°F for the rest of the day. We might also want to add certain extra nutrients in the middle of the day, while still maintaining a slightly acidic pH. From the perspective outside of each growing-plan object, a client must be able to establish the details of a plan, modify a plan, and inquire about a plan, as shown in Figure 2–8. (Note that abstractions are likely to evolve over the lifetime of a project. As details begin to be fleshed out, a responsibility such as "establish plan" could turn into multiple responsibilities, such as "set temperature," "set pH," and so forth. This is to be expected as more knowledge of client requirements is gained, designs mature, and implementation approaches are considered.)

Our decision is also that we will not require a growing plan to carry out its plan: We will leave this as the responsibility of a different abstraction (e.g., a `Plan Controller`). In this manner, we create a clear *separation of concerns* among the logically different parts of the system, so as to reduce the conceptual size of each individual abstraction. For example, there might be an object that sits at the

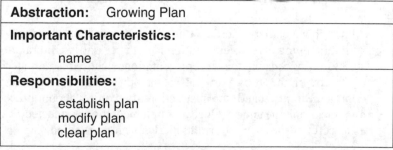

Related Candidate Abstractions: Crop, Conditions, Plan Controller

Figure 2–8 Abstraction of a `Growing Plan`

boundary of the human/machine interface and translates human input into plans. This is the object that establishes the details of a growing plan, so it must be able to change the state of a `Growing Plan` object. There must also be an object that carries out the growing plan, and it must be able to read the details of a plan for a particular time.

As this example points out, no object stands alone; every object collaborates with other objects to achieve some behavior.[1] Our design decisions about how these objects cooperate with one another define the boundaries of each abstraction and thus the responsibilities and protocol of each object.

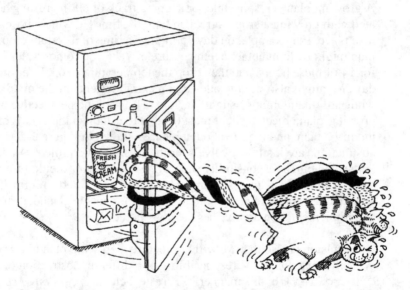

Objects collaborate with other objects to achieve some behavior.

The Meaning of Encapsulation

Although we earlier described our abstraction of the `Growing Plan` as a time/ action mapping, its implementation is not necessarily a literal table or map data structure. Indeed, whichever representation is chosen is immaterial to the client's contract with the `Growing Plan`, as long as that representation upholds the contract. Simply stated, the abstraction of an object should precede the decisions about its implementation. Once an implementation is selected, it should be treated as a secret of the abstraction and hidden from most clients.

---

1. Stated another way, with apologies to the poet John Donne, no object is an island (although an island may be abstracted as an object).

Encapsulation hides the details of the implementation of an object.

Abstraction and encapsulation are complementary concepts: Abstraction focuses on the observable behavior of an object, whereas encapsulation focuses on the implementation that gives rise to this behavior. Encapsulation is most often achieved through information hiding (not just data hiding), which is the process of hiding all the secrets of an object that do not contribute to its essential characteristics; typically, the structure of an object is hidden, as well as the implementation of its methods. "No part of a complex system should depend on the internal details of any other part" [50]. Whereas abstraction "helps people to think about what they are doing," encapsulation "allows program changes to be reliably made with limited effort" [51].

Encapsulation provides explicit barriers among different abstractions and thus leads to a clear separation of concerns. For example, consider again the structure of a plant. To understand how photosynthesis works at a high level of abstraction, we can ignore details such as the responsibilities of plant roots or the chemistry of cell walls. Similarly, in designing a database application, it is standard practice to write programs so that they don't care about the physical representation of data but depend only on a schema that denotes the data's logical view [52]. In both of these cases, objects at one level of abstraction are shielded from implementation details at lower levels of abstraction.

"For abstraction to work, implementations must be encapsulated" [53]. In practice, this means that each class must have two parts: an interface and an implementation. The interface of a class captures only its outside view, encompassing our abstraction of the behavior common to all instances of the class. The implementation of a class comprises the representation of the abstraction as well as the mechanisms that achieve the desired behavior. The interface of a class is the one place where we assert all of the assumptions that a client may make about any instances of the class; the implementation encapsulates details about which no client may make assumptions.

To summarize, we define encapsulation as follows:

> Encapsulation is the process of compartmentalizing the elements of an abstraction that constitute its structure and behavior; encapsulation serves to separate the contractual interface of an abstraction and its implementation.

Britton and Parnas call these encapsulated elements the "secrets" of an abstraction [54].

Examples of Encapsulation

To illustrate the principle of encapsulation, let's return to the problem of the Hydroponics Gardening System. Another key abstraction in this problem domain is that of a heater. A heater is at a fairly low level of abstraction, and thus we might decide that there are only three meaningful operations that we can perform on this object: turn it on, turn it off, and find out if it is running.

Separation of Concerns

We do not make it a responsibility of the `Heater` abstraction to maintain a fixed temperature. Instead, we choose to give this responsibility to another object (e.g., the `Heater Controller`), which must collaborate with a temperature sensor and a heater to achieve this higher-level behavior. We call this behavior *higher-level* because it builds on the primitive semantics of temperature sensors and heaters and adds some new semantics, namely, *hysteresis*, which prevents the heater from being turned on and off too rapidly when the temperature is near boundary conditions. By deciding on this separation of responsibilities, we make each individual abstraction more cohesive.

All a client needs to know about the class `Heater` is its available interface (i.e., the responsibilities that it may execute at the client's request—see Figure 2–9).

Turning to the inside view of the `Heater`, we have an entirely different perspective. Suppose that our system engineers have decided to locate the computers that control each greenhouse away from the building (perhaps to avoid the harsh environment) and to connect each computer to its sensors and actuators via serial lines. One reasonable implementation for the `Heater` class might be to use an electromechanical relay that controls the power going to each physical heater, with the relays in turn commanded by messages sent along these serial lines. For example, to turn on a heater, we might transmit a special command string, followed by a number identifying the specific heater, followed by another number used to signal turning the heater on.

Abstraction:	Heater
Important Characteristics:	
location status	
Responsibilities:	
turn on turn off provide status	

Related Candidate Abstractions: Heater Controller, Temperature Sensor

Figure 2–9 Abstraction of a `Heater`

Suppose that for whatever reason our system engineers choose to use memory-mapped I/O instead of serial communication lines. We would not need to change the interface of the `Heater`, yet the implementation would be very different. The client would not see any change at all as the client sees only the `Heater` interface. This is the key point of encapsulation. In fact, the client should not care what the implementation is, as long as it receives the service it needs from the `Heater`.

Let's next consider the implementation of the class `GrowingPlan`. As we mentioned earlier, a growing plan is essentially a time/action mapping. Perhaps the most reasonable representation for this abstraction would be a dictionary of time/action pairs, using an open hash table. We need not store an action for every hour, because things don't change that quickly. Rather, we can store actions only for when they change, and have the implementation extrapolate between times.

In this manner, our implementation encapsulates two secrets: the use of an open hash table (which is distinctly a part of the vocabulary of the solution domain, not the problem domain) and the use of extrapolation to reduce our storage requirements (otherwise we would have to store many more time/action pairs over the duration of a growing season). No client of this abstraction need ever know about these implementation decisions because they do not materially affect the outwardly observable behavior of the class.

Intelligent encapsulation localizes design decisions that are likely to change. As a system evolves, its developers might discover that, in actual use, certain operations take longer than is acceptable or that some objects consume more space than is available. In such situations, the representation of an object is often changed so that more efficient algorithms can be applied or so that one can optimize for space by calculating rather than storing certain data. This ability to change the representation of an abstraction without disturbing any of its clients is the essential benefit of encapsulation.

Hiding is a relative concept: What is hidden at one level of abstraction may represent the outside view at another level of abstraction. The underlying representation of an object can be revealed, but in most cases only if the creator of the abstraction explicitly exposes the implementation, and then only if the client is willing to accept the resulting additional complexity. Thus, encapsulation cannot stop a developer from doing stupid things; as Stroustrup points out, "Hiding is for the prevention of accidents, not the prevention of fraud" [56]. Of course, no programming language prevents a human from literally seeing the implementation of a class, although an operating system might deny access to a particular file that contains the implementation of a class.

The Meaning of Modularity

"The act of partitioning a program into individual components can reduce its complexity to some degree. . . . Although partitioning a program is helpful for this reason, a more powerful justification for partitioning a program is that it creates a number of well-defined, documented boundaries within the program. These boundaries, or interfaces, are invaluable in the comprehension of the program" [57]. In some languages, such as Smalltalk, there is no concept of a module, so the class forms the only physical unit of decomposition. Java has packages that contain classes. In many other languages, including Object Pascal, C++, and Ada, the module is a separate language construct and therefore warrants a separate set of design decisions. In these languages, classes and objects form the logical structure of a system; we place these abstractions in modules to produce the system's physical architecture. Especially for larger applications, in which we may have many hundreds of classes, the use of modules is essential to help manage complexity.

Modularity packages abstractions into discrete units.

"Modularization consists of dividing a program into modules which can be compiled separately, but which have connections with other modules. We will use the definition of Parnas: 'The connections between modules are the assumptions which the modules make about each other'" [58]. Most languages that support the module as a separate concept also distinguish between the interface of a module and its implementation. Thus, it is fair to say that modularity and encapsulation go hand in hand.

Deciding on the right set of modules for a given problem is almost as hard a problem as deciding on the right set of abstractions. Zelkowitz is absolutely right when he states that "because the solution may not be known when the design stage starts, decomposition into smaller modules may be quite difficult. For older applications (such as compiler writing), this process may become standard, but for new ones (such as defense systems or spacecraft control), it may be quite difficult" [59].

Modules serve as the physical containers in which we declare the classes and objects of our logical design. This is no different than the situation faced by the electrical engineer designing a computer motherboard. NAND, NOR, and NOT gates might be used to construct the necessary logic, but these gates must be physically packaged in standard integrated circuits. Lacking any such standard software parts, the software engineer has considerably more degrees of freedom—as if the electrical engineer had a silicon foundry at his or her disposal.

For tiny problems, the developer might decide to declare every class and object in the same package. For anything but the most trivial software, a better solution is to group logically related classes and objects in the same module and to expose only those elements that other modules absolutely must see. This kind of modularization is a good thing, but it can be taken to extremes. For example, consider an application that runs on a distributed set of processors and uses a message-passing mechanism to coordinate the activities of different programs. In a large system, such as a command and control system, it is common to have several hundred or even a few thousand kinds of messages. A naive strategy might be to define each message class in its own module. As it turns out, this is a singularly poor design decision. Not only does it create a documentation nightmare, but it makes it terribly difficult for any users to find the classes they need. Furthermore, when decisions change, hundreds of modules must be modified or recompiled. This example shows how information hiding can backfire [60]. Arbitrary modularization is sometimes worse than no modularization at all.

In traditional structured design, modularization is primarily concerned with the meaningful grouping of subprograms, using the criteria of coupling and cohesion. In object-oriented design, the problem is subtly different: The task is to decide where to physically package the classes and objects, which are distinctly different from subprograms.

Our experience indicates that there are several useful technical as well as non-technical guidelines that can help us achieve an intelligent modularization of classes and objects. As Britton and Parnas have observed, "The overall goal of the decomposition into modules is the reduction of software cost by allowing modules to be designed and revised independently. . . . Each module's structure should be simple enough that it can be understood fully; it should be possible to change the implementation of other modules without knowledge of the implementation of other modules and without affecting the behavior of other modules; [and] the ease of making a change in the design should bear a reasonable relationship to the likelihood of the change being needed" [61]. There is a pragmatic edge to these guidelines. In practice, the cost of recompiling the body of a module is relatively small: Only that unit need be recompiled and the application relinked. However, the cost of recompiling the interface of a module is relatively high. Especially with strongly typed languages, one must recompile the module interface, its body, all other modules that depend on this interface, the modules that depend on these modules, and so on. Thus, for very large programs (assuming that our development environment does not support incremental compilation), a change in a single module interface might result in much longer compilation time. Obviously, a development manager cannot often afford to allow a massive "big bang" recompilation to happen too frequently. For this reason, a module's interface should be as narrow as possible, yet still satisfy the needs of the other modules that use it. Our style is to hide as much as we can in the implementation of a module. Incrementally shifting declarations from a module's implementation to its interface is far less painful and destabilizing than ripping out extraneous interface code.

The developer must therefore balance two competing technical concerns: the desire to encapsulate abstractions and the need to make certain abstractions visible to other modules. "System details that are likely to change independently should be the secrets of separate modules; the only assumptions that should appear between modules are those that are considered unlikely to change. Every data structure is private to one module; it may be directly accessed by one or more programs within the module but not by programs outside the module. Any other program that requires information stored in a module's data structures must obtain it by calling module programs" [62]. In other words, strive to build modules that are cohesive (by grouping logically related abstractions) and loosely coupled (by minimizing the dependencies among modules). From this perspective, we may define modularity as follows:

> Modularity is the property of a system that has been decomposed into a set of cohesive and loosely coupled modules.

Thus, the principles of abstraction, encapsulation, and modularity are synergistic. An object provides a crisp boundary around a single abstraction, and both encapsulation and modularity provide barriers around this abstraction.

Two additional technical issues can affect modularization decisions. First, since modules usually serve as the elementary and indivisible units of software that can be reused across applications, a developer might choose to package classes and objects into modules in a way that makes their reuse convenient. Second, many compilers generate object code in segments, one for each module. Therefore, there may be practical limits on the size of individual modules. With regard to the dynamics of subprogram calls, the placement of declarations within modules can greatly affect the locality of reference and thus the paging behavior of a virtual memory system. Poor locality happens when subprogram calls occur across segments and lead to cache misses and page thrashing that ultimately slow down the whole system.

Several competing nontechnical needs may also affect modularization decisions. Typically, work assignments in a development team are given on a module-by-module basis, so the boundaries of modules may be established to minimize the interfaces among different parts of the development organization. Senior designers are usually given responsibility for module interfaces, and more junior developers complete their implementation. On a larger scale, the same situation applies with subcontractor relationships. Abstractions may be packaged so as to quickly stabilize the module interfaces as agreed upon among the various companies. Changing such interfaces usually involves much wailing and gnashing of teeth—not to mention a vast amount of paperwork—so this factor often leads to conservatively designed interfaces. Speaking of paperwork, modules also usually serve as the unit of documentation and configuration management. Having ten modules where one would do sometimes means ten times the paperwork, and so, unfortunately, sometimes the documentation requirements drive the module design decisions (usually in the most negative way). Security may also be an issue. Most code may be considered unclassified, but other code that might be classified secret or higher is best placed in separate modules.

Juggling these different requirements is difficult, but don't lose sight of the most important point: Finding the right classes and objects and then organizing them into separate modules are largely independent design decisions. The identification of classes and objects is part of the logical design of the system, but the identification of modules is part of the system's physical design. One cannot make all the logical design decisions before making all the physical ones, or vice versa; rather, these design decisions happen iteratively.

Examples of Modularity

Let's look at modularity in the Hydroponics Gardening System. Suppose we decide to use a commercially available workstation where the user can control the system's operation. At this workstation, an operator could create new growing plans, modify old ones, and follow the progress of currently active ones. Since one of our key abstractions here is that of a growing plan, we might therefore create a module whose purpose is to collect all of the classes associated with individual growing plans (e.g., FruitGrowingPlan, GrainGrowingPlan). The implementations of these GrowingPlan classes would appear in the implementation of this module. We might also define a module whose purpose is to collect all of the code associated with all user interface functions.

Our design will probably include many other modules. Ultimately, we must define some main program from which we can invoke this application. In object-oriented design, defining this main program is often the least important decision, whereas in traditional structured design, the main program serves as the root, the keystone that holds everything else together. We suggest that the object-oriented view is more natural, for, as Meyer observes, "Practical software systems are more appropriately described as offering a number of services. Defining these systems by single functions is usually possible, but yields rather artificial answers. . . . Real systems have no top" [63].

The Meaning of Hierarchy

Abstraction is a good thing, but in all except the most trivial applications, we may find many more different abstractions than we can comprehend at one time. Encapsulation helps manage this complexity by hiding the inside view of our abstractions. Modularity helps also, by giving us a way to cluster logically related abstractions. Still, this is not enough. A set of abstractions often forms a hierarchy, and by identifying these hierarchies in our design, we greatly simplify our understanding of the problem.

We define hierarchy as follows:

> Hierarchy is a ranking or ordering of abstractions.

The two most important hierarchies in a complex system are its class structure (the "is a" hierarchy) and its object structure (the "part of" hierarchy).

Examples of Hierarchy: Single Inheritance

Inheritance is the most important "is a" hierarchy, and as we noted earlier, it is an essential element of object-oriented systems. Basically, inheritance defines a relationship among classes, wherein one class shares the structure or behavior defined in one or more classes (denoting single inheritance and multiple inheritance, respectively). Inheritance thus represents a hierarchy of abstractions, in which a subclass inherits from one or more superclasses. Typically, a subclass augments or redefines the existing structure and behavior of its superclasses.

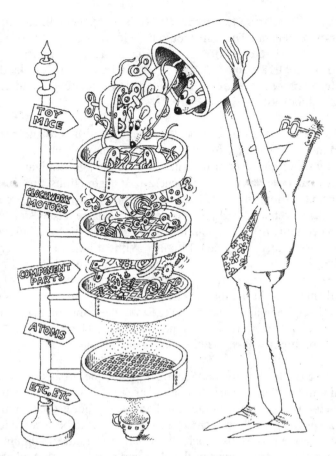

Abstractions form a hierarchy.

Semantically, inheritance denotes an "is a" relationship. For example, a bear "is a" kind of mammal, a house "is a" kind of tangible asset, and a quick sort "is a" particular kind of sorting algorithm. Inheritance thus implies a generalization/specialization hierarchy, wherein a subclass specializes the more general structure or behavior of its superclasses. Indeed, this is the litmus test for inheritance: If B is not a kind of A, then B should not inherit from A.

Consider the different kinds of growing plans we might use in the Hydroponics Gardening System. An earlier section described our abstraction of a very generalized growing plan. Different kinds of crops, however, demand specialized growing plans. For example, the growing plan for all fruits is generally the same but is quite different from the plan for all vegetables, or for all floral crops. Because of this clustering of abstractions, it is reasonable to define a standard fruit-growing plan that encapsulates the behavior common to all fruits, such as the knowledge of when to pollinate or when to harvest the fruit. We can assert that FruitGrowingPlan "is a" kind of GrowingPlan.

In this case, `FruitGrowingPlan` is more specialized, and `GrowingPlan` is more general. The same could be said for `GrainGrowingPlan` or `VegetableGrowingPlan`, that is, `GrainGrowingPlan` "is a" kind of `GrowingPlan`, and `VegetableGrowingPlan` "is a" kind of `GrowingPlan`. Here, `GrowingPlan` is the more general superclass, and the others are specialized subclasses.

As we evolve our inheritance hierarchy, the structure and behavior that are common for different classes will tend to migrate to common superclasses. This is why we often speak of inheritance as being a generalization/specialization hierarchy. Superclasses represent generalized abstractions, and subclasses represent specializations in which fields and methods from the superclass are added, modified, or even hidden. In this manner, inheritance lets us state our abstractions with an economy of expression. Indeed, neglecting the "is a" hierarchies that exist can lead to bloated, inelegant designs. "Without inheritance, every class would be a free-standing unit, each developed from the ground up. Different classes would bear no relationship with one another, since the developer of each provides methods in whatever manner he chooses. Any consistency across classes is the result of discipline on the part of the programmers. Inheritance makes it possible to define new software in the same way we introduce any concept to a newcomer, by comparing it with something that is already familiar" [64].

There is a healthy tension among the principles of abstraction, encapsulation, and hierarchy. "Data abstraction attempts to provide an opaque barrier behind which methods and state are hidden; inheritance requires opening this interface to some extent and may allow state as well as methods to be accessed without abstraction" [65]. For a given class, there are usually two kinds of clients: objects that invoke operations on instances of the class and subclasses that inherit from the class. Liskov therefore notes that, with inheritance, encapsulation can be violated in one of three ways: "The subclass might access an instance variable of its superclass, call a private operation of its superclass, or refer directly to superclasses of its superclass" [66]. Different programming languages trade off support for encapsulation and inheritance in different ways. C++ and Java offer great flexibility. Specifically, the interface of a class may have three parts: private parts, which declare members that are accessible only to the class itself; protected parts, which declare members that are accessible only to the class and its subclasses; and public parts, which are accessible to all clients.

Examples of Hierarchy: Multiple Inheritance

The previous example illustrated the use of single inheritance: the subclass `FruitGrowingPlan` had exactly one superclass, the class `GrowingPlan`. For certain abstractions, it is useful to provide inheritance from multiple superclasses.

For example, suppose that we choose to define a class representing a kind of plant. Our analysis of the problem domain might suggest that flowering plants and fruits and vegetables have specialized properties that are relevant to our application. For example, given a flowering plant, its expected time to flower and time to seed might be important to us. Similarly, the time to harvest might be an important part of our abstraction of all fruits and vegetables. One way we could capture our design decisions would be to make two new classes, a `Flower` class and a `FruitVegetable` class, both subclasses of the class `Plant`. However, what if we need to model a plant that both flowered and produced fruit? For example, florists commonly use blossoms from apple, cherry, and plum trees. For this abstraction, we would need to invent a third class, `FlowerFruitVegetable`, that duplicated information from the `Flower` and `FruitVegetable` classes.

A better way to express our abstractions and thereby avoid this redundancy is to use multiple inheritance. First, we invent classes that independently capture the properties unique to flowering plants and to fruits and vegetables. These two classes have no superclass; they stand alone. These are called *mixin classes* because they are meant to be mixed together with other classes to produce new subclasses.

For example, we can define a `Rose` class (see Figure 2–10) that inherits from both `Plant` and `FlowerMixin`. Instances of the subclass `Rose` thus include the structure and behavior from the class `Plant` together with the structure and behavior from the class `FlowerMixin`.

Similarly, a `Carrot` class could be as shown in Figure 2–11. In both cases, we form the subclass by inheriting from two superclasses.

Now, suppose we want to declare a class for a plant such as the cherry tree that has both flowers and fruit. This would be conceptualized as shown in Figure 2–12.

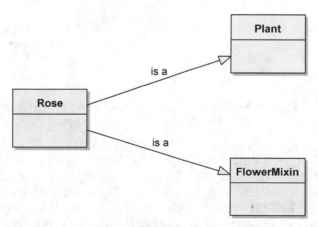

Figure 2–10 The `Rose` Class, Which Inherits from Multiple Superclasses

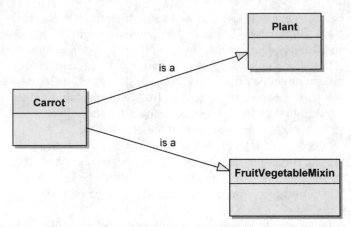

Figure 2–11 The `Carrot` Class, Which Inherits from Multiple Superclasses

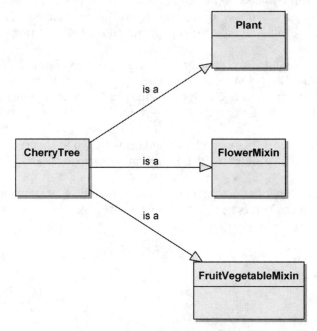

Figure 2–12 The `CherryTree` Class, Which Inherits from Multiple Superclasses

Multiple inheritance is conceptually straightforward, but it does introduce some practical complexities for programming languages. Languages must address two issues: clashes among names from different superclasses and repeated inheritance. Clashes will occur when two or more superclasses provide a field or operation with the same name or signature as a peer superclass.

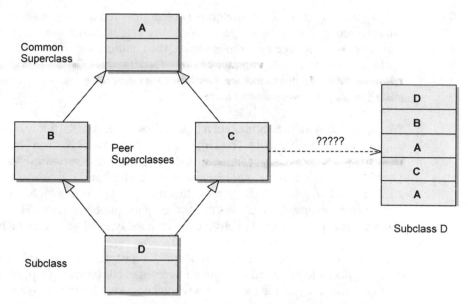

Figure 2–13 The Repeated Inheritance Problem

Repeated inheritance occurs when two or more peer superclasses share a common superclass. In such a situation, the inheritance lattice will be diamond-shaped, so the question arises, does the leaf class (i.e., subclass) have one copy or multiple copies of the structure of the shared superclass? (See Figure 2–13.) Some languages prohibit repeated inheritance, some unilaterally choose one approach, and others, such as C++, permit the programmer to decide. In C++, virtual base classes are used to denote a sharing of repeated structures, whereas nonvirtual base classes result in duplicate copies appearing in the subclass (with explicit qualification required to distinguish among the copies).

Multiple inheritance is often overused. For example, cotton candy is a kind of candy, but it is distinctly not a kind of cotton. Again, the litmus test for inheritance applies: If B is not a kind of A, then B should not inherit from A. Ill-formed multiple inheritance lattices should be reduced to a single superclass plus aggregation of the other classes by the subclass, where possible.

Examples of Hierarchy: Aggregation

Whereas these "is a" hierarchies denote generalization/specialization relationships, "part of" hierarchies describe aggregation relationships. For example, consider the abstraction of a garden. We can contend that a garden consists of a collection of plants together with a growing plan. In other words, plants are "part of" the garden, and the growing plan is "part of" the garden. This "part of" relationship is known as *aggregation*.

Aggregation is not a concept unique to object-oriented development or object-oriented programming languages. Indeed, any language that supports record-like structures supports aggregation. However, the combination of inheritance with aggregation is powerful: Aggregation permits the physical grouping of logically related structures, and inheritance allows these common groups to be easily reused among different abstractions.

When dealing with hierarchies such as these, we often speak of levels of abstraction, a concept first described by Dijkstra [67]. In terms of its "is a" hierarchy, a high-level abstraction is generalized, and a low-level abstraction is specialized. Therefore, we say that a `Flower` class is at a higher level of abstraction than a `Plant` class. In terms of its "part of" hierarchy, a class is at a higher level of abstraction than any of the classes that make up its implementation. Thus, the class `Garden` is at a higher level of abstraction than the type `Plant`, on which it builds.

Aggregation raises the issue of ownership. Our abstraction of a garden permits different plants to be raised in a garden over time, but replacing a plant does not change the identity of the garden as a whole, nor does removing a garden necessarily destroy all of its plants (they are likely just transplanted). In other words, the lifetime of a garden and its plants are independent. In contrast, we have decided that a `GrowingPlan` object is intrinsically associated with a `Garden` object and does not exist independently. Therefore, when we create an instance of `Garden`, we also create an instance of `GrowingPlan`; when we destroy the `Garden` object, we in turn destroy the `GrowingPlan` instance.

The Meaning of Typing

The concept of a type derives primarily from the theories of abstract data types. As Deutsch suggests, "A type is a precise characterization of structural or behavioral properties which a collection of entities all share" [68]. For our purposes, we will use the terms *type* and *class* interchangeably.[2] Although the concepts of a type and a class are similar, we include typing as a separate element of the object

---

2. A type and a class are not exactly the same thing; some languages distinguish these two concepts. For example, early versions of the language Trellis/Owl permitted an object to have both a class and a type. In Smalltalk, objects of the classes `SmallInteger`, `LargeNegativeInteger`, and `LargePositiveInteger` are all of the same type, `Integer`, although not of the same class [69]. For most mortals, however, separating the concepts of type and class is utterly confusing and adds very little value. It is sufficient to say that a class implements a type.

model because the concept of a type places a very different emphasis on the meaning of abstraction. Specifically, we state the following:

> Typing is the enforcement of the class of an object, such that objects of different types may not be interchanged, or at the most, they may be interchanged only in very restricted ways.

Typing lets us express our abstractions so that the programming language in which we implement them can be made to enforce design decisions.

A given programming language may be strongly typed, weakly typed, or even untyped, yet still be called object-oriented. For example, Eiffel is strongly typed, meaning that type conformance is strictly enforced: Operations cannot be called on an object unless the exact signature of that operation is defined in the object's class or superclasses.

The idea of conformance is central to the notion of typing. For example, consider units of measurement in physics [71]. When we divide distance by time, we expect some value denoting speed, not weight. Similarly, dividing a unit of force by temperature doesn't make sense, but dividing force by mass does. These are both examples of strong typing, wherein the rules of our domain prescribe and enforce certain legal combinations of abstractions.

Strong typing prevents mixing of abstractions.

Strong typing lets us use our programming language to enforce certain design decisions and so is particularly relevant as the complexity of our system grows. However, there is a dark side to strong typing. Practically, strong typing introduces semantic dependencies such that even small changes in the interface of a base class require recompilation of all subclasses.

There are two general solutions to these problems. First, we could use a type-safe container class that manipulates only objects of a specific class. This approach addresses the first problem, wherein objects of different types are incorrectly mingled. Second, we could use some form of runtime type identification; this addresses the second problem of knowing what kind of object you happen to be examining at the moment. In general, however, runtime type identification should be used only when there is a compelling reason because it can represent a weakening of encapsulation. As we will discuss in the next section, the use of polymorphic operations can often (but not always) mitigate the need for runtime type identification.

As Tesler points out, there are a number of important benefits to be derived from using strongly typed languages:

- Without type checking, a program in most languages can 'crash' in mysterious ways at runtime.
- In most systems, the edit-compile-debug cycle is so tedious that early error detection is indispensable.
- Type declarations help to document programs.
- Most compilers can generate more efficient object code if types are declared. [72]

Untyped languages offer greater flexibility, but even with untyped languages, as Borning and Ingalls observe, "In almost all cases, the programmer in fact knows what sorts of objects are expected as the arguments of a message, and what sort of object will be returned" [73]. In practice, the safety offered by strongly typed languages usually more than compensates for the flexibility lost by not using an untyped language, especially for programming-in-the-large.

Examples of Typing: Static and Dynamic Typing

The concepts of *strong and weak* typing and *static and dynamic* typing are entirely different. Strong and weak typing refers to *type consistency*, whereas static and dynamic typing refers to the *time* when names are bound to types. Static typing (also known as *static binding* or *early binding*) means that the types of all variables and expressions are fixed at the time of compilation; dynamic typing (also known as *late binding*) means that the types of all variables and expressions are not known until runtime. A language may be both strongly and statically typed (Ada), strongly typed yet supportive of dynamic typing (C++, Java), or untyped yet supportive of dynamic typing (Smalltalk).

Polymorphism is a condition that exists when the features of dynamic typing and inheritance interact. Polymorphism represents a concept in type theory in which a single name (such as a variable declaration) may denote objects of many different classes that are related by some common superclass. Any object denoted by this name is therefore able to respond to some common set of operations [74]. The opposite of polymorphism is *monomorphism*, which is found in all languages that are both strongly and statically typed.

Polymorphism is perhaps the most powerful feature of object-oriented programming languages next to their support for abstraction, and it is what distinguishes object oriented programming from more traditional programming with abstract data types. As we will see in the following chapters, polymorphism is also a central concept in object-oriented design.

The Meaning of Concurrency

For certain kinds of problems, an automated system may have to handle many different events simultaneously. Other problems may involve so much computation that they exceed the capacity of any single processor. In each of these cases, it is natural to consider using a distributed set of computers for the target implementation or to use multitasking. A single process is the root from which independent dynamic action occurs within a system. Every program has at least one thread of control, but a system involving concurrency may have many such threads: some that are transitory and others that last the entire lifetime of the system's execution. Systems executing across multiple CPUs allow for truly concurrent threads of

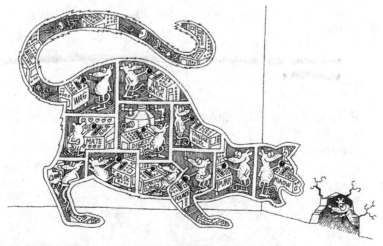

Concurrency allows different objects to act at the same time.

control, whereas systems running on a single CPU can only achieve the illusion of concurrent threads of control, usually by means of some time-slicing algorithm.

We also distinguish between *heavyweight* and *lightweight* concurrency. A heavyweight process is one that is typically independently managed by the target operating system and so encompasses its own address space. A lightweight process usually lives within a single operating system process along with other lightweight processes, which share the same address space. Communication among heavyweight processes is generally expensive, involving some form of interprocess communication; communication among lightweight processes is less expensive and often involves shared data.

Building a large piece of software is hard enough; designing one that encompasses multiple threads of control is much harder because one must worry about such issues as deadlock, livelock, starvation, mutual exclusion, and race conditions. "At the highest levels of abstraction, OOP can alleviate the concurrency problem for the majority of programmers by hiding the concurrency inside reusable abstractions" [76]. Black et al. therefore suggest that "an object model is appropriate for a distributed system because it implicitly defines (1) the units of distribution and movement and (2) the entities that communicate" [77].

Whereas object-oriented programming focuses on data abstraction, encapsulation, and inheritance, concurrency focuses on process abstraction and synchronization [78]. The object is a concept that unifies these two different viewpoints: Each object (drawn from an abstraction of the real world) may represent a separate thread of control (a process abstraction). Such objects are called *active*. In a system based on an object-oriented design, we can conceptualize the world as consisting of a set of cooperative objects, some of which are active and thus serve as centers of independent activity. Given this conception, we define concurrency as follows:

> Concurrency is the property that distinguishes an active object from one that is not active.

Examples of Concurrency

Let's consider a sensor named `ActiveTemperatureSensor`, whose behavior requires periodically sensing the current temperature and then notifying the client whenever the temperature changes a certain number of degrees from a given setpoint. We do not explain how the class implements this behavior. That fact is a secret of the implementation, but it is clear that some form of concurrency is required.

In general, there are three approaches to concurrency in object-oriented design. First, concurrency is an intrinsic feature of certain programming languages, which provide mechanisms for concurrency and synchronization. In this case, we may create an active object that runs some process concurrently with all other active objects.

Second, we may use a class library that implements some form of lightweight processes. Naturally, the implementation of this kind is highly platform-dependent, although the interface to the library may be relatively portable. In this approach, concurrency is not an intrinsic part of the language (and so does not place any burdens on nonconcurrent systems) but appears as if it were intrinsic, through the presence of these standard classes.

Third, we may use interrupts to give us the illusion of concurrency. Of course, this requires that we have knowledge of certain low-level hardware details. For example, in our implementation of the class `ActiveTemperatureSensor`, we might have a hardware timer that periodically interrupts the application, during which time all such sensors read the current temperature and then invoke their callback function as necessary.

No matter which approach to concurrency we take, one of the realities about concurrency is that once you introduce it into a system, you must consider how active objects synchronize their activities with one another as well as with objects that are purely sequential. For example, if two active objects try to send messages to a third object, we must be certain to use some means of mutual exclusion, so that the state of the object being acted on is not corrupted when both active objects try to update its state simultaneously. This is the point where the ideas of abstraction, encapsulation, and concurrency interact. In the presence of concurrency, it is not enough simply to define the methods of an object; we must also make certain that the semantics of these methods are preserved in the presence of multiple threads of control.

The Meaning of Persistence

An object in software takes up some amount of space and exists for a particular amount of time. Atkinson et al. suggest that there is a continuum of object existence, ranging from transitory objects that arise within the evaluation of an expression to objects in a database that outlive the execution of a single program. This spectrum of object persistence encompasses the following:

- Transient results in expression evaluation
- Local variables in procedure activations
- Own variables [as in ALGOL 60], global variables, and heap items whose extent is different from their scope
- Data that exists between executions of a program
- Data that exists between various versions of a program
- Data that outlives the program [79]

Traditional programming languages usually address only the first three kinds of object persistence; persistence of the last three kinds is typically the domain of database technology. This leads to a clash of cultures that sometimes results in very strange architectures: Programmers end up crafting ad hoc schemes for storing objects whose state must be preserved between program executions, and database designers misapply their technology to cope with transient objects [80].

An interesting variant of Atkinson et al.'s "Data that outlives the program" is the case of Web applications where the application may not be connected to the data it is using through the entire transaction execution. What changes may happen to data provided to a client application or Web service while disconnected to the data source, and how should resolution of the two be handled? Frameworks like Microsoft's ActiveX Data Object for .NET (ADO.NET) have arisen to help address such distributed, disconnected scenarios.

Unifying the concepts of concurrency and objects gives rise to concurrent object-oriented programming languages. In a similar fashion, introducing the concept of persistence to the object model gives rise to object-oriented databases. In practice, such databases build on proven technology, such as sequential, indexed, hierarchical, network, or relational database models, but then offer to the programmer the abstraction of an object-oriented interface, through which database queries and other operations are completed in terms of objects whose lifetimes transcend the lifetime of an individual program. This unification vastly simplifies the development of certain kinds of applications. In particular, it allows us to apply the same design methods to the database and nondatabase segments of an application.

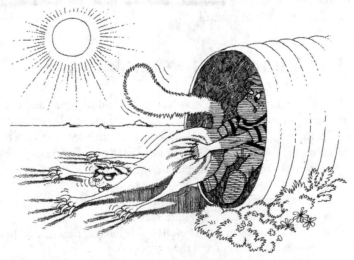

Persistence saves the state and class of an object across time or space.

Some object-oriented programming languages provide direct support for persistence. Java provides Enterprise Java Beans (EJBs) and Java Data Objects. Smalltalk has protocols for streaming objects to and from storage (which must be redefined by subclasses). However, streaming objects to flat files is a naive solution to persistence that does not scale well. Persistence may be achieved through a modest number of commercially available object-oriented databases [81]. A more typical approach to persistence is to provide an object-oriented skin over a relational database. Customized object-relational mappings can be created by the individual developer. However, that is a very challenging task to do well. Frameworks are available to ease this task, such as the open source framework Hibernate [85]. Commercial object-relational mapping software is available. This approach is most appealing when there is a large capital investment in relational database technology that would be risky or too expensive to replace.

Persistence deals with more than just the lifetime of data. In object-oriented databases, not only does the state of an object persist, but its class must also transcend any individual program, so that every program interprets this saved state in the same way. This clearly makes it challenging to maintain the integrity of a database as it grows, particularly if we must change the class of an object.

Our discussion thus far pertains to persistence in time. In most systems, an object, once created, consumes the same physical memory until it ceases to exist. However, for systems that execute on a distributed set of processors, we must sometimes be concerned with persistence across space. In such systems, it is useful to think of objects that can move from machine to machine and that may even have different representations on different machines.

To summarize, we define persistence as follows:

> Persistence is the property of an object through which its existence transcends time (i.e., the object continues to exist after its creator ceases to exist) and/or space (i.e., the object's location moves from the address space in which it was created).

2.4 Applying the Object Model

As we have shown, the object model is fundamentally different from the models embraced by the more traditional methods of structured analysis, structured design, and structured programming. This does not mean that the object model abandons all of the sound principles and experiences of these older methods. Rather, it introduces several novel elements that build on these earlier models. Thus, the object model offers a number of significant benefits that other models simply do not provide. Most importantly, the use of the object model leads us to construct systems that embody the five attributes of well-structured complex systems noted in Chapter 1: hierarchy, relative primitives (i.e., multiple levels of abstraction), separation of concerns, patterns, and stable intermediate forms. In our experience, there are five other practical benefits to be derived from the application of the object model.

Benefits of the Object Model

First, the use of the object model helps us to exploit the expressive power of object-based and object-oriented programming languages. As Stroustrup points out, "It is not always clear how best to take advantage of a language such as C++. Significant improvements in productivity and code quality have consistently been achieved using C++ as 'a better C' with a bit of data abstraction thrown in where it is clearly useful. However, further and noticeably larger improvements have been achieved by taking advantage of class hierarchies in the design process. This is often called object-oriented design and this is where the greatest benefits of using C++ have been found" [82]. Our experience has been that, without the application of the elements of the object model, the more powerful features of languages such as Smalltalk, C++, Java, and so forth are either ignored or greatly misused.

Second, the use of the object model encourages the reuse not only of software but of entire designs, leading to the creation of reusable application frameworks [83]. We have found that object-oriented systems are often smaller than equivalent non-object-oriented implementations. Not only does this mean less code to write and maintain, but greater reuse of software also translates into cost and schedule benefits. However, reuse does not just happen. If reuse is not a primary goal of your project, it is unlikely that it will be achieved. Plus, designing for reuse may cost you more when initially implementing the reusable component. The good news is that the initial cost will be recovered in the subsequent uses of that component.

Third, the use of the object model produces systems that are built on stable intermediate forms, which are more resilient to change. This also means that such systems can be allowed to evolve over time, rather than be abandoned or completely redesigned in response to the first major change in requirements.

Chapter 7, Pragmatics, explains further how the object model reduces the risks inherent in developing complex systems. This fourth benefit accrues primarily because integration is spread out across the lifecycle rather than occurring as one major event. The object model's guidance in designing an intelligent separation of concerns also reduces development risk and increases our confidence in the correctness of our design.

Finally, the object model appeals to the workings of human cognition. As Robson suggests, "Many people who have no idea how a computer works find the idea of object-oriented systems quite natural" [84].

Open Issues

To effectively apply the elements of the object model, we must next address several open issues.

- What exactly are classes and objects?
- How does one properly identify the classes and objects that are relevant to a particular application?
- What is a suitable notation for expressing the design of an object-oriented system?
- What process can lead us to a well-structured object-oriented system?
- What are the management implications of using object-oriented design?

These issues are the themes of the next five chapters.

Summary

- The maturation of software engineering has led to the development of object-oriented analysis, design, and programming methods, all of which address the issues of programming-in-the-large.
- There are several different programming paradigms: procedure-oriented, object-oriented, logic-oriented, rule-oriented, and constraint-oriented.
- An abstraction denotes the essential characteristics of an object that distinguish it from all other kinds of objects and thus provide crisply defined conceptual boundaries, relative to the perspective of the viewer.
- Encapsulation is the process of compartmentalizing the elements of an abstraction that constitute its structure and behavior; encapsulation serves to separate the contractual interface of an abstraction and its implementation.
- Modularity is the property of a system that has been decomposed into a set of cohesive and loosely coupled modules.
- Hierarchy is a ranking or ordering of abstractions.
- Typing is the enforcement of the class of an object, such that objects of different types may not be interchanged or, at the most, may be interchanged only in very restricted ways.

- Concurrency is the property that distinguishes an active object from one that is not active.
- Persistence is the property of an object through which its existence transcends time and/or space.

Chapter 3

Classes and Objects

Both the engineer and the artist must be intimately familiar with the materials of their trade. Oils versus watercolors, steel versus aluminum, bolts versus nails, object versus classes—each of these materials serves similar functions (e.g., bolts and nails are both fasteners), yet each has its own specific properties and uses. The architect may not know the most efficient way to drive a nail (that is a specific skill of the carpenter), but the architect must understand when it is appropriate to use nails or bolts or glue or welds. To ignore such fundamental considerations can yield disastrous results.

When we use object-oriented methods to analyze or design a complex software system, our basic building blocks are classes and objects. Since we have thus far provided only informal definitions of these two elements, in this chapter we turn to a detailed study of the nature of classes, objects, and their relationships, and along the way we provide several rules of thumb for crafting quality abstractions and mechanisms.

3.1 The Nature of an Object

The ability to recognize physical objects is a skill that humans learn at a very early age. A brightly colored ball will attract an infant's attention, but typically, if you hide the ball, the child will not try to look for it; when the object leaves her field of vision, as far as she can determine, it ceases to exist. It is not until near the age of one that a child normally develops what is called the *object concept*, a skill that is of critical importance to future cognitive development. Show a ball to a one-year-old and then hide it, and she will usually search for it even though it is not visible. Through the object concept, a child comes to realize that objects have a permanence and identity apart from any operations on them [1].

What Is and What Isn't an Object

In Chapter 1, we informally defined an object as a tangible entity that exhibits some well-defined behavior. From the perspective of human cognition, an object is any of the following:

- A tangible and/or visible thing
- Something that may be comprehended intellectually
- Something toward which thought or action is directed

We add to our informal definition the idea that an object models some part of reality and is therefore something that exists in time and space. In software, the term *object* was first formally applied in the Simula language; objects typically existed in Simula programs to simulate some aspect of reality [2].

Real-world objects are not the only kinds of objects that are of interest to us during software development. Other important kinds of objects are inventions of the design process whose collaborations with other such objects serve as the mechanisms that provide some higher-level behavior [3]. Jacobson et al. define *control objects* as "the ones that unite courses of events and thus will carry on communication with other objects" [62]. This leads us to the more refined definition of Smith and Tockey, who suggest that "an object represents an individual, identifiable item, unit, or entity, either real or abstract, with a well-defined role in the problem domain" [4].

Consider for a moment a manufacturing plant that processes composite materials for making such diverse items as bicycle frames and airplane wings. Manufacturing plants are often divided into separate shops: mechanical, chemical, electrical, and so forth. Shops are further divided into cells, and in each cell we have some collection of machines, such as die stamps, presses, and lathes. Along a manufacturing line, we might find vats containing raw materials, which are used in a chemical process to produce blocks of composite materials, and which in turn are formed and shaped to produce bicycle frames, airplane wings, and other end items. Each of the tangible things we have mentioned thus far is an object. A lathe has a crisply defined boundary that separates it from the block of composite material it operates on; a bicycle frame has a crisply defined boundary that distinguishes it from the cell of machines that produced the frame itself.

Some objects may have crisp conceptual boundaries yet represent intangible events or processes. For example, a chemical process in a manufacturing plant may be treated as an object because it has a crisp conceptual boundary, interacts with certain other objects through a well-ordered collection of operations that unfolds over time, and exhibits a well-defined behavior. Similarly, consider a CAD/CAM system for modeling solids. Where two solids such as a sphere and a cube intersect, they may form an irregular line of intersection. Although it does not exist apart from the sphere or cube, this line is still an object with crisply defined conceptual boundaries.

An object has state, exhibits some well-defined behavior,
and has a unique identity.

Some objects may be tangible yet have fuzzy physical boundaries. Objects such as rivers, fog, and crowds of people fit this definition.[1] Just as the person holding a hammer tends to see everything in the world as a nail, so the developer with an object-oriented mindset begins to think that everything in the world is an object. This perspective is a little naive because some things are distinctly not objects. For example, attributes such as beauty or color are not objects, nor are emotions such as love and anger. On the other hand, these things are all potentially properties of other objects. For example, we might say that a man (an object) loves his wife (another object), or that a particular cat (yet another object) is gray.

---

1. This is true only at a sufficiently high level of abstraction. To a person walking through a fog bank, it is generally futile to distinguish "my fog" from "your fog." However, consider a weather map: A fog bank over San Francisco is a distinctly different object than a fog bank over London.

Thus, it is useful to say that an object is something that has crisply defined boundaries, but this is not enough to guide us in distinguishing one object from another, nor does it allow us to judge the quality of our abstractions. Our experience therefore suggests the following definition.

> An object is an entity that has state, behavior, and identity. The structure and behavior of similar objects are defined in their common class. The terms *instance* and *object* are interchangeable.

We will consider the concepts of state, behavior, and identity in more detail in the sections that follow.

State

Consider a vending machine that dispenses soft drinks. The usual behavior of such objects is that when someone puts money in a slot and pushes a button to make a selection, a drink emerges from the machine. What happens if a user first makes a selection and then puts money in the slot? Most vending machines just sit and do nothing because the user has violated the basic assumptions of their operation. Stated another way, the vending machine was in a state (of waiting for money) that the user ignored (by making a selection first). Similarly, suppose that the user ignores the warning light that says, "Correct change only," and puts in extra money. Most machines are user-hostile; they will happily swallow the excess money.

In each of these circumstances, we see how the behavior of an object is influenced by its history: The order in which one operates on the object is important. The reason for this event- and time-dependent behavior is the existence of state within the object. For example, one essential state associated with the vending machine is the amount of money currently entered by a user but not yet applied to a selection. Other important properties include the amount of change available and the quantity of soft drinks on hand.

From this example, we may form the following low-level definition.

> The state of an object encompasses all of the (usually static) properties of the object plus the current (usually dynamic) values of each of these properties.

Another property of a vending machine is that it can accept money. This is a static (i.e., fixed) property, meaning that it is an essential characteristic of a vending machine. In contrast, the actual quantity of money accepted at any given moment represents the dynamic value of this property and is affected by the order of operations on the machine. This quantity increases as a user inserts money and then decreases when a product is vended. We say that values are "usually dynamic" because in some cases values are static. For example, the serial number of a vending machine is a static property and value.

A property is an inherent or distinctive characteristic, trait, quality, or feature that contributes to making an object uniquely that object. For example, one essential property of an elevator is that it is constrained to travel up and down and not horizontally. Properties are usually static because attributes such as these are unchanging and fundamental to the nature of the object. We say "usually static" because in some circumstances the properties of an object may change. For example, consider an autonomous robot that can learn about its environment. It may first recognize an object that appears to be a fixed barrier, only to learn later that this object is in fact a door that can be opened. In this case, the object created by the robot as it builds its conceptual model of the world gains new properties as new knowledge is acquired.

All properties have some value. This value might be a simple quantity, or it might denote another object. For example, part of the state of an elevator might have the value 3, denoting the current floor on which the elevator is located. In the case of the vending machine, its state encompasses many other objects, such as a collection of soft drinks. The individual drinks are in fact distinct objects; their properties are different from those of the machine (they can be consumed, whereas a vending machine cannot), and they can be operated on in distinctly different ways. Thus, we distinguish between objects and simple values: Simple quantities such as the number 3 are "atemporal, unchangeable, and non-instantiated," whereas objects "exist in time, are changeable, have state, are instantiated, and can be created, destroyed, and shared" [6].

The fact that every object has state implies that every object takes up some amount of space, be it in the physical world or in computer memory.

We may say that all objects within a system encapsulate some state and that all of the state within a system is encapsulated by objects. Encapsulating the state of an object is a start, but it is not enough to allow us to capture the full intent of the abstractions we discover and invent during development (refer to Example 3–1, which shows how a simple abstraction may evolve). For this reason, we must also consider how objects behave.

Example 3–1

Consider an abstraction of an employee record. Figure 3–1 depicts this abstraction using the Unified Modeling Language notation for a class. (For more on the UML notation, see Chapter 5.)

Each part of this abstraction denotes a particular property of our abstraction of an employee. This abstraction is not an object because it does not represent a

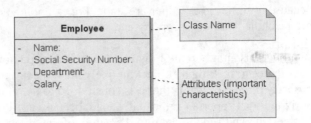

Figure 3–1 `Employee` Class with Attributes

specific instance. When made specific, we may have, for example, two distinct objects: `Tom` and `Kaitlyn`, each of which takes up some amount of space in memory (see Figure 3–2).

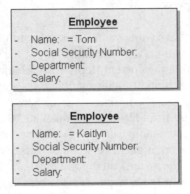

Figure 3–2 Employee Objects `Tom` and `Kaitlyn`

None of these objects shares its space with any other object, although each of them has the same properties; thus, their states have a common representation.

It is good engineering practice to encapsulate the state of an object rather than expose it. For example, we might change the abstraction (class) as shown in Figure 3–3.

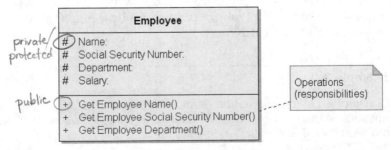

Figure 3–3 `Employee` Class with Protected Attributes and Public Operations

This abstraction is slightly more complicated than the previous one, but it is superior for a number of reasons. Specifically, its internal representation is hidden (protected, indicated by #) from all other outside clients. If we change its representation, we will have to recompile some code, but semantically, no outside client will be affected by this change (in other words, existing code will not break).

Also, we have captured certain decisions about the problem space by explicitly stating some of the operations (responsibilities) that clients may perform on objects of this class. In particular, we grant all clients the (public, indicated by +) right to retrieve the name, social security number, and department of an employee. We will discuss visibility (i.e., public, protected, private, and package) later in this chapter.

Behavior

No object exists in isolation. Rather, objects are acted on and themselves act on other objects. Thus, we may say the following:

> Behavior is how an object acts and reacts, in terms of its state changes and message passing.

In other words, the behavior of an object represents its outwardly visible activity.

An operation is some action that one object performs on another in order to elicit a reaction. For example, a client might invoke the operations append and pop to grow and shrink a queue object, respectively. A client might also invoke the operation length, which returns a value denoting the size of the queue object but does not alter the state of the queue itself.

In Java, operations that clients may perform on an object are typically declared as methods. In languages such as C++, which derive from more procedural ancestors, we speak of one object invoking the member function of another. In pure object-oriented languages such as Smalltalk, we speak of one object passing a message to another. Generally, a message is simply an operation that one object performs on another, although the underlying dispatch mechanisms are different. For our purposes, the terms *operation* and *message* are interchangeable.

Message passing is one part of the equation that defines the behavior of an object; our definition for behavior also notes that the state of an object affects its behavior as well. Consider again the vending machine example. We may invoke some operation to make a selection, but the vending machine will behave differently depending on its state. If we do not deposit change sufficient for our selection, the machine will probably do nothing. If we provide sufficient change, the machine will take our change and then give us our selection (thereby altering its state). Thus, we may say that the behavior of an object is a function of its state as well as the operation performed on it, with certain operations having the side effect of altering the object's state. This concept of side effect thus leads us to refine our definition of state.

The state of an object represents the cumulative results of its behavior.

Most interesting objects do not have state that is static; rather, their state has properties whose values are modified and retrieved as the object is acted on. The behavior of an object is embodied in the sum of its operations. Next we will discuss operations, how they relate to an object's roles, and how they enable objects to meet their responsibilities.

Operations

An operation denotes a service that a class offers to its clients. In practice, we have found that a client typically performs five kinds of operations on an object.[2] The three most common kinds of operations are the following:

- Modifier: an operation that alters the state of an object
- Selector: an operation that accesses the state of an object but does not alter the state
- Iterator: an operation that permits all parts of an object to be accessed in some well-defined order

Two other kinds of operations are common; they represent the infrastructure necessary to create and destroy instances of a class.

- Constructor: an operation that creates an object and/or initializes its state
- Destructor: an operation that frees the state of an object and/or destroys the object itself

In C++, constructors and destructors are declared as part of the definition of a class, whereas in Java there are constructors, but no destructors. In Smalltalk, such operations are typically part of the protocol of a metaclass (i.e., the class of a class).

---

2. Lippman suggests a slightly different categorization: manager functions, implementer functions, helping functions (all kinds of modifiers), and access functions (equivalent to selectors) [7].

Roles and Responsibilities

Collectively, all of the methods associated with a particular object comprise its protocol. The protocol of an object thus defines the envelope of an object's allowable behavior and so comprises the entire static and dynamic view of the object. For most nontrivial abstractions, it is useful to divide this larger protocol into logical groupings of behavior. These collections, which thus partition the behavior space of an object, denote the roles that an object can play. A role is a mask that an object wears [8] and so defines a contract between an abstraction and its clients.

Objects can play many different roles.

"Responsibilities are meant to convey a sense of the purpose of an object and its place in the system. The responsibilities of an object are all the services it provides for all of the contracts it supports" [9]. In other words, we may say that the state and behavior of an object collectively define the roles that an object may play in the world, which in turn fulfill the abstraction's responsibilities.

Indeed, most interesting objects play many different roles during their lifetime. Consider the following examples [10].

- A bank account may have the role of a monetary asset to which the account owner may deposit or withdraw money. However, to a taxing authority, the account may play the role of an entity whose dividends must be reported on annually.

- To a trader, a share of stock represents an entity with value that may be bought or sold; to a lawyer, the same share denotes a legal instrument to which are attached certain rights.
- In the course of one day, the same person may play the role of mother, doctor, gardener, and movie critic.

The roles played by objects are dynamic yet can be mutually exclusive. In the case of the share of stock, its roles overlap slightly, but each role is static relative to the client that interacts with the share. In the case of the person, her roles are quite dynamic and may change from moment to moment.

Objects play many different roles during their lifetimes.

As we will discuss further in later chapters, we often start our analysis of a problem by examining the various roles that an object plays. During design, we refine these roles by inventing the particular operations that carry out each role's responsibilities.

Objects as Machines

The existence of state within an object means that the order in which operations are invoked is important. This gives rise to the idea that each object is like a tiny, independent machine [11]. Indeed, for some objects, this event and time ordering of operations is so pervasive that we can best formally characterize the behavior of such objects in terms of an equivalent finite state machine. In Chapter 5, we will show a particular notation for hierarchical finite state machines that we may use for expressing these semantics.

Continuing the machine metaphor, we may classify objects as either active or passive. An active object is one that encompasses its own thread of control, whereas a passive object does not. Active objects are generally autonomous, meaning that they can exhibit some behavior without being operated on by another object. Passive objects, on the other hand, can undergo a state change only when explicitly acted on. In this manner, the active objects in our system serve as the roots of control. If our system involves multiple threads of control, we will usually have multiple active objects. Sequential systems, on the other hand, usually have exactly one active object, such as a main object responsible for managing an event loop that dispatches messages. In such architectures, all other objects are passive, and their behavior is ultimately triggered by messages from the one active object. In other kinds of sequential system architectures (such as transaction-processing systems), there is no obvious central active object, so control tends to be distributed throughout the system's passive objects.

Identity

Khoshafian and Copeland offer the following definition for identity: "Identity is that property of an object which distinguishes it from all other objects" [12].

They go on to note that "most programming and database languages use variable names to distinguish temporary objects, mixing addressability and identity. Most database systems use identifier keys to distinguish persistent objects, mixing data value and identity." The failure to recognize the difference between the name of an object and the object itself is the source of many kinds of errors in object-oriented programming.

Example 3–2 demonstrates the importance of maintaining the identity of the objects you create and shows how easily the identity can be irrecoverably lost.

Example 3–2

Consider a class that denotes a display item. A display item is a common abstraction in all GUI-centric systems: It represents the base class of all objects that have a visual representation on some window and so captures the structure and behavior common to all such objects. Clients expect to be able to draw, select, and move display items, as well as query their selection state and location. Each display item has a location designated by the coordinates x and y.

Let us assume we instantiate a number of `DisplayItem` classes as indicated in Figure 3–4a. Specifically, the manner in which we instantiate these classes sets aside four locations in memory whose names are `item1`, `item2`, `item3`, and `item4`, respectively. Here, `item1` is the name of a distinct `DisplayItem` object, but the other three names each denote a pointer to a `DisplayItem` object. Only `item2` and `item3` actually point to distinct `DisplayItem` objects (because in their declarations we allocated a new `DisplayItem` object); `item4` designates no such object. Furthermore, the names of the objects pointed to by `item2` and `item3` are anonymous: We can refer to these distinct objects only indirectly, via their pointer value.

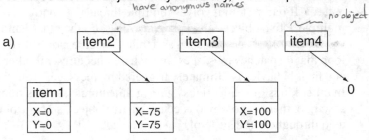

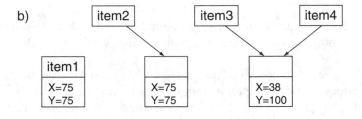

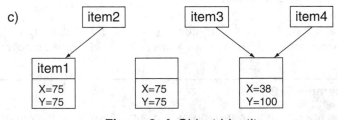

Figure 3–4 Object Identity

The unique identity (but not necessarily the name) of each object is preserved over the lifetime of the object, even when its state is changed. This is like the Zen question about a river: Is a river the same river from one day to the next, even though the same water never flows through it? For example, let's move item1. We can access the object designated by item2, get its location, and move item1 to that same location.

Also, if we equate item4 to item3, we can now reference the object designated by item3 by using item4 also. Using item4 we can then move that object to a new location, say, X=38, Y=100. Figure 3–4b illustrates these results. Here we see that item1 and the object designated by item2 both have the same location state and that item4 now also designates the same object as does item3. Notice that we use the phrase "the object designated by item2" rather than saying "the object item2." The first phrase is more precise, although we will sometimes use these phrases interchangeably.

Although item1 and the object designated by item2 have the same state, they represent distinct objects. Also, note that we have changed the state of the object designated by item3 by operating on it through its new indirect name, item4. This is a situation we call *structural sharing*, meaning that a given object can be named in more than one way; in other words, there are aliases to the object. Structural sharing is the source of many problems in object-oriented programming. Failure to recognize the side effects of operating on an object through aliases often leads to memory leaks, memory-access violations, and, even worse, unexpected state changes. For example, if we destroyed the object designated by item3, then item4's pointer value would be meaningless; this is a situation we call a *dangling reference.*

Consider also Figure 3–4c, which illustrates the results of modifying the value of the item2 pointer to point to item1. Now item2 designates the same object as item1. Unfortunately, we have introduced a memory leak: The object originally designated by item2 can no longer be named, either directly or indirectly, and so its identity is lost. In languages such as Smalltalk and Java, such objects will be garbage-collected and their storage reclaimed automatically, but in languages such as C++, their storage will not be reclaimed until the program that created them finishes. Especially for long-running programs, memory leaks such as this are either bothersome or disastrous.[3]

---

3. Consider the effects of a memory leak in software controlling a satellite or a pacemaker. Restarting the computer in a satellite several million miles away from earth is quite inconvenient. Similarly, the unpredictable occurrence of automatic garbage collection in a pacemaker's software is likely to be fatal. For these reasons, real-time system developers often steer away from the unrestrained allocation of objects on the heap.

3.2 Relationships among Objects

An object by itself is intensely uninteresting. Objects contribute to the behavior of a system by collaborating with one another. "Instead of a bit-grinding processor raping and plundering data structures, we have a universe of well-behaved objects that courteously ask each other to carry out their various desires" [13]. For example, consider the object structure of an airplane, which has been defined as "a collection of parts having an inherent tendency to fall to earth, and requiring constant effort and supervision to stave off that outcome" [14]. Only the collaborative efforts of all the component objects of an airplane enable it to fly.

The relationship between any two objects encompasses the assumptions that each makes about the other, including what operations can be performed and what behavior results. We have found that two kinds of object relationships are of particular interest in object-oriented analysis and design, namely:

1. Links
2. Aggregation

Links

The term *link* derives from Rumbaugh et al., who define it as a "physical or conceptual connection between objects" [16]. An object collaborates with other objects through its links to these objects. Stated another way, a link denotes the specific association through which one object (the client) applies the services of another object (the supplier), or through which one object may navigate to another.

Figure 3–5 illustrates several different links. In this figure, a line between two object icons represents the existence of a link between the two and means that messages may pass along this path. Messages are shown as small directed lines representing the direction of the message, with a label naming the message itself. For example, in Figure 3–5 we show part of a simplified flow control system. This may be controlling the flow of water through a pipe in a manufacturing plant. You can see that the `FlowController` object has a link to a `Valve` object. The `Valve` object has a link to the `DisplayPanel` object in which its status will be displayed. Only across these links may one object send messages to another.

Message passing between two objects is typically unidirectional, although it may occasionally be bidirectional. In our example, the `FlowController` object

invokes operations on the `Valve` object (to change its setting) and the
`DisplayPanel` (to change what it displays), but these objects do not themselves operate on the `FlowController` object. This separation of concerns is
quite common in well-structured object-oriented systems. Notice also that
although message passing is initiated by the client (such as `FlowController`)
and is directed toward the supplier (such as the `Valve` object), data may flow in
either direction across a link. For example, when `FlowController` invokes
the operation `adjust` on the `Valve` object, data (i.e., the setting to change to)
flows from the client to the supplier. However, if `FlowController` invokes a
different operation, `isClosed`, on the `Valve` object, the result (i.e., whether
the valve is in the fully closed position) passes from the supplier to the client.

As a participant in a link, an object may play one of three roles.

1. Controller: This object can operate on other objects but is not operated on
    by other objects. In some contexts, the terms *active object* and *controller* are
    interchangeable.
2. Server: This object doesn't operate on other objects; it is only operated on
    by other objects.
3. Proxy: This object can both operate on other objects and be operated on by
    other objects. A proxy is usually created to represent a real-world object in
    the domain of the application.

the communicator

In the context of Figure 3–5, `FlowController` acts as a controller object,
`DisplayPanel` acts as a server object, and `Valve` acts as a proxy. Example 3–3
illustrates how responsibilities can be properly separated across a group of collaborating objects.

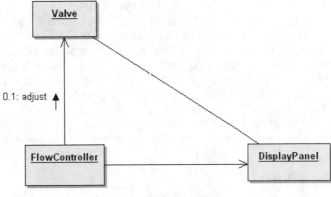

Figure 3–5 Links

Example 3–3

In many different kinds of industrial processes, certain reactions require a temperature ramp, wherein we raise the temperature of some substance, hold it at that temperature for a fixed period, and then let it cool to ambient temperature. Different processes require different profiles: Some objects (such as telescope mirrors) must be cooled slowly, whereas other materials (such as steel) must be cooled rapidly. This abstraction of a temperature ramp has a sufficiently well-defined behavior that it warrants the creation of a class. Thus we provide the class `TemperatureRamp`, which is conceptually a time/temperature mapping (see Figure 3–6).

Actually, the behavior of this abstraction is more than just a literal time/temperature mapping. For example, we might set a temperature ramp that requires the temperature to be 250°F at time 60 (one hour into the temperature ramp) and 150°F at time 180 (three hours into the process), but then we would like to know what the temperature should be at time 120. This requires linear interpolation, which is therefore another behavior (i.e., interpolate) we expect of this abstraction.

One behavior we explicitly do not require of this abstraction is the control of a heater to carry out a particular temperature ramp. Rather, we prefer a greater separation of concerns, wherein this behavior is achieved through the collaboration of three objects: a temperature ramp instance, a heater, and a temperature controller (see Figure 3–6). The operation `process` provides the central behavior of this abstraction; its purpose is to carry out the given temperature ramp for the heater at the given location.

A comment regarding our style: At first glance, it may appear that we have devised an abstraction whose sole purpose is to wrap a functional decomposition inside a class to make it appear noble and object-oriented. The operation `schedule` suggests that this is not the case. Objects of the class `TemperatureController` have sufficient knowledge to determine when a particular profile should be scheduled, so we expose this operation as an additional behavior of our abstraction. In some high-energy industrial processes (such as steel making), heating a substance is a costly event, and it is important to take into account any lingering heat from a previous process, as well as the normal cool-down of an unattended heater. The operation `schedule` exists so that clients can query a `TemperatureController` object to determine the next optimal time to process a particular temperature ramp.

Visibility

Consider two objects, A and B, with a link between the two. In order for A to send a message to B, B must be visible to A in some manner. During our analysis of a problem, we can largely ignore issues of visibility, but once we begin to devise concrete implementations, we must consider the visibility across links because our decisions here dictate the scope and access of the objects on each side of a link. We will discuss this further later in this chapter.

Synchronization

Whenever one object passes a message to another across a link, the two objects are said to be synchronized. For objects in a completely sequential application, this synchronization is usually accomplished by simple method invocation. However, in the presence of multiple threads of control, objects require more sophisticated message passing in order to deal with the problems of mutual exclusion that can occur in concurrent systems. As we described earlier, active objects embody their own thread of control, so we expect their semantics to be guaranteed in the presence of other active objects. However, when one active object has a link to a passive one, we must choose one of three approaches to synchronization.

1. Sequential: The semantics of the passive object are guaranteed only in the presence of a single active object at a time.
2. Guarded: The semantics of the passive object are guaranteed in the presence of multiple threads of control, but the active clients must collaborate to achieve mutual exclusion.
3. Concurrent: The semantics of the passive object are guaranteed in the presence of multiple threads of control, and the supplier guarantees mutual exclusion.

Aggregation

Whereas links denote peer-to-peer or client/supplier relationships, aggregation denotes a whole/part hierarchy, with the ability to navigate from the whole (also called the *aggregate*) to its parts. In this sense, aggregation is a specialized kind of association. For example, as shown in Figure 3–6, the object Temperature-Controller has a link to the object TemperatureRamp as well as to Heater. The object TemperatureController is thus the whole, and Heater is one of its parts. The notation shown for an aggregation relationship will be further explained in Chapter 5.

By implication, an object that is a part of another object has a link to its aggregate. Across this link, the aggregate may send messages to its parts. Given the object TemperatureController, it is possible to find its corresponding Heater. Given an object such as Heater, it is possible to navigate to its enclosing object (also called its *container*) if and only if this knowledge is a part of the state of Heater.

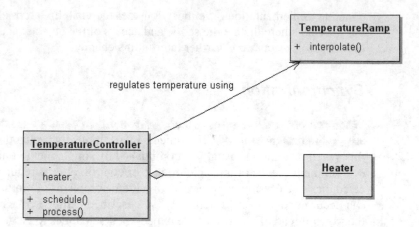

Figure 3–6
Aggregation

Aggregation may or may not denote physical containment. For example, an airplane is composed of wings, engines, landing gear, and so on: This is a case of physical containment. On the other hand, the relationship between a shareholder and his or her shares is an aggregation relationship that does not require physical containment. The shareholder uniquely owns shares, but the shares are by no means a physical part of the shareholder. Rather, this whole/part relationship is more conceptual and therefore less direct than the physical aggregation of the parts that form an airplane.

There are clear trade-offs between links and aggregation. Aggregation is sometimes better because it encapsulates parts as secrets of the whole. Links are sometimes better because they permit looser coupling among objects. Intelligent engineering decisions require careful weighing of these two factors.

3.3 The Nature of a Class

The concepts of a class and an object are tightly interwoven, for we cannot talk about an object without regard for its class. However, there are important differences between these two terms.

What Is and What Isn't a Class

Whereas an object is a concrete entity that exists in time and space, a class represents only an abstraction, the "essence" of an object, as it were. Thus, we may speak of the class Mammal, which represents the characteristics common to all mammals. To identify a particular mammal in this class, we must speak of "this mammal" or "that mammal."

In everyday terms, *Webster's Third New International Dictionary* defines a class as "a group, set, or kind marked by common attributes or a common attribute; a group division, distinction, or rating based on quality, degree of competence, or condition" [17].

In the context of object-oriented analysis and design, we define a class as follows:

> A class is a set of objects that share a common structure, common behavior, and common semantics.

A single object is simply an instance of a class.

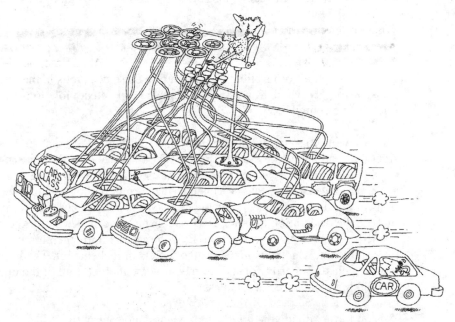

A class represents a set of objects that share a common structure and a common behavior.

What isn't a class? An object is not a class. Objects that share no common structure and behavior cannot be grouped in a class because, by definition, they are unrelated except by their general nature as objects.

It is important to note that the class—as defined by most programming languages—is a necessary but insufficient vehicle for decomposition. Sometimes abstractions are so complex that they cannot be conveniently expressed in terms of a single class declaration. For example, at a sufficiently high level of abstraction, a GUI framework, a database, and an entire inventory system are all conceptually individual objects, none of which can be expressed as a single class.[4] Instead, it is far better for us to capture these abstractions as a cluster of classes whose instances collaborate to provide the desired structure and behavior. Stroustrup calls such a cluster a component [18].

Interface and Implementation

Meyer [19] and Snyder [20] have both suggested that programming is largely a matter of "contracting": The various functions of a larger problem are decomposed into smaller problems by subcontracting them to different elements of the design. Nowhere is this idea more evident than in the design of classes.

Whereas an individual object is a concrete entity that performs some role in the overall system, the class captures the structure and behavior common to all related objects. Thus, a class serves as a sort of binding contract between an abstraction and all of its clients. By capturing these decisions in the interface of a class, a strongly typed programming language can detect violations of this contract during compilation.

This view of programming as contracting leads us to distinguish between the outside view and the inside view of a class. The interface of a class provides its outside view and therefore emphasizes the abstraction while hiding its structure and the secrets of its behavior. This interface primarily consists of the declarations of all the operations applicable to instances of this class, but it may also include the declaration of other classes, constants, variables, and exceptions as needed to complete the abstraction. By contrast, the implementation of a class is its inside view, which encompasses the secrets of its behavior. The implementation of a class primarily consists of the implementation of all of the operations defined in the interface of the class.

We can further divide the interface of a class into four parts:

1. Public: a declaration that is accessible to all clients
2. Protected: a declaration that is accessible only to the class itself and its subclasses

---

4. One might be tempted to express such abstractions in a single class, but the granularity for reuse and change is too coarse. Having a "fat" interface is bad practice because most clients will want to reference only a small subset of the services provided. Furthermore, changing one part of a huge interface obsolesces every client, even those that don't care about the parts that changed. Nesting classes doesn't eliminate these problems; it only defers them.

3. **Private:** a declaration that is accessible only to the class itself
4. **Package:** a declaration that is accessible only by classes in the same package

The detailed semantics of these forms of visibility can vary based on the implementation language used.

Visibility and Friendship

Different programming languages provide different mixtures of public, protected, private, and package parts, which developers can choose among to establish specific access rights for each part of a class's interface and thereby exercise control over what clients can see and what they can't see (i.e., visibility).

In particular, C++ allows a developer to make explicit distinctions among all four of these different parts.[5] The C++ *friendship* mechanism permits a class to distinguish certain privileged classes that are given the rights to see the class's protected and private parts. Friendships break a class's encapsulation and so, as in life, must be chosen carefully. Java does not have friendship. Instead, Java has a somewhat similar type of visibility called *package access*, where all classes in the same package can access each other. Aside from friendship, public, protected, and private access operate in Java as they do in C++. By contrast, Ada permits declarations to be public or private but not protected. In Smalltalk, all instance variables are private, and all methods are public. In Object Pascal, both fields and operations are public and hence unencapsulated.

The constants and variables that form the representation of a class are known by various terms, depending on the particular language we use. For example, Smalltalk uses the term *instance variable*, Object Pascal and Java use the term *field*, C++ uses the term *data member*. We will use these terms interchangeably to denote the parts of a class that serve as the representation of its instance's state.

The state of an object must have some representation in its corresponding class and so is typically expressed as constant and variable declarations placed in the protected or private part of a class's interface. In this manner, the representation common to all instances of a class is encapsulated, and changes to this representation do not functionally affect any outside clients.

---

5. The C++ `struct` is a special case, in the sense that a `struct` is a kind of class with all of its elements public.

Class Lifecycle

We may come to understand the behavior of a simple class just by understanding the semantics of its distinct public operations in isolation. However, the behavior of more interesting classes (such as moving an instance of the class `DisplayItem` or scheduling an instance of the class `TemperatureController`) involves the interaction of their various operations over the lifetime of each of their instances. As described earlier in this chapter, the instances of such classes act as little machines, and since all such instances embody the same behavior, we can use the class to capture these common event- and time-ordered semantics. As we discuss in Chapter 5, we may describe such dynamic behavior for certain interesting classes by using finite state machines.

3.4 Relationships among Classes

Consider for a moment the similarities and differences among the following classes of objects: flowers, daisies, red roses, yellow roses, petals, and ladybugs. We can make the following observations.

- A daisy is a kind of flower.
- A rose is a (different) kind of flower.
- Red roses and yellow roses are both kinds of roses.
- A petal is a part of both kinds of flowers.
- Ladybugs eat certain pests such as aphids, which may be infesting certain kinds of flowers.

From this simple example we conclude that classes, like objects, do not exist in isolation. Rather, for a particular problem domain, the key abstractions are usually related in a variety of interesting ways, forming the class structure of our design [21].

We establish relationships between two classes for one of two reasons. First, a class relationship might indicate some sort of sharing. For example, daisies and roses are both kinds of flowers, meaning that both have brightly colored petals, both emit a fragrance, and so on. Second, a class relationship might indicate some kind of semantic connection. Thus, we say that red roses and yellow roses are more alike than are daisies and roses, and daisies and roses are more closely related than are petals and flowers. Similarly, there is a symbiotic connection between ladybugs and flowers: Ladybugs protect flowers from certain pests, which in turn serve as a food source for the ladybug.

In all, there are three basic kinds of class relationships [22]. The first of these is generalization/specialization, denoting an "is a" relationship. For instance, a rose is a kind of flower, meaning that a rose is a specialized subclass of the more general class, flower. The second is whole/part, which denotes a "part of" relationship. Thus, a petal is not a kind of a flower; it is a part of a flower. The third is association, which denotes some semantic dependency among otherwise unrelated classes, such as between ladybugs and flowers. As another example, roses and candles are largely independent classes, but they both represent things that we might use to decorate a dinner table.

Association

Of these different kinds of class relationships, associations are the most general but also the most semantically weak. The identification of associations among classes is often an activity of analysis and early design, at which time we begin to discover the general dependencies among our abstractions. As we continue our design and implementation, we will often refine these weak associations by turning them into one of the other more concrete class relationships.

Semantic Dependencies

As Example 3–4 suggests, an association only denotes a semantic dependency and does not state the direction of this dependency (unless otherwise stated, an association implies bidirectional navigation, as in our example), nor does it state the exact way in which one class relates to another (we can only imply these semantics by naming the role each class plays in relationship with the other). However, these semantics are sufficient during the analysis of a problem, at which time we need only to identify such dependencies. Through the creation of associations, we come to capture the participants in a semantic relationship, their roles, and their cardinality.

Example 3–4

For a vehicle, two of our key abstractions include the vehicle and wheels. As shown in Figure 3–7, we may show a simple association between these two classes: the class `Wheel` and the class `Vehicle`. (Arguably, an aggregation would be better.) By implication, this association suggests bidirectional navigation. Given an instance of `Wheel`, we should be able to locate the object denoting its `Vehicle`, and given an instance of `Vehicle`, we should be able to locate all the wheels.

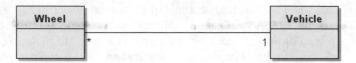

Figure 3–7 Association

Here we show a one-to-many association: Each instance of `Wheel` relates to one `Vehicle`, and each instance of `Vehicle` may have many `Wheels` (noted by the *).

Multiplicity

Our example introduced a one-to-many association, meaning that for each instance of the class `Vehicle`, there are zero (a boat, which is a vehicle, has no wheels) or more instances of the class `Wheel`, and for each `Wheel`, there is exactly one `Vehicle`. This denotes the multiplicity of the association. In practice, there are three common kinds of multiplicity across an association:

1. One-to-one
2. One-to-many
3. Many-to-many

A one-to-one relationship denotes a very narrow association. For example, in retail telemarketing operations, we would find a one-to-one relationship between the class `Sale` and the class `CreditCardTransaction`: Each sale has exactly one corresponding credit card transaction, and each such transaction corresponds to one sale. Many-to-many relationships are also common. For example, each instance of the class `Customer` might initiate a transaction with several instances of the class `SalesPerson`, and each such salesperson might interact with many different customers. As we will discuss further in Chapter 5, there are variations on these three common forms of multiplicity.

Inheritance

Inheritance, perhaps the most semantically interesting of these concrete relationships, exists to express generalization/specialization relationships. In our experience, however, inheritance is an insufficient means of expressing all of the rich relationships that may exist among the key abstractions in a given problem domain. An alternate approach to inheritance involves a language mechanism called *delegation*, in which objects delegate their behavior to related objects.

Example 3–5

After space probes are launched, they report back to ground stations with information regarding the status of important subsystems (such as electrical power and propulsion systems) and different sensors (such as radiation sensors, mass spectrometers, cameras, micrometeorite collision detectors, and so on). Collectively, this relayed information is called *telemetry data*. Telemetry data is commonly transmitted as a bitstream consisting of a header, which includes a timestamp and some keys identifying the kind of information that follows, plus several frames of processed data from the various subsystems and sensors. This appears to be a straightforward aggregation of different kinds of data.

This critical data needs to be encapsulated. Otherwise, there is nothing to prevent a client from changing the value of important data such as `timestamp` or `currentPower`. Likewise, the representation of this data is exposed, so if we were to change the representation (e.g., by adding new elements or changing the bit alignment of existing ones), every client would be affected. At the very least, we would certainly have to recompile every reference to this structure. More importantly, such changes might violate the assumptions that clients had made about this representation and cause the logic in our program to break.

Lastly, suppose our analysis of the system's requirements reveals the need for several hundred different kinds of telemetry data, including electrical data that encompassed the preceding information and also included voltage readings from various test points throughout the system. We would find that declaring these additional structures would create a considerable amount of redundancy, in terms of both replicated structures and common functions.

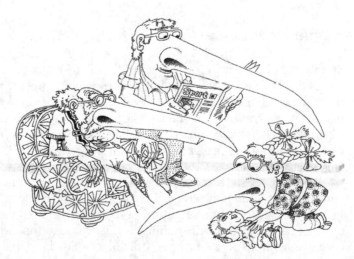

A subclass may inherit the structure and behavior of its superclass.

A slightly better way to capture our decisions would be to declare one class for each kind of telemetry data. In this manner, we could hide the representation of each class and associate its behavior with its data. Still, this approach does not address the problem of redundancy.

A far better solution, therefore, is to capture our decisions by building a hierarchy of classes, in which specialized classes inherit the structure and behavior defined by more generalized classes, as shown in Figure 3–8.

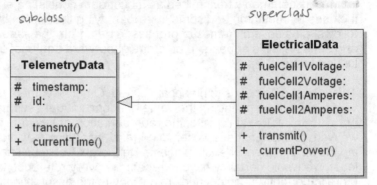

Figure 3–8 `ElectricalData` Inherits from the Superclass `TelemetryData`

As for the class `ElectricalData`, this class inherits the structure and behavior of the class `TelemetryData` but adds to its structure (the additional voltage data), redefines its behavior (the function `transmit`) to transmit the additional data, and can even add to its behavior (the function `currentPower`, a function to provide the current power level).

Single Inheritance

Simply stated, inheritance is a relationship among classes wherein one class shares the structure and/or behavior defined in one (single inheritance) or more (multiple inheritance) other classes. We call the class from which another class inherits its *superclass*. In Example 3–5, `TelemetryData` is a superclass of `ElectricalData`. Similarly, we call a class that inherits from one or more classes a *subclass*; `ElectricalData` is a subclass of `TelemetryData`. Inheritance therefore defines an "is a" hierarchy among classes, in which a subclass inherits from one or more superclasses. This is in fact the litmus test for inheritance. Given classes A and B, if A is not a kind of B, then A should not be a subclass of B. In this sense, `ElectricalData` is a specialized kind of the more generalized class `TelemetryData`. The ability of a language to support this kind of inheritance distinguishes object-oriented from object-based programming languages.

A subclass typically augments or restricts the existing structure and behavior of its superclasses. A subclass that augments its superclasses is said to use inheritance for extension. For example, the subclass `GuardedQueue` might extend the behavior of its superclass `Queue` by providing extra operations that make instances of this class safe in the presence of multiple threads of control. In contrast, a subclass that constrains the behavior of its superclasses is said to use inheritance for restriction. For example, the subclass `UnselectableDisplayItem` might constrain the behavior of its superclass, `DisplayItem,` by prohibiting clients from selecting its instances in a view. In practice, it is not always so clear whether or not a subclass augments or restricts its superclass; in fact, it is common for a subclass to do both.

Figure 3–9 illustrates the single inheritance relationships deriving from the superclass `TelemetryData`. Each directed line denotes an "is a" relationship. For example, `CameraData` "is a" kind of `SensorData`, which in turn "is a" kind of `TelemetryData`.

This is identical to the hierarchy one finds in a semantic net, a tool often used by researchers in cognitive science and artificial intelligence to organize knowledge about the world [25]. Indeed, as we discuss further in Chapter 4, designing a suitable inheritance hierarchy among abstractions is largely a matter of intelligent classification.

We expect that some of the classes in Figure 3–9 will have instances and some will not. For example, we expect to have instances of each of the most specialized classes (also known as *leaf classes* or *concrete classes*), such as `ElectricalData` and `SpectrometerData`. However, we are not likely to have any instances of the intermediate, more generalized classes, such as `SensorData` or even `TelemetryData`. Classes with no instances are called *abstract classes*. An abstract class is written with the expectation that its subclasses will add to its structure and behavior, usually by completing the implementation of its (typically) incomplete methods.

There is a very real tension between inheritance and encapsulation. To a large degree, the use of inheritance exposes some of the secrets of an inherited class. Practically, this means that to understand the meaning of a particular class, you must often study all of its superclasses, sometimes including their inside views.

Inheritance means that subclasses inherit the structure of their superclass. Thus, in Example 3–5, the instances of the class `ElectricalData` include the data members of the superclass (such as `id` and `timestamp`), as well as those of the more specialized classes (such as `fuelCell1Voltage, fuelCell2Voltage, fuelCell1Amperes, and fuelCell2Amperes`).

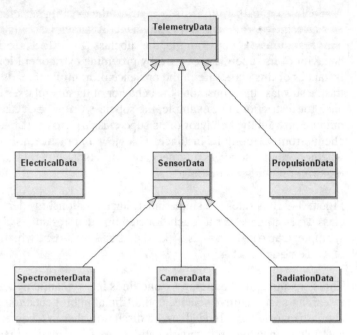

Figure 3–9 Single Inheritance

Subclasses also inherit the behavior of their superclasses. Thus, instances of the class ElectricalData may be acted on with the operations currentTime (inherited from its superclass), currentPower (defined in the class itself), and transmit (redefined in the subclass).

Polymorphism

For the class TelemetryData, the function transmit may transmit the identifier of the telemetry stream and its timestamp. But the same function for the class ElectricalData may invoke the TelemetryData transmit function and also transmit its voltage and current values.

This behavior is due to polymorphism. In a generalization, such operations are called *polymorphic*. Polymorphism is a concept in type theory wherein a name may denote instances of many different classes as long as they are related by some common superclass. Any object denoted by this name is thus able to respond to some common set of operations in different ways. With polymorphism, an operation can be implemented differently by the classes in the hierarchy. In this manner, a subclass can extend the capabilities of its superclass or override the parent's operation, as ElectricalData does in Example 3–5.

The concept of polymorphism was first described by Strachey [29], who spoke of ad hoc polymorphism, by which symbols such as + could be defined to mean different things. We call this concept *overloading*. In C++, one may declare functions having the same names, as long as their invocations can be distinguished by their signatures, consisting of the number and types of their arguments (in C++, unlike Ada, the type of a function's returned value is not considered in overload resolution). By contrast, Java does not permit overloaded operators. Strachey also spoke of parametric polymorphism, which today we simply call polymorphism.

Without polymorphism, the developer ends up writing code consisting of large case or switch statements.[6] Without it, we cannot create a hierarchy of classes for the various kinds of telemetry data; rather, we have to define a single, monolithic variant record encompassing the properties associated with all the kinds of data. To distinguish one variant from another, we have to examine the tag associated with the record.

To add another kind of telemetry data, we would have to modify the variant record and add it to every case statement that operated on instances of this record. This is particularly error-prone and, furthermore, adds instability to the design.

In the presence of inheritance, there is no need for a monolithic type since we may separate different kinds of abstractions. As Kaplan and Johnson note, "Polymorphism is most useful when there are many classes with the same protocols" [30]. With polymorphism, large case statements are unnecessary because each object implicitly knows its own type.

Inheritance without polymorphism is possible, but it is certainly not very useful.

Polymorphism and late binding go hand in hand. In the presence of polymorphism, the binding of a method to a name is not determined until execution. In C++, the developer may control whether a member function uses early or late binding. Specifically, if the method is declared as virtual, then late binding is employed, and the function is considered to be polymorphic. If this virtual declaration is omitted, then the method uses early binding and thus can be resolved at the time of compilation. Java simply performs late binding without the need for an explicit declaration such as `virtual`. How an implementation selects a particular method for execution is described in the sidebar, Invoking a Method.

---

6. This is in fact the litmus test for polymorphism. The existence of a switch statement that selects an action based on the type of an object is often a warning sign that the developer has failed to apply polymorphic behavior effectively.

Invoking a Method

In traditional programming languages, invoking a subprogram is a completely static activity. In Pascal, for example, for a statement that calls the subprogram P, a compiler will typically generate code that creates a new stack frame, places the proper arguments on the stack, and then changes the flow of control to begin executing the code associated with P. However, in languages that support some form of polymorphism, such as Smalltalk and C++, invoking an operation may require a dynamic activity because the class of the object being operated on may not be known until runtime. Matters are even more interesting when we add inheritance to the situation. The semantics of invoking an operation in the presence of inheritance without polymorphism is largely the same as for a simple static subprogram call, but in the presence of polymorphism, we must use a much more sophisticated technique.

Consider the class hierarchy in Figure 3–10, which shows the base class DisplayItem along with three subclasses named Circle, Triangle, and Rectangle. Rectangle also has one subclass, named SolidRectangle. In the class DisplayItem, suppose that we define the instance variable theCenter (denoting the coordinates for the center of the displayed item), along with the following operations as in our earlier example:

- draw   Draw the item.
- move   Move the item.
- location   Return the location of the item.

The operation location is common to all subclasses and therefore need not be redefined, but we expect the operations draw and move to be redefined since only the subclasses know how to draw and move themselves.

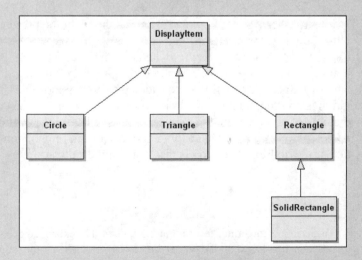

Figure 3–10 DisplayItem Class Diagram

The class `Circle` must include the instance variable `theRadius` and appropriate operations to `set` and `retrieve` its value. For this subclass, the redefined operation `draw` draws a circle of the given radius, centered on `theCenter`. Similarly, the class `Rectangle` must include the instance variables `theHeight` and `theWidth`, along with appropriate operations to `set` and `retrieve` their values. For this subclass, the operation `draw` draws a rectangle with the given height and width, again centered on `theCenter`. The subclass `SolidRectangle` inherits all characteristics of the class `Rectangle` but again redefines the behavior of the operation `draw`. Specifically, the implementation of `draw` for the class `SolidRectangle` first calls `draw` as defined in its superclass `Rectangle` (to draw the outline of the rectangle) and then fills in the shape. The invocation of `draw` demands polymorphic behavior.

Suppose now that we have some client object that wishes to draw all of the subclasses. In this situation, the compiler cannot statically generate code to invoke the proper `draw` operation because the class of the object being operated on is not known until runtime. Let's consider how various object-oriented programming languages deal with this situation.

Because Smalltalk is a typeless language, method dispatch is completely dynamic. When the client sends the message `draw` to an item found in the list, here is what happens.

- The item object looks up the message in its class's message dictionary.
- If the message is found, the code for that locally defined method is invoked.
- If the message is not found, the search for the method continues in the superclass.

This process continues up the superclass hierarchy until the message is found or until we reach the topmost base class, `Object`, without finding the message. In the latter case, Smalltalk ultimately passes the message `doesNotUnderstand` to signal an error.

The key to this algorithm is the message dictionary, which is part of each class's representation and is therefore hidden from the client. This dictionary is created when the class is created and contains all the methods to which instances of this class may respond. Searching for the message is time-consuming; method lookup in Smalltalk takes about 1.5 times as long as a simple subprogram call. All production-quality Smalltalk implementations optimize method dispatch by supplying a cached message dictionary, so that commonly passed messages may be invoked quickly. Caching typically improves performance by 20% to 30% [31].

The operation `draw` defined in the subclass `SolidRectangle` poses a special case. We said that its implementation of `draw` first calls `draw` as defined in the superclass `Rectangle`. In Smalltalk, we specify a superclass method by using the keyword `super`. Then, when we pass the message `draw` to `super`, Smalltalk uses the same method-dispatch algorithm as mentioned earlier, except that the search begins in the superclass of the object instead of its class.

Studies by Deutsch suggest that polymorphism is not needed about 85% of the time, so message passing can often be reduced to simple procedure calls [32]. Duff notes that in such cases, the developer often makes implicit assumptions that permit an early binding of the object's class [33]. Unfortunately, typeless languages such as Smalltalk have no convenient means for communicating these implicit assumptions to the compiler.

More strongly typed languages such as C++ do let the developer assert such information. Because we want to avoid method dispatch wherever possible but must still allow for the occurrence of polymorphic dispatch, invoking a method in these languages proceeds a little differently than in Smalltalk.

In C++, the developer can decide whether a particular operation is to be bound late by declaring it to be `virtual`; all other methods are considered to be bound early, and thus the compiler can statically resolve the method call to a simple subprogram call.

To handle virtual member functions, most C++ implementations use the concept of a *vtable*, which is defined for each object requiring polymorphic dispatch, when the object is created (and thus when the class of the object is fixed). This table typically consists of a list of pointers to virtual functions. For example, if we create an object of the class `Rectangle`, then the vtable will have an entry for the virtual function `draw`, pointing to the closest implementation of `draw`. If, for example, the class `DisplayItem` included the virtual function `Rotate`, which was not redefined in the class `Rectangle`, then the vtable entry for `Rotate` would point to the implementation of `Rotate` in the class `DisplayItem`. In this manner, runtime searching is eliminated: Referring to a virtual member function of an object is just an indirect reference through the appropriate pointer, which immediately invokes the correct code without searching [34].

Multiple Inheritance

With single inheritance, each subclass has exactly one superclass. However, as Vlissides and Linton point out, although single inheritance is very useful, "it often forces the programmer to derive from one of two equally attractive classes. This limits the applicability of predefined classes, often making it necessary to duplicate code. For example, there is no way to derive a graphic that is both a circle and a picture; one must derive from one or the other and reimplement the functionality of the class that was excluded" [40].

Consider for a moment how one might organize various assets such as savings accounts, real estate, stocks, and bonds. Savings accounts and checking accounts are both kinds of assets typically managed by a bank, so we might classify both of them as kinds of bank accounts, which in turn are kinds of assets. Stocks and bonds are managed quite differently than bank accounts, so we might classify stocks, bonds, mutual funds, and the like as kinds of securities, which in turn are also kinds of assets.

However, there are many other equally satisfactory ways to classify savings accounts, real estate, stocks, and bonds. For example, in some contexts, it may be useful to distinguish insurable items such as real estate and certain bank accounts (which, in the United States, are insured up to certain limits by the Federal Deposit Insurance Corporation). It may also be useful to identify assets that return a dividend or interest, such as savings accounts, checking accounts, and certain stocks and bonds.

Unfortunately, single inheritance is not expressive enough to capture this lattice of relationships, so we must turn to multiple inheritance.[7] Figure 3–11 illustrates such a class structure. Here we see that the class `Security` is a kind of `Asset` as well as a kind of `InterestBearingItem`. Similarly, the class `BankAccount` is a kind of `Asset`, as well as a kind of `InsurableItem` and `InterestBearingItem`.

Designing a suitable class structure involving inheritance, and especially involving multiple inheritance, is a difficult task. This is often an incremental and iterative process. Two problems present themselves when we have multiple inheritance: How do we deal with name collisions from different superclasses, and how do we handle repeated inheritance?

Name collisions are possible when two or more different superclasses use the same name for some element of their interfaces, such as instance variables and methods. For example, suppose that the classes `InsurableItem` and `Asset` both have attributes named `presentValue`, denoting the present value of the item. Since the class `RealEstate` inherits from both of these classes, what does

---

7. In fact, this is the litmus test for multiple inheritance. If we encounter a class lattice wherein the leaf classes can be grouped into sets denoting orthogonal behavior (such as insurable and interest-bearing items), and these sets overlap, this is an indication that, within a single inheritance lattice, no intermediate classes exist to which we can cleanly attach these behaviors without violating our abstraction of certain leaf classes by granting them behaviors that they should not have. We can remedy this situation by using multiple inheritance to mix in these behaviors only where we want them.

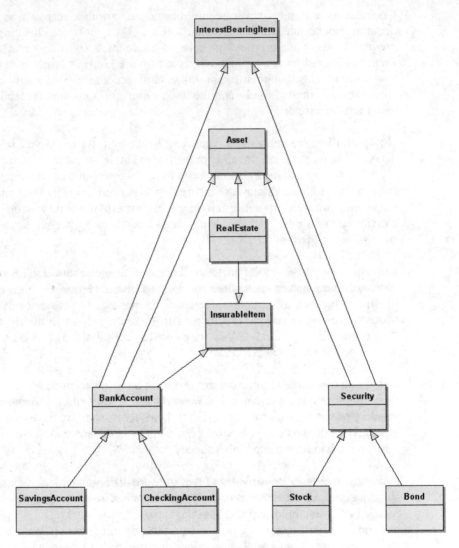

Figure 3–11 Multiple Inheritance

it mean to inherit two operations with the same name? This in fact is the key difficulty with multiple inheritance: Clashes may introduce ambiguity in the behavior of the multiply inherited subclass.

There are three basic approaches to resolving this kind of clash. First, the language semantics might regard such a clash as illegal and reject the compilation of the class. Second, the language semantics might regard the same name introduced by different classes as referring to the same attribute. Third, the language semantics might permit the clash but require that all references to the name fully qualify the source of its declaration.

P2   The second problem is repeated inheritance, which Meyer describes as follows: "One of the delicate problems raised by the presence of multiple inheritance is what happens when a class is an ancestor of another in more than one way. If you allow multiple inheritance into a language, then sooner or later someone is going to write a class D with two parents B and C, each of which has a class A as a parent—or some other situation in which D inherits twice (or more) from A. This situation is called repeated inheritance and must be dealt with properly" [41]. As an example, suppose that we define the (ill-conceived) MutualFund class as a subclass of the classes Stock and Bond. This class introduces repeated inheritance of the class Security, which is a superclass of both Stock and Bond (see Figure 3–11).

S2   There are various approaches to dealing with the problem of repeated inheritance. First, we can treat occurrences of repeated inheritance as illegal. Second, we can permit duplication of superclasses but require the use of fully qualified names to refer to members of a specific copy. Third, we can treat multiple references to the same class as denoting the same class. Different languages handle this approach differently.

The existence of multiple inheritance gives rise to a style of classes called *mixins*. Mixins derive from the programming culture surrounding the language Flavors: One would combine (mix in) little classes to build classes with more sophisticated behavior. "A mixin is syntactically identical to a regular class, but its intent is different. The purpose of such a class is solely to . . . [add] functions to other flavors [classes]—one never creates an instance of a mixin" [44]. In Figure 3–11, the classes InsurableItem and InterestBearingItem are mixins. Neither of these classes can stand alone; rather, they are used to augment the meaning of some other class. Thus, we may define a mixin as a class that embodies a single, focused behavior and is used to augment the behavior of some other class via inheritance. The behavior of a mixin is usually completely orthogonal to the behavior of the classes with which it is combined. A class that is constructed primarily by inheriting from mixins and does not add its own structure or behavior is called an *aggregate class*.

Aggregation

We also need aggregation relationships, which provide the whole/part relationships manifested in the class's instances. Aggregation relationships among classes have a direct parallel to aggregation relationships among the objects corresponding to these classes.

So if A is destroyed, B will be destroyed too

A

TemperatureController

part of Temp Cont

B

Heater

Figure 3–12 Aggregation

As we show in Figure 3–12, the class `TemperatureController` denotes the whole, and the class `Heater` is one of its parts. This corresponds exactly to the aggregation relationship among the instances of these classes illustrated earlier in Figure 3–6.

Physical Containment

In the case of the class `TemperatureController`, we have aggregation as containment by value, a kind of physical containment meaning that the `Heater` object does not exist independently of its enclosing `TemperatureController` instance. Rather, the lifetimes of these two objects are intimately connected: When we create an instance of `TemperatureController`, we also create an instance of the class `Heater`. When we destroy our `TemperatureController` object, by implication we also destroy the corresponding `Heater` object.

A less direct kind of aggregation is also possible, called *composition*, which is containment by reference. In this case, the class `TemperatureController` still denotes the whole, and an instance of the class `Heater` is still one of its parts, although that part must now be accessed indirectly. Hence, the lifetimes of these two objects are not so tightly coupled as before: We may create and destroy instances of each class independently.

A → B True
B → A False

Aggregation asserts a direction to the whole/part relationship. For example, the `Heater` object is a part of the `TemperatureController` object, and not vice versa. Of course, as we described in an earlier example, aggregation need not require physical containment. For example, although shareholders own stocks, a shareholder does not physically contain the owned stocks. Rather, the lifetimes of these objects may be completely independent, although there is still conceptually a whole/part relationship (each share is always a part of the shareholder's assets). Representation of this aggregation can be very indirect.

This is still aggregation, although not physical containment. Ultimately, the litmus test for aggregation is this: If and only if there exists a whole/part relationship between two objects, we must have an aggregation relationship between their corresponding classes.

Multiple inheritance is often confused with aggregation. When considering inheritance versus aggregation, remember to apply the litmus test for each. If you cannot honestly affirm that there is an "is a" relationship between two classes, aggregation or some other relationship should be used instead of inheritance.

Dependencies

Aside from inheritance, aggregation, and association, there is another group of relationships called *dependencies*. A dependency indicates that an element on one end of the relationship, in some manner, depends on the element on the other end of the relationship. This alerts the designer that if one of these elements changes, there could be an impact to the other. There are many different kinds of dependency relationships (refer to the Object Management Group's latest UML specification for the full list [45]). You will often see dependencies used in architectural models (one system component, or package, is dependent on another) or at the implementation level (one module is dependent on another).

3.5 The Interplay of Classes and Objects

Classes and objects are separate yet intimately related concepts. Specifically, every object is the instance of some class, and every class has zero or more instances. For practically all applications, classes are static; therefore, their existence, semantics, and relationships are fixed prior to the execution of a program. Similarly, the class of most objects is static, meaning that once an object is created, its class is fixed. In sharp contrast, however, objects are typically created and destroyed at a furious rate during the lifetime of an application.

Relationships between Classes and Objects

For example, consider the classes and objects in the implementation of an air traffic control system. Some of the more important abstractions include planes, flight plans, runways, and air spaces. By their very definition, the meanings of these classes and objects are relatively static. They must be static, for otherwise one could not build an application that embodied knowledge of such commonsense facts as that planes can take off, fly, and then land, and that two planes should not occupy the same space at the same time. Conversely, the instances of these classes are dynamic. At a fairly slow rate, new runways are built, and old ones are deactivated. Faster yet, new flight plans are filed, and old ones are filed away. With great frequency, new planes enter a particular air space, and old ones leave.

The Role of Classes and Objects in Analysis and Design

During analysis and the early stages of design, the developer has two primary tasks:

1. Identify the classes that form the vocabulary of the problem domain
2. Invent the structures whereby sets of objects work together to provide the behaviors that satisfy the requirements of the problem

Collectively, we call such classes and objects the *key abstractions* of the problem, and we call these cooperative structures the *mechanisms* of the implementation.

During these phases of development, the developer must focus on the outside view of these key abstractions and mechanisms. This view represents the logical framework of the system and therefore encompasses the class structure and object structure of the system. In the later stages of design and then moving into implementation, the task of the developer changes: The focus is on the inside view of these key abstractions and mechanisms, involving their physical representation.

3.6 On Building Quality Classes and Objects

Ingalls suggests that "a system should be built with a minimum set of unchangeable parts; those parts should be as general as possible; and all parts of the system should be held in a uniform framework" [51]. With object-oriented development, these parts are the classes and objects that make up the key abstractions of the system, and the framework is provided by its mechanisms.

In our experience, the design of classes and objects is an incremental, iterative process. Frankly, except for the most trivial abstractions, we have never been able to define a class exactly right the first time. It takes time to smooth the conceptual jagged edges of our initial abstractions. Of course, there is a cost to refining these abstractions, in terms of recompilation, understandability, and the integrity of the fabric of our system design. Therefore, we want to come as close as we can to being right the first time.

Measuring the Quality of an Abstraction

How can one know if a given class or object is well designed? We suggest five meaningful metrics:

less coupling and more cohesion

5 metrics to check if class / object is well designed

1. Coupling
2. Cohesion
3. Sufficiency
4. Completeness
5. Primitiveness

Coupling is a notion borrowed from structured design, but with a liberal interpretation it also applies to object-oriented design. Stevens, Myers, and Constantine define coupling as "the measure of the strength of association established by a connection from one module to another. Strong coupling complicates a system since a module is harder to understand, change, or correct by itself if it is highly interrelated with other modules. Complexity can be reduced by designing systems with the weakest possible coupling between modules" [52]. A counterexample to good coupling is given by Page-Jones in his description of a modular stereo system in which the power supply is located in one of the speaker cabinets [53].

Coupling with regard to modules still applies to object-oriented analysis and design, but coupling with regard to classes and objects is equally important. However, there is tension between the concepts of coupling and inheritance because inheritance introduces significant coupling. On the one hand, weakly coupled classes are desirable; on the other hand, inheritance—which tightly couples superclasses and their subclasses—helps us to exploit the commonality among abstractions.

The idea of cohesion also comes from structured design. Simply stated, cohesion measures the degree of connectivity among the elements of a single module (and for object-oriented design, a single class or object). The least desirable form of cohesion is coincidental cohesion, in which entirely unrelated abstractions are thrown into the same class or module. For example, consider a class comprising the abstractions of dogs and spacecraft, whose behaviors are quite unrelated. The most desirable form of cohesion is functional cohesion, in which the elements of a class or module all work together to provide some well-bounded behavior. Thus, the class Dog is functionally cohesive if its semantics embrace the behavior of a dog, the whole dog, and nothing but the dog.

Closely related to the ideas of coupling and cohesion are the criteria that a class or module should be sufficient, complete, and primitive. By sufficient, we mean that the class or module captures enough characteristics of the abstraction to permit meaningful and efficient interaction. To do otherwise renders the component useless. For example, if we are designing the class Set, it is wise to include an operation that removes an item from the set, but our wisdom is futile if we neglect an operation that adds an item. In practice, violations of this characteristic are detected very early; such shortcomings rise up almost every time we build a client that must use this abstraction.

By complete, we mean that the interface of the class or module captures all of the meaningful characteristics of the abstraction. Whereas sufficiency implies a minimal interface, a complete interface is one that covers all aspects of the abstraction. A complete class or module is thus one whose interface is general enough to be commonly usable to any client. Completeness is a subjective matter, and it can be overdone. Providing all meaningful operations for a particular abstraction overwhelms the user and is generally unnecessary since many high-level operations can be composed from low-level ones. For this reason, we also suggest that classes and modules be primitive.

Primitive operations are those that can be efficiently implemented only if given access to the underlying representation of the abstraction. Thus, adding an item to a set is primitive because to implement this operation Add, the underlying representation must be visible. On the other hand, an operation that adds four items to a set is not primitive because it can be implemented just as efficiently on the more primitive Add operation, without having access to the underlying representation. Of course, efficiency is also a subjective measure. An operation is indisputably primitive if we can implement it only through access to the underlying representation. An operation that could be implemented on top of existing primitive operations, but at the cost of significantly more computational resources, is also a candidate for inclusion as a primitive operation.

Choosing Operations

Crafting the interface of a class or module is plain hard work. Typically, we make a first attempt at the design of a class, and then, as we and others create clients, we find it necessary to augment, modify, and further refine this interface. Eventually, we may discover patterns of operations or patterns of abstractions that lead us to invent new classes or to reorganize the relationships among existing ones.

We often can identify patterns of abstraction, structure, or behavior.

Functional Semantics

Within a given class, it is our style to keep all operations primitive, so that each exhibits a small, well-defined behavior. We call such methods *fine-grained*. We also tend to separate methods that do not communicate with one another. In this manner, it is far easier to construct subclasses that can meaningfully redefine the behavior of their superclasses. The decision to contract out a behavior to one versus many methods may be made for two competing reasons: Lumping a particular behavior in one method leads to a simpler interface but larger, more complicated methods; spreading a behavior across methods leads to a more complicated interface but simpler methods. As Meyer observes, "A good designer knows how to find the appropriate balance between too much contracting, which produces fragmentation, and too little, which yields unmanageably large modules" [54].

It is common in object-oriented development to design the methods of a class as a whole because all these methods cooperate to form the entire protocol of the abstraction. Thus, given some desired behavior, we must decide in which class to place it. Halbert and O'Brien offer the following criteria to be considered when making such a decision [55].

- Reusability: Would this behavior be more useful in more than one context?
- Complexity: How difficult is it to implement the behavior?
- Applicability: How relevant is the behavior to the type in which it might be placed?
- Implementation knowledge: Does the behavior's implementation depend on the internal details of a type?

We usually choose to declare the meaningful operations that we may perform on an object as methods in the definition of that object's class (or superclass).

Time and Space Semantics

Once we have established the existence of a particular operation and defined its functional semantics, we must decide on its time and space semantics. This means that we must specify our decisions about the amount of time it takes to complete an operation and the amount of storage it needs. Such decisions are often expressed in terms of best, average, and worst cases, with the worst case specifying an upper limit on what is acceptable.

Earlier, we also mentioned that whenever one object passes a message to another across a link, the two objects must be synchronized in some manner. In the presence of multiple threads of control, this means that message passing is much more than a subprogram-like dispatch. In most of the languages we use, synchronization among objects is simply not an issue because our programs contain exactly one thread of control, meaning that all objects are sequential. We speak of message passing in such situations as simple because its semantics are most akin to simple subprogram calls. However, in languages that support concurrency, we must concern ourselves with more sophisticated forms of message passing, so as to avoid the problems created if two threads of control act on the same object in unrestrained ways. As we described earlier, objects whose semantics are preserved in the presence of multiple threads of control are either guarded or synchronized objects.

Choosing Relationships

Choosing the relationships among classes and among objects is linked to the selection of operations. If we decide that object X sends message M to object Y, then either directly or indirectly, Y must be accessible to X; otherwise, we could not name the operation M in the implementation of X. By accessible, we mean the ability of one abstraction to see another and reference resources in its outside view. Abstractions are accessible to one another only where their scopes overlap and only where access rights are granted (e.g., private parts of a class are accessible only to the class itself and its friends). Coupling is thus a measure of the degree of accessibility.

The Law of Demeter

One useful guideline in choosing the relationships among objects is called the Law of Demeter, which states that "the methods of a class should not depend in any way on the structure of any class, except the immediate (top-level) structure of their own class. Further, each method should send messages to objects belonging to a very limited set of classes only" [56]. The basic effect of applying this law is the creation of loosely coupled classes, whose implementation secrets are encapsulated. Such classes are fairly unencumbered, meaning that to understand the meaning of one class, you need not understand the details of many other classes.

In looking at the class structure of an entire system, we may find that its inheritance hierarchy is wide and shallow, narrow and deep, or balanced. Class structures that are wide and shallow usually represent forests of free-standing classes that can be mixed and matched [57]. Class structures that are narrow and deep represent trees of classes that are related by a common ancestor [58]. There are advantages and disadvantages to each approach. Forests of classes are more loosely coupled, but they may not exploit all the commonality that exists. Trees of classes exploit this commonality, so that individual classes are smaller than in forests. However, to understand a particular class, it is usually necessary to understand the meaning of all the classes it inherits from or uses. The proper shape of a class structure is highly problem-dependent.

We must make similar trade-offs among inheritance, aggregation, and dependency relationships. For example, should the class Car inherit, contain, or use the classes named Engine and Wheel? In this case, we suggest that an aggregation relationship is more appropriate than an inheritance relationship. Meyer states that between the classes A and B, "inheritance is appropriate if every instance of B may also be viewed as an instance of A. The client relationship is appropriate when every instance of B simply possesses one or more attributes of A" [59]. From another perspective, if the behavior of an object is more than the sum of its individual parts, creating an aggregation relationship rather than an inheritance relationship between the appropriate classes is probably superior.

Mechanisms and Visibility

Deciding on the relationship among objects is mainly a matter of designing the mechanisms whereby these objects interact. The question the developer must ask is simply this: Where does certain knowledge go? For example, in a manufacturing plant, materials (called lots) enter manufacturing cells to be processed. As they enter certain cells, we must notify the room's manager to take appropriate action. We now have a design choice: Is the entry of a lot into a room an operation on the room, an operation on the lot, or an operation on both? If we decide that it is an operation on the room, the room must be visible to the lot. If we decide that it is an operation on the lot, the lot must be visible to the room because the lot must know what room it is in. Lastly, if we consider this to be an operation on both the room and the lot, we must arrange for mutual visibility. We must also decide on some visibility relationship between the room and the manager (and not the lot and the manager); either the manager must know the room it manages, or the room must know of its manager.

Choosing Implementations

Only after we stabilize the outside view of a given class or object do we turn to its inside view. This perspective involves two different decisions: a choice of representation for a class or object and the placement of the class or object in a module.

Representation

The representation of a class or object should almost always be one of the encapsulated secrets of the abstraction. This makes it possible to change the representation (e.g., to alter the time and space semantics) without violating any of the functional assumptions that clients may have made. As Wirth wisely states, "The choice of representation is often a fairly difficult one, and it is not uniquely determined by the facilities available. It must always be taken in light of the operations that are to be performed upon the data" [60]. For example, given a class whose objects denote a set of flight-plan information, do we optimize the representation for fast searching or for fast insertion and deletion? We cannot optimize for both, so our choice must be based on the expected use of these objects. Sometimes it is not easy to choose, and we end up with families of classes whose interfaces are virtually identical but whose implementations are radically different, in order to provide different time and space behavior.

One of the more difficult trade-offs when selecting the implementation of a class is between computing the value of an object's state versus storing it as a field. For example, suppose we have the class Cone, which includes the method Volume. Invoking this method returns the volume of the object. As part of the representation of this class, we are likely to use fields for the height of the cone and the radius of its base. Should we have an additional field in which we store the volume of the object, or should the method Volume just calculate it every time [61]? If we want this method to be fast, we should store the volume as a field. If space efficiency is more important to us, we should calculate the value. Which representation is better depends entirely on the particular problem. In any case, we should be able to choose an implementation independently of the class's outside view; indeed, we should even be able to change this representation without its clients caring.

Packaging

Similar issues apply to the declaration of classes and objects within modules. The competing requirements of visibility and information hiding usually guide our design decisions about where to declare classes and objects. Generally, we seek to build functionally cohesive, loosely coupled modules. Many nontechnical factors influence these decisions, such as matters of reuse, security, and documentation. Like the design of classes and objects, module design is not to be taken lightly. As Parnas, Clements, and Weiss note with regard to information hiding, "Applying this principle is not always easy. It attempts to minimize the expected cost of software over its period of use and requires that the designer estimate the likelihood of changes. Such estimates are based on past experience and usually require knowledge of the application area as well as an understanding of hardware and software technology" [63].

Summary

- An object has state, behavior, and identity.
- The structure and behavior of similar objects are defined in their common class.
- The state of an object encompasses all of the (usually static) properties of the object plus the current (usually dynamic) values of each of these properties.
- Behavior is how an object acts and reacts in terms of its state changes and message passing.
- Identity is the property of an object that distinguishes it from all other objects.
- A class is a set of objects that share a common structure and a common behavior.
- The three kinds of relationships include association, inheritance, and aggregation.
- Key abstractions are the classes and objects that form the vocabulary of the problem domain.
- A mechanism is a structure whereby a set of objects work together to provide a behavior that satisfies some requirement of the problem.
- The quality of an abstraction may be measured by its coupling, cohesion, sufficiency, completeness, and primitiveness.

Chapter 4

Classification

Classification is the means whereby we order knowledge. In object-oriented design, recognizing the sameness among things allows us to expose the commonality within key abstractions and mechanisms and eventually leads us to smaller applications and simpler architectures. Unfortunately, there is no golden path to classification. To the reader accustomed to finding cookbook answers, we unequivocally state that there are no simple recipes for identifying classes and objects. There is no such thing as the "perfect" class structure, nor the "right" set of objects. As in any engineering discipline, our design choices are a compromise shaped by many competing factors.

Fortunately, there exists a vast legacy of experience with classification in other disciplines. From more classical approaches, techniques of object-oriented analysis have emerged that offer several useful recommended practices and rules of thumb for identifying the classes and objects relevant to a particular problem. These heuristics are the focus of this chapter.

4.1 The Importance of Proper Classification

The identification of classes and objects is a challenging part of object-oriented analysis and design. Our experience shows that identification involves both discovery and invention. Through discovery, we come to recognize the key abstractions and mechanisms that form the vocabulary of our problem domain. Through invention, we devise generalized abstractions as well as new mechanisms that specify how objects collaborate. Ultimately, discovery and invention are both problems of classification, and classification is fundamentally a problem of finding sameness. When we classify, we seek to group things that have a common structure or exhibit a common behavior.

Intelligent classification is actually a part of all good science. As Michalski and Stepp observe, "An omnipresent problem in science is to construct meaningful classifications of observed objects or situations. Such classifications facilitate human comprehension of the observations and the subsequent development of a scientific theory" [2]. The same philosophy applies to engineering. In the domain of building architecture and city planning, Alexander notes that, for the architect, "his act of design, whether humble, or gigantically complex, is governed entirely by the patterns he has in his mind at that moment, and his ability to combine these patterns to form a new design" [3]. Not surprisingly, then, classification is relevant to every aspect of object-oriented design.

Classification helps us to identify generalization, specialization, and aggregation hierarchies among classes. By recognizing the common patterns of interaction among objects, we come to invent the mechanisms that serve as the soul of our implementation. Classification also guides us in making decisions about modularization. We may choose to place certain classes and objects together in the same module or in different modules, depending on the sameness we find among these declarations. Coupling and cohesion also indicate a type of sameness. Classification also plays a role in allocating processes to processors. We place certain processes together in the same processor or different processors, depending on packaging, performance, or reliability concerns.

The Difficulty of Classification

In the previous chapter, we defined an object as something that has a crisply defined boundary. However, the boundaries that distinguish one object from another are often quite fuzzy. For example, look at your leg. Where does your knee begin, and where does it end? In recognizing human speech, how do we know that certain sounds connect to form a word and are not instead a part of any surrounding words? Consider also the design of a word processing system. Do characters constitute a class, or are whole words a better choice? How do we treat arbitrary, noncontiguous selections of text? Also, what about sentences, paragraphs, or even whole documents: Are these classes of objects relevant to our problem?

The fact that intelligent classification is difficult is hardly new information. Since there are parallels to the same problems in object-oriented design, consider for a moment the problems of classification in two other scientific disciplines: biology and chemistry.

Until the eighteenth century, the prevailing scientific thought was that all living organisms could be arranged from the most simple to the most complex, with the measure of complexity being highly subjective (not surprisingly, humans were usually placed at the top of this list). In the mid-1700s, however, the Swedish botanist Carolus Linnaeus suggested a more detailed taxonomy for categorizing organisms, according to what he called *genus* and *species*.

A century later, Darwin proposed the theory that natural selection was the mechanism of evolution, whereby present-day species evolved from older ones. Darwin's theory depended on an intelligent classification of species. As Darwin himself states, naturalists "try to arrange the species, genera, and families in each class, on what is called the natural system. But what is meant by this system? Some authors look at it merely as a scheme for arranging together those living objects which are most alike, and for separating those which are most unlike" [4]. In contemporary biology, classification denotes "the establishment of a hierarchical system of categories on the basis of presumed natural relationships among organisms" [5]. The most general category in a biological taxonomy is the kingdom, followed in order of increasing specialization, by phylum, subphylum, class, order, family, genus, and, finally, species.

To a computer scientist, biology may seem to be a stodgily mature discipline, with well-defined criteria for classifying organisms. This is simply not the case. "Surprisingly, scientists have a better understanding of how many stars there are

Classification is the means whereby we order knowledge.

in the galaxy than how many species there are on Earth. Estimates of global species diversity have varied from 2 million to 100 million species, with a best estimate of somewhere near 10 million, and only 1.4 million have actually been named" [65]. Furthermore, different criteria for classifying the same organisms yield different results. Martin suggests that "it all depends on what you want classification to do. If you want it to reflect precisely the genetic relatedness among species, that will give you one answer. But if you want it instead to say something about levels of adaptation, then you will get another" [8]. The moral here is that even in scientifically rigorous disciplines, classification is highly dependent on the reason for the classification.

Similar lessons may be learned from chemistry [9]. In ancient times, all substances were thought to be some combination of earth, air, fire, and water. By today's standards (unless you are an alchemist), these do not represent very good classifications. In the mid-1600s, the chemist Robert Boyle proposed that elements were the primitive abstractions of chemistry, from which more complex compounds could be made. It wasn't until over a century later, in 1789, that the chemist Lavoisier published the first list of elements, containing some 23 items, some of which were later discovered not to be elements at all. The discovery of new elements continued and the list grew, but finally, in 1869, the chemist Mendeleyev proposed the periodic law that gave a precise criteria for organizing all known elements and could predict the properties of those yet undiscovered. The periodic law was not the final story in the classification of the elements. In the early 1900s, elements with similar chemical properties but different atomic weights were discovered, leading to the idea of isotopes of elements.

The lesson here is simple: As Descartes states, "The discovery of an order is no easy task. . . . yet once the order has been discovered there is no difficulty at all in knowing it" [10]. The best software designs look simple, but as experience shows, it takes a lot of hard work to design a simple architecture.

The Incremental and Iterative Nature of Classification

We have not said all this to defend lengthy software development schedules, although to the manager or end user, it does sometimes seem that software engineers need centuries to complete their work. Rather, we have told these stories to point out that intelligent classification is intellectually hard work and that it best comes about through an incremental and iterative process. As Shaw has observed, in software engineering, "The development of individual abstractions often follows a common pattern. First, problems are solved ad hoc. As experience accumulates, some solutions turn out to work better than others, and a sort of folklore is passed informally from person to person. Eventually, the useful solutions are understood more systematically, and they are codified and analyzed. This enables the development of models that support automatic implementation and theories that allow the generalization of the solution. This in turn enables a more sophisticated level of practice and allows us to tackle harder problems—which we often approach *ad hoc*, starting the cycle over again" [11].

Different observers will classify the same object in different ways.

The incremental and iterative nature of classification directly impacts the construction of class and object hierarchies in the design of a complex software system. In practice, it is common to assert a certain class structure early in a design and then revise this structure over time. At later stages in the design, once clients have been built that use this structure, we will obtain insights as to the quality of our classification. On the basis of this experience, we may decide to create new subclasses from existing ones (derivation). We may split a large class into several smaller ones (factorization), or create one larger class by uniting smaller ones (composition). Occasionally, we may even discover previously unrecognized commonality and proceed to devise a new class (abstraction) [12].

Why, then, is classification so hard? We suggest that there are two important reasons. First, there is no such thing as a "perfect" classification, although certainly some classifications are better than others. As Coombs, Raiffa, and Thrall state, "There are potentially at least as many ways of dividing up the world into object systems as there are scientists to undertake the task" [13]. Any classification is relative to the perspective of the observer doing the classification. Second, intelligent classification requires a tremendous amount of creative insight. Birtwistle, Dahl, Myhrhaug, and Nygard observe that "sometimes the answer is evident, sometimes it is a matter of taste, and at other times, the selection of suitable components is a crucial point in the analysis" [15]. This fact recalls the riddle, "Why is a laser beam like a goldfish? . . . because neither one can whistle" [16]. Only a creative mind can find sameness among such otherwise unrelated things.

4.2 Identifying Classes and Objects

The problem of classification has been the concern of countless philosophers, linguists, cognitive scientists, and mathematicians since before the time of Plato. It is reasonable to study their experiences and apply what we learn to object-oriented design.

Classical and Modern Approaches

Historically, there have been only three general approaches to classification:

1. Classical categorization
2. Conceptual clustering
3. Prototype theory [17]

Classical Categorization

In the classical approach to categorization, "All the entities that have a given property or collection of properties in common form a category. Such properties are necessary and sufficient to define the category" [18]. For example, married people constitute a category: One is either married or not, and the value of this property is sufficient to decide to which group a particular person belongs. On the other hand, tall people do not form a category, unless we can agree to some absolute criteria for what distinguishes the property of tall from short.

Classical categorization comes to us first from Plato, and then from Aristotle through his classification of plants and animals, in which he uses a technique much akin to the contemporary children's game of Twenty Questions (Is it an animal, mineral, or vegetable? Does it have fur or feathers? Can it fly? Does it smell?) [20]. Later philosophers, most notably Aquinas, Descartes, and Locke, adopted this approach. As Aquinas stated, "We can name a thing according to the knowledge we have of its nature from its properties and effects" [21].

The classical approach to categorization is also reflected in modern theories of child development. Piaget observed that around the age of one, a child typically develops the concept of object permanence; shortly thereafter, the child acquires skills in classifying these objects, first using basic categories such as dogs, cats, and toys [22]. Later, the child discovers more general categories (such as animals) and more specific ones (such as beagles) [23].

To summarize, the classical approach uses related properties as the criteria for sameness among objects. Specifically, one can divide objects into disjoint sets depending on the presence or absence of a particular property. Minsky suggests that "the most useful sets of properties are those whose members do not interact too much. This explains the universal popularity of that particular combination of properties: size, color, shape, and substance. Because these attributes scarcely interact at all with one another, you can put them together in any combination whatsoever to make an object that is either large or small, red or green, wooden or glass, and having the shape of a sphere or a cube" [24]. In a general sense, properties may denote more than just measurable characteristics; they may also encompass observable behaviors. For example, the fact that a bird can fly but a fish cannot is one property that distinguishes an eagle from a salmon.

The particular properties that should be considered in a given situation are highly domain-specific. For instance, the color of a car may be important for the purposes of inventory control in an automobile manufacturing plant, but it is not at all relevant to the software that controls the traffic lights within a metropolitan area. This is in fact why we say that there are no absolute measures of classification, although a given class structure may be better suited to one application than another. As James suggests, "No one scheme of classification, more than any other, represents the real structure or order of nature. Nature indifferently submits to any and all divisions which we wish to make among existing things. Some classifications may be more significant than others, but only by reference to our interests, not because they represent reality more accurately or adequately" [25].

Classical categorization permeates much of contemporary Western thought, but, as our earlier example of classifying tall and short people suggests, this approach is not always satisfactory. Kosko observes that "natural categories tend to be messy: Most birds fly, but some do not. Chairs can consist of wood, plastic, or metal and can have almost any number of legs, depending on the whim of the designer. It seems practically impossible to come up with a property list for any natural category that excludes all examples that are not in the category and includes all examples that are in the category" [26]. These are indeed fundamental problems for classical categorization, which conceptual clustering and prototype theory attempt to resolve.

Conceptual Clustering

Conceptual clustering is a more modern variation of the classical approach and largely derives from attempts to explain how knowledge is represented. As Stepp and Michalski state, "In this approach, classes (clusters of entities) are generated by first formulating conceptual descriptions of these classes and then classifying the entities according to the descriptions" [27]. For example, we may state a concept such as "a love song." This is a concept more than a property, for the "love songness" of any song is not something that may be measured empirically. However, if we decide that a certain song is more of a love song than not, we place it in this category. Thus, conceptual clustering represents more of a probabilistic clustering of objects.

Conceptual clustering is closely related to fuzzy (multivalue) set theory, in which objects may belong to one or more groups, in varying degrees of fitness. Conceptual clustering makes absolute judgments of classification by focusing on the "best fit."

A Problem of Classification

Figure 4–1 contains ten items, labeled *A* to *J*, each of which represents a train. Each train includes an engine (on the right) and from two to four cars, each shaped differently and holding different loads. Before reading further, spend the next few minutes arranging these trains into any number of groups you deem meaningful. For example, you might create three groups: one for trains whose engines have all black wheels, one for trains whose engines have all white wheels, and one for trains whose engines have black and white wheels.

This problem comes from the work by Stepp and Michalski on conceptual clustering [19]. As in real life, there is no "right" answer. In their experiments, subjects came up with 93 different classifications. The most popular classification was by the length of the train, forming three groups (trains with two, three, and four cars). The second most popular classification was by engine wheel color, as we suggested. Of these 93 classifications, about 40 of them were totally unique.

Our use of this example confirms Stepp and Michalski's study. Most of our subjects have used the two most popular classifications, although we have encountered some rather creative groupings. For example, one subject arranged these trains into two groups: one group represented trains labeled by letters containing straight lines (*A*, *E*, *F*, *H*, and *I*) and the other group represented trains labeled by letters containing curved lines. This is truly an example of nonlinear thinking: creative, albeit bizarre.

Once you have completed this task, let's change the requirements (again, as in real life). Suppose that circles represent toxic chemicals, rectangles represent lumber, and all other shapes of loads represent passengers. Try classifying the trains again, and see how this new knowledge changes your classification.

Among our subjects, the clustering of trains changed significantly. Most subjects classified trains according to whether or not they carried toxic loads. We conclude from this simple experiment that more knowledge about a domain makes it easier to achieve an intelligent classification.

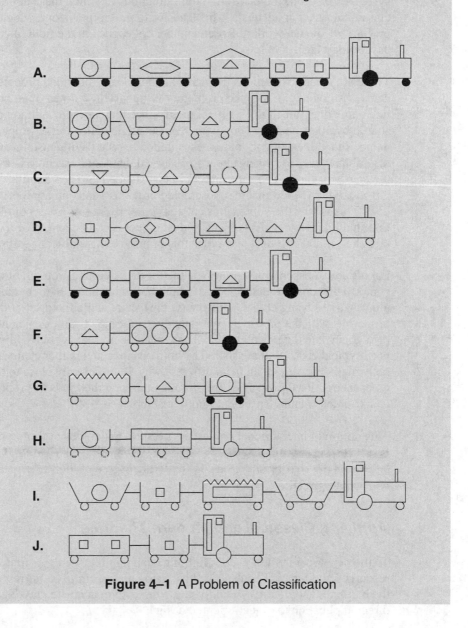

Figure 4–1 A Problem of Classification

Prototype Theory

Classical categorization and conceptual clustering are sufficiently expressive to account for most of the classifications we need in the design of complex software systems. However, there are still some situations in which these approaches to classification are inadequate. This leads us to prototype theory, which derives primarily from the work of Rosch and her colleagues in the field of cognitive psychology [28].

There are some abstractions that have neither clearly bounded properties nor concepts. As Lakoff explains the problem, "Wittgenstein pointed out that a category like game does not fit the classical mold, since there are no common properties shared by all games. . . . Though there is no single collection of properties that all games share, the category of games is united by what Wittgenstein calls family resemblances. . . . Wittgenstein also observed that there was no fixed boundary to the category game. The category could be extended and new kinds of games introduced, provided that they resembled previous games in appropriate ways" [29]. This is why the approach is called prototype theory: a class of objects is represented by a prototypical object, and an object is considered to be a member of this class if and only if it resembles this prototype in significant ways.

Lakoff and Johnson apply prototype theory to the earlier problem of classifying chairs. They observe that "we understand beanbag chairs, barber chairs, and contour chairs as being chairs, not because they share some fixed set of defining properties with the prototype, but rather because they bear a sufficient family resemblance to the prototype. . . . There need be no fixed core of properties of prototypical chairs that are shared by both beanbag and barber chairs, yet they are both chairs because each, in its different way, is sufficiently close to the prototype. Interactional properties are prominent among the kinds of properties that count in determining sufficient family resemblance" [30].

This notion of interactional properties is central to the idea of prototype theory. In conceptual clustering, we group things according to distinct concepts. In prototype theory, we group things according to the degree of their relationship to concrete prototypes.

Applying Classical and Modern Theories

To the developer in the trenches fighting changing requirements amidst limited resources and tight schedules, our discussion may seem to be far removed from the battlefields of reality. Actually, these three approaches to classification have direct application to object-oriented design.

In our experience, we identify classes and objects first according to the properties relevant to our particular domain. Here, we focus on identifying the structures and behavior that are part of the vocabulary of our problem space. Many such abstractions are usually available for the picking [31]. If this approach fails to yield a satisfactory class structure, we next consider clustering objects by concepts (or refining our initial domain-based classification by concepts). Here, we focus our attention on the behavior of collaborating objects. If either of these two approaches fails to capture our understanding of the problem domain, we consider classification by association, through which clusters of objects are defined according to how closely each resembles some prototypical object.

p.126

More directly, these three approaches to classification provide the theoretical foundation of object-oriented analysis, which offers a number of pragmatic practices and rules of thumb that we may apply to identify classes and objects in the design of a complex software system.

Object-Oriented Analysis

The boundaries between analysis and design are fuzzy, although the focus of each is quite distinct. In analysis, the focus is to fully analyze the problem at hand and to model the world by discovering the classes and objects that form the vocabulary of the problem domain. In design, we invent the abstractions and mechanisms in our models that provide the design of the solution to be built.

In the following sections, we examine a number of proven approaches for analysis that are relevant to object-oriented systems.

Classical Approaches

A number of methodologists have proposed various sources of classes and objects, derived from the requirements of the problem domain. We call these approaches *classical* because they derive primarily from the principles of classical categorization.

For example, Shlaer and Mellor suggest that candidate classes and objects usually come from one of the following sources [32]:

- Tangible things   Cars, telemetry data, pressure sensors
- Roles   Mother, teacher, politician
- Events   Landing, interrupt, request
- Interactions   Loan, meeting, intersection

From the perspective of database modeling, Ross offers a similar list [33]:

- People — Humans who carry out some function
- Places — Areas set aside for people or things
- Things — Physical objects, or groups of objects, that are tangible
- Organizations — Formally organized collections of people, resources, facilities, and capabilities having a defined mission, whose existence is largely independent of individuals
- Concepts — Principles or ideas not tangible per se; used to organize or keep track of business activities and/or communications
- Events — Things that happen, usually to something else at a given date and time, or as steps in an ordered sequence

Coad and Yourdon suggest yet another set of sources of potential objects [34]:

- Structure — "Is a" and "part of" relationships
- Other systems — External systems with which the application interacts
- Devices — Devices with which the application interacts
- Events remembered — A historical event that must be recorded
- Roles played — The different roles users play in interacting with the application
- Locations — Physical locations, offices, and sites important to the application
- Organizational units — Groups to which users belong

At a higher level of abstraction, Coad introduces the idea of subject areas, which are basically logical groups of classes that relate to some higher-level system function.

Behavior Analysis

Whereas these classical approaches focus on tangible things in the problem domain, another school of thought in object-oriented analysis focuses on dynamic behavior as the primary source of classes and objects.[1] These approaches are

---

1. Shlaer and Mellor extended their earlier work to focus on behavior as well. In particular, they studied the lifecycle of each object as a means of understanding the boundaries [35].

more akin to conceptual clustering: We form classes based on groups of objects that exhibit similar behavior.

Wirfs-Brock, Wilkerson, and Wiener, for example, emphasize responsibilities, which denote "the knowledge an object maintains and the actions an object can perform. Responsibilities are meant to convey a sense of the purpose of an object and its place in the system. The responsibilities of an object are all the services it provides for all of the contracts it supports" [36]. In this manner, we group things that have common responsibilities, and we form hierarchies of classes involving superclasses that embody general responsibilities and subclasses that specialize their behavior.

Rubin and Goldberg offer an approach to identifying classes and objects derived from system functions. As they suggest, "the approach we use emphasizes first understanding what takes place in the system. These are the system behaviors. We next assign these behaviors to parts of the system, and try to understand who initiates and who participates in these behaviors. . . . Initiators and participants that play significant roles are recognized as objects, and are assigned the behavioral responsibilities for these roles" [37].

Rubin's concept of system behavior is closely related to the idea of function points, first suggested in 1979 by Albrech. A function point is "defined as one end-user business function" [38]. A business function represents some kind of output, inquiry, input, file, or interface. Although the information-system roots of this definition show through, the idea of a function point generalizes to all kinds of automated systems: A function point is any relevant outwardly visible and testable behavior of the system.

Domain Analysis

The principles we have discussed thus far are typically applied to the development of single, specific applications. Domain analysis, on the other hand, seeks to identify the classes and objects that are common to all applications within a given domain, such as patient record tracking, bond trading, compilers, or missile avionics systems. If you are in the midst of a design and stuck for ideas as to the key abstractions that exist, a narrow domain analysis can help by pointing you to the key abstractions that have proven useful in other related systems. Domain analysis works well because, except for special situations, there are very few truly unique kinds of software systems.

The idea of domain analysis was first suggested by Neighbors. We define domain analysis as "an attempt to identify the objects, operations, and relationships [that] domain experts perceive to be important about the domain" [39]. Moore and Bailin suggest the following steps in domain analysis.

- Construct a strawman generic model of the domain by consulting with domain experts.
- Examine existing systems within the domain and represent this understanding in a common format.
- Identify similarities and differences between the systems by consulting with domain experts.
- Refine the generic model to accommodate existing systems. [40]

Domain analysis may be applied across similar applications (vertical domain analysis), as well as to related parts of the same application (horizontal domain analysis). For example, when starting to design a new patient-monitoring system, it is reasonable to survey the architecture of existing systems to understand what key abstractions and mechanisms were previously employed and to evaluate which were useful and which were not. Similarly, an accounting system must provide many different kinds of reports. By considering these reports within the same application as a single domain, a domain analysis can lead the developer to an understanding of the key abstractions and mechanisms that serve all the different kinds of reports. The resulting classes and objects reflect a set of key abstractions and mechanisms generalized to the immediate report generation problem; therefore, the resulting design is likely to be simpler than if each report had been analyzed and designed separately.

Who exactly is a domain expert? Often, a domain expert is simply a user, such as a train engineer or dispatcher in a railway system, or a nurse or doctor in a hospital. A domain expert typically will not be a software developer; more commonly, he or she is simply a person who is intimately familiar with all the elements of a particular problem. A domain expert speaks the vocabulary of the problem domain.

Some managers may be concerned with the idea of direct communication between developers and end users (for some, even more frightening is the prospect of letting an end user see a developer!). For highly complex systems, domain analysis may involve a formal process, using the resources of multiple domain experts and developers over a period of many months. Such a formal analysis is not necessary on all projects, particularly smaller projects. Often, all it takes to clear up a design problem is a brief meeting between a domain expert and an architect or developer. It is truly amazing to see what a little bit of domain knowledge can do to enable intelligent design decisions. Indeed, we find it highly useful to have many such meetings throughout the design of a system. Domain analysis is rarely a monolithic activity; it is better focused if we consciously choose to analyze a little and then design a little.

Use Case Analysis

In isolation, the practices of classical analysis, behavior analysis, and domain analysis all depend on a large measure of personal experience on the part of the analyst. For the majority of development projects, this is unacceptable because such a process is neither deterministic nor predictably successful.

However, there is one practice that can be coupled with all three of these earlier approaches, to drive the process of analysis in a meaningful way. That practice is use case analysis, first formalized by Jacobson. Jacobson et al. define a use case as "A behaviourally related sequence of transactions performed by an actor in a dialogue with the system to provide some measurable value to the actor" [41].

Briefly, we can apply use case analysis as early as requirements analysis, at which time end users, other domain experts, and the development team enumerate the scenarios that are fundamental to the system's operation. (We need not elaborate on these scenarios at first; we can simply enumerate them.) These scenarios collectively describe the system functions of the application. Analysis then proceeds by a study of each scenario, possibly using storyboarding techniques similar to practices in the television and movie industry [42]. As the team walks through each scenario, they must identify the objects that participate in the scenario, the responsibilities of each object, and the ways those objects collaborate with other objects, in terms of the operations each invokes on the other. In this manner, the team is forced to craft a clear separation of concerns among all abstractions. As the development process continues, these initial scenarios are expanded to consider exceptional conditions as well as secondary system behaviors. The results from these secondary scenarios introduce new abstractions or add, modify, or reassign the responsibilities of existing abstractions. Scenarios also serve as the basis of system tests.

CRC Cards

CRC cards emerged as a simple yet marvelously effective way to analyze scenarios.[2] First proposed by Beck and Cunningham as a tool for teaching object-oriented programming [44], CRC cards have proven to be a useful development tool that facilitates brainstorming and enhances communication among developers. A CRC card is nothing more than a 3×5 index card,[3] on which the analyst writes—in pencil—the name of a class (at the top of the card), its responsibilities

---

2. CRC stands for Class/Responsibilities/Collaborators.

3. If your software development budget can handle it, buy 5×7 cards. Cards with lines are nice, and a sprinkling of colored cards shows that you are a very cool developer.

(on one half of the card), and its collaborators (on the other half of the card). One card is created for each class identified as relevant to the scenario. As the team members walk through the scenario, they may assign new responsibilities to an existing class, group certain responsibilities to form a new class, or (most commonly) divide the responsibilities of one class into more fine-grained ones and perhaps distribute these responsibilities to a different class.

CRC cards can be spatially arranged to represent patterns of collaboration. As viewed from the dynamic semantics of the scenario, the cards are arranged to show the flow of messages among prototypical instances of each class; as viewed from the static semantics of the scenario, the cards are arranged to represent generalization/specialization or aggregation hierarchies among the classes.

Informal English Description

A radical alternative to classical object-oriented analysis was first proposed by Abbott, who suggests writing an English description of the problem (or a part of a problem) and then underlining the nouns and verbs [45]. The nouns represent candidate objects, and the verbs represent candidate operations on them.

Abbott's approach is useful because it is simple and because it forces the developer to work in the vocabulary of the problem space. However, it is by no means a rigorous approach, and it definitely does not scale well to anything beyond fairly trivial problems. Human language is a terribly imprecise vehicle of expression, so the quality of the resulting list of objects and operations depends on the writing skill of its author. Furthermore, any noun can be verbed, and any verb can be nouned; therefore, it is easy to skew the candidate list to emphasize either objects or operations.

Structured Analysis

Some organizations have tried to use the products of structured analysis as a front end to object-oriented design. This technique appears appealing only because a large number of analysts are skilled in structured analysis, and computer-aided software engineering (CASE) tools exist that support the automation of these methods. Personally, we discourage the use of structured analysis as a front end to object-oriented design.

This approach starts with an essential model of the system, as described by data flow diagrams and the other products of structured analysis. These diagrams provide a reasonably formal model of the problem. From this model, we may proceed to identify the meaningful classes and objects in our problem domain in three different ways.

①

McMenamin and Palmer suggest starting with an analysis of the data dictionary and proceeding to analyze the model's context diagram. As they state, "With your list of essential data elements, think about what they tell you or what they describe. If they were adjectives in a sentence, for instance, what nouns would they modify? The answers to this question make up the list of candidate objects" [47]. These candidate objects typically derive from the surrounding environment, from the essential inputs and outputs, and from the products, services, and other resources managed by the system.

②

The next two techniques involve analyzing individual data flow diagrams. Given a particular data flow diagram (using the terminology of Ward and Mellor [48]), candidate objects may be derived from the following:

- External entities
- Data stores
- Control stores
- Control transformations

Candidate classes derive from two sources:

- Data flows
- Control flows

③

This leaves us with data transformations, which we assign either as operations on existing objects or as the behavior of an object we invent to serve as the agent responsible for this transformation.

Seidewitz and Stark suggest another technique, which they call *abstraction analysis*. Abstraction analysis focuses on the identification of central entities, which are similar in nature to central transforms in structured design. As they state, "In structured analysis, input and output data are examined and followed inwards until they reach the highest level of abstraction. The processes between the inputs and the outputs form the central transform. In abstraction analysis a designer does the same, but also examines the central transform to determine which processes and states represent the best abstract model of what the system does" [49]. After identifying the central entity in a particular data flow diagram, abstraction analysis proceeds to identify all the supporting entities by following the afferent and efferent data flows from the central entity and grouping the processes and states encountered along the way. In practice, Seidewitz and Stark have found abstraction analysis a difficult technique to apply successfully, and as an alternative they recommend object-oriented analysis methods [50].

We must strongly emphasize that structured design, as normally coupled with structured analysis, is entirely orthogonal to the principles of object-oriented design. Our experience indicates that using structured analysis as a front end to object-oriented design often fails when the developer is unable to resist the urge to fall back into the abyss of the structured design mindset. Another very real danger is the fact that many analysts tend to write data flow diagrams that reflect a design rather than an essential model of the problem. It is tremendously difficult to build an object-oriented system from a model that is so obviously biased toward algorithmic decomposition. This is why we prefer object-oriented analysis as the front end to object-oriented design: There is simply less danger of polluting the design with preconceived algorithmic notions.

If you must use structured analysis as a front end, for whatever honorable reasons,[4] we suggest that you stop writing data flow diagrams as soon as they start to smell of a design instead of an essential model. Also, it is a healthy practice to walk away from the products of structured analysis once the design is fully under way. Remember that the products of development, including data flow diagrams, are not ends in themselves; they should be viewed simply as tools along the way that aid the developer's intellectual comprehension of the problem and its implementation. One typically writes a data flow diagram and then invents the mechanisms that implement the desired behavior. Practically speaking, the very act of design changes the developer's understanding of the problem. Thus, only the products of structured analysis that are at a sufficiently high level of abstraction should be retained. They capture an essential model of the problem and so lend themselves to any number of different designs.

4.3 Key Abstractions and Mechanisms

A *key abstraction* is a class or object that forms part of the vocabulary of the problem domain. The primary value of identifying such abstractions is that they give boundaries to our problem; they highlight the things that are in the system and therefore relevant to our design, and they suppress the things that are outside the system and therefore superfluous.

In the previous chapter, we used the term *mechanism* to describe any structure whereby objects collaborate to provide some behavior that satisfies a requirement of the problem. Whereas the design of a class embodies the knowledge of how individual objects behave, a mechanism is a design decision about how collections of objects cooperate. Mechanisms thus represent patterns of behavior.

Let us now discuss the identification and refinement of these key abstractions and mechanisms.

---

4. Political and historical reasons are distinctly not honorable.

Identifying Key Abstractions

The identification of key abstractions is highly domain-specific. As Goldberg states, the "appropriate choice of objects depends, of course, on the purposes to which the application will be put and the granularity of information to be manipulated" [51].

As we mentioned earlier, the identification of key abstractions involves two processes: discovery and invention. Through discovery, we come to recognize the abstractions used by domain experts; if the domain expert talks about it, the abstraction is usually important [52]. Through invention, we create new classes and objects that are not necessarily part of the problem domain but are useful artifacts in the design or implementation. For example, a customer using an automated teller speaks in terms of accounts, deposits, and withdrawals; these words are part of the vocabulary of the problem domain. A developer of such a system uses these same abstractions but must also introduce new ones, such as databases, screen managers, lists, queues, and so on. These key abstractions are artifacts of the particular design, not of the problem domain.

Refining Key Abstractions

Once we identify a certain key abstraction as a candidate, we must evaluate it according to the metrics described in the previous chapter. As Stroustrup suggests, "Often this means that the programmer must focus on the questions: how are objects of this class created? Can objects of this class be copied and/or destroyed? What operations can be done on such objects? If there are no good answers to such questions, the concept probably wasn't 'clean' in the first place, and it might be a good idea to think a bit more about the problem and the proposed solution instead of immediately starting to 'code around' the problems" [53].

Given a new abstraction, we must place it in the context of the existing class and object hierarchies we have designed. Practically speaking, this is neither a top-down nor a bottom-up activity. As Halbert and O'Brien observe, "You do not always design types in a type hierarchy by starting with a supertype and then creating the subtypes. Frequently, you create several seemingly disparate types, realize they are related, and then factor out their common characteristics into one or more supertypes. . . . several passes up and down are usually required to produce a complete and correct program design" [54]. This is not a license to hack, but an observation, based on experience, that object-oriented design is both incremental and iterative. Stroustrup makes a similar observation when he notes that "the most common reorganizations of a class hierarchy are factoring the common part of two classes into a new class and splitting a class into two new ones" [55].

Placing classes and objects at the right levels of abstraction is difficult. Sometimes we may find a general subclass and so may choose to move it up in the class structure, thus increasing the degree of sharing. This is called *class promotion* [56]. Similarly, we may find a class to be too general, thus making inheritance by a subclass difficult because of the large semantic gap. This is called a *grainsize conflict* [57]. In either case, we strive to identify cohesive and loosely coupled abstractions, so as to mitigate these two situations.

LOOK AT THE QUADRUPED RECLINING ON THE VERANDA

Classes and objects should be at the right level of abstraction: neither too high nor too low.

Naming Key Abstractions

Naming things properly—so that they reflect their semantics—is often treated lightly by most developers yet is important in capturing the essence of the abstractions we are describing. Software should be written as carefully as English prose, with consideration given to the reader as well as to the computer [58]. Consider for a moment all the names we may need just to identify a single object: We have the name of the object itself, the name of its class, and the name of the module in which that class is declared. Multiply this by thousands of objects and possibly hundreds of classes, and you have a very real problem.

We offer the following suggestions.

- Objects should be named with proper noun phrases, such as `theSensor` or just simply `shape`.

- Classes should be named with common noun phrases, such as `Sensor` or `Shape`.
- The names chosen should reflect the names used and recognized by the domain experts, whenever possible.
- Modifier operations should be named with active verb phrases, such as `draw` or `moveLeft`.
- Selector operations should imply a query or be named with verbs of the form "to be," such as `extentOf` or `isOpen`.
- The use of underscores and styles of capitalization are largely matters of personal taste. No matter which cosmetic style you use, at least have your programs be self-consistent.

Identifying Mechanisms

Consider a system requirement for an automobile: Pushing the accelerator should cause the engine to run faster, and releasing the accelerator should cause the engine to run slower. How this actually comes about is absolutely immaterial to the driver. Any mechanism may be employed as long as it delivers the required behavior, and thus which mechanism is selected is largely a matter of design choice. More specifically, any of the following designs might be considered.

- A mechanical linkage connects the accelerator directly to the fuel injectors.
- An electronic mechanism connects a pressure sensor below the accelerator to a computer that controls the fuel injectors (a drive-by-wire mechanism).
- No linkage exists. The gas tank is placed on the roof of the car, and gravity causes fuel to flow to the engine. Its rate of flow is regulated by a clip around the fuel line; pushing on the accelerator pedal eases tension on the clip, causing the fuel to flow faster (a low-cost mechanism).

Which mechanism a developer chooses from a set of alternatives is most often a result of other factors, such as cost, reliability, manufacturability, and safety.

Just as it is rude for a client to violate the interface of another object, so it is socially unacceptable for objects to step outside the boundaries of the rules of behavior dictated by a particular mechanism. Indeed, it would be surprising for a driver if stepping on an accelerator turned on the car's lights instead of causing the engine to run faster.

Whereas key abstractions reflect the vocabulary of the problem domain, mechanisms are the soul of the design. During the design process, the developer must consider not only the design of individual classes but also how instances of these classes work together. Again, the use of scenarios drives this analysis process.

Mechanisms are the means whereby objects collaborate to provide some higher-level behavior.

Once a developer decides on a particular pattern of collaboration, the work is distributed among many objects by defining suitable methods in the appropriate classes. Ultimately, the protocol of an individual class encompasses all the operations required to implement all the behavior and all the mechanisms associated with each of its instances.

Mechanisms thus represent strategic design decisions, as does the design of a class structure. In contrast, however, the interface of an individual class is more of a tactical design decision. These strategic decisions must be made explicitly; otherwise, we will end up with a mob of relatively uncooperative objects, all pushing and shoving to do their work with little regard for other objects. The most elegant, lean, and fast programs embody carefully engineered mechanisms.

Mechanisms as Patterns

Mechanisms are actually one in a spectrum of patterns we find in well-structured software systems. At the low end of the food chain, we have idioms. An idiom is an expression peculiar to a certain programming language or application culture, representing a generally accepted convention for use of the language.[5] For exam-

---

5. One defining characteristic of an idiom is that ignoring or violating the idiom has immediate social consequences: You are branded as a yahoo or, worse, an outsider, unworthy of respect.

ple, in CLOS, no programmer would use underscores in function or variable names, although this is common practice in Ada [59]. Part of the effort in learning a programming language is learning its idioms, which are usually passed down as folklore from programmer to programmer. However, as Coplien points out, idioms play an important role in codifying low-level patterns. He notes that "many common programming tasks [are] idiomatic" and therefore identifying such idioms allows "using C++ constructs to express functionality outside the language proper, while giving the illusion of being part of the language" [60].

Whereas idioms are part of a programming culture, at the high end of the food chain, we have frameworks. A framework is a collection of classes that provides a set of services for a particular domain; a framework thus exports a number of individual classes and mechanisms that clients can use or adapt. Frameworks represent reuse in the large. They are often the product of commercial ventures, such as Microsoft's .NET Framework, or open source efforts such as Apache Software Foundation's Struts framework and the JUnit testing framework (Erich Gamma and Kent Beck), among many others.

Examples of Mechanisms

Consider the drawing mechanism commonly used in graphical user interfaces. Several objects must collaborate to present an image to a user: a window, a view, the model being viewed, and some client that knows when (but not how) to display this model. The client first tells the window to draw itself. Since it may encompass several subviews, the window next tells each of its subviews to draw themselves. Each subview in turn tells its model to draw itself, ultimately resulting in an image shown to the user. In this mechanism, the model is entirely decoupled from rendering of the window and view in which it is presented. This is the model-view-controller paradigm (MVC pattern) [61]. A similar mechanism is employed in almost every object-oriented graphical user interface framework.

Mechanisms thus represent a level of reuse that is higher than the reuse of individual classes. For example, the MVC paradigm is used extensively in the Smalltalk user interface. The MVC paradigm in turn builds on another mechanism, the dependency mechanism, which is embodied in the behavior of the Smalltalk base class Model and thus pervades much of the Smalltalk class library.

Examples of mechanisms and patterns may be found in virtually every domain. For example, the structure of an operating system may be described at the highest level of abstraction according to the mechanism used to dispatch programs. In artificial intelligence, a variety of mechanisms have been explored for the design of reasoning systems. One of the most widely used paradigms is the blackboard mechanism, in which individual knowledge sources independently update a blackboard. There is no central control in such a mechanism, but any change to the blackboard may trigger an agent to explore some new problem-solving path [63]. Coad has similarly identified a number of common mechanisms in object-oriented systems, including patterns of time association, event logging, and broadcasting [64]. In each case, these mechanisms manifest themselves not as individual classes but as the structure of collaborating classes.

This completes our study of classification and of the concepts that serve as the foundation of object-oriented design. The next three chapters focus on notation, process, and pragmatics.

Summary

- The identification of classes and objects is a fundamental issue in object-oriented analysis and design; identification involves both discovery and invention.
- Classification is fundamentally a problem of clustering.
- Classification is an incremental and iterative process, made difficult because a given set of objects may be classified in many equally proper ways.
- The three approaches to classification include classical categorization (classification by properties), conceptual clustering (classification by concepts), and prototype theory (classification by association with a prototype).
- Scenarios are a powerful tool of object-oriented analysis and can be used in approaches such as classical analysis, behavior analysis, domain analysis, and use case analysis.
- Key abstractions reflect the vocabulary of the problem domain and may either be discovered from the problem domain or invented as part of the design.
- Mechanisms denote strategic design decisions regarding the collaborative activity of many different kinds of objects.

Method

> Which innovation leads to a successful design and which to a failure is not completely predictable. Each opportunity to design something new, either bridge or airplane or skyscraper, presents the engineer with choices that may appear countless. The engineer may decide to copy as many seemingly good features as he can from existing designs that have successfully withstood the forces of man and nature, but he may also decide to improve upon those aspects of prior designs that appear to be wanting.
>
> HENRY PETROSKI
> *To Engineer Is Human*

For any technology to become successful in the marketplace, certain things need to happen. A critical mass of users, who have proven success using the technology, needs to develop. This attracts investment in that technology area by others. For that critical mass to develop, a common language is very beneficial so that knowledge in that technology domain can easily be taught, exchanged, and disseminated.

In order for the technology to do well in the mainstream market, a key part of the knowledge to be disseminated is how the technology can be successfully used or developed (i.e., what is the process) and how this all can be done efficiently and effectively. That is what this section addresses: a common, standard language (the Unified Modeling Language), a process, and the pragmatics of object-oriented analysis and design.

Chapter 5

Notation

The act of drawing a diagram does not constitute analysis or design. A diagram simply captures a statement of a system's behavior (for analysis), or the vision and details of an architecture (for design). If you follow the work of any engineer—software, civil, mechanical, chemical, architectural, or whatever—you will soon realize that the one and only place that a system is conceived is in the mind of the designer. As this design unfolds over time, it is often captured on such high-tech media as whiteboards, napkins, and the backs of envelopes [1].

5.1 The Unified Modeling Language

Having a well-defined and expressive notation is important to the process of software development. First, a standard notation makes it possible for an analyst or developer to describe a scenario or formulate an architecture and then unambiguously communicate those decisions to others. Draw an electrical circuit, and the symbol for a transistor will be understood by virtually every electrical engineer in the world. Similarly, if an architect in New York City drafts the plans for a house, a builder in San Francisco will have little trouble understanding where to place doors, windows, and electrical outlets, given the details of the blueprints. Second, as Whitehead states in his seminal work on mathematics, "By relieving the brain of all unnecessary work, a good notation sets it free to concentrate on more advanced problems" [2]. Third, an expressive notation makes it possible to eliminate much of the tedium of checking the consistency and correctness of these decisions by using automated tools. As a report by the Defense Science Board states, "Software development is and always will be a labor-intensive technology. . . . Although our machines can do the dog-work and can help us keep track of our edifices, concept development is the quintessentially human activity. . . . The part of software development that will not go away is the crafting of conceptual structures; the part that can go away is the labor of expressing them" [3].

A Brief Historical Perspective

The Unified Modeling Language (UML) is the primary modeling language used to analyze, specify, and design software systems. As object-oriented programming languages began to see use in the software industry, as cited in Chapter 2, object-oriented methodologies began to appear. From the late 1980s and well into the 1990s, numerous methodologies arose and were subsequently modified and refined. Many of these were strong in certain areas, weaker in others. This gave rise to methodologists adopting useful facets from other methodologies into their own. This reflected what the object-oriented practitioners were doing in the working world. While the practitioners may have been, for the most part, following a particular methodology, as other useful ideas entered the marketplace, they would weave these ideas into their daily work.

In the mid-1990s, Booch, Rumbaugh, and Jacobson joined forces at Rational Software Corporation and began to meld their respective methodologies to create what would be the first version of the UML. They then began to work with other methodologists and companies to propose a standard modeling language to the Object Management Group (OMG), a consortium that creates and maintains standards for the computer industry. In November 1997 the OMG adopted the UML as a standard. Since then the OMG has assumed the stewardship and ongoing development of the UML.

There have been numerous revisions of the UML since its adoption. UML 2.0 is the version discussed in this text. Many books have chronicled the detailed history of the development of the UML. For more information, see Appendix B, Further Reading.

Models and Multiple Views

As in many other disciplines (e.g., electronics, chemistry, architecture, music) that have their unique notations for representing the artifacts they create, the UML is used to model (i.e., represent) the system being built. Taken in total, the UML model that you build will represent, to a certain level of fidelity, the real system that will be constructed. However, it is impossible to capture all the subtle details of a complex software system in just one large diagram. The UML has numerous types of diagrams, each providing a certain view of your system. As Kleyn and Gingrich observe, "One must understand both the structure and the function of the objects involved. One must understand the taxonomic structure of the class objects, the inheritance mechanisms used, the individual behaviors of objects, and the dynamic behavior of the system as a whole. The problem is somewhat analogous to that of viewing a sports event such as tennis or a football game. Many different camera angles are required to provide an understanding of the action taking place. Each camera reveals particular aspects of the action that could not be conveyed by one camera alone" [4].

For example, consider an application comprising several hundred classes. It is impossible and in fact unnecessary to produce a single diagram that shows all of these classes and all of their relationships. Rather, we would use several class diagrams, each of which presents one view of the model. One diagram might show the inheritance lattice of certain key classes; another might show the transitive closure of all classes used by one particular class. At times when the model is stable (what we speak of as a *steady state*), all such diagrams remain semantically consistent with one another and with the model. For example, if in a given interaction (which we describe in an object diagram), object A passes the message M to object B, then M must be defined for B's class either directly or indirectly. In a corresponding class diagram, there must be an appropriate relationship between the classes of A and B, such that instances of A's class can in fact invoke message M on instances of class B.

Across all diagrams, all entities with the same name are considered to be references to the same model item. For example, if class C appears in two different diagrams for the same system, both are references to the same class C. The exception to this rule is for operations, whose names may be overloaded.

Diagram Taxonomy

UML diagrams can be classified into two groups: structure diagrams and behavior diagrams (see Figure 5–1). This dichotomy parallels the discussion of complexity in Chapter 1. System complexity is driven both by the number and organization of elements in the system (i.e., structure) and the manner in which all these elements collaborate to perform their function (i.e., behavior).

Structure Diagrams

These diagrams are used to show the static structure of elements in the system. They may depict such things as the architectural organization of the system, the physical elements of the system, its runtime configuration, and domain-specific elements of your business, among others. The UML structure diagrams include the following:

UML Diagrams

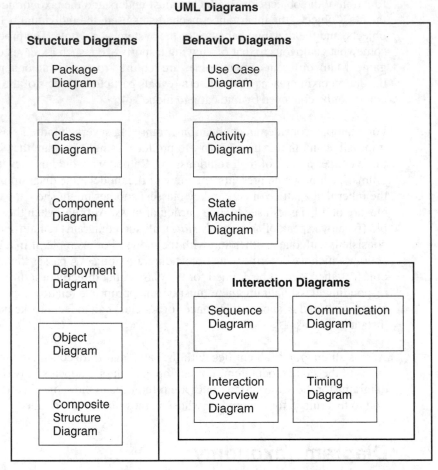

Figure 5–1 The Diagrams of the UML

- Package diagram
- Class diagram
- Component diagram
- Deployment diagram
- Object diagram
- Composite structure diagram

Structure diagrams are often used in conjunction with behavior diagrams to depict a particular aspect of your system. Each class may have an associated state machine diagram that indicates the event-driven behavior of the class's instances. Similarly, in conjunction with an object diagram representing a scenario, we may provide an interaction diagram to show the time or event ordering of messages as they are evaluated.

2) *Behavior Diagrams*

The diagrams we have introduced thus far are largely static. However, events happen dynamically in all software-intensive systems: Objects are created and destroyed, objects send messages to one another in an orderly fashion, and in some systems, external events trigger operations on certain objects. Not surprisingly, describing dynamic behavior in a static medium such as a sheet of paper is a difficult problem, but it confronts virtually every scientific discipline. In object-oriented development, we express the dynamic behavioral semantics of a problem or its implementation through the following additional diagrams:

- Use case diagram
- Activity diagram
- State machine diagram
- Interaction diagrams
  - Sequence diagram
  - Communication diagram
  - Interaction overview diagram
  - Timing diagram

use to express dynamic behavioral semantics of a problem

We will present the UML elements that comprise these diagrams later in this chapter.

The Use of Diagrams in Practice

The fact that the UML is a detailed specification does not mean that every aspect of it must be used at all times. In fact, a proper subset of this notation is sufficient to express the semantics of a large percentage of analysis and design issues. We will highlight this subset during our presentation of the notation in this chapter. Why, then, bother with the detail beyond this subset? Quite simply, such detail is necessary to express certain important tactical decisions (as we'll show in the Applications section of this book). Additionally, some detail exists in the infra-structure of the UML, of interest to tool vendors, which facilitates the creation of forward-engineering and reverse-engineering tools. Such internal details enable the integration of front-end CASE tools that support this notation together with software development environments that focus on manipulating the products of the object-oriented programming language.

As Weinberg notes, "In other design fields, such as architecture, the rough sketch is the most frequently used graphic device, and precise detailed drawings are rarely used at all until the creative part of the design work is finished" [5]. Remember, a notation is only a vehicle for capturing the reasoning about the behavior and architecture of a system; a notation is not an end in itself. Therefore, you should apply only those elements of the notation that are necessary to convey the intended meaning, and nothing more. Just as it is dangerous to overspecify a set of requirements, so it is dangerous to overspecify a solution to a problem. For example, on a blueprint, an architect may show the general location of a light switch in a room, but its exact location will not be established until the construction manager and owner do an electrical walkthrough, after the house has been framed. It would be foolish to specify the precise three-dimensional coordinates of the light switch on the blueprint (unless, of course, this detail is functionally important to the owner; perhaps the owner's family is significantly taller or shorter than average). Thus, if the analysts, designers, and implementers of a relatively small software system are highly skilled and have already established a close working relationship, rough sketches may suffice (although it will still be necessary to leave a legacy of the architectural vision for the sake of the system's maintainers). In practice, this is rarely the case. If, on the other hand, the system is large and software-intensive, or the implementers are not quite so skilled, or if the developers are separated by geography, time, or contract, more detail will be required during the development process.

Conceptual, Logical, and Physical Models

The models of your system may present various levels of detail as your system development progresses and matures over time. The conceptual model captures the system in terms of the domain entities that exist (or will exist) and their association with other such entities of your system. The conceptual level of modeling is performed using the terminology of your business domain and should be technology-agnostic. The logical view of a system takes the concepts created in the conceptual model and establishes the existence and meaning of the key abstractions and mechanisms that will determine the system's architecture and overall design. The physical model of a system describes the concrete software and hardware composition of the system's implementation. Obviously, the physical model is technology-specific.

On a given project, over time, the system's design will evolve from conceptual, through logical, to physical levels of maturity. Which diagrams are used at various points in the development lifecycle varies. Some diagrams are used only early in the development lifecycle. Some are used, at varying levels of detail, throughout the lifecycle. Usage can also vary depending on the type of system you are building. For example, a stockbroker's investment trading system would use many more state machine diagrams and timing diagrams than a simple checkbook application would.

For a given project, the products of analysis and design are expressed through these models. Collectively, these different models are semantically rich: They are expressive enough to allow a developer to capture all of the interesting strategic and tactical decisions that need to be made during the analysis of a system as well as during the formulation of its architecture, and they are complete enough to serve as blueprints for implementation in almost any object-oriented programming language.

The Role of Tools

The notation described in this chapter can be used manually, although for larger applications it cries out for automated tool support. Given automated support for any notation, one of the things that tools can do is help bad designers create ghastly designs much more quickly than they ever could without them. Great designs come from great designers, not from great tools. Tools simply empower the individual, freeing him or her to concentrate on the truly creative aspects of analysis or design. Thus, there are some things that tools can do well and some things that tools cannot do at all.

Tools can provide consistency checking, constraint checking, completeness checking, and analysis, and they can help a developer browse through the products of analysis and design in unconstrained ways. For example, while looking at a component diagram, a developer might want to study a particular mechanism; he or she can use a tool to locate all the classes allocated to a particular component. While looking at a sequence diagram describing a scenario, the developer might want to see the inheritance lattice. If this scenario involved an active object, the developer might use a tool to find the processor to which this thread of control is allocated and then view an animation of its class's state machine on that processor. Freed from the tedium of keeping all the details of the analysis and design consistent, developers who use such tools can focus on the creative parts of the development process.

On the other hand, a tool cannot tell us that we ought to invent a new class so as to simplify our class structure; that takes human insight. We might consider trying to use some expert system as such a tool, but this requires (1) a person who is an expert both in object-oriented development and in the problem domain and (2) the ability to articulate classification heuristics, as well as a great deal of common-sense knowledge. We don't expect such comprehensive, all-knowing tools to replace designers in the near future; in the meantime, we have real systems to create.

The Products of Object-Oriented Development

Typically, the analysis of a system will include sets of use case and activity diagrams (to express the behavior of the system through scenarios), class diagrams (to express the roles and responsibilities of agents that provide the system's behavior), and interaction and/or state machine diagrams (to show the event-ordered behavior of these agents). Similarly, the architecture of a system may include sets of package diagrams, class diagrams, object diagrams, component diagrams, and deployment diagrams, as well as their corresponding dynamic views.

End-to-end connectivity exists among these diagrams, permitting us to trace requirements from implementation back to specification. Starting with a deployment diagram, a node may host an artifact that manifests a component that is defined in some component diagram. This component diagram may encompass the definition of a collection of classes whose definitions we will find in the appropriate class diagram. Finally, the definitions of individual classes point to our use cases and requirements because these classes in general directly reflect the vocabulary of the problem space.

Scaling Up and Scaling Down

We have found the UML applicable both to small systems consisting of just a dozen or so classes and to ones consisting of several thousand classes. As we will see in the next two chapters, this notation is particularly applicable to an incremental, iterative approach to development. You do not create a diagram and then walk away from it, treating it as some sacred, immutable artifact. Rather, these diagrams evolve during the design process as new design decisions are made and more detail is established.

We have also found this notation to be largely language-independent. It applies to any of a wide spectrum of object-oriented programming languages.

The Syntax and Semantics of the UML

The purpose of the remainder of this chapter is to describe the syntax and semantics of the UML for object-oriented analysis and design. We will provide a few small examples of this notation, using the problem of the Hydroponics Gardening System that we introduced in Chapter 2. This chapter does not explain the development process during which UML diagrams are developed; that is the topic of Chapter 6.

To give a sense of their relationships, we present the UML 2.0 diagrams in an order in which one might typically develop them. We believe this to be more useful than, for example, presenting all structure diagrams followed by all behavior diagrams. Specifically, the diagrams are presented in the following order:

- Section 5.2: package diagrams
- Section 5.3: component diagrams
- Section 5.4: deployment diagrams

- Section 5.5: use case diagrams
- Section 5.6: activity diagrams
- Section 5.7: class diagrams
- Section 5.8: sequence diagrams
- Section 5.9: interaction overview diagrams
- Section 5.10: composite structure diagrams
- Section 5.11: state machine diagrams
- Section 5.12: timing diagrams
- Section 5.13: object diagrams
- Section 5.14: communication diagrams

In Section III of this book, each chapter presents a different type of application and focuses on a certain set of diagrams that would be most appropriate for the application at the point in the overall lifecycle that we describe.

UML 2.0 Information Sources

The UML 2.0 notation is quite extensive and complex, as a review of the OMG UML 2.0 Specification clearly confirms. Effective practical use of the specification requires turning to additional resources, such as this chapter. If, after reading the OMG UML 2.0 Specification and this chapter, you desire a further level of explanation or detail, we suggest reviewing *The Unified Modeling Language Reference Manual, Second Edition.* Appendix B lists other UML 2.0 resources.

5.2 Package Diagrams

While performing object-oriented analysis and design, you need to organize the artifacts of the development process to clearly present the analysis of the problem space and the associated design. The specific reasons will vary but will focus either on physically structuring the visual model itself or on clearly representing the model elements through multiple views. The benefits of organizing the OOAD artifacts include the following [42]:

- Provides clarity and understanding in a complex systems development
- Supports concurrent model use by multiple users
- Supports version control
- Provides abstraction at multiple levels—from systems to classes in a component
- Provides encapsulation and containment; supports modularity

The primary means to accomplish this organization is the UML package diagram, which provides us the ability to represent grouped UML elements.

The essential elements of a package diagram are packages, their visibility, and their dependencies.

Essentials: The Package Notation

The UML package is one of the two primary notations used on a package diagram. The other one is the dependency relationship, which we will describe later. The notation for the package is a rectangle with a tab on the top left. UML 2.0 specifies that the name of the package is placed in the interior of the rectangle if the package contains no UML elements. If it does contain elements, the name should be placed within the tab. A tool-specific implementation of the naming guidelines appears in Figure 5–2, which provides a black-box perspective of the HydroponicsGardeningSystem package that does not show its contained elements [45, 46].

When there are fewer elements to be shown because fewer exist or because we have a focused concern, we can use the appropriate notation (package, use case, class, component, and so on) to show these constituent pieces within the containing package. Figure 5–3 again shows the HydroponicsGardeningSystem package, but with two of its contained elements represented as packages themselves. In the representation on the left, we show the Planning and Greenhouse

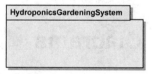

Figure 5–2 The Package Notation for HydroponicsGardeningSystem

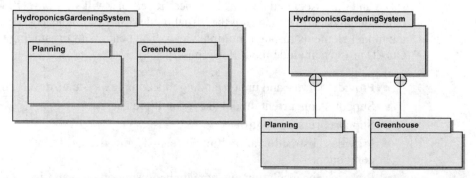

Figure 5–3 The Package Notation for Contained Elements

packages as physically contained packages inside the `HydroponicsGardening-System` package. On the right appears an alternate notation for the containment relationship [47, 48].

Essentials: Visibility of Elements

Access to the services provided by a group of collaborating classes within a package—or more generically, to any elements within a package—is determined by the visibility of the individual elements, including nested packages. The visibility of the elements, defined by the containing package to be either public or private, applies both to contained elements and to those that are imported. The concept of importing elements will be discussed later in this section.

Visibility is defined from the perspective of the containing package, which provides the namespace for its contained elements. Because the package provides the namespace, every contained element has a unique name, at least among other elements of its type. As an example, this means that no two classes contained within the same namespace may have the same name [49, 50]. We will discuss this concept further when we look at import and access.

Elements with public visibility can be thought of as part of the package's interface because these elements are visible to all other elements. Those elements with private visibility are not visible outside the containing package. The definition of public and private visibility is provided here, along with the corresponding notation shown in parentheses [51, 52]:

- Public (+)   Visible to elements within its containing package, including nested packages, and to external elements
- Private (-)   Visible only to elements within its containing package and to nested packages

On a visual diagram, this visibility notation is placed in front of the element name, as shown in Figure 5–4. The `GardeningPlan` class has public visibility

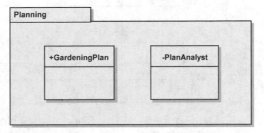

Figure 5–4 The Visibility of Elements within `Planning` Package

to permit other elements to access it, while the `PlanAnalyst` class has private visibility.

Essentials: The Dependency Relationship

If an element has the appropriate visibility to afford access, a dependency relationship to it can be shown representing this access. This dependency relationship is the other primary notation on a package diagram, as we mentioned earlier when discussing the package notation itself. A dependency shows that an element is dependent on another element as it fulfills its responsibilities within the system.

Dependencies between UML elements (including packages), as shown in Figure 5–5, are represented as a dashed arrow with an open arrowhead. The tail of the arrow is located at the element having the dependency (*client*), and the arrowhead is located at the element that supports the dependency (*supplier*). Dependencies may be labeled to highlight the type of dependency between the elements by

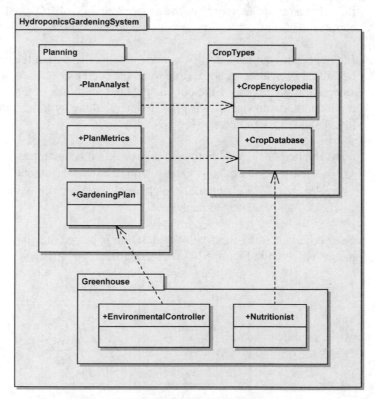

Figure 5–5 The Dependency Notation for
`HydroponicsGardeningSystem`

placing the dependency type—denoted by a keyword—within guillemets (« »), for example, «import». Package-specific dependencies include import, access, and merge; dependencies between packages due to the relationships of contained elements include trace, derive, refine, permit, and use [53].

If multiple contained element dependencies exist between packages, these dependencies are aggregated at the package level. A package-level dependency may be labeled with a keyword, denoting type, inside guillemets (« ») ; however, if the contained dependencies are of different types, the package-level dependency is not labeled. Figure 5–6 shows the dependencies of Figure 5–5 elevated to the containing package level. Note that the two individual element dependencies between the Planning and CropTypes packages have been aggregated to the level of the containing package [54].

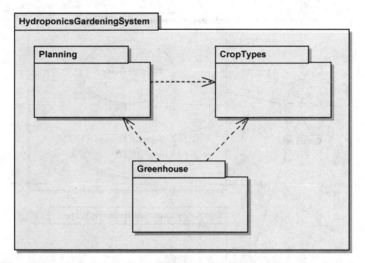

Figure 5–6 Aggregation of Contained Element Dependencies

Essentials: Package Diagrams

So far, we've discussed what could be referred to as the constituent pieces of a package diagram:

- Package notation
- Element visibility
- Dependency relationship

The package diagram is the UML 2.0 structure diagram that contains packages as the primary represented UML element and shows dependencies between the packages.

However, the package notation can be used to show the structuring and containment of many different model elements, such as classes, as shown earlier in Figures 5–4 and 5–5. It can also be used on UML diagrams that are not structure diagrams. We alluded to this earlier when we mentioned that a package can be used to organize use cases. This might be done for the sake of clarity in a very large system or to partition work. An example appears in Figure 5–7, where packages are used to group use cases of the `HydroponicsGardeningSystem` to facilitate their specification among two groups with different expertise—operations and support [55]. We'll discuss actors and use cases in depth later in this chapter.

The elements grouped in a package should typically be related in some manner, such as the subsystems within a system, use cases related to a particular aspect of

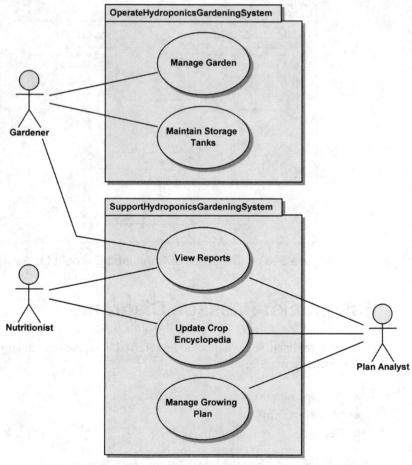

Figure 5–7 The Package Notation Used for Partitioning

the system, or classes that collaborate to provide a usable subset of system functionality [56].

What are the criteria for deciding how to package elements? There are many different ways to organize a system with packages—by architectural layer, by subsystem, by user (for use cases), and so on. Good packages are loosely coupled and highly cohesive; that is, we should see more interaction among the elements within a package and less between the packages. We should also strive not to extend generalization hierarchies or aggregations across packages. Similarly, don't break use case include or extend relationships across packages [57]—again, this will become clearer after our discussion of classes and use cases later in this chapter.

Every element contained within a namespace may be referred to with a qualified name in the format of `package name::element name`. Elements are permitted to have the same name as long as they belong to different namespaces (reside in different packages) [58, 59]. This leads us into the advanced concepts of import and access.

Advanced Concepts: Import and Access

Import and access are really two sides of the same coin—import is a public package import, whereas access is a private package import. What this really means is that in an import, other elements that have visibility into the importing package can see the imported items. But, when a package performs an access, no other elements can see those elements that have been added to the importing package's namespace. These items are private; they are not visible outside the package that performed the access [60, 61].

At this point, you're probably wondering why we would perform a package import or package access. Doing so gives us the ability to refer to the public elements of another namespace by using unqualified names; the importing package adds the names of the imported elements to its namespace. However, if any of the imported elements are of the same type and have the same name as an owned element, they are not added to the importing namespace. Similarly, if any elements imported from multiple different namespaces are of the same type and have the same name, they are not added to the importing namespace [62, 63].

The import of a package's elements can be broad or focused—all the elements or just selected ones may be imported. Look back at Figure 5–5, which shows the `PlanAnalyst` class with a dependency on the `CropEncyclopedia` class. Because the `Planning` package does not import or access the `CropTypes` package, `PlanAnalyst` must use the qualified name `HydroponicsGardeningSystem::CropTypes::CropEncyclopedia` to reference the `CropEncyclopedia` class.

To indicate that the Planning package imports the CropTypes package, a dependency is shown from Planning to CropTypes and is labeled with «import», for a *public* package import, as shown in Figure 5–8. This means that both PlanAnalyst and PlanMetrics can access the CropEncyclopedia and CropDatabase classes with their unqualified names. This is true for PlanMetrics because its namespace (Plans package) provides it access to the elements of outer packages within which it is nested.

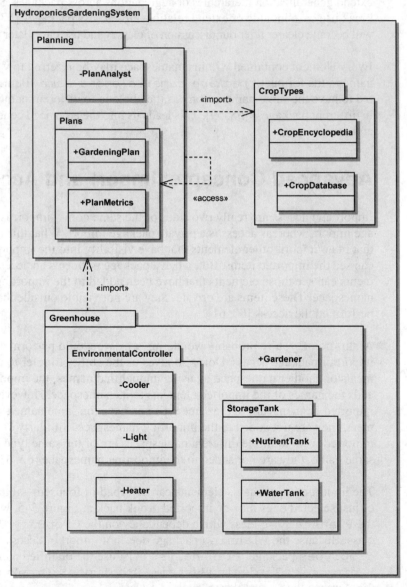

Figure 5–8 Package Import in the HydroponicsGardeningSystem

Figure 5–8 also shows the `Planning` package performing a private import of the `Plans` package, as illustrated by the dependency labeled with «`access`». This is necessary to allow the `PlanAnalyst` class to access the `GardeningPlan` and `PlanMetrics` classes with unqualified names. But, since an access dependency is private, the `Greenhouse` package's import of the `Planning` package doesn't provide the `Greenhouse` package elements, such as the `Gardener` class, with the ability to reference `GardeningPlan` and `PlanMetrics` with unqualified names. In addition, the elements of the `Greenhouse` package can't even see the `PlanAnalyst` class because it has private visibility.

Looking inside the `Greenhouse` package, the `Gardener` class must use the qualified names of the elements within the `StorageTank` package because its namespace does not import the package. For example, it must use the name `StorageTank::WaterTank` to reference the `WaterTank` class. Taking this one more step, we look at the elements within the `EnvironmentalController` package. They all have private visibility. This means they are not visible outside their namespace, that is, the `EnvironmentalController` package.

To summarize, an unqualified name (often called a *simple name*) is the name of the element without any path information telling us how to locate it within our model. This unqualified name can be used to access the following elements in a package [64, 65]:

- Owned elements
- Imported elements
- Elements within outer packages

A nested package can use an unqualified name to reference the contents of its containing package, through all levels of nesting. However, if an element in an outer package is of the same type and has the same name as one within the inner package, a qualified name must be used. The access situation from a containing package's perspective is quite different, though—the package is required to import its nested packages to reference their elements with unqualified names [66, 67].

5.3 Component Diagrams

A component represents a reusable piece of software that provides some meaningful aggregate of functionality. At the lowest level, a component is a cluster of classes that are themselves cohesive but are loosely coupled relative to other clusters. Each class in the system must live in a single component or at the top level of the system. A component may also contain other components.

Components are a type of structured classifier whose collaborations and internal structure can be shown on a component diagram. A component, collaborating with other components through well-defined interfaces to provide a system's functionality, may itself be comprised of components that collaborate to provide its own functionality. Thus, components may be used to hierarchically decompose a system and represent its logical architecture. This logical perspective of a component is new with UML 2.0. Previously, a component was regarded as a physical item that was deployed within a system. Now, a component may be manifested by an artifact that is deployed on a node [68, 69].

The essential elements of a component diagram are components, their interfaces, and their realizations.

Essentials: The Component Notation

Since a component is a structured classifier, its detailed assembly can be shown with a composite structure using parts, ports, and connectors. Figure 5–9 shows the notation used to represent a component. Its name, `EnvironmentalControlSystem` in this case, is included within the classifier rectangle in bold lettering, using the specific naming convention defined by the development team. In addition, one or both of the component tags should be included: the keyword label «`component`» and the component icon shown in the upper right-hand corner of the classifier rectangle [70, 71].

On the boundary of the classifier rectangle, we have seven ports, which are denoted by small squares. Ports have public visibility unless otherwise noted. Components may also have hidden ports, which are denoted by the same small squares, but they are represented totally inside the boundary of the composite structure, with only one edge touching its internal boundary. Hidden ports may be used for capabilities such as test points that are not to be publicly available. Ports

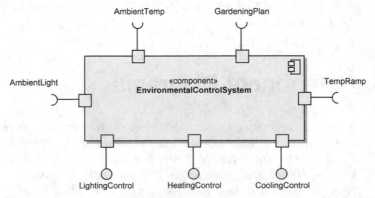

Figure 5–9 The Component Notation for `EnvironmentalControlSystem`

are used by the component for its interactions with its environment, and they provide encapsulation to the structured classifier. These seven ports are unnamed but should be named, in the format of *port name* : *Port Type*, when needed for clarity. The port type is optional when naming a port [72, 73].

To the ports shown in Figure 5–9, we have connected interfaces, which define the component's interaction details. The interfaces are shown in the ball-and-socket notation. Provided interfaces use the ball notation to specify the functionality that the component will provide to its environment; LightingControl is an example of a provided interface. Required interfaces use the socket notation to specify the services that the component requires from its environment; AmbientTemp is one of the required interfaces [74, 75].

This representation of EnvironmentalControlSystem is considered a black-box perspective since we see only the functionality required or provided by the component at its boundary. We are not able to peer inside and see the encapsulated components or classes that actually provide the functionality.

A one-to-one relationship between ports and interfaces is not required; ports can be used to group interfaces, as shown in Figure 5–10. This may be done, for example, to provide clarity in a very complex diagram or to represent the intention of having one port through which certain types of interactions will take place. In Figure 5–10, the ambient measurements of light and temperature are received at one port. Similarly, the gardening plan and temperature ramp information provided by the staff of the Hydroponics Gardening System are received at a single port. Note that the interface names are separated by a comma when using this notation. On these complex ports, we could alternately show separate interfaces such that one port would contain two required interfaces, one named AmbientLight and the other named AmbientTemp, and the other port would contain a required interface named GardeningPlan and another one named TempRamp [76, 77].

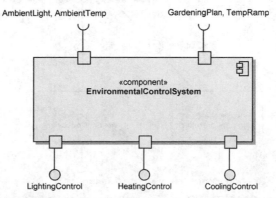

Figure 5–10 The Component Notation with Interface Grouping

Essentials: The Component Diagram

During development, we use component diagrams to indicate the logical layering and partitioning of our architecture. In them, we represent the interdependencies of components, that is, their collaborations through well-defined interfaces to provide a system's functionality. Figure 5–11 shows the component diagram for `EnvironmentalControlSystem`. This white-box perspective shows the four encapsulated components that provide its functionality: `Environmental Controller`, `LightingController`, `HeatingController`, and `CoolingController` [78, 79].

As in Figure 5–9, the ball-and-socket notation is used to specify the required and provided interfaces of each of the components. The interfaces between the components are called *assembly connectors*; they are also known as *interface connectors*. Though the assembly connectors are shown in the ball-and-socket notation, we could have used a straight line to represent each connection. However, this would not be as informative. The interface between `Environmental Controller` and `CoolingController` is shown with a dependency to illustrate another form of representation. This dependency is actually redundant because the interface names are the same: `CoolControl` [80, 81].

Previously, we mentioned the reusable nature of components. For example, as long as another component fulfills the requirements of `LightingController`'s

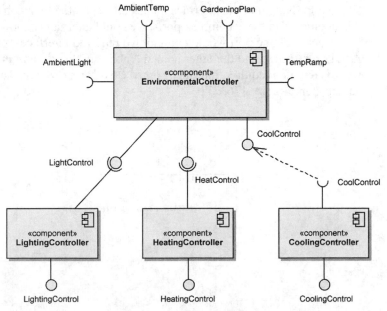

Figure 5–11 The Component Diagram for `EnvironmentalControlSystem`

interfaces, it may replace `LightingController` within `Environmental ControlSystem`. This property of components means that we may more easily upgrade our system as needed. In fact, the entire contents of `Environmental ControlSystem` may be replaced, as long as its required and provided interface requirements are met by its contained components.

Essentials: Component Interfaces

If we need to show more details about a component's interfaces, we may provide an interface specification, as shown in Figure 5–12. In our case, the specification focuses on only two of the seven interfaces of `EnvironmentalController`: `CoolControl` and `AmbientTemp` [82, 83].

`EnvironmentalController` realizes the `CoolControl` interface; this means that it provides the functionality specified by the interface. This functionality is starting, stopping, setting the temperature, and setting the fan speed for any component using the interface, as shown by the contained operations. These operations may be further detailed with parameters and return types, if needed. The `CoolingController` component (shown in Figure 5–11) requires the functionality of this interface.

Figure 5–12 also shows the dependency of the `EnvironmentalController` component on the `AmbientTemp` interface. Through this interface, `EnvironmentalController` acquires the ambient temperature that it requires to fulfill its responsibilities within the `EnvironmentalControl System` component.

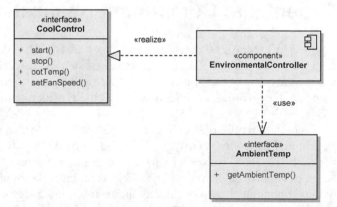

Figure 5–12 The Specification of Two Interfaces for
`EnvironmentalController`

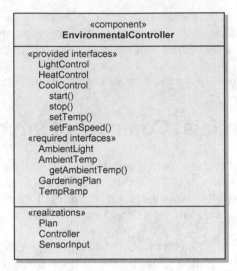

Figure 5–13 An Alternate Notation for `EnvironmentalController`'s Interfaces and Realizations

In Figure 5–13, we show an alternate notation for the interfaces of `EnvironmentalController`. Here we see the three provided interfaces listed under the heading «provided interfaces». For the `CoolControl` interface specified in Figure 5–12, we have provided the associated operations. Likewise, the required interfaces are shown under the heading «required interfaces», along with three classes listed under the «realizations» heading [84, 85]. We discuss the concept of realizations in the next section.

Essentials: Component Realizations

Figure 5–13 specifies that the `EnvironmentalController` component is realized by the classes `Plan`, `Controller`, and `SensorInput`. These three classes provide all of the functionality advertised by its provided interfaces. But, in doing so, they require the functionality specified by its required interfaces [86, 87].

This realization relationship between the `EnvironmentalController` component and the `Plan`, `Controller`, and `SensorInput` classes is shown in Figure 5–14. Here, we see a realization dependency from each of the classes to `EnvironmentalController`. This same information may be represented with a containment relationship, as shown in Figure 5–15; each of the classes is physically contained by the `EnvironmentalController` component. The naming convention used for these internal classifiers is tool-specific. Also, note the associations between the classes and the specification of multiplicity [88].

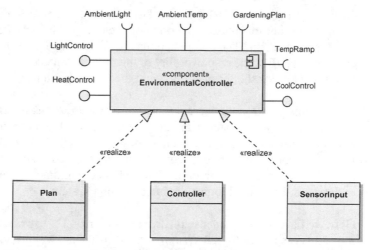

Figure 5–14 The Realization Dependencies for `EnvironmentalController`

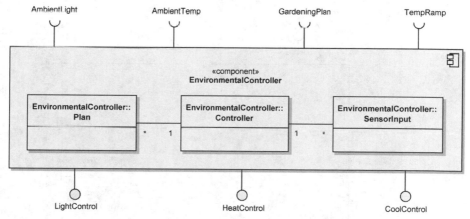

Figure 5–15 The Containment Representation of
`EnvironmentalController`'s Realization

Advanced Concepts: A Component's Internal Structure

The internal structure of a component may be shown by using an internal structure diagram; Figure 5–16 shows just such a diagram for the `Environmental ControlSystem` subsystem. In this example, we have changed its keyword label from «component», as shown in Figure 5–9, to «subsystem» because it is comprised of four components of some complexity that are logically related. Of course, this is a judgment call; the label could reasonably be left as «component». In addition, Figure 5–16 contains a notation that we haven't encountered yet, the «delegate» label on the lines between the interfaces of the internal components and the ports on the edge of the Environmental ControlSystem. These connections provide the means to show which internal component fulfills the responsibility of the provided interfaces and which internal component needs the services shown in the required interfaces [89, 90].

Subsystems partition the logical model of a system. A subsystem is an aggregate containing other subsystems and other components. Each component in the system must live in a single subsystem or at the top level of the system. In practice, a large system has one top-level component diagram, consisting of the subsystems at the highest level of abstraction. Through this diagram a developer comes to understand the general logical architecture of a system.

Here we have more of a sense of EnvironmentalControlSystem as a reusable component (or subsystem, if you wish) than we did with Figure 5–11. We use ports at its boundary and show that the responsibility for fulfilling the "contract" of an interface has been delegated to one or more of the component's

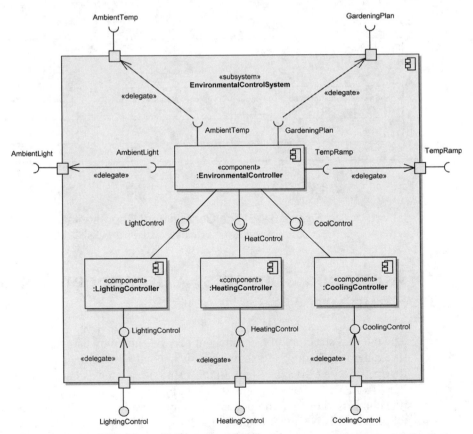

Figure 5–16 The Internal Structure of EnvironmentalControlSystem

contained parts. However, remember that these contained parts may require services from the environment of the `EnvironmentalControlSystem` component, such as a gardening plan to meet this contract.

To be specific, `:EnvironmentalController` requires `GardeningPlan`, which specifies the environmental needs (lighting, heating, and cooling) of the Hydroponics Gardening System. The needs of this required interface are delegated to an unnamed port, to which is attached the `GardeningPlan` interface. In this manner, we know that we must provide the `EnvironmentalControlSystem` component with a gardening plan if we intend to use its services. We also recognize that we must provide it with `AmbientLight`, `AmbientTemp`, and `TempRamp` services.

The connectors of `EnvironmentalControlSystem` provide its communication links to its environment, as well as the means for its parts to communicate internally. In Figure 5–16, the type of connectors new to our view of `Environmental ControlSystem` are the *delegation connectors* to which we've alluded. Through these connectors, the responsibilities (provided interfaces) of `EnvironmentalControlSystem`, as well as its requirements (required interfaces), are communicated. For example, the `:LightingController` component opaquely provides the `LightingControl` services. A user of `EnvironmentalControlSystem` would not likely have this white-box perspective of the subsystem [91, 92].

5.4 Deployment Diagrams

A deployment diagram is used to show the allocation of artifacts to nodes in the physical design of a system. A single deployment diagram represents a view into the artifact structure of a system. During development, we use deployment diagrams to indicate the physical collection of nodes that serve as the platform for execution of our system.

The three essential elements of a deployment diagram are artifacts, nodes, and their connections.

Essentials: The Artifact Notation

An artifact is a physical item that implements a portion of the software design. It is typically software code (executable) but could also be a source file, a document, or another item related to the software code. Artifacts may have relationships with other artifacts, such as a dependency or a composition [20, 21].

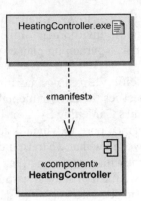

Figure 5–17 The Artifact Notation
for `HeatingController.exe`

The notation for an artifact consists of a class rectangle containing the name of the artifact, the keyword label «artifact», and an optional icon that looks like a sheet of paper with the top right-hand corner folded over. Figure 5–17 shows the `HeatingController.exe` artifact, without the optional icon.

The name of this artifact includes the extension `.exe`, indicating that it is an executable (i.e., software code). The `HeatingController.exe` artifact has a dependency relationship to the `HeatingController` component, labeled with «manifest». This means that it physically implements the component, thereby connecting the implementation to the design. An artifact may manifest more than one component [22].

Essentials: The Node Notation

A node is a computational resource, typically containing memory and processing, on which artifacts are deployed for execution. Nodes may contain other nodes to represent complex execution capability; this is shown by nesting or using a composition relationship. There are two types of nodes: devices and execution environments [23, 24].

A device is a piece of hardware that provides computational capabilities, such as a computer, a modem, or a sensor. An execution environment is software that provides for the deployment of specific types of executing artifacts; examples include «database» and «J2EE server». Execution environments are typically hosted by a device [25].

Figure 5–18 shows the three-dimensional cube icon that we use to represent a node, in this case, the `PC` and `ApplicationServer` nodes. The icon may be adorned with a symbol to provide additional visual specification of the node type. There are no particular constraints on node names because they denote hardware, not software, entities.

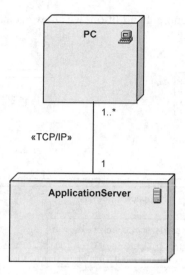

Figure 5–18 Notations
for Two Nodes

Nodes communicate with one another, via messages and signals, through a communication path indicated by a solid line. Communication paths are usually considered to be bidirectional, although if a particular connection is unidirectional, an arrow may be added to show the direction. Each communication path may include an optional keyword label, such as «http» or «TCP/IP», that provides information about the connection. We may also specify multiplicity for each of the nodes connected via a communication path.

In Figure 5–18, the communication between the PC and ApplicationServer nodes is bidirectional. A communication path usually represents some direct hardware coupling, such as a USB cable, an Ethernet connection, or even a path to shared memory. However, the path could also represent more indirect couplings, such as satellite-to-ground or mobile phone communications. In our case, it represents a bidirectional connection using TCP/IP protocols. We've specified the connection of one or more PC nodes to one ApplicationServer node.

Essentials: The Deployment Diagram

In Figure 5–19, we provide an example of a deployment diagram drawn primarily from the physical architecture of the Environmental Control System within the Hydroponics Gardening System. Here we see that our system architects have decided to decompose this portion of our system into a network of two nodes (PC and ApplicationServer) and two devices (LightMeter and Thermometer). If you compare this deployment diagram to the component diagram of EnvironmentalControlSystem (presented earlier in Figure 5–11), you will see that it does not account for all of its interfaces; we omitted some to somewhat simplify our example. In addition, we show each artifact implementing exactly one component.

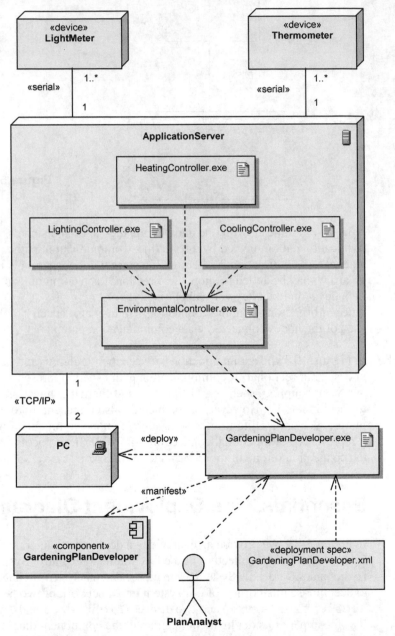

Figure 5–19 The Deployment Diagram for `EnvironmentalControlSystem`

The deployment of the `EnvironmentalController.exe`, `LightingController.exe`, `HeatingController.exe`, and `CoolingController.exe` artifacts on the `ApplicationServer` node is indicated by containment. Another way to denote deployment is shown by the dependency from the `GardeningPlanDeveloper.exe` artifact to the `PC` node labeled with «`deploy`». A third way to denote deployment is through textually listing the artifacts within the node icon; this is especially useful for larger or more complex deployment diagrams [26, 27].

We have three unnamed dependencies within Figure 5–19 between artifacts: from the `LightingController.exe`, `HeatingController.exe`, and `CoolingController.exe` artifacts to the `EnvironmentalController.exe` artifact. These denote the dependencies between the components that they implement, rather than deployment onto a node.

We also have another dependency, from the `EnvironmentalController.exe` artifact to the `GardeningPlanDeveloper.exe` artifact. This relates back to the interface on the `EnvironmentalController` component, which requires a gardening plan. Here we see that the gardening plan will be developed by `PlanAnalyst` using the `GardeningPlanDeveloper.exe` artifact, which manifests the `GardeningPlanDeveloper` component. Note that `PlanAnalyst` may perform this task from either of two `PC` nodes.

The two devices, `LightMeter` and `Thermometer`, provide the ambient light and ambient temperature sensor readings required by the `EnvironmentalController.exe` artifact in support of its provision of functionality to the system. One item we have yet to discuss is the `GardeningPlanDeveloper.xml` deployment specification, which has a dependency relationship to the `GardeningPlanDeveloper.exe` artifact. This deployment specification describes deployment properties of the artifact, such as its execution and transaction specifics [28].

5.5 Use Case Diagrams

Evidence over the years has shown that some of the most common reasons software projects fail center around poor or nonexistent communication between the key stakeholders. This is particularly critical when there is lack of alignment between the development organization and the line of business. The business people may know that they have a certain problem that needs to be solved, but the development organization may receive only a general description of what the business wants, with few specific requirements. Would you build your home that way? In one of the most pathological cases we've seen, people in one business organization viewed communicating with developers as demeaning and potentially harmful to their business careers.

Sometimes development people will have specifications but will have no idea what the business's goals are, that is, why they are building the system. Does the business, interested in being a low-cost provider, want the system to reduce costs? Or is the goal to provide high-quality, personalized service? Does the business want to be faster or to be innovative? If the development organization does not understand the business goals, when given a choice of approaches during design and implementation, developers could make technical decisions that directly conflict with the business goals.

There is a strong need for an approach to system development that allows the development organization to understand what the business wants while not being cumbersome to the business staff (after all, their primary job is to run the daily operation of the business). Use case diagrams give us that capability. Use case diagrams are used to depict the context of the system to be built and the functionality provided by that system. They depict who (or what) interacts with the system. They show what the outside world wants the system to do.

Essentials: Actors

Actors are entities that interface with the system. They can be people or other systems. Actors, which are external to the system they are using, are depicted as stylized stick figures. Figure 5–20 shows two actors for the Hydroponics Gardening System we discussed earlier.

One way to think of actors is to consider the roles the actors play. In the real world, people (and systems) may serve in many different roles; for example, a person can be a salesperson, a manager, a father, an artist, and so forth.

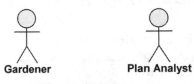

Gardener   **Plan Analyst**

Figure 5–20 Actors

Essentials: Use Cases

Use cases represent *what* the actors want your system to do for them. Figure 5–21 depicts some use cases, shown as ovals, for the Hydroponics Gardening System. Use cases are not just any capability that your system may provide. A use case must be a *complete* flow of activity, from the *actor's point of view*, that provides *value* to the actor. As defined by Jacobson et al. [16]:

> A use case is a specific way of using the system by using some part of the functionality. . . . A use case is thus a special sequence of related transactions performed by an actor and the system in a dialogue. . . . Each use case is a complete course of events in the system from a user's perspective.

Essentials: The Use Case Diagram

To show which actors use which use cases, you can create a use case diagram by connecting them via basic associations, shown by lines, as in Figure 5–22.

The associations in the use case diagram indicate which actors initiate which use cases. Here we see that only the `Gardener` actor can maintain the storage tanks, but all the actors may view reports.

Specifying Use Case Details

So how do we specify the details of the functionality provided by use cases? How do we specify the complete course of events? The optimal way is to use additional UML models (such as activity diagrams, which we will discuss later in this chapter) and textual specifications. There are many different formats for use case specifications in the UML literature. Most include the following information at a minimum: the name of the use case; its purpose, in the form of a short description; the optimistic flow (i.e., the flow of events that will occur if everything goes right in the use case); and one or more pragmatic flows (i.e., those flows where things don't occur as you intended).

Figure 5–21 Use Cases

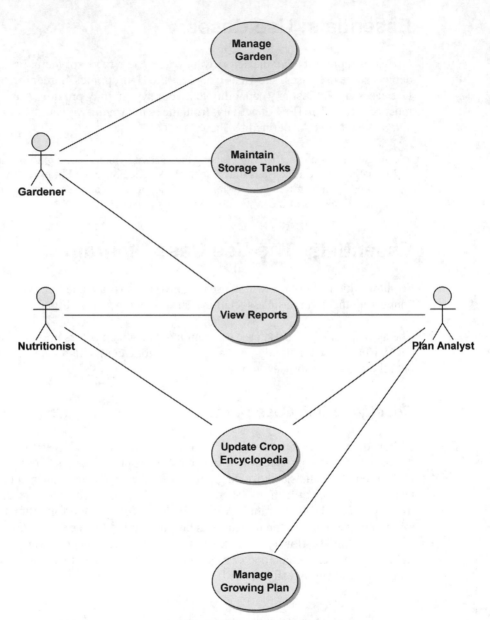

Figure 5–22 A Use Case Diagram

An Example Use Case Specification

Let us look at an example for the use case `Maintain Storage Tanks`.

Use Case Specification

Use case name: `Maintain Storage Tanks`

Use case purpose: This use case provides the ability to maintain the fill levels of the contents of the storage tanks. This use case allows the actor to maintain specific sets of water and nutrient tanks.

Optimistic flow:

    A. Actor examines the levels of the storage tanks' contents.

    B. Actor determines that tanks need to be refilled.

    C. Normal hydroponics system operation of storage tanks is suspended by the actor.

    D. Actor selects tanks and sets fill levels.

For each selected tank, steps E through G are performed.

    E. If tank is heated, the system disables heaters.

        1. Heaters reach safe temperature.

    F. The system fills tank.

    G. When tank is filled, if tank is heated, the system enables heaters.

        1. Tank contents reach operating temperature.

    H. Actor resumes normal hydroponics system operation.

Pragmatic flows:

Conditions triggering alternate flow:

Condition 1: There is insufficient material to fill tanks to the levels specified by the actor.

    D1. Alert actor regarding insufficient material available to meet tank setting. Show amount of material available.

    D2. Prompt actor to choose to end maintenance or reset fill levels.

    D3. If reset chosen, perform step D.

    D4. If end maintenance chosen, perform step H.

    D5. Else, perform step D2.

Condition 2: . . .

Other useful information may also be added to the specification, such as preconditions (what must be true prior to executing the use case), postconditions (what will be true after executing the use case), limitations, assumptions, and so forth. For example, in our hydroponics system, there is a limitation that the nutrient and water tanks for a given crop must be refilled, as a pair, during the same maintenance activity. This is a business operations decision (limitation) established in order to not disrupt the proportions of nutrient and water being provided to the crop.

Overall, a use case specification should not be very long—it should be only a few pages. If your specifications are very long, you should reconsider whether your use case is doing too much. It may be that it is actually more than one use case. Also, for practical reasons, you cannot include all possible things that could trigger an alternate flow. Include the most important or critical alternates. Do not include every possible error condition, such as when the operator enters data in the wrong format (let the user interface handle that type of exception).

Advanced Concepts: «include» and «extend» Relationships

Two relationships used primarily for organizing use case models are both powerful and commonly misused: the «include» and «extend» relationships. These relationships are used between use cases.

«include» Relationships

In our hydroponics example, we have an Update Crop Encyclopedia use case. During analysis, we determine that the Nutritionist actor using that use case will have to see what is in the crop encyclopedia prior to updating it. This is why the Nutritionist can invoke the View Reports use case. The same is true for the Gardener actor whenever invoking Maintain Storage Tanks. Neither actor should be executing the use cases blindly. Therefore, the View Report use case is a common functionality that both other use cases need. This can be depicted on the use case model via an «include» relationship, as shown in Figure 5–23.

This diagram states, for example, that the Update Crop Encyclopedia use case includes the View Reports use case. This means that View Reports must be executed when Update Crop Encyclopedia is executed. Update Crop Encyclopedia would not be considered complete without View Reports.

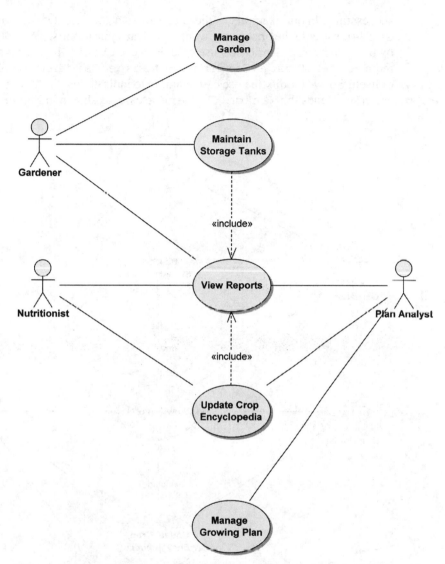

Figure 5–23 A Use Case Diagram Showing «include» Relationships

Where an included use case is executed, it is indicated in the use case specification as an inclusion point. The inclusion point specifies where, in the flow of the including use case, the included use case is to be executed.

«extend» Relationships

While developing your use cases, you may find that certain activities might be performed as part of the use case but are not mandatory for that use case to run successfully. In our example, as the `Gardener` actor executes the `Manage Garden` use case, he or she may want to look at some reports. This could be done by using the `View Reports` use case. However, `View Reports` is not required when `Manage Garden` is run. `Manage Garden` is complete in and of itself. So, we modify the use case diagram to indicate that the `View Reports` use case extends the `Manage Garden` use case, as shown in Figure 5–24.

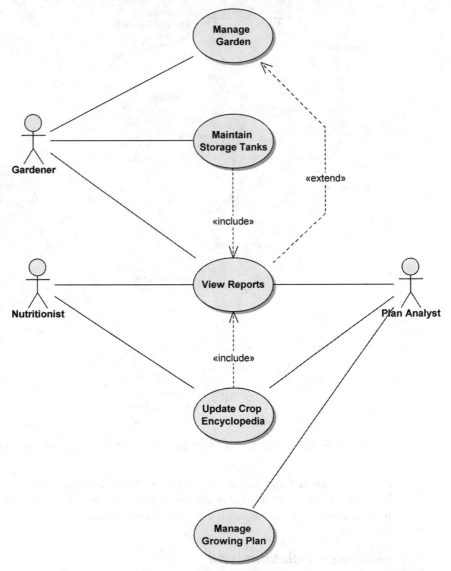

Figure 5–24 A Use Case Diagram Showing an `<<extend>>` Relationship

Where an extending use case is executed, it is indicated in the use case specification as an extension point. The extension point specifies where, in the flow of the including use case, the extending use case is to be executed. Note also that the extension points can be shown on the use case diagram, as indicated in Figure 5–25.

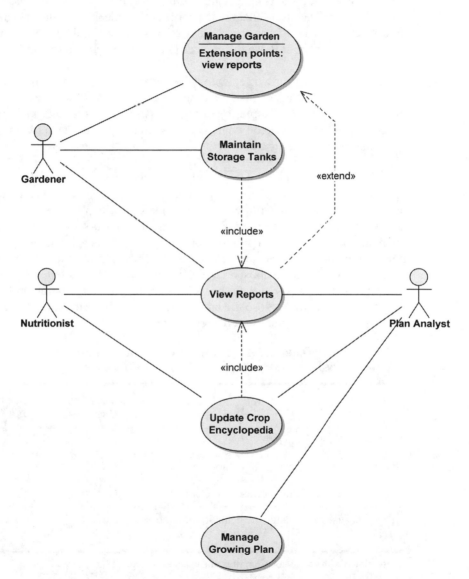

Figure 5–25 A Use Case Diagram Showing an Extension Point

The Dangers of «include» and «extend» Relationships

While these two concepts are very useful for specifying common functionality («include») and simplifying more complex use case flows («extend»), as we indicated earlier, these concepts are commonly misused during use case modeling. The primary cause is that some people are not clear about the semantic differences between «include» and «extend». Maksimchuk and Naiburg provide a concise summary of those differences [17], as summarized in Table 5–1.

Another common error we see with these relationships is violation of basic use case principles. Included and extending use cases are still use cases and must conform to the use case principles cited earlier; a use case represents a *complete* flow of activity of *what* the actor wants your system to do from the *actor's point of view* that provides *value* to the actor.

If you stick to these principles strongly, you will avoid yet another error: use of these relationships to "functionally decompose" use cases. This is the most prevalent problem we see regarding use case models, in which people break down use cases into smaller and smaller pieces, using «include» or «extend» to tie them all together. This problem is rooted in a software development culture where Structured Analysis/Structured Design (SA/SD) approaches were very prevalent. These approaches decomposed large development problems into smaller pieces. Doing this will quickly violate the use case principles noted in the previous paragraph. You will quickly lose the advantages of the object model of development that we noted in the first four chapters of this book.

Table 5–1 Key Differences between «include» and «extend» Relationships[a]

	Included Use Case	Extending Use Case
Is this use case optional?	No	Yes
Is the base use case complete without this use case?	No	Yes
Is the execution of this use case conditional?	No	Yes
Does this use case change the behavior of the base use case?	No	Yes

a. Reprinted with permission from Maksimchuk and Naiburg [17].

Advanced Concepts: Generalization

Generalization relationships, as described in Chapter 3, can also be used to relate use cases. As with classes, use cases can have common behaviors that other use cases (i.e., child use cases) can modify by adding steps or refining others. For example, Figure 5–26 shows the use cases for purchasing various tickets.

`Purchase Ticket` contains the basic steps necessary for purchasing any tickets, while the child use cases specialize `Purchase Ticket` for the specific kinds of tickets being purchased.

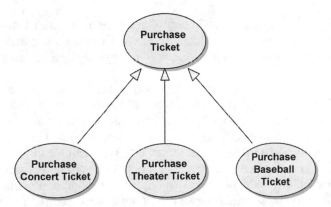

Figure 5–26 A Use Case Generalization

5.6 Activity Diagrams

In the previous section, we described the flow of a use case with text (the use case specification). Textual descriptions have several advantages: They are easy to create and change (no complex tools are required), they can be created anywhere (all you need is paper and a pencil), they can be easily used and shared by business and development staff alike, and so forth. However, complex use cases, business processes, and algorithms can be difficult to comprehend when captured in text. A visual representation of complex flows is much more powerful. We can see potential problems visually that a stack of textual specifications could never reveal.

We know of one project for which a complex production process was documented in reams of formal specifications that were developed and maintained by a company serving as the program office for the project. These specifications were also reviewed by other companies, which served as the implementers of the process. Even with all this rigor and control, when a basic visual diagram was made of the product flow, multiple dead ends in the production process were quickly revealed.

Activity diagrams provide visual depictions of the flow of activities, whether in a system, business, workflow, or other process. These diagrams focus on the activities that are performed and who (or what) is responsible for the performance of those activities.

The elements of an activity diagram are action nodes, control nodes, and object nodes. There are three types of control nodes: initial and final (final nodes have two varieties, activity final and flow final), decision and merge, and fork and join.[1]

Essentials: Actions

Actions are the elemental unit of behavior in an activity diagram. Activities can contain many actions which are what activity diagrams depict. Figure 5–27 shows an action that can be performed in our hydroponics example.

Note the rake symbol inside the action notation at its bottom right-hand corner. This denotes that this action is a `callBehavior` type action, which is one of the predefined actions in UML 2 that are "primitive actions that model manipulation of objects and links as well as computation and communication among objects" [101]. The `callBehavior` type action calls an activity whose definition is composed of action nodes, control nodes, and object nodes. Consequently, the majority of actions used in our activity diagram modeling would be of this type, at least in higher-level activity diagrams. So, as a practical matter, we may want to use the rake symbol only when we have actually defined that activity to be called.

Figure 5–27 The Notation for an Action

Essentials: Starting and Stopping

Since an activity diagram shows a process flow, that flow must start and stop somewhere. The starting point (the initial node) for an activity flow is shown as a solid dot, and the stopping point (the activity final node) is shown as a bull's-eye.

---

1. Conrad Bock's series of five articles ("UML 2 Activity and Action Models") provides a detailed look into this subject. See Section L of the Classified Bibliography.

Figure 5–28 Initial and Final Nodes for a Simple Activity Diagram

Figure 5–28 depicts a simple activity diagram composed of one action, Check Tank Levels.

Another type of final node is the flow final node, which is denoted by a circle with a nested "X" symbol. The flow final node, used to stop a single flow without stopping the entire activity, is depicted in the discussion of the merge node.

Essentials: Decision and Merge Nodes

Decision and merge nodes control the flow in an activity diagram. Each node is represented by a diamond shape with incoming and outgoing arrows. A decision node has one incoming flow and multiple outgoing flows. Its purpose is to direct the one incoming flow into one (and only one) of the node's outgoing flows. The outgoing flows usually have guard conditions that determine which outgoing path is selected. Figure 5–29 shows the guard condition [all levels within tolerance] and the alternative [else]. There is no waiting or synchronization at a decision node.

Merge nodes take multiple input flows and direct any and all of them to one outgoing flow. There is no waiting or synchronization at a merge node. In Figure 5–30, whenever any of the three incoming flows reach the merge point (shown as

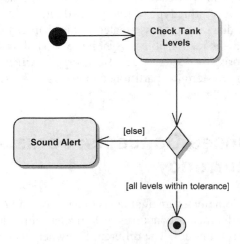

Figure 5–29 A Decision Node

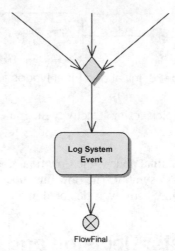

Figure 5–30 A Merge Node with a Flow Final Node

a diamond), each will be routed through it to the Log System Event action. Thus, multiple events will be logged. Figure 5–30 also shows the flow final node that we discussed earlier.

Essentials: Partitions

The elements in an activity diagram can be grouped by using partitions. The purpose of a partition is to indicate where the responsibility lies for performing specific activities. In a business model, the partitions may be business units, divisions, or organizations. For systems, the partitions may be other systems or subsystems. In application modeling, the partitions may be objects in the application. (However, this type of fine-grained interaction is more often shown in a sequence diagram, discussed later in this chapter.) Each partition may be named to indicate the responsible party. Figure 5–31 shows how the various activities that comprise the Maintain Storage Tanks use case of our Hydroponics Gardening System are partitioned to the Gardener, WaterTank, and NutrientTank.

Advanced Concepts: Forks, Joins, and Concurrency

Fork and join nodes are analogous to decision and merge nodes, respectively. The critical difference is concurrency. Forks have one flow in and multiple flows out, as do decision nodes. The difference is, where a decision node selects a single outbound flow, a single flow into a fork results in multiple outbound flows. All

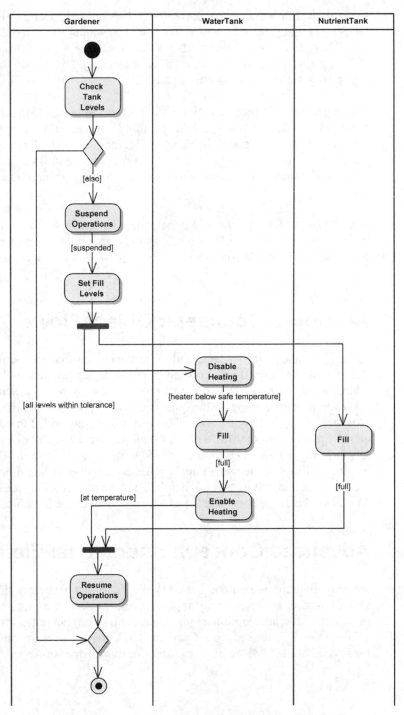

Figure 5–31 An Activity Diagram with Partitions

the outbound flows occur concurrently. In Figure 5–31, a single flow goes from the Set Fill Levels action into the fork, which is the first thick horizontal line. Thereafter, the NutrientTank flow (with the Fill action) and the WaterTank flow (with the Disable Heating, Fill, and Enable Heating actions) both occur in parallel.

A join has multiple incoming flows and a single outbound flow, similar to merge nodes. However, with a join, all the incoming flows must be completed before the outbound flow commences. In Figure 5–31, the second thick horizontal line is a join. Both of the incoming flows, NutrientTank and WaterTank, must be complete before the outbound flow continues to the Resume Operations action.

(Similar to the concept of a join, where there are multiple flows into an action, whether control or object flow, all flows must arrive at the action before it can begin. When an action completes, all flows [control and object] out of the action are begun.)

Advanced Concepts: Object Flows

In some situations, it may be useful to see the objects that are manipulated during the execution of an activity. You can show the objects in an activity diagram by adding an object flow. (We do not recommend this for all your activity diagrams, however, because adding all the objects would likely make the diagrams too complex and unwieldy.) Figure 5–32 shows an object flow added to our previous activity diagram. In the WaterTank partition, two object nodes (rectangles labeled :WaterTank) have been added to the flow. This shows that, after the heating is disabled, the water tank is below its low operational limit and that, after the Fill action, the water tank is full. The WaterTank object's states of [below low limit] and [full] are shown under the object name.

Advanced Concepts: Additional Elements

Activity diagrams are among the UML diagrams that have very rich semantics. Other interesting elements may appear on activity diagrams (e.g., additional types of object nodes, interruptible regions, pins, and so on) but not nearly as frequently as those we discussed earlier. If you want to learn more about activity diagrams, read some of the UML references listed for this chapter in Appendix B.

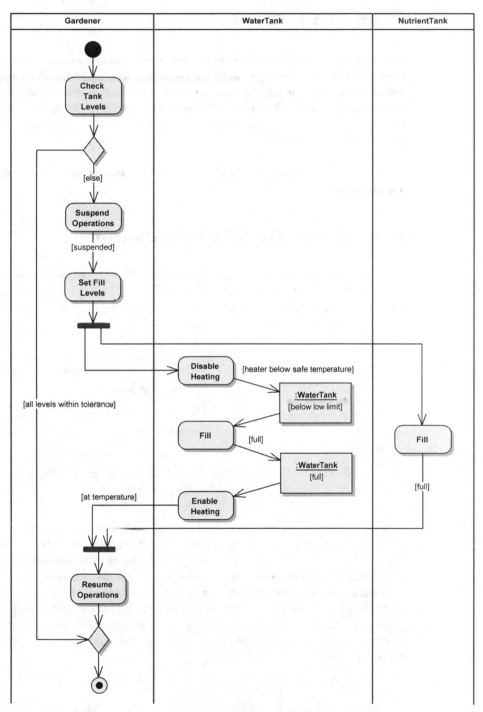

Figure 5–32 An Activity Diagram with Object Nodes

5.7 Class Diagrams

A class diagram is used to show the existence of classes and their relationships in the logical view of a system. A single class diagram represents a view of the class structure of a system. During analysis, we use class diagrams to indicate the common roles and responsibilities of the entities that provide the system's behavior. During design, we use class diagrams to capture the structure of the classes that form the system's architecture.

The two essential elements of a class diagram are classes and their basic relationships.

Essentials: The Class Notation

Figure 5–33 shows the icon used to represent a class in a class diagram and an example from our Hydroponics Gardening System. The class icon consists of three compartments, with the first occupied by the class name, the second by the attributes, and the third by the operations.

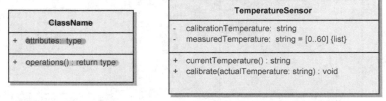

Figure 5–33 A General Class Icon and an Example for the Gardening System

A name is required for each class and must be unique to its enclosing namespace. By convention, the name begins in capital letters, and the space between multiple words is omitted. Again by convention, the first letter of the attribute and operation names is lowercase, with subsequent words starting in uppercase, and spaces are omitted just as in the class name. Since the class is the namespace for its attributes and operations, an attribute name must be unambiguous in the context of the class. So must an operation name, according to the rules in the chosen implementation language. The format of the attribute and operation specifications is shown here [29]:

- Attribute specification format:
  ```
  visibility attributeName : Type [multiplicity] =
  DefaultValue {property string}
  ```

- Operation specification format:

  visibility operationName (parameterName : Type) :
  ReturnType {property string}

We will discuss the concept of visibility (public, private, protected, or package) in an upcoming subsection. The type, for both attributes and operations, is the name of a class or data type. We will also discuss multiplicity of an attribute a little later; for now, note from Figure 5–33 that in the TemperatureSensor class, the multiplicity of [0..60] on the measuredTemperature attribute indicates an array of 0 to 60 temperature measurements. The default value for an attribute is the value to be given at creation time, if none was provided. The property string listed in braces provides additional properties such as {list} shown after the measuredTemperature attribute in the TemperatureSensor class. In this case, the keyword list means that the temperature measurements will be ordered and may be nonunique. This provides the means to see the time ordering of the measurements and to permit a repetition in measured temperature. In the format of an operation, the combination of *parameterName : Type* is repeated as needed to accommodate the number of arguments.

For certain class diagrams, it is useful to expose some of the attributes and operations associated with a class. We say "some" because for all but the most trivial class, it is clumsy and indeed unnecessary to show all such members in a diagram. In this sense, the attributes and operations that we show represent an elided view of the class's entire specification, which serves as the single point of declaration for all of its members. If we need to show many such members, we may magnify the class icon; if we choose to show no such members at all, we may drop the separating lines and show only the class name.

As a general principle for the notation, the syntax for items such as attributes and operations may be tailored to use the syntax for the chosen implementation language. This simplifies the notation by isolating the peculiarities of various languages.

As we described in Chapter 3, an abstract class is one for which no instances may be created. Because such classes are so important to engineering good class inheritance trees, there is a special way to designate an abstract class, as shown in Figure 5–34. Specifically, we italicize the class name to show that we may have only instances of its subclasses. Similarly, to denote that an operation is abstract, we simply italicize the operation name; this means that this operation may be implemented differently by all instances of its subclasses. In the Hydroponics Gardening System, we have food items that have a specific vitamin content and caloric equivalent, but there is not a type of food called "food item." Hence, the FoodItem class is abstract. Figure 5–34 also shows the subclass Tomato, which represents a concrete (instantiable) food item grown in the greenhouse [30]. We explain the meaning of the relationships among the classes in the next section.

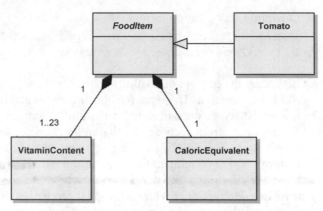

Figure 5–34 Abstract Class Adornment

Essentials: Class Relationships

Classes rarely stand alone; instead, they collaborate with other classes in a variety of ways. The essential connections among classes include association, generalization, aggregation, and composition, whose icons we summarize in Figure 5–35. Each such relationship may include a textual label that documents the name of the relationship or suggests its purpose, or the association ends may have names—but typically both are not used at the same time.

The association icon connects two classes and denotes a semantic connection. Associations are often labeled with noun phrases, such as `Analyzes` in Figure 5–35, denoting the nature of the relationship. A class may have an association to itself (called a *reflexive association*), such as the collaboration among instances of the `PlanAnalyst` class. Note here the use of both the association end names and the association name to provide clarity. It is also possible to have more than one association between the same pair of classes. Associations may be further adorned with their multiplicity, as described in Chapter 3, using the syntax in the following examples:

- `1`   Exactly one
- `*`   Unlimited number (zero or more)
- `0..*`   Zero or more
- `1..*`   One or more
- `0..1`   Zero or one
- `3..7`   Specified range (from three through seven, inclusive)

The multiplicity adornment is applied to the target end of an association and denotes the number of links between each instance of the source class and instances of the target class. Unless explicitly adorned, the multiplicity of a rela-

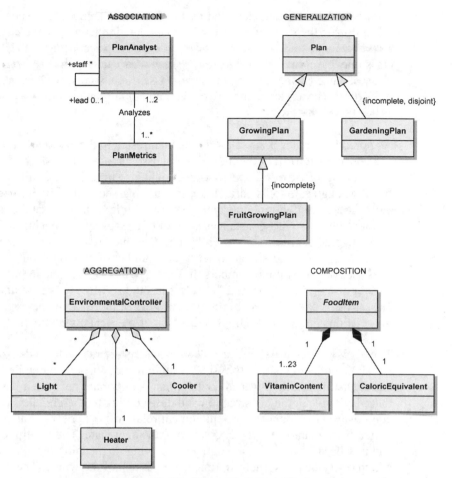

Figure 5–35 Class Relationship Icons

tionship should be considered unspecified. It is best to always show multiplicity so there is no misunderstanding.

The remaining three essential class relationships are drawn as refinements of the more general association icon. Indeed, during development, this is exactly how relationships tend to evolve. We first assert the existence of a semantic connection between two classes and then, as we make tactical decisions about the exact nature of their relationship, often refine them into generalization, aggregation, or composition relationships.

The generalization icon denotes a generalization/specialization relationship (the "is a" relationship, described in Chapter 3) and appears as an association with a closed arrowhead. The arrowhead points to the superclass, and the opposite end of the association designates the subclass. The GrowingPlan class in

Figure 5–35 is the superclass and its subclass is the `FruitGrowingPlan`. According to the rules of the chosen implementation language, the subclass inherits the structure and behavior of its superclass. Also according to these rules, a class may have one (single inheritance) or more (multiple inheritance) superclasses; name clashes among the superclasses are also resolved according to the rules of the chosen language. Also, generalization relationships may not have multiplicity adornments.

As noted in Chapter 3, aggregation, as manifested in the "part of" relationship, is a constrained form of the more general association relationship. The aggregation icon denotes a whole/part hierarchy and also implies the ability to navigate from the aggregate to its parts. It appears as an association with an unfilled diamond at the end denoting the aggregate (the whole). The class at the other end denotes the class whose instances are part of the aggregate object. Reflexive and cyclic aggregation is possible. This whole/part hierarchy does not mean physical containment: A professional society has a number of members, but by no means does the society own its members. In Figure 5–35, we see that an individual `EnvironmentalController` class has the `Light`, `Heater`, and `Cooler` classes as its parts. The multiplicity of `*` (zero or more) at the aggregate end of the relationship further highlights this lack of physical containment.

The choice of aggregation is usually an analysis or architectural design decision; the choice of composition (physical containment) is usually a detailed, tactical issue. Distinguishing physical containment is important because it has semantics that play a role in the construction and destruction of an aggregate's parts. The composition icon denoting a containment relationship appears as an association with a filled diamond at the end denoting the aggregate. The multiplicity at this end is `1` because the parts are defined as having no meaning outside the whole, which owns the parts; their lifetime is tied to that of the whole. The *FoodItem* class in Figure 5–35 physically contains the `VitaminContent` and `CaloricEquivalent` classes.

Consider another example. In Figure 5–36, we see the class `CropHistory`, whose instances physically contain `*` instances of the class `NutrientSchedule` and `*` instances of the class `ClimateEvent`. Composition implies that the construction and destruction of these parts occurs as a consequence of the construction and destruction of the aggregate. By contrast, each instance of `CropHistory` does not physically contain one instance of `Crop`. This means that the lifetimes of the two objects are independent, although the one is still considered a part of the other.

The icons described thus far constitute the essential elements of all class diagrams. Collectively, they provide the developer with a notation sufficient to describe the fundamentals of a system's class structure.

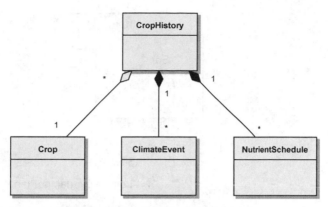

Figure 5–36 Physical Containment

Advanced Concepts: Template (Parameterized) Classes

The elements we have presented thus far constitute the essential parts of the class notation. However, there are often a number of strategic and tactical decisions that we must capture that require an extension of this basic notation. As a general rule, stick to the essential elements of the notation, and apply only those advanced concepts necessary to express analysis or design details that are essential to visualizing or understanding the system.

Some object-oriented programming languages, C++ for example, provide for template (parameterized) classes. A template class denotes a family of classes whose structure and behavior are defined independent of the formal class parameters. We must match these formal parameters with actual ones (the process of binding) to form a concrete class in this family; by concrete class, we mean one that may have instances.

Template classes are sufficiently different than plain classes to warrant a special adornment. As the example in Figure 5–37 shows, a template class is depicted as a simple class, but with a dashed-line box in the upper right-hand corner, which contains its formal parameters. A bound class is also shown as a simple class. The binding relationship between a template class and its bound class is shown as a dashed arrow, pointing to the template class, with the keyword «bind» attached. The actual parameters, bound to the formal parameters of the template, are shown along with the keyword in the form of <*Formal Parameter* → *Actual Parameter*>. In Figure 5–37, we see the PlanSet class being bound to the Set template class with the GardeningPlan class as the actual parameter replacing the formal parameter, Item.

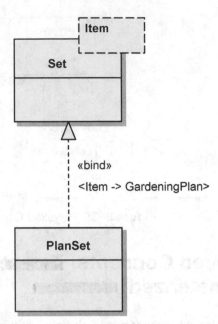

Figure 5–37 A Template Class and Its Bound Class

A template class may not have any instances and may not itself be used as a template. A bound class defines a new class distinct from all other concrete classes in the same family whose actual parameters differ.

Advanced Concepts: Visibility

In Section 5.2, Package Diagrams, we discussed the concept of visibility from the view of whether the elements contained by a package could be seen outside that package. A class also provides an enclosing namespace for its contained elements. Here, we will look at the visibility of class associations, attributes, and operations.

All interesting object-oriented programming languages provide a clear separation between the interface and implementation of a class. As we described in Chapter 3, most also permit the developer to specify finer-grained access to the interface as well. For example, in C++, members may be public (accessible to all clients), protected (accessible only to subclasses, friends, or the class itself), or private (accessible only to the class itself or its friends). Also in C++, certain elements might be a part of a class's implementation and thus inaccessible even to friends of the class; this is referred to as implementation visibility.

We may specify visibility by adorning the appropriate element with the following symbols [43]:

- **Public (+)**   Visible to any element that can see the class
- **Protected (#)**   Visible to other elements within the class and to subclasses
- **Private (-)**   Visible to other elements within the class
- **Package (~)**   Visible to elements within the same package

We denote association visibility by placing these visibility symbols on the association end names to indicate access to the target end from the source end of the association. For example, in Figure 5–38, we see that the association end names (database and crop) between the CropDatabase and GrainCrop classes are both public. This means that either class can access the other. In contrast, look at the visibility of the association end names between the GrainCrop class and the GrainYieldPredictor class; GrainCrop is private to the GrainYieldPredictor class.

Another advanced concept to note here is that of association directionality. During analysis we regard associations as bidirectional logical connections between analysis classes. During design we turn our focus to issues such as navigability of an association. The unidirectional association from the GrainCrop class to the GrainYieldPredictor class typically means that some method of GrainCrop uses the services of GrainYieldPredictor in its implementation.

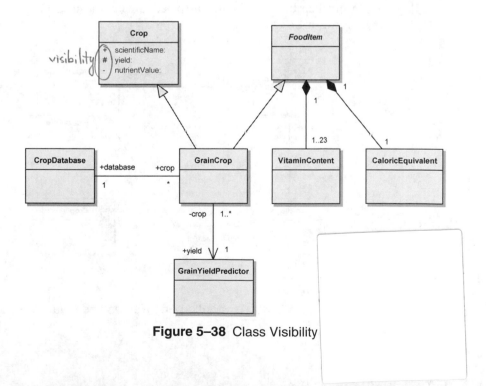

Figure 5–38 Class Visibility

These visibility symbols also apply to nested entities in all their forms. Specifically, in a class icon we may indicate the accessibility of attributes and operations by prefixing one of the visibility symbols to their names. For example, in Figure 5–38, we see that the class `Crop` has one public attribute (`scientificName`), one protected attribute (`yield`), and one private attribute (`nutrientValue`).

Advanced Concepts: Association End Names and Qualifiers

In the previous chapter, we described the importance of identifying the various roles an object plays in its collaboration with other objects. Briefly, the role of an abstraction is the face it presents to the world at a given moment. A role denotes the purpose or capacity wherein one class associates with another. As the example in Figure 5–39 shows, this role is depicted with an association end name (role name in UML 1), placed adjacent to the class offering the role. Here we see that the classes `PlanAnalyst` and `Nutritionist` are both contributors to the `CropEncyclopedia` class; this means that they both add information to the encyclopedia. The `PlanAnalyst` class is a user as well by virtue of looking up information in the encyclopedia. In each case, the client's role identifies the particular behavior and protocol that it uses with its supplier while acting in that role. Note also the reflexive association for the class `PlanAnalyst`: Here we show that multiple instances of this class may collaborate with one another and that they have a particular protocol they use when collaborating, which is distinguished from their behavior in their association with, for instance, `CropEncyclopedia`.

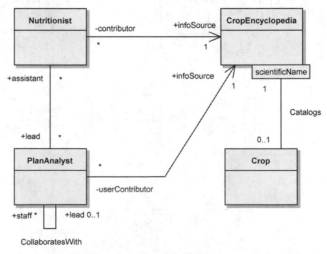

Figure 5–39 Association End Names and Qualifiers

Our example also shows an association between the classes `CropEncyclopedia` and `Crop`, but with a different kind of adornment representing a qualifier, shown as a small rectangle at the `CropEncyclopedia` end of the association. A qualifier is an attribute whose value uniquely identifies a single target object.

In this example, the class `CropEncyclopedia` uses the attribute `scientificName` as a qualifier to navigate to individual entries in the set of items managed by instances of `CropEncyclopedia`. In general, a qualifier must be an attribute of the object that is a part of the aggregate object at the target end of the association. Multiple qualifiers are possible, but qualifier values must be unique. Without a qualifier, the multiplicity on the `Crop` end of the association would be zero or more (*).

Advanced Concepts: Constraints

A constraint is the expression of some semantic condition that must be preserved. Stated another way, a constraint is an invariant of a class or relationship that must be preserved while the system is in a steady state. We emphasize *steady state* because there may be transitory circumstances wherein the state of the system is changing (and thus is temporarily in a self-inconsistent state), during which time it is impossible to preserve all the system's constraints. Constraints are guarantees that apply only when the state of the system is stable. Preconditions and postconditions are examples of constraints that apply while a system is in a steady state, that is, at the specific points in time when an operation is invoked and when it is completed [31].

During the process of designing the system, we must ensure that it will be able to meet the constraints placed on it. We will apply the constraints to a variety of model elements; typically, any model element may be constrained. We use an adornment for constraints that consists of an expression, surrounded by braces ({ }), adjacent to the class or relationship for which the constraint applies. This expression can be represented in a natural language (textual) or in a more formal language such as a programming language or the UML Object Constraint Language (OCL). One benefit of a more formal language is that some tools provide the means of verifying compliance with the constraint when using a formal language. Usually we see development teams textually specifying a constraint, which requires them to have some agreed-upon style of specification [32].

The placement of a constraint in a visual diagram depends on the number of diagram elements affected by the constraint. Table 5–2 provides general guidelines. However, of course, we are constrained by the particular tool we are using.

Table 5–2 Placement of Constraints[a]

Number of Diagram Elements	Constraint Placement
One	1. In note attached to element by dashed line.
	2. Near element.
Two	1. In note attached to each element by dashed line.
	2. Near dashed line connecting elements. Dashed line may have arrowhead on the end pointing to first position in the collection.
Three or more	1. In note attached to each element by dashed line.
	2. For associations (including generalizations, aggregations, and compositions), attached to dashed line crossing the associations.

a. Based on Rumbaugh, Jacobson, and Booch [33].

Constraints applied to generalization associations indicate whether the classifiers in the relationship are complete and disjoint by the use of the four constraints—complete or incomplete and disjoint or overlapping—as defined here [34].

- **Complete**: An instance of the supertype is an instance of at least one of the subtypes.
- **Incomplete**: An instance of the supertype is <u>not</u> an instance of at least one of the subtypes.
- **Disjoint**: There are no common instances among the classifiers.
- **Overlapping**: There are common instances among the classifiers.

Looking back to Figure 5–35, we see examples of these constraints. The {incomplete} constraint on the generalization of the Plan class indicates that there are more types of plans than just the growing plan and gardening plan. This means that an instance of the Plan class might not be an instance of either the GrowingPlan or GardeningPlan classes. The {disjoint} constraint indicates that a plan can't be both a growing plan and a gardening plan, at least in the way we've defined our plans; that is, an instance of the GrowingPlan class can't also be an instance of the GardeningPlan class.

We can see other types of constraints on a class diagram specifically related to the class itself. These include constraints on the class attributes, as discussed earlier regarding Figure 5–33, where we have the {list} constraint on the measuredTemperature attribute in the TemperatureSensor class.

This specifies that the temperature measurements will be ordered and might be nonunique.

As the example in Figure 5–40 indicates, we may apply constraints to individual classes, whole associations, and participants in an association. In this diagram, we see a cardinality constraint on the class `EnvironmentalController`, stating that there may be no more than seven instances of this class in the system.

The `Cooler` class has a different kind of constraint. Here we see a statement of hysteresis in the cooler's operation—a cooler may not be restarted sooner than five minutes after it was last shut down. We attach this constraint to the `Cooler` class because we mean this to be an invariant preserved by instances of the class themselves.

In this diagram we also find two different kinds of association constraints. In the association between the `EnvironmentalController` and `Light` classes, we require that individual lights be uniquely indexed with respect to one another in the context of this association. We also have an exclusive-or constraint `{xor}` that spans the controller's association with the `Heater` and `Cooler` classes,

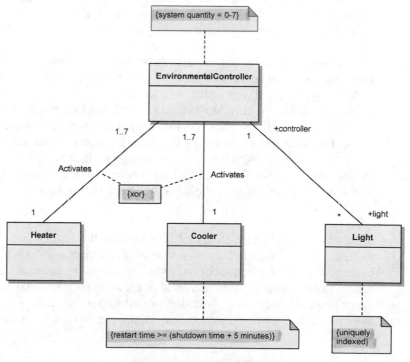

Figure 5–40 Constraints

Refinement of Class Relationships

Earlier, when discussing class relationship icons, we saw that generalization, aggregation, and composition are refinements of the more general association relationship between classes. Specifically, when we looked at aggregation, Figure 5–35 presented the `EnvironmentalController` class as the aggregate whole with the `Light`, `Heater`, and `Cooler` classes as its pieces. Now, in Figure 5–40, we see the aggregations replaced by general association relationships. What's going on here? Well, Figure 5–40 could represent an earlier analysis perspective of the relationship between these classes. Later in our development efforts, as we made tactical decisions about the exact nature of the relationship, we could have refined the relationships into aggregations, as shown in Figure 5–35, where we possibly regard the `EnvironmentalController` class more as a subsystem comprised of the `Light`, `Heater`, and `Cooler` classes. We might then need to add an additional class to provide the actual control functionality within our subsystem, such as a `Controller` class.

stating the invariant that the `EnvironmentalController` class may not activate the heater and the cooler at the same time. We place this as a constraint on the association rather than as a constraint on `Heater` or `Cooler` because it is an invariant that cannot be preserved by heaters or coolers themselves.

Constraints are also useful for the expression of secondary classes, attributes, and associations. For example, consider the classes `Adult` and `Child`, both of which might be subclasses of the abstract class `Person`. For the `Person` class, we might provide the attribute `dateOfBirth`, and we might also include an attribute named `age`, perhaps because age is important in our model of the real world. However, the `age` attribute is secondary: It can be computed from `dateOfBirth`. Thus, in our model, we might include both attributes but include an attribute constraint that states this derivation. It is a tactical decision as to which attribute derives from the other, but our constraint can record whatever decision we make.

Similarly, we might have an association between the `Adult` and `Child` classes named `Parent`. We might also include another association named `Caretaker` because it suits the purposes of our model (perhaps we are modeling the legal relationships between parent and child in the analysis of a social welfare system). `Caretaker` is secondary; it derives from the consequences of the `Parent` association, and we might state this invariant as a constraint on the `Caretaker` association.

Advanced Concepts: Association Classes and Notes

The final advanced concept specific to class diagrams concerns itself with the problem of modeling properties of associations; the notational solution to this specific problem generalizes to diagram elements that may be applied to every diagram in the notation.

Consider the example shown in Figure 5–41. Here we see a many-to-many association between Crop and Nutrient, meaning that every crop depends on N nutrients, and each nutrient may be applied to N different crops. The NutrientSchedule class is really a property of this many-to-many relationship, whose instances denote a specific mapping of a crop and its nutrients. To indicate this semantic fact, we draw a dashed line from the Crop-to-Nutrient association (the attributed association) to its property, the NutrientSchedule class (the association's attribute). A given unique association may have at most one such attribute, which is called an *association class*, and the name of such an association must match the name of the class used as its attribute.

The very idea of attributing associations has a generalization. Specifically, during analysis and design, there are a myriad of seemingly random assumptions and decisions that each developer may collect; these insights are often lost because there is usually no convenient place to collect them, save for keeping them in the head of the developer—a decidedly unreliable practice. Thus, it is useful to add arbitrary notes to any element of any diagram, whose text captures these assumptions and decisions. In Figure 5–41, we have two such notes. The note attached to

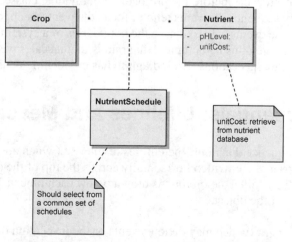

Figure 5–41 Association Classes and Notes

the `NutrientSchedule` class tells us something about the expected unique-ness of its instances. The other note, attached to the `Nutrient` class, captures our expectation of how the `unitCost` attribute will be populated.

For such notes we use a distinctive note-shaped icon and connect it to the element it affects by using a dashed line as before. Largely a tool issue, notes may contain any information, including plain text, fragments of code, or references to other documents. A note may be unconnected to any diagram element, meaning that it applies to the diagram as a whole.

5.8　Sequence Diagrams

A sequence diagram is used to trace the execution of a scenario in the same con-text as a communication diagram. (Communication diagrams are discussed later in this chapter.) Indeed, to a large degree, a sequence diagram is simply another way to represent a communication diagram.

Essentials: Objects and Interactions

In Figure 5–42, we provide a sequence diagram that duplicates most of the semantics of the communication diagram shown. The advantage of using a sequence diagram is that it is easier to read the passing of messages in relative order. Sequence diagrams are often better than object diagrams (to be discussed later in this chapter) for capturing the semantics of scenarios early in the develop-ment lifecycle, before the protocols of individual classes have been identified. Early sequence diagrams tend to focus on events as opposed to operations because events help to define the boundaries of a system under development. The advantage of using an object diagram is that it scales well to many objects with complex invocations. Each diagram has compelling benefits.

Essentials: Lifelines and Messages

In sequence diagrams, the entities of interest (which are the same as for object diagrams) are written horizontally across the top of the diagram. A dashed verti-cal line, called the *lifeline*, is drawn below each object. These indicate the exist-ence of the object.

Messages (which may denote events or the invocation of operations) are shown horizontally. The endpoints of the message icons connect with the vertical lines

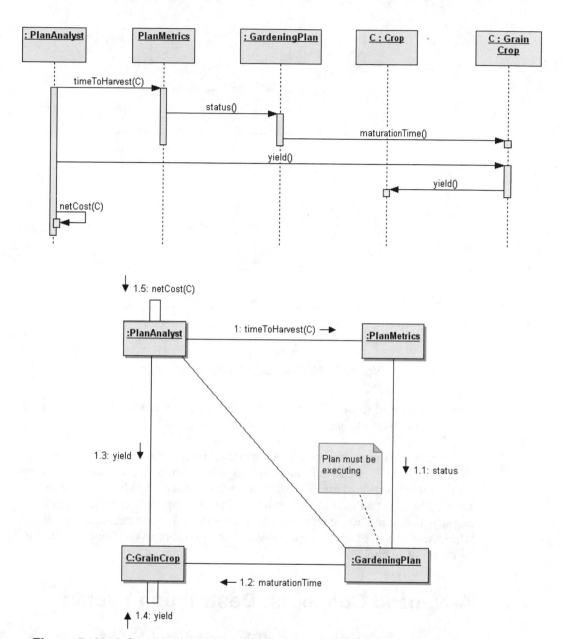

Figure 5–42 A Sequence Diagram (Top) and Its Related Communication Diagram (Bottom)

that connect with the entities at the top of the diagram. Messages are drawn from the sender to the receiver. Ordering is indicated by vertical position, with the first message shown at the top of the diagram, and the last message shown at the bottom. As a result, sequence numbers aren't needed.

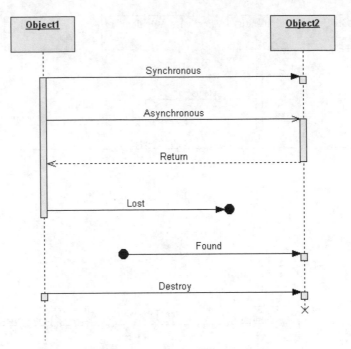

Figure 5–43 Notations for Types of Messages

The notation used for messages (i.e., the line type and arrowhead type) indicates the type of message being used, as shown in Figure 5–43.

A synchronous message (typically an operation call) is shown as a solid line with a filled arrowhead. An asynchronous message has a solid line with an open arrowhead. A return message uses a dashed line with an open arrowhead. A lost message (a message that does not reach its destination) appears as a synchronous message that terminates at an endpoint (a black dot). A found message (a message whose sender is not known) appears as a synchronous message that originates at an endpoint symbol.

Advanced Concepts: Destruction Events

A destruction event indicates when an object is destroyed. It is shown as an X at the end of a lifeline. See the `Object2` lifeline in Figure 5–43 for an example. If this object is involved in a composition, the other involved objects may also be destroyed.

Sequence diagrams are conceptually very simple; however, you can add other elements to make them more expressive in the presence of certain complicated patterns of interaction.

Advanced Concepts: Execution Specification

Simple sequence diagrams may not indicate the focus of control as messages are passed. For example, if object A sends messages X and Y to other objects, it may not be clear whether X and Y are independent messages from A or whether they have been invoked as part of the same enclosing message Z. As we show in Figures 5–42 and 5–43, to clarify such situations, we may adorn the vertical lines descending from each object in a sequence diagram with a box representing the relative time that the flow of control is focused in that object. For example, in Figure 5–44, we see that the anonymous instance of the GardeningPlan object is the ultimate focus of control, and its behavior of carrying out a climatic plan invokes other methods, which in turn call other methods that eventually return control back to the GardeningPlan object.

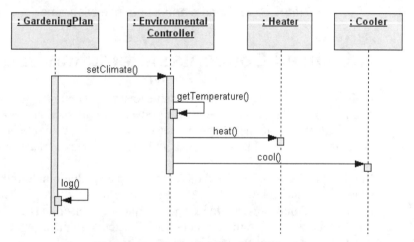

Figure 5–44 Execution Specification

Scripts

Although not officially part of UML 2.0, you may see the use of descriptive text on sequence diagrams. For complex scenarios that involve conditions or iterations, sequence diagrams can be enhanced by the use of scripts. As we see in the example in Figure 5–45, a script may be written to the left of a sequence diagram, with the steps of the script aligning with the message invocations.

Scripts may be written using free-form or structured English text or using the syntax of the chosen implementation language.

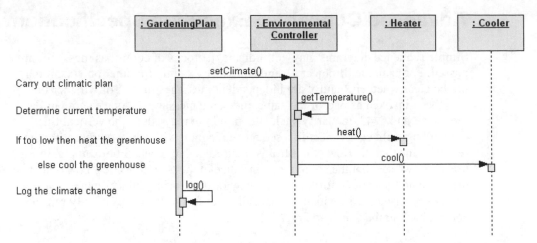

Figure 5–45 Scripts and Sequence Diagrams

Advanced Concepts: Interaction Use

UML 2.0 has various constructs available to simplify complex sequence diagrams. The first we will discuss is the *interaction use*. An interaction use is merely a way to indicate on a sequence diagram that we want to reuse an interaction that is defined elsewhere. This is shown, as in Figure 5–46, as a frame labeled `ref`.

In this case, we have modified our earlier sequence diagram to introduce a login sequence, required before the `PlanAnalyst` uses the system. The frame, labeled `ref`, indicates that the `Login` sequence is inserted (i.e., copied) where this fragment is placed in this sequence. The actual login sequence would be defined on another sequence diagram.

Advanced Concepts: Control Constructs

Just as we saw fragments being used to simplify sequence diagrams, they can similarly be used to indicate flow control constructs on sequence diagrams. For example, Figure 5–47 shows the introduction of a loop in our sequence diagram.

Note that the frame is named with the interaction operator `loop`. The sequence execution within this frame is controlled by the condition [For each Gardening Plan].

Now let us assume that we have many `GardeningPlan` objects, some active, some inactive (past plans that are now saved just for informational purposes). We

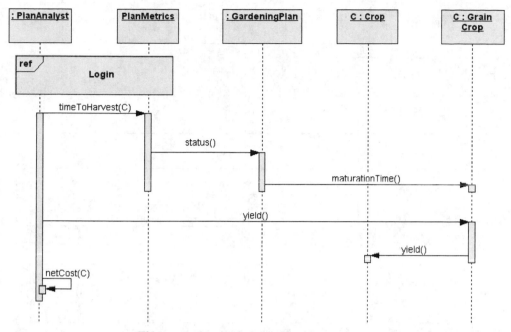

Figure 5–46 An Interaction Use, `Login`

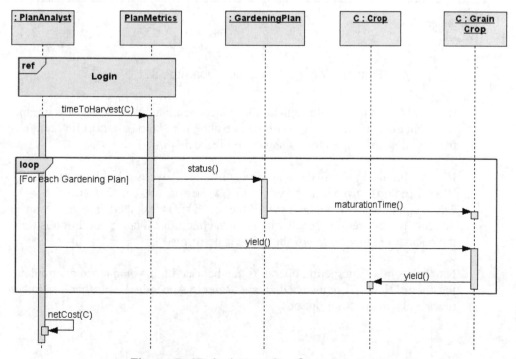

Figure 5–47 An Interaction Operator, `loop`

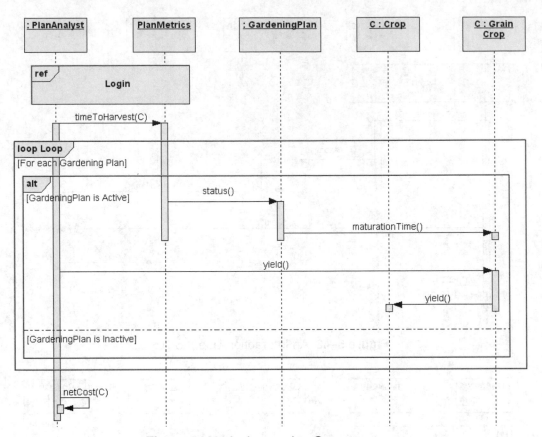

Figure 5–48 An Interaction Operator, `alt`

would not want to loop through all those inactive plans. We just want to use the ones that are currently active. This can be done with an `alt` (short for "alternatives") interaction operator, as shown in Figure 5–48.

Here within the loop, an alternate choice is made, governed by the conditions `[GardeningPlan is Active]` and `[GardeningPlan is Inactive]`. These conditions select which part of the sequence is executed. The `alt` frame is divided into two regions, each with its own condition. When a condition is true, the behavior in that region of the frame is performed.

Numerous other interaction operators can be used in this manner to manipulate the control flow of a sequence diagram. Refer to Appendix B, Further Reading, to investigate all the other options.

5.9 Interaction Overview Diagrams

Interaction overview diagrams are a combination of activity diagrams and interaction diagrams that are intended to provide an overview of the flow of control between interaction diagram elements. Though any type of interaction diagram (sequence, communication, or timing) may be used, the sequence diagram will likely be the most prevalent.

The essential elements of the interaction overview diagram are the frames, the flow of control elements, and the interaction diagram elements.

Essentials: Frames

The interaction overview diagram is typically surrounded by a frame; however, the frame is optional when the context is clear. In Figure 5–49, we see the surrounding frame with the name `sd MaintainTemperature lifelines :EnvironmentalController, :Heater, :Cooler` in the compartment in the upper left-hand corner. The meaning of this name is as follows:

- `sd`: a tag that indicates this is an interaction diagram
- `MaintainTemperature`: a name describing the purpose of the diagram
- `lifelines :EnvironmentalController, :Heater, :Cooler`: an optional list of contained lifelines

This interaction overview diagram contains flow of control elements and three frames, `EvaluateTemperature`, `Heat`, and `Cool`, which we discuss in the next subsections.

Essentials: Flow of Control Elements

The flow of control within an interaction overview diagram is provided by a combination of activity diagram elements to provide for both alternate and parallel paths. The alternate path control is provided by combinations of a decision node, where the appropriate path is chosen, and a corresponding merge node (as appropriate) to bring the alternate paths together.

This combination appears twice in Figure 5–49. First, a decision node is used to choose a path based on whether the temperature of the Hydroponics Gardening System is within bounds (therefore, requiring no action) or out of bounds, which requires either heating or cooling. The interaction constraint `[lower bound < = temp < = upper bound]` is used to choose the appropriate path. The second

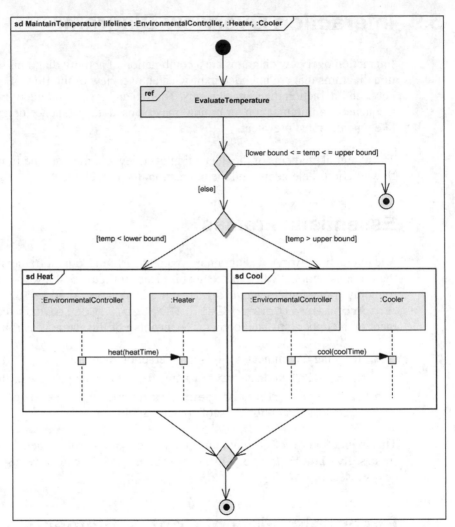

Figure 5–49 The Interaction Overview Diagram for `MaintainTemperature`

combination of a decision node and a merge node controls whether heating or cooling is applied by using the two interaction constraints, `[temp < lower bound]` and `[temp > upper bound]`.

Flow of control within parallel paths is provided by combinations of a fork node, to split into parallel paths, and a corresponding join node to bring the parallel paths together. One important concern with parallel paths is that tokens from all paths must arrive at the join node before the flow is allowed to continue. This requires us to ensure that, wherever an interaction constraint may block flow along a path, there is an alternate path for the token to proceed [35].

Essentials: Interaction Diagram Elements

The interaction overview diagram contains two types of elements to provide the interaction diagram information, either an interaction or an interaction use. The interaction is any type of interaction diagram that provides the nested details of the interaction; these are typically sequence diagrams. They can be anonymous or named, as in Figure 5–49, which shows the `Heat` and `Cool` interactions.

The interaction use references an interaction diagram rather than providing its details. Figure 5–49 contains an example, the `EvaluateTemperature` interaction use. The details of `EvaluateTemperature` would show how concerns, such as the following, would be managed:

- Periodicity of temperature readings
- Protection of compressors by not restarting the `:Cooler` sooner than five minutes since shutdown
- Temperature adjustments based on time of day
- Temperature ranges for different crops

5.10 Composite Structure Diagrams

Composite structure diagrams provide a way to depict a structured classifier with the definition of its internal structure. This internal structure is comprised of parts and their interconnections, all within the namespace of the composite structure. Structured classifiers can be nested, so each part could be another structured classifier. In addition to representing a component, a structured classifier can also represent a class. Thus, the composite structure diagram is useful during design to decompose classes into their constituent parts and model their runtime collaborations [36, 37].

The essential elements of a composite structure are its parts, ports, interfaces, and connectors.

Essentials: Composite Structure Parts

The composite structure diagram for the Hydroponics Gardening System's `WaterTank` is shown in Figure 5–50. Its name is placed in the top compartment; the specific naming convention should be defined by the development team. `WaterTank` contains the `Heater` and `Tank` parts, which collaborate to provide its functionality, that of providing appropriately heated water for the gardeners to use.

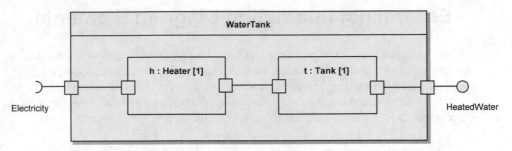

Figure 5–50 The Composite Structure Diagram for `WaterTank`

The name of a composite structure part uses the format of *role name : Class Name [multiplicity]*, where the role name defines the role played by a part within the composite structure. Though showing the multiplicity is optional, we include it in Figure 5–50 to make clear that `WaterTank` consists of one `Heater` and one `Tank`.

Essentials: Composite Structure Ports and Interfaces

The composite structure and its parts interface with their external environment through ports, denoted by a small square on the boundary of the part or composite structure. In Figure 5–50, we see that `Heater` and `Tank` both have ports through which they interact with each other to provide the functionality of `WaterTank`. In addition, `WaterTank` has a port through which it receives electricity for the `Heater` and a port through which it provides the heated water from the `Tank` to its environment.

Using ports for all interactions provides encapsulation to the structured classifier. These ports have public visibility unless otherwise noted. Hidden ports are denoted by a small square that appears totally inside the composite structure, with only one edge touching its boundary. These ports may be used for capabilities such as test points that are not to be publicly available. The name and multiplicity of ports is optional, but they should be provided where needed for clarity. Port names are in the format *port name : Port Type [multiplicity]*. The port type is optional when naming a port [38, 39].

To these ports, we connect the interfaces that define the details of the composite structure's interactions. These interfaces are commonly shown in the ball-and-socket notation. A required interface uses the socket notation to denote the services expected from its external environment, whereas the ball notation denotes the services it offers through its provided interfaces. As part of `WaterTank`, `Heater` receives electricity from the Hydroponics Gardening System, and `Tank` provides heated water to the gardeners.

Essentials: Composite Structure Connectors

Connectors within composite structure diagrams provide the communication links between the composite and its environment, as well as the means for its parts to communicate internally. In Figure 5–50 we have three connectors between its ports; the two that connect to the boundary of the composite are called *delegation connectors*, and the one between `Heater` and `Tank` is called an *assembly connector* (also known as an *interface connector*). Here we have `Heater` providing heat to `Tank` to fulfill its service need. Although Figure 5–50 shows the assembly connector in the straight line notation of the delegation connectors, we could have used the ball-and-socket notation to represent this connection. Naming the connectors is optional; those in Figure 5–50 are not named because clarity here doesn't require names [40].

Advanced Concepts: Collaborations

A collaboration is a type of structured classifier that specifies the runtime interactions of classifier instances. It differs from the composite structure in that it is not instantiated and does not actually own these instances but defines the roles that classifier instances must assume and the connectors over which they collaborate to provide the functionality of interest. Collaborations may be nested, and the concept of abstraction supports our focus at a level of detail pertinent to our particular concerns. The details of a collaboration may be expressed with the use of an interaction diagram [41, 44].

The collaboration's primary use is to define templates, that is, patterns of roles joined by connectors. At runtime, classifier instances will be bound to these roles so they may cooperate to provide the functionality defined by the collaboration. For example, Figure 5–51 shows the `TemperatureControl` collaboration defining a pattern for controlling the temperature within the Hydroponics Gardening System. In this pattern, `TemperatureController` uses `TemperatureRamp`, which defines the precise temperature variations required over time to support the needs of a crop [93, 94].

The name of a collaboration, shown inside the dashed oval that encapsulates the collaboration, may be partitioned from the role definitions by a horizontal dashed line (not shown here). In this collaboration, we have two defined roles, `TemperatureController` and `TemperatureRamp`, joined by a connector.

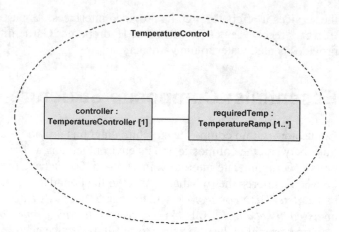

Figure 5–51 The `TemperatureControl` Collaboration

Since the connector is unnamed, it will be realized by a temporary runtime means such as a property or an argument. If it were named, it would be realized by an instance of an actual association, that is, a link [95, 96].

Roles are labeled with a name and type in the format of `role name : Role Type [multiplicity]`. The role name describes a particular classifier instance that may fulfill this role, and the role type is a constraint on this classifier instance. We have shown the role names, role types, and multiplicity for the `TemperatureController` and `TemperatureRamp` roles [97, 98].

A role defines the properties that a structured classifier must have to participate in the collaboration. The typing of a role by interfaces means that any classifier instance complying with the interface can fulfill the role, regardless of its internal design or implementation. The classifier instance may have functionality beyond that required in a particular role, thereby giving it the ability to fulfill multiple roles in a single collaboration or even roles in different collaborations at the same time [99, 100].

5.11 State Machine Diagrams

State machines are well known in industries that use real-time processing. State machine diagrams are used to design and understand time-critical systems, in which the consequences of improper timing are severe. Medical devices, financial trading systems, satellite command and control systems, and weapon systems are typical examples where state machine diagrams can play an important role in understanding how systems behave in reaction to key events.

A state machine diagram expresses behavior as a progression through a series of states, triggered by events, and the related actions that may occur. Such state machines are also known as behavioral state machines. State machine diagrams are typically used to describe the behavior of individual objects. However, they can also be used to describe the behavior of larger elements of any system. (Remember from Chapter 1 that the selected level of abstraction in a complex system is relative to the observer.) State machine diagrams are cousins to activity diagrams. However, state machine diagrams focus on the states and transitions between those states versus the flow of activities.

Not every class has significant event-ordered behavior, so we supply state machine diagrams only for those classes that exhibit such behavior. We may also provide state machine diagrams that show the event-ordered behavior of the system as a whole. During analysis, we may use state machine diagrams to indicate the dynamic behavior of the system. During design, we use state machine diagrams to capture the dynamic behavior of individual classes or of collaborations of classes.

The two essential elements of a state machine diagram are states and state transitions.

Essentials: Initial, Final, and Simple States

The state of an object represents the cumulative results of its behavior. For example, when a telephone is first installed, it is in the idle state, meaning that no previous behavior is of great interest and that the phone is ready to initiate or receive calls. When we pick up the handset, the phone is off-hook and in the dialing state. In this state, we do not expect the phone to ring; we expect to be able to initiate a conversation with someone on another telephone. When the phone is on-hook, if it rings and we pick up the handset, the phone is now in the receiving state, and we expect to be able to converse with the person who called.

At any given point in time, the state of an object encompasses all of its (usually static) properties, together with the current (usually dynamic) values of each of these properties. By properties, we mean the totality of the object's attributes and relationships with other objects. We can generalize the concept of an individual object's state to apply to the object's class because all instances of the same class live in the same state space, which encompasses an indefinite yet finite number of possible (although not always desirable or expected) states.

When an object is in a given state, it can do the following:

- Execute an activity
- Wait for an event

- Fulfill a condition
- Do some or all of the above

In every state machine diagram, there must be exactly one default initial state, which we designate by writing an unlabeled transition to the state from a special icon, shown as a filled circle. Less often, we need to designate a stop state. Usually, a state machine associated with a class or the system as a whole never reaches a stop state; the state machine just goes out of existence when the enclosing object is destroyed. We designate a stop state by drawing an unlabeled state transition from the state to a special icon, shown as a filled circle inside a slightly larger unfilled circle. Initial and final states are technically called *pseudostates*. Figure 5–52 depicts the elements for a duration timer in our hydroponics system. For simple states, the state name is shown in the rounded rectangle depicting the state. Here we have two simple states for our timer—Initializing and Timing. Simple states have no substates (we will discuss substates in an upcoming subsection).

Figure 5–52 Notations for Simple States

Essentials: Transitions and Events

The movements between states are called transitions. On a state machine diagram, transitions are shown by directed arrows between states. Each state transition connects two states. Figure 5–53 shows a transition from the initial state to the state named Initializing, from Initializing to Timing, and from Timing to the final state. Moving between states is referred to as *firing the transition*. A state may have a state transition to itself, and it is common to have many different state transitions from the same state, although each such transition must be unique, meaning that there will never be any circumstances that would trigger more than one state transition from the same state.

Figure 5–53 Transitions for the Duration Timer

There are various ways to control the firing of a transition. A transition that has no annotation is referred to as a *completion transition*. This simply means that when the source state completes, the transition automatically fires, and the target state is entered. You can see this in Figure 5–53 between the Initializing state and the Timing state. When the duration timer is initialized, it immediately begins timing.

In other cases, certain events have to occur for the transition to fire. Such events are annotated on the transition. An event is some occurrence that may cause the state of a system to change. For example, in the Hydroponics Gardening System, the following events play a role in the system's behavior.

- A new crop is planted.
- A crop becomes ready to harvest.
- The temperature in a greenhouse drops because of inclement weather.
- A cooler fails.
- Time passes.

Each of the first four events is likely to trigger some action, such as starting or stopping the execution of a specific gardening plan, turning on a heater, or sounding an alarm to the gardener. The passage of time is another issue: Although the passing of seconds or minutes may not be significant to our system (observable plant growth is generally on much longer scales of time), the passage of hours or days may be a signal to our system to turn lights on or off or to change the temperature in the greenhouse, in order to create an artificial day necessary for plant growth. In Figure 5–54, we develop the duration timer state diagram. Here you see that the timer execution can be put into a Paused state and timing resumed through the occurrence of pause and resume events, respectively.

While transitions often show how an object moves between states, they may also be recursive, showing an exit from and reentry into the same state.

The UML elements described thus far constitute the essential elements of all state transition diagrams. Collectively, they provide a notation sufficient to describe simple, flat, finite state machines, suitable for applications with a limited number

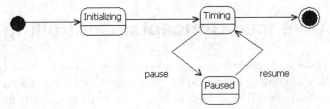

Figure 5–54 Additional States and Transition Events for the Duration Timer

of states. Systems that have a large number of states or that exhibit particularly complicated event-ordered behavior involving conditional transitions or transitions based on previously entered states require the use of the more advanced concepts for state transition diagrams. We will discuss these now.

Advanced Concepts: State Activities—Entry, Do, and Exit Activities

Activities may be associated with states. In particular, we may specify some activity that is to be carried out at certain points in time with respect to a state.

- Perform an activity upon entry of the state.
- Do an activity while in the state.
- Perform an activity upon exit of the state.

Figure 5–55 shows an example of this concept. Here we see that upon entering the `Timing` state, we start the timer (indicated by the icon of an arrow next to two parallel lines), and upon exiting this state (indicated by the icon of an arrow between two parallel lines), we stop the timer (note that these icons are tool specific). While in this state, we measure the time duration (indicated by the circular arrow).

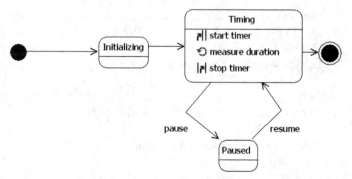

Figure 5–55 Entry, Do, and Exit Activities

Advanced Concepts: Controlling Transitions

As we said earlier, there are ways to exercise finer control over state transitions than just having events on the transition. Conditions can be specified to control the transition. These conditions act as guards so that when an event occurs, the condition will either allow the transition (if the condition is true) or disallow the transition (if the condition is false).

Another way to control transition behavior is to use effects. An effect is a behavior (e.g., an activity, an action) that occurs when a specified event occurs. Thus, when a transition event occurs, the transition fires and the effect also occurs. Each of these refinements can be used in combination with the others.

Let us expand our duration timer example to show the use of effects. One important event that could happen in our hydroponics system is that a cooler could fail. Rather than just hope that this does not happen, we will change our basic timer to a duration timer used to measure the total operational time during which the cooler is running. The purpose is to alert us to perform maintenance on the cooler after it has been in operation for a certain period of time. We hope that regular maintenance will prevent a failure of the cooler. So we enhance our state machine diagram as shown in Figure 5–56.

In this diagram, you can see that the timeout transition has been replaced with a condition. This condition specifies that when the duration exceeds the maintenance time, the timer transitions into the `Sounding Alarm` state, alerting us to the need for maintenance. The use of an event, condition, and effect in combination is shown on the transition from `Sounding Alarm` to `Timing`. Here, once the maintenance is complete, we want to clear the alarm condition and resume timing. There is a `clear` event, but it is guarded by the condition that the cooler must be back online first (before timing is resumed), shown in brackets. If the

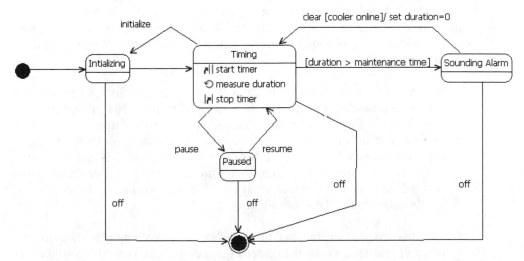

Figure 5–56 The Enhanced State Machine Diagram for the Duration Timer

cooler is not online, the transition does not fire. If it is, the effect occurs (the duration timer is set to zero, as shown after the slash), the transition fires, and timing begins again.

The order of evaluation in conditional state transitions is important. Given state S with transition T on event E with condition C and effect A, the following order applies.

1. Event E occurs.
2. Condition C is evaluated.
3. If C evaluates true, then transition T is triggered, and effect A is invoked.

This means that if a condition evaluates false, the state transition may not be triggered until the event occurs again and the condition is reevaluated. Side effects in evaluating the condition or in carrying out an exit action will not affect the triggering of a state transition. For example, suppose that event E occurs, and condition C evaluates true, but then the execution of the exit action changes the world so that C no longer evaluates true. The state transition will still be triggered.

Advanced Concepts: Composite States and Nested States

Up to this point, we have been discussing simple states and transitions between them. In larger, more complex systems, state machine diagrams can get very large, tangled, and unwieldy. The ability to nest states gives depth to state machine diagrams; this is a key feature of state machine diagrams that mitigates the combinatorial explosion of states and state transitions that often occurs in complex systems.

In Figure 5–57, we have nested the states Timing, Sounding Alarm, and Paused. This nesting is depicted with a surrounding boundary known as a *region*. The enclosing boundary is called a *composite state*. Thus we now have a composite state named Operating that contains the nested states Timing, Sounding Alarm, and Paused. Note also that this diagram is visually simplified in that there is now only one transition from the composite state Operating to the final state. This means that when any of the nested states' off events occur, the transition to the final state fires.

Nesting may be to any depth, and thus substates may be composite states to other lower-level substates. Given the composite state Operating with its three substates, the semantics of nesting implies an XOR (exclusive OR) relationship. If the system is in the Operating state (the composite state), it must also be in exactly one of the three substates: Timing, Sounding Alarm, or Paused.

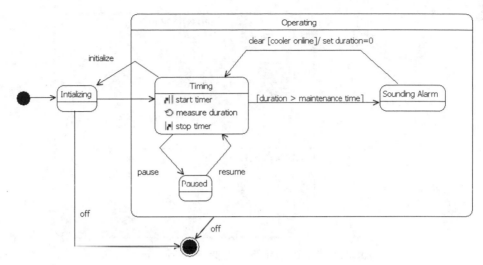

Figure 5–57 Composite and Nested States

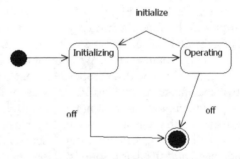

Figure 5–58 A Higher-Level View of the State Machine Diagram for the Duration Timer

For simplicity in drawing state transition diagrams with depth, we may zoom in or zoom out relative to a particular state. Zooming out elides substates, and zooming in reveals substates. When we zoom out of Figure 5–57, we get a state machine diagram that is much easier to understand (see Figure 5–58).

Advanced Concepts: Concurrency and Control

Concurrent behavior can be depicted in state machine diagrams by simply partitioning a composite state into two or more sub-regions by using dotted lines. Each sub-region within the composite state represents behavior that will occur concurrently. Figure 5–59 shows a state with three concurrent sub-regions.

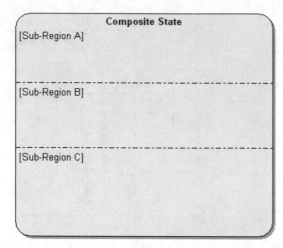

Figure 5–59 Concurrent Sub-Regions in a State Machine Diagram

For our example, when the cooler is overdue for maintenance, the duration timer sounds an alarm. Earlier, in Figure 5–56, we showed this by having the state machine transition into the Sounding Alarm state. Let us say that, instead of just sounding the alarm, we want the system to also capture how long the cooler remains overdue for maintenance. We show this in Figure 5–60 by replacing the Sounding Alarm state with a composite state, Maintenance Overdue, that contains two concurrent states: Sounding Alarm and Timing Maintenance Overdue (which captures how long the cooler has been overdue for maintenance). Thus, when the transition into the Maintenance Overdue composite state occurs, both substates start and run concurrently, that is, the overdue maintenance timer starts and the alarm sounds. (Note that we have removed the transition that allows the alarm to be turned off without bringing the cooler back online; see the off transition from the Sounding Alarm state in Figure 5–56.) This helps ensure the alarm will not just be silenced without performing the maintenance.

Control flow into and out of concurrent states can be depicted in various ways using the UML, each with its own precise meaning. You must be careful to make sure that how you diagram the flow correctly represents your intent. Let us examine this with a generic composite state, as shown in Figure 5–61.

You can transition into a composite state in various ways. For example, you can have a transition to the composite state, as shown in Figure 5–62. In this case, the concurrent submachines would all activate and begin to operate concurrently. Each individual sub-region would execute beginning at the default initial state (pseudostate) for that sub-region. While it is not necessary, we recommend overtly showing the initial states in the sub-region for clarity.

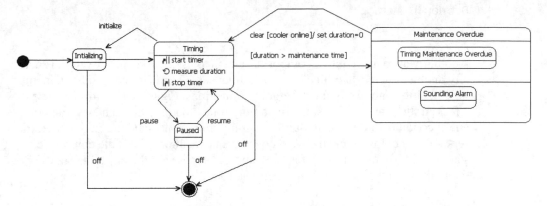

Figure 5–60 The Composite `Maintenance Overdue` State with Concurrent Sub-Regions

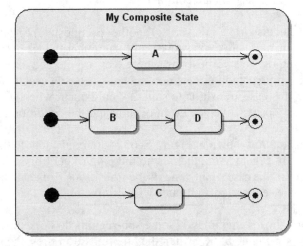

Figure 5–61 A Generic Composite State with Concurrent Sub-Regions

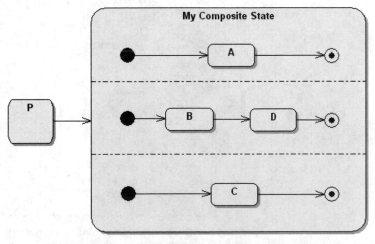

Figure 5–62 A Transition into a Composite State

Another way to move into a composite state is to use a fork. A fork vertex is actually another pseudostate (like initial and final states) and is used to split an incoming transition into two or more outgoing transitions. Figure 5–63 shows the use of a fork in this manner. The single incoming transition may have an event and or a guard condition on it. The multiple outgoing transitions may not. In our case, the fork splits the flow of control, and concurrent execution within the composite state would begin with substates A, B, and C, as these are the target substates of the multiple outgoing transitions from the fork.

Similar constructs can be used when exiting a compound, concurrent state. Figure 5–64 shows a transition from the composite state to a subsequent state. The single completion transition from the composite state fires when all of the prior substates (A, D, and C) are complete.

You can also use a join vertex (another pseudostate) to perform a similar merging of control. Figure 5–65 shows multiple transitions from the individual concurrent sub-regions to a vertical bar, where they are merged into one outgoing transition. This single outgoing transition may also have an event and a guard condition on it. In this case, transition to state S would occur when all the joined substates (A, D, and C) are active, the event occurs, and the condition is satisfied.

The situation shown in Figure 5–65 is not equivalent to that shown in Figure 5–66. In Figure 5–66, there is no merging of control as there is when joins are used. In this case, if any one of the transitions from substates A, D, or C fire, all the other concurrent substates will terminate.

Along those same lines, if some sub-regions do not explicitly participate in a join (see Figure 5–67), when the join transition fires, the nonparticipating

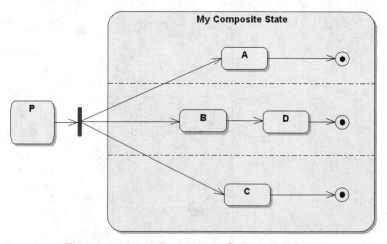

Figure 5–63 A Fork into a Composite State

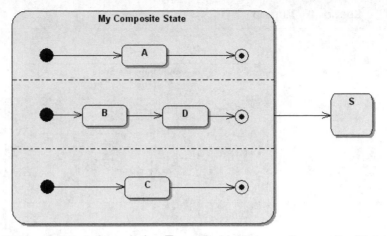

Figure 5–64 A Completion Transition Leaving a Composite State

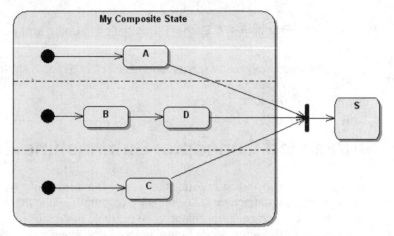

Figure 5–65 A Join Leaving a Composite State

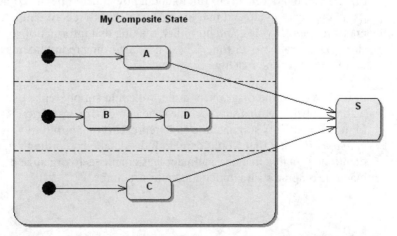

Figure 5–66 Individual Transitions Leaving a Composite State

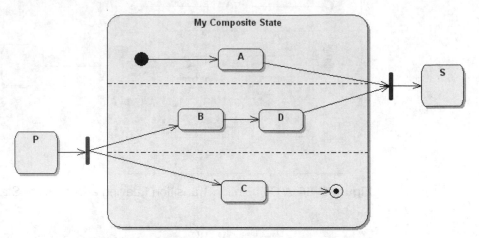

Figure 5–67 Partial Participation in Joins and Forks

sub-regions will be forced to terminate. Conversely, if some sub-regions do not explicitly participate in a fork, the nonparticipating sub-regions will execute starting at their initial states [18, 19].

Advanced Concepts: Submachine State

Along with simple and composite states, there is a third major type of state: a submachine state. Submachine states are used to simplify state machine diagrams or to contain common behavior that may be reusable in various diagrams. For example, refer back to Figure 5–56. Let us suppose that much more needs to be done when the maintenance time is exceeded than just sounding the alarm. Let us say that a second timer needs to run to count how much time the cooler has exceeded its maintenance cycle and that the system needs to record temperature, coolant pressure, on/off cycles, and humidity, making that information available as graphs showing the values over time. These new recording requirements could result in a quite complex state machine diagram.

In order to keep the diagrams simple, we could simply replace the Sounding Alarm substate with a submachine state named Operating:Recording (see Figure 5–68). This submachine state represents *an entirely separate state machine diagram* that would depict all the detailed recording requirements just mentioned. In this manner, submachines enable us to organize complex state machine diagrams into understandable structures.

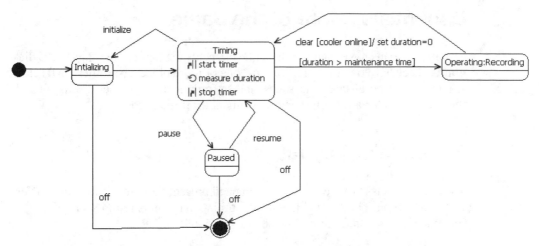

Figure 5–68 Using a Submachine State in the State Machine Diagram for the Duration Timer

Advanced Concepts: Additional State Machine Diagram Elements

State machine diagrams may be the most semantically rich diagram type in the UML. They can be very, very complex. Many more elements than we have described can be used in state machine diagrams (e.g., entry and exit points, shallow and deep history, protocol state machines, and so forth). If you have the need or desire to explore these very dark corners of the UML, Appendix B, Further Reading, provides some useful references.

5.12 Timing Diagrams

Anyone who has worked on logic circuit design, any electrical engineer, or even any electronic hobbyist will recognize timing diagrams. Similar diagrams have been used for decades in these and other industries where it's critical to understand the behaviors and timing of the system elements.

Timing diagrams are a type of interaction diagram. Their purpose is to show how the states of an element or elements change over time and how events change those states.

Essentials: More of the Same

Timing diagrams have many of the same elements that appear in other UML diagrams. They have one or more lifelines, one or more objects (or other UML classifier), two or more states, messages, and so forth. Refer to earlier discussions of these elements for a refresher on their semantics, if required.

Essentials: Layout

Timing diagrams take the UML elements and present them to the user in a different organization. The general layout of a timing diagram is reminiscent of a sequence diagram laid on its side (see Figure 5–69).

Timing diagrams have one or more lifelines (which look like a horizontal partition) for each object in the diagram. The lifeline name (i.e., the object name) is shown in the lifeline. The possible states of the object are listed inside the lifeline. Also, a timeline shows how the object changes from one state to another. Events that drive the state changes are shown along the timeline. The horizontal axis shows time and may also show tick marks to help the reader of the diagram better understand specific timing. For example, Figure 5–70 shows a simple timing dia-

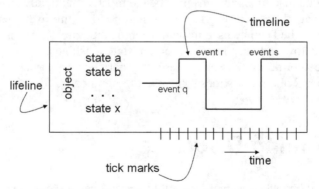

Figure 5–69 A Generic Timing Diagram

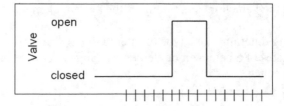

Figure 5–70 A Timing Diagram for the `Valve` Object

gram for a `Valve` object that is controlled to fill the `WaterStorageTank` object in our Hydroponics Gardening System.

As you can see, `Valve` has two simple states: `open` and `closed`. Alone, this timing diagram provides little insight into the operation of the system. (In fact, this timing diagram can be considered incomplete.) When does the valve open and close? What events cause those changes in state?

Essentials: Events

Events (or other stimuli such as messages) that cause state changes are shown in the lifeline near the timeline of the object. In Figure 5–71, two events have been added, that is, `TankLow` and `TankFull`, which cause changes in the state of the valve.

Essentials: Constraints

Constraints can be used to specify conditions or limits that restrict the change of state shown on a timing diagram. In Figure 5-72, we show a timing diagram with

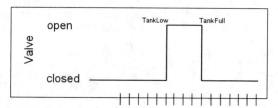

Figure 5–71 A Timing Diagram for `Valve` That Includes Events

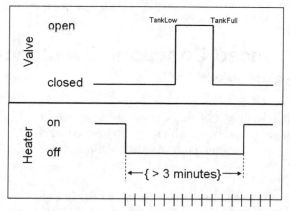

Figure 5–72 A Timing Diagram for Two Objects That Includes a Constraint

both the `Valve` and the `Heater` objects represented. This diagram shows the relationship between the state of `Heater` and the state of `Valve`.

Here we see a constraint on `Heater` that restricts how quickly the heater can be turned back on. (This type of constraint may be in place to prevent rapid or repeated switching of the heater's heating elements on and off, which would typically reduce its operational life.) The constraint indicates that once the heater is turned off, at least three minutes must pass before the heater is turned back on.

Advanced Concepts: Alternate Representations

In cases where timing diagrams have many lifelines, or objects that have many states, instead of using a timeline as we did in the previous figures, we can use a more compact representation, as shown in Figure 5–73. States are shown within the hexagons, and the state changes occur between them.

Instead of the change of state being indicated as a rise and fall of a timeline, the state changes are merely shown progressing along the horizontal axis.

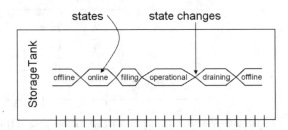

Figure 5–73 Using a Compact Representation Instead of Timelines on a Timing Diagram

Advanced Concepts: Events versus Messages

As stated earlier, not only can events drive state changes, but other stimuli such as messages can, too. So which should be used when? The subtle difference in this case is that an event has a specific location in space and time, which is not true for messages.

For example, the two events shown earlier in Figure 5–71, `TankLow` and `TankFull`, physically occur in the actual storage tank. Instead of using these events, we could use messages to open or close the valve. Say that the gardener

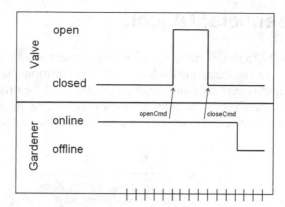

Figure 5–74 Using Messages Instead of Events on a Timing Diagram

decides to add more water to the water storage tank, even though the tank's level is not physically low. The gardener simply wants to increase the amount of water in the tank. In this case, using a message would be better than using an event. Figure 5–74 shows two messages (openCmd and closeCmd) that command the valve to open, thus filling the tank, and close, to stop the filling, respectively.

Either messages or events can be used in UML diagrams to express a designer's intent clearly. But when in doubt, the best course of action is to check the semantics of the elements in question (i.e., messages versus events) and use them appropriately. UML diagrams are not just sketches. Each element has a specific meaning and an appropriate usage.

5.13 Object Diagrams

An object diagram is used to show the existence of objects and their relationships in the logical design of a system. Stated another way, an object diagram represents a snapshot in time of an otherwise transitory stream of events over a certain configuration of objects. Object diagrams are thus prototypical—each one represents the structural relationships that may occur among a given set of class instances. In this sense, a single object diagram represents a view of the object structure of a system. During analysis, object diagrams are often used to indicate the semantics of primary and secondary scenarios that provide a trace of the system's behavior. During design, object diagrams are often used to illustrate the semantics of mechanisms in the logical design of a system. Regardless of the development phase, object diagrams present concrete examples that assist in the visualization of the associated class diagrams.

The two essential elements of object diagrams are objects and their relationships.

Essentials: Objects

Figure 5–75 shows the icon we use to represent an object in an object diagram. Similar to class diagrams, a horizontal line partitions the text inside the icon into two regions, one denoting the object's name and the other providing an optional view of the object's attributes and their values. Here, though, we see a tool-specific implementation that does not use a horizontal line to completely partition the two regions.

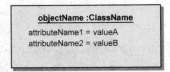

Figure 5–75 A Generic Object Icon

The name of an object may be written in any of the three following forms:

- *objectName*   Object name only
- *:ClassName*   Object class only
- *objectName :ClassName*   Object name and class

All forms of an object name are underlined to clearly distinguish them from a class name. If we never specify the class of an object, either explicitly by using the above syntax or implicitly through the object's specification, the object's class is considered anonymous. If we specify only a class name, the object is said to be anonymous; each such icon without an object name denotes a distinct anonymous object.

For some objects, it may be useful to expose a portion or all of their attributes. We say "some" because objects represent only a view of the object structure. The name of each of these attributes must refer to an attribute defined in the object's class or any of its superclasses. The syntax includes the ability to specify a value for each attribute, as shown in Figure 5–75. We do not show class properties, such as operations, since they are shared by all instances of the class.

Essentials: Object Relationships

As explained in Chapter 3, objects interact through their links to other objects, as shown in Figure 5–76, which is an object diagram corresponding to the class diagram of Figure 5–39. A link is an instance of an association, analogous to an object being an instance of a class.

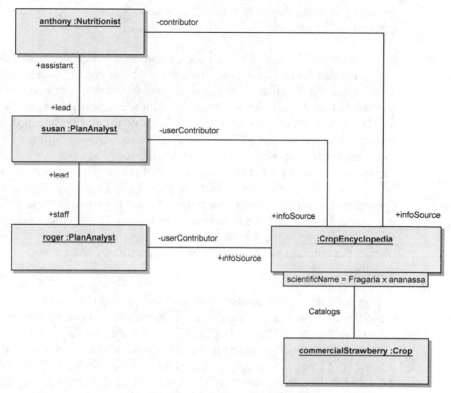

Figure 5–76 Object Relationships

A link may exist between two objects if and only if there is an association between their corresponding classes. This class association may manifest itself in any way, meaning that the class relationship could be a plain association, a generalization, an aggregation, or a composition. The existence of an association between two classes therefore denotes a path of communication (i.e., a link) between instances of the classes, whereby one object may send messages to another. All classes implicitly have an association to themselves, and hence it is possible for an object to send a message to itself.

Advanced Concepts: End Names and Qualifiers

We've discussed objects and their relationships, which constitute the essential parts of the notation for object diagrams. However, a number of particularly knotty development issues require slightly more than this basic notation. As we warned in our discussion on class diagrams, we must again emphasize that these advanced features should be applied only as necessary to capture the intended semantics of a scenario.

In an earlier section, we noted that associations in a class diagram may be adorned with a role denoting the purpose or capacity wherein one class associates with another. For certain object diagrams, it is useful to restate this role on the corresponding link between two objects. Often, this adornment helps to explain why one object is operating on another. Figure 5–76 provides an example of this advanced feature. Here we see that a `PlanAnalyst` object (Susan) both uses information from and contributes information to an anonymous `CropEncyclopedia` object, and does so while acting in the role of `userContributor`, as denoted by the end name on the link. When comparing Figure 5–76 to Figure 5–39 (from our class diagram discussion), we notice that we have two instances of the `PlanAnalyst` class; one is Susan, in the role of `lead`, collaborating with the other one, Roger, in the role of `staff`. Susan is also in the role of `lead` with respect to the relationship with Anthony (a `Nutritionist` object), who is assisting Susan.

In Figure 5–39, we saw a class adornment called a *qualifier* whose value uniquely identifies a single object, out of many, at the target end of an association. Specifically, the class `CropEncyclopedia` uses the attribute `scientificName` as a qualifier to navigate to individual entries in the set of items managed by instances of `CropEncyclopedia`. Here in Figure 5–76, our instance of crop is a `commercialStrawberry`, which was selected by using `Fragaria × ananassa`[2] as the `scientificName` qualifier.

Using the same representation as for class diagrams, additional notations that we may represent on object diagrams include constraint, keyword label, navigation, and link name.

5.14 Communication Diagrams

If you are familiar with the earlier versions of the UML, you may recognize communication diagrams by their pre-UML 2.0 name—collaboration diagrams. A communication diagram is a type of interaction diagram that focuses on how objects are linked and what messages they pass as they participate in a specific interaction.

---

2. Fragaria × ananassa is known by a number of common names, including commercial strawberry, garden strawberry, cultivated strawberry, and just plain strawberry.

Essentials: Objects, Links, and Messages

A link may exist between two objects if and only if there is an association between their corresponding classes. The existence of an association between two classes denotes a path of communication (i.e., a link) between instances of the classes, whereby one object may send messages to another.

Given object A with a link L to object B, A may invoke any operation that is applicable to B's class and accessible to A; the reverse is true for operations invoked by B on A. We will refer to the object that invokes the operation as the *client* and whichever object provides the operation as the *supplier*. In general, the sender of a message knows the receiver, but the receiver does not necessarily know the sender.

In the steady state, there must be consistency between the class structure and the object structure of a system. If we show an operation M being invoked across link L on object B, then B's specification (or the specification of an appropriate super-class) must contain the declaration of M.

Figure 5–77 shows an example of a communication diagram for the Hydroponics Gardening System. The intent of this diagram is to illustrate the interaction for the execution of a common system function, namely, the determination of a predicted net cost-to-harvest for a specific crop.

As shown in Figure 5–77, we may adorn a link with one or more messages. We indicate the direction of a message by adorning it with a directed line, pointing to the destination object. An operation invocation is the most common kind of message (the other type would be a signal). An operation invocation may include actual parameters that match the signature of the operation, such as the `timeToHarvest` message that appears in Figure 5–77.

Essentials: Sequence Expressions

Carrying out the predicted net cost-to-harvest system function requires the collaboration of several different objects. To show an explicit ordering of events, we prefix a sequence number (starting at 1) to a message. This sequence expression indicates the relative ordering of messages. Messages with lower sequence numbers are dispatched before messages with higher sequence numbers. The sequence numbers in Figure 5–77 specify the order of messages for that example.

Using a nested decimal numbering scheme (e.g., 4.1.5.2), we can show how some messages are nested within the next higher-level procedure call. Each integer term indicates the level of nesting within the interaction. Integer terms at the same level

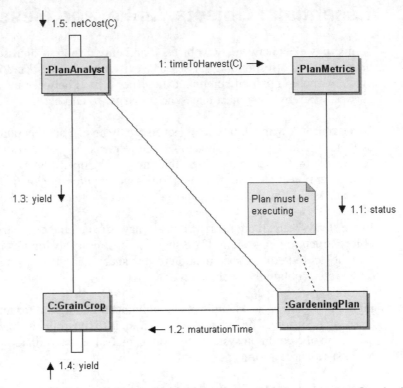

Figure 5–77 A Communication Diagram for the Hydroponics Gardening System

indicate the sequence of the messages at that level. In Figure 5–77, message 1.3 follows message 1.2, which follows message 1.1, and all are nested calls within the timeToHarvest call activation (i.e., message 1).

We see from this diagram that the action of the scenario begins with some PlanAnalyst object invoking the operation timeToHarvest() on PlanMetrics. Note that the object C is passed as an actual argument to this operation. Subsequently, PlanMetrics calls status() on a certain unnamed GardeningPlan object; our diagram includes a development note indicating that we must check that the given plan is in fact executing. The GardeningPlan object in turn invokes the operation maturationTime() on the selected GrainCrop object, asking for the time the crop is expected to mature. After this selector operation completes, control then returns to the PlanAnalyst object, which then calls yield(), which in turn propagates this operation to the C:GrainCrop object. Control again returns to the PlanAnalyst object, which completes the scenario by invoking the operation netCost() on itself.

(This diagram also indicates a link between the `PlanAnalyst` and `GardeningPlan` objects. Although no messages are passed, the presence of this link highlights the existence of a semantic dependency between the two objects.)

Figure 5–78 shows the same sequence of messages as in Figure 5–77. However, the nesting of the messages is different. Here, messages 1.1 and 1.2 are nested within the `timeToHarvest` message (1), and message 2.1 is nested within the `yield` message (2). The same functionality is provided, but the structure of control differs.

The sequence expression may also contain a name to indicate concurrent messages at a specific level of nesting. For example, using the names *a* and *b*, messages 7.2a and 7.2b would be concurrent within the activation of message 7.2. Each would have its own thread of control.

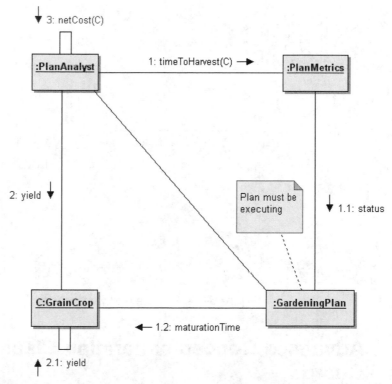

Figure 5–78 A Variant of Figure 5–77, Showing Different Sequence Numbers

Advanced Concepts: Messages and Synchronization

Albeit slightly contrived, the example in Figure 5–79 illustrates the different kinds of message synchronization that may appear in a communication diagram. The message startup() is an example of a simple call and is represented with a directed line with a solid arrowhead. This indicates a synchronous message. In the cases of the startup() and isReady() messages, the client must wait for the supplier to completely process the message before control can resume.

In the case of the message turnOn(), the semantics are different. This is an example of an asynchronous message, indicated by the open arrowhead. Here the client sends the event to the supplier for processing, the supplier queues the message, and the client then proceeds without waiting for the supplier. Asynchronous message passing is akin to interrupt handling.

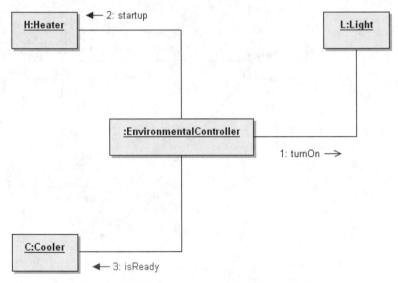

Figure 5–79 Objects and Synchronization

Advanced Concepts: Iteration Clauses and Guards

Additional information can be added to the sequence expression to refine how execution occurs. An iteration clause optionally can be added to indicate a series of messages to be sent. The manner in which the iteration clause is specified is up

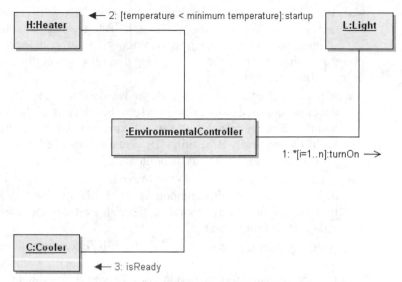

Figure 5–80 Iteration Clause and Guard Adornments on a Communication Diagram

to the individual, although using pseudocode would seem a good choice. Figure 5–80 shows an iteration clause added to the turnOn() message. The adornment is shown as an asterisk followed by the iteration clause in brackets. This example indicates that the turnOn message is to be sent sequentially, 1 to n times. If the messages were to be sent concurrently, the asterisk would be followed by a double bar (i.e., *||[i=1..n]).

Guard conditions can also adorn messages. The notation is similar to an iteration clause, but without the asterisk. The guard condition is placed within brackets, as shown in Figure 5–80 for the startup message. This condition indicates that the message will be executed when the guard condition is true, in this case, when the temperature is below the minimum temperature desired. The manner in which the guard is expressed is up to the individual.

Summary

- Designing is not the act of drawing a diagram; a diagram simply captures a design.
- In the design of a complex system, it is important to view the design from multiple perspectives: namely, its conceptual, logical, and physical models and its structural and behavioral semantics.

- The UML includes thirteen diagrams: package diagram, component diagram, deployment diagram, use case diagram, activity diagram, class diagram, sequence diagram, interaction overview diagram, composite structure diagram, state machine diagram, timing diagram, object diagram, and communication diagram.

- A package diagram provides the means to organize the artifacts of the development process to clearly present the analysis of the problem space and the associated design. The specific reasons will be varied but will either focus on physically structuring the visual model itself or on clearly representing the model elements through multiple views.

- A component diagram shows the internal structure of components and their dependencies with other components. This diagram provides the representation of components, collaborating through well-defined interfaces, to provide system functionality.

- A deployment diagram shows the allocation of artifacts to nodes in the physical design of a system. A single deployment diagram represents a view into the artifact structure of a system. During development, we use deployment diagrams to indicate the physical collection of nodes that serve as the platform for execution of our system.

- A use case diagram depicts the context of the system to be built and the functionality provided by that system. Use case diagrams depict who (or what) interacts with the system. They show what the outside world wants the system to do.

- An activity diagram provides the visual depiction of the flow of activities, whether in a system, business, workflow, or other process. These diagrams focus on the activities performed and who (or what) is responsible for the performance of those activities.

- A class diagram shows the existence of classes and their relationships in the logical design of a system. During analysis, class diagrams indicate the common roles and responsibilities of the entities that provide the system's behavior. During design, class diagrams capture the structure of the classes that form the system's architecture.

- A sequence diagram traces the execution of a scenario in the same context as an object diagram. To a large degree, a sequence diagram is simply another way to represent an object diagram.

- An interaction overview diagram is a combination of activity diagrams and interaction diagrams intended to provide an overview of the flow of control between diagram elements. Though any type of interaction diagram may be used, the sequence diagram is most prevalent.

- A composite structure diagram provides a way to depict a structured classifier with the definition of its internal structure. This diagram is also useful during design to decompose classes into their constituent parts and model their runtime collaborations.

- A state machine diagram is used to design and understand time-critical systems. A state machine diagram expresses behavior as a progression through a series of states, triggered by events, and the related actions that may occur. These are also known as behavioral state machines.
- A timing diagram is a type of interaction diagram. Its purpose is to show how the states of an element or elements change over time and how events change those states.
- An object diagram shows the existence of objects and their relationships in the logical design of a system. A single object diagram represents a view of the object structure of a system and is typically used to represent a scenario.
- A communication diagram is a type of interaction diagram that focuses on how objects are linked and the messages they pass, as they participate in a specific interaction.

Chapter 6

Process

The amateur software engineer is always in search of magic, some sensational method or tool whose application promises to render software development trivial. It is the mark of the professional software engineer to know that no such panacea exists. Amateurs often want to follow cookbook steps; professionals know that such approaches to development usually lead to inept design products, born of a progression of lies, and behind which developers can shield themselves from accepting responsibility for earlier misguided decisions. The amateur software engineer either ignores documentation altogether or follows a process that is documentation-driven, worrying more about how these paper products look to the customer than about the substance they contain. The professional acknowledges the importance of creating certain documents but never does so at the expense of making sensible architectural innovations.

The process of object-oriented analysis and design cannot be described in a cookbook, yet it is sufficiently well defined as to offer a predictable and repeatable process for the mature software development organization. In this chapter, we examine the analysis and design process in detail (and the overall software development process in general) as we consider the purposes, products, steps, and measures of each of the analysis and design activities.

6.1 First Principles

We begin our discussion of process by covering some first principles—those traits that tend to characterize successful projects.

Traits of Successful Projects

A successful software project is one in which the deliverables satisfy and possibly exceed the customer's expectations, the development occurred in a timely and economical fashion, and the result is resilient to change and adaptation. By this measure, we have observed several traits[1] that are common to virtually all of the successful object-oriented systems we have encountered and noticeably absent from the ones that we count as failures:

- Existence of a strong architectural vision
- Application of a well-managed iterative and incremental development lifecycle

Strong Architectural Vision

A strong architectural vision is something that is common to virtually all of the successful object-oriented systems we have encountered. So, what is architecture? The IEEE Recommended Practice for Architectural Description of Software Intensive Systems (referred to as IEEE 1471) defines architecture as the "fundamental organization of a system embodied in its components, their relationships to each other, and to the environment, and the principles guiding its design and evolution" [42]. There are numerous other definitions for architecture in use today, most definitions indicate that architecture is concerned with both structure and behavior, is concerned with significant decisions only, may conform to an architectural style, is influenced by its stakeholders and its environment, and embodies decisions based on rationale [41].

A system that has a sound architecture is one that has conceptual integrity, and as Brooks firmly states, "conceptual integrity is the most important consideration in system design" [1]. In some ways, the architecture of a system is largely irrele-

---

1. Some may argue that there are many other traits of successful projects, and we agree. However, in this chapter, we have chosen these traits to focus on as they have a direct effect on object-oriented analysis and design processes.

vant to its end users. However, having a "clean internal structure" is essential to constructing a system that is understandable, can be extended and reorganized, and is maintainable and testable [2]. It is only through having a clear sense of a system's architecture that it becomes possible to discover common abstractions and mechanisms. Exploiting this commonality ultimately leads to the construction of systems that are simpler and therefore smaller and more reliable. Neglecting an architectural vision leaves us with the software equivalent of sludge.

Just as there is no right way to classify abstractions, there is no right way to craft the architecture of a given system. For any application domain, there are certainly some profoundly stupid ways, and occasionally some very elegant ways, to design the architecture of a solution. How then do you distinguish a good architecture from a bad one? Fundamentally, good architectures tend to be object-oriented and structured by using components. This is not to say that all object-oriented architectures are good, or that only object-oriented architectures are good. However, as we discussed in Chapters 1 and 2, it can be shown that the application of the principles that underlie object-oriented decomposition tend to yield architectures that exhibit the desirable properties of organized complexity.

Good software architectures tend to have several attributes in common.

- They are constructed in well-defined layers of abstraction, each layer representing a coherent abstraction, provided through a well-defined and controlled interface, and built on equally well-defined and controlled facilities at lower levels of abstraction.
- There is a clear separation of concerns between the interface and implementation of each layer, making it possible to change the implementation of a layer without violating the assumptions made by its clients.
- The architecture is simple: Common behavior is achieved through common abstractions and common mechanisms.

Architectures constructed in this way tend to be less complex and more robust and resilient. They also enable more effective reuse.

Agile processes tend to deemphasize the importance of establishing the architecture up front. Instead, they describe concepts such as simple design, emergent design, refactoring, and "serendipitous" architecture [47]. In such processes, the architecture evolves over time. As we discuss in an upcoming section, Toward a Rational Development Process, the approach you choose depends on your context. In any case, when in the lifecycle the architecture is developed and how it is developed does not downplay the importance of having an architectural vision. Without such a vision, the system is harder to evolve and maintain over time.

Iterative and Incremental Lifecycle

For a few limited application domains, the problem being solved may already be well defined, with many different implementations currently fielded. Here, it is possible to almost completely codify the development process: The designers of a new system in such a domain already understand what the important abstractions are, they already know what mechanisms ought to be employed, and they generally know the range of behavior expected of such a system. Creativity is still important in such a process, but here the problem is sufficiently constrained as to already address most of the system's strategic decisions. In such circumstances, it is possible to achieve radically high rates of productivity because most of the development risk has been eliminated [6]. The more you know about the problem to be solved, the easier it is to solve.

Most industrial-strength software problems are not like this. Most involve the balancing of a unique set of functional and performance requirements, and this task demands the full creative energies of the development team. Under such circumstances, it is impossible to provide a cookbook process. Software development, like any human activity that requires creativity and innovation, demands an iterative and incremental process that relies on the experience, intelligence, and talent of each team member.[2]

Iterative and incremental development is where the functionality of the system is developed in a successive series of releases (iterative) of increasing completeness (incremental). A release may be external (available to the customer) or internal (not available to the customer). The selection of what functionality is developed in each iteration is driven by the mitigation of project risks, with the most critical risks being addressed first. The experience and results gained as a result of one iteration are applied to the next iteration. With each iteration, you gradually refine your strategic and tactical decisions, ultimately converging on a solution that meets the end user's real (and usually unstated) requirements and yet is simple, reliable, and adaptable.

The iterative and incremental approach is at the heart of most modern software development methods, including agile methods like Extreme Programming (XP)

---

2. The "Day in the Life" empirical study led by Booch reinforces these observations. This experiment was conducted on Tuesday, March 27, 2001, and it involved 50 developers from around the world. Booch studied a group of developers, observing what they did with their time and how they employed tools. From these studies, he noted that "Individuals and teams must cope with high degrees of uncertainty, ambiguity, and chaos, while at the same time, demanding creativity, predictability, and repeatability. . . . Development is a team sport. . . . The importance of team productivity will supersede the importance of individual programmer productivity" [40].

and SCRUM. It is extremely well suited to the object-oriented paradigm and offers a number of benefits relative to risk management. As Gilb so aptly states, "evolutionary[3] delivery is devised to give us early warning signals to impending unpleasant realities" [15].

The following are some advantages of an iterative development approach [45].

- Requirements changes are accommodated. Each iteration focuses on a specific set of requirements.
- There is no "big bang" integration effort at the end of the project. Each iteration involves the integration of the elements included in the release. Integration is progressive and continual.
- Risks are addressed early. Early iterations mitigate key risks and allow for the identification of new risks earlier in the lifecycle, when they are more easily addressed.
- Tactical changes to the product are possible. Changes can be made to the product and/or early releases of the product are possible in order to counter a competitor's move.
- Reuse is facilitated. Key components of the architecture are actually built early, so the identification of reusable elements, as well as the opportunity to reuse existing elements, is easier.
- Defects can be found earlier and corrected. Testing is performed during every iteration, so defects can be found early and corrected in subsequent iterations instead of being found at the end of the project, when there may not be time to fix them (or the impact of fixing the defects is too big).
- Project personnel are employed more effectively. Iterative development encourages a model in which team members play multiple roles during an iteration, as opposed to a pipeline organization in which analysts hand off to designers, who hand off to programmers, who hand off to testers, and so on. An iterative approach leverages the expertise of the team members and eliminates handoffs.
- Team members learn along the way. Each iteration offers team members the opportunity to learn from past experiences ("practice makes perfect"). Issues in one iteration can be addressed in later iterations.
- The development process can be refined and improved. Each iteration results in an assessment of what worked and what didn't with regard to process and organization. The results of these assessments can be used to improve the process for the next iteration.

---

3. In evolutionary development, the solution evolves over time instead of being defined and then frozen up front. Evolutionary development fits very well with incremental and iterative development because each iteration provides an opportunity to evolve the system by using feedback from the previous iteration.

Now that we have looked at some traits that tend to distinguish successful projects, let's take a look at the range of processes currently available and some strategies for arriving at a rational process.

Toward a Rational Development Process

Parnas and Clements once said, "we will never find a process that allows us to design software in a perfectly rational way" [9] because of the need for creativity and innovation during the development process. However, they went on to say, "the good news is that we can fake it. . . . [Because] designers need guidance, we will come closer to a rational process if we try to follow the process rather than proceed on an ad hoc basis. When an organization undertakes many software projects, there are advantages to having a standard procedure. . . . If we agree on an ideal process, it becomes much easier to measure the progress that the project is making." As we noted earlier, it is important to have a well-managed incremental and iterative lifecycle: well-managed in the sense that the process can be controlled and measured, yet not so rigid that it fails to provide sufficient degrees of freedom to encourage creativity and innovation. In this section, we discuss the range of process styles available today and provide some recommendations on how to select the process style that best meets the needs of your project and your organization.

In the software development community today, there is a plethora of software development processes to choose from—the Rational Unified Process (RUP), XP, SCRUM, Crystal, and so on. Which software development process you choose has a profound impact on how you plan and develop your software development projects and may even determine the success or failure of those projects. Thus, such a decision should not be taken lightly. The good news is that the choice of which process to use is not a binary decision. In fact, we like to think of all software development processes as existing somewhere on a process continuum, with agile on one end and plan-driven on the other.[4] The location of a specific process on the continuum is based on its key themes and its overall strategy.

With agile processes, the primary goal is to deliver a system to the customer that meets their current needs in the shortest amount of time. The process is just a means to an end. Thus, agile processes tend to have the following characteristics:

- Lightweight and sparse, less ceremony (do only what is absolutely necessary and no more)

---

4. Boehm and Turner provide a detailed discussion of the differences between agile and plan-driven processes [38].

- Reliant on the tacit knowledge of the team members (rather than on well-documented processes)
- Tactically focused rather than strategic (don't build for the future as that future is unknown)
- Iterative and incremental (deliver parts of the system in several cycles)
- Heavily reliant on customer collaboration (customers are active participants in requirements definition and validation)
- Self-organizing and managing (the teams figure out the best way to work)
- Emergent as opposed to predetermined (the process evolves out of actually executing the process as opposed to being planned or defined up front)

Agile processes release the software development teams from following a strict set of steps and allow developers to concentrate their creative energies on the system under development.

With plan-driven processes, in addition to delivering the desired system to the customer in an acceptable time frame, another important goal is the definition and validation of a predictable, repeatable software development process. The process is not just a means to an end but is considered an end in itself. In other words, in addition to the system requested by the customer, the software development process itself and its artifacts are key results. Thus, plan-driven processes tend to have these characteristics:

- More heavyweight, more ceremony (follow prescriptive activities resulting in well documented artifacts)
- Reliant on well-documented processes (as opposed to the tacit knowledge of the team members)
- Strategically focused rather than tactically focused (establish a strong architectural framework that can accommodate future changes)
- Reliant on a customer contract (develop and agree on a contract that describes up front what is to be built)
- Managed and controlled (follow detailed plans with explicit milestones and verification points both within and across teams)[5]
- Defined up front and then continually improved (include explicit process improvement procedures and infrastructure)

There is a common misconception that agile means no process and all creativity and that plan-driven means all process and no creativity. This is not an accurate

---

5. Plan-driven processes are not necessarily iterative and incremental (a project can apply a strictly waterfall plan-driven process), but they can be (and we recommend that they should be).

representation of either process style. Agile does not mean lack of process. Agile processes are designed to rapidly handle changes to both the application being developed and the process itself. Agile processes are not, by definition, more creative and innovative than plan-driven ones. Iterative and incremental plan-driven processes that allow time for prototyping provide plenty of room for creativity and innovation.

The choice of which software development process is right for your project is best determined by using a two-phase approach. You first figure out where you (your organization and your project) are on the process continuum, and then you select the process style that will serve as the overall guiding framework for your development process. Then you customize and configure that process framework to include techniques from the other process styles so that the resulting development process achieves the balance between agile and plan-driven techniques that reflects your position on that continuum. For example, if you are closer to the agile end of the continuum, the overall framework or strategy that you will follow in your process will be agile. Then, depending on how far you are to the right (toward the plan-driven end), the more of the plan-driven techniques you will adopt, refine, and include in your process. It is also important to note that the style of process you use may vary depending on where you are in the lifecycle. Early lifecycle phases may require more agility, whereas later lifecycle phases may require more rigor.

To figure out where you are on the process continuum, compare the characteristics of your project with the characteristics of the different process styles, and select the process style with the closest match. Table 6–1 lists the project characteristics commonly associated with the process styles on each end of the continuum.

When deciding on how agile or how plan-driven you need to be, just as with software development, let risk be a guiding factor. What are the risks faced by your project? Select a process style and supporting techniques that address those risks. Is it more risky to use the process or more risky to live without it? Always strive to reduce risk. No matter what process you choose, it should be treated as a recipe that can be adjusted to fit your project's personal tastes, available ingredients, time available, and intended consumers. In the end, all projects need to meet customer needs and be responsive to change in order to maintain relevancy. Thus, every project could benefit from a little agility (which enables flexibility and fosters creativity and invention) as well as a little discipline (which provides predictability, repeatability, and consistency). Using the terms of Parnas and Clements mentioned earlier, this is how you can fake a rational design process for building object-oriented systems.

Table 6–1 Agile and Plan-Driven Project Characteristics

Agile	Plan-Driven
■ Project is small (5–10 people[a]).	■ Project is large (more than 10 people).
■ Experienced teams with a wide range of abilities and skills take part.	■ Teams include varied capabilities and skill sets.
■ Teams are self-starters, independent leaders, and others who are self-directing.	■ Teams are geographically distributed and/or outsourced.
■ Project is an in-house project, and the team is co-located.	■ Project is of strategic importance (e.g., an enterprise initiative); scope crosses the organization.
■ System is new, with lots of unknowns.	■ System is well understood, with a familiar scope and feature set.
■ Requirements must be discovered.	■ Requirements are fairly stable (low change rates) and can be determined in advance.
■ Requirements and environment are volatile, with high change rates.	
■ End-user environment is flexible.	■ System is large and complex, with critical safety or high reliability requirements.
■ Relationship with customer is close and collaborative.	
■ Customer is readily available, dedicated, and co-located.	■ Project stakeholders have a weak relationship with the development team.
■ High trust environment exists within the development teams, between the development teams, and with the customer.	■ External legal concerns (e.g., contracts, liability, formal certification against specific industry standards) exist
■ Rapid value and high-responsiveness are required.	■ Focus is on strong, quantitative process improvement.
	■ Definition and management of process are important.
	■ Predictability and stability of process are important.

a. For a discussion on team size for agile projects, see Boehm and Turner [38].

Once your process is defined, your process work is not done. The process should be refined throughout the development lifecycle as issues arise (ideally, after every iteration). Process activities that worked well should be retained, and those that did not should be eliminated. (And then, rinse and repeat.) Continual process improvement based on practical experience executing the process should be the goal.

The remainder of this chapter describes a framework for the software development process that has been tuned to the construction of object-oriented systems. The software development process is described from two perspectives—the overall software development lifecycle (the macro process) and the analysis and design process (the micro process). The discussion of the macro process sets the context for the micro process, which is the true focus of this chapter.

A key point in the definition of the macro and micro processes is the strong separation of concerns between them. The macro process is concerned with the overall software development lifecycle, and the micro process is concerned with specific analysis and design techniques—the techniques you use to get from requirements to implementation. The choice of lifecycle style (e.g., waterfall, iterative, agile, plan-driven, and so on) affects the macro process, and the choice of analysis and design techniques (e.g., structured, object-oriented, and so on) affects the micro process. Thus, whether you choose an agile or a plan-driven process as your macro process, the object-oriented analysis and design tips and techniques described in the micro process section can be applied equally well.

6.2 The Macro Process: The Software Development Lifecycle

The macro process is the overall software development lifecycle that serves as the controlling framework for the micro process (which we'll describe later in this chapter). It represents the activities of the entire development team, and as such, the macro process dictates a number of measurable products and activities that permit the development team to meaningfully assess risk and make early corrections to the micro process, so as to better focus the team's analysis and design activities.

As we noted earlier, there is a continuum of software development lifecycle styles currently available to choose from—from waterfall to iterative, from agile to plan-driven, and many possibilities in between. The selection of a lifecycle style directly affects the size and shape of the macro process (e.g., the definition and number of phases, the recommended iteration duration, the average number of iterations, and so on).

In this section, we will describe an example of a plan-driven macro process that directly supports the two traits we discussed at the beginning of this chapter: a strong architectural focus and an iterative development lifecycle. The macro process we describe is the RUP lifecycle [51]. This will provide a baseline against which we will compare other possible lifecycles. For a detailed comparison of the lifecycles for different agile methods, see Larman [46].

Overview

The purpose of the macro process is to guide the overall development of the system, ultimately leading to the production system. The scope of the macro process is from the identification of an idea to the first version of the software system that implements that idea.

The development of subsequent versions of the system, whether for evolutionary or maintenance purposes, is accomplished by executing another instance of the macro process (another lifecycle). The size and shape of the maintenance lifecycle is a variant of the initial development lifecycle. For more information on the maintenance lifecycle, see the Post-Transition Software Evolution and Maintenance sidebar.

In an iterative and incremental macro process, which is the style we will concentrate on in this section, the macro process defines the system in an evolutionary way through successive refinements, ultimately leading to the production system. The primary product of such a process is a stream of executable releases (iterations) representing successive refinements (increments) of the system. Secondary products include behavioral prototypes[6] used to explore alternative designs or to further analyze the dark corners of the system's functionality, as well as documentation used to record design decisions and rationale.[7]

The macro software development process can be described in terms of two dimensions, content and time—what is done and when it is done. The content dimension includes roles, tasks, and work products and can be described in terms of disciplines, or areas of concern, which logically group the content. The time dimension shows the lifecycle aspects of the process and can be described in terms of milestones, phases, and iterations.

---

6. For more information on behavioral prototypes, see the Prototyping in the Software Development Process sidebar.

7. Many developers balk at "unnecessary documentation" because they don't feel it benefits them. However, it is important to note that the audience for documentation is rarely the current development team but is usually people external to the team (such as integrators, database administrators, project managers, operational support teams, technical help desk staff, and so on) or people who will join the team in the future. Thus, documentation should be created only if it will be read in the future. When it is developed, documentation should evolve along with the system rather than being treated as a separate milestone and should be a natural, semiautomatically generated artifact of the process.

Post-Transition Software Evolution and Maintenance

Once a software system has been delivered (post-transition), changes to the deployed system will most likely be needed. Those changes may be to provide new or improved features (evolution) or to fix discovered defects (maintenance). The issue of maintaining an operational system without breaking what is already there is a real concern.

Lehman and Belady have made some cogent observations regarding the maturation of a deployed software system.

- A program that is used in a real-world environment necessarily must change or become less and less useful in that environment (the law of continuing change).
- As an evolving program changes, its structure becomes more complex unless active efforts are made to avoid this phenomenon (the law of increasing complexity). [31]

Refinement of deployed software systems is especially important in agile development. In fact, one of the key principles of agile development is "to satisfy the customer through early and continuous delivery of valuable software" [35]. With agile processes, deployed systems are continually refactored to simplify their structure without breaking any existing implementations (e.g., all tests must still pass).

Changes to a deployed software system can be developed and delivered by reexecuting a lifecycle that is similar to the original software development lifecycle, except that the size and shape of a maintenance lifecycle (i.e., what phases are needed and the number of iterations in each phase) depend on what needs to be accomplished in the release. Some maintenance releases involve simple localized changes and no architectural innovation (i.e., they include mainly a Transition phase), but others require some thinking with regard to scope and business value, as well as architecture and risk (i.e., they include both Inception and Elaboration phases). Such maintenance releases are considered more major, and their lifecycles look something more like the complete end-to-end process. For a discussion of maintenance lifecycles, see Kruchten [44].

The products of evolution and maintenance lifecycles are similar to those of the original release lifecycle, with the addition of a list of change requests. Immediately upon release of the production system, its developers and end users will probably already have a set of improvements or modifications they would like to carry out in subsequent production releases, which for business reasons did not make it into the initial production release. Additionally, as more users exercise the system, new bugs and patterns of use will be uncovered that the quality assurance team could not anticipate. (Users are amazingly creative when it comes to exercising a system in unexpected ways.) A change request list serves as the vehicle for collecting defects and enhancement requirements, so that they can be prioritized for future releases.

The activities performed after transition are similar to those required during the development of a system. However, in addition to the usual software development activities, post-transition release planning involves prioritizing the change requests, assessing their impact and cost of development, and assigning the changes to a release. Also, many operational problems must be resolved within 24 hours (or fewer!). Thus, patches must be delivered outside of the normal release mechanism. Configuring and testing such changes as well as integrating them into the current development release can be significant project activities.

The Macro Process Content Dimension— Disciplines

The macro process involves the following disciplines, executed in the following relative order.

1. *Requirements*: Establish and maintain agreement with the customers and other stakeholders on what the system should do. Define the boundaries of (delimit) the system.
2. *Analysis and design*: Transform the requirements into a design of the system, which serves as a specification of the implementation in the selected implementation environment. This includes evolving a robust architecture for the system and establishing the common mechanisms that must be used by disparate elements of the system.
3. *Implementation*: Implement, unit test, and integrate the design, resulting in an executable system.
4. *Test*: Test the implementation to make sure that it fulfills the requirements (i.e., the requirements have been implemented appropriately). Validate through concrete demonstration that the software product functions as designed.
5. *Deployment*: Ensure that the software product (including the tested implementation) is available for its end users.

The following disciplines are executed throughout the lifecycle.

- *Project management*: Manage the software development project, including planning, staffing, and monitoring the project, as well as managing the risks.

Prototyping in the Software Development Process

Prototyping serves multiple purposes in the software development process. Before discussing the role of prototyping, let's first define what we mean by a prototype, specifically, a behavioral prototype. A behavioral prototype explores some isolated element of the system, such as a new algorithm, a user interface model, or a database schema. Its purpose is the rapid exploration of design alternatives, so that areas of risk can be resolved early without endangering the production releases. Such prototypes are, by their very nature, incomplete and only marginally engineered, and they are meant to be thrown away after they have served their purposes.

The first use of a behavioral prototype is usually during the early phases of the software development lifecycle when you are trying to understand what can be built and what technologies you can leverage to build it. For every significant new system, there should be some proof-of-concept, manifesting itself in the form of a quick-and-dirty prototype. Obviously, for applications on a massive scale (such as ones that have national significance or multinational implications), the prototyping effort itself may be a large undertaking. That is to be expected and, in fact, encouraged. It is far better to discover during proof-of-concept that assumptions of functionality, performance, size, or complexity were wrong, rather than later, when abandoning the current development path could prove to be financially or socially disastrous.

Behavioral prototypes can also be used throughout the software development lifecycle to better understand the semantics of the system's behavior. Typically, a team uses behavioral prototypes to storyboard user interface semantics and present them to end users for early feedback, or to do performance trade-offs for the implementation of specific mechanisms.

Any and all programming paradigms should support the development of proofs-of-concept in order to help teams better understand an idea and to uncover risks. However, it is often the case that, in the presence of a reasonably rich object-oriented application framework, developing prototypes is often faster than alternative approaches. It is not unusual to see proofs-of-concept developed in one language (such as Smalltalk) and the end product developed in another (such as Java).

Prototypes should not be allowed to directly evolve into the production system, unless there is a strong compelling reason. Convenience for the sake of meeting a short-term schedule is distinctly not a compelling reason: This decision represents a false economy that optimizes for short-term development and ignores the cost of ownership of the software. When developing prototypes, it is important to establish clear criteria for the goals and completion of each prototype. Upon completion, decide on an approach to integrate the results of the prototyping effort into the current, or subsequent, releases.

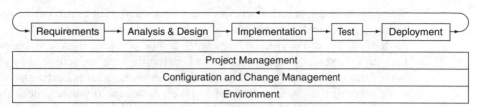

Figure 6–1 The Macro Development Process Disciplines

- *Configuration and change management*: Identify the configuration items, control changes to those items, and manage configurations of those items.
- *Environment*: Provide the software development environment, including both processes and tools that support the development team.

Figure 6–1 shows the relative order and iterative nature of the macro process disciplines. Each cycle through the disciplines constitutes an iteration of the macro process.

It is important to emphasize that while the disciplines tend to be executed in the order shown (requirements, then analysis and design, then implementation, and so on), the macro process does not have to be a waterfall process (though it can be). In a waterfall macro process, just one pass is made through the disciplines—the requirements for the entire system are defined, followed by the analysis and design for the entire system, and so on. In an iterative and incremental macro process, there are multiple passes through the disciplines, and the scope of the work performed in each discipline during each pass depends on where you are in the overall development process. This will become clearer when we discuss milestones and phases.

Many elements of the macro process are simply sound software management practices and apply equally well to object-oriented as well as non-object-oriented systems. These include basic practices such as requirements management, configuration management, testing and quality assurance, code walkthroughs, and documentation.

Now that we have looked at the content dimension of the macro process, let's turn our attention to the time dimension, which can be described in terms of milestones, phases, and iterations.

The Macro Process Time Dimension— Milestones and Phases

In an iterative and incremental macro process, the disciplines are repeated. However, there is more to an iterative development process than a stream of iterations.

There must be an overall framework in which the iterations are performed that represents the strategic plan for the project and drives the goals and objectives of each of the iterations. Such a framework can be provided by a series of well-defined milestones, where objectives of each milestone are achieved by executing one or more iterations.[8] At each milestone, an assessment is performed to determine whether the objectives have been met. A satisfactory assessment allows the project to continue with the next phase to achieve the next milestone.

The milestones ensure that the iterations make progress and converge on a solution, rather than just iterating indefinitely. They should be viewed not as dates on a project schedule but as quality or maturity gateways, such that achieving these milestones means that a project has reached a specific level of maturity and an increased level of understanding of the evolving plans, specifications, and completed solutions. If the date originally set for one of these milestones is reached and the project is not at the indicated level of maturity and understanding, then the milestone date should slip—the date is the flexible part, not the milestone criteria.

Figure 6–2 shows how milestones and iterations fit together in an iterative and incremental macro process, as well as the phases that the milestones delineate.

In the following subsections we describe each of these phases in detail.

Inception

This subsection covers the purpose, activities, work products, and milestone of the Inception phase.

Purpose   The purpose of the Inception phase is to ensure that the project is both valuable and feasible (scope and business value). For any truly new piece of software, or even for the novel adaptation of an existing system, at some moment in the mind of the developer, the architect, the analyst, or the end user, an idea for some application springs forth. This idea may represent a new business venture, a new complementary product in an existing product line, or perhaps a new set of features for an existing software system. It is not the purpose of the Inception phase to completely define this idea. Rather, this phase's purpose is to establish the vision for the idea and validate its assumptions. Even for the refinement of an existing system, there is still value in the Inception phase. In such cases, Inception is brief but still focuses on ensuring business value and technical feasibility.

---

8. A waterfall-based macro process also has milestones, but those milestones represent the completion of each of the disciplines for the entire system (e.g., requirements complete, analysis and design complete, and so on).

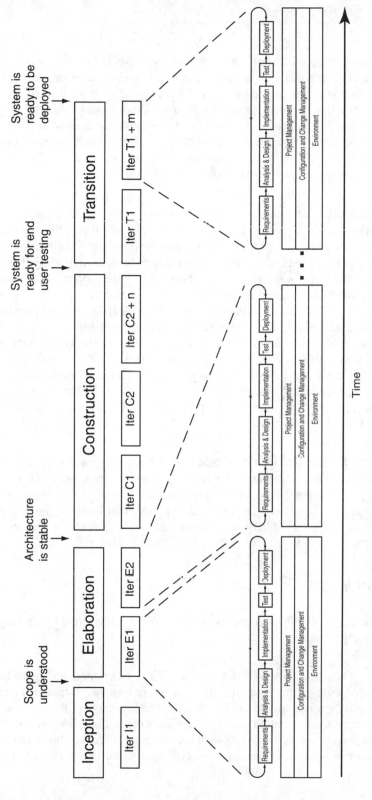

Figure 6–2 Macro Process Milestones, Phases, and Iterations

Activities   During the Inception phase, you establish and prioritize the core requirements of the system, obtain agreement with the customer on what is to be built, make sure you understand the key risks associated with building the system, and decide what development environment to use (both process and tools). Remember the earlier discussion on selecting a process that is most appropriate for the current context? Inception is when that decision is made, the development process is customized, and tools are selected to support the process. There is nothing inherently object-oriented about the Inception phase.

Work Products   The primary work products of the Inception phase are a vision of what is to be built, behavioral prototypes, an initial risk list, the identification of the key architectural mechanisms, and the development environment. The vision provides a clear description of what is to be built, including its scope, key features, and impacts on and relationships with existing systems, as well as any existing constraints that must be considered. The prototypes serve as proofs-of-concept that the system is buildable. The risk list identifies critical items that must be mitigated early in the lifecycle to increase the probability of success. The architectural mechanisms define the general capabilities of the system that support the basic system functionality (e.g., user interface paradigms, error detection and handling, persistency, memory management, interprocess communication, transaction management and security, and so on). The development environment includes the development process to be followed and the development tools that will support the process.

Milestone: Scope Is Understood   The Inception phase is successfully completed when there is a clear understanding of what is to be built (the overall scope and key requirements of the system), an understanding of the relative priority of those requirements, and a strong business reason for building the system. In addition, there is agreement between the customer and the development organization on the scope of the system and the overall timeline for delivery.

Elaboration

This subsection covers the purpose, activities, work products, and milestone of the Elaboration phase.

Purpose   Once the scope of what is to be built is understood and agreed to, attention turns to developing the overall architecture framework that will provide the foundation for all the iterations that follow. The intent is to identify architectural flaws early and to establish common policies that yield a simpler architecture. The Elaboration phase is when such architectural discovery takes place, choices are made, and the architecture evolves across multiple iterations. This evolution is driven by the mitigation of the highest risks and the implementation of the requirements with the highest priority and the most architectural significance.

Activities   The Elaboration phase involves making architectural decisions, establishing the architectural framework, implementing the framework, testing the framework, and refining the framework based on the results of the testing. The evolution of the architecture is largely a matter of trying to satisfy a number of competing constraints, including functionality, time, and space: One is always limited by the most restrictive constraint. For example, if the weight of the computer is a critical factor (as it is in spacecraft design), the weight of individual memory chips must be considered, and in turn the amount of memory permitted by the weight allowance limits the size of the program that may be loaded. Relax any given constraint, and other design alternatives become possible; tighten any constraint, and certain designs become intractable. By evolving the architecture of a software system rather than taking a more monolithic approach to development, you can identify which constraints are really important and which are delusions. Early in the Elaboration phase, you typically do not know enough to understand where the performance bottlenecks will arise in the system. By actually building the key architectural elements and measuring the results via testing, the development team can better understand how to tune the architecture over time.

Work Products   During the Elaboration phase, the architecture is validated by creating a series of executable architectural releases that partially satisfy the semantics of the key end-user scenarios (the architecturally significant scenarios). These scenarios are those that exercise and test the main system elements and their collaborations, as well as those that investigate identified areas of risk. These architectural releases denote a vertical slice through the entire architecture, capturing important (but incomplete) semantics of all significant system elements. Thus, the result of the Elaboration phase not only provides an architecture document but also includes actual releases of the system that serve as tangible manifestations of the architecture design itself. An architectural release should be executable, thus allowing the architecture to be instrumented, studied, and evaluated precisely. These architectural releases become the foundation of the evolving production system.

Milestone: Architecture Is Stable   The Elaboration phase is successfully completed when the architecture has been validated (by actual testing and formal review) against all of the key system requirements, both functional and nonfunctional, and when all risks have been sufficiently mitigated in order to predictably determine the cost and schedule for completing the development of the system. A key indicator that the architecture has stabilized (and that the Elaboration phase is successfully completed) is that the rate of change of key architectural interfaces and mechanisms has slowed considerably, if not been eliminated entirely. Measuring the rate of change of architectural interfaces and mechanisms is the primary measure of architectural stability [30]. Localized changes are to be expected throughout the software lifecycle, but if key architectural elements are being changed often, this indicates some architectural problems, which should be recognized as an area of risk and an indication that Elaboration is still in process.

Construction

This subsection covers the purpose, activities, work products, and milestone of the Construction phase.

Purpose   Once the architecture has stabilized, the focus shifts from understanding the problem and identifying key elements of the solution to the development of a deployable product. The Construction phase is when you move from discovery into production, where production can be thought of as "a controlled methodological process of raising product quality to the point where the product can be shipped" [24].

Activities   During the Construction phase, the development of the system is completed, based on the baselined architecture produced during the Elaboration phase.

Work Products   During the iterations of the Construction phase, a series of executable releases are produced that satisfy the semantics of the remaining end-user scenarios. These releases can be instrumented, studied, and evaluated precisely as they incrementally grow in scope and evolve into the production system.

Milestone: System Is Ready for End-User Testing   The Construction phase is successfully completed when the functionality and quality of the releases are sufficient to deploy to the end user for some end-user testing. Some primary measures of goodness during this phase include to what degree you satisfied the requirements of the releases, as well as the quality of those releases. An important indication of quality during this phase includes defect-discovery rates. Defect-discovery rates are a measure of how rapidly new errors are being detected [29]. By investing in quality assurance early in the development process, it is possible to establish measures of quality for each release, which the management team can use to identify areas of risk and also to calibrate the development team. After each release, the defect-discovery rate generally surges. A stagnant defect-discovery rate usually indicates undiscovered errors. An offscale defect-discovery rate is an indication that the architecture has not yet stabilized or that new elements in a given release are incorrectly designed or implemented. In either case, the system is not ready for end-user testing, and these measures should be used to adjust the focus of subsequent releases.

Transition

This subsection covers the purpose, activities, work products, and milestone of the Transition phase.

Purpose   The Transition phase is when you ensure that the software is acceptable to its end users.

Activities   During the Transition phase, the product is provided to the user community for evaluation and testing (e.g., alpha testing, beta testing, and so on). The development team then incorporates the feedback received. The focus of Transition is on fine-tuning the product; addressing configuration, installation, and usability issues; and addressing issues raised by the early adopters. Supporting documentation also undergoes final development, as does any applicable training material. Any production-related issues, such as packaging and marketing materials, are also handled. The resulting product then undergoes acceptance testing. It is important to note that even though testing has been performed throughout the lifecycle, end-user testing and final acceptance testing is still important as such testing ensures that the developed product fulfills its acceptance criteria at both the development and target installation sites.

Work Products   The work products produced during the Transition phase include the packaged product, any supporting documentation, training materials, and marketing materials.

Milestone: System Is Ready to Be Deployed   The Transition phase is successfully completed when the functionality and quality of the releases are sufficient to make the product available to end users (the system has passed acceptance testing). The primary measure of goodness is similar to that in the Construction phase, a reduced rate of reported defects. However, in this phase, early adopters are reporting the defects.

Phases in Agile Methods

Agile methods also include the concept of phases. In this sidebar, we summarize the phases defined in some of the available agile methods [46].

The XP lifecycle includes five phases.

1. *Exploration*: Determine feasibility, understand key "stories" for the first release, and develop exploratory prototypes.
2. *Planning*: Agree on the date and stories for the first release.

3. *Iterations to release*: Implement and test selected stories in a series of iterations. Refine the iteration plan.
4. *Productionizing*: Prepare supporting materials (documentation, training, marketing), and deploy the operational system.
5. *Maintenance*: Fix and enhance the deployed system.

The SCRUM lifecycle includes four phases.

1. *Planning*: Establish the vision, set expectations, secure funding, and develop exploratory prototypes.
2. *Staging*: Prioritize and plan for the first iteration. Develop exploratory prototypes.
3. *Development*: Implement requirements in a series of sprints, and refine the iteration plan.
4. *Release*: Prepare supporting materials (documentation, training, marketing), and deploy the operational system.

As you can see, the phases defined in both plan-driven and agile methods are quite similar. Specifically, all the methods we have described include phases for:

- Envisioning, feasibility, and scoping
- Release and iteration planning
- Implementing and testing
- Productizing and deploying

Now that we have looked at some examples of macro process phases and milestones, it is time to turn our attention to what occurs within each of the phases—the iterations.

The Macro Process Time Dimension— Iterations

As shown in Figure 6–3, in an iterative macro process, the milestones are achieved by executing one or more iterations, and those iterations may involve activities in any and all of the disciplines. However, the relative time spent in the different disciplines varies depending on what phase the iteration occurs in. If the iteration is in the Inception phase, more time would be spent on requirements; if the iteration is in the Elaboration phase, more time would be spent on analysis and design (specifically, architecture); if the iteration is in the Construction phase, more time would be spent on implementation and testing; and so on. Of course, some disciplines, such as configuration and change management, environment, and project management, are performed throughout the lifecycle.

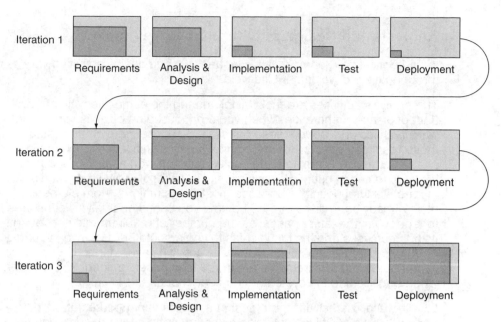

Figure 6–3 The Shifting Focus of Iterations

Figure 6–3 illustrates how the focus of a project shifts across successive iterations. The size of the boxes within each of the disciplines illustrates the relative time spent performing the activities within that discipline. For a discussion on how the analysis and design activities change throughout an iterative and incremental lifecycle, see the Analysis and Design and Iterative Development sidebar.

At the end of each iteration, a postmortem should be held to assess the iteration in terms of the state of the system being built, as well as in terms of the state of the development environment and team. Each iteration should be seen as an opportunity to adjust the course of the project, either by adjusting the functionality mapped to subsequent iterations and/or by refining the environment to improve those areas that are not working well.

The concept of an iteration is pretty much the same across most software development methods. What differs is the recommended duration for each iteration [46].

- XP recommends that iterations be one or two weeks long, if possible.
- SCRUM specifies that all iterations (sprints) should be 30 days long.
- RUP recommends that iterations be two to six weeks long.

As noted earlier, a key deliverable of the macro process is a series of sequential, evolutionary releases. Thus, we conclude this section on the macro process with a discussion of release planning.

Analysis and Design and Iterative Development

In an iterative development lifecycle, analysis and design activities vary throughout the development lifecycle.

The analysis activities are most visible during the earlier lifecycle phases (Inception and Elaboration) when you are focused on establishing the software architecture. During these phases, you concentrate on analyzing those requirements considered architecturally significant. During the later phases, when you complete the implementation, you analyze any remaining requirements, but this analysis is not as extensive as what you did during architectural definition because most of the major system elements have already been discovered. The time you spend on analysis continues to taper off in the later phases, as the number of requirements not yet analyzed decreases and the focus shifts to implementation. However, you may need to perform some minimal analysis activities even during later phases if changes to the requirements are introduced based on feedback received when transitioning the system to the user, though this is unlikely.

Like the analysis activities, the design activities vary throughout the development lifecycle. Design activities can start in the early phases when you are establishing the scope of the system if you decide, for example, that you will base your solution on a set of existing software elements. These activities then pick up in the early iterations of architectural definition, when you concentrate on designing the major (or architecturally significant) elements of the system. As you move into the later lifecycle phases, design activities taper off, and the focus is more on what you could categorize as being peripheral or supporting elements.

Release Planning

During release planning, you define what the releases are and what they will contain. The purpose of release planning is to identify a controlled series of releases, each growing in its functionality, ultimately encompassing the requirements of the complete production system. The primary input to release planning is the scope of what is to be built, as well as any constraining factors (e.g., cost, time, quality). The activities performed during release planning include establishing the project's heartbeat, prioritizing requirements, allocating requirements to iterations, tagging an iteration release as external or internal, and finally developing detailed iteration plans. The result of release planning is a development plan, which identifies the stream of releases, team activities, and risk assessments. Now let's look at each of the release-planning activities in a little more detail.

The first step when planning the releases involves establishing the heartbeat of the project—deciding on the average duration for the iterations (i.e., deciding on the spacing of the releases). The duration of an iteration is an important factor when deciding just how much you think you can accomplish in a single iteration. Iteration release dates should be sufficiently separated to allow adequate development time and to synchronize releases with other development activities, such as documentation and field testing. For a small project involving six to twelve months of end-to-end development time, this might mean a release every two to six weeks. For a modest-sized project involving twelve to eighteen months of end-to-end development time, this might mean a release every two to three months. For more complex projects that require much greater development effort, this might mean a release every six months or so. More extended release schedules are suspect because they do not force closure of the micro process and may hide areas of risk that are being intentionally or unintentionally ignored.

Once you know about how long your iterations are going to be, the next step during release planning is to prioritize the system requirements to be delivered, both functional and nonfunctional. These priorities will be used when determining what requirements are allocated to what iteration.

Requirements are prioritized based on a number of factors. These factors may include the following:

- Benefit to stakeholders (e.g., how important the requirement is to the end user, or how important it is to demonstrate a consistent part of the system functionality to the project's sponsor)
- Architectural impact and coverage (e.g., whether the requirement involves key aspects of the architecture such as access to databases, integration with legacy systems, and so on)
- Risks mitigated by addressing the requirement (e.g., whether the requirement includes access to an external system whose interface is not well understood)

Depending on where you are in the development lifecycle, each of these factors may have a different weight. For example, what's considered high priority during the Elaboration phase is different than what is considered high priority during the Construction phase (during Elaboration, architectural significance has more weight). It is important to note that requirements are not prioritized only once. Their relative priorities should be evaluated every iteration and adjusted where necessary, based on the current project status, new requirements, discovery of new risks, and mitigation of existing risks. Due to the multiple factors affecting priority, prioritizing requirements is best accomplished by a team that includes a user representative, a domain expert, an analyst, an architect, and quality assurance personnel.

Once the requirements have been prioritized, the requirements are allocated to a series of iteration releases, with the highest-priority requirements allocated to the earlier iterations. Each iteration should have a planned capability that is demonstrable and should have clear evaluation criteria that will be used to assess the success of the iteration. The content of an iteration release is determined by the scope of the iteration, which in turn is determined by where the iteration is in the software life-cycle (i.e., what phase it is in).

Each iteration results in a release that may be internal or external; the final release is an external release that represents the production system. The determination of whether a release is internal or external depends on the overall lifecycle phase. Early in the development process, the releases are generally internal. Major executable releases are turned over by the development team to quality assurance personnel, who can begin to test the release against the scenarios established during requirements, thereby gathering information on the completeness, correctness, and robustness of the release. This early data gathering aids in identifying problems of quality, which are more easily addressed during evolution of the subsequent release. Later in the development process, more releases tend to be external, as executable releases are turned over to select end users (the alpha and beta customers) in a controlled manner. By "controlled," we mean that the development team carefully sets expectations for each release and identifies aspects that it wishes to have evaluated. In general, there may be more internal releases to the development team, with only a few executable releases turned over to external parties. The internal releases represent a sort of continuous integration of the system and exist to force closure on some key system areas.

Note that the act of creating a release is relatively costly (especially for an external release), so other constraining factors such as time, quality, and scope may place limits on the number and duration of the releases. In such cases, quality can be used as a bargaining chip when forced to deliver some fixed unit of cost, time, or scope. This is particularly significant for a fixed-price contract.

The final activity of release planning is the development of detailed iteration plans. During iteration planning, detailed project plans are developed for the current iteration, and development resources needed to achieve the release are identified. Unlike the overall release plan (which is defined up front and identifies the key milestones, a proposed number of iterations, and a high-level understanding of their content), detailed iteration plans are developed just in time (when the iteration is to begin). This allows project managers to account for the inevitable schedule adjustments needed as the development progresses. "Unjustifiable precision—in requirements or plans—has proven to be a substantial yet subtle recurring obstacle to success. Most of the time, early precision is just plain dishonest and serves to provide a façade for more progress of more quality than actually exists" [50].

With iterative development, release planning is ongoing and risk-driven. After each iteration, the remaining development plan should be reexamined and adjusted, as necessary. Often, this involves some reprioritization of requirements, small adjustments to dates, or migration of functionality from one iteration to another. Periodic risk assessments should be performed throughout the lifecycle and the development plan adjusted to tackle the risky things first so that those risks can be eliminated or reduced. This helps the team to manage future strategic and tactical trade-offs. Facing up to the presence of risks early in the development process makes it far easier to make pragmatic architectural trade-offs later.

6.3 The Micro Process: The Analysis and Design Process

In the previous section, we discussed the overall software development process (the macro process). In this section, we cover the analysis and design process (the micro process) by looking at what activities are performed and what work products are produced.

Overview

As shown in Figure 6–4, the analysis and design process is performed in the context of an overall software development process. The macro process drives the scope of the micro process, provides inputs to the micro process, and consumes the outputs of the micro process. Specifically, the micro process takes the requirements provided by the macro process (and any analysis and design specifications produced by previous iterations of the micro process) and produces design specifications (most notably, the architecture) that are implemented, tested, and deployed in the macro process.

Just as we described the macro process in terms of two dimensions, time and content, we will describe the micro process in terms of its two key dimensions—

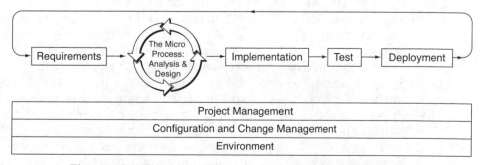

Figure 6–4 The Micro Process within the Macro Process

levels of abstraction and content (activities and work products). We then discuss how the activities performed and the work products produced are affected by the levels of abstraction.

Levels of Abstraction

In the micro process, the traditional phases of analysis and design are intentionally blurred and instead are performed at different levels of abstraction along a continuum. Analysis takes the system requirements and produces an initial solution, and design takes the results of analysis and produces a specification that can be efficiently implemented. The analysis is considered complete when it accurately represents the system requirements, is consistent, and can serve as a good basis for design. The design is considered complete when it is detailed enough to be implemented and tested. As Mellor et al. state, "the purpose of analysis is to provide a description of a problem. The description must be complete, consistent, readable, and reviewable by diverse interested parties, [and] testable against reality" [16]. In our terms, the purpose of analysis is to provide a model of the system's behavior.

Analysis focuses on behavior, not form. In analysis, you seek to model the world by identifying the elements that form the vocabulary of the problem domain and describing their roles, responsibilities, and collaborations. During analysis, it is inappropriate to pursue issues of representation or implementation. Rather, analysis must yield a statement of what the system does, not how it does it. Any intentional statements of "how" during analysis should be viewed as useful only for the purpose of exposing the behavior of the system and not as testable requirements of the design. Analysis is about understanding the problem to be solved a little better. Analysis is a critical part of the overall software development process and, if performed well, will result in a more robust and understandable design, with a clear separation of concerns and a balanced division of responsibility between system elements.

In design, you invent the elements that provide the behavior that the analysis elements require. You begin the design process as soon as you have some reasonably complete model of the behavior of the system. It is important to avoid premature designs, wherein development begins before analysis reaches closure. It is equally important to avoid delayed designing, wherein the organization thrashes while trying to complete a perfect and hence unachievable analysis model (a condition commonly referred to as analysis paralysis). During analysis, you should not expect to devise an exhaustive understanding of the system's behavior. Indeed, it is neither possible nor desirable to carry out a complete analysis before allowing design to commence. The very act of building a system raises questions of behavior that no reasonable amount of analysis can efficiently uncover. It is sufficient that you accomplish an analysis of all the primary behaviors of the system, with a sprinkling of secondary behaviors considered as well to ensure that no essential patterns of behavior are missed.

Since architecture plays such an important part of the overall solution, we need to understand the separation of concerns when developing the architecture versus the individual components during analysis and design. Architecture is primarily concerned with the relationships between the parts of the systems (e.g., components), their responsibilities, interfaces, and collaboration. In contrast, analysis and design of system components focus on the internals of those components and how they will satisfy the requirements levied on them that result from the architectural analysis and design. Figure 6–5 summarizes what should be the focus of analysis and design, when done from both architectural and component perspectives.

The architecture describes the structural decisions and essence of the system. Thus, the architectural concern is more strategic in nature, whereas component analysis and design are more tactical. What you focus on depends on whether you are concerned with the architecture or with the components that are part of that architecture.

Analysis and design are performed at multiple levels of abstraction throughout the development lifecycle. The number of levels cannot be specified a priori. This depends primarily on the size of your system. In fact, you may at times discover,

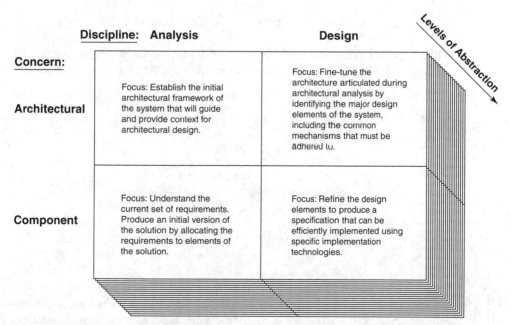

Figure 6–5 The Varying Focus of Analysis and Design, Depending on Perspective

for example, that the component you were trying to analyze is too large. You may have to take a step back and perform another round of architectural analysis on that component in order to partition it into further components (or subcomponents) that are more manageable and can be better analyzed.

Now let's look at the activities performed during the micro process and the work products they produce.

Activities

The micro process consists of the following set of activities, which are performed for a specific scope and at a specific level of abstraction.

- *Identify the elements*:[9] Discover (or invent) the elements to work with. Define the object-oriented decomposition.
- *Define the collaborations between the elements*: Describe how the identified elements collaborate to provide the system's behavioral requirements.
- *Define the relationships between the elements*: Define the relationships between the elements that support the element collaborations.
- *Define the semantics of the elements*: Establish the behavior and attributes of the identified elements. Prepare the elements for the next level of abstraction.

These micro process activities are shown in Figure 6–6.

While these activities are shown as being performed sequentially, in practice they are performed in parallel. For example, you may identify the elements and their

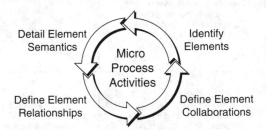

Figure 6–6 The Micro Process Activities

9. Throughout this chapter, we will use the term *element* to refer to the "things" we are working with at the current level of abstraction. Thus, an element may be an analysis class, a component, a design class, and so on. For more information on the elements identified during analysis and design, see Table 6–2.

collaborations at the same time. You may also identify behaviors and attributes when defining the element collaborations. The ability to do this comes with experience. Think of performing the micro process in a series of passes through the activities for the current scope; however, you can minimize the number of passes as you become more experienced at applying the process.

We will discuss each of the micro process activities in more detail later in this chapter. Now let's take a look at the products of the micro process.

Products

As you would expect, the primary products of the micro process reflect the different analysis and design concerns.

- The *architecture description* describes the system's architecture, including descriptions of common mechanisms. The description includes the architecturally significant aspects of the analysis/design model.
- The *analysis/design model* includes the analysis and design elements of the software solution and their organization, as well as the realizations that describe how the system's behavioral requirements are realized in terms of those elements.

As with the analysis/design model, choosing to what level of detail the architecture is described depends on the system being developed and what type of development process you have selected. Once documented, the architecture needs to be communicated to the development team. After all, it describes the system's architectural vision, whose importance we discussed in an earlier subsection, Strong Architectural Vision. For recommendations on how to document the software architecture, see the Documenting the Software Architecture sidebar.

There are essential benefits to creating an analysis/design model as part of the micro process. First, maintaining an analysis/design model helps to establish a common and consistent vocabulary that can be used throughout the project. The analysis/design model serves as the central repository for the elements, their semantics, and their relationships as development progresses. Over time, the analysis/design model is refined by adding new elements, eliminating irrelevant elements, and consolidating similar elements. In this way, the team continues to evolve a consistent language of expression. Also, having a central repository for the elements in a system not only ensures that those elements are consistent but also can serve as an efficient vehicle for browsing through all the elements of a project in arbitrary ways. This feature is particularly useful when new members of the development team must quickly orient themselves to the solution already under development. An analysis/design model also permits architects to take a global view of the project, which may lead to the discovery of commonalities that otherwise might be missed. As you can probably guess, the use of the UML to represent the analysis/design model enhances these benefits even more. Not only do you realize the typical benefit of "a picture is worth a thousand words," but visually representing the analysis/design model helps to uncover inconsistencies between the elements. (For information on using the UML to represent object-oriented analysis and design elements, see Chapter 5.)

The choice of whether to maintain separate analysis and design models depends on the system being developed and what type of development process you have chosen.[10] A separate analysis model may be useful if the system being developed will live for decades, will have multiple variants, or is designed for multiple target environments, each with its own design architecture. In such cases, the analysis model is maintained as an abstraction (platform-independent representation) of the individual (platform-specific) design models. In fact, this is one of the foundation principles of Model Driven Architecture (MDA) as espoused by the Object Management Group [48]. A separate analysis model may also be maintained to provide a conceptual overview of a complex system; however, a well-documented architecture can serve this same purpose. It can be very costly to maintain a high degree of fidelity between the analysis model and the design model. When deciding whether a separate analysis model is needed, keep in mind the extra work required to ensure that the analysis and design models remain consistent and balance that cost against the benefits of having a separate model that provides a conceptual view of the system. Alternatively, the analysis model can be considered a temporary artifact that evolves into a design model (in such cases, the analysis model is considered an "initial" design model).

Documenting the Software Architecture

Documenting the architecture of a system has considerable value to the architects themselves and to the system's stakeholders. The value is not only in the resulting documentation but also in the documenting process itself. The architecture is the part of design that is shared across many stakeholders, not just the development team. Deployment designers, network designers, application support and operations personnel, help desk staff, and even project managers will read the software architecture documentation, but few if any of these folks will read the detailed software design notes. The software architecture documentation provides an excellent overview of the key aspects of the system and supports the confirmation that the system meets its requirements. Documenting the architecture

---

10. For more information on the software development process, see the Toward a Rational Development Process section.

forces you to consider very carefully the different aspects of the architecture. In this sidebar, we provide some suggestions for how to think about and document the software architecture.

As we discussed earlier, architecture describes a set of key design decisions, rules, and patterns, as well as a set of constraints that define a framework in which the design and implementation of the system takes place. Software architecture involves multiple perspectives, so the architecture description should also include multiple perspectives. As described in IEEE 1471 [42], an architect can define his or her own viewpoints and views to communicate the architecture of the system, where a viewpoint describes:

- One or more system models and views (projections) of those models
- The stakeholders interested in the views
- The stakeholders' concerns that should be addressed through the views

The software architecture should be represented by using a set of relevant views defined by viewpoints, where a viewpoint serves as a guide for a view. These architectural views include those development artifacts that are considered architecturally significant from a particular viewpoint.

The following is a simple set of views that can be used to describe a software architecture. This set of views, first proposed by Kruchten [43], is known as the 4+1 architecture view model.

- *Requirements View (also known as the Use Case View)*: The Requirements View describes the architecturally significant requirements, both functional and nonfunctional. The architecturally significant functional requirements tend to drive the definition of the architecturally significant use case scenarios that are analyzed early in the software lifecycle. The architecturally significant nonfunctional requirements include any system-wide architectural qualities (e.g., usability, resilience, performance, size, scalability, security, privacy, comprehensibility) and economic and technology constraints (e.g., use of off-the-shelf products, integration with legacy software, reuse strategy, required development tools, team structure and schedule), as well as regulatory constraints (e.g., adherence to specific standards and controls). It is these nonfunctional requirements that tend to be the most architecturally significant, and they drive the definition of the architectural mechanisms documented in the Logical View.

- *Logical View*: The Logical View contains the architecturally significant analysis and design elements, their relationships, and their organization into components, packages, and layers, as well as a few selected realizations that illustrate how these architecturally significant elements work together to provide the architecturally significant scenarios described in the Requirements View. The Logical View also describes the key mechanisms and patterns that shape the system structure.

- *Implementation View*: The Implementation View describes the key implementation elements (executables, directories) and their relationships. This view is important because the structure of the implementation has a major impact on concurrent development, configuration management, and integration and testing.
- *Process View*: The Process View describes the independent threads of control in the system and what logical elements participate in these threads.
- *Deployment View*: The Deployment View describes the various system nodes (such as computers, routers, and virtual machines/containers) and the allocation of the architecturally significant logical, implementation, or process elements to these nodes.

The "4+1" name of this set of views refers to the debate over whether requirements should be considered an architectural view. The Requirements View is included in the architectural description in order to describe the subset of the requirements that shape the architecture and to allow the qualities of the architecture to be expressed. Thus, requirements are critical to the architecture, and it is recommended that you call out the architecturally significant ones as part of the architecture description and trace those requirements to the other architectural views.

As Booch, Rumbaugh, and Jacobson point out, each of the architectural views can stand alone so that different stakeholders can focus on the architectural areas that most concern them [39]. These five architectural views also interact with one another (e.g., nodes from the Deployment View hold elements from the Implementation View that, in turn, represent the physical realization of the elements from the Logical and Process Views).

An architect should feel free to add as many views as needed to describe the software architecture (e.g., a Data View or a User Experience View) and to remove views that do not apply.

Numerous other architecture frameworks, both simple and complex, have the common characteristic of using views and viewpoints. Some of the more notable are the Zachman framework [32], the Department of Defense Architecture Framework (DoDAF) [33], and the Federal Enterprise Architecture (FEA) [34].

In some cases, depending on your project and the process you are using, it may make sense to collect all architectural information into an actual software architecture document (SAD). The SAD becomes the primary artifact where the architecture of a system is described, and it contains references to all other architecturally significant artifacts. If someone wants to understand the architecture of a system, the SAD is the place to start. The SAD should show how the key architectural concerns are addressed, so it is best organized to follow the architectural views just discussed. The SAD should be reviewed with the entire team and updated as the architecture evolves.

The Micro Process and Levels of Abstraction

The micro process applies equally to the project architect and to the application engineer, the difference being the level of abstraction considered. From the perspective of the architect, the micro process offers a framework for evolving the architecture and exploring alternative designs; from the perspective of the engineer, the micro process offers guidance in making the myriad tactical decisions that are part of the daily fabrication and adaptation of the architecture.

The details of what is performed during the micro process activities depend on the current concern (i.e., architectural or component; refer to Figure 6–5). The following list further describes the focus of the micro process activities for each of the concerns defined earlier.

- When performing *architectural analysis*, the micro process activities focus on creating an initial version of the architecture that leverages any existing reference architectures or architectural frameworks, as well as identifying other existing assets that could be used as the building blocks. This includes the overall structure of the system, its key abstractions, and its mechanisms. In fact, it's not a bad idea to develop a high-level understanding of each of the architectural views. The results of architectural analysis are used to drive architectural design.
- During *architectural design*, the initial architecture developed from the architectural analysis is refined based on what was learned during architectural analysis. The micro process activities focus on refining the identified analysis elements, the design elements, and their responsibilities and interactions. The design elements defined at this level represent the key building blocks of the overall architectural framework, and their relationships determine the overall structure of the system. The analysis mechanisms are also refined into design mechanisms that leverage specific technologies, and the impact of concurrency and distribution on the architecture are considered much more closely. Reuse also plays an important role, as the opportunity and impact of incorporating existing design elements (and their associated implementation) are explored.
- In *component analysis*, the micro process activities focus on identifying the analysis elements and their responsibilities and interactions. These analysis elements represent the first approximation of the system components that are then used during component design to identify the design elements. It is important to remember that the nature of the micro process analysis activities are to provide us with an analysis perspective of the component, and you should avoid the temptation to design the component at this stage, since this entails additional concerns that will be addressed during design.
- During *component design*, the micro process activities focus on refining the design of the component by defining it in terms of design classes that can be

directly implemented by the selected implementation technology. During detailed design, you continue refining the design classes by working out the details of their content, behavior, and relationships. The refinement should stop when there is enough detail for the design classes to be implemented. This is followed by implementation, which is part of the macro process.

While it may appear that the micro process is a clean, full-breadth walk down a path from high-level abstractions to lower-level abstractions, that is not the really the case.

As shown earlier in Figure 6–4, you start the micro process with a set of requirements from the macro process (e.g., use cases, scenarios, function points, user stories, and supplementary specifications).[11] You then execute several iterations of the micro process, with each iteration taking its inputs that are at some level of abstraction and producing a realization of these inputs at the next level of abstraction. The end result of the micro process iterations is a detailed design realization of the original requirements that is fed back into the macro process for implementation.

During the micro process iterations, the selection of what elements to take to a lower level of abstraction at any point in time is opportunistic and risk-based. For example, when performing architectural design, for a certain scope, you may "go deep" (e.g., perform component design) for a set of elements that you don't know much about, in order to reduce risk, and then pop back up again to continue your architecture design work. Let's take a closer look at an example and see if we can clarify what we mean.

Imagine that we are in an Elaboration phase iteration of the macro process, and the architecturally significant requirements that are in scope for that iteration are ready to be taken through the analysis and design process (the micro process). The following scenario describes what may happen during the micro process.

1. Architectural analysis is performed for all of the architecturally significant scenarios. The result is a set of architecturally significant analysis elements.
2. Architectural design occurs, using all of the architectural analysis elements as input. During this iteration, a design element is discovered that is not that well understood, so component analysis and design is executed *for that element*. As a result, some refinements are needed to the element *at the architectural design level*. The result of these iterations is a set of architecturally significant design elements.

---

11. No matter which type of requirements representation is used, it is important that the requirements accurately document what the system needs to do from the perspective of the user, including both functional and nonfunctional requirements. In this chapter, we use the term *scenario* to refer to this user-focused view of the requirements.

3. Component analysis is performed for each of the architecturally significant scenarios, using the architectural design elements as input. The result of these iterations is a set of design elements that support the architecturally significant scenarios.

4. Component design is executed for each of the architecturally significant elements from component analysis.

5. Additional micro process iterations are executed at lower levels of abstraction (e.g., moving from the enterprise level to system, subsystem, component, and subcomponent levels, and so forth).

The result of these iterations is a set of detailed design elements that are ready for implementation in the macro process. Figure 6–7 summarizes the relationship between the macro process, the micro process, and the micro process iterations.

Now that we have completed our discussion of the micro process and levels of abstraction, we can examine each of the micro process activities in more detail and discuss what is performed, what is produced, and how to assess the quality of what is produced.

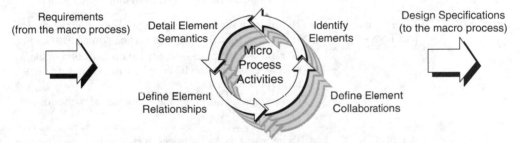

Figure 6–7 Micro Process Iterations

Identifying Elements

The identification of elements is a key activity when devising an object-oriented decomposition of a system. Thus, the purpose of this first micro process activity is to identify the key elements that will be used to describe the solution at a particular level of abstraction. We use the word *identify* rather loosely here. The activity is really an evolution of elements from one level of abstraction to the next. Identifying elements at one level of abstraction involves evolving the previous level, which results in new and different elements. The elements identified at one level of abstraction are then used as the primary inputs to the identification of elements at the next level.

While performing this activity, it is important to maintain a delicate balance between identifying the elements and refining their semantics. This element identification activity should focus just on identifying the elements and describing them at a high level (a brief description). The micro process activities that follow will progressively refine the semantics of the identified elements.

Products

The primary product of this micro process activity is the analysis/design model, which includes the identified elements and their basic description at a particular level of abstraction. Table 6–2 summarizes the elements identified during the different analysis and design activities.

Table 6–2 Elements Identified During Analysis and Design Activities

Focus	Identified Elements	Purpose and Comments
Architectural analysis	Key abstractions	■ To form the vocabulary of the problem domain. Identifying key abstractions up front reduces the possibility that key concepts will be defined in conflicting ways later, when elements are identified from individual requirements.
	Architectural partitions	■ To represent separate areas of concern within the system and to cluster analysis elements (i.e., components). ■ To represent the high-level logical organization of the system. Partitions can be based on an existing architectural framework. In a layered architecture, the architectural partitions are the layers.
	Analysis mechanisms	■ To represent the key services, infrastructure, and common policies you might need going forward. Some of these are foundational, meaning that they address domain-independent issues such as memory management, error detection and handling, persistence, interprocess communication, transaction management, and security. Others are domain-specific and include idioms and mechanisms that are germane to that domain, such as control policies in real-time systems or transaction and database management in information systems. Analysis mechanisms are described in broad terms that are not implementation-specific. ■ To support consistency across the analysis activities (as opposed to having one analyst come up with one solution while another analyst comes up with a different solution). Identifying common mechanisms early on mitigates the risk that a poor tactical design decision about common policies will be made that could negatively affect the overall architecture.

Focus	Identified Elements	Purpose and Comments
Architectural design	Architecturally significant design elements	■ To encapsulate business behavior and/or to provide access to and management of system data. ■ To represent specifications that can be efficiently implemented by using specific implementation technologies.
	Architectural partitions	■ To refine the original architectural logical partitions defined during architectural analysis. ■ To cluster design elements.
	Design mechanisms	■ To refine the analysis mechanisms to specific technologies.
Component analysis	Analysis classes[a]	■ To represent the initial object-oriented composition of the desired solution that provides the desired behavior. ■ To describe separate elements with cohesive responsibility.
Component design	Design classes	■ Same purposes as for architectural design, except here we work at a lower level of abstraction (i.e., component design elements vs. architectural design elements). These design elements are refined and specified to a level of detail that enables implementation.

a. Some may disagree with the use of the word *classes* in this context. However, the important idea is not what they are called but what they represent.

Steps

In Chapter 4, we described specific classification techniques for identifying object-oriented elements (i.e., classical object-oriented analysis, behavior analysis, domain analysis, use case analysis, CRC cards, informal English description, and structured analysis). As described in that chapter, the identification of object-oriented elements usually involves two activities: discovery and invention. During analysis, identification is mostly driven by discovery, whereas in design, invention plays a bigger part. During analysis, designers work in conjunction with domain experts to identify the elements. They must be good at discovering abstractions, capable of looking at the problem domain and finding meaningful analysis elements. During design, architects and designers identify elements and must be skilled in crafting new design elements that derive from the solution domain.

During design, some elements identified during analysis may turn out to be actual classes, and others may turn out to be simply attributes of, or synonyms for, other abstractions. In addition, some of the analysis elements you identify early in the lifecycle may be wrong, but that is not necessarily a bad thing. During analysis, it is important to keep such decisions open to refinement as development progresses. Many of the tangible things and roles that you encounter early in the lifecycle will carry through all the way to implementation because they are so fundamental to your conceptual model of the problem. As you learn more about the problem, you will probably change the boundaries of certain elements by real-locating responsibilities, combining similar elements, and—quite often—dividing larger elements into groups of collaborating ones, thus forming some of the mechanisms of your solution. In summary, analysis elements are often quite fluid and changeable, and they can evolve greatly before they solidify during design.

The overall approach for identifying elements is generally the same for all levels of abstraction; what differs is your starting point (what abstractions you already have), what you concentrate on (architecturally significant elements or not), and how far you go (whether you look inside a design element and identify the elements that comprise it). For example, when performing architectural design, you use the results of architectural analysis as a starting point, you concentrate on the archi-tecturally significant design elements, and you may also consider the elements that comprise those architecturally significant elements to make sure that you understand each element's behavior well enough to reduce risk. When performing component analysis and design, you use the results of architectural analysis and design as a starting point, and you identify any remaining design elements needed to specify the implementation, including more fine-grained design elements that comprise the more coarse-grained elements (e.g., the classes that will provide the behavior of a component).

The identification of elements is then repeated recursively in order to invent more fine-grained abstractions that you can use to construct higher-level ones and to discover commonality among existing abstractions, which you can then exploit to simplify the system's architecture. When identifying design elements, the design elements with the largest granularity are usually identified first because they define the core of the logical structure of the system and are composed of the smaller granularity elements. However, in reality, design elements at different lev-els of granularity may be identified at the same time, though there are obvious sequential dependencies (e.g., you cannot identify classes that specify the imple-mentation of a particular component until that component has been identified).

The following analysis classes are excellent candidates for being refined into design elements.

- Analysis classes with a nontrivial set of responsibilities.
- Groups of analysis classes that represent information that should be man-aged together. Elements whose information should be managed together should belong to the same design element, and the responsibilities that involve manipulating that information should belong to that design element.
- Groups of analysis classes that collaborate to provide a specific behavioral requirement or related behavioral requirements (e.g., the analysis classes

participating in the same or related realizations). Collaborating elements
should belong to the same design element.

■ Groups of analysis classes that have the same responsibilities. Similar (or
related) responsibilities should belong to the same design element.

In addition to looking at the analysis elements as inspiration for the design elements, the refinement of analysis elements into design elements is also driven by
the application of selected architectural and/or design patterns (especially those
that reflect your selected architectural style), as well as general design principles.
Some examples of patterns include IBM's patterns for eBusiness [52], architecture patterns [53], and design patterns [55]. Some examples of design principles
include the enterprise component design principles described in Cheesman and
Daniels [54] and the best practices of developing business components described
in Herzum and Sims [56].

When identifying elements, it is always wise to investigate similar systems at
similar levels of abstraction. In this way, you benefit from the experience of other
projects that had to make similar development decisions. In general, during the
element identification step, it is important to identify the opportunity and the
impact of incorporating (reusing) existing elements, making sure that the
intended context for a potential reusable asset is consistent with your context.

The logical partitions identified during architectural analysis are usually based on
the selection of a specific architectural pattern. These partitions are refined during
design as design elements are identified and clustered. Some partitioning guidelines include clustering elements that support the same function. Functions that
build on one another should fall into different partitions; functions that collaborate to yield behaviors at a similar level of abstraction should fall into partitions,
which represent peer services. These decisions have strategic implications. In
some cases, this clustering is done from the top down, by taking a global view of
the system and partitioning it into abstractions that denote major system services
that are logically cohesive and/or likely to change independently. This architecture may also be refined from the bottom up, as clusters of classes that are semantically close are identified. As existing design partitions become bloated, or as
new clusters become evident, you may choose to introduce a new design partition
or reorganize the allocation of existing ones. Such refactoring is a key practice in
agile processes.

The mechanisms identified during architectural analysis are considered placeholders for the common policies and infrastructure that are needed to support all
elements of the system. These analysis mechanisms are identified by looking at
the key services that might be needed, and are characterized in broad terms. (For
more information on how to identify mechanisms, see Chapter 4.) During architectural design, you make decisions on how the analysis mechanisms will be

designed and implemented. Thus, analysis mechanisms are refined into design mechanisms, and their descriptions become more detailed. Specifically, design mechanisms are described in terms of specific abilities provided by the selected implementation technology.

If elements are to be maintained at different levels of abstraction (i.e., separate analysis and design elements), as opposed to the elements at one level of detail just morphing into elements at the next level, it is wise, from the viewpoint of requirements management and change management, to maintain traceability between the different levels of abstraction. Establishing and maintaining traceability is critical to effective and accurate impact assessment.

Milestones and Measures

You successfully complete the micro process activity of identifying elements for a specific scope at a specific level of abstraction when you have an ample set of abstractions, consistently named and described. Another measure of goodness is that you have a reasonably stable analysis/design model for that scope at that level of abstraction. In other words, the analysis/design model is not changing wildly each time you iterate through the micro process. For example, the discovery of architecturally significant design elements late in the project's lifecycle indicates a flaw in requirements, analysis, or the discussed aspects of the design. A rapidly changing analysis/design model is a sign either that the development team has not yet achieved focus or that the architecture is in some way flawed. As development proceeds, you can track stability in lower-level parts of the architecture by following the local changes in collaborative abstractions.

Defining Element Collaborations

The purpose of the second micro process activity, defining element collaborations, is to describe how the identified elements work together to provide the system's behavioral requirements. In this activity, we refine the identified elements through an intelligent and measurable distribution of responsibilities.

Products

The primary products of this micro process activity are the realizations that indicate how the identified elements collaborate to perform the behavioral requirements that are in scope. Realizations describe how a set of behavioral requirements are realized in terms of elements at a specific level of abstraction collaborating with one another. Realizations reflect an explicit distribution of responsibilities among the collaborating elements and provide the link between the behavioral requirements and the software solution. Realizations are initially described in terms of analysis elements and then later in terms of design elements.

The realizations and the supporting element responsibilities are documented in the analysis/design model. The level of detail and the representation used depend on the level of abstraction with which you are working. During analysis, you might use freeform descriptions for the responsibilities. Usually a phrase or a single sentence is sufficient; anything more suggests that a given responsibility is overly complex and ought to be divided into smaller parts. During design, you may create specifications for each element that state the named operations that form the protocol of each element. During detailed design, these operations are formally captured as interfaces with complete signatures in the selected implementation language. The collaborations themselves may be documented by using simple diagrams that show which elements collaborate with each other. UML interaction diagrams (specifically, sequence and communication diagrams) are very effective for representing these collaborations. In addition, for those elements whose states drive how they collaborate with other elements, you may include state machine diagrams that capture the key state changes. UML state machine diagrams are very effective for representing these state machines. For more information on specifying an element's semantics, see the upcoming Detailing Element Semantics section. For more information on using the UML, see Chapter 5.

Steps

Analyzing behavioral requirements is an excellent technique for allocating the work to be performed to the identified elements. The following steps describe an approach for defining the semantics of a set of elements at a specific level of abstraction.

1. *Analyze the behavior*, allocating responsibilities to the elements that participate in providing the behavior (i.e., the elements identified during the previous micro process step). Consider exceptional behavior as well as expected behavior. Where the lifecycle of certain elements is significant or essential, develop a state machine for the element. The result of this step is a realization of the behavior in terms of the participating elements and their collaborations.
2. *Scavenge for patterns* among the realizations, and express these patterns in terms of more abstract, generalized realizations.

This approach applies equally well at all levels of abstraction, whether you are analyzing the system's behavior expressed as use cases/scenarios (analysis), analyzing a component's behavior expressed as responsibilities/interfaces (design), or analyzing the behavior of an architectural mechanism expressed in a textual description (analysis and design).

Now let's look at each of these steps in a little more detail.

Behavior Analysis   Behavior analysis can be used to understand how a set of behavioral requirements are provided by the elements of the solution. The primary product of scenario analysis is a set of realizations. A realization can be developed by using the techniques of use case analysis (highly recommended), behavior analysis, or CRC cards, as described in Chapter 4.

A typical order of events when analyzing a scenario can be summarized as follows.

1. Select a scenario or a set of scenarios from the behavioral requirements to be considered.
2. Identify the elements relevant to the scenario. (The elements themselves may have already been identified during the previous micro process activity.)
3. Walk through the scenario, assigning responsibilities to each element in order to accomplish the desired behavior. As needed, assign attributes that represent structural elements required to carry out certain responsibilities. *Note*: In this step it is important to focus on behavior, not structure. Attributes represent structural elements, so there is a danger, especially early in analysis, of binding implementation decisions too early by requiring the presence of certain attributes. Attributes should be identified at this point only insofar as they are essential to building a conceptual model of the scenario.
4. As scenario analysis proceeds, reallocate responsibilities so that there is a reasonably balanced distribution of behavior. Where possible, reuse or adapt existing responsibilities. Splitting large responsibilities into smaller ones is a very common action; less often, but still possible, trivial responsibilities are assembled into larger behaviors. The analysis of individual scenarios may result in disparate responsibilities being allocated to the same element. Split such elements into multiple elements, each with a consistent and cohesive set of responsibilities.
5. During design, concurrency and distribution must also be considered in these realizations; where there are opportunities for concurrency, you must specify the actors, agents, and servers, as well as the means of synchronization among them. Along the way, you may discover the need to introduce new paths among objects and to eliminate or consolidate unused or redundant ones.

When analyzing a scenario, you may find that the state (or lifecycle) of one or more of the elements plays a significant role in affecting the overall flow of the scenario. In such cases, it is worth the time to take a closer look at the externally visible state changes that the element may experience and to make sure that the scenario flow can accommodate those state changes. An accurate way to capture the element's key states and state transitions is to use a state machine diagram.

Pattern Scavenging   This step recognizes the importance of commonality. As you identify the semantics of your elements, you must be sensitive to patterns of behavior, which represent opportunities for reuse.

A typical order of events for scavenging patterns may be the following.

1. Given the complete set of realizations at this level of abstraction, look for patterns of interaction among the participating elements. Such collaborations may represent implicit idioms or mechanisms, which should be examined to ensure there are no gratuitous differences. Nontrivial patterns of collaboration should be explicitly documented as strategic decisions so that they can be reused rather than reinvented. This activity preserves the integrity of the architectural vision.
2. Given the set of responsibilities generated at this level of abstraction, look for patterns of behavior. Common roles and responsibilities should be unified in the form of common elements with common responsibilities.
3. When working at lower levels of abstraction, as concrete operations are being specified, look for patterns within operation signatures. Remove any gratuitous differences, and introduce common classes when such signatures are found to be repetitious.

When you find patterns of collaboration, express them in terms of more abstract, generalized realizations.

Milestones and Measures

You successfully complete the micro process activity of defining element collaborations when you have a consistent set of elements and responsibilities that provide the required functional behavior of the system within a particular scope at a specific level of abstraction and that offer a sensible and balanced separation of responsibilities between those elements.

As a result of this activity, you should have developed and validated realizations that represent the fundamental behaviors considered in scope. By *fundamental*, we mean behaviors that are central to the application's purpose. Measures of goodness with regard to the realizations include completeness and simplicity. Each realization must accurately reflect the semantics of the individual elements participating in the realization. A good set of realizations will cover all primary scenarios and a statistically interesting set of secondary ones. We neither expect nor desire a realization for every scenario. It is sufficient to consider only primary and some secondary scenarios. In addition, a good set of realizations will also discover patterns of behavior, ultimately yielding a solution structure that exploits all that is common among different scenarios.

With regard to the individual element responsibilities, keep in mind that the focus of this activity is on the collaboration and on the identification of "who does what." At this point, it is enough to just capture the element responsibilities. At the higher levels of abstraction, you may use an informal statement of responsibilities. At the lower levels of abstraction, you may want to use more precisely stated semantics, but don't go into too much detail here as the explicit definition of the semantics of the individual elements is the purpose of the fourth micro process activity, as described in the upcoming Detailing Element Semantics section.

The following list gives a few simple and useful checkpoints for evaluating the results of this activity.

- Elements should have balanced responsibilities. A single element should not be "doing it all."
- Elements should have consistent responsibilities. When an element's responsibilities are disjoint, it should be split into two or more elements.
- There should not be two elements with identical or very similar responsibilities.
- The responsibilities defined for each element should support the flows in which the element participates.
- Responsibilities that are neither simple nor clear suggest that the given abstraction is not yet well defined.

At this point, we have identified the elements and have defined how those elements collaborate to provide the required behavior. Now it is time for us to turn our attention to the relationships between the elements that enable and support those collaborations.

Defining Element Relationships

The purpose of the third micro process activity is to define the relationships between the elements that support the element collaborations defined in the previous micro process activity. Defining the element relationships establishes the shape of the solution. Specifically, at the architectural levels of abstraction, the relationships between the key elements and the key partitions define the overall structure of the system and form the basis for all other relationships between system elements. Identifying the relationships is done to solidify the boundaries of each element and to clearly represent which elements collaborate with each other.

This activity formalizes the separation of concerns among elements that was initially established when defining the element collaborations.

Products

The primary products of this micro process activity are the relationships between the elements at the current level of abstraction. The defined relationships are added to the evolving analysis/design model.

Even though these relationships will ultimately be expressed in a concrete form (namely, through programming languages), we recommend that you represent them visually, using either UML diagrams or freeform diagrams. Visual diagrams offer a broader view of the architecture and let you express relationships that are not enforced by the linguistics of programming languages. These diagrams help you visualize and reason about relationships that may cross entities that are conceptually and physically distant. As a result of producing these diagrams, you may discover previously hidden patterns of interaction, which you could seek to exploit. This may also lead to a local tweaking of the inheritance lattice.

It is not desirable, nor is it possible, to produce a comprehensive set of diagrams that express every conceivable view of the relationships among elements. Rather, we recommend that you focus on the interesting ones, where our measure of *interesting* encompasses any set of related elements whose relationships are an expression of some fundamental architectural decision or that express a detail necessary to complete a blueprint for implementation. One set of diagrams that you may want to consider developing are diagrams associated with the realizations produced as part of the previous micro process activity of defining element collaborations. Such diagrams would contain the elements participating in the realization, along with their relationships, and would represent the structural aspects of the realization.

Steps

In general, there are two steps associated with defining element relationships:

1. *Identification of associations*, the initial identification of a semantic connection between elements
2. *Refinement of associations* into more semantically rich relationships (e.g., aggregations, dependencies, and so on)

The identification of associations is primarily an analysis and early design activity. During architectural analysis, you define the relationships between the high-level architectural partitions and between the key abstractions. During architectural design, you perform this activity in order to specify the relationships between the key components, as well as the high-level clustering of design elements into design partitions. During component analysis, you perform this activity in order to specify the relationships among analysis elements (including associations and certain important inheritance and aggregation relationships).

A typical order of events for identifying element associations might be the following.

1. Collect a set of elements that exist at a given level of abstraction or are associated with a particular scenario/realization.
2. Consider the presence of a semantic relationship between any two elements, and establish an association if such a dependency exists. The need for navigation from one element to another and/or the need to elicit some behavior from an element are both cause for introducing associations. If two elements must collaborate between each other, there should be a relationship between them.
3. For each association, if not redundant with the element names, specify the role of each participant, as well as any relevant multiplicity or other kind of constraint. Include such details only if they are obvious, as refining of these relationships is the purpose of the next step.
4. Validate your decisions by walking through scenarios and ensuring that the associations in place are necessary and sufficient to provide the navigation and behavior among elements participating in each scenario.

As we explained in Chapter 3, associations are the most semantically weak relationship: They represent only some sort of general dependency. However, during analysis and early design, this is often sufficient, for it captures enough interesting details about the relationship between two abstractions, yet prevents us from making premature statements of detailed design.

The refinement of associations is both an analysis and a design activity. During analysis, you may evolve certain associations into other, more semantically precise and concrete relationships to reflect your increasing understanding of the problem domain. During design, you similarly transform associations as well as add new concrete relationships in order to provide a blueprint for implementation. Aggregation, composition, and dependency are the main kinds of relationships of interest, together with additional properties such as names, roles, multiplicity, and so on.

A typical order of events for refining the element relationships might be the following.

1. Look for a collection of elements already clustered by some set of associations (e.g., the elements participating in a specific realization), and consider

the semantics of each of those relationships, refining the type of relationship as necessary. Does the relationship represent a simple usage of another object? If so, the association should be refined into a dependency relationship. Does the association represent a particular structural relationship between the respective elements? If so, the association should be refined into an aggregation or a composition relationship. Each of the existing relationships should be examined with the goal of identifying and documenting the nature of these relationships.

2. Look for patterns of structure among the elements. If found, consider creating new elements that capture this common structure, and introduce them either through inheritance (place the classes in the context of an existing inheritance lattice, or fabricate a lattice if an appropriate one does not already exist) or through aggregation.

3. Look for patterns of behavior among the elements. If found, consider the possibility of introducing common parameterized elements that perform the common behavior.

4. Consider the navigability of existing associations, and constrain them if possible. Use unidirectional relationships if bidirectional navigation is not a desired property.

5. As development proceeds, introduce details such as statements of role, multiplicity, and so on. It is not desirable to state every detail; just include information that represents an important analysis or design position or that is necessary for implementation.

Milestones and Measures

You successfully complete the micro process activity of defining element relationships when you have specified the relationships among the elements at a specific level of abstraction.

One thing to look for at this phase is the consistency of the relationships between the elements participating in a realization. Specifically, for each realization, the relationships between the participating elements and the required collaborations between elements must be consistent (if there is collaboration, there must be a relationship).

Measures of goodness include cohesion, coupling, and completeness. In reviewing the relationships you identify during this activity, you seek to have logically cohesive and loosely coupled elements. In addition, you seek to identify all of the important relationships at a given level of abstraction, so that the next level of abstraction does not require you to introduce new significant relationships or perform unnatural acts to use the ones you have already specified. If you find that your elements and relationships are awkward to specify, that is an indication that you have not yet devised a meaningful set of relationships among your elements.

Detailing Element Semantics

Up to this point, we have focused mainly on how the elements collaborate. Now we will take a closer look at the semantics of the individual elements from the bottom up, making sure that they are consistent and well understood.

The purpose of this fourth micro process activity is to clarify the behavior and attributes of each identified element at a specific level of abstraction, to define semantics that are consistent across all scenarios the element participates in, and to make sure that sufficient information is provided for each element in order to take that element to the next level of abstraction. In this activity, the element semantics are refined *at the current level of abstraction* in sufficient enough detail to enable the identification of elements at the next level of abstraction. For example, during analysis, the purpose of detailing the element semantics is to refine the analysis elements' semantics to include enough information to enable the identification of design elements. During design, the purpose of detailing the element semantics is to refine the design elements' semantics to include enough detail to support implementation.

The placement of this activity as the last activity in the micro process is intentional: The micro process focuses first on behavior and collaboration between elements and defers decisions about the detailed semantics of the individual elements until as late as possible. This strategy avoids premature decisions that can ruin opportunities for smaller, simpler architectures and also allows for the freedom to change internal representations as needed for reasons of efficiency, while limiting the disruption to the existing architecture. Whereas the first three activities of the micro process focus on an outside view of the elements and how they collaborate, this final activity focuses on each of the elements individually, clearly specifying each element's external view and providing additional details that will drive the development of the internal view.

Products

The primary product of this micro process activity is a refined analysis/design model that includes more detailed semantics for the elements. Both the level of detail and the representation used to document the element's semantics depend on the level of abstraction you are working in.

During analysis, the results of this activity are relatively abstract. You are not so concerned about making representation decisions; rather, you are more interested in discovering new abstractions to which you can delegate responsibility. Detailing the semantics at the analysis level may involve developing more detailed descriptions of those responsibilities in the form of activity diagrams that describe the overall flow. For those elements whose responsibilities involve event-driven or state-ordered behavior, you may want to include state machines that capture the dynamic semantics of each element's protocols.[12]

During design, and especially in later stages of detailed design, you must increasingly make concrete decisions regarding representation. As you begin to refine the protocol of individual elements, you may name specific operations, ignoring their full signatures. As soon as practical, you may attach full signatures for each operation. During design, you may also specify that certain algorithms should be used. When working at the lower levels of abstraction, and as you make further bindings to the given implementation language (i.e., during detailed design), the detailed semantics may even include pseudocode or executable code. Once you produce formal class interfaces, you can begin to use programming tools to test and enforce the design decisions. The primary benefit of the more formal products of this step is that they force the developer to consider the pragmatics of each abstraction's protocol. The inability to specify clear semantics is a sign that the abstractions themselves are flawed.

Steps

Detailing an element's semantics involves the selection of the structures and algorithms that describe the structure and the behavior of the element. A typical order of events for detailing an element's semantics might be the following.

1. Enumerate the element's roles and responsibilities. Collect and consolidate the results from the individual realizations produced earlier while defining element collaborations (the second micro process activity). Use these realizations to help you identify the responsibilities of the participating elements. Determine the responsibilities of an element by looking at all of the incoming collaborations to that element in the realizations. (The responsibilities of an element are all the things that other elements can ask it to do.)

2. Describe each responsibility in more detail. Produce activity or sequence diagrams to describe overall flow, produce state machine diagrams to describe state behavior, and so on. Wherever possible, recommend a suitable algorithm for each responsibility/operation. During design, consider introducing helper operations to divide complex algorithms into less complicated, reusable parts. Consider the trade-offs of storing versus calculating certain states of an element.

---

12. A protocol specifies that certain operations are to be invoked in a specific order. For all but the most trivial classes, operations rarely stand alone; each has preconditions that must be satisfied, often by invoking other operations.

3. During design, consider inheritance. Select the appropriate abstract classes (or create new ones, if the problem is sufficiently general), and adjust the inheritance lattice as required. Consider the elements to which you might delegate responsibility. For an optimal fit, this may require a minor readjustment of the responsibilities and/or protocol of the lower-level elements. If the element's semantics cannot be provided through inheritance, instantiation, or delegation, consider a suitable representation at the next level of abstraction (e.g., if you are at the design level, this may include primitives in the implementation language). Keep in mind the importance of operations from the perspective of the element's clients, and select a representation that optimizes for the expected patterns of use. Remember that it is not possible to optimize for every use, however. As you gain empirical information from successive releases, you can identify which elements are not time and/or space efficient, and alter their implementation locally, with little concern that you will violate the assumptions clients make about your abstraction.

4. As responsibilities are defined for each element, consider the attributes that the element must have in order to fulfill these responsibilities.

5. During design, devise a sufficient set of operations that satisfy these responsibilities. Where possible, try to reuse operations for conceptually similar roles and responsibilities. In the case of an individual class, responsibilities are documented as operations on the class; in the case of a component, responsibilities represent the services provided by the component and are documented as operations on the component's interface.

   ■ Consider each operation in turn, and ensure that it is primitive. If not, isolate and expose its more primitive operations. Composite operations may be retained in the element itself (if the operation is sufficiently common, or for reasons of efficiency) or migrated to a common class (especially if the operation is likely to change often). Decomposing operations enables you to potentially find more commonality.

   ■ Consider the needs for construction, copying, and destruction [13]. It is better to have a common strategic policy for these behaviors, rather than allowing individual classes to follow their own idiom, unless there is a compelling reason to do so.

   ■ Consider the need for completeness. Add other primitive operations that are not necessarily required for the immediate clients but whose presence rounds out the element and therefore would probably be used by future clients. Realizing that it is impossible to have perfect completeness, lean more toward simplicity than complexity.

While detailing the responsibilities of the element, you may discover new elements that support the detailed descriptions (e.g., when more fully describing an element's responsibility, you may find that you missed a key piece of information, so you might identify a new element to represent that information). Document those elements and their responsibilities, and repeat the steps just described for those elements.

When defining the semantics of individual elements during analysis, commonality among elements may become apparent, and it may be very tempting to start defining very elaborate inheritance relationships among the elements in order to reflect common behavior and common structure. However, it is important to avoid looking for inheritance relationships too soon: Introducing inheritance prematurely often leads to loss of type integrity. The use of inheritance is generally considered a design activity because at that point you have a more detailed understanding of the semantics of the design elements and thus are in a better position to place them in an inheritance lattice. During design, commonality encountered among classes can be represented in a generalization/specialization hierarchy. When defining this inheritance lattice, be sensitive to balance (the lattice should not be too tall or too short, neither too wide nor too skinny). Where patterns of structure or behavior appear among these classes, reorganize the lattice to maximize commonality (but not at the expense of simplicity). For additional considerations when constructing an inheritance hierarchy, see Chapter 3.

In the early stages of development, before inheritance has been used, documenting the semantics of the individual elements is isolated. However, once you have inheritance lattices in place, documenting an element's semantics must also address placement of operations in the hierarchy. When considering the operations associated with a given element, it is important to decide at what level in the inheritance hierarchy the operation is best placed. Operations that may be used by a set of peer classes should be refactored to a common superclass, possibly by introducing a new intermediate class.

When detailing an element's semantics, be sure to *stay at the current level of abstraction*. Identifying elements at the next level of abstraction occurs during the first activity in the next iteration of the micro process (or during implementation in the macro process).

Milestones and Measures

You successfully complete the micro process activity of detailing the element semantics when you have a more complete understanding of the semantics of the elements at a specific level of abstraction (i.e., you have provided enough detail to move to the next level of abstraction) and when you have specified those semantics in a form that is consistent with that level of abstraction. As the last activity in the micro process, the ultimate objective is to have a set of crisp abstractions that are tightly cohesive and loosely coupled.

Evaluating the success of this activity involves looking at the semantics of the individual elements. As a result of this activity, you should have a reasonably sufficient, primitive, and complete set of semantics for each element at a specific level of abstraction. You should have provided enough detail for each of the elements to enable the identification of elements at the next level of abstraction. For example, during analysis, you successfully complete this activity when you have an informal statement of responsibilities and attributes of the analysis elements and you know enough to move to design. During design, you successfully complete this activity when you have more precisely stated semantics (e.g., operations and attributes) that are detailed enough to be implemented and tested (meaning their structure and use can be defined by the selected implementation language). This does not necessarily mean that the elements must be expressed in vivid detail, just that there is sufficient information for a competent implementer to be able to do their job.

The primary measure of goodness for this activity is simplicity. Element semantics that are complex, awkward, or inefficient are an indication that the element itself is lacking or that you have chosen a poor representation.

This completes our discussion of the micro process activities and also completes this chapter on the software development process. It is our hope that you now have an appreciation for the separation of concerns between the overall software development lifecycle (the macro process) and the analysis and design activities (the micro process), as well as an understanding of how these processes support each other. It is crucial to the success of your software development project that you choose a specific development process and configure it to meet the specific needs of your project, at both the macro and the micro process levels.

Summary

- Successful projects are usually characterized by the existence of a strong architectural vision and the application of a well-managed iterative and incremental development lifecycle.
- Architecture describes the significant decisions that have been made with regard to both structure and behavior and usually reflects an architectural style. A strong architectural vision enables the construction of systems that are simpler, are more robust and resilient, enable more effective reuse, and are easier to maintain.
- Iterative and incremental development occurs when the functionality of the system is delivered in a successive series of releases (either internal or external) of increasing completeness, with each release being an iteration. The selection of what functionality is developed in each iteration is driven by the mitigation of project risks; the most critical risks are addressed first. The iterative and incremental approach is at the heart of most modern software development methods, including agile methods, as it is a very effective technique for managing risk and change.

- All software development processes exist somewhere on a process continuum, with agile methods on one end and plan-driven techniques on the other. The choice of the right software development process for a particular project is driven by the project's (and the organization's) characteristics and involves configuring a development process that reflects a balance between agile and plan-driven processes that matches the project's position on that continuum.

- In this chapter, the software development process framework is described from two perspectives—the overall software development lifecycle (the macro process) and the analysis and design process (the micro process). The choice of lifecycle style (e.g., waterfall, iterative, agile, plan-driven, and so on) affects the macro process, and the choice of analysis and design techniques (e.g., structured, object-oriented, and so on) affects the micro process. Whether you choose an agile or a plan-driven process as your macro process, the object-oriented analysis and design tips and techniques described in the micro process section can be applied equally well.

- The purpose of the micro process is to take the requirements provided by the macro process (and possibly the analysis and design specifications produced by previous iterations of the micro process) and produce analysis and design specifications that are fed back into the macro process. Ultimately, the micro process produces specifications for the implementation that are built, tested, and deployed in the macro process.

- The micro process is comprised of four key activities (identify elements, define element collaborations, define element relationships, and detail element semantics). Each iteration of the micro process involves iterating through these activities for a set of behavioral requirements at a specific level of abstraction. The basic steps and the resulting products are about the same for all levels of abstraction; what differs is the level of detail (lower levels of abstraction result in more detailed products).

Chapter 7

Pragmatics

Software development today is a multibillion-dollar, competitive, worldwide business, stretching from North America through Western and Eastern Europe and into Asia and the Pacific Rim. In spite of the tools available to support the major functions in object-oriented development—requirements management, configuration management, design, code, and test—there are still too many failures. Schedules are missed. Costs are overrun. Functionality is not provided. Tens to hundreds of millions of dollars are lost on single development efforts. An unfortunate example is the FBI's Virtual Case File system, which was intended to be an important tool in fighting terrorism. After more than three years in development, in April 2005 "the bureau had to scrap the US $170 million project, including $105 million worth of unusable code" [1]. On March 16, 2006, the FBI awarded a $305 million contract to develop the Sentinel system to replace the Virtual Case File system [2]. This is but one example of far too many failed software developments [3].

Compounding matters is the fact that designing software is not an exact science. Consider the design of a complex database using entity-relationship modeling, one of the foundations of object-oriented design. As Hawryszkiewycz observes, "Although this sounds fairly straightforward, it does involve a certain amount of personal perception of the importance of various objects in the enterprise. The result is that the design process is not deterministic: different designers can produce different enterprise models of the same enterprise" [4].

We may reasonably conclude that no matter how sophisticated the development method, no matter how well-founded its theoretical basis, we cannot ignore the practical aspects of designing systems for the real world.

This means that we must consider sound management practices with regard to such issues as staffing, release management, and quality assurance. To the technologist, these are intensely dull topics; to the professional software engineer, these are realities that must be faced if one wants to be successful in building complex software systems. Thus, this chapter focuses on the pragmatics[1] of object-oriented development and examines the impact of the object model on various management practices.

7.1 Management and Planning

In the presence of an iterative and incremental lifecycle, it is of paramount importance to have strong project leadership that actively manages and directs a project's activities. Too many projects go astray because of a lack of focus, and the presence of a strong management team mitigates this problem.

Risk Management

Ultimately, the responsibility of the software development manager is to manage nontechnical risks, while the technical risks are typically the responsibility of the project architect. Technical risks in object-oriented systems include problems such as the selection of an inheritance structure that offers the best compromise between usability and flexibility, or the choice of mechanisms that yield acceptable performance while simplifying the system's architecture. Nontechnical risks encompass issues such as supervising the timely delivery of software from a third-party vendor, or managing the relationship between the customer and the development team so as to facilitate the discovery of the system's real requirements during analysis.

As we described in the previous chapter, the micro process of object-oriented development is inherently unstable and requires active planning to force closure. Fortunately, the macro process of object-oriented development is designed to lead to closure by providing a number of tangible products that management can study to ascertain the health of the project, together with controls that permit management to redirect the team's resources as necessary. The macro process's evolutionary approach to development means that there are opportunities to identify problems early in the lifecycle and meaningfully respond to these risks before they jeopardize the success of the project.

---

1. *Webster's New World College Dictionary* defines *pragmatic* as "concerned with actual practice, not with theory or speculation; practical."

Many of the basic practices of software development management, such as task planning and walkthroughs, are unaffected by object-oriented technology. What is different about managing an object-oriented project, however, is that the tasks scheduled and the products reviewed are different than for non-object-oriented systems.

Task Planning

In any modest- to large-sized project, it is reasonable to have periodic team meetings to discuss work completed and activities for the coming work period. Some minimal frequency of meetings is necessary to foster communication among team members; too many meetings destroy productivity and in fact are a sign that the project has lost its way. Object-oriented software development requires that individual developers have unscheduled critical masses of time in which they can think, innovate, develop, and meet informally with other team members as necessary to discuss detailed technical issues. The management team must plan for this unstructured time.

Team meetings provide a simple yet effective vehicle for fine-tuning schedules in the micro process, as well as for gaining insight into risks looming on the horizon. These meetings may result in small adjustments to work assignments, so as to ensure steady progress: No project can afford for any of its developers to sit idle while waiting for other team members to stabilize their part of the architecture. This is particularly true for object-oriented systems, wherein class and mechanism design pervades the architecture. Development can come to a standstill if certain key classes are in flux.

On a broader scale, task planning involves scheduling the deliverables of the macro process. Between evolutionary releases, the management team must assess both the imminent and longer-term risks to the project, focus development resources as necessary to attack those risks,[2] and then manage the next iteration of the micro process that yields a stable system satisfying the required use case scenarios scheduled for that release. Task planning at this level most often fails because of overly optimistic schedules [5]. Development that was viewed as a "simple matter of programming" expands to weeks or months of work; schedules are thrown out the window when developers working on one part of the system assume certain protocols from other parts of the system but are then blindsided by delivery of incompletely or incorrectly fabricated classes. Even more insidious, schedules may be mortally wounded by the appearance of performance problems that must be worked around, often by corrupting certain tactical design decisions.

---

2. Gilb notes that "if you do not actively attack the risks, they will actively attack you" [6].

The key to not being at the mercy of overly optimistic planning is the calibration of the development team and its tools; this is a continuous process. Typically, task planning goes like this. First, the management team directs the energies of a developer to a specific part of the system, for example, the design of a set of classes for interfacing to a relational database. The developer considers the scope of the effort and returns with an estimate of time to complete, which management then relies on to schedule other developers' activities. The problem is that these estimates are not always reliable because they usually represent best-case conditions. One developer might quote one week of effort for some task, whereas another developer might quote one month for the same task. When the work is actually carried out, it might take both developers three weeks, the first developer having underestimated the effort (the common problem of most developers), and the second developer having set much more realistic estimates (usually because he or she understood the difference between actual work time versus calendar time, which often gets filled with a multitude of nonfunctional activities). In order to develop schedules in which the team can have confidence, it is therefore necessary for the management team to devise multiplicative factors for each developer's estimates. This is not an indication of management not trusting its developers: It is a simple acknowledgment of the reality that most developers are focused on technical issues, not planning issues. Management must help its developers learn to do effective planning, a skill that is typically acquired through battlefield experience. Adequate training and estimation guidelines are a necessity in the effort to reduce ineffective planning.

The process of object-oriented development explicitly helps to develop these calibration factors. Its iterative and incremental lifecycle means that there are many intermediate milestones established early in the project, which management can use to gather data on each developer's track record for setting and meeting schedules. As evolutionary development proceeds, this means that management over time will gain a better understanding of the real productivity of each of its developers, and developers can gain experience in estimating their own work more accurately. The same lesson applies to tools: With the emphasis on early delivery of architectural releases, the process of object-oriented development encourages the early use of tools, which leads to the identification of their limitations before it is too late to change course.

Development Reviews

Development reviews are another well-established practice that every development team should employ. As with task planning, the conduct of software development reviews is largely unaffected by object-oriented technology. However, relative to non-object-oriented systems, what is reviewed is a different matter.

Management must take steps to strike a balance between too many and too few development reviews. In all but the most safety-critical systems, it is simply not economical to review every aspect of the design. Therefore, management must direct the scarce resources of its team to review those aspects of the system that represent strategic development issues. For object-oriented systems, this suggests conducting formal reviews based on use case scenarios as well as the system's architecture, with many more informal reviews focused on smaller tactical issues. The scenarios chosen should include the primary scenarios and those alternate scenarios where system response is critical.

As described in the previous chapter, use case scenarios are a primary product of the analysis phase of object-oriented development and serve to capture the desired behavior of the system in terms of the functionality it provides, from the users' perspective. Formal reviews of use case scenarios are led by the team's analysts (who have use case development expertise), together with domain experts or other end users, and are witnessed by other developers, including quality assurance personnel (testers). Such reviews are best conducted throughout the analysis phase, rather than waiting to carry out one massive review at the end of analysis, when it is already too late to do anything useful to redirect the analysis effort. Experience shows that even nondevelopers can understand use case scenarios presented through text or visual diagrams such as activity or sequence diagrams.[3] Ultimately, such reviews help to establish a common vocabulary among a system's developers and its users. Letting other members of the development team witness these reviews exposes them to the real requirements of the system early in the development process.

Architectural reviews should focus on the overall structure of the system, including its class structure and mechanisms. As with use case scenario reviews, architectural reviews should be conducted throughout the project, led by the project's architect or other designers. Early reviews focus on sweeping architectural issues, whereas later reviews may focus on a certain component or specific pervasive mechanisms. The central purpose of such reviews is to validate designs early in the lifecycle. In so doing, we also help to communicate the vision of the architecture. A secondary purpose of such reviews is to increase the visibility of the architecture so as to create opportunities for discovering patterns of classes or collaborations of objects, which may then be exploited over time to simplify the architecture.

Informal reviews should be carried out periodically, in accordance with the development process, and generally involve the peer review of certain components or lower-level mechanisms. The purpose of such reviews is to validate these tactical

---

3. We have encountered use of the notation in reviews involving such diverse non-developer groups as astronomers, biologists, meteorologists, physicists, and bankers.

decisions; their secondary purpose is to provide a vehicle for more senior developers to instruct junior members of the team.

7.2 Staffing

Staffing for object-oriented development is similar to that for traditional software development. The differences tend to be associated with the timing of these resources within the development cycle. For example, architects and designers play a critical role early in the process due to its iterative and incremental nature.

Resource Allocation

One of the more delightful aspects of managing object-oriented projects is that, in the steady state, there is usually a reduction in the total amount of resources needed and a shift in the timing of their deployment relative to more traditional methods, such as a single waterfall. The operative phrase here is *in the steady state*, with an experienced team. Generally speaking, the first object-oriented project undertaken by an organization will require more resources than for non-object-oriented methods, primarily because of the learning curve inherent in adopting any new technology. The essential resource benefits of the object model will not show themselves until the second or third project, at which time the development team is more adept at object-oriented analysis and design, from architecture through class design and harvesting of common abstractions and mechanisms, and the management team is more comfortable with driving the iterative and incremental development process.

For analysis, resource requirements do not typically change much when employing object-oriented methods. However, because the object-oriented process places an emphasis on architectural design, we tend to accelerate the deployment of architects and other designers to much earlier in the development process, sometimes even engaging them during later phases of analysis to begin architectural exploration. During later increments, fewer resources are typically required, mainly because the ongoing work tends to leverage common abstractions and mechanisms invented earlier during architectural design or previous increments. Testing may also require fewer resources, primarily because adding new functionality to a class or mechanism is achieved mainly by modifying a structure that is known to behave correctly in the first place. Thus, testing tends to begin earlier in the lifecycle and manifests itself as a cumulative rather than a monolithic activity. Integration usually requires fewer resources, compared with traditional methods, mainly because integration happens incrementally throughout the development lifecycle, rather than occurring in one "big bang" event. Thus, in the steady state with an experienced team, the net of all the human resources required for object-oriented development is typically less than that required for traditional approaches. Furthermore, when we consider the cost of ownership of object-oriented software, the total lifecycle costs are often less because the resulting product tends to be of far better quality and so is much more resilient to change.

Development Team Roles

It is important to remember that software development is ultimately a human endeavor. Developers are not interchangeable parts, and the successful deployment of any complex system requires the unique and varied skills of a focused team of people.

Experience suggests that the object-oriented development process requires a subtly different partitioning of skills, compared with traditional methods. We have found the following three roles to be central to the technical development team for an object-oriented project:

1. Project architect
2. Component lead
3. Application engineer

The project architect is the visionary and is responsible for evolving and maintaining the system's architecture. For small to medium-sized systems, architectural design is typically the responsibility of a few particularly insightful individuals. For larger projects, this may be the shared responsibility of a larger team. The project architect is not necessarily the most senior developer, but rather is the one best qualified to make strategic decisions, usually as a result of his or her extensive experience in building similar kinds of systems. Because of this experience, architects intuitively know the common architectural patterns relevant to a given domain and the performance issues that apply to certain architectural variants. In addition to analysis and design experience, architects should have programming experience and be well versed in the notation, process, and tools of object-oriented development because they must ultimately express their architectural vision in terms of clusters of classes and collaborations of objects.

It is generally bad practice to hire an outside architect who, metaphorically speaking, storms in on a white horse, proclaims some architectural vision, and then rides away while others suffer the consequences of these decisions. It is far better to actively engage an architect during analysis and then retain that architect throughout most if not all of the system's evolution. Thus, the architect will become more familiar with the actual needs of the system and over time will be subject to the implications of his or her architectural decisions. In addition, by keeping responsibility for architectural integrity in the hands of one person or a small team of developers, we increase our chances of developing a more resilient architecture.

Component leads are the primary abstractionists of the project. A component lead is responsible for the design of an entire component. In conjunction with the project architect, each lead must devise, defend, and negotiate the interface of a specific component and then direct its implementation. A component lead is therefore the ultimate owner of a cluster of classes and its associated mechanisms and is also responsible for its testing and release during the evolution of the system.

Component leads must be well versed in the notation and process of object-oriented development. They may be better designers and programmers than the project architect but lack the architect's broad experience. On the average, component leads constitute about a third to a half of the development team.

Application engineers are the less senior developers in a project and usually carry out one of two responsibilities. Certain application engineers are responsible for the implementation of a component, under the supervision of its component lead. This activity may involve some class design but generally involves implementing and then unit testing the classes and mechanisms invented by other designers on the team. Other application engineers are then responsible for taking the classes designed by the architect and component leads and assembling them to carry out the use case scenarios of the system. In a sense, these engineers are responsible for writing small programs in the domain-specific language defined by the classes and mechanisms of the architecture. Another approach to accomplishing this work is to have the application engineers responsible for even more of the detailed class design while ensuring they have sufficient supervision and mentoring from the component lead.

Application engineers are familiar with but not necessarily experts in the notation and process of object-oriented development; however, they are very good programmers who understand the idioms and idiosyncrasies of the given programming languages. On the average, half or more of the development team consists of application engineers.

This breakdown of skills addresses the staffing problem faced by most software development organizations, which usually have only a handful of really good designers and many more less-experienced ones. The social benefit of this approach to staffing is that it offers a career path to the more junior people on the team: Specifically, junior developers work under the guidance of more senior developers in a mentor/apprentice relationship. As junior developers gain experience in using well-designed classes, over time they learn to design their own quality classes. The corollary to this arrangement is that not every developer needs to be an expert abstractionist but can grow in those skills over time.

In larger projects, a number of other distinct development roles are required to carry out the work. Some of the roles listed here (such as the system administrator) are indifferent to the use of object-oriented technology, although some of them are especially relevant to the object model (such as the reuse engineer).

- Project manager
  Responsible for the active management of the project's deliverables, tasks, resources, and schedules

- Analyst
  Responsible for evolving and interpreting the end user's requirements; must be an expert in the problem domain, yet must not be isolated from the rest of the development team

- Reuse engineer
  Responsible for managing the project's repository of classes, components, and designs; through participation in reviews and other activities, actively seeks opportunities for commonality and causes them to be exploited; acquires (e.g., through commercial libraries), produces, and adapts classes and components for general use within the project or the entire organization

- Quality assurance
  Responsible for measuring the products of the development process; generally directs system-level testing of all prototypes and production releases

- Integration manager
  Responsible for assembling compatible versions of released components in order to form a deliverable release; maintains the configurations of released products

- Documenter
  Responsible for producing end-user documentation of the product and its architecture

- Toolsmith
  Responsible for creating and adapting software tools that facilitate the production of the project's deliverables

- System administrator
  Responsible for managing the physical computing resources used by the project

Of course, not every project requires all of these roles. For small projects, many of these responsibilities may be shared by the same person; for larger projects, each role may represent an entire organization. For even larger projects, there may be additional roles such as an enterprise architect, a methodologist, a configuration management lead, and a business analyst. Some of these, such as the methodologist, might not be dedicated to just one project [29].

Experience indicates that object-oriented development makes it possible to use smaller development teams, compared with traditional methods. Indeed, it is not impossible for a team of roughly 30–40 developers to produce several hundred thousand lines of production-quality code in a single year. However, we agree with Boehm, who observes that "the best results occur with fewer and better people" [7]. Unfortunately, trying to staff a project with fewer people than traditional folklore suggests are needed may produce resistance. Such an approach infringes on the attempts of some managers to build empires. Other managers like to hide behind large numbers of employees because more people represent more power. Furthermore, if a project fails, there are more subordinates on whom to heap the blame.

Just because a project applies the most sophisticated design method or the latest fancy tool doesn't mean a manager has the right to abdicate responsibility for hiring designers who can think or to let a project run on autopilot [8].

7.3 Release Management

Release management concerns for object-oriented development are like those for traditional software development; they provide a foundation to support the development process. The development team must manage the configuration of the system being developed while integrating and testing the pieces of developed software, from classes to components and finally to the entire software system.

Configuration Management and Version Control

Consider the plight of an individual developer, who might be responsible for implementing a particular component. He or she must have a working version of that component, that is, a version under development. In order to proceed with further development, at least the interfaces of all imported components must be available. As this working version becomes stable, it is released to an integration team, which is responsible for collecting a set of compatible components for the entire system. Eventually, this collection of components is frozen and baselined and made part of an internal release. This internal release thus becomes the current operational release, visible to all active developers who need to further refine their particular part of its implementation. In the meantime, the individual developer can work on a newer version of his or her component. Thus, development can proceed in parallel, with stability made possible because of well-defined and well-guarded component interfaces.

Implicit in this model is the idea that a cluster of classes, not the individual class, is the primary unit of version control. Experience suggests that managing versions of classes is too fine a granularity since no class stands alone. Rather, it is better to version related groups of classes. This does not mean that we don't version control classes, just that this is not our primary focus. Practically speaking, this means versioning components since groups of classes map to components. At higher levels within the software system, one would version subsystems composed of multiple lower-level components.

At any given point in the evolution of a system, multiple versions of a particular component may exist: There might be a version for the current release under development, one for the current internal release, and one for the latest customer release. This intensifies the need for reasonably powerful configuration management and version control tools.

Source code is not the only development product that should be placed under configuration management. The same concepts apply to all the other products of object-oriented development, such as use case specifications, visual models, and software architecture documents.

Integration

Industrial-strength projects require the development of families of programs. At any given time in the development process, there will be multiple prototypes and production releases, as well as development and test scaffolding. Often, each developer will have his or her own executable view of the system under development.

As explained in the previous chapter, the nature of the iterative and incremental process of object-oriented development means that there should not be a single "big bang" integration event (although this may happen in projects that are in trouble). Instead, there will generally be many smaller integration events, each marking the creation of another prototype or architectural release. Each such release is generally incremental in nature, having evolved from an earlier stable release. As Davis et al. observe, "when using incremental development, software is deliberately built to satisfy fewer requirements initially, but is constructed in such a way as to facilitate the incorporation of new requirements and thus achieve higher adaptability" [9]. From the perspective of the ultimate user of the system, the macro process generates a stream of executable releases, each with increasing functionality, eventually evolving into the final production system. From the perspective of those inside the organization, many more releases are actually constructed, and only some are frozen and baselined to stabilize important system interfaces. This strategy tends to reduce development risk because it accelerates the discovery of architectural and performance problems early in the development process.

For a modest-sized project, an organization may produce an internal release every two to three months. For more complex projects that require much greater development effort, this might mean a release every six months or so, according to the needs of the project. In the steady state, a release consists of a set of compatible components along with their associated documentation. Building a release is possible whenever the major components of a project are stable enough and work together well enough to provide some new level of functionality.

Testing

The principle of continuous integration applies as well to testing, which should also be a continuous activity during the development process. In the context of object-oriented architectures, testing must encompass at least three dimensions.

1. *Unit testing* involves testing individual classes and mechanisms. It is the responsibility of the application engineer who implemented the structure.
2. *Component testing*, which involves integration testing a complete component, is the responsibility of the component lead. Component tests can be used as regression tests for each newly released version of the component. Note that the term *component* is generic and can mean a single component in a small project or a collection of components, sometimes referred to as a *subsystem*, in a larger project.
3. *System testing* involves integration testing the system as a whole and is the responsibility of the quality assurance team. System tests are also typically used as regression tests by the integration team when assembling new releases.

Testing at each level should focus on the external behavior of the item being tested; a secondary purpose of testing is to push the limits of the system in order to understand how it fails under certain conditions.

7.4 Reuse

One of the most acclaimed benefits of object-oriented development is reuse, but it is one that requires management commitment to realize the benefits of reusing the many artifacts of the development process.

Elements of Reuse

Any artifact of software development can be reused, including use case scenarios (for both requirements and testing), design, code, and documentation. As noted in Chapter 3, classes serve as the primary linguistic vehicle for reuse: Classes may be subclassed to specialize or extend the base class. Also, as explained in Chapter 4, we can reuse patterns of classes, objects, and designs in the form of idioms, mechanisms, and frameworks. Reuse of collaborating classes, in the form of components, typically offers the most benefit. Framework reuse and pattern reuse are at a higher level of abstraction than the reuse of individual classes and so provide greater leverage (but are harder to achieve).

It is dangerous and misleading to quote figures for levels of reuse [10]. In successful projects, we have encountered reuse factors as high as 70% (meaning that almost three-fourths of the software in the system was taken intact from some other source) and as low as 0%. The degree of reuse should not be viewed as a quota to achieve because potential reuse appears to vary wildly by domain and is affected by many nontechnical factors, including schedule pressure, the nature of subcontractor relationships, and security considerations.

Ultimately, any amount of reuse is better than none because reuse represents a savings of resources that would otherwise be used to reinvent some previously solved problem.

Institutionalizing Reuse

Reuse within a project or even within an entire organization doesn't just happen—it must be institutionalized. This means that opportunities for reuse must be actively sought out and rewarded. Indeed, this is why we include pattern scavenging as an explicit activity in the micro process.

An effective reuse program is best achieved by making specific individuals responsible for leading the reuse activity, while making everyone responsible for participating. This activity involves identifying opportunities for commonality, usually discovered through architectural reviews, and exploiting these opportunities, usually by producing new components or adapting existing ones, and championing their reuse among developers. This approach requires the explicit rewarding of reuse. Even simple rewards are highly effective in fostering reuse; for example, peer recognition of the author or reuser is often useful.

In addition to developing assets to be reused, we can purchase commercial class and component libraries to assist us with our development. However, we must still develop an effective design, within the framework of the architecture, to use these commercial library assets. It is not simply a matter of plugging together the classes or components [30].

Ultimately, reuse costs resources in the short term but pays off in the long term. A reuse activity will be successful only in an organization that takes a long-term view of software development and optimizes resources for more than just the current project.

7.5 Quality Assurance and Metrics

Software quality assurance involves "the systematic activities providing evidence of the fitness for use of the total software product" [11]. Quality assurance seeks to give us quantifiable measures of goodness for the quality of a software system. Many such traditional measures are directly applicable to object-oriented systems.

Software Quality

Schulmeyer and McManus define software quality as "the fitness for use of the total software product" [12]. Software quality doesn't just happen: It must be engineered into the system. Indeed, the use of object-oriented technology doesn't automatically lead to quality software; it is still possible to design bad software with object-oriented analysis and design techniques and to write very bad software using object-oriented programming languages.

This is why we place such an emphasis on software architecture in the process of object-oriented development. A simple, adaptable architecture is central to any quality software; its quality is made complete by carrying out simple and consistent tactical design decisions that support the strategic design decisions.

As we described earlier, development reviews and other kinds of inspections are important practices even in object-oriented systems and provide insights into the software's quality. Perhaps the most important quantifiable measure of goodness is the defect-discovery rate. During the evolution of the system, we track software defects according to their severity and location. The defect-discovery rate is thereby a measure of how quickly errors are being discovered, which we plot against time. As Dobbins observes, "the actual number of errors is less important than the slope of the line" [13]. A project that is under control will have a bell-shaped curve, with the defect-discovery rate peaking at around the midpoint of the test period and then falling off to some, hopefully, very low rate. A project that is out of control will have a curve that tails off very slowly or not at all.

One of the reasons that the macro process of object-oriented development works so well is that it permits the early and continuous collection of data about the defect-discovery rate. For each incremental release, we can perform a system test and plot the defect-discovery rate versus time. Even though early releases will have less functionality, we still expect to see a bell-shaped curve for every release in a healthy project.

Defect density is another relevant quality measure. Measuring defects per thousand source lines of code (KSLOC) is the traditional approach and is still generally applicable to object-oriented systems. In healthy projects, defect density tends to "reach a stable value after approximately 10,000 lines of code have been inspected and will remain almost unchanged no matter how large the code volume is thereafter" [14].

In object-oriented systems, we have also found it useful to measure defect density in terms of the numbers of defects per class. With this measure, the 80/20 rule seems to apply: 80% of the software defects will be found in 20% of the system's classes [15].

Object-Oriented Metrics

The British physicist Lord Kelvin, after whom the Kelvin temperature scale was named, said the following about measurement: "When you can measure what you are speaking about, and express it into numbers, you know something about it; but when you cannot measure it, when you cannot express it in numbers, your knowledge is of a meager and unsatisfactory kind. It may be the beginning of knowledge, but you have scarcely in your thoughts advanced to the stage of science."[4] Our concern with object-oriented metrics is specifying ones that provide meaningful measures to support the analysis and design of software systems.

Metrics to assist us in this endeavor fall into one of two categories, process metrics or product metrics. Process metrics, sometimes called project metrics, assist the management team in assessing progress with respect to the object-oriented development process being used. Examples of process metrics include the number of person-hours expended, the amount of work accomplished, and the number of project dollars spent—all compared to what was planned. We can also look at metrics more specific to object-oriented development, such as those recommended by Lorenz and Kidd [16]:

---

4. Lord William Thomson Kelvin is said to have made this statement in *Popular Lectures and Addresses* during 1891–1894. He also supposedly said that "Heavier-than-air flying machines are impossible." We will agree with his first statement.

- Application size
  - Number of scenario scripts (NSS)
  - Number of key classes (NKC)
  - Number of support classes (NSC)
  - Number of subsystems (NOS)
- Staffing size
  - Person-days per class (PDC)
  - Classes per developer (CPD)
- Scheduling
  - Number of major iterations (NMI)
  - Number of contracts completed (NCC)

We tend to measure development progress by counting the classes in the logical design, or the components in the physical design, that are completed and working. As we described in the previous chapter, another measure of progress is the stability of key interfaces (that is, how often they change). At first, the interfaces of all key abstractions will change daily, if not hourly. Over time, the most important interfaces will stabilize first, the next most important interfaces will stabilize second, and so on. Toward the end of the development lifecycle, only a few insignificant interfaces will need to be changed since most of the emphasis is on getting the already designed classes and components to work together. Occasionally, a few changes may be needed in a critical interface, but such changes are usually upwardly compatible. Even so, such changes are made only after careful thought about their impacts. These changes can then be incrementally introduced into the production system as part of the usual release cycle.

Our primary focus here is on product metrics (sometimes called design metrics) that help the development team assess the artifacts of their analysis and design efforts, rather than on process metrics. We have found that appropriate product metrics can help the architect and component leads assess the quality of the design. For example, they will be able to know whether design guidelines, such as the range for the depth of the inheritance tree, are being met. Acquiring and analyzing applicable quantitative measures against these metrics on a variety of projects over time will provide a historical database that can be used as a point of comparison for the measures being analyzed on current projects.

Chidamber and Kemerer suggest a number of language-independent design metrics that are directly applicable to object-oriented systems [17]:

- Weighted methods per class (WMC)
- Depth of inheritance tree (DIT)
- Number of children (NOC)
- Coupling between object classes (CBO)

- Response for a class (RFC)
- Lack of cohesion in methods (LCOM)

Weighted methods per class gives the sum of the complexities of each of the methods of an individual class. If all the method complexities are considered to be equally complex, this becomes a measure of the number of methods per class. However, this measure is truly useful when we assign relative complexity values to each of the methods; however, for the sake of flexibility, Chidamber and Kemerer did not provide the means to define this complexity. In general, a class with significantly more methods than its peers is more complex, tends to be more application-specific, and often hosts a greater number of defects [17].

The depth of the inheritance tree and number of children are measures of the shape and size of the class structure. As we described in Chapter 3, well-structured object-oriented systems tend to be architected as forests of classes, rather than as one very large inheritance tree. The depth of the inheritance tree, measured from the subject class to its highest-level parent class, gives a measure of the impact to it from inheriting functionality. Therefore, a deeper inheritance tree increases the complexity of a class, due to the functionality it inherits.

Looking down the inheritance tree, we see the number of children for the subject class. The more children a class has, the greater its impact on the software system's design, due to the reuse it produces [17].

Coupling between objects is a measure of their connectedness to other objects and thus is a measure of their class's encumbrance. As with traditional measures of coupling, we seek to design loosely coupled objects, which have a greater potential for reuse.

Response for a class is a measure of the methods that its instances can execute in response to a message call. In general, a class that has significantly more methods that can be invoked, compared with its peers, is more complex.

Lack of cohesion in methods is a measure of the unity of the class's abstraction. A class with low cohesion among its methods suggests an accidental or inappropriate abstraction; such a class should generally be reabstracted into more than one class or its responsibilities delegated to other existing classes [17].

In his text on software quality engineering, Kan discusses examples of how to apply the product metrics proposed by Lorenz (and later by Lorenz and Kidd in 1994) and those proposed by Chidamber and Kemerer. The eleven Lorenz design metrics include several object-oriented design guidelines and rules of thumb for their application. Kan found that the rules of thumb "are very useful. They were derived based on experiences from industry OO projects. They provide a threshold for comparison and interpretation" [18].

With respect to the Chidamber and Kemerer metrics (the CK metrics) applied in several studies, Kan found that "more empirical studies need to be accumulated before preferable threshold values of the CK metrics can be determined" [18]. In fact, Chidamber and Kemerer said that the threshold values should be determined for each development site. Kan did find that "In practical use, the metrics can be used to flag out-lying classes for special attention" [18].

More recently, Kemerer and Darcy provided several examples of the application of the CK metrics suite and offered observations about its practical application. From study of these applications, they made several observations about object-oriented metrics [19].

- Such metrics have been successfully applied in several domains.
- They consistently demonstrated relationships to quality factors (e.g., cost, defects, reuse, and maintainability).
- A generally useful set consists of size (WMC), coupling (CBO or RFC), and cohesion (LCOM).
- The relationship between metrics and outcome predictions should be calculated for local influences.

There is still disagreement about how object-oriented design principles contribute to software quality; consequently, there is still much debate about what constitutes an appropriate set of object-oriented metrics. We believe the metrics presented here provide a reasonable set of measures to assist the architect and component leads in assessing the quality of their object-oriented design.

7.6 Documentation

In addition to code, there are development artifacts that are critical to the complete lifecycle of a software system. These artifacts, such as requirements and design, must be documented to support the development process and the operation and maintenance of the system.

Development Legacy

The development of a software system involves much more than writing its raw source code. Certain products of development offer ways to give the management team and users insight into the progress of the project. We also seek to leave behind a legacy of analysis and design decisions for the eventual maintainers of the system. The products of object-oriented analysis and design are visual models in which we create numerous views in the form of diagrams. These views include sets of use case diagrams, activity diagrams, class diagrams, state machine diagrams, sequence diagrams, and component diagrams. Collectively, with appropriate guidelines, we can use these diagrams to offer traceability back to the system's requirements. Use case diagrams (along with use case specifications) show the high level functionality specified by the requirements, while the activity diagrams detail the use case scenarios. Class diagrams represent key abstractions that form the vocabulary of the problem domain. Classes with complex state-related behavior are examined in state machine diagrams. Sequence diagrams show the collaboration of objects as they provide system functionality. Component diagrams show the mapping of classes to components.

Documentation Contents

The documentation of a system's architecture and implementation is important, but the production of such documents should never drive the development process: Documentation is an essential, albeit secondary, product of the development process. It is also important to remember that documents are living products that should be allowed to evolve together with the iterative and incremental evolution of the project's releases. Together with the design and generated code, delivered documents serve as the basis of most formal and informal reviews.

What must be documented? Obviously, end-user documentation must be produced, instructing the user on the installation and operation of each release.[5] In addition, analysis documentation must be produced to capture the semantics of the system's required functionality as viewed through use case scenarios. We must also generate architectural and implementation documentation, to communicate the vision and details of the architecture to the development team and to preserve information about all relevant strategic decisions, so the system can readily be adapted and evolved over time.

In general, the essential documentation (not necessarily on paper) of a system's architecture and implementation should include the following:

- Documentation of the high-level system architecture
- Documentation of the key abstractions and mechanisms in the architecture
- Documentation of scenarios that illustrate the as-built behavior of key aspects of the system

---

5. It is an unwritten rule that for personal productivity software, a system that requires a user to constantly refer to a manual is user-hostile. Object-oriented user interfaces in particular should be designed so that their use is intuitive and self-consistent, in order to minimize or eliminate the need for end-user documentation.

The worst possible documentation to create for an object-oriented system is a stand-alone description of the semantics of each method on a class-by-class basis. This approach tends to generate a great deal of useless documentation that no one reads or trusts, and it fails to document the more important architectural issues that transcend individual classes, namely, the collaborations among classes and objects—and especially among components. It is far better to document these higher-level structures in UML diagrams and then refer developers to the interfaces of certain important classes for tactical details.

7.7 Tools

Object-oriented development practices change the tools needed by the development team during analysis and design. The development of complex object-oriented systems changes the picture entirely: Trying to build a large software system with a minimal tool set is equivalent to building a multistory building with stone hand tools. Since object-oriented analysis and design highlights key abstractions and mechanisms, we need tools that can focus on richer semantics. In addition, the rapid development of releases defined by the macro process of object-oriented development requires tools that offer rapid turnaround for the analysis and design cycle.

It is important to choose tools that scale well. A tool that works for one developer designing a small stand-alone application will not necessarily scale to production releases of more complex applications. Indeed, for every tool, there will be a threshold beyond which the tool's capacity is exceeded, causing its benefits to be greatly outweighed by its liabilities and clumsiness.

Kinds of Tools

We have identified three primary tools applicable to object-oriented analysis and design. The first is a visual modeling tool supporting the UML notation. Such a tool can be used during analysis to capture the semantics of use case scenarios, as well as early in the development process to capture strategic and tactical design decisions, maintain control over the design products, and coordinate the design activities of a team of developers. Indeed, visual modeling tools can be used throughout the lifecycle, as the design evolves into a production implementation. Such tools are also useful during systems maintenance. Specifically, we have found it possible to reverse-engineer many of the interesting aspects of an object-oriented system, producing at least the class structure and component architecture of the system as built. Without this feature, designers may generate marvelous visual representations of the design, only to find that they are out of date once the implementation proceeds because programmers fiddled with the implementation without updating the design. Reverse engineering makes it less likely that design documentation will ever get out of step with the actual implementation.

Next, especially for larger projects, one must have software configuration management and version control tools. Such tools support the development team as they collaborate and share assets throughout the entire software development lifecycle. These assets include all artifacts of the analysis and design process, from use case diagrams through class and sequence diagrams that provide the design of the architecture and the components that collaborate within the architecture. As mentioned earlier, these components are the best unit of configuration management, especially from a reuse perspective.

The third tool we have found important with object-oriented analysis and design is a class library tool. Many languages have predefined class libraries or commercially available class libraries. As a project matures, the library grows as domain-specific reusable software classes and components are added over time. It does not take long for such a library to grow to enormous proportions, which makes it difficult for a developer to find a class or component that meets his or her needs. If the perceived cost (usually inflated) of *finding* a certain component is higher than the perceived cost (usually underestimated) of *creating* that component from scratch, all hope of reuse is lost. For this reason, it is important to have at least some minimal library tool that allows designers to locate classes and components according to different criteria and add useful classes and components to the library as they are developed.

These three tools often have integrations providing the development team with a more seamless access to their aggregate capabilities. Though the primary function of an integrated development environment (IDE) is to provide a programming environment, it may also provide a foundation through which visual modeling, configuration management and version control, and class library tools collaborate.

Organizational Implications

This need for powerful tools creates a demand for two specific roles within the development organization: a reuse engineer and a toolsmith. Among other things, the duties of the reuse engineer are to maintain the class library for a project. Without active effort, such a library can become a vast wasteland of junk classes that no developer would ever want to walk through. Also, it is often necessary to be proactive to encourage reuse, and the reuse engineer can facilitate this process by scavenging the products of current design efforts. The duties of a toolsmith are to create domain-specific tools and tailor existing ones for the needs of a project. For example, a project might need common test scaffolding to test certain aspects of a user interface, or it might need a customized class browser. A toolsmith is in the best position to craft these tools, usually from components already in the class library. Such tools can also be used for later development efforts. However, in the best of cases where an integrated tool suite is available, the role of toolsmith would not be needed. The system administrator could mange the integrated suite.

A manager already faced with scarce human resources may lament that powerful tools, as well as designated reuse engineers and toolsmiths, are an unaffordable luxury. We do not deny this reality for some resource-constrained projects. However, in many other projects, we have found that these activities go on anyway, usually in an ad hoc fashion. We advocate explicit investments in tools and people to make these ad hoc activities more focused and efficient; doing so adds real value to the overall development effort.

7.8 Special Topics

There are several topics of special concern to people practicing object-oriented analysis and design. Domain-specific issues include the development of effective user interfaces and the integration of legacy functionality, from data to entire systems. Another special concern to most everyone involved is how to effectively adopt object-oriented technologies.

Domain-Specific Issues

We have found that certain application domains warrant special architectural consideration. One of these is the design of an effective user interface, which is still much more of an art than a science. For this domain, the use of prototyping is absolutely essential. Feedback must be gathered early and often from end users, so as to evaluate the gestures, error behavior, and other paradigms of user interaction. The generation of use case scenarios is also effective in driving the analysis of the user interface.

Some applications involve a major database component; other applications may require integration with databases whose schemas cannot be changed, usually because large amounts of data already populate the database (the problem of legacy data). For such domains, the principle of separation of concerns is directly applicable: It is best to encapsulate the access to all such databases inside the confines of well-defined interface classes. This principle is particularly important when mixing object-oriented decomposition with relational database technology.

Consider also real-time systems. Real-time means different things in different contexts: It might denote subsecond response is user-centered systems and submicrosecond response in data acquisition and control applications. It is important to realize that even for hard real-time systems, not every component of the system must (or can) be optimized. Indeed, for many complex systems, the greater risk is whether or not the system can be completed, not whether it will perform within its performance requirements. For this reason, we warn against premature optimization. Focus on producing simple architectures, and the evolutionary generation of releases will illuminate the performance bottlenecks of the system early enough to take corrective action.

We refer to a legacy system as one for which there is a large capital investment that cannot economically or safely be abandoned. However, such systems may have intolerable maintenance costs, which require that they be replaced over time. Fortunately, coping with legacy systems is much like coping with databases: We encapsulate access to the facilities of the legacy system within the context of well-defined interface classes and, over time, migrate the coverage of the object-oriented architecture to replace certain functionality currently provided by the legacy system. Of course, it is essential to begin with an architectural vision of how the final system will look, so that the incremental replacement of the legacy system will not end up as an inconsistent patchwork of software.

Adopting Object-Oriented Technology

As Stix and Mosley report, "As the information systems community responds to the market's demand for object technologists, many cognitive issues need to be addressed. . . . two major challenges software practitioners are confronted with are: understanding objects and understanding how to design. Furthermore, the evidence gathered suggests that programming constructs and design are two independent skill sets that must be learned concurrently to effectively implement and achieve the benefits of object technology" [20].

How do we develop this object-oriented design capability? We recommend the following ideas.

- Provide formal training to developers and managers in:
  - The Unified Modeling Language
  - The object-oriented analysis and design process to be used by the project
  - The tools to be used by the project
  - The languages and libraries to be used by the project
- Use object-oriented development in a low-risk project first, and allow the team to learn by:
  - Using experienced OOAD consultants as mentors for the project team
  - Growing expertise within these team members and using them to seed other projects and act as mentors for the object-oriented approach

- Expose the developers and managers to examples of well-designed object-oriented systems

In our experience, it takes only a few weeks for a professional developer to master the syntax and semantics of a new programming language. It may take several more weeks for the same developer to begin to appreciate the importance and power of classes and objects. However, we have seen a very different situation with the mastering of object-oriented design concepts and applications. Maksimchuk and Naiburg make this case from the perspective of what they refer to as the Training Trap: "A programming language might be object-oriented, but learning an object-oriented language does not mean you will learn the concepts for good object-oriented design using the UML" [21]. It may take as many as six months of experience for that developer to mature into a competent class designer. This is not necessarily a bad thing, for in any discipline, it takes time to master the art.

We have found that learning by example is often an efficient and effective approach. Once an organization has accumulated a critical mass of applications developed in an object-oriented style, introducing new developers and managers to object-oriented development is far easier. Developers may start as analysts and grow into a design role as they become more skilled in object-oriented techniques; or, they may start as designers, using the well-structured abstractions that already exist. Over time, developers who have studied and used these components under the supervision of more experienced people gain sufficient experience to develop a meaningful conceptual framework of the object model and become effective designers.

7.9 The Benefits and Risks of Object-Oriented Development

The benefits of object-oriented development have been touted for years and are quite real. However, without the successful application of an object-oriented development process, one will become more familiar with the risks.

The Benefits of Object-Oriented Development

The adopters of object-oriented technology usually embrace these practices for one of two reasons. First, they seek a competitive advantage, such as reduced time-to-market, greater product flexibility, or schedule predictability. Second, they may have problems that are so complex that they don't seem to have any other solution.

In Chapter 2, we suggested that the use of the object model leads us to construct systems that embody the five attributes of well-structured complex systems: hierarchy, relative primitives (i.e., multiple levels of abstraction), separation of concerns, patterns, and stable intermediate forms. The object model forms the conceptual framework for the notation and process of object-oriented development, and thus these benefits are true of the method itself. In that chapter, we also noted the benefits that flow from the following characteristics of the object model (and thus from object-oriented development):

- Appeals to the working of human cognition
- Leads to systems that are more resilient to change
- Encourages the reuse of software components
- Reduces development risk
- Exploits the expressive power of object-oriented programming languages

A number of case studies reinforce these findings; in particular, they point out that the object-oriented approach can reduce development time and the size of the resulting source code, better in some cases than in others [22, 23, 24].

The Risks of Object-Oriented Development

On the darker side of object-oriented development, we find the risks. An innovative study of these risks is presented in an article by Hantos, where "Bertrand Meyer's classic OO technology concepts are mapped into Barry Boehm's Top 10 methodology-neutral software risks to illustrate potential areas of exposure" [25]. From Meyer's work [26], Hantos developed the following list of object-oriented concepts, to be mapped into Boehm's risks [25]:

- A unique way to define architecture and data structure instances
- Information hiding through abstraction and encapsulation
- Inheritance to organize related elements
- Polymorphism to perform operations that can automatically adapt to the type of structure they operate on
- Specialized analysis and design methods
- Object-oriented languages
- Environments that facilitate the creation of object-oriented systems
- Design by contract, a powerful technique to circumvent module boundary and interface problems

- Memory management that can automatically reclaim unused memory
- Distributed objects to facilitate the creation of powerful distributed systems
- Object databases to move beyond the data-type limitations of relational database management systems

For the other side of his mapping, he took Boehm's Top 10 Software Risks [27], along with an updated list from Boehm [28], to develop the following eight risks [25]:

1. Personnel shortfalls
2. Unrealistic schedules, budgets, or processes
3. Shortfalls in commercial off-the-shelf products, external components, or legacy software
4. Mismatches in requirements or user interface
5. Shortfalls in architecture, performance, or quality
6. Continuing stream of requirements changes
7. Shortfalls in externally performed tasks
8. Straining computer science

Hantos provides a detailed explanation of each of the eight risks and how the object-oriented concepts he listed either increase the particular risk within the software development project or help to mitigate it.

For a simple visual perspective of the results, he summarizes his study in a single mapping diagram; we see that Boehm's classical software development risks pertain to object-oriented software development, as they do to other approaches. On the positive side, Hantos shows that several of the object-oriented development concepts described by Meyer help to mitigate software risks. Specifically, the concept of "architecture and instances" helps to mitigate the risks of a "continuing stream of requirements changes" and of "shortfalls in externally performed tasks." The concept of "abstraction and encapsulation" also helps to mitigate the risk of a "continuing stream of requirements changes [25]."

If we recall our study of these object-oriented concepts, we can understand their risk-mitigating effects. Requirements changes, especially ones continuing throughout a development project, have the potential to wreak havoc. But, by focusing on an appropriate logical and physical structuring (architecture) of the system classes and components, we can provide a compartmentalization of structure and behavior to reduce the ripple effect of requirements change throughout our system. Any system development shortfalls by the project team are similarly compartmentalized.

Understanding the potential risks in a software development project—and how object-oriented concepts potentially contribute to or mitigate them—is essential as we develop risk management plans for our software development projects.

Summary

- The successful development and deployment of a complex software system involves much more than just generating code.
- Many of the basic practices of software development management, such as walkthroughs, are unaffected by object-oriented technology.
- In the steady state, object-oriented projects typically require a reduction in resources during development; the roles required of these resources are subtly different than for non-object-oriented systems.
- In object-oriented analysis and design, using an iterative approach, there should never be a single "big bang" integration event; the unit of configuration management for releases should be the component, not the individual class.
- Reuse must be institutionalized to be successful.
- Defect-discovery rate and defect density are useful measures for the quality of an object-oriented system. Other useful measures include various process and product metrics.
- Documentation should never drive the development process.
- Object-oriented development requires different tools than does non-object-oriented systems development.
- The transition by an organization to the use of the object model requires a change in mindset; it is critical that the development team understand object-oriented analysis and design techniques. Object-oriented software development is not just about programming.
- There are many benefits to object-oriented technology as well as risks; good risk management can assist in realizing the former while minimizing the latter.

Applications

To build a theory, one needs to know a lot about the basic phenomena of the subject matter. We simply do not know enough about these, in the theory of computation, to teach the subject very abstractly. Instead, we ought to teach more about the particular examples we now understand thoroughly, and hope that from this we will be able to guess and prove more general principles.

MARVIN MINSKY
"Form and Content in Computer Science"

Methods are a wonderful thing, but from the perspective of the practicing engineer, the most elegant notation or process ever devised is entirely useless if it does not help us build systems for the real world. The previous chapters have been but a prelude to this section of the book, in which we now apply object-oriented analysis and design to the pragmatic construction of software systems. We have chosen a set of applications from widely varying domains, encompassing navigation, command and control, cryptanalysis, data acquisition, and Web business application design, each of which involves its own unique set of problems.

We will present the application of object-oriented analysis and design techniques by successively moving through the phases in the macro process in each of the five application chapters. The chapters progress from Inception through Elaboration to Construction. (Transition is for the most part beyond the scope of this book. However, we present some interesting post-transition considerations.) That is, each of the chapters will primarily emphasize a specific part of the macro lifecycle and the applicable analysis and design (i.e., micro process) techniques. We believe this provides a more interesting approach than simply focusing on a single problem through all the steps of object-oriented analysis and design.

Each chapter focuses on the particular aspects of development shown here but also includes other aspects as necessary to provide context and a better understanding of the chapter's primary focus.

- Chapter 8 (satellite-based navigation)   focuses on system architecture
- Chapter 9 (control system)   focuses on system requirements
- Chapter 10 (cryptanalysis)   focuses on analysis
- Chapter 11 (data acquisition)   focuses on analysis to preliminary design
- Chapter 12 (Web modeling)   focuses on detailed design and implementation

Each of these chapters could expand to fill an entire book on its own. Thus, we cannot address every phase, every activity, and every step in the process. However, we strive to address those key aspects that are most interesting and important.

The relationship of the disciplines of object-oriented analysis and design and the specific diagrams that should be used is not rigid or prescriptive. Certain diagrams are typically seen more in one phase than another. Use case diagrams are seen much more often in the early phases of a project lifecycle. Some diagrams you will rarely, if ever, encounter on a real project. However, as you will see in the following chapters, certain types of diagrams are used throughout the project lifecycle. The difference is in the level of abstraction that the diagrams capture. For example, early in the lifecycle, component diagrams may capture very large, coarse elements (e.g., systems or subsystems). Later in the lifecycle, component diagrams can be used to capture fine-grained implementation elements (e.g., software executables). You will see the refinement in the level of abstraction as you progress through the application chapters.

Chapter 8

System Architecture: Satellite-Based Navigation

The object-oriented analysis and design principles and process presented earlier in this book, as well as the UML 2.0 notation discussed in Chapter 5, apply just as well to the development of the highest-level system architecture as to the development of software. With system architecture, though, rather than developing the structure and design of classes, we are concerned with understanding the system requirements and using that knowledge to partition the larger system into its constituent segments. However, we must remember that the concerns at this level typically are quite abstract, huge in scope and impact, and uninvolved with implementation or technology details. If we understand this and take the right steps when designing the architecture, we're more likely to create a system with long-term viability—it will be more operable, maintainable, and extensible, as it should be.

In this chapter, we show how we would approach the development of the system architecture for the hypothetical Satellite Navigation System (SNS) by logically partitioning the required functionality. To keep this problem manageable, we develop a simplified perspective of the first and second levels of the architecture, where we define the constituent segments and subsystems, respectively. In doing so, we show a representative subset of the process steps and artifacts developed, but not all of them. Showing a more complete perspective of the specification of any of these individual segments and their subsystems could easily require a complete book. However, the approach that we show could be applied more completely across an architectural level (e.g., segment or subsystem) and through the multiple levels of the Satellite Navigation System's architecture.

We chose this domain because it is technically complex and very interesting, more so than a simple system invented solely as an example problem. Today there are two principal satellite-based navigation systems in existence, the U.S. Global Positioning System (GPS) and the Russian Global Navigation Satellite System (GLONASS). In addition, a third system called Galileo is being developed by the European Union.

8.1 Inception

The first steps in the development of the system architecture are really systems engineering steps, rather than software engineering, even for purely or mostly software systems. Systems engineering is defined by the International Council on Systems Engineering (INCOSE) as "an interdisciplinary approach and means to enable the realization of successful systems" [1]. INCOSE further defines system architecture, which is our focus here, as "the arrangement of elements and subsystems and the allocation of functions to them to meet system requirements" [2].

Our focus here is to determine *what* we must build for our customer by defining the boundary of the problem, determining the mission use cases, and then determining a subset of the system use cases by analyzing one of the mission use cases. In this process, we develop use cases from the functional requirements and document the nonfunctional requirements and constraints. But before we jump into our requirements analysis, read the sidebar to get an introduction to the Global Positioning System.

Requirements for the Satellite Navigation System

The process of building systems to help solve our customer's problems begins with determining *what* we must build. The first step is to use whatever documentation of the problem or need our customer has given us. For our system, we have been given a vision statement and associated high-level requirements and constraints.

An Introduction to the Global Positioning System

The Global Positioning System provides anyone possessing a GPS receiver with the ability to know his or her position on the earth regardless of the location, the time of day, or the weather.[1] GPS satellites, in orbits at 11,000 nautical miles above the earth, are controlled and monitored from ground stations around the world. From the launch of the first GPS satellite in 1978 to the 24th in 1994, which completed the system, GPS has been a boon to worldwide navigation [3].

Navigation has progressed from the ways the earliest people remembered and recognized landmarks as they lived their daily lives to the many technological developments on the way to GPS today. Along this path, people have used maps of the earth and stars, compasses, sextants, chronometers, and current ground-based radio navigation systems such as LORAN (long-range navigation) [4].

The GPS architecture consists of three segments: Control, User, and Space. The Control Segment is comprised of six ground stations, with the master control station located at Schriever Air Force Base in Colorado. The receivers that assist many of us in our navigation efforts constitute the User Segment, which receives position information from the 24 satellites that comprise the constellation of the Space Segment [5].

GPS receivers calculate their distance from the satellites by using time and position data broadcast by the satellites. Specifically, "If we know our exact distance from a satellite in space, we know we are somewhere on the surface of an imaginary sphere with a radius equal to the distance to the satellite radius. If we know our exact distance from two satellites, we know that we are located somewhere on the line where the two spheres intersect. And, if we take a third and a fourth measurement from two more satellites, we can find our location. The GPS receiver processes the satellite range measurements and produces its position" [6].

The Global Positioning System has numerous uses, both military and civilian. Most people are familiar with its use by military personnel for navigation on land, at sea, and in the air. It is also used on weapon systems such as the cruise missile for precise real-time navigation in support of targeting. But it's the civilian applications that have crept into many people's lives. GPS is used by emergency services to quickly provide support to people in need. It was used during the construction of the English Channel Tunnel to ensure that separate teams digging from England and France met in the middle at the precise location. It's even used in numerous personal activities such as driving, geocaching,[2] and hiking [7].

---

1. The Aerospace Corporation developed the *GPS Primer—A Student Guide to the Global Positioning System,* which is the source of this introductory information. Additional information can be found in the Aerospace Corporation's Summer 2002 issue of *Crosslink*, which focuses on satellite navigation and the GPS.

2. You can find the Official Global GPS Cache Hunt Site at www.geocaching.com/.

Vision:

- Provide effective and affordable Satellite Navigation System services for our customers.

Functional requirements:

- Provide SNS services
- Operate the SNS
- Maintain the SNS

Nonfunctional requirements:

- Level of reliability to ensure adequate service guarantees
- Sufficient accuracy to support current and future user needs
- Functional redundancy in critical system capabilities
- Extensive automation to minimize operational costs
- Easily maintained to minimize maintenance costs
- Extensible to support enhancement of system functionality
- Long service life, especially for space-based elements

Constraints:

- Compatibility with international standards
- Maximal use of commercial-off-the-shelf (COTS) hardware and software

Obviously, this is a highly simplified statement of requirements, but it does provide the very basic specification for a satellite-based navigation system. In practice, detailed requirements for a system as large as this come about only after the viability of a solution is demonstrated, and then only after many hundreds of person-months of analysis involving the participation of numerous domain experts and the eventual users and clients of the system. Ultimately, the requirements for a large system may encompass thousands of pages of documentation (and, hopefully, visual models), specifying not only the general behavior of the system but also intricate details such as the screen layouts to be used for human/machine interaction.

Defining the Boundaries of the Problem

Though minimal, the requirements and constraints do permit us to take an important first step in the design of the system architecture for the Satellite Navigation System—the definition of its context, as shown in Figure 8–1. This context diagram provides us with a clear understanding of the environment within which the SNS must function. Actors, representing the external entities that interact with the system, include people, other systems that provide services, and the actual envi-

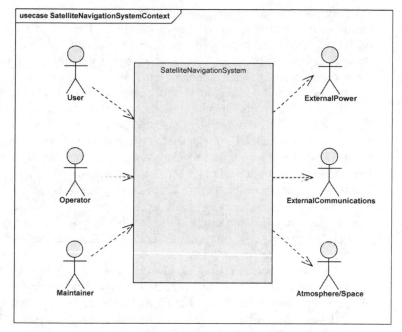

Figure 8–1 The Satellite Navigation System Context Diagram

ronment. Dependency arrows show whether the external entity is dependent on the SNS or the SNS is dependent on it.

It is quite clear that the User, Operator, and Maintainer actors are dependent on the SNS for its services as they use its navigation information, operate it, and maintain it, respectively. Though the Satellite Navigation System will have the capability to generate its own power as a backup for ground-based systems, primary power services will be provided by an external system, the ExternalPower actor. In a similar manner, we have an ExternalCommunications actor that provides purchased communications services to the SNS, as primary in some cases and backup to the internally provided system communications in other cases. We've prefixed the names for these two actors with "External" to clearly separate them from internal system power and communications services.

The remaining actor, Atmosphere/Space, may seem rather odd until we consider that it is the transmission medium for communications between the Satellite Navigation System's ground-based and space-based assets; therefore, it is a service provider. Its state certainly affects the quality of these communications. Another way to regard this actor is from the perspective of the constraint "Compatibility with international standards." Numerous national and international regulations and treaties govern satellite transmissions; thus, we have important reasons to specify this actor.

A critical point about our context diagram is the actual boundary of the system, that is, what is inside our system and what is not. Some may question our placing of the `Operator` and `Maintainer` actors outside the boundary of the `SatelliteNavigationSystem` package. By doing so, we've taken the viewpoint of a particular stakeholder, our customer, whose focus is that the system be used to provide navigation information to the user. The customer's focus is not on the broader corporate enterprise within which the SNS operates, unlike the `User` actor, who would likely regard the `Operator` and `Maintainer` as inside the system. Clearly, one's perspective is the key point here. For example, if we were providing a complete turnkey system that included operation and maintenance services, we would place the `Operator` and `Maintainer` actors inside the boundary of the `SatelliteNavigationSystem` package.

We've seen numerous variations in the presentation of a context diagram, some very elaborate and some very simple. The more elaborate ones tend to provide detailed information about the information that flows, in both directions, between the actors and the system being developed. Where a system is being developed within a more mature environment, perhaps as a replacement for an existing system, this type of information is known earlier in the development cycle, and thus some development teams choose to represent it here.

The particulars are much less important than having the development team choose a style, document it, and then follow it so clarity and understanding are ensured. However, we prefer our approach to presenting a context diagram because it simply and clearly conveys the high-level concept of the system being a container of functionality that interacts with entities in its external environment. In these interactions, the system provides services to some entities and receives services from others. This is the critical understanding that is so important in the beginning of development.

In addition to the functional requirements, we've been given high-level nonfunctional requirements that apply to portions of the functional capability or to the system as a whole. These nonfunctional requirements concern reliability, accuracy, redundancy, automation, maintainability, extensibility, and service life. Also, we see that there are some design constraints on the development of the SNS. We maintain the nonfunctional requirements and design constraints in a textual document called a *supplementary specification*; it is also used to maintain the functional requirements that apply to more than one use case. Another critical document that we must begin at this point is the *glossary*; it is important that the development team agrees on the definition of terms and then use them accordingly.

Even from these highly elided system requirements, we can make two observations about the process of developing the Satellite Navigation System.

1. The architecture must be allowed to evolve over time.
2. The implementation must rely on existing standards to the greatest extent practical.

Obviously, we cannot carry out a complete analysis or design of the Satellite Navigation System (or even the architecture) in a single chapter, much less a single book. Since our intent here is to explore how our notation and process scale up to the development of a system's architecture, we focus on the problem of designing the first and second levels of the architecture, where we define the constituent segments and subsystems, respectively. We develop these architectural levels by logically partitioning the required functionality used by the Operator actor. As stated in the chapter introduction, we show only a representative subset of the process steps and artifacts developed.

After reviewing both the vision and the requirements, we (the architecture team) realize that the functional requirements provided to us are really containers (packages, in the UML) for numerous mission-level use cases that define the functionality that must be provided by the Satellite Navigation System. These mission use case packages provide us a high-level functional context for the SNS, as shown in Figure 8–2. These packages contain the mission use cases that show how the users, operators, and maintainers of the SNS interact with the system to fulfill their missions. Since we are using object-oriented analysis and design techniques and the UML 2.0 notation to perform a systems engineering rather than a software engineering task, how we've used the notation in Figure 8–2 may be slightly unfamiliar. However, we believe it clearly presents the desired information and thus ensures understanding.

Determining Mission Use Cases

The vision statement for the system is rather open ended: a system to "Provide effective and affordable Satellite Navigation System services for our customers." The task of the architect, therefore, requires judicious pruning of the problem space, so as to leave a problem that is solvable. A problem such as this one could easily suffer from analysis paralysis, so we must focus on providing navigation services that are of the most general use, rather than trying to make this a navigation system that is everything for everybody (which would likely turn out to provide nothing useful for anyone). We begin by developing the mission use cases for the SNS.

Large projects such as this one are usually organized around some small, centrally located team responsible for establishing the overall system architecture, with the actual development work subcontracted out to other companies or different teams within the same company. Even during analysis, system architects usually have in

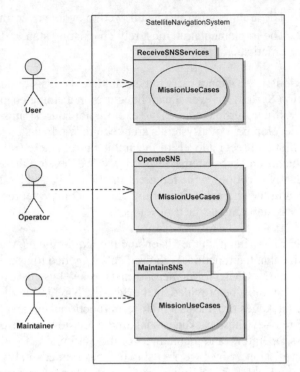

Figure 8–2 Packages for the SNS Mission Use Cases

mind some conceptual model that divides the elements of the implementation. Based on our experience in building satellite-based systems and in their operation and maintenance, we believe the highest-level logical architecture consists of four segments: Ground, Launch, Satellite, and User.

One may argue that this is design, not analysis, but we counter by saying that one must start constraining the design space at some point. Indeed, it is difficult to ascertain whether this logical architecture represents system requirements or a system design. Regardless of this issue, system architecture at this stage of development is principally object-oriented. For example, the architecture shows complex objects such as the Ground Segment and the Satellite Segment, each of which performs a major function in the system. This is just as we discussed in Chapter 4: In large systems, the objects at the highest levels of abstraction tend to be clustered along the lines of major system functions. How we identify and refine these objects during analysis is little different than how we do so during design.

Even before we have a conceptual architecture at the level of a package diagram like the one shown in Figure 8–3, we can begin our analysis by working with domain experts to articulate the primary mission use cases that detail the system's

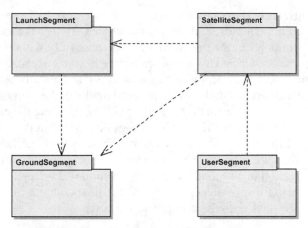

Figure 8–3 The SNS Logical Architecture

desired behavior. We say "even before" because, even though we have a notion of the architecture of the SNS, we should begin our analysis from a black-box perspective so as not to unnecessarily constrain its architecture. That is, we analyze the required functionality to determine the mission use cases for the SNS first, rather than for the individual SNS segments. Then, we allocate this use case functionality to the individual segments, in what is termed a white-box perspective of the Satellite Navigation System.

In their *Unified Modeling Language Reference Manual*, Rumbaugh, Jacobson, and Booch state that "An activity diagram is helpful in understanding the high-level execution behavior of a system, without getting involved in the internal details of message passing required by a collaboration diagram"[8].[3] Therefore, activity diagrams are our primary tool in analyzing the mission use cases and thereby illustrating the expected behavior of the system. Some development teams use sequence or communication diagrams for this purpose, but we believe those diagrams are more suitable for design efforts at lower levels within our architectural hierarchy. In our analysis, we focus only on the success scenarios of our mission use cases; the numerous alternate scenarios are left to another day.

The term *success scenario* might not be a familiar one. The well-worn ATM example helps with this explanation. One use case for the ATM is `Withdraw Cash`. This is typically what we want to do at one of these machines. In withdrawing cash, we interact with the ATM through many different steps: swipe card, enter PIN, choose withdrawal, choose amount, and so on. None of these steps embodies the end goal (withdraw cash) to us, so they are not really use cases

---

3. In UML 2.0, the collaboration diagram is called a communication diagram.

themselves. The `Withdraw Cash` use case (and all use cases) contains many different scenarios, each an individual path through the use case functionality. We first think about the one in which we successfully withdraw cash; hence, the term *success scenario*. This is also called the *primary scenario*. The alternate or secondary scenarios deal with the situations that typically branch off a primary scenario. For example, we're proceeding down the primary scenario of `Withdraw Cash` and get to the point of selecting the amount of cash we want. The ATM responds that we've requested more than the withdrawal amount permitted in one day. Oops! It requests that we select another amount, which we do, and then we get our cash (much less than originally desired, though). This is an illustration of a secondary scenario. It followed the path of a primary (success) scenario for several steps, veered off to deal with our amount problem, and then jumped back onto the primary scenario.

Hopefully, we've cleared rather than muddied the waters with this explanation. One more point, though—with respect to real-time systems such as the Satellite Navigation System, it is important to understand that much of its functionality is embodied within the secondary scenarios. These can be thought of as the portion of the iceberg that is below the water level yet critical to the complete and safe operation of the system. That is, the secondary scenarios are hidden in the sense that they are usually given much less attention, but they can cripple a system just as the portion of the iceberg below the water level can sink a ship. In short, our analysis must include the secondary scenarios. The amount of system functionality embodied in the secondary scenarios varies but is typically substantial in such systems. We won't consider it here—however, we must in our actual system development efforts.

Now, getting back to the task at hand, we develop the mission use cases of the `OperateSNS` mission use case package. Based on our analysis of the overall operation of the SNS, we define four corresponding mission use cases:

- `Initialize Operations`
- `Provide Normal Operations`
- `Provide Special Operations`
- `Terminate Operations`

Our specification of these mission use cases depends primarily on the domain expertise of our development team. In addition to past experience, simulations and prototypes are often invaluable tools in this analysis process. Typically, though, our analysis employs activity diagram modeling such as that which we perform to develop the system use cases in the following subsection. Figure 8–4 depicts the result of our analysis to develop the mission use cases for the

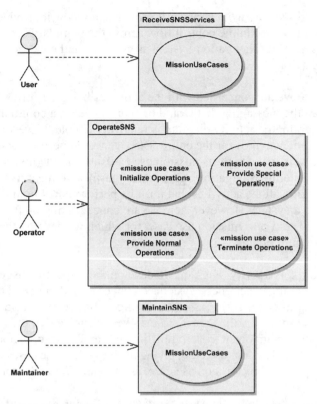

Figure 8–4 Refining the `OperateSNS` Mission Use Case Package

`OperateSNS` mission use case package. For the remainder of this chapter, our efforts focus on analyzing the `Initialize Operations` mission use case to determine the activities that the system must perform to provide the operator with the ability to initialize the operation of the Satellite Navigation System.

Determining System Use Cases

As stated previously, we develop an activity diagram of the `Initialize Operations` mission use case functionality to determine the encapsulated system use cases. In developing this activity diagram, we do not attempt to use our notion of the segments that comprise the SNS (refer back to Figure 8–3). We take this approach because we do not wish to constrain our analysis of SNS operations by presupposing possible architectural solutions to the problem at hand. We focus on the SNS as though it were a black box into which we could not peer and thus could see only *what* services it provides, not *how* it provides those services. We are interested in the control flow across the boundary between the operator and the Satellite Navigation System as we analyze the system's high-level execution behavior.

Since we are concerned with the activities being performed by the SNS, rather than the messaging that would be represented in a communication or sequence diagram, the activity diagram is relatively simple. If we wanted to define the system activities for the entire SNS, we would perform activity diagram–based analysis for each of its mission use cases to find the myriad of activities that the Satellite Navigation System must perform to meet its requirements. Try to imagine all the activities that must be performed 24 hours a day to operate such a system. However, here we are concentrating on the `Initialize Operations` mission use case, for which we develop the activity diagram shown in Figure 8–5.

From this activity diagram, we develop the respective list of system use cases by making experienced systems engineering judgments. For example, we decide to combine the actions `Prepare for Launch` and `Launch` into one system use case, `Launch Satellite`. We determine that the remaining actions embody significant system functionality and therefore should each represent an individual system use case, giving us the system use cases for the `Initialize Operations` mission use case, as shown in Table 8–1 on page 347.

Figure 8–6 shows the system use cases of Table 8–1 in an updated use case diagram. Here we have used the `InitializeOperations` package to contain the system use cases that we developed from the `Initialize Operations` mission use case. The other three mission use cases that embody functionality for operating the SNS are shown with the keyword label of «`mission use case`». We find this modeling approach to be useful and clear; however, each development team needs to determine and document its chosen techniques.

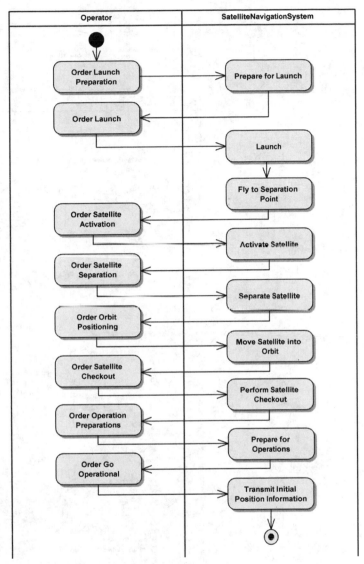

Figure 8–5 The Black-Box Activity Diagram for `Initialize Operations`

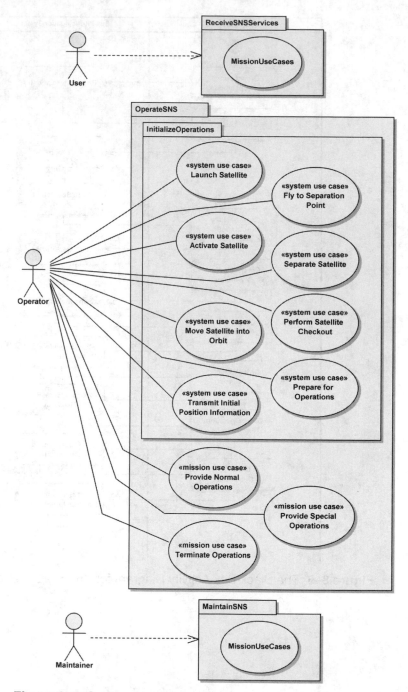

Figure 8–6 System Use Cases for `Initialize Operations`

Table 8–1 System Use Cases for *Initialize Operations*

System Use Case	Use Case Description
Launch Satellite	Prepare the launcher and its satellite payload for launch, and perform the launch.
Fly to Separation Point	Fly the launcher to the point at which the satellite payload will be separated. This involves the use and separation of multiple launcher stages.
Activate Satellite	Perform the activation of the satellite in preparation for its deployment from the launcher.
Separate Satellite	Deploy the satellite from the launcher.
Move Satellite into Orbit	Use the satellite bus propulsion capability to position the satellite into the correct orbital plane.
Perform Satellite Checkout	Perform the in-orbit checkout of the satellite's capabilities.
Prepare for Operations	Perform the final preparations prior to going operational.
Transmit Initial Position Information	Go operational and transmit initial position information to the users of the SNS.

8.2 Elaboration

Our attention turns to the system architecture that provides the foundation for realizing the requirements contained in the system use cases developed in the previous section. In the first two subsections, we introduce two architectural issues: the concerns when developing a good architecture and the activities performed when developing an architecture.

This discussion leads us into the subsequent two subsections (Validating the Proposed System Architecture, followed by Allocating Nonfunctional Requirements and Specifying Interfaces), where we perform what might be termed a macro-level analysis of the SNS system architecture. Our goal is to validate the proposed SNS architecture prior to analyzing the segments and specifying their architectures of collaborating subsystems. We use the same use case analysis techniques employed earlier to develop the system use cases, but we analyze all the use cases at the same time, rather than individually. This shortcut is perfectly valid during our behavioral prototyping but is *not* valid when actually allocating system use case functionality to the individual segments.

After the behavioral prototyping is complete, we stipulate the SNS architecture and its deployment in the next subsection. From there, we resume our actual system architectural analysis effort to decompose the Satellite Navigation System's architecture into its segments and their contained subsystems.

Developing a Good Architecture

As we discussed in Chapter 6, there are numerous methods of developing the architecture of a system. Some ways are very elegant; unfortunately, some are profoundly stupid. How do we know the difference between a good architecture and a bad one?

Good architectures tend to exhibit object-oriented characteristics. This doesn't mean, quite obviously, that as long as we use object-oriented techniques, we are assured of developing a good architecture. But, as we discussed in Chapters 1 and 2, applying the principles that underlie object-oriented decomposition tends to yield architectures that exhibit the desirable properties of organized complexity. Good architectures, whether system or software, typically have several attributes in common.

- They are constructed in well-defined layers of abstraction, each layer representing a coherent abstraction, provided through a well-defined and controlled interface, and built on equally well-defined and controlled facilities at lower levels of abstraction.
- There is a clear separation of concerns between the interface and implementation of each layer, making it possible to change the implementation of a layer without violating the assumptions made by its clients.
- The architecture is simple: Common behavior is achieved through common abstractions and common mechanisms.

Simply (or not so simply) developing a good architecture for the Satellite Navigation System is not enough; we must effectively communicate this architecture to all of its stakeholders. The Creating Architectural Descriptions sidebar explains how we may go about this task.

Defining Architectural Development Activities

The analysis and design micro process presented in Chapter 6 defines a set of development activities that are performed at each abstraction level within a system. The activities generally define the systems engineering tasks necessary to

Creating Architectural Descriptions

In the Documenting the Software Architecture sidebar presented in Chapter 6, we explained how documenting the architecture of a system has considerable value to the architects and to the other system stakeholders. We also discussed IEEE Standard 1471-2000, the IEEE Recommended Practice for Architectural Description of Software-Intensive Systems, and the 4+1 views proposed by Kruchten that present five views of software architecture: Use Case View, Logical View, Implementation View, Process View, and Deployment View.

Although IEEE Standard 1471-2000 focuses on software architecture, "it is equally applicable to any system; hence appropriate for use as a part of systems engineering to describe system architectures," according to Maier, Emery, and Hilliard [9]. In addition, they state that "A particularly important application of ANSI/IEEE 1471-2000 in systems engineering may be to reconcile and harmonize the wide array of architecture frameworks now becoming popular" [10]. They go on to compare the viewpoints for several of the more commonly used architecture frameworks: 4+1, ISO RM-ODP, DoDAF, and Zachman.

Similarly, the 4+1 views proposed by Kruchten also apply to systems engineering, according to Krikorian, who presents "Augmented 4+1 views" in which Kruchten's views are defined from the perspective of systems engineering, with appropriate activities and artifacts defined [11].

develop the system architecture for the Satellite Navigation System and are presented here, reworded for our focus.

- Identify the architectural elements at the given level of abstraction to further establish the problem boundaries and begin the object-oriented decomposition.
- Identify the semantics of the elements, that is, establish their behavior and attributes.
- Identify the relationships among the elements to solidify their boundaries and collaborators.
- Specify the interface of the elements and then their refinement in preparation for analysis at the next level of abstraction.

This set of activities makes quite clear that our primary concerns when developing the SNS architecture are the definition of its elements (segments and subsystems), their responsibilities, their collaborations, and their interfaces. These provide the architect with a framework for evolving the architecture and exploring alternative designs. One point to keep in mind is that these activities are typically performed in parallel, rather than sequentially. For example, identifying the relationships among elements might help us to better establish their behavior and attributes. In the following subsections, we define the segments of the Satellite Navigation System, the functionality they provide, their collaborations with each other, and their interfaces.

Validating the Proposed System Architecture

We recommend that the system architects be given the opportunity to experiment with alternative system decompositions, so that we can have a fairly high level of confidence that our global design decisions are sound. This may involve modeling, simulation, or prototyping on a very large scale. These models, simulations, and prototypes can then be carried on through the maturation of this system, as vehicles for regression testing.

In this and the following subsection, we perform a macro-level analysis of the SNS system architecture to validate our assumptions and decisions before proceeding further. We want to ensure that any problems with the architecture are found now, rather than later. In the same manner that requirements changes are simpler and less expensive to accommodate earlier in the development lifecycle, so are architecture changes. We focus on the `Initialize Operations` functionality because, for example, this has been a problematic area in previous developments.

We must add a note of caution here: Though the basic techniques we use in this section and the next are very similar to those used when developing the actual architecture of the system, we apply them very differently here. We focus on drilling very quickly through several architectural levels to study some broader system concerns that we have with respect to the `Initialize Operations` mission use case. The models that we derive here are not used as part of our specification of the actual system architecture.

Far too often the initial architectural decisions are not validated because architecture teams are not aware of the utility of this step or because of the rush to move on in the development. This being the case, teams often immediately proceed to decompose the system use cases to develop segment use cases that are allocated to the segment architecture teams. The segment architecture teams then repeat the process to define subsystem use cases. Eventually, the architecture teams may attempt to recompose these use cases up through the architectural levels to determine whether everything holds together at each architectural level. Unfortunately, if it does not, it is too late. Any fixes at this late stage would likely be much more difficult, time consuming, and costly. This is why performing a macro-level analysis *before* developing the segment use cases is advantageous. This same process should be regarded as necessary by the segment architecture teams, for the very same reasons, when they begin their analyses.

The first step is to review the results of our previous work, assess where we stand, and plan the path forward. With our domain experts, we evaluate the SNS logical architecture (refer back to Figure 8–3) and the black-box activity diagram for the `Initialize Operations` mission use case (refer back to Figure 8–5), from both functional and nonfunctional perspectives. We believe that we've captured the functionality correctly, yet we are not sure about several of the nonfunctional requirements. We have the requirement to ensure that the SNS has functional redundancy in critical system capabilities. At this level in our system architecture, we are laying out the structure of the segments, not designing their internal architectures. So, here we must ensure redundancy across segments.

To meet this requirement for functional redundancy, we choose to make two strategic system architecture decisions. First, we will have backup hardware for mission-essential equipment within the SNS Ground Segment. This equipment will be run in a hot-swappable mode where both primary and backup are active at the same time. The backup will be able to quickly replace the primary in the event of a problem that renders the primary incapable of performing its mission. Second, we will use the same hot-swappable equipment approach with the SNS Launch Segment to ensure redundant functionality. With our Satellite Segment, we will take advantage of the fact that there is redundancy across the multiple satellites in the constellation and that there will be spare satellites either on orbit or ready to be launched. This is in addition to the functional redundancy within each satellite that its designers must provide to meet the SNS nonfunctional requirement. For the User Segment, the functional redundancy requirement will be met by simply providing a replacement for the entire User Segment. As with the Satellite Segment, the designers of this segment need to focus on internal segment redundancy, as appropriate.

Beginning with the black-box activity diagram for `Initialize Operations` presented earlier in Figure 8–5, we allocate the system functionality, shown in the `SatelliteNavigationSystem` partition, to one or more of its constituent segments: Ground, Launch, Satellite, or User. Our goal is to allocate segment use cases, derived from the system use cases, to each of the segments. This way we see SNS functionality provided by a collaborative effort of its segments. If we assign use cases appropriately, the individual segments exhibit core object-oriented principles, as follows.

- *Abstraction*: Segments provide crisply defined conceptual boundaries, relative to the perspective of the viewer.
- *Encapsulation*: Segments compartmentalize their subsystems, which provide structure and behavior. Segments are black boxes to the other segments.

- *Modularity*: Segments are organized into a set of cohesive and loosely coupled subsystems.
- *Hierarchy*: Segments exhibit a ranking or ordering of abstractions.

For a system with the complexity of SNS, this part of the analysis process could easily take months to complete to any reasonable level of detail.[4] This is one of the reasons that we strongly suggest validating architectural decisions first by trying a quick-and-dirty proof-of-concept (e.g., modeling, simulation, or prototyping) to see if this part of the analysis is on the right track. The architecture team should not attempt to generate a complete list of use cases (no amount of time is sufficient) but should study some percentage of the more architecturally significant ones here.

As we walk through each of the actions shown in Figure 8–5, we must continually ask ourselves a number of questions. Which segment, or segments, should be responsible for a certain action? Does a segment have sufficient knowledge to carry out an action directed to it, or must it delegate the behavior? Is the segment trying to do too much? Is it performing actions that are not really related in some manner? What could go wrong? That is to say, what happens if certain preconditions are violated, or if postconditions cannot be satisfied?

Isn't it interesting just how similar these questions are to those we'd be asking ourselves if we were performing software engineering? Remember what we said in the introduction to this chapter?

> The object-oriented analysis and design principles and process presented earlier in this book, as well as the UML 2.0 notation discussed in Chapter 5, apply just as well to the development of the highest-level system architecture as to the development of software.

Earlier, we performed a black-box analysis of SNS system-level functionality. Now, we focus on the internal structure of the SNS—the segments that comprise this system and the functionality that each must provide collaboratively, so that the SNS is able to meet its requirements. We accomplish this task by performing a white-box analysis of the system use case functionality listed earlier in Table 8–1. We peer inside the SNS and determine *how* it provides the required services.

There is something to be aware of before we proceed; a constraint such as "Shall use the Proteus-4 launcher" would certainly impact the allocation of functional responsibility that we intend to make. To carry this thought further, when the

---

4. But beware of analysis paralysis: If the system analysis cycle takes longer than the window of opportunity for the business, then abandon hope, all ye who follow this path, for you will eventually be out of business.

Satellite Segment design team is designing the architecture of its segment, the team would be impacted by a constraint such as "Shall use the Gamma II(B) satellite bus."[5] We explore this concern further in the Allocation of Functionality sidebar.

Allocation of Functionality

Eventually, we must translate the system requirements into requirements for the hardware, software, and manual operation elements of the Satellite Navigation System, so that different organizations, each with different skills, can proceed in parallel to attack their particular part of the problem. During these efforts, the architecture team is always promoting and preserving the system's architectural vision.

The allocation of functionality is a concern of the system architect throughout the development because allocation can be done at any level in the abstraction, from the highest level in the system architecture to the lowest. The following list provides examples to illustrate this assertion.

- *System*: We could allocate the functionality of the entire Satellite Navigation System to another development effort. For example, a codevelopment effort could be pursued with the European Space Agency in the development of Galileo.
- *Segment*: A prime example of allocation at the segment level is subcontracting the entire launch effort. Numerous companies provide this type of service. This would mean, of course, that we would not be developing the Launch Segment but would be defining the interfaces to it with the subcontractor team.
- *Subsystem*:[6] We could envision allocation at this level in the SNS involving the utilization of a commercially available satellite bus subsystem in the development of the Satellite Segment.
- *Component*: This is the level within the SNS architecture at which we would most likely allocate requirements to hardware, software, or manual operations. For example, the User Interface Subsystem of the User Segment would likely consist of two components, one hardware (an LCD screen) and one software (used to control the User Segment).

---

5. A satellite bus provides infrastructure type services (e.g., power and communications) to onboard payloads that provide specialized capabilities, such as providing position information.

6. In discussing the subsystem and component levels of the SNS architecture at this time, we have given a glimpse into the future.

Previously, we listed eight SNS system use cases in Table 8–1, which we developed from the actions in the `SatelliteNavigationSystem` partition of Figure 8–5. If we were actually developing the system architecture, rather than performing a quick look analysis as we are here, we would develop an individual activity diagram for each of these use cases and apportion the activity diagram actions across the segments such that they exhibit the four core object-oriented principles that we discussed previously. But, to give us a broader perspective of the functionality in this macro-level analysis, instead we analyze all eight system use cases on one activity diagram. This is easily accomplished because we aren't trying to drive too much deeper into the details; rather, we are concerned with allocating portions of the use case functionality to the segments.

With the realization of our four logical SNS segments in hand (refer back to Figure 8–3), we begin our work with the domain experts to allocate the functionality denoted in the actions. If we didn't have a notion of the system architecture at this point, we could allocate the functionality to partitions with generic names such as `SegmentOne`, `SegmentTwo`, and `SegmentThree`. In each partition, we would then allocate the actions such that each of the segments is defined as a specialist in providing closely related capabilities, as it collaborates with the other segments to provide the Satellite Navigation System functionality—here, initializing operations. This allocation would be continued during the analysis of multiple use case scenarios to build a more complete picture of the segments' functionality, thus supporting the choice of a meaningful name for each segment.

This approach is analogous to how we would want to design good classes, as we discussed in Chapter 3. There we said that one might measure the quality of an abstraction and suggested five metrics. Two of them—coupling and cohesion—are central concerns with regard to the key abstractions of the Satellite Navigation System's architecture, that is, its segments. We are specifying the SNS segments such that they are loosely coupled; we want them to stand "alone" with only the minimal number of connections necessary to support their collaboration to provide SNS functionality.

Cohesion is the other measure by which we may judge the quality of our chosen abstractions. Cohesion measures the degree of connectivity among the elements that comprise a single segment. The least desirable form of cohesion is coincidental cohesion, in which entirely unrelated abstractions are thrown into an SNS segment. The most desirable form of cohesion is functional cohesion, in which the elements of a segment all work together to provide some well-bounded behavior.

By stepping through a few of the actions in Figure 8–5 together, we'll see how we arrived at the white-box activity diagram of Figure 8–7. The `Launch Satellite` system use case consisted of two actions, `Prepare for Launch` and `Launch`. It's fairly obvious that the `GroundSegment` and `LaunchSegment` should be providing this capability. The `GroundSegment` needs to perform its preparations for launch and also command the LaunchSegment to do its preparations. After preparations are complete, the Operator orders the GroundSegment to launch, which then commands the LaunchSegment to do so. From the SNS system use case Launch Satellite, we have derived several actions each for the GroundSegment and the LaunchSegment. We continue this analysis process with the remaining system use cases in the Initialize Operations package to develop the complete activity diagram shown in Figure 8–7.

The white-box activity diagram for Initialize Operations presents the results of analyzing only a portion of the functionality contained within the OperateSNS mission use case package. What remains are all the preparatory activities that lead up to this point and all the activities that occur afterward, which are contained within the other three mission use cases: Provide Normal Operations, Provide Special Operations, and Terminate Operations. However, these are not our focus in this macro-level analysis. If they were, we would repeat our analysis techniques to specify this behavior and thereby develop a more complete picture of how the segments cooperate to provide the Satellite Navigation System's operational capability.

This capability would include preparatory activities such as activating the Ground and Launch Segments, checking the integrity of the satellite, and mating the satellite with the launcher. In addition to this capability, we would find that the Ground Segment performs many activities during normal operations, including the following:

- Continuously monitoring and reporting system status
- Continuously evaluating satellite flight dynamics and managing station keeping
- Monitoring for and reporting on alarms
- Managing events, including initialization and termination
- Optimizing satellite operations: estimating propellant and extending satellite life
- Recovering from power failure
- Managing satellite quality of service
- Developing operational procedures (routine and emergency)

We wouldn't be done at this point because the system functionality embodied in the MaintainSNS and ReceiveSNSServices mission use case packages of Figures 8–2 and 8–6 would also need to be analyzed to completely define the architecture of the Satellite Navigation System. However, we'll continue here with our analysis of the Initialize Operations capability for our quick look.

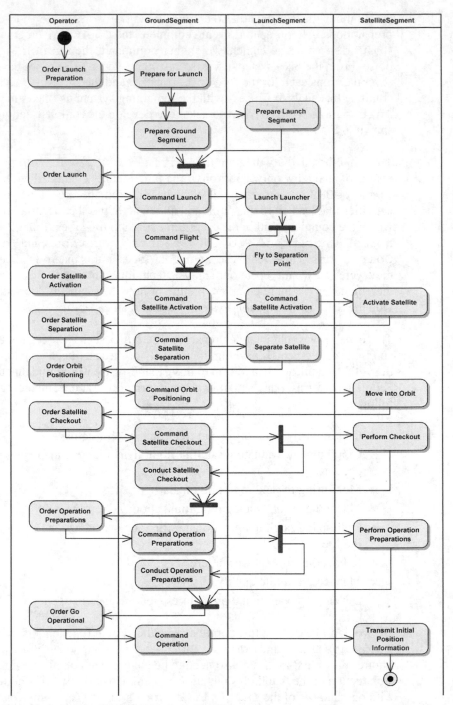

Figure 8–7 The White-Box Activity Diagram for `Initialize Operations`

The next step is to define use cases for each of the SNS segments, from the activity diagram in Figure 8–7. We do this by focusing on one partition at a time and determining which actions encompass reasonable use case functionality, by themselves or in combinations. Let's start with the GroundSegment partition. We decide that the first three actions—Prepare for Launch, Prepare Ground Segment, and Command Launch—provide the functionality for a use case we name Control Launch. The next action, Command Flight, is significant in its scope, so we define a single use case named Control Flight to enclose its behavior. We continue this approach for the entire GroundSegment partition and then repeat it for the LaunchSegment and SatelliteSegment partitions. Table 8–2 shows the resulting segment use cases and their constituent actions for the white-box Initialize Operations activity diagram in Figure 8–7.

Table 8–2 Segment Use Cases for *Initialize Operations*

SNS Segment	Segment Use Case	Segment Use Case Action
GroundSegment	Control Launch	Prepare for Launch
		Prepare Ground Segment
		Command Launch
	Control Flight	Command Flight
	Command Satellite Activation	Command Satellite Activation
	Command Satellite Separation	Command Satellite Separation
	Control Orbit Positioning	Command Orbit Positioning
	Command Satellite Checkout	Command Satellite Checkout
		Conduct Satellite Checkout
	Conduct Operation Preparations	Command Operation Preparations
		Conduct Operation Preparations
	Command Operation	Command Operation

(continued)

Table 8–2 Segment Use Cases for *Initialize Operations* *(Continued)*

SNS Segment	Segment Use Case	Segment Use Case Action
LaunchSegment	Launch	Prepare Launch Segment
		Launch Launcher
	Fly to Separation Point	Fly to Separation Point
	Command Satellite Activation	Command Satellite Activation
	Separate Satellite	Separate Satellite
SatelliteSegment	Activate Satellite	Activate Satellite
	Maneuver to Orbit	Move into Orbit
	Prepare for Operations	Perform Checkout
		Perform Operation Preparations
	Transmit Initial Position Information	Transmit Initial Position Information

Allocating Nonfunctional Requirements and Specifying Interfaces

During the analysis of the `Initialize Operations` functionality, we received an additional nonfunctional requirement on the Satellite Navigation System: "The time from the beginning of launch preparation to the beginning of the satellite transmitting navigation information shall be less than 7 days." Why might we be given such a requirement? Perhaps our customer doesn't want to use the approach of replacing malfunctioning satellites with on-orbit spares,[7] preferring to be able to launch a replacement satellite and have it operational within a week of need. The task we face is apportioning the 7 days (168 hours) among the use cases shown in Table 8–2 and any additional ones, such as mating the satellite

---

7. Replacing a malfunctioning satellite can be accomplished by using a satellite that was previously launched into space as a spare. It sits in space, like a sports player on the bench waiting to fill in for an injured player.

to the launcher, so that the entire timeline spans fewer than 168 hours, as our customer specified.

A reasonable question at this point is "How do we do this?" Well, there are two primary issues here, apportioning the nonfunctional requirement and documenting the result. Allocating the appropriate portion of the performance requirement (168 hours) to each segment use case relies a great deal on domain expertise. In addition to using the experience of the domain experts and development teams, we employ other techniques such as simulation to determine the impact of alternate allocation schemes. For our example, 48 of the 168 hours have been allocated to the `Initialize Operations` segment use cases shown in Table 8–2. The remaining 120 hours have been allocated to all the preparatory activities, which include activating the Ground Segment, activating the Launch Segment, checking the satellite integrity, and mating the satellite with the launcher.

The second issue, how to document the results, depends largely on the requirements and visual-modeling tools that the team is using and, of course, on the development process. Many tools do provide a way to document the results, but the information is usually in a requirements database that has a reference to the activities in the visual model or is buried under a tab within a properties box for an activity. While this is useful for running reports and performing statistical analysis, it doesn't provide the visual representation that we prefer, especially at this level in our development efforts. Here, we've chosen to use a table, specifically, Table 8–3, to clearly present the results of our effort to allocate the 48 hours across the segment use cases. These same techniques would be used to allocate other nonfunctional requirements across all the segment use cases that we would eventually specify.

The nonfunctional requirements allocated to a segment use case are then, at the next lower level in the architecture hierarchy, apportioned across its constituent subsystem use cases, employing the same techniques used at the segment level. Our techniques for allocating functional and nonfunctional requirements can be applied recursively from one level to the next in the architectural hierarchy—from the system to the segments, to their subsystems, and so forth.

We might then ask about potential requirements alluded to by the design constraints we've been given:

- Compatibility with international standards
- Maximal use of COTS hardware and software

The constraint "Compatibility with international standards" drove our specification of the external actor `Atmosphere/Space`, as discussed earlier. We must interact with the national and international agencies that regulate the use of the

Table 8–3 Launch Time Allocations for *Initialize Operations*[a]

SNS Segment	Segment Use Case	Allocated Time (hours:minutes)
GroundSegment	Control Launch	11:22
	Control Flight	0:17
	Command Satellite Activation	0:01
	Command Satellite Separation	0:01
	Control Orbit Positioning	0:05
	Command Satellite Checkout	16:30
	Conduct Operation Preparations	4:30
	Command Operation	0:01
LaunchSegment	Launch	11:30
	Fly to Separation Point	0:17
	Command Satellite Activation	0:01
	Separate Satellite	0:04
SatelliteSegment	Activate Satellite	0:03
	Maneuver to Orbit	13:45
	Prepare for Operations	21:29
	Transmit Initial Position Information	0:03[b]

a. If you have real-world experience in these activities, please forgive our crude allocations. Our domain experts were at lunch. Though the allocated times add up to about 80 hours, the actual clock time expended is within the 48 hours intended. This is possible because a number of actions are performed in parallel, as shown in Figure 8–7.

b. These 3 minutes denote the time it takes the Satellite System to begin transmitting position information, once commanded. Also, 40 minutes (of the 48 hours) have been allocated to the eight activities shown in the Operator partition in Figure 8–7.

airwaves to determine, for example, the specific frequencies at which we may communicate with the Satellite Segment, as well as the frequencies at which it may transmit position information. This means that the Ground Segment, Launch Segment (at least during the flight phase), and Satellite Segment now must fulfill the external interface responsibilities of the Satellite Navigation System. We point out these issues because in the focus on functional capability, constraints (and nonfunctional requirements) may be considered far too late in the development cycle or sometimes even overlooked.

The subject of external interfaces is one other point that we have not really touched on here, due to our focus on developing the logical architecture of the Satellite Navigation System by analyzing its functionality. The techniques to develop and document interface specifications should be familiar to those who have done any type of system or software development. The Satellite Navigation System has interfaces with those actors shown in Figure 8–1: User, Operator, Maintainer, ExternalPower, ExternalCommunications, and Atmosphere/Space. Clearly, we must perform some level of functional analysis prior to attempting the specification of the interfaces for the User, Operator, and Maintainer actors. In addition, human/machine interface specialists would be critical team members in this task. Interfaces to ExternalPower and ExternalCommunications actors could be specified quite early because of the standards dictating the provision of power and communications. The final external interface, the one to the Atmosphere/Space actor, is largely specified by national and international governments and agencies through regulations and treaties that govern satellite transmissions.

Stipulating the System Architecture and Its Deployment

The notion of the SNS logical architecture that we presented earlier in Figure 8–3 has withstood the test of our behavioral prototyping efforts. Consequently, Figure 8–3 represents the logical view of the first-level SNS architecture, as does the component diagram shown in Figure 8–8. With UML 2.0, the component diagram may be used to hierarchically decompose a system, and thus it here represents the highest-level abstraction of the Satellite Navigation System architecture, that is, its segments and their relationships. Figure 8–8 illustrates two ways to represent the interface between segments, the ball-and-socket notation (LaunchSupport interface) and the dashed dependency line connecting the required and provided interfaces (PositionInformation interfaces).

Looking back at Figure 8–1, we see that three of the system actors are not accounted for by the SNS interfaces shown in Figure 8–8: ExternalPower, ExternalCommunications, and Atmosphere/Space. These actors

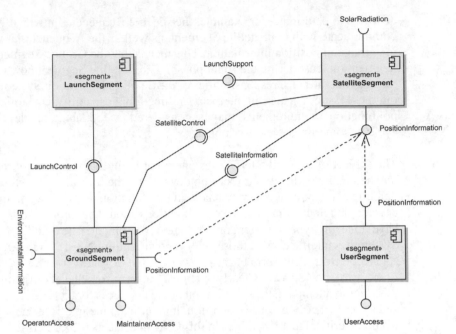

Figure 8–8 The Component Diagram for the Satellite Navigation System

provide important services to the Satellite Navigation System; however, they are not central to our focus on developing its logical architecture.

Figure 8–9 shows the deployment of the components represented in Figure 8–8 onto the architectural nodes of our system. These components are the segments of the SNS and are represented as UML 2.0 artifacts. We recognize that this is not a typical use of the notation; typically, we would deploy software artifacts (such as code, a source file, a document, or another item relating to the code) onto processing nodes. However, this diagram clearly presents the information, and some non-standard usage is unavoidable when using the UML 2.0 notation for systems engineering. The interfaces through which the Operator, Maintainer, and User actors interact with the Satellite Navigation System are contained within its segments, so we've chosen to illustrate these relationships with dependencies.

Previously, we decided that our approach to providing functional redundancy was to run backups for mission-essential equipment at both the GroundSegment and LaunchSegment in a hot-swappable mode, where both primary and backup are active at the same time. In developing the SNS architecture, we've come to realize that a better approach to meeting the requirement for functional redundancy is to distribute the GroundSegment at two geographically dispersed sites and to do the same for the LaunchSegment. This protects us from

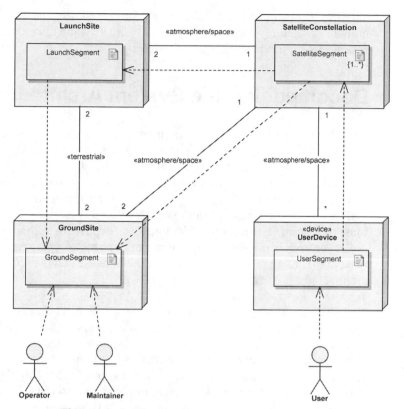

Figure 8–9 The Deployment of SNS Segments

a complete loss of segment functionality due to natural disasters, for example. This design decision is represented by the multiplicities of 2 on the communication association between the GroundSite and LaunchSite nodes. Similar to what we originally proposed with backup equipment, we now have backup sites that are prepared to assume the role of primary when commanded.

Another aspect of the SNS design that requires explanation is the Satellite Constellation node and the SatelliteSegment artifact(s) that it hosts. The SatelliteConstellation node is essentially the set of Satellite Navigation System satellites and their locations in space as they provide position information to the UserSegment artifacts. The SatelliteConstellation node provides support to its hosted SatelliteSegment artifacts, such as gravity (an external system actor that we overlooked?) to help keep the satellites in their proper orbit and both the atmosphere and outer space to provide a communications medium for the satellites. The multiplicity of {1..*} on the SatelliteSegment artifact denotes that there is at least one satellite in the constellation. Our customer has not yet determined the coverage area for the

Satellite Navigation System.[8] When this is resolved, we will determine the actual number of satellites necessary to provide "effective and affordable Satellite Navigation System services" for the SNS users.

Decomposing the System Architecture

Now that we've validated our assumptions and decisions surrounding the Satellite Navigation System's architecture with respect to the `Initialize Operations` system use case, we can proceed with the specification of its segments and their subsystems. If we had encountered any problems, we would have modified the architecture as needed. Before we move on, we must emphasize one critical point with respect to the results of our macro-level analysis—our behavioral prototype must be discarded; it has served its intended purpose. In the same manner that prototype code is not the foundation for deliverable software, neither is our behavioral prototype the foundation for the Satellite Navigation System's architecture.

The SNS logical architecture diagram shown earlier in Figure 8–3 is useful but incomplete because each segment in this diagram is far too large to be developed by a small team of developers. We must zoom inside each of the segments and further decompose them into their nested subsystems. This is accomplished by applying the same analysis techniques—but applied more completely—that we used to prototype the Satellite Navigations System's architecture of segments for the `Initialize Operations` functionality, as depicted in the component diagram shown in Figure 8–8. These techniques are repeated through all the levels of abstraction in the Satellite Navigation System—from the system to the segments, to their subsystems, and so forth—to determine the use cases for each element at every level in the system's architecture. As we do this, the nonfunctional requirements are apportioned across the use cases, allocated to each element at every level in the system decomposition. Our analysis techniques are presented here for completeness.

1. Perform black-box analysis for each system use case to determine its actions.
2. Perform white-box analysis of these system actions to allocate them across segments.

---

8. This indecision is definitely a major source of risk (technical and nontechnical) to the program. To help our customer nail down this critical requirement, we can use simulations to determine the optimal number of satellites for a desired coverage. For those interested in this subject area, the Summer 2002 edition of the Aerospace Corporation's *Crosslink* publication (available at www.aero.org/publications/crosslink/summer2002/index.html) contains two pertinent articles: "Orbit Determination and Satellite Navigation" and "Optimizing Performance Through Constellation Management."

3. Define segment use cases from these allocated system actions.

4. Perform black-box analysis for each segment use case to determine its actions.

5. Perform white-box analysis of these segment actions to allocate them across subsystems.

6. Define subsystem use cases from these allocated segment actions.

A perspective of the black-box and white-box system analysis approach that we've used is provided in the Similar Architectural Analysis Techniques sidebar.

Normally, when applying our analysis techniques, we would complete each step, across that entire architectural level of the system, before proceeding to the next step. In other words, for step 1 we would do the black-box analysis for *all* the system use cases, *before* proceeding to step 2. Then we would do the white-box analysis of *all* the system actions *before* proceeding to step 3, and so on.

However, due to the size constraints of a chapter in a book, our example of decomposing the system architecture continues to focus on only part of the entire system—the Launch Satellite system use case. We make note of this so that you do not read the steps we performed (listed below) and assume that you should drill down vertically from one system use case to system activities to segment use cases to segment activities to subsystems, and so on, and then repeat for the next system use case. That would be an ineffective approach. The steps numbered above are to be applied horizontally across each architectural level of the system to provide a complete, holistic view of the system that can be validated at any point along the way.

Similar Architectural Analysis Techniques

For many years, systems engineers have been using techniques—very similar to what we describe—to analyze system functionality and allocate portions of it to the elements of a system's architecture. These techniques of black-box and white-box analysis have been used successfully to develop the complex architectural hierarchies for systems such as the Global Positioning System.

In their book *The Object Advantage*, Jacobson et al. present use cases and their application to the analysis of enterprise systems through the concepts of superordinate and subordinate use cases [12]. The IBM Rational Unified Process for Systems Engineering (RUP SE) essentially combines these approaches through systems engineering extensions to RUP. Systems engineers have been effectively employing the concepts of use cases and black-box/white-box analysis for a number of years.

We continued our analysis—not shown here—by performing the following activities:

- Performed black-box analysis for the Launch Satellite system use case to determine its actions
- Performed white-box analysis of these system actions to allocate them across segments
- Defined GroundSegment use cases from these allocated system actions
- Performed black-box analysis for the GroundSegment's Control Launch use case to determine its actions
- Performed white-box analysis of the GroundSegment's Control Launch actions to allocate them across its subsystems

Figure 8–10 presents the results of this analysis. We see the actions that each of the GroundSegment subsystems must perform as they collaborate to provide the GroundSegment functionality of controlling the launch. Through such analyses, we can develop the architecture of each of the Satellite Navigation System's segments. The following pages present the resulting segment architectures.

The architecture of the GroundSegment is composed of five subsystems: ControlCenter, TT&C (tracking, telemetry, and command), SensorStation, Gateway, and UserInterface, as shown in Figure 8–11. The Control Center subsystem essentially provides the command and control functionality for the whole of the Satellite Navigation System, with support from the TT&C subsystem and the SensorStation subsystem. The TT&C subsystem provides the means to monitor and control the SatelliteSegment, while the SensorStation subsystem provides position information being provided by the SatelliteSegment and the environmental conditions. The Gateway subsystem provides the means for the ControlCenter subsystem to communicate with the LaunchSegment and SatelliteSegment to control launch activities and satellite operations, respectively. Finally, the UserInterface subsystem provides GroundSegment functionality access to the Operator and Maintainer actors.

Figure 8–12 presents the logical architecture for the LaunchSegment, which is composed of three subsystems: LaunchCenter, Launcher, and Gateway. The LaunchCenter subsystem provides the command and control functionality for the LaunchSegment, similar to that provided by the ControlCenter subsystem of the GroundSegment. The Launcher subsystem provides all the capability necessary to place the SatelliteSegment into its initial orbit. The Gateway subsystem here, as in the GroundSegment, enables the Launch-Center to receive launch control support from the GroundSegment and to provide launch support to the Launcher.

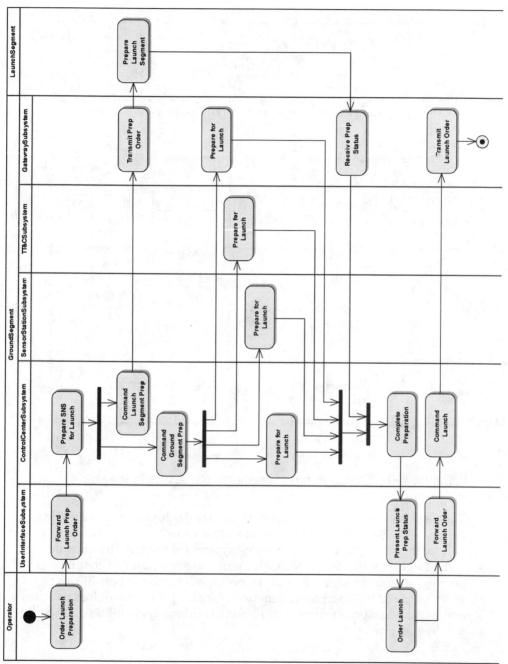

Figure 8–10 The White-Box Activity Diagram for Control Launch

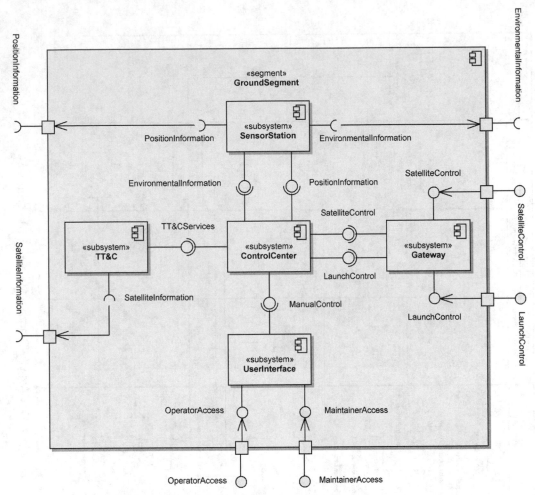

Figure 8–11 The Logical Architecture of the `GroundSegment`

The `SatelliteSegment` decomposes into two subsystems, as shown in Figure 8–13. The `SatelliteBus` subsystem provides the infrastructure support for the `NavigationPayload` subsystem. On its body structure, the `SatelliteBus` hosts equipment that provides power, attitude control, and propulsion, to name a few services. This equipment makes it possible for the `NavigationPayload` equipment (including a high-accuracy clock and position signal generation) to provide the position information to the Satellite Navigation System users.

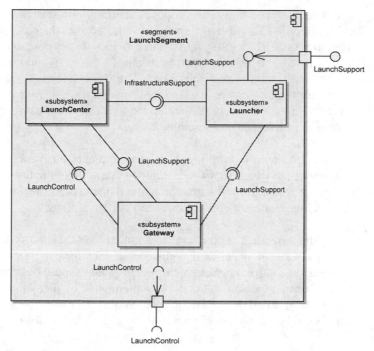

Figure 8–12 The Logical Architecture of the `LaunchSegment`

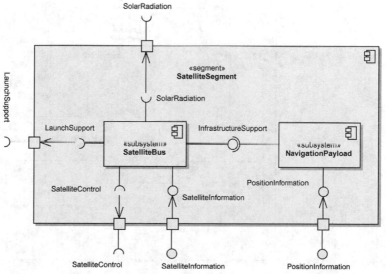

Figure 8–13 The Logical Architecture of the `SatelliteSegment`

The UserSegment also decomposes naturally into several subsystems, shown in Figure 8–14. The Receiver subsystem receives the position information from the SatelliteSegment and provides this as position data to the Processor subsystem, which translates this to navigation information for use by the UserInterface subsystem. The UserInterface provides the means for the User to access and make use of the UserSegment navigation services through a variety of specialized user interfaces using, for example, push buttons, touch screens, and audible alerts.

This design leaves us with four top-level segments, each encompassing several subsystems, to which we have allocated system functionality provided by combinations of hardware, software, and manual operations. In some cases, these allocations may be clear to the experienced system architect.

As we discussed in Chapter 7, these segments and their subsystems form the units for work assignments as well as the coarse units for configuration management and version control. Each segment or subsystem should be owned by one organization, team, or person, yet may be implemented by many more. The owner directs the detailed design and implementation of the element and manages its interface relative to other elements at the same level of abstraction. Thus, the

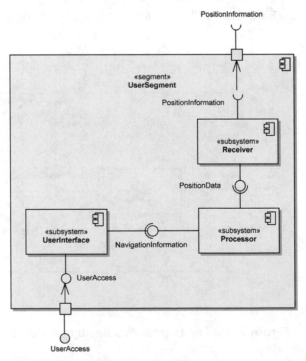

Figure 8–14 The Logical Architecture of the UserSegment

management of a very large development program is made possible by taking a very complex problem and decomposing it into successively smaller ones.

We have now met the goal of this chapter—we have shown that object-oriented analysis and design principles and process and the UML 2.0 notation apply just as well to the development of the highest-level system architecture as to the development of software.

8.3 Construction

At the end of the Elaboration phase, as we pointed out in Chapter 6, a stable architecture of our system should have been developed. Any modifications to the system architecture that are required as a result of activities in the Construction phase are likely limited to those of lower-level architectural elements, not the segments and subsystems of the Satellite Navigation System that have been our concern. In line with the stated intent of this chapter—to show the approach to developing the SNS system architecture by logically partitioning the required functionality to define the constituent segments and subsystems—we do not show any architectural development activities in this phase.

8.4 Post-Transition

The Satellite Navigation System's original nonfunctional requirements included two that caused us to develop a flexible architecture: extensibility and long service life. This long service life dictates, in addition to many other aspects, a design that is extensible to ensure the reliable provision of desired functionality. As there are more users of the Satellite Navigation System, and as we adapt this design to new implementations, they will discover new, unanticipated uses for existing mechanisms, creating pressure to add new functionality to the system. We now investigate how well our SNS design has met these requirements as we add new functionality and also change the system's target hardware.

Adding New Functionality

Let's consider an addition to our requirements, namely, the capability to also use the position information transmissions from other systems, such as GPS, GLONASS, and Galileo. This would add greatly to the availability and accuracy of the positioning capability of our system throughout the world. Fortunately, this is accommodated with minimal change to the Satellite Navigation System since its impact is isolated to the User Segment. Also fortunate is the fact that our existing User Segment can be easily upgraded to provide this capability, by changing the `Receiver` subsystem and upgrading the firmware in the `Processor` subsystem. Thus, adding this functionality has done very little to our existing design. This is indeed quite common in well-structured object-oriented systems: A significant addition to the requirements for the system can be dealt with fairly easily by building new applications on existing mechanisms.

What about an even more radical change? Suppose our customer wanted to introduce the capability to support search and rescue (SAR) missions by receiving distress beacons with our Satellite Navigation System.[9] How would this new requirement affect our architecture? After analysis, we see that the greatest impact is to the Satellite Segment, but there is also some impact to the Ground Segment. This is not unexpected. If we had thought ahead to this requirement, we would have added the capability to receive these specific signals (or perhaps a range of signals), and there would be no design impact to the Satellite Segment, just the operational impact of using the functionality. Otherwise, we would need to add an additional subsystem to the Satellite Segment that would provide this capability. With respect to the Ground Segment, the impact is merely being able to relay information about the reception of the distress beacon to the appropriate civil authorities. This would likely involve minor software or operational modifications to the `ControlCenter` and `TT&C` subsystems.

Again, this large change would have minimal impact to the overall SNS architecture. Unfortunately, the difficulty of making modifications to space-based assets forces the system architects to be very far-reaching in their vision for the system. But even in the worst-case situation here, we would be able to add the SAR capability to Satellite Segment elements being developed in the future, with minimal impact on the existing architecture or functionality.

Changing the Target Hardware

Hardware technology is still moving at a faster pace than our ability to generate software. Furthermore, it is likely that a number of political and historical reasons will cause us to make certain hardware and software choices early in the develop-

---

9. The Galileo program is adding this type of capability from the outset to assist the Cospas-Sarsat Program (www.cospas-sarsat.org/) in its mission of supporting SAR missions throughout the world. In fact, the Galileo program believes that its contribution to this effort will provide near real-time acquisition of distress beacons and location to within several meters.

ment process that we may later regret.[10] For this reason, the target hardware for large systems becomes obsolete far earlier than does its software.

For example, after several years of operational use, we might decide we need to replace the entire `ControlCenter` subsystem of the Ground Segment. How might this affect our existing architecture? If we have kept our subsystem interfaces at a high level of abstraction during the evolution of our system, this hardware change would affect our software in only minimal ways. Since we chose to encapsulate all design decisions regarding the specifics of the `ControlCenter` subsystem, no other subsystem was ever defined to depend on the specific characteristics of a given workstation, for example; the subsystem encapsulates all such hardware secrets. This means that the behavior of workstations is hidden in the `ControlCenter` subsystem. Thus, this subsystem acts as an abstraction firewall, which shields all other clients from the intricacies of our particular computing technology.

In a similar fashion, a radical change in telecommunications standards would affect our implementation, but only in limited ways. Specifically, our design ensures that only the `Gateway` subsystem knows about network communications. Thus, even a fundamental change in networking would never affect any higher-level client; the `Gateway` subsystem shields them from the perversity of the real world.

None of the changes we have introduced rends the fabric of our existing architecture. This is indeed the ultimate mark of a well-architected, object-oriented system.

---

10. For example, our project might have chosen a particular hardware or software product from a third-party vendor, only to later discover that the product didn't live up to its promises. Even worse, we might find that the only supplier of a critical product went out of business. In such cases, the project manager usually has one of two choices: (1) run screaming into the night, or (2) choose another product, and hope that the system's architecture is resilient enough to accommodate the change. The use of object-oriented analysis and design helps us to achieve (2), although it is sometimes still very satisfying to carry out (1).

Chapter 9

Control System: Traffic Management

The economics of software development have progressed to the point where many more kinds of applications are now automated than ever before, ranging from embedded microcomputers that control a myriad of automobile functions to tools that eliminate much of the drudgery associated with producing an animated film to systems that manage the distribution of interactive video services to millions of consumers. The distinguishing characteristic of all these larger systems is that they are extremely complex. Building systems so that their implementation is small is certainly an honorable task, but reality tells us that certain large problems demand large implementations. For some massive applications, it is not unusual to find software development organizations that employ several hundred programmers who must collaborate to produce millions of lines of code against a set of requirements that are guaranteed to be unstable during development. Such projects rarely involve the development of single programs; they more often encompass multiple, cooperative programs that must execute across a distributed target system consisting of many computers connected to one another in a variety of ways. To reduce development risk, such projects usually involve a central organization that is responsible for systems architecture and integration; the remaining work may be subcontracted to other companies or to other in-house organizations. Thus, the development team as a whole never assembles as one; it is typically distributed over space and—because of the personnel turnover common in large projects—over time.

Developers who are content with writing small, stand-alone, single-user, window-based tools may find the problems associated with building massive applications staggering—so much so that they view it as folly even to try. However, the actuality of the business and scientific world is such that complex software systems must be built. Indeed, in some cases, it is folly not to try. Imagine using a manual system to control air traffic around a major metropolitan center or to manage the life-support system of a manned spacecraft or the accounting activities of a multinational bank. Successfully automating such systems not only addresses the very real problems at hand but also leads to a number of tangible and intangible benefits, such as lower operational costs, greater safety, and increased functionality. Of course, the operative word here is *successfully.* Building complex systems is plain hard work and requires the application of the best engineering practices we know, along with the creative insight of a few great designers.

This chapter tackles the development of such a problem.

9.1 Inception

To most people living in the United States, trains are an artifact of an era long past; in Europe and in many parts of Asia, the situation is entirely the opposite. Trains are an essential part of their transportation networks; tens of thousands of kilometers of track carry people and goods daily, both within cities and across national borders. In all fairness, trains do provide an important and economical means of transporting goods within the United States. Additionally, as major metropolitan centers grow more crowded, light rail transport is increasingly providing an attractive option for easing congestion and addressing the problems of pollution from internal combustion engines.

Still, railroads are a business and consequently must be profitable. Railroad companies must delicately balance the demands of frugality and safety and the pressures to increase traffic against efficient and predictable train scheduling. These conflicting needs suggest an automated solution to train traffic management, including computerized train routing and monitoring of all elements of the train system. Such automated and semiautomated train systems exist today in Sweden, Great Britain, West Germany, France, Japan [1], Canada, and the United States. The motivation for each of these systems is largely economic and social: Lower operating costs and more efficient use of resources are the goals, with improved safety as an integral by-product.

In this section, we begin our analysis of the fictitious Train Traffic Management System (TTMS) by specifying its requirements and the system use cases that further describe the required functionality.

Requirements for the Train Traffic Management System

Our experience with developing large systems has been that an initial statement of requirements is never complete, often vague, and always self-contradictory. For these reasons, we must consciously concern ourselves with the management of uncertainty during development, and therefore we strongly suggest that the development of such a system be deliberately allowed to evolve over time in an incremental and iterative fashion. As we pointed out in Chapter 6, the very process of development gives both users and developers better insight into what requirements are really important—far better than any paper exercise in writing requirements documents in the absence of an existing implementation or prototype. Also, since developing the software for a large system may take several years, software requirements must be allowed to change to take advantage of rapidly changing hardware technology.[1] It is undeniably futile to craft an elegant software architecture targeted to a hardware technology that is guaranteed to be obsolete by the time the system is fielded. This is why we suggest that, whatever mechanisms we craft as part of our software architecture, we should rely on existing standards for communications, graphics, networking, and sensors. For truly novel systems, it is sometimes necessary to pioneer new hardware or software technology. This adds risk to a large project, however, which already involves a customarily high risk. Software development clearly remains the technology of highest risk in the successful deployment of any large automated application, and our goal is to limit this risk to a manageable level, not to increase it.

This is a very large and highly complex system that in reality would not be specified by simple requirements. However, for this chapter, the requirements that follow will suffice for the purposes of our analysis and design effort. In the real world, a problem such as this could easily suffer from analysis paralysis because there would be many thousands of requirements, both functional and nonfunctional, with a myriad of constraints. Quite clearly, we would need to focus our efforts on the most critical elements and prototype candidate solutions within the operational context of the system under development.

---

1. In fact, for many such systems of this complexity, it is common to have to deal with many different kinds of computers. Having a well-thought-out and stable architecture mitigates much of the risk of changing hardware in the middle of development, an event that happens all too often in the face of the rapidly changing hardware business. Hardware products come and go, and therefore it is important to manage the hardware/software boundary of a system so that new products can be introduced that reduce the system's cost or improve its performance, while at the same time preserving the integrity of the system's architecture.

The Train Traffic Management System has two primary functions: train routing and train systems monitoring. Related functions include traffic planning, failure prediction, train location tracking, traffic monitoring, collision avoidance, and maintenance logging. From these functions, we define eight use cases, as shown in the following list.

- `Route Train`: Establish a train plan that defines the travel route for a particular train.
- `Plan Traffic`: Establish a traffic plan that provides guidance in the development of train plans for a time frame and geographic region.
- `Monitor Train Systems`: Monitor the onboard train systems for proper functioning.
- `Predict Failure`: Perform an analysis of train systems' condition to predict probabilities of failure relative to the train plan.
- `Track Train Location`: Monitor the location of trains using TTMS resources and the Navstar Global Positioning System (GPS).
- `Monitor Traffic`: Monitor all train traffic within a geographic region.
- `Avoid Collision`: Provide the means, both automatic and manual, to avoid train collisions.
- `Log Maintenance`: Provide the means to log maintenance performed on trains.

These use cases establish the basic functional requirements for the Train Traffic Management System, that is, they tell us *what* the system must do for its users. In addition, we have nonfunctional requirements and constraints that impact the requirements specified by our use cases, as listed here.

Nonfunctional requirements:
- Safely transport passengers and cargo
- Support train speeds up to 250 miles per hour
- Interoperate with the traffic management systems of operators at the TTMS boundary
- Ensure maximum reuse of and compatibility with existing equipment
- Provide a system availability level of 99.99%
- Provide complete functional redundancy of TTMS capabilities
- Provide accuracy of train position within 10.0 yards
- Provide accuracy of train speed within 1.5 miles per hour
- Respond to operator inputs within 1.0 seconds
- Have a designed-in capability to maintain and evolve the TTMS

Constraints:

- Meet national standards, both government and industry
- Maximize use of commercial-off-the-shelf (COTS) hardware and software

Now that we have our core requirements defined, at least at a very high level, we must turn our attention to understanding the users of the Train Traffic Management System. We find that we have three types of people who interact with the system: `Dispatcher`, `TrainEngineer`, and `Maintainer`. In addition, the Train Traffic Management System interfaces with one external system, `Navstar GPS`. These actors play the following roles within the TTMS.

- `Dispatcher` establishes train routes and tracks the progress of individual trains.
- `TrainEngineer` monitors the condition of and operates the train.
- `Maintainer` monitors the condition of and maintains train systems.
- `Navstar GPS` provides geolocation services used to track trains.

Determining System Use Cases

Figure 9–1 shows the use case diagram for the Train Traffic Management System. In it, we see the system functionality used by each of the actors. We also see that we have «include» and «extend» relationships used to organize relationships between several of the use cases. The functionality of the use case `Monitor Train Systems` is extended by the use case `Predict Failure`. During the course of monitoring systems, a failure prediction analysis (`condition: {request Predict Failure}`) can be requested for a particular system that is operating abnormally or may have been flagged with a yellow condition indicating a problem requiring investigation. This occurs at the `Potential Failure` extension point.

The functionality of the `Monitor Traffic` use case is also extended, by that of the `Avoid Collision` use case. Here, when monitoring train traffic, an actor has optional system capability to assist in the avoidance of a collision—at the `Potential Collision` extension point. This assistance can support both manual and automatic interventions. `Monitor Traffic` always includes the functionality of the `Track Train Location` use case to have a precise picture of the location of all train traffic. This is accomplished by using both TTMS resources and the Navstar GPS.

We may specify the details of the functionality provided by each of these use cases in textual documents called use case specifications. We have chosen to focus on the two primary use cases, `Route Train` and `Monitor Train`

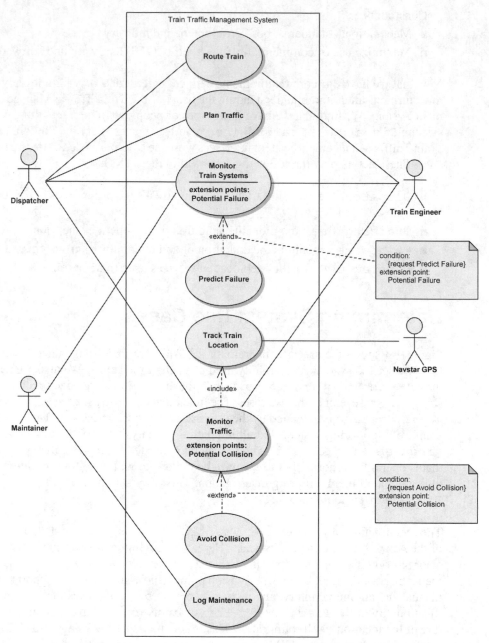

Figure 9–1 The Use Case Diagram for the Train Traffic Management System

`Systems`, in the following use case specifications. The format of the use case specification is a general one that provides setup information along with the primary scenario and one or more alternate scenarios.

It should be noted that these use case specifications focus on the boundary-level interaction between the users of the system and the Train Traffic Management System itself. This perspective is often referred to as a black-box view since the internal functioning of the system is not seen externally. This view is used when we are concerned with *what* the system does, not *how* the system does it.

Use case name: `Route Train`

Use case purpose: The purpose of this use case is to establish a train plan that acts as a repository for all the pertinent information associated with the route of one particular train and the actions that take place along the way.

Point of contact: Katarina Bach

Date modified: 9/5/06

Preconditions: A traffic plan exists for the time frame and geographic region (territory) relevant to the train plan being developed.

Postconditions: A train plan has been developed for a particular train to detail its travel route.

Limitations: Each train plan will have a unique ID within the system. Resources may not be committed for utilization by more than one train plan for a particular time frame.

Assumptions: A train plan is accessible by dispatchers for inquiry and modification and accessible by train engineers for inquiry.

Primary scenario:
  A. The Train Traffic Management System (TTMS) presents the dispatcher with a list of options.
  B. The dispatcher chooses to develop a new train plan.
  C. The TTMS presents the template for a train plan to the dispatcher.
  D. The dispatcher completes the train plan template, providing information about locomotive ID(s), train engineer(s), and waypoints with times.
  E. The dispatcher submits the completed train plan to the TTMS.
  F. The TTMS assigns a unique ID to the train plan and stores it. The TTMS makes the train plan accessible for inquiry and modification.
  G. This use case ends.

Alternate scenarios:

Condition triggering an alternate scenario:

Condition 1: Develop a new train plan, based on an existing one.

B1. The dispatcher chooses to develop a new train plan, based on an existing one.

B2. The dispatcher provides search criteria for existing train plans.

B3. The TTMS provides the search results to the dispatcher.

B4. The dispatcher chooses an existing train plan.

B5. The dispatcher completes the train plan.

B6. The primary scenario is resumed at step E.

Condition triggering an alternate scenario:

Condition 2: Modify an existing train plan.

B1. The dispatcher chooses to modify an existing train plan.

B2. The dispatcher provides search criteria for existing train plans.

B3. The TTMS provides the search results to the dispatcher.

B4. The dispatcher chooses an existing train plan.

B5. The dispatcher modifies the train plan.

B6. The dispatcher submits the modified train plan to the TTMS.

B7. The TTMS stores the modified train plan and makes it accessible for inquiry and modification.

B8. This use case ends.

Use case name: Monitor Train Systems

Use case purpose: The purpose of this use case is to monitor the onboard train systems for proper functioning.

Point of contact: Katarina Bach

Date modified: 9/5/06

Preconditions: The locomotive is operating.

Postconditions: Information concerning the functioning of onboard train systems has been provided.

Limitations: None identified.

Assumptions: Monitoring of onboard train systems is provided when the locomotive is operating. Audible and visible indications of system problems, in addition to those via video display, are provided.

Primary scenario:

A. The Train Traffic Management System (TTMS) presents the train engineer with a list of options.

B. The train engineer chooses to monitor the onboard train systems.

C. The TTMS presents the train engineer with the overview status information for the train systems.

D. The train engineer reviews the overview system status information.

E. This use case ends.

Alternate scenarios:

Condition triggering an alternate scenario:

Condition 1: Request detailed monitoring of a system.

E1. The train engineer chooses to perform detailed monitoring of a system that has a yellow condition.

E2. The TTMS presents the train engineer with the detailed system status information for the selected system.

E3. The train engineer reviews the detailed system status information.

E4. The primary scenario is resumed at step B..

Extension point—Potential Failure:

Condition 2: Request a failure prediction analysis for a system.

E3-1. The train engineer requests a failure prediction analysis for a system.

E3-2. The TTMS performs a failure prediction analysis for the selected system.

E3-3. The TTMS presents the train engineer with the failure prediction analysis for the system.

E3-4. The train engineer reviews the failure prediction analysis.

E3-5. The train engineer requests that the TTMS alert the maintainer of the system that might fail.

E3-6. The TTMS alerts the maintainer of that system.

E3-7. The maintainer requests the failure prediction analysis for review.

E3-8. The TTMS presents the maintainer with the failure prediction analysis.

E3-9. The maintainer reviews the analysis and determines that the yellow condition is not severe enough to warrant immediate action.

E3-10. The maintainer requests that the TTMS inform the train engineer of this determination.

E3-11. The TTMS provides the train engineer with the determination of the maintainer.

E3-12. The train engineer chooses to perform detailed monitoring of the selected system.

E3-13. The alternate scenario is resumed at step E3.

Even though the requirements for the Train Traffic Management System are very simplified, we still have not completely specified them, and they are somewhat vague. This is not unlike what we've encountered while developing large, complex systems in the real world. As we've discussed previously, effectively managing ever-changing requirements is critical to having a successful development process, which we should all define as providing the right functionality, on time, and within budget. But don't think that our goal is to stop requirements from changing; we can't and we shouldn't want to do this. We can understand this if we focus on the rapid pace of functional enhancements made to hardware technology that, usually along with decreased cost, provide ever more solutions to our software development problems. Just look at the incredibly capable and complex software that can be run on today's personal computers, with their processors running at multigigahertz speeds and sporting gigabytes of random access memory (RAM).

So, how do we accommodate changing requirements, especially over development time frames that may encompass several years? We've found that using an iterative and incremental development process is one of the key means to managing the risks associated with changing requirements in such a large automated system. Another is designing an architecture that remains flexible throughout the development. Yet another is maximizing the use of COTS hardware and software, as one of the TTMS constraints directs us to do. As we proceed through this chapter, our prime focus will be on developing an architecture that can accommodate change.

9.2 Elaboration

Our attention now turns to developing the overall architecture framework for the Train Traffic Management System. We begin by analyzing the required system functionality that leads us into the definition of the TTMS architecture. From there, we begin our transition from systems engineering to the disciplines of hardware and software engineering. We conclude this section by describing the key abstractions and mechanisms of the TTMS.

Analyzing System Functionality

Now that the requirements for the Train Traffic Management System have been specified, our focus turns to *how* the system's aggregate parts provide this required functionality. This perspective is often referred to as a white-box view since the internal functioning of the system is seen externally. We use activity diagrams to analyze the various use case scenarios to develop this further level of detail.

Let's begin by looking at Figure 9–2, which analyzes the primary scenario of the Route Train use case. This activity diagram is relatively straightforward and follows the course of the use case scenario. Here we see the interaction of the Dispatcher actor and the RailOperationsControlSystem, which we've designated as the primary command and control center for the TTMS, as the Dispatcher creates a new TrainPlan object.

When determining the constituent elements of the TTMS, we must of course consider the requirements, both functional and nonfunctional, and the constraints. But we also have two competing technical concerns: the desire to encapsulate abstractions and the need to make certain abstractions visible to other elements. In other words, we must strive to design elements that are cohesive (by grouping logically related abstractions) and loosely coupled (by minimizing the dependencies among elements). Therefore, we define modularity as the property of a system that has been decomposed into a set of cohesive and loosely coupled elements.

In contrast to Figure 9–2, the activity diagram of Figure 9–3 is a bit more complicated because we've illustrated the first alternate scenario of the Monitor Train Systems use case, where the TrainEngineer chooses to perform a detailed monitoring of the LocomotiveAnalysisandReporting system, which has a yellow condition. Here we see that the constituent elements of the TTMS providing this capability are the OnboardDisplay system, the LocomotiveAnalysisandReporting system, the EnergyManagement system, and the DataManagement unit.

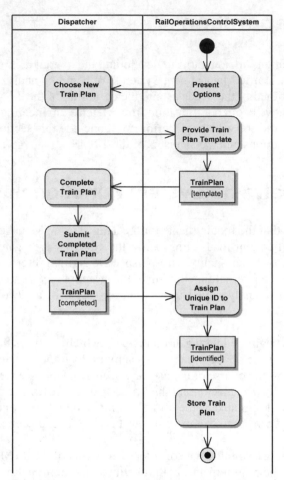

Figure 9–2 The `Route Train` Primary Scenario

We see that the `OnboardDisplay` system is the interface between the
`TrainEngineer` and the TTMS. As such, it receives the `TrainEngineer`'s
request to monitor the train systems and then requests the appropriate data from
each of the other three systems. The overview level of status information is provided to the `TrainEngineer` for review. At this point, the `TrainEngineer`
could remain at the overview level, which would end the primary scenario. In the
alternate scenario, however, the `TrainEngineer` requests a more detailed
review from the `LocomotiveAnalysisandReporting` system because it
has presented a yellow condition indicating some type of problem that requires
attention. In response, the `OnboardDisplay` system retrieves the detailed data
from the system for presentation. After reviewing this information, the
`TrainEngineer` returns to monitoring the overview level of system status
information.

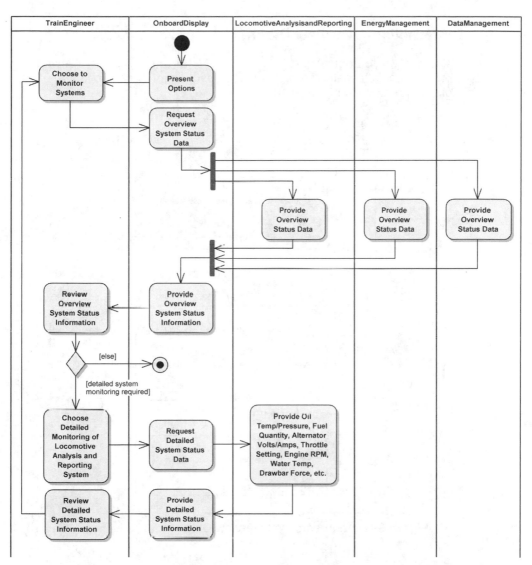

Figure 9–3 A `Monitor Train Systems` Alternate Scenario

It is a matter of project convention whether we regard the activity diagram in Figure 9–3 as representing one (alternate) or two (primary and alternate) separate scenarios. The second alternate scenario we described earlier details the extension of the `Monitor Train Systems` use case functionality with that of the `Predict Failure` use case. This scenario could be appended to Figure 9–3 to provide a more complete picture of system capability by detailing the actions whereby the `TrainEngineer` requests a failure prediction analysis (`condition:` `{request Predict Failure}`) be run on the problematic system. In fact, we show this perspective in the Interaction Overview Diagram sidebar.

Interaction Overview Diagram

Another way to depict the `Monitor Train Systems` use case—with its primary and alternate scenarios—is by using an interaction overview diagram, as shown in Figure 9–4.

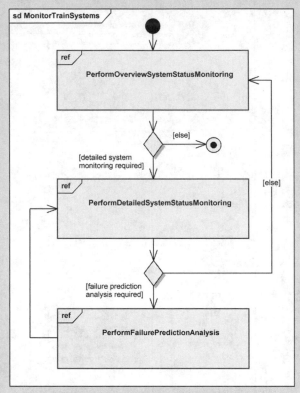

Figure 9–4 An Interaction Overview Diagram for `Monitor Train Systems`

True to its name, this diagram shows a higher-level overview of the complete `Monitor Train Systems` use case functionality. This interaction overview diagram shows a flow among interaction occurrences, indicated by the three frames annotated with `ref` in their upper-left corners. In place of the reference to interaction diagrams, we could show the actual interactions to provide the details for each of the scenarios: `Perform Overview System Status Monitoring`, `Perform Detailed System Status Monitoring`, and `Perform Failure Prediction Analysis`.

The interaction overview diagram can use any type of interaction—
sequence, communication, timing, or another interaction overview—to
show this detail. As we see here, this diagram can be used to map the flow
from one interaction to another, which can be useful if you have long, complicated interactions.

Defining the TTMS Architecture

A much more thorough analysis of the functionality required by all the use case
scenarios, including the impact of the nonfunctional requirements and constraints,
leads us to a block diagram for the Train Traffic Management System's major elements, as shown in Figure 9–5 [2]. The locomotive analysis and reporting system

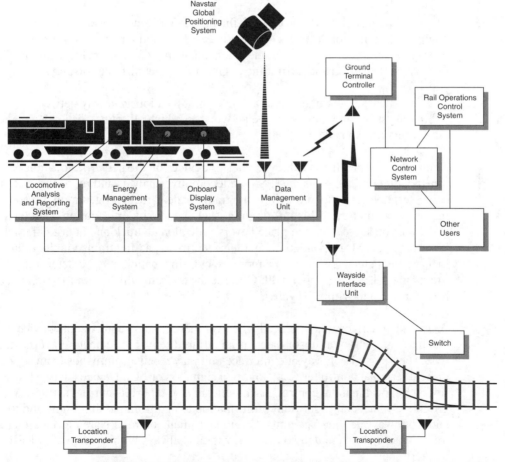

Figure 9–5 The Train Traffic Management System

includes several digital and analog sensors for monitoring locomotive conditions, including oil temperature, oil pressure, fuel quantity, alternator volts and amperes, throttle setting, engine RPM, water temperature, and drawbar force. Sensor values are presented to the train engineer via the onboard display system and to dispatchers and maintainers elsewhere on the network. Warning or alarm conditions are registered whenever certain sensor values fall outside of the normal operating range. A log of sensor values is maintained to support maintenance and fuel management.

The energy management system advises the train engineer in real time as to the most efficient throttle and brake settings. Inputs to this system include track profile and grade, speed limits, schedules, train load, and power available, from which the system can determine fuel-efficient throttle and brake settings that are consistent with the desired schedule and safety concerns. Suggested throttle and brake settings, track profile and grade, and train position and speed are made available for display on the onboard display system.

The onboard display system provides the human/machine interface for the train engineer. Information from the locomotive analysis and reporting system, the energy management system, and the data management unit are made available for display. Soft keys exist to permit the engineer to select different displays.

The data management unit serves as the communications gateway between all onboard systems and the rest of the network, to which all trains, dispatchers, and other users are connected.

Train location tracking is achieved via two devices on the network: location transponders and the Navstar GPS. The locomotive analysis and reporting system can determine the general location of a train via dead reckoning, simply by counting wheel revolutions. This information is augmented by information from location transponders, which are placed every mile along a track and at critical track junctions. These transponders relay their identity to passing trains via their data management units, from which a more exact train location may be determined. Trains may also be equipped with GPS receivers, from which train location may be determined to within 10 yards.

A wayside interface unit is placed wherever there is some controllable device (such as a switch) or a sensor (such as an infrared sensor for detecting overheated wheel bearings). Each wayside interface unit may receive commands from a local ground terminal controller (e.g., to turn a signal on or off). Devices may be overridden by local manual control. Each unit can also report its current setting. A ground terminal controller relays information to and from passing trains and to and from wayside interface units. Ground terminal controllers are placed along a track, spaced close enough so that every train is always within range of at least one terminal.

Every ground terminal controller relays its information to a common network control system. Connections between the network control system and each ground terminal controller may be made via microwave link, landlines, or fiber optics, depending on the remoteness of each ground terminal controller. The network control system monitors the health of the entire network and can automatically route information in alternate ways in the event of equipment failure.

The network control system is ultimately connected to one or more dispatch centers, which comprise the rail operations control system and other users. At the rail operations control system, dispatchers can establish train routes and track the progress of individual trains. Individual dispatchers control different territories; each dispatcher's control console may be set up to control one or more territories. Train routes include instructions for automatically switching trains from track to track, setting speed restrictions, setting out or picking up cars, and allowing or denying train clearance to a specific track section. Dispatchers may note the location of track work along train routes for display to train engineers. Trains may be stopped from the rail operations control system (manually by dispatchers or automatically) when hazardous conditions are detected (such as a runaway train, track failure, or a potential collision condition). Dispatchers may also call up any information available to individual train engineers, as well as send movement authority, wayside device settings, and plan revisions.

It should be apparent that track layouts and wayside equipment may change over time; in addition, the numbers of trains and their routes may change daily. The Train Traffic Management System must therefore be designed to permit incorporation of new sensor, network, and processor technology. Our nonfunctional requirement—to have a designed-in capability to maintain and evolve the TTMS—makes it very clear that we must design an architecture that has the flexibility to evolve over time. In addition, both of our constraints tell us that the system must rely on national standards (government and industry), while maximizing the use of COTS hardware and software.

From Systems Engineering to Hardware and Software Engineering

Up to this point in our development, we performed systems engineering, rather than hardware or software engineering activities, as we analyzed scenarios of the use cases that specify the primary functional requirements for the Train Traffic Management System. From this analysis, we were able to specify a block diagram of its major elements to define a candidate TTMS system architecture. As we continue our development, the architecture of lower-level hardware and software elements will evolve based on the concepts that our system architects likely have in mind. Eventually we decide what portions of the system functionality will be fulfilled by hardware, software, or manual operations. At that point, development becomes even more of a collaborative effort among the systems, hardware, software, and operational engineering teams.

The block diagram in Figure 9–5 presents a candidate architecture developed using an object-oriented approach, the clear consequence of this being the component nature of the architecture. We see the elements of the TTMS exhibiting cohesion and loose coupling while performing major functions in the system. As we further our analysis of the system's functionality, we may continue to use activity diagrams (especially when working with domain experts), which provide a clear perspective of the work being done by each of the system's elements as they collaborate in the system scenarios. More specific detail of the interactions is required as we proceed through the lower levels of the architectural hierarchy; consequently, we will more likely use sequence diagrams, class diagrams, and prototypes to examine the required system behavior.

In Figure 9–6, we provide a sequence diagram that captures one simple scenario for the automated processing of a daily train order and provides more detail into the inner workings of the Train Traffic Management System than does the activity diagram presented earlier in Figure 9–2. We assume this scenario begins essentially at the conclusion of Figure 9–2, where a new train plan has been created. Here we see just the major events that transpire and the interactions of the system elements. Later in our development, we must begin to document element details such as attribute definitions, operation signatures, and association specifications.

After completing our systems engineering analysis of the TTMS functionality (through its architectural levels), we must allocate the system requirements to hardware, software, and even operational elements. We say "even operational"

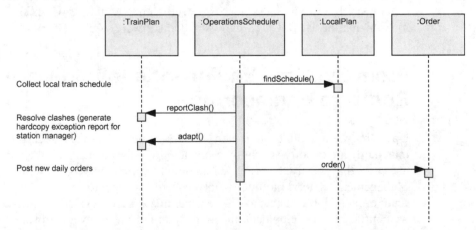

Figure 9–6 A Scenario for Processing Daily Train Orders

because all too often we think that everything can and should be automated. Certainly, that is a typical goal, but we must understand that some functionality, especially in safety-critical areas, should employ (and must by law in some cases) a human-in-the-loop design. In some cases, the allocation of requirements to hardware or software is fairly obvious; for example, software is the right implementation vehicle for describing train schedules. For both the onboard display system and the displays in the rail operations control centers, one might use off-the-shelf terminals or workstations. These allocation decisions are driven by many criteria, including reuse issues, commercially available items, and the experience and preferences of the system architects. When choosing commercially available items, such as the many sensors in the system, we have allocated those element design decisions to the engineers at the vendor companies. In general, though, we will lean toward software where we need the most flexibility and will choose hardware where performance is vital.

For the purposes of our problem, we assume that an initial hardware architecture has been chosen by the system architects. This choice need not be considered irreversible, but at least it gives us a starting point in terms of where to allocate software requirements. As we proceed with analysis and then design, we need the freedom to trade off hardware and software: We might later decide that additional hardware is needed to satisfy some requirement or that certain functions can be performed better through software than hardware.

Figure 9–7 illustrates the target deployment hardware for the Train Traffic Management System, using the notation for deployment diagrams. This hardware architecture parallels the block diagram of the system shown earlier in Figure 9–5. Specifically, there is one computer on each train, encompassing the locomotive analysis and reporting system, the energy management system, the onboard display system, and the data management unit. Each location transponder is connected to a transmitter, through which messages may be sent to passing trains; no computer is associated with a location transponder. On the other hand, each collection of wayside devices (each of which encompasses a wayside interface unit and its switches) is controlled by a wayside computer that may communicate via its transmitter and receiver with a passing train or a ground terminal controller. Communications between transmitters and receivers may be made via microwave link, landlines, or fiber optics, as discussed earlier. Each ground terminal controller ultimately connects to a local area network, one for each dispatch center (encompassing the rail operations control system). Because of the need for uninterrupted service, we have chosen to place two computers at each dispatch center: a primary computer and a backup computer that we expect will be brought online whenever the primary computer fails. During idle periods, the backup computer can be used to service the computational needs of other, lower-priority users.

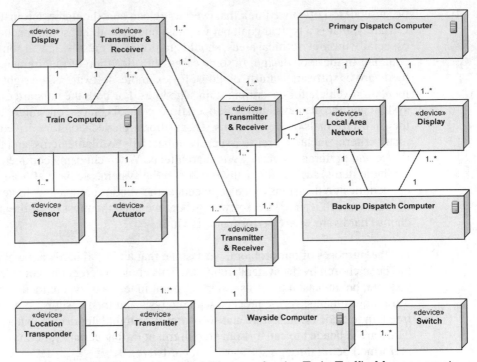

Figure 9–7 The Deployment Diagram for the Train Traffic Management System

When operational, the Train Traffic Management System may involve hundreds of computers, including one for each train, one for each wayside interface unit, and two at each dispatch center. The deployment diagram shows the presence of only a few of these computers since the configurations of similar computers are completely redundant.

The key to maintaining sanity during the development of any complex project is to engineer sound and explicit interfaces among the key elements of the system. This is particularly important when defining hardware and software interfaces. At the start, interfaces can be loosely defined, but they must quickly be formalized so that different parts of the system can be developed, tested, and released in parallel. Well-defined interfaces also make it far easier to make hardware/software trade-offs as opportunities arise, without disrupting already completed parts of the system. Furthermore, we cannot expect all of the developers in a large, possibly globally distributed, development organization to have a complete view and understanding of all parts of the system. We must therefore leave the specification of these key abstractions and mechanisms to our best architects.

Key Abstractions and Mechanisms

A study of the requirements for the Train Traffic Management System suggests that we really have four different subproblems to solve:

1. Networking
2. Database
3. Human/machine interface
4. Real-time analog and digital device control

How did we come to identify these problems as those involving the greatest development risk?

The thread that ties this system together is a distributed communications network. Messages pass by radio from transponders to trains, between trains and ground terminal controllers, between trains and wayside interface units, and between ground terminal controllers and wayside interface units. Messages must also pass between dispatch centers and individual ground terminal controllers. The safe operation of this entire system depends on the timely and reliable transmission and reception of messages.

Additionally, this system must keep track of the current locations and planned routes of many different trains simultaneously. We must keep this information current and self-consistent, even in the presence of concurrent updates and queries from around the network. This is basically a distributed database problem.

The engineering of the human/machine interfaces poses a different set of problems. Specifically, the users of this system are principally train engineers and dispatchers, none of whom are necessarily skilled in using computers. The user interface of an operating system such as UNIX or Windows might be acceptable to a professional software engineer, but it is often regarded as user-hostile by end users of applications such as the Train Traffic Management System. All forms of user interaction must therefore be carefully engineered to suit this domain-specific group of users.

Lastly, the Train Traffic Management System must interact with a variety of sensors and actuators. No matter what the device, the problems of sensing and controlling the environment are similar and so should be dealt with in a consistent manner by the system.

Each of these four subproblems involves largely independent issues. Our system architects need to identify the key abstractions and mechanisms involved in each, so that we can assign experts in each domain to tackle their particular subproblem in parallel with the others. Note that this is not a problem of analysis or design:

Our analysis of each problem will impact our architecture, and our designs will uncover new aspects of the problem that require further analysis. Development is thus unavoidably iterative and incremental.

If we do a brief domain analysis across these four subproblem areas, we find that there are three common high-level key abstractions:

1. Trains: including locomotives and cars
2. Tracks: encompassing profile, grade, and wayside devices
3. Plans: including schedules, orders, clearances, authority, and crew assignments

Every train has a current location on the tracks, and each train has exactly one active plan. Similarly, the number of trains at each point on the tracks may be zero or one; for each plan, there is exactly one train, involving many points on the tracks.

Continuing, we may devise a key mechanism for each of the four nearly independent subproblems:

1. Message passing
2. Train schedule planning
3. Displaying information
4. Sensor data acquisition

These four mechanisms form the soul of our system. They represent approaches to what we have identified as the areas of highest development risk. It is therefore essential that we deploy our best system architects here to experiment with alternative approaches and eventually settle on a framework from which more junior developers may compose the rest of the system.

9.3 Construction

Architectural design involves the establishment of the central class structure of the system, plus a specification of the common collaborations that animate these classes. Focusing on these mechanisms early directly attacks the elements of highest risk in the system and concretely captures the vision of the system's architects. Ultimately, the products of this phase serve as the framework of classes and collaborations on which the other functional elements of the final system build.

In this section, we start by examining the semantics of each of this system's four key mechanisms: message passing, train schedule planning, displaying information, and sensor data acquisition. This leads into a discussion of release management, which supports our iterative and incremental development process. We conclude this section by analyzing how developing a system architecture supports the specification of the TTMS subsystems.

Message Passing

By *message*, we do not mean to imply method invocation, as in an object-oriented programming language; rather, we are referring to a concept in the vocabulary of the problem domain, at a much higher level of abstraction. For example, typical messages in the Train Traffic Management System include signals to activate wayside devices, indications of trains passing specific locations, and orders from dispatchers to train engineers. In general, these kinds of messages are passed at two different levels within the TTMS:

1. Between computers and devices
2. Among computers

Our interest is in the second level of message passing. Because our problem involves a geographically distributed communications network, we must consider issues such as noise, equipment failure, and security.

We can make a first cut at identifying these messages by examining each pair of communicating computers, as shown in our previous deployment diagram (refer back to Figure 9–7). For each pair, we must ask three questions.

1. What information does each computer manage?
2. What information should be passed from one computer to the other?
3. At what level of abstraction should this information be?

There is no determinate solution for these questions. Rather, we must use an iterative approach until we are satisfied that the right messages have been defined and that there are no communications bottlenecks in the system (perhaps because of too many messages over one path, or messages being too large or too small).

It is absolutely critical at this level of design to focus on the substance, not the form, of these messages. Too often, we have seen system architects start off by selecting a bit-level representation for messages. The real problem with prematurely choosing such a low-level representation is that it is guaranteed to change and thus disrupt every client that depends on a particular representation. Furthermore, at this point in the design process, we cannot know enough about how these messages will be used to make intelligent decisions about time- and space-efficient representations.

By focusing on the substance of these messages, we mean to urge a focus on the outside view of each class of messages. In other words, we must decide on the roles and responsibilities of each message and what operations we can meaningfully perform on each message.

The class diagram in Figure 9–8 captures our design decisions regarding some of the most important messages in the Train Traffic Management System. Note that all messages are ultimately instances of a generalized abstract class named `Message`, which encompasses the behavior common to all messages. Three lower-level classes represent the major categories of messages, namely, `Train StatusMessage`, `TrainPlanMessage`, and `WaysideDeviceMessage`. Each of these classes is further specialized. Indeed, our final design might include dozens of such specialized classes, at which time the existence of these intermediate classes becomes even more important; without them, we would end up with many unrelated—and therefore difficult to maintain—components representing each distinct specialized class. As our design unfolds, we are likely to discover other important groupings of messages and so invent other intermediate classes. Fortunately, reorganizing our class hierarchy in this manner tends to have minimal semantic impact on the clients that ultimately use the base classes.

As part of the architectural design, we would be wise to stabilize the interface of the key message classes early. We might start with a domain analysis of the more interesting base classes in this hierarchy, in order to formulate the roles and responsibilities of all such classes.

Once we have designed the interface of the more important messages, we can write programs that build on these classes to simulate the creation and reception of streams of messages. We can use these programs as a temporary scaffolding to test different parts of the system during development and before the pieces with which they interface are completed.

The class diagram in Figure 9–8 is unquestionably incomplete. In practice, we find that we can identify the most important messages first and let all others evolve as we uncover the less common forms of communication. Using an object-oriented architecture allows us to add these messages incrementally without disrupting the existing design of the system because such changes are generally upwardly compatible.

Once we are satisfied with this class structure, we can begin to design the message-passing mechanism itself. Here we have two competing goals for the mechanism: It must provide for the reliable delivery of messages and yet do so at a high enough level of abstraction so that clients need not worry about how message delivery takes place. Such a message-passing mechanism allows its clients to make simplifying assumptions about how messages are sent and received.

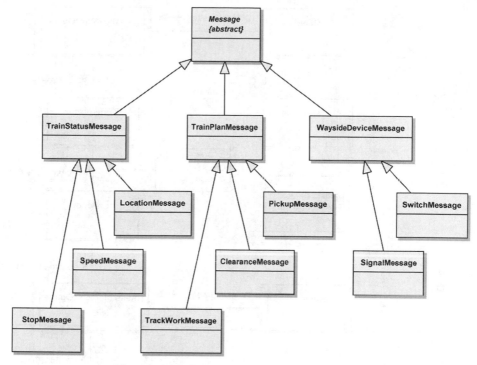

Figure 9–8 The Message Class Diagram

Figure 9–9 provides a scenario that captures our design of the message-passing mechanism. As this diagram indicates, to send a message, a client first creates a new message m and then broadcasts it to its node's message manager, whose responsibility is to queue the message for eventual transmission. Notice that our design uses four objects that are active (have their own thread of control), as indicated by the extra vertical lines within the object notation: Client, messageMgr :Queue, messageMgr' :Queue, and Receiver. Notice also that the message manager receives the message to be broadcast as a parameter and then uses the services of a Transporter object to reduce the message to its canonical form and broadcast it across the network.

As this diagram suggests, we choose to make this an asynchronous operation— indicated by the open-headed arrow—because we don't want to make the client wait for the message to be sent across a radio link, which requires time for encoding, decoding, and perhaps retransmission because of noise. Eventually, some Listener object on the other side of the network receives this message and presents it in a canonical form to its node's message manager, which in turn creates a parallel message and queues it. A receiver can block at the head of its message

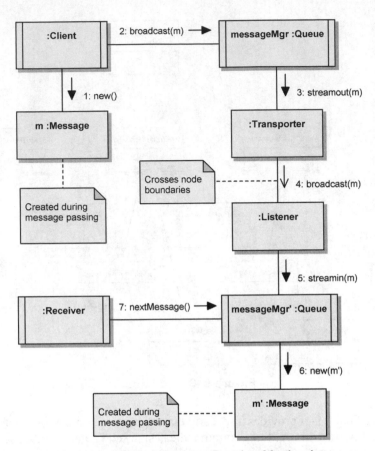

Figure 9–9 The Message-Passing Mechanism

manager's queue, waiting for the next message to arrive, which is delivered as a parameter to the operation `nextMessage()`, a synchronous operation.

Our design of the message manager places it at the application layer in the ISO Open Systems Interconnection (OSI) model for networks [3]. This allows all message-sending clients and message-receiving clients to operate at the highest level of abstraction, namely, in terms of application-specific messages.

We expect the final implementation of this mechanism to be a bit more complex. For example, we might want to add behaviors for encryption and decryption and introduce codes to detect and correct errors, so as to ensure reliable communication in the presence of noise or equipment failures.

Train Schedule Planning

As we noted earlier, the concept of a train plan is central to the operation of the Train Traffic Management System. Each train has exactly one active plan, and each plan is assigned to exactly one train and may involve many different orders and locations on the track.

Our first step is to decide exactly what parts constitute a train plan. To do so, we need to consider all the potential clients of a plan and how we expect each of them to use that plan. For example, some clients might be allowed to create plans, others might be allowed to modify plans, and still others might be allowed only to read plans. In this sense, a train plan acts as a repository for all the pertinent information associated with the route of one particular train and the actions that take place along the way, such as picking up or setting out cars.

Figure 9–10 captures our strategic decisions regarding the structure of the TrainPlan class. We use a class diagram to show the parts that compose a train plan (much as a traditional entity-relationship diagram would do). Thus, we see that each train plan has exactly one crew and may have many general orders and

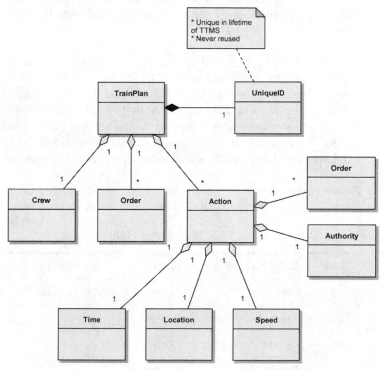

Figure 9–10 The TrainPlan Class Diagram

many actions. We expect these actions to be time ordered, with each action composed of information such as time, a location, speed, authority, and orders. For example, a specific train plan might consist of the actions shown in Table 9–1.

As the diagram in Figure 9–10 indicates, the `TrainPlan` class has a `UniqueId`, whose purpose is to provide a number for uniquely identifying each `TrainPlan` instance. Because of the complexity of the information here, classes in this diagram that might otherwise be considered an attribute of a class are really stand-alone classes. For example, the `UniqueID` class is not merely an identification number; it contains various attributes and operations necessary to meet stringent national and international regulations. Another example is that crews have restrictions placed on their work—they may work only at certain locations or must adhere to speed restrictions in certain locations at particular times.

As we did for the `Message` class and its subclasses, we can design the most important elements of a train plan early in the development process; its details will evolve over time, as we actually apply plans to various kinds of clients.

The fact that we may have a plethora of active and inactive train plans at any one time confronts us with the database problem we spoke of earlier. The class diagram in Figure 9–10 can serve as an outline for the logical schema of this database. The next question we might therefore ask is simply, where are train plans kept?

In a more perfect world, with no communication noise or delays and infinite computing resources, our solution would be to place all train plans in a single, centralized database. This approach would yield exactly one instance of each train plan. However, the real world is much more perverse, so this solution is not practical. We must expect communication delays, and we don't have unlimited processor cycles. Thus, having to access a plan located in the dispatch center from a train would not at all satisfy our real-time and near real-time requirements.

However, we can create the illusion of a single, centralized database in our software. Basically, our solution is to have a database of train plans located on the

Table 9–1 Actions a Train Plan Might Contain

Time	Location	Speed	Authority	Orders
0800	Pueblo	As posted	See yardmaster	Depart yard
1100	Colorado Springs	40 mph		Set out 30 cars
1300	Denver	45 mph		Set out 20 cars
1600	Pueblo	As posted		Return to yard

computers at the dispatch center, with copies of individual plans distributed as needed at sites around the network. For efficiency, then, each train computer could retain a copy of its current plan. Thus, onboard software could query this plan with negligible delay. If the plan changed, either as a result of dispatcher action or (less likely) by the decision of the train engineer, our software would have to ensure that all copies of that plan were updated in a timely fashion.

The way this scenario plays out is a function of our train schedule planning mechanism, shown in Figure 9–11. The primary version of each train plan resides in a centralized database at a dispatch center, with zero or more mirror-image copies scattered about the network. Whenever some client requests a copy of a particular train plan (via the operation get(), invoked with a value of UniqueId as an argument), the primary version is cloned and delivered to the client as a parameter, and the network location of the copy is recorded in the database. Now, suppose that a client on a train needed to make a change to a particular plan, perhaps as a result of some action by the train engineer. Ultimately, this client would invoke operations on its copy of the train plan and so modify its state. These operations would also send messages to the centralized database, to modify the state of the primary version of the plan in the same way. Since we record the location in the network of each copy of a train plan, we can also broadcast messages to the centralized repository that force a corresponding update to the state of all remaining copies. To ensure that changes are made consistently across the network, we

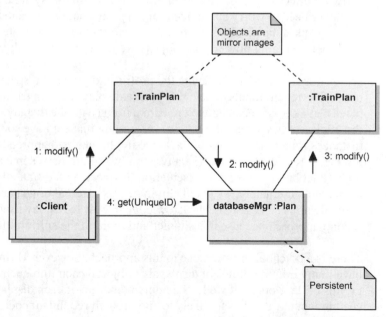

Figure 9–11 Train Schedule Planning

could employ a record-locking mechanism, so that changes would not be committed until all copies and the primary version were updated.

This mechanism applies equally well if some client at the dispatch center initiates the change, perhaps as a result of some dispatcher action. First, the primary version of the plan would be updated, and then changes to all copies would be broadcast throughout the network, using the same mechanism. In either case, how exactly do we broadcast these changes? The answer is that we use the message-passing mechanism devised earlier. Specifically, we would need to add to our design some new train plan messages and then build our train plan mechanism on this lower-level message-passing mechanism.

Using commercial, off-the-shelf database management systems on the dispatch computers allows us to address any requirements for database backup, recovery, audit trails, and security.

Displaying Information

Using off-the-shelf technology for our database needs helps us to focus on the domain-specific parts of our problem. We can achieve similar leverage for our display needs by using standard graphics facilities. Using off-the-shelf graphics software effectively raises the level of abstraction in our system, so that developers never need to worry about manipulating the visual representation of displayable objects at the pixel level. Still, it is important to encapsulate our design decisions regarding how various objects are represented visually.

For example, consider displaying the profile and grade of a specific section of track. Our requirements dictate that such a display may appear in two different places: at a dispatch center and onboard a train (with the display focusing only on the track that lies ahead of the train). Assuming that we have some class whose instances represent sections of track, we might take two approaches to representing the state of such objects visually. First, we might have some display manager object that builds a visual representation by querying the state of the object to be displayed. Alternately, we could eliminate this external object and have each displayable object encapsulate the knowledge of how to display itself. We prefer this second approach because it is simpler and more in the spirit of the object model.

There is a potential disadvantage to this approach, however. Ultimately, we might have many different kinds of displayable objects, each implemented by different groups of developers. If we let the implementation of each displayable object proceed independently, we are likely to end up with redundant code, different implementation styles, and a generally unmaintainable mess. A far better solution is to do a domain analysis of all the kinds of displayable objects, determine what visual elements they have in common, and devise an intermediate set of class util-

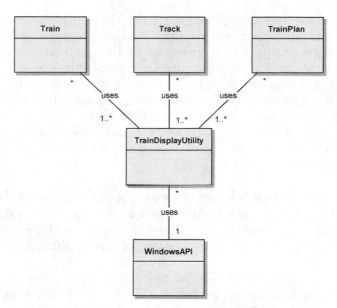

Figure 9–12 Class Utilities for Displaying

ities that provide display routines for these common picture elements. These class utilities in turn can build on lower-level, off-the-shelf graphics packages.

Figure 9–12 illustrates this design, showing that the implementation of all displayable objects shares common class utilities. These utilities in turn build on lower-level Windows interfaces, which are hidden from all of the higher-level classes. Pragmatically, interfaces such as the Windows API cannot easily be expressed in a single class. Therefore, our diagram is a bit of a simplification: It is more likely that our implementation will require a set of peer class utilities for the Windows API as well as for the train display utilities.

The principal advantage of this approach is that it limits the impact of any lower-level changes resulting from hardware/software trade-offs. For example, if we find that we need to replace our display hardware with more or less powerful devices, we need only reimplement the routines in the `TrainDisplayUtility` class. Without this collection of routines, low-level changes would require us to modify the implementation of every displayable object.

Sensor Data Acquisition

As our requirements suggest, the Train Traffic Management System includes many different kinds of sensors. For example, sensors on each train monitor the oil temperature, fuel quantity, throttle setting, water temperature, drawbar load, and so on. Similarly, active sensors in some of the wayside devices report among other things the current positions of switches and signals. The kinds of values returned by the various sensors are all different, but the processing of different sensor data is all very much the same. Furthermore, most sensors must be sampled periodically. If a value is within a certain range, nothing special happens other than notifying some client of the new value. If this value exceeds certain preset limits, a different client might be warned. Finally, if this value goes far beyond its limits, we might need to sound some sort of alarm and notify yet another client to take drastic action (e.g., when locomotive oil pressure drops to dangerous levels).

Replicating this behavior for every kind of sensor not only is tedious and error-prone but also usually results in redundant code. Unless we exploit this commonality, different developers will end up inventing multiple solutions to the same problem, leading to the proliferation of slightly different sensor mechanisms and, in turn, a system that is more difficult to maintain. It is highly desirable, therefore, to do a domain analysis of all periodic, nondiscrete sensors, so that we might invent a common sensor mechanism for all kinds of sensors. We might use an architecture that encompasses a hierarchy of sensor classes and a frame-based mechanism that periodically acquires data from these sensors.

Release Management

Since we are using an incremental development approach, we will investigate the employment of release management techniques and further analyze the system's architecture and the specification of its subsystems.

We start the incremental development process by first selecting a small number of interesting scenarios, taking a vertical slice through our architecture, and then implementing enough of the system to produce an executable product that at least simulates the execution of these scenarios.

For example, we might select just the primary scenarios of three use cases: `Route Train`, `Monitor Train Systems`, and `Monitor Traffic`. Together, the implementation of these three scenarios requires us to touch almost every critical architectural interface, thereby forcing us to validate our strategic assumptions. Once we successfully pass this milestone, we might then generate a stream of new releases, according to the following sequence.

1. Create a train plan based on an existing one; modify a train plan.
2. Request detailed monitoring of a system with a yellow condition; request a failure prediction analysis; request maintainer review of a failure prediction analysis.

3. Manually avoid a collision; request automated assistance in avoiding a colli-
    sion; track train traffic using either TTMS resources or Navstar GPS.

For a 12- to 18-month development cycle, this probably means generating a reasonably stable release every 3 months or so, each building on the functionality of
the other. When we are done, we will have covered every scenario in the system.

The key to success in this strategy is risk management, whereby for each release
we identify the highest development risks and attack them directly. For control
system applications such as this one, this means introducing testing of positive
control early (so that we identify any system control holes early enough that we
can do something about them). As our sequence of releases suggests, this also
means broadly selecting scenarios for each release from across the functional
elements of the system, so that we are not blindsided by unforeseen gaps in our
analysis.

System Architecture

The software design for very large systems must often commence before the target hardware is completed. Software design frequently takes far longer than hardware design, and in any case, trade-offs must be made against each along the way.
This implies that hardware dependencies in the software must be isolated to the
greatest extent possible, so that software design can proceed in the absence of a
stable target environment. It also implies that the software must be designed with
the idea of replaceable subsystems in mind. In a command and control system
such as the Train Traffic Management System, we might wish to take advantage
of new hardware technology that has matured during the development of the system's software.

We must also have an early and intelligent physical decomposition of the system's
software, so that subcontractors working on different parts of the system can work
in parallel. Often many nontechnical reasons drive the physical decomposition of
a large system. Perhaps the most important of these concerns the assignment of
work to independent teams of developers. Subcontractor relationships are usually
established early in the life of a complex system, often before there is enough
information to make sound technical decisions regarding proper subsystem
decomposition.

How do we select a suitable subsystem decomposition? The highest-level objects
are often clustered around functional lines. Again, this is not orthogonal to the
object model because by the term *functional*, we do not mean algorithmic abstractions, embodying simple input/output mappings. We are speaking of scenarios
that represent outwardly visible and testable behaviors, resulting from the cooperative action of logical collections of objects. Thus, the highest-level abstractions

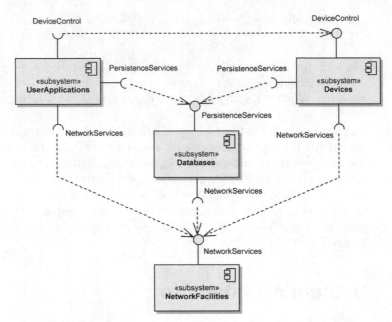

Figure 9–13 The Top-Level Component Diagram for the Train Traffic Management System

and mechanisms that we first identify are good candidates around which to organize our subsystems. We may assert the existence of such subsystems first and then evolve their interfaces over time.

The component diagram shown in Figure 9–13 represents our design decisions regarding the top-level system architecture of the Train Traffic Management System. Here we see a layered architecture that encompasses the functions of the four subproblems we identified earlier, namely, networking, database, the human/machine interface, and real-time device control.

Subsystem Specification

If we focus on the outside view of any of these subsystems, we find that it has all the characteristics of an object. It has a unique, albeit static, identity; it embodies a significant amount of state; and it exhibits very complex behavior. Subsystems serve as the repositories of other subsystems and eventually classes; thus, they are best characterized by the resources they export through their provided interfaces, such as the NetworkServices provided by the NetworkFacilities subsystem shown in Figure 9–13.

The component diagram in Figure 9–13 is merely a starting point for the specification of the TTMS subsystem architecture. These top-level subsystems must be further decomposed through multiple architectural levels of nested subsystems. Looking at the `NetworkFacilities` subsystem, we decompose it into two other subsystems, a private `RadioCommunication` subsystem and a public `Messages` subsystem. The private subsystem hides the details of software control of the physical radio devices, while the public subsystem provides the functionality of the message-passing mechanism we designed earlier.

The subsystem named `Databases` builds on the resources of the subsystem `NetworkFacilities` and implements the train plan mechanism we created earlier. We choose to further decompose this subsystem into two public subsystems, representing the major database elements in the system. We name these nested subsystems `TrainPlanDatabase` and `TrackDatabase`, respectively. We also expect to have one private subsystem, `DatabaseManager`, whose purpose is to provide all the services common to the two domain-specific databases.

In the `Devices` subsystem, we choose to group the software related to all wayside devices into one subsystem and the software associated with all onboard locomotive actuators and sensors into another. These two subsystems are available to clients of the `Devices` subsystem, and both are built on the resources of the `TrainPlanDatabase` and `Messages` subsystems. Thus, we have designed the `Devices` subsystem to implement the sensor mechanism we described earlier.

Finally, we choose to decompose the top level `UserApplications` subsystem into several smaller ones, including the subsystems `EngineerApplications` and `DispatcherApplications`, to reflect the different roles of the two main users of the Train Traffic Management System. The subsystem `Engineer Applications` includes resources that provide all the train-engineer/machine interaction specified in the requirements, including the functionality of the locomotive analysis and reporting system and the energy management system. We include the subsystem `DispatcherApplications` to encompass the software that provides the functionality of all dispatcher/machine interactions. Both `EngineerApplications` and `DispatcherApplications` share common private resources, as provided from the subsystem `Displays`, which embodies the display mechanism we described earlier.

This design leaves us with four top-level subsystems, encompassing several smaller ones, to which we have allocated all of the key abstractions and mechanisms we invented earlier. These subsystems are allocated to development teams that will design and implement them, maintaining adherence to the defined interfaces through which each subsystem will collaborate with other subsystems at the same level of abstraction.

This approach to decomposing a large and complex problem affords us different views of the system while it is being developed. A system release is thus composed of compatible versions of each subsystem, and we may have many such releases: one for each developer, one for our quality assurance team, and perhaps one for early customer use. Individual developers can create their own stable releases into which they integrate new versions of the software for which they are responsible, before releasing it to the rest of the team.

The key to making this work is the careful engineering of subsystem interfaces. Once engineered, these interfaces must be rigorously guarded. How do we determine the outside view of each subsystem? We do so by looking at each subsystem as an object. Thus, we ask the same questions we ask of much more primitive objects: What state does this object embody, what operations can clients meaningfully perform on it, and what operations does it require of other objects?

For example, consider the subsystem `TrainPlanDatabase`. It builds on three other subsystems (`Messages`, `TrainDatabase`, and `TrackDatabase`) and has several important clients, namely, the four subsystems, `WaysideDevices`, `LocomotiveDevices`, `EngineerApplications`, and `Dispatcher Applications`. The `TrainPlanDatabase` embodies a relatively straightforward state, specifically, the state of all train plans. Of course, the twist is that this subsystem must support the behavior of the distributed train plan mechanisms. Thus, from the outside, clients see a monolithic database, but from the inside, we know that this database is really distributed and must therefore be constructed on top of the message-passing mechanism found in the subsystem `Messages`.

What services does the `TrainPlanDatabase` provide? All the usual database operations seem to apply: adding records, deleting records, modifying records, and querying records. We would eventually capture all of these design decisions that make up this subsystem in the form of classes that provide the declarations of all these operations.

At this stage in the design, we would continue the design process for each subsystem. Again, we expect that these interfaces will not be exactly right at first; we must allow them to evolve over time. Happily, as for smaller objects, our experience suggests that most of the changes we will need to make to these interfaces will be upwardly compatible, assuming that we did a good job up front in characterizing the behavior of each subsystem in an object-oriented manner.

9.4 Post-Transition

A safe and useful control system is a work in progress. This is not to say that we never get to the point where we have a stable system—in fact, we must with every delivery. Rather, the reality is that for systems that are central to a business such as rail transportation, the hardware and software must adapt as the rules of the business change; otherwise, our system becomes a liability rather than a competitive asset. Though the dominant risk in changes to a system like the Train Traffic Management System is technical, there are political and social risks as well. By having a resilient object-oriented architecture, the development organization at least offers the company many degrees of freedom in being able to adapt nimbly to the changing regulatory environment and marketplace.

For the Train Traffic Management System, we can envision a significant addition to our requirements, namely, payroll processing. Specifically, suppose that our analysis shows that train company payroll is currently being supported by a piece of hardware that is no longer being manufactured and that we are at great risk of losing our payroll processing capability because a single serious hardware failure would put our accounting system out of action forever. For this reason, we might choose to integrate payroll processing with the Train Traffic Management System. At first, it is not difficult to conceive how these two seemingly unrelated problems could coexist; we could simply view them as separate applications, with payroll processing running as a background activity.

Further examination shows that there is actually tremendous value to be gained from integrating payroll processing. You may recall from our earlier discussion that, among other things, train plans contain information about crew assignments. Thus, it is possible for us to track actual versus planned crew assignments, and from this we can calculate hours worked, amount of overtime, and so on. By getting this information directly, our payroll calculations will be more precise and certainly timelier.

What does adding this functionality do to our existing design? Very little. Our approach would be to add one more subsystem, representing the functionality of payroll processing, inside the `UserApplications` subsystem. At this location in the architecture, such a subsystem would have visibility to all the important mechanisms on which it could build. This is indeed quite common in well-structured object-oriented systems: A significant addition in the requirements for the system can be dealt with fairly easily by building new applications on existing mechanisms.

An even more significant change would be to inject expert system technology into our system by building a dispatcher's assistant that could provide advice about appropriate traffic routing and emergency responses. What would be the impact to the system's architecture?

Again, there would be very little impact. Our solution would be to add a new subsystem between the subsystems `TrainPlanDatabase` and `Dispatcher Applications` because the knowledge base embodied by this expert system parallels the contents of the `TrainPlanDatabase`; furthermore, the subsystem `DispatcherApplications` is the sole client of this expert system. We would need to invent some new mechanisms to establish the manner in which advice is presented to the ultimate user. For example, we might use a blackboard architecture.

One fascinating characteristic of architectures is that—if well engineered—they tend to reach a sort of critical mass of functionality and adaptability. In other words, if we have selected the right element functionality and structure, we will find that users soon discover means to evolve the system functionality in ways its designers never imagined or expected. As we discover patterns in the ways that clients use our system, it makes sense to codify these patterns by formally making them a part of the architecture. A sign of a well-designed architecture is that we can introduce these new patterns by reusing existing mechanisms and thus preserving its design integrity.

Chapter 10

Artificial Intelligence: Cryptanalysis

Sentient creatures exhibit a vastly complex set of behaviors that spring from the mind through mechanisms that we only poorly understand. For example, think about how you solve the problem of planning a route through a city to run a set of errands. Consider also how, when walking through a dimly lit room, you are able to recognize the boundaries of objects and avoid stumbling. Furthermore, think about how you can focus on one conversation at a party while dozens of people are talking simultaneously. None of these kinds of problems lends itself to a straightforward algorithmic solution. Optimal route planning is known to be an NP-complete problem. Navigating through dark terrain involves deriving understanding from visual input that is (very literally) fuzzy and incomplete. Identifying a single speaker from dozens of sources requires that the listener distinguish meaningful data from noise and then filter out all unwanted conversations from the remaining cacophony.

Researchers in the field of artificial intelligence have pursued these and similar problems to improve our understanding of human cognitive processes. Activity in this field often involves the construction of intelligent systems that mimic certain aspects of human behavior. Erman, Lark, and Hayes-Roth point out that:

intelligent systems differ from conventional systems by a number of attributes, not all of which are always present:

- They pursue goals which vary over time.
- They incorporate, use, and maintain knowledge.
- They exploit diverse, ad hoc subsystems embodying a variety of selected methods.

- They interact intelligently with users and other systems.
- They allocate their own resources and attention. [1]

Any one of these properties is sufficiently demanding to make the crafting of intelligent systems a very difficult task. When we consider that intelligent systems are being developed for a variety of domains that affect both life and property, such as for medical diagnosis or aircraft routing, the task becomes even more demanding because we must design these systems so that they are never actively dangerous: Artificial intelligences rarely embody any kind of commonsense knowledge.

Although the field has at times been oversold by an overly enthusiastic press, the study of artificial intelligence has given us some very sound and practical ideas, among which we count approaches to knowledge representation and the evolution of common problem-solving architectures for intelligent systems, including rule-based expert systems and the blackboard model [2]. In this chapter, we turn to the design of an intelligent system that solves cryptograms using a blackboard framework in a manner that parallels the way a human would solve the same problem. As we will see, the use of object-oriented development is very well suited to this domain.

10.1 Inception

Our problem is one of cryptanalysis, the process of transforming ciphertext back to plaintext. In its most general form, deciphering cryptograms is an intractable problem that defies even the most sophisticated techniques. Happily, our problem is relatively simple because we limit ourselves to single substitution ciphers.

Cryptanalysis Requirements

Cryptography "embraces methods for rendering data unintelligible to unauthorized parties" [3]. Using cryptographic algorithms, messages (plaintext) may be transformed into cryptograms (ciphertext) and back again.

One of the most basic kinds of cryptographic algorithms, employed since the time of the Romans, is called a substitution cipher. With this cipher, every letter of the plaintext alphabet is mapped to a different letter. For example, we might shift every letter to its successor: A becomes B, B becomes C, Z wraps around to become A, and so on. Thus, the plaintext

```
CLOS is an object-oriented programming language
```

may be enciphered to the cryptogram

```
DMPT jt bo pckfdu-psjfoufe qsphsbnnjoh mbohvbhf
```

Most often, the substitution of letters is jumbled. For example, A becomes G, B becomes J, and so on. As an example, consider the following cryptogram:

```
PDG TBCER CQ TCK AL S NGELCH QZBBR SBAJG
```

Hint: The letter C represents the plaintext letter O.

It is a vastly simplifying assumption to know that only a substitution cipher was employed to encode a plaintext message; nevertheless, deciphering the resulting cryptogram is not an algorithmically trivial task. Deciphering sometimes requires trial and error, wherein we make assumptions about a particular substitution and then evaluate their implications. For example, we may start with the one- and two-letter words in the cryptogram and hypothesize that they stand for common words such as I and a, or it, in, is, of, or, and on. By substituting the other occurrences of these ciphered letters, we may find hints for deciphering other words. For instance, if there is a three-letter word that starts with o, the word might reasonably be one, our, or off.

We can also use our knowledge of spelling and grammar to attack a substitution cipher. For example, an occurrence of double letters is not likely to represent the sequence qq. Similarly, we might try to expand a word ending with the letter g to the suffix ing. At a higher level of abstraction, we might assume that the sequence of words it is is more likely to occur than the sequence if is. Also, we might assume that the structure of a sentence typically includes a noun and a verb. Thus, if our analysis has identified a verb but no actor or agent, we might start a search for adjectives and nouns.

Sometimes we may have to backtrack. For example, we might have assumed that a certain two-letter word was or, but if the substitution for the letter r causes contradictions or blind alleys in other words, we might have to try the word of or on instead and consequently undo other assumptions we had based on this earlier substitution.

This leads us to the overarching requirement of our problem: to devise a system that, given a cryptogram, transforms it back to its original plaintext, assuming that only a simple substitution cipher was employed.

Defining the Boundaries of the Problem

As part of our analysis, let's walk through a scenario of solving a simple crypto-gram. Spend the next few minutes solving the following problem, and as you proceed, record how you did it (no fair reading ahead!):

```
Q AZWS DSSC KAS DXZNN DASNN
```

As a hint, we note that the letter W represents the plaintext V.

Trying an exhaustive search is pretty much senseless. Assuming that the plaintext alphabet encompasses only the 26 uppercase English characters, there are 26! (approximately 4.03×10^{26}) possible combinations. Thus, we must try something other than a brute force attack. An alternate technique is to make an assumption based on our knowledge of sentence, word, and letter structure and then follow this assumption to its natural conclusions. Once we can go no further, we choose the next most promising assumption that builds on the first one, and so on, as long as each succeeding assumption brings us closer to a solution. If we find that we are stuck, or we reach a conclusion that contradicts a previous one, we must back-track and alter an earlier assumption.

Here is our solution, showing the results at each step.

1. According to the hint, we may directly substitute V for W.

   ```
   Q AZVS DSSC KAS DXZNN DASNN
   ```

2. The first word is small, so it is probably either an A or an I; let's assume that it is an A.

   ```
   A AZVS DSSC KAS DXZNN DASNN
   ```

3. The third word needs a vowel, and it is likely to be the double letters. It is probably neither II nor UU, and it can't be AA because we have already used an A. Thus, we might try EE.

   ```
   A AZVE DEEC KAE DXZNN DAENN
   ```

4. The fourth word is three letters long and ends in an E; it is likely to be the word THE.

   ```
   A HZVE DEEC THE DXZNN DHENN
   ```

5. The second word needs a vowel, but only an I, O, or U (we've already used A and E). Only the I gives us a meaningful word.

   ```
   A HIVE DEEC THE DXINN DHENN
   ```

6. There are few four-letter words that have a double E, including DEER, BEER, and SEEN. Our knowledge of grammar suggests that the third word should be a verb, and so we select SEEN.

   ```
   A HIVE SEEN THE SXINN SHENN
   ```

7. This sentence is not making any sense (hives cannot see), so we probably made a bad assumption somewhere along the way. The problem seems to lie with the vowel in the second word, so we might consider reversing our initial assumption.

   `I HAVE SEEN THE SXANN SHENN`

8. Let's attack the last word. The double letters can't be `SS` (we've used an `S`, and besides, `SHESS` doesn't make any sense), but `LL` forms a meaningful word.

   `I HAVE SEEN THE SXALL SHELL`

9. The fifth word is part of a noun phrase and so is probably an adjective (`STALL`, for example, is rejected on this account). Searching for words that fit the pattern `S?ALL` yields `SMALL`.

   `I HAVE SEEN THE SMALL SHELL`

Thus, we have reached a solution.

We may make the following observations about this problem-solving process.

- We applied many different sources of knowledge, such as knowledge about grammar, spelling, and vowels.
- We recorded our assumptions in one central place and applied our sources of knowledge to these assumptions to reason about their consequences.
- We reasoned opportunistically. At times, we reasoned from general to specific rules (if the word is three letters long and ends in `E`, it is probably `THE`), and at other times, we reasoned from the specific to the general (`?EE?` might be `DEER`, `BEER`, or `SEEN`, but since the word must be a verb and not a noun, only `SEEN` satisfies our hypothesis).

From these problem-solving observations, we can identify some key abstractions. Key abstractions are analysis elements of our solution that begin to establish the initial architectural framework. The three bullets identify multiple knowledge sources, a central place for assumptions or hypotheses, and a control component that opportunistically controls the problem solving.

What we have described is a problem-solving approach known as a *blackboard model*. The blackboard model was first proposed by Newell in 1962 and later incorporated by Reddy and Erman into the Hearsay and Hearsay II projects, both of which dealt with the problems of speech recognition [4]. The blackboard model proved to be useful in this domain, and the framework was soon applied successfully to other domains, including signal interpretation, the modeling of three-dimensional molecular structures, image understanding, and planning [5]. Blackboard frameworks have proven to be particularly noteworthy with regard to the representation of declarative knowledge and are space and time efficient when compared with alternate approaches [6].

The blackboard framework is an architectural pattern that can be applied as a result of the analysis of our problem-solving algorithm. The framework can be represented in terms of classes and mechanisms that describe how instances of those classes collaborate.

The Architecture of the Blackboard Framework

Englemore and Morgan explain the blackboard model by analogy to the problem of a group of people solving a jigsaw puzzle:

> Imagine a room with a large blackboard and around it a group of people each holding over-size jigsaw pieces. We start with volunteers who put on the blackboard (assume it's sticky) their most "promising" pieces. Each member of the group looks at his pieces and sees if any of them fit into the pieces already on the blackboard. Those with the appropriate pieces go up to the blackboard and update the evolving solution. The new updates cause other pieces to fall into place, and other people go to the blackboard to add their pieces. It does not matter whether one person holds more pieces than another. The whole puzzle can be solved in complete silence; that is, there need be no direct communication among the group. Each person is self-activating, knowing when his pieces will contribute to the solution. No a priori established order exists for people to go up to the blackboard. The apparent cooperative behavior is mediated by the state of the solution on the blackboard. If one watches the task being performed, the solution is built incrementally (one piece at a time) and opportunistically (as an opportunity for adding a piece arises), as opposed to starting, say, systematically from the left top corner and trying each piece. [7]

As Figure 10–1 indicates, the blackboard framework consists of three elements: a blackboard, multiple knowledge sources, and a controller that mediates among these knowledge sources [8]. Notice how the following description describes the key abstractions identified from the problem space. According to Nii, "the purpose of the blackboard is to hold computational and solution-state data needed by and produced by the knowledge sources. The blackboard consists of objects from the solution space. The objects on the blackboard are hierarchically organized into levels of analysis. The objects and their properties define the vocabulary of the solution space" [9].

As Englemore and Morgan explain, "The domain knowledge needed to solve a problem is partitioned into knowledge sources that are kept separate and independent. The objective of each knowledge source is to contribute information that will lead to a solution to the problem. A knowledge source takes a set of current information on the blackboard and updates it as encoded in its specialized knowledge. The knowledge sources are represented as procedures, sets of rules, or logic assertions" [10].

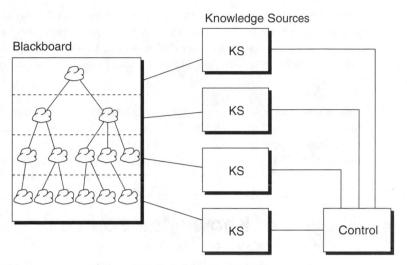

Figure 10–1 A Blackboard Framework

Knowledge sources, or KSs for short, are domain-specific. In speech recognition systems, knowledge sources might include agents that can reason about phonemes, morphemes, words, and sentences. In image recognition systems, knowledge sources would include agents that know about simple picture elements, such as edges and regions of similar texture, as well as higher-level abstractions representing the objects of interest in each scene, such as houses, roads, fields, cars, and people. Generally speaking, knowledge sources parallel the hierarchical structure of objects on the blackboard. Furthermore, each knowledge source uses objects at one level as its input and then generates and/or modifies objects at another level as its output. For instance, in a speech recognition system, a knowledge source that embodies knowledge about words might look at a stream of phonemes (at a low level of abstraction) to form a new word (at a higher level of abstraction). Alternately, a knowledge source that embodies knowledge about sentence structure might hypothesize the need for a verb (at a high level of abstraction); by filtering a list of possible words (at a lower level of abstraction), this knowledge source can verify the hypothesis.

These two approaches to reasoning represent forward-chaining and backward-chaining, respectively. Forward-chaining involves reasoning from specific assertions to a general assertion, and backward-chaining starts with a hypothesis, then tries to verify the hypothesis from existing assertions. This is why we say that control in the blackboard model is opportunistic: Depending on the circumstances, a knowledge source might be selected for activation that uses either forward- or backward-chaining.

Knowledge sources usually embody two elements, namely, preconditions and actions. The preconditions of a knowledge source represent the state of the blackboard in which the knowledge source shows an interest. For example, a precondition for a knowledge source in an image recognition system might be the discovery of a relatively linear region of picture elements (perhaps representing a road). Triggering a precondition causes the knowledge source to focus its attention on this part of the blackboard and then take action by processing its rules or procedural knowledge.

Under these circumstances, polling is unnecessary: When a knowledge source thinks it has something interesting to contribute, it notifies the blackboard controller. Figuratively speaking, it is as if each knowledge source raises its hand to indicate that it has something useful to do; then, from among eager knowledge sources, the controller calls on the one that looks the most promising.

Analysis of Knowledge Sources

Let's return to our specific problem and consider the knowledge sources that can contribute to a solution. As is typical with most knowledge-engineering applications, the best strategy is to sit down with an expert in the domain and record the heuristics that this person applies to solve the problems in the domain. For our present problem, this might involve trying to solve a number of cryptograms and recording our thinking process along the way.

Our analysis suggests that 13 knowledge sources are relevant; they appear with the knowledge they embody in the following list:

- Common prefixes   Common word beginnings such as `re`, `anti`, and `un`
- Common suffixes   Common word endings such as `ly`, `ing`, `es`, and `ed`
- Consonants   Nonvowel letters
- Direct substitution   Hints given as part of the problem statement
- Double letters   Common double letters, such as `tt`, `ll`, and `ss`
- Letter frequency   Probability of the appearance of each letter
- Legal strings   Legal and illegal combinations of letters, such as `qu` and `zg`, respectively
- Pattern matching   Words that match a specified pattern of letters
- Sentence structure   Grammar, including the meanings of noun and verb phrases
- Small words   Possible matches for one-, two-, three-, and four-letter words
- Solved   Whether or not the problem is solved, or if no further progress can be made
- Vowels   Nonconsonant letters
- Word structure   The location of vowels and the common structure of nouns, verbs, adjectives, adverbs, articles, conjunctives, and so on

From an object-oriented perspective, each of these 13 knowledge sources represents a candidate class in our architecture: Each instance embodies some state (its knowledge), each exhibits certain class-specific behavior (a suffix knowledge source can react to words suspected of having a common ending), and each is uniquely identifiable (a small-word knowledge source exists independent of the pattern-matching knowledge source).

We may also arrange these knowledge sources in a hierarchy. Specifically, some knowledge sources operate on sentences, others on letters, still others on contiguous groups of letters, and the lowest-level ones on individual letters. Indeed, this hierarchy reflects the objects that may appear on the blackboard: sentences, words, strings of letters, and letters.

10.2 Elaboration

We are now ready to design a solution to the cryptanalysis problem using the blackboard framework we have described. This is a classic example of reuse-in-the-large, in that we are able to reuse a proven architectural pattern as the foundation of our design.

The architecture of the blackboard framework suggests that among the highest-level objects in our system are a blackboard, several knowledge sources, and a controller. Our next task is to identify the domain-specific classes and objects that specialize these general key abstractions.

Blackboard Objects

The blackboard is an elaborate structure of multiple levels of abstractions. The abstractions are captured as objects that appear hierarchically on a blackboard structure. The hierarchical object structure parallels the different levels of abstractions of the knowledge sources. The knowledge sources use the blackboard as a global source of input data, partial solutions, alternatives, final solutions, and control information.

To begin the design of the blackboard's hierarchical structure, we identify the following classes:

- Sentence   A complete cryptogram
- Word   A single word in the cryptogram
- CipherLetter   A single letter of a word

Knowledge sources must also share knowledge about the assumptions each makes, so we include the following class of blackboard objects:

- `Assumption` An assumption made by a knowledge source

Finally, it is important to know what plaintext and ciphertext letters in the alphabet have been used in assumptions made by the knowledge sources, so we include the following class:

- `Alphabet` The plaintext alphabet, the ciphertext alphabet, and the mapping between the two

Is there anything in common among these five classes? We answer with a resounding yes: Each one of these classes represents objects that may be placed on a blackboard, and that very property distinguishes them from, for example, knowledge sources and controllers. Thus, we invent the `BlackboardObject` class as the superclass of every object that may appear on a blackboard. Figure 10–2 shows our preliminary design of the `Blackboard` abstraction.

Looking at the `BlackboardObject` class from its outside view, we may define two applicable operations:

- `register` Add the object to the blackboard.
- `resign` Remove the object from the blackboard.

Why do we define `register` and `resign` as operations on instances of `BlackboardObject`, instead of on the `Blackboard` itself? This situation is not unlike telling an object to draw itself in a window. The litmus test for deciding where to place these kinds of operations is whether or not the class itself has sufficient knowledge or responsibility to carry out the operation. In the case of

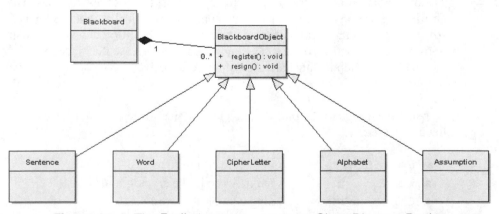

Figure 10–2 The Preliminary `Blackboard` Class Diagram Design

`register` and `resign`, this is indeed the case: The `BlackboardObject` is the only abstraction with detailed knowledge of how to attach or remove itself from the `Blackboard` (although it certainly does require collaboration with the `BlackboardObject`). In fact, it is an important responsibility of this abstraction that each `BlackboardObject` be self-aware as it is attached to the `Blackboard` because only then can it begin to participate in opportunistically solving the problem on the `Blackboard`.

Dependencies and Affirmations

Individual sentences, words, and cipher letters have another thing in common: Each has certain knowledge sources that depend on it. A given knowledge source may express an interest in one or more of these objects, and therefore, a sentence, word, or cipher letter must maintain a reference to each such knowledge source, so that when an assumption about the object changes, the appropriate knowledge sources can be notified that something interesting has happened. To provide this mechanism, we introduce a simple abstract class: `Dependent`.

To design the `Dependent` class, we include an object that represents a collection of knowledge sources:

- `references`   Collection of knowledge sources

In addition, the following operations are defined for this class:

- `add`   Add a reference to the knowledge source.
- `remove`   Remove a reference to the knowledge source.
- `numberOfDependents` Return the number of dependents.
- `notify`   Broadcast an operation of each dependent.

The operation `notify` has the semantics of a passive iterator, meaning that when we invoke it, we can supply an operation that we wish to perform on every dependent in the collection.

Dependency is an independent property that can be mixed in with other classes. For example, a `CipherLetter` is a `BlackboardObject` as well as a `Dependent`, so we can combine these two abstractions to achieve the desired behavior. Using an abstract class in this way increases the reusability and separation of concerns in our architecture.

`CipherLetter` and `Alphabet` have another property in common: Instances of both of these classes may have assumptions made about them (and remember that an `Assumption` object is also a kind of `BlackboardObject`). For example, a certain knowledge source might assume that the ciphertext letter K represents the plaintext letter P. As we get closer to solving our problem, we might make the unchangeable assertion that G represents J. Thus we need to include a class that maintains the assumptions and assertions about the associated object. This class we will identify as `Affirmation`.

In our architecture, we will make affirmations only about individual letters, as in `CipherLetter` and `Alphabet`. As our earlier scenario implied, cipher letters represent single letters about which statements might be made, and alphabets comprise many letters, each of which might have different statements made about them. Defining `Affirmation` as an independent class thus captures the common behavior across these two disparate classes.

We define the following operations for instances of the `Affirmation` class:

- `make`   Make a statement.
- `retract`   Retract a statement.
- `ciphertext` Given a plaintext letter, return its ciphertext equivalent.
- `plaintext`   Given a ciphertext letter, return its plaintext equivalent.

Further analysis suggests that we should clearly distinguish between the two roles played by a statement: An assumption, which represents a temporary mapping between a ciphertext letter and its plaintext equivalent, and an assertion, which is a permanent mapping, meaning that the mapping is defined and therefore not changeable. During the solution of a cryptogram, knowledge sources will make many assumptions, and as we move closer to a final solution, these mappings eventually become assertions. To model these changing roles, we will refine the previously identified class `Assumption` and introduce a new subclass named `Assertion`, both of whose instances are managed by instances of the class `Affirmation` as well as placed on the blackboard. We begin by completing the signature of the operations `make` and `retract` to include an `Assumption` or `Assertion` argument, and then add the following selectors:

- `isPlainLetterAsserted`   A selector: Is the plaintext letter defined?
- `isCipherLetterAsserted`   A selector: Is the ciphertext letter defined?
- `plainLetterHasAssumption`   A selector: Is there an assumption about the plaintext letter?
- `cipherLetterHasAssumption`   A selector: Is there an assumption about the ciphertext letter?

Assumption objects are a kind of BlackboardObject because they represent state that is of general interest to all knowledge sources. Member objects will need to be declared to represent the following properties:

- target   The blackboard object about which the assumption was made
- creator   The knowledge source that created the assumption
- reason   The reason the knowledge source made the assumption
- plainLetter   The plaintext letter about which the assumption is being made
- cipherLetter   The assumed value of the plaintext letter

The need for each of these properties is largely derived from the very nature of an assumption: A particular knowledge source makes an assumption about a plaintext/ciphertext mapping and does so for a certain reason (usually because some rule was triggered). The need for the first member, target, is less obvious. We include it because of the problem of backtracking. If we ever have to reverse an assumption, we must notify all blackboard objects for which the assumption was originally made, so that they in turn can alert the knowledge sources they depend on (via the dependency mechanism) that their meaning has changed.

Next, we declare the subclass of Assumption named Assertion. The classes Assumption and Assertion share the following operation, among others:

- isRetractable   A selector: Is the mapping temporary?

All Assumption objects answer true to the predicate isRetractable, whereas all Assertion objects answer false. Additionally, once made, an assertion can neither be restated nor retracted.

Figure 10–3 provides a class diagram that illustrates the collaboration of the Dependent and Affirmation classes. Pay particular attention to the roles each abstraction plays in the various associations. For example, a Knowledge-Source is the creator of an Assumption and is also the referencer of a CipherLetter. Because a role represents a different view than an abstraction presents to the world, we would expect to see a different protocol between knowledge sources and assumptions than between knowledge sources and letters.

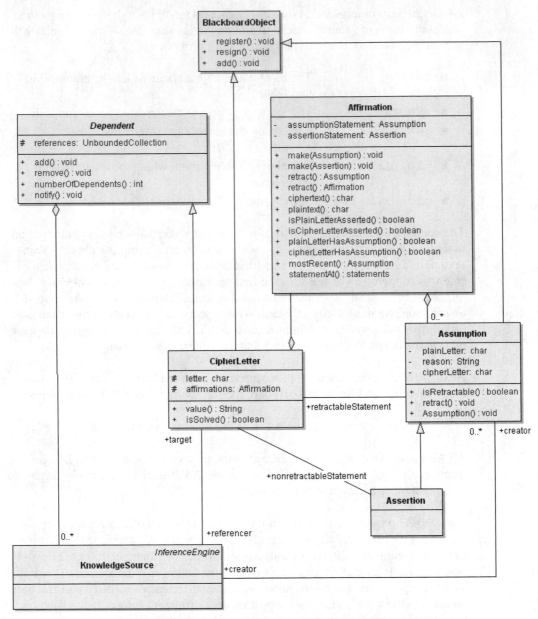

Figure 10–3 Dependency and Affirmation Classes

10.3 Construction

Let's continue our design of the Sentence, Word, and CipherLetter classes, followed by the Alphabet class, by doing a little isolated class design.

Designing the Blackboard Objects

A sentence is quite simple: It is a BlackboardObject as well as a Dependent, and it denotes a list of words that compose the sentence.

We make the superclass Dependent abstract[1] (Figure 10–4) because we expect there may be other Sentence subclasses that try to inherit from Dependent as well. By marking this inheritance relationship abstract, we cause such subclasses to share a single Dependent superclass.

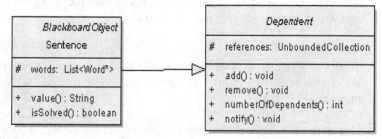

Figure 10–4 The Sentence Class Design with the Abstract Dependent Class

In addition to the operations register and resign defined by its superclass BlackboardObject, plus the four operations defined in Dependent, we add the following two sentence-specific operations:

- value   Return the current value of the sentence.
- isSolved   Return true if there is an assertion for all words in the sentence.

At the start of the problem, value returns a string representing the original cryptogram. Once isSolved evaluates as true, the operation value may be used to retrieve the plaintext solution. Accessing value before isSolved is true will yield partial solutions.

---

1. In UML 2.0, an abstract class is represented with the class name in italics. A keyword {abstract} may also be placed in the property list.

Just like the `Sentence` class, a `Word` is a kind of `BlackboardObject` as well as a kind of `Dependent`. Furthermore, a `Word` denotes a list of letters. To assist the knowledge sources that manipulate words, we include a reference from a word to its sentence, as well as from a word to the previous and next words in the sentence.

As we did for the `Sentence` operations, we define the following two operations for the class `Word`:

- `value`   Return the current value of the word.
- `isSolved` Return true if there is an assertion for every letter in the word.

We may next define the class `CipherLetter`. An instance of this class is a kind of `BlackboardObject` and a kind of `Dependent`. In addition to its inherited behaviors, each `CipherLetter` object has a value (such as the ciphertext letter H) together with a collection of assumptions and assertions regarding its corresponding plaintext letter. We can use the class `Affirmation` to collect these statements. Figure 10–5 illustrates the addition of the design of `CipherLetter` and `Word` in our architecture framework.

Notice that we include the selectors `value` and `isSolved`, similar to our design of `Sentence` and `Word`. We must also eventually provide operations for the clients of `CipherLetter` to access its assumptions and assertions in a safe manner.

One comment about the member object affirmations: We expect this to be a collection of assumptions and assertions ordered according to their time of creation, with the most recent statement in this collection representing the current assumption or assertion. The reason we choose to keep a history of all assumptions is to permit knowledge sources to look at earlier assumptions that were rejected, so that they can learn from earlier mistakes. This decision influences our design decisions about the `Affirmation` class, to which we add the following operations:

- `mostRecent`   A selector: returns the most recent assumption or assertion
- `statementAt` A selector: returns the nth statement

Now that we have refined its behavior, we can next make a reasonable implementation decision about the `Affirmation` class. Specifically, we can include the protected member object `statements`, which is defined as a collection of assumptions.

Consider next the class named `Alphabet`. This class represents the entire plaintext and ciphertext alphabet, plus the mappings between the two. This information is important because each knowledge source can use it to determine which

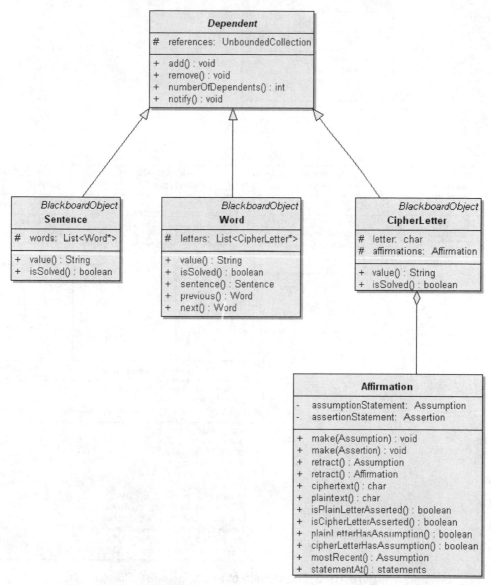

Figure 10–5 The Design of the `CipherLetter` and `Word` Classes

mappings have been made and which are yet to be done. For example, if we already have an assertion that the ciphertext letter C is really the letter M, then an alphabet object records this mapping so that no other knowledge source can apply the plaintext letter M. For efficiency, we need to query about the mapping both ways: Given a ciphertext letter, return its plaintext mapping, and given a plaintext letter, return its ciphertext mapping. Figure 10–6 illustrates the addition of the design of the Alphabet class.

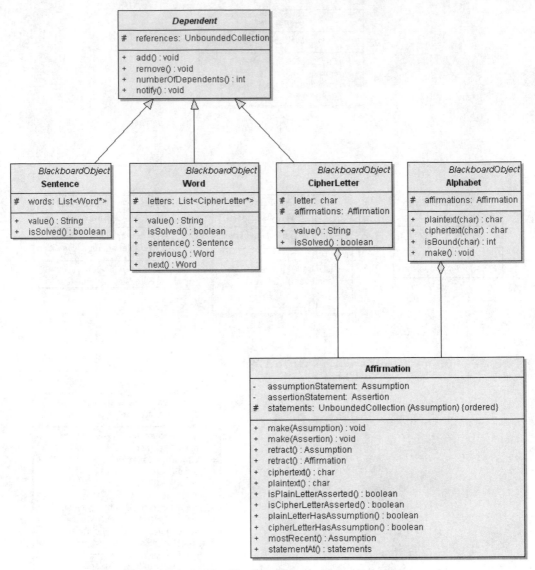

Figure 10–6 The Design of the `Alphabet` Class

Just as for the `CipherLetter` class, we also include a protected member object `affirmations` and provide suitable operations to access its state.

Now we are ready to define the `Blackboard` class. This class has the simple responsibility of collecting instances of the `BlackboardObject` class and its subclasses. Thus we may design `Blackboard` as a type of instance of a `DynamicCollection`. We have chosen to inherit from rather than contain an instance of the `DynamicCollection` class because `Blackboard` passes our test for inheritance: A `Blackboard` is indeed a kind of collection.

The `Blackboard` class provides operations such as `add` and `remove`, which it inherits from the `Collection` class. Our design includes five operations specific to the blackboard.

- `reset`   Clean the blackboard.
- `assertProblem`   Place an initial problem on the blackboard.
- `connect`   Attach the knowledge source to the blackboard.
- `isSolved`   Return true if the sentence is solved.
- `retrieveSolution`   Return the solved plaintext sentence.

The second operation is needed to create a dependency between a blackboard and its knowledge sources.

In Figure 10–7, we summarize our design of the classes that collaborate with `Blackboard`. In this diagram, notice that we show the `Blackboard` class as both instantiating and inheriting from the template class `DynamicCollection`. This diagram also clearly shows why introducing the `Dependent` class as an abstract class was a good design decision. Specifically, `Dependent` represents a behavior that encompasses only a partial set of `BlackboardObject` subclasses. By making `Dependent` abstract, we increase its chances of being reused.

Designing the Knowledge Sources

In a previous section, we identified 13 knowledge sources relevant to this problem. Just as we did for the `Blackboard` objects, we can design a class structure encompassing these knowledge sources and thereby elevate all common characteristics to more abstract classes.

Designing Specialized Knowledge Sources

Assume for the moment the existence of an abstract class called `Knowledge Source`, whose purpose is much like that of the class `BlackboardObject`. Rather than treat each of the 13 knowledge sources as a direct subclass of this more general class, it is useful to first perform a domain analysis and see if there are any clusters of knowledge sources. Indeed, there are such groups: Some knowledge sources operate on whole sentences, others on whole words, others on contiguous strings of letters, and still others on individual letters. We may capture these design decisions by creating the following subclasses:

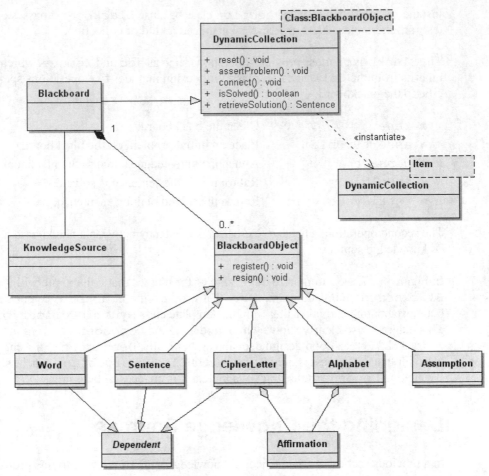

Figure 10–7 The Refined `Blackboard` Class Diagram Design

- `SentenceKnowledgeSource`   Rules associated with sentences
- `WordKnowledgeSource`   Rules associated with words
- `LetterKnowledgeSource`   Rules associated with letters
- `StringKnowledgeSource`   Rules associated with strings

For each of these classes, we may provide another level of specification. For example, the subclasses of the class `SentenceKnowledgeSource` include the following:

- `SentenceStructureKnowledgeSource`   Rules specific to sentence structure
- `SolvedKnowledgeSource`   Solved cryptogram sentence

Similarly, the subclasses of the intermediate class `WordKnowledgeSource` include these:

■ `WordStructureKnowledgeSource`	Rules specific to word structure
■ `SmallWordKnowledgeSource`	Rules specific to small words
■ `PatternMatchingKnowledgeSource`	Rules for matching patterns of words

The last class requires some explanation. In our earlier list of the 13 knowledge sources, we said that the purpose of a pattern-matching knowledge source was to propose words that fit a certain pattern. We can use regular expression pattern-matching symbols such as:

■ Any item	`?`
■ Not item	`~`
■ Closure item	`*`
■ Start group	`{`
■ Stop group	`}`

With these symbols, we might give an instance of this class the pattern `?E~{A E I O U}`, thereby asking it to give us from its dictionary all the three-letter words starting with any letter, followed by an `E`, and ending with any letter except a vowel. All instances of this class share a dictionary of words, and each instance has its own regular expression pattern-matching agent. The detailed behavior of this class is not important to us at this point in our design, so we will defer the invention of the remainder of its interface and implementation.

Continuing, we may declare the following subclasses of the class `String KnowledgeSource`:

■ `CommonPrefixKnowledgeSource`	Rules specific to prefixes
■ `CommonSuffixKnowledgeSource`	Rules specific to suffixes
■ `DoubleLetterKnowledgeSource`	Rules for double letters, e.g., `oo`, `ll`, and so on
■ `LegalStringKnowledgeSource`	Rules specific to what makes legal strings

Lastly, we can introduce the following subclasses of the class `LetterKnowledgeSource`:

- `DirectSubstitutionKnowledgeSource`   Rules specific to substitution of letters
- `VowelKnowledgeSource`   Rules specific for vowels
- `ConsonantKnowledgeSource`   Rules specific for consonants
- `LetterFrequencyKnowledgeSource`   Rules specific to frequency of letters

Figure 10–8 illustrates the hierarchical structure of `KnowledgeSource`.

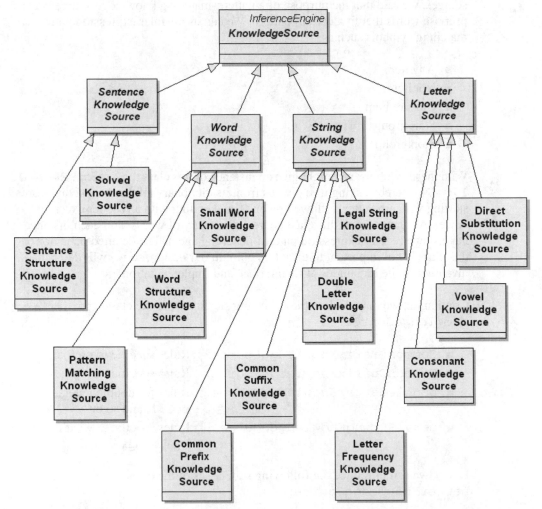

Figure 10–8 The Generalization Hierarchy of the `KnowledgeSource` Class

Generalizing the Knowledge Sources

Analysis suggests that only two primary operations apply to all these specialized classes:

- `reset`   Restart the knowledge source.
- `evaluate`   Evaluate the state of the blackboard.

The reason for this simple interface is that knowledge sources are relatively autonomous entities: We point one to an interesting `Blackboard` object and then tell it to evaluate its rules according to the current global state of the `Blackboard`. As part of the evaluation of its rules, a given knowledge source might do any one of several things.

- Propose an assumption about the substitution cipher.
- Discover a contradiction among previous assumptions, and cause the offending assumption to be retracted.
- Propose an assertion about the substitution cipher.
- Tell the controller that it has some interesting knowledge to contribute.

These are all general actions that are independent of the specific kind of knowledge source. To generalize even further, these actions represent the behavior of an inference engine. Therefore, we create the class `InferenceEngine` that, given a set of rules, evaluates those rules either to generate new rules (forward-chaining) or to prove some hypothesis (backward-chaining). When designing the constructor for `InferenceEngine`, the basic responsibility is to create an instance of this class and populate it with a set of rules, which it then uses for evaluation.

In fact, this class has only one critical operation that it makes visible to knowledge sources:

- `evaluate`   Evaluate the rules of the inference engine.

This then is how knowledge sources collaborate: Each specialized knowledge source defines its own knowledge-specific rules and delegates responsibility for evaluating these rules to the `InferenceEngine` class. More precisely, we may say that the operation `KnowledgeSource::evaluate` ultimately invokes the operation `InferenceEngine::evaluate`, the results of which are used to carry out any of the four actions we listed earlier. In Figure 10–9, we illustrate a common scenario of this collaboration.

The sequence diagram illustrates the following steps in this scenario:

1. Select a `KnowledgeSource` for action.
2. Evaluate the `KnowledgeSource` against the state of the `Blackboard`.

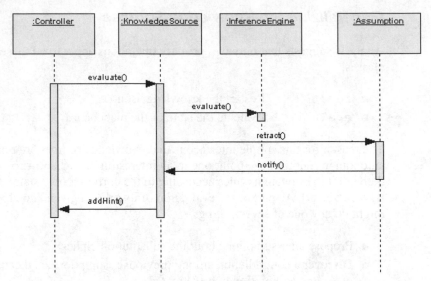

Figure 10–9 A Scenario for Evaluating Knowledge Source Rules

3. Take some action, such as retracting an `Assumption`.
4. Notify all dependent `KnowledgeSource` objects that the assumption has been retracted.
5. Tell the `Controller` that the `KnowledgeSource` has a new hint to offer in solving the blackboard problem.

What exactly is a rule? A rule might be composed for the common suffix knowledge source using a pattern-matching algorithm that recognizes a common suffix pattern such as `*I??`. Given a string of letters matching the regular expression pattern `*I??`, the candidate suffixes may include `ING`, `IES`, and `IED`.

In terms of its class structure, we may thus say that a knowledge source is a kind of inference engine. Additionally, each knowledge source must have some association with a blackboard object, for that is where it finds the objects on which it operates. Finally, each knowledge source must have an association to a controller, with which it collaborates by sending hints of solutions; in turn, the controller might trigger the knowledge source from time to time. Figure 10–10 illustrates these design decisions.

We also introduce the collection `pastAssumptions`, so that the knowledge source can keep track of all the assumptions and assertions it has ever made, in order to learn from its mistakes.

Instances of the `Blackboard` class serve as a repository of `Blackboard` objects. For a similar reason, we need a `KnowledgeSources` class, denoting the entire collection of knowledge sources for a particular problem.

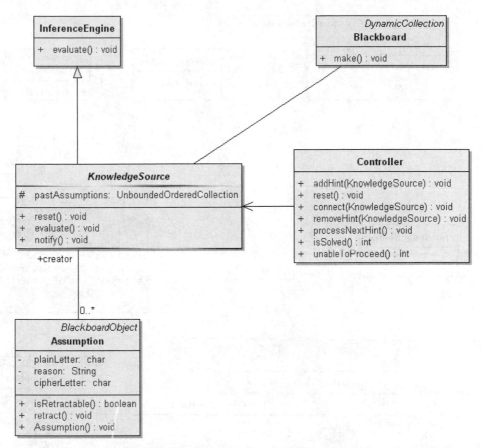

Figure 10–10 The Preliminary Design of `KnowledgeSource`

One of the responsibilities of this class is that when we create an instance of `KnowledgeSources`, we also create the 13 individual `KnowledgeSource` objects. We may perform three operations on instances of this class:

- `restart`   Restart the knowledge sources.
- `startKnowledgeSource`   Give a specific knowledge source its initial conditions.
- `connect`   Attach the knowledge source to the blackboard or to the controller.

Figure 10–11 provides the refined design of the class structure of the `KnowledgeSource` classes, according to these design decisions.

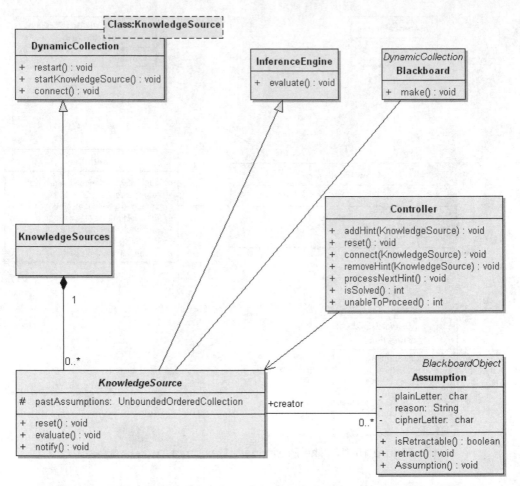

Figure 10–11 The Refined Design of the `KnowledgeSource` Class Diagram

Designing the Controller

Consider for a moment how the controller and individual knowledge sources interact. At each stage in the solution of a cryptogram, a particular knowledge source might discover that it has a useful contribution to make and so gives a hint to the controller. Conversely, the knowledge source might decide that its earlier hint no longer applies and so may remove the hint. Once all knowledge sources have been given a chance, the controller selects the most promising hint and activates the appropriate knowledge source by invoking its `evaluate` operation.

How does the controller decide which knowledge source to activate? We may devise a few suitable rules.

- An `Assertion` has a higher priority than an `Assumption`.
- The `SolvedKnowledgeSource` provides the most useful hints.
- The `PatternMatchingKnowledgeSource` provides higher-priority hints than the `SentenceStructureKnowledgeSource`.

A controller thus acts as an agent responsible for mediating among the various knowledge sources that operate on a blackboard.

The controller must have an association to its knowledge sources, which it can access through the appropriately named class `KnowledgeSources`. Additionally, the controller must have as one of its properties a collection of hints, ordered in accordance with the above rules of prioritization. In this manner, the controller can easily select for activation the knowledge source with the most interesting hint to offer.

Engaging in a little more isolated class design, we offer the following operations for the `Controller` class.

- `reset`   Restart the controller.
- `addHint`   Add a knowledge source hint.
- `removeHint`   Remove a knowledge source hint.
- `processNextHint` Evaluate the next-highest-priority hint.
- `isSolved`   A selector: Return true if the problem is solved.
- `unableToProceed` A selector: Return true if the knowledge sources are stuck.
- `connect`   Attach the controller to the knowledge source.

The controller is in a sense driven by the hints it receives from various knowledge sources. As such, finite state machines are well suited for capturing the dynamic behavior of this class.

For example, consider the state transition diagram shown in Figure 10–12. Here we see that a controller may be in one of five major states: `Initializing`, `Selecting`, `Evaluating`, `Stuck`, and `Solved`. The controller's most interesting activity occurs between the `Selecting` and `Evaluating` states. While selecting, the controller naturally transitions from the state `Creating Strategy` to `Processing Hint` and eventually to `Selecting KS`. If a knowledge source is in fact selected, then the controller transitions to the `Evaluating` state, wherein it first is in `Updating Blackboard`. It transitions to `Connecting` if objects are added and to `Backtracking` if assumptions are retracted, at which time it also notifies all dependents.

The controller unconditionally transitions to `Stuck` if it cannot proceed and to `Solved` if it finds a solved blackboard problem.

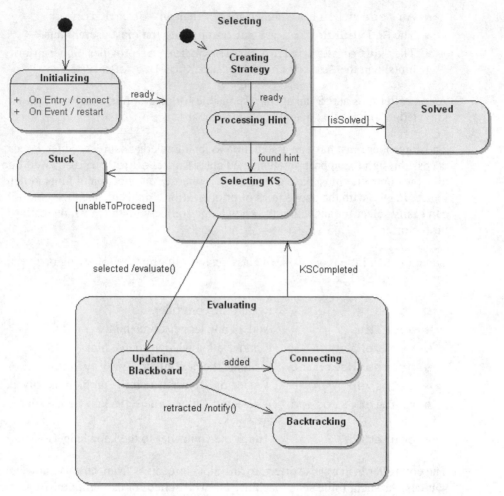

Figure 10–12 The Controller State Machine

Integrating the Blackboard Framework

Now that we have defined the key abstractions for our domain, we may continue by putting them together to form a complete application. We will proceed by implementing and testing a vertical slice through the architecture and then by completing the system one mechanism at a time.

Integrating the Topmost Objects

Figure 10–13 is a composite structure diagram that captures our design of the topmost object in the system, paralleling the structure of the generic blackboard

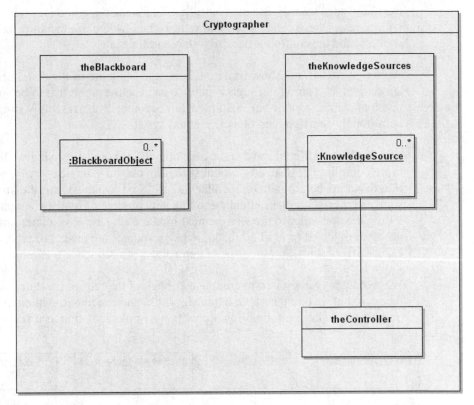

Figure 10–13 The Cryptanalysis Composite Structure Diagram

framework shown earlier in Figure 10–1. In Figure 10–13, we show the physical containment of blackboard objects by the collection `theBlackboard` and knowledge sources by the collection `theKnowledgeSources`, using a shorthand style identical to that for showing nested classes.

In this diagram, we introduce an instance of a new class that we call `Cryptographer`. The intent of this class is to serve as an aggregate encompassing the blackboard, the knowledge sources, and the controller. In this manner, our application might provide several instances of this class and thus have several blackboards running simultaneously.

We define two primary operations for the `Cryptographer` class:

- `reset` Restart the blackboard.
- `decipher` Solve the given cryptogram.

The behavior we require as part of this class's constructor is to create the dependencies between the blackboard and its knowledge sources, as well as between the knowledge sources and the controller. The `reset` method is similar, in that it simply resets these connections and returns the blackboard, the knowledge sources, and the controller back to a stable initial state.

Although we will not show its details here, the signature of the `decipher` operation includes a string, through which we provide the ciphertext to be solved. In this manner, the root of our main program becomes embarrassingly simple, as is common in well-designed object-oriented systems.

The implementation of the `decipher` operation is, not surprisingly, slightly more complicated. Basically, we must first invoke the `assertProblem` operation to set up the problem on the blackboard. Next, we must start the knowledge sources by bringing their attention to this new problem. Finally, we must loop, telling the controller to process the next hint at each new pass, either until the problem is solved or until all the knowledge sources are unable to proceed. Figure 10–14 illustrates the flow of control using a sequence diagram.

We would be best advised to complete enough of the relevant architectural interfaces so that we could complete this algorithm and execute it. Although at this point it would have minimal functionality, its implementation as a vertical slice

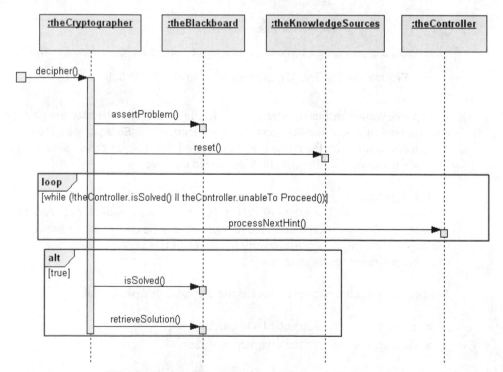

Figure 10–14 The `decipher` Sequence Diagram

through the architecture would force us to validate certain key architectural decisions.

Continuing, let's look at two of the key operations used in `decipher`, namely, `assertProblem` and `retrieveSolution`. The `assertProblem` operation is particularly interesting because it must generate an entire set of `Blackboard` objects. In the form of a simple pseudocode script, our algorithm is as follows.

```
trim all leading and trailing blanks from the string
return if the resulting string is empty
create a sentence object
add the sentence to the blackboard
create a word object (this will be the leftmost word in the
    sentence)
add the word to the blackboard
add the word to the sentence
for each character in the string, from left to right
   if the character is a space
      make the current word the previous word
         create a word object
         add the word to the blackboard
         add the word to the sentence
      else
         create a cipher-letter object
         add the letter to the blackboard
         add the letter to the word
```

The purpose of design is simply to provide a blueprint for implementation. This script supplies a sufficiently detailed algorithm, so we need not show its complete implementation.

The operation `retrieveSolution` is far simpler; we simply return the value of the sentence on the blackboard. Calling `retrieveSolution` before `isSolved` evaluates true will yield partial solutions.

Implementing the Assumption Mechanism

At this point, we have implemented the mechanisms that allow us to set and retrieve values for `Blackboard` objects. The next major function point involves the mechanism for making assumptions about `Blackboard` objects. This is a particularly significant issue because assumptions are dynamic (meaning that they are routinely created and destroyed during the process of forming a solution), and their creation or retraction triggers controller events.

Figure 10–15 illustrates the primary scenario of when a knowledge source states an assumption. As this communication diagram shows, once the KnowledgeSource creates an Assumption, it notifies the Blackboard, which in turn makes the Assumption for its Alphabet and then for each BlackboardObject to which the Assumption applies. Using the dependency mechanism, the affected BlackboardObject in turn might notify any dependent KnowledgeSource.

In its most naive implementation, retracting an assumption simply undoes the work of this mechanism. For example, to retract an assumption about a cipher letter, we just pop its collection of assumptions, up to and including the assumption we are retracting. In this manner, the given assumption and all assumptions that built on it are undone.

A more sophisticated mechanism is possible. For example, suppose that we made an assumption that a certain one-letter word is really just the letter I (assuming we need a vowel). We might make a later assumption that a certain double-letter word is NN (assuming we need a consonant). If we then find we must retract the first assumption, we probably don't have to retract the second one. This approach requires us to add a new behavior to the Assumption class so that it can keep track of what assumptions are dependent on others. We can reasonably defer this enhancement until much later in the evolution of this system because adding this behavior has no architectural impact.

Adding New Knowledge Sources

Now that we have the key abstractions of the blackboard framework in place, and once the mechanisms for stating and retracting assumptions are working, our next

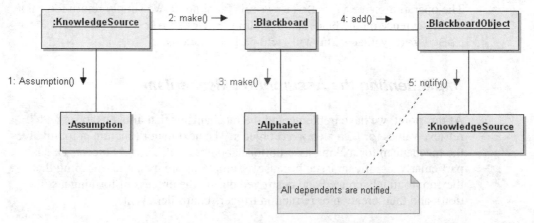

Figure 10–15 The Assumption Mechanism

step is to implement the `InferenceEngine` class since all knowledge sources depend on it. As we mentioned earlier, this class has only one really interesting operation, namely, `evaluate`. We will not show its details here because this particular method reveals no new important design issues.

Once we are confident that our inference engine works properly, we may incrementally add each knowledge source. We emphasize the use of an incremental process for two reasons.

1. For a given knowledge source, it is not clear what rules are really important until we apply them to real problems.
2. Debugging the knowledge base is far easier if we implement and test smaller related sets of rules, rather than trying to test them all at once.

Fundamentally, implementing each knowledge source is largely a problem of knowledge engineering. For a given knowledge source, we must confer with an expert (perhaps a cryptologist) to decide which rules are meaningful. As we test each knowledge source, our analysis may reveal that certain rules are useless, others are either too specific or too general, and perhaps some are missing. We may then choose to alter the rules of a given knowledge source or even add new sources of knowledge.

As we implement each knowledge source, we may discover the existence of common rules as well as common behavior. For example, we might notice that the `WordStructureKnowledgeSource` and the `SentenceStructure KnowledgeSource` classes share a common behavior, in that both must know how to evaluate rules regarding the legal ordering of certain constructs. The former knowledge source is interested in the arrangement of letters; the latter is interested in the arrangement of words. In either case, the processing is the same. Thus, it is reasonable for us to alter the knowledge source class structure by developing a new abstract class, called `StructureKnowledgeSource`, in which we place this common behavior.

This new knowledge source class hierarchy highlights the fact that evaluating a set of rules is dependent on both the kind of knowledge source as well as the kind of blackboard object. For example, given a specific knowledge source, it might use forward-chaining on one kind of `Blackboard` object and backward-chaining on another. Furthermore, given a specific `Blackboard` object, how it is evaluated will depend on which knowledge source is applied.

10.4 Post-Transition

In this section, we consider an improvement to the functionality of the cryptanalysis system and observe how our design weathers the change.

System Enhancements

In any intelligent system, it is important to know what the final answer is to a problem, but it is often equally important to know how the system arrived at this solution. Thus, we desire our application to be introspective: It should keep track of when knowledge sources were activated, what assumptions were made and why, and so on, so that we can later question it, for example, about why it made an assumption, how it arrived at another assumption, and when a particular knowledge source was activated.

To add this new functionality, we need to do two things. First, we must devise a mechanism for keeping track of the work that the controller and each knowledge source perform, and second, we must modify the appropriate operations so that they record this information. Basically, the design calls for the knowledge sources and the controller to register what they did in some central repository.

Let's start by inventing the classes needed to support this mechanism. First, we might define the class `Action`, which serves to record what a particular knowledge source or controller did. Figure 10–16 presents the design of the `Action` class as it fits into our architectural design.

For example, if the controller selected a particular knowledge source for activation, it would create an instance of this class, set the `who` argument to itself, set the `what` argument to the knowledge source, set the `why` argument to some explanation (perhaps including the current priority of the hint), and set `when` this occurred.

The first part of our task is done, and the second part is almost as easy. Consider for a moment where important events take place in our application. As it turns out, five primary kinds of operations are affected:

1. Methods that state an assumption
2. Methods that retract an assumption
3. Methods that activate a knowledge source
4. Methods that cause rules to be evaluated
5. Methods that register hints from a knowledge source

Actually, these events are largely constrained to two places in the architecture: as part of the controller's finite state machine and as part of the assumption mechanism. Our maintenance task, therefore, involves touching all the methods that play a role in these two places, a task that is tedious but by no means rocket science. Indeed, the most important discovery is that adding this new behavior requires no significant architectural change.

To complete our work here, we must also implement a class that can answer who, what, when, and why questions from the user. The design of such an object is not terribly difficult because all the information it needs to know may be found as the state of instances of the class actions.

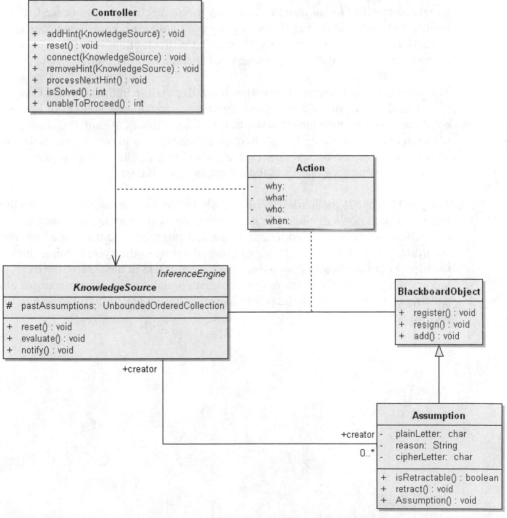

Figure 10–16 Additional Functionality Provided through the `Action` Class Design

Changing the Requirements

Once we have a stable implementation in place, many new requirements can be incorporated with minimal changes to our design. Let's consider three kinds of new requirements:

1. The ability to decipher languages other than English
2. The ability to decipher using transposition ciphers as well as single substitution ciphers
3. The ability to learn from experience

The first change is fairly easy because the fact that our application uses English is largely immaterial to our design. Assuming the same character set is used, it is mainly a matter of changing the rules associated with each knowledge source. Actually, changing the character set is not that difficult either because even the `Alphabet` class is not dependent on what characters it manipulates.

The second change is much harder, but it is still possible in the context of the blackboard framework. Basically, our approach is to add new sources of knowledge that embody information about transposition ciphers. Again, this change does not alter any existing key abstraction or mechanism in our design; rather, it involves the addition of new classes that use existing facilities, such as the `InferenceEngine` class and the assumption mechanism.

The third change is the hardest of all, mainly because machine learning is on the fringes of our knowledge in artificial intelligence. As one approach, when the controller discovers it can no longer proceed, it might ask the user for a hint. By recording this hint, along with the actions that led up to the system being stuck, the blackboard application can avoid a similar problem in the future. We can incorporate this simplistic learning mechanism without vastly altering any of our existing classes; as with all the other changes, this one can build on existing facilities.

Chapter 11

Data Acquisition: Weather Monitoring Station

For many scientific systems, the automatic collection of data is usually acquired through the use of sensors or devices. This data acquisition typically involves the processing of signals and waveforms to obtain the desired information. The components of a data acquisition system include the appropriate sensors that convert any measured parameter to an electrical signal, which is acquired by data acquisition hardware. Control software is developed that interprets the signals for analysis and display.

Using object-oriented techniques to design a data acquisition system allows us to isolate the hardware that measures and collects the data from the application that then analyzes the information. A robust architecture can be defined to allow for sensors and devices to be added or replaced without disturbing the architecture of the control application. Applying interfaces that act as a skin overlaying the hardware allows for isolation of the measuring devices from the application that processes the information. In this chapter, we provide an example of a data acquisition system, in our case, a Weather Monitoring System. The Weather Monitoring System uses sensors and devices that measure the weather conditions that are analyzed and displayed. This example illustrates an object-oriented solution to a real-time control processing application that provides a reusable component architecture that can isolate the hardware from the application.

11.1 Inception

Our Weather Monitoring System is a simple application, encompassing only a handful of classes. Indeed, at first glance, the object-oriented novice might be tempted to tackle this problem in an inherently non-object-oriented manner by considering the flow of data and the various input/output mappings involved. However, as we shall see, even a system as small as this one lends itself well to an object-oriented architecture, and in so doing exposes some of the basic principles of the object-oriented development process.

Requirements for the Weather Monitoring Station

This system shall provide automatic monitoring of various weather conditions. Specifically, it must measure the following:

- Wind speed and direction
- Temperature
- Barometric pressure
- Humidity

The system shall also provide these derived measurements:

- Wind chill
- Dew point temperature
- Temperature trend
- Barometric pressure trend

The system shall have a means of determining the current time and date, so that it can report the highest and lowest values of any of the four primary measurements during the previous 24-hour period.

The system shall have a display that continuously indicates all eight primary and derived measurements, as well as the current time and date. Through the use of a keypad, the user may direct the system to display the 24-hour high or low value of any one primary measurement, together with the time of the reported value.

The system shall allow the user to calibrate its sensors against known values and to set the current time and date.

Defining the Boundaries of the Problem

We begin our analysis by considering the hardware on which our software must execute. This is inherently a problem of systems analysis, involving manufacturability and cost issues that are far beyond the scope of this text. To bound our problem and thus allow us to expose the issues of its software analysis and design, we will make the following strategic assumptions.

- The processor (i.e., CPU) may take the form of a PC or a handheld device.
- Time and date are supplied by a clock.
- Temperature, barometric pressure, and humidity are measured via remote sensors.
- Wind direction and speed are measured from a boom encompassing a wind vane (capable of sensing wind from any of 16 directions) and cups (which advance a counter for each revolution).
- User input is provided through a keypad.
- The display is an off-the-shelf LCD graphic device.
- A timer interrupts the computer every 1/60 second.

Figure 11–1 provides a deployment diagram that illustrates this hardware platform.

We have chosen to throw some hardware at this problem so that we might better focus on the system's software. Obviously, we could require more software by doing less in hardware (e.g., by eliminating some of the hardware for the user input and graphics device), but in this particular application, changing the hardware/software boundary is largely immaterial to our object-oriented architecture. Indeed, one of the characteristics of an object-oriented system is that it tends to speak in the vocabulary of its problem space and so represents a virtual machine that parallels our abstraction of the problem's key entities. Changing the details of the system's hardware impacts only our abstraction of the lower layers of the system.

The details of hardware interfaces can be easily insulated from our software abstractions by wrapping a class around each such interface. For example, we might devise a simple class for accessing the current time and date. We begin by doing a little isolated class analysis, in which we consider what roles and responsibilities this abstraction should encompass.[1] Thus, we might decide that

---

1. Actually, instead of first setting out to design a new class from scratch, we should start by looking for an existing class that already satisfies our needs. A time and data class is certainly a good candidate for reuse. However, for the purposes of this chapter, we will assume that no such class could be found.

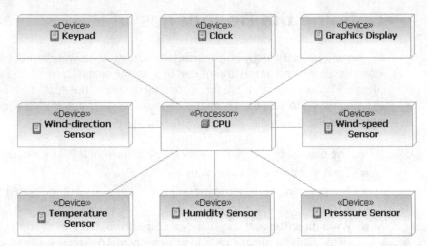

Figure 11–1 The Deployment Diagram for the Weather Monitoring System

this class is responsible for keeping track of the current time in hours, minutes, and seconds, as well as the current month, day, and year. Our analysis might decide to turn these responsibilities into two services, denoted by the operations `currentTime` and `currentDate`, respectively. The operation `currentTime` returns a string in the following format:

```
13:56:42
```

showing the current hour, minute, and second. The operation `currentDate` returns a string in the following format:

```
6-10-93
```

showing the current month, day, and year.

Further analysis suggests that a more complete abstraction would allow a client to chose either a 12- or 24-hour format for the time, which we may provide in the form of an additional modifier named `setFormat`.

By specifying the behavior of this abstraction from the perspective of its public clients, we have devised a clear separation between its interface and implementation. The basic idea here is to build the outside view of each class as if we had complete control over its underlying platform, then implement the class as a bridge to its real inside view. Thus, the implementation of a class at the system's hardware/software boundary serves to bolt the outside view of the abstraction to its underlying platform, which is often constrained by system decisions that are out of the hands of the software engineer. Of course, the gap between an abstraction's outside and inside views must not be so wide as to require a thick and inefficient implementation to glue the two views together.

One responsibility of our time and date class must therefore include setting the date and time. Carrying out this responsibility requires a new set of services to set the time and date, which we provide via the operations setHour, setMinute, setSecond, setDay, setMonth, and setYear.

We may summarize our abstraction of a time/date class as follows.

Class name:
    TimeDate
Responsibility:
    Keep track of the current time and date.
Operations:
    currentTime
    currentDate
    setFormat
    setHour
    setMinute
    setSecond
    setMonth
    setDay
    setYear
Attributes:
    time
    date

Instances of this class have a dynamic lifecycle, which we can express in the state transition diagram shown in Figure 11–2. Here we see that upon initialization, an instance of this class resets its time and date attributes and then unconditionally enters the Running state, where it begins in 24-hour mode. Once in the Running state, receipt of the operation setFormat toggles the object between 12- and 24-hour mode. No matter what its nested state, however, setting the time or date causes the object to renormalize its attributes. Similarly, requesting its time or date causes the object to calculate a new string value.

We have specified the behavior of this abstraction in enough detail that we can offer it for use in scenarios with other clients we might discover during analysis. Before we consider these scenarios, let's specify the behavior of the other tangible objects in our system.

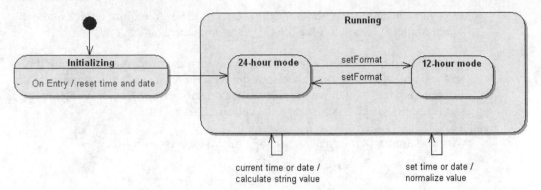

Figure 11–2 The `TimeDate` Lifecycle

The class `Temperature Sensor` serves as an analog to the hardware temperature sensors in our system. Isolated class analysis yields the following first cut at this abstraction's outside view.

Class name:
    `Temperature Sensor`
Responsibility:
    Keep track of the current temperature.
Operations:
    `currentTemperature`
    `setLowTemperature`
    `setHighTemperature`
Attribute:
    `temperature`

The operation `currentTemperature` is self-explanatory. The other two operations derive directly from our requirements, which obligate us to provide a mechanism for calibrating each sensor. For the moment, we will assume that each temperature sensor value is represented by a fixed-point number, whose low and high points can be calibrated to fit known actual values. We translate intermediate numbers to their actual temperatures by simple linear interpolation between these two points, as illustrated in Figure 11–3.

The careful reader may wonder why we have proposed a class for this abstraction, when our requirements imply that there is exactly one temperature sensor in the system. That is indeed true, but in anticipation of reusing this abstraction, we choose to capture it as a class, thereby decoupling it from the particulars of this one system. In fact, the number of temperature sensors monitored by a particular

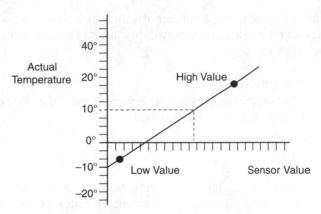

Figure 11-3 `Temperature Sensor` Calibration

system is largely immaterial to our architecture, and by devising a class, we make it simple for other programs in this family of systems to manipulate any number of sensors.

We can express our abstraction of the barometric pressure sensor in the following specification.

Class name:
    `Pressure Sensor`
Responsibility:
    Keep track of the current barometric pressure.
Operations:
    `currentPressure`
    `setLowPressure`
    `setHighPressure`
Attribute:
    `pressure`

A review of the system's requirements reveals that we may have missed one important behavior for this and the previous class, `Temperature Sensor`. Specifically, our requirements compel us to provide a means for reporting the temperature and pressure trends. For the moment (because we are doing analysis, not design), we will be content to focus on the nature of this behavior and, most important, on deciding which abstraction we should make responsible for this behavior.

For both the `Temperature Sensor` and the `Pressure Sensor`, we can express the trends as floating-point numbers between –1 and 1, representing the slope of a line fitting a number of values over some interval of time.[2] Thus, we may add the following responsibility and its corresponding operation to both of these classes.

Responsibility:
Report the temperature or pressure trend as the slope of a line fitting the past values over the given interval.
Operation:
`trend`

Because this behavior is common to both the `Temperature Sensor` and `Pressure Sensor` classes, our analysis suggests the invention of a common superclass, which we will call `Trend Sensor`, responsible for providing this common behavior.

For completeness, we should point out that there is an alternative view of the world that we might have chosen in our analysis. Our decision was to make this common behavior a responsibility of the sensor class itself. We could have decided to make this behavior a part of some external agent that periodically queried the particular sensor and calculated its trend, but we rejected this approach because it was unnecessarily complex. Our original specification of the `Temperature Sensor` and `Pressure Sensor` classes suggested that each abstraction had sufficient knowledge to carry out this trend-reporting behavior, and by combining responsibilities (albeit in the form of a superclass), we end up with a simple and conceptually cohesive abstraction.

Our abstraction of the humidity sensor can be expressed in the following specification.

Class name:
`Humidity Sensor`
Responsibility:
Keep track of the current humidity, expressed as a percentage of saturation from 0% to 100%.
Operations:
`currentHumidity`
`setLowHumidity`
`setHighHumidity`

---

2. A value of 0 means that the temperature or pressure is stable. A value of 0.1 denotes a modest rise; a value of –0.3 denotes rapidly declining values. A value approaching –1 or 1 suggests an environmental cataclysm, which is beyond the scope of the scenarios our system is expected to handle properly.

Attribute:

    humidity

The Humidity Sensor has no responsibility for calculating its trend and is therefore not a subclass of Trend Sensor.

A review of the system's requirements suggests some behavior common to the classes Temperature Sensor, Pressure Sensor, and Humidity Sensor. In particular, our requirements compel us to provide a means of reporting the highest and lowest values of each of these sensors during a 24-hour period. We defer deciding how to carry out this responsibility because that is an issue of design, not analysis. However, because this behavior is common to all three sensor classes, our analysis suggests the invention of a common superclass, which we call Historical Sensor, responsible for providing this common behavior.

Class name:

    Historical Sensor

Responsibility:

    Report the highest and lowest values over a 24-hour period.

Operations:

    highValue
    lowValue
    timeOfHighValue
    timeOfLowValue

Humidity Sensor is a direct subclass of Historical Sensor, as is Trend Sensor, which serves as an intermediate abstract class, bridging our abstractions of Historical Sensor and the concrete classes Temperature Sensor and Pressure Sensor.

Our abstraction of the wind-speed sensor can be expressed in the following specification.

Class name:

    WindSpeed Sensor

Responsibility:

    Keep track of the current wind speed.

Operations:

    currentSpeed
    setLowSpeed
    setHighSpeed

Attribute:

    speed

Our requirements suggest that we cannot detect the current wind speed directly; rather, we must calculate its value by taking the number of revolutions of the cups on the boom, dividing by the interval over which those revolutions were counted, and then applying a scaling value appropriate to the particular boom assembly. Needless to say, this calculation is one of the secrets of this class; clients could care less how `currentSpeed` is calculated, as long as this operation satisfies its contract and delivers meaningful values.

A quick domain analysis of the last four concrete classes (`Temperature Sensor`, `Pressure Sensor`, `Humidity Sensor`, and `WindSpeed Sensor`) reveals yet another behavior in common: Each of these classes knows how to calibrate itself by providing a linear interpolation against two known data points. Rather than replicating this behavior in all four classes, we instead choose to make this behavior the responsibility of an even higher superclass, which we call `Calibrating Sensor`, whose specification includes the following.

Class name:
   Calibrating Sensor
Responsibility:
   Provide a linear interpolation of values, given two known data points.
Operations:
   currentValue
   setHighValue
   setLowValue

`Calibrating Sensor` is an immediate superclass of `Historical Sensor`.[3]

Our final concrete sensor for wind direction is a bit different because it requires neither calibration nor history. We may express our abstraction of this entity in the following specification.

Class name:
   WindDirection Sensor
Responsibility:
   Keep track of the current wind direction, in terms of points along a compass rose.
Operation:
   currentDirection

---

3. This hierarchy passes our litmus test for inheritance: a `Temperature Sensor` is a kind of `Trend Sensor`, which is also a kind of `Historical Sensor`, which in turn is a kind of `Calibrating Sensor`.

Attribute:
```
direction
```

To unify our sensor abstractions, we generate the abstract base class `Sensor`, which serves as the immediate superclass to both the classes `WindDirection Sensor` and `Calibrating Sensor`. Figure 11–4 illustrates this complete hierarchy.

Although not part of the sensor hierarchy, our abstraction of the keypad for user input has a simple specification.

Class name:
```
Keypad
```
Responsibility:
Keep track of the last user input.
Operation:
```
lastKeyPress
```
Attribute:
```
key
```

Notice that this class has no knowledge of the meaning of any particular key: Instances of this class know only that one of several keys was pressed. We delegate responsibility for interpreting the meaning of these keys to a different class, which we will identify when we apply these concrete boundary classes to our scenarios.

Our abstraction of an `LCD Device` class serves to insulate our software from the particular hardware we might use. To decouple our software from the particular graphics hardware we might use, our analysis leads us to prototype some common displays for the Weather Monitoring System, and then determine our interface needs.

Figure 11–5 provides such a prototype. Here, we have omitted the required display of wind chill and dew point, as well as such details as how to display the 24-hour high or low value of primary measurements. Nonetheless, some patterns emerge: We need to display only text (in two different sizes and two different styles), circles, and lines (of varying thickness). Additionally, we note that some elements of our display are static (such as the label TEMP), while others are dynamic (such as the wind direction). We choose to display both static and dynamic elements via software. In this manner, we lessen the burden on our hardware by eliminating the need for special labels on the LCD itself, but we require slightly more of our software.

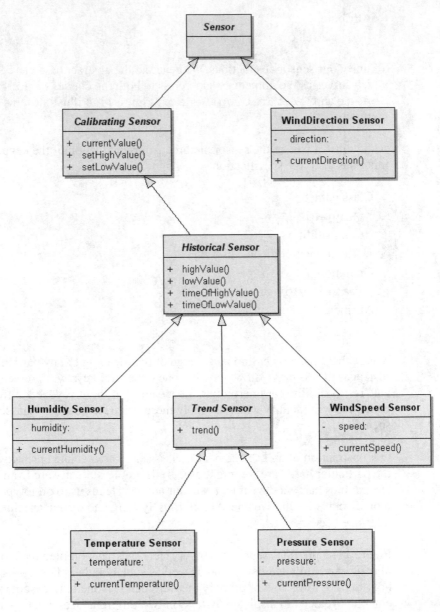

Figure 11–4 The Hierarchy of the `Sensor` Class

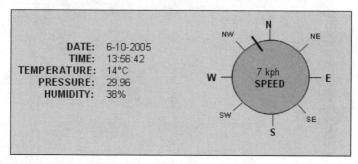

Figure 11–5 The Display for the Weather Monitoring System

We can translate these requirements into the following class specification.

Class name:

   `LCD Device`

Responsibility:

   Manage the LCD device and provide services for displaying certain graphics elements.

Operations:

   `drawText`
   `drawLine`
   `drawCircle`
   `setTextSize`
   `setTextStyle`
   `setPenSize`

As with the class `Keypad`, the class `LCD Device` has no knowledge of the meaning of the elements it manipulates. Instances of this class know only how to display text and lines; they do not know what these figures represent. This separation of concerns leaves us with loosely coupled abstractions (which is what we desire), but it does require that we find some agent responsible for mediating between the raw sensors and the display. We defer the invention of this new abstraction until we study some scenarios applicable to this system.

The final boundary class we need to consider is that of the timer. We will make the simplifying assumption that there is exactly one timer per system, whose behavior is to interrupt the computer every 1/60 of a second and, in so doing, to invoke an interrupt service routine. This is a particularly grungy detail, and it would be best if we could hide this implementation detail from the rest of our software abstractions. We can do so by devising a class that uses a callback function and exports only static members (so that we constrain our system to have exactly one timer).

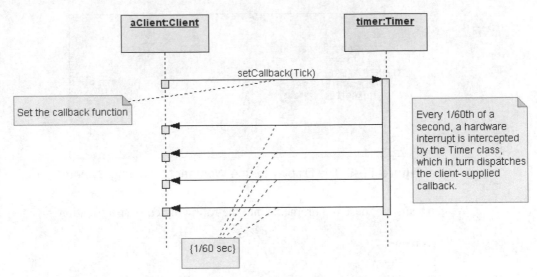

Figure 11–6 The `Timer` Interaction Diagram

Figure 11–6 provides a sequence diagram that illustrates a use case for this abstraction. Here we see how the timer and its client collaborate: The client begins by supplying a callback function, and every 1/60 of a second, the timer calls that function. In this manner, we decouple the client from knowing about how to intercept timed events, and we decouple the timer from knowing what to do when such an event occurs. The primary responsibility that this protocol places on the client is simply that the execution of its callback function must always take less than 1/60 of a second; otherwise, the timer will miss an event.

By intercepting time events, the `Timer` class serves as an active abstraction, meaning that it is at the root of a thread of control. We may express our abstraction of this class in the following specification.

> Class name:
>   Timer
> Responsibility:
>   Intercept all timed events and dispatch a callback function accordingly.
> Operation:
>   setCallback()

Scenarios

Now that we have established the abstractions at the boundaries of our system, we continue our analysis by studying several scenarios of its use. We begin by enu-

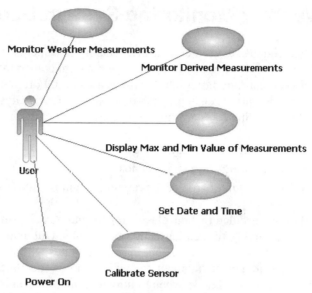

Figure 11–7 Primary Use Cases for the Weather Monitoring System

merating a number of primary use cases (Figure 11–7), as viewed from the point of view of the clients of this system:

- Monitoring basic weather measurements, including wind speed and direction, temperature, barometric pressure, and humidity
- Monitoring derived measurements, including wind chill, dew point, temperature trend, and barometric pressure trend
- Displaying the highest and lowest values of a selected measurement
- Setting the time and date
- Calibrating a selected sensor
- Powering up the system

We add to this list two secondary use cases:

- Power failure
- Sensor failure

11.2 Elaboration

Let's examine a number of these scenarios in order to illuminate the behavior—but not the design—of the system.

Weather Monitoring System Use Cases

Monitoring basic weather measurements is the principal function point of the Weather Monitoring System. One of our system constraints is that we cannot take measurements any faster than 60 times a second. Fortunately, most interesting weather conditions change much more slowly. Our analysis suggests that the following sampling rates are sufficient to capture changing conditions:

- Wind direction: every 0.1 second
- Wind speed: every 0.5 seconds
- Temperature, barometric pressure, and humidity: every 5 minutes

Earlier, we decided that the classes representing each primary sensor should have no responsibility for dealing with timed events. Our analysis therefore requires that we devise an external agent that collaborates with these sensors to carry out this scenario. For the moment, we will defer our specification of the behavior of this agent (how it knows when to initiate a sample is an issue of design, not analysis). The interaction diagram shown in Figure 11–8 illustrates this scenario. Here we see that when the agent begins sampling, it polls each sensor in turn but intentionally skips certain sensors in order to sample them at a slower rate. By polling each sensor rather than letting each sensor act as a thread of control, the execution of our system is more predictable because our agent can control the flow of events. Because this name reflects its place in the behavior of the system, we will make this agent an instance of the class Sampler.

We must continue this scenario by asking which of these objects in the interaction diagram is then responsible for displaying the sampled values on the one instance of our LCD Device class. Ultimately, we have two choices: We can have each sensor be responsible for displaying itself (the common pattern used in MVC-like architectures), or we can have a separate object be responsible for this behavior. For this particular problem, we choose the latter option because it allows us to

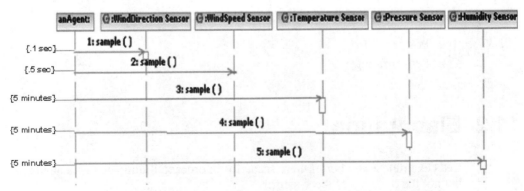

Figure 11–8 A Scenario for Monitoring Basic Measurements

encapsulate all our design decisions about the layout of our display in one class.[4]
Thus, we add the following class specification to our products of analysis.

Class name:
   Display Manager
Responsibility:
   Manage the layout of items on the LCD device.
Operations:
   drawStaticItems
   displayTime
   displayDate
   displayTemperature
   displayHumidity
   displayPressure
   displayWindChill
   displayDewPoint
   displayWindSpeed
   displayWindDirection
   displayHighLow

The operation drawStaticItems exists to draw the unchangeable parts of
the display, such as the compass rose used for indicating the wind direction.
We will also assume that the operations displayTemperature and
displayPressure are responsible for displaying their corresponding
trends (therefore, as we move into implementation, we must provide a suitable
signature for these operations).

Figure 11–9 provides a class diagram illustrating the abstractions that must collaborate to carry out this scenario. Note that we also indicate the role that each
abstraction plays in its association with other classes.

There is one important side effect from our decision to include the class Display
Manager.[5] Specifically, internationalizing our software, that is, adapting it to

---

4. The dominant problem here is where we display each item, not how each item looks.
Because this is a decision that is likely to change, it is best for us to encapsulate in one class
all the knowledge about where to display each item on the LCD device. Changing our assumptions about front panel layout therefore requires that we touch only one class instead of many.

5. Is this an analysis decision or a design decision? The question can be argued in either
direction, although such arguments are largely academic in the face of having to deliver
production software. If a decision advances our understanding of the system's desired behavior and in addition leads us to an elegant architecture, we don't really care what it is called.

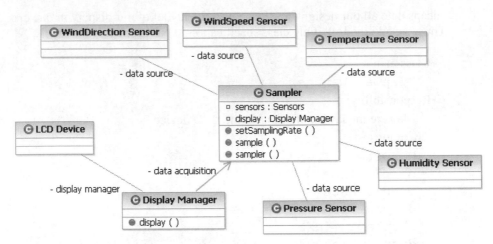

Figure 11–9 The `Sampler` and `Display Manager` Classes

different countries and languages, becomes much easier given this design decision because the knowledge about how elements are named and thus labeled on the display (such as TEMP and WIND) is part of the secrets of this one class.

Internationalization leads us to consider an issue about which the requirements are silent: Should the system display temperature in Centigrade or Fahrenheit? Similarly, should the system display wind speed in kilometers per hour (kph) or miles per hour (mph)? Ultimately, our software should not constrain us. Because we seek end-user flexibility, we must add an operation `setMode` to both the `Temperature Sensor` and `WindSpeed Sensor` classes. We must also add a new responsibility to each of these classes, which makes their instances construct themselves in a known stable state. Finally, we must modify the signature of the operation `Display Manager::drawStaticItems` accordingly, so that when we change units of measurement, the display manager can update the front panel display if needed.

This discovery leads us to add one more scenario for consideration in our analysis, namely:

■ Setting the unit of measurement for temperature and wind speed

We will defer considering this scenario until we study the other use cases that deal with user interaction.

Monitoring the derived measurements for temperature and pressure trends can be achieved through the protocol we have already established for the `Temperature Sensor` and `Pressure Sensor` classes. However, to complete this scenario for all derived measurements, we are now led to discover two new classes, which we call Wind Chill and Dew Point, responsible for calculating their respective values. Neither of these abstractions represents sensors because they do not denote any tangible device in the system. Rather, each one acts as an agent that collaborates with two other classes to carry out its responsibilities. Specifically, the Wind Chill conspires with the Temperature Sensor and WindSpeed Sensor, and the Dew Point conspires with the Temperature Sensor and Humidity Sensor. In turn, Wind Chill and Dew Point collaborate with Sampler, using the same mechanism as Sampler uses to monitor all the primary weather measurements. Figure 11–10 illustrates the classes involved in this scenario; basically, this class diagram is just a slightly different view of the system than the one shown in Figure 11–9.

Why do we define Wind Chill and Dew Point as classes, instead of just carrying out their calculation through a simple nonmember function? The answer is that this situation passes our litmus test for object-oriented abstractions: Instances of both Wind Chill and Dew Point provide some behavior (namely, the calculation of their respective values) and encapsulate some state (each must maintain an association with a particular instance of two different concrete sensors), and each has a unique identity (each particular wind-speed sensor/temperature sensor association must have its own Wind Chill object). By "objectifying" these seemingly algorithmic abstractions, we also end up with a more reusable architecture: Both Wind Chill and Dew Point can be lifted from this particular application because each presents a clear contract to its clients, and each offers a clear separation of concerns relative to all the other abstractions.

Moving on, we next consider the various scenarios that relate to user interaction with the Weather Monitoring System. Deciding on the proper user gestures for

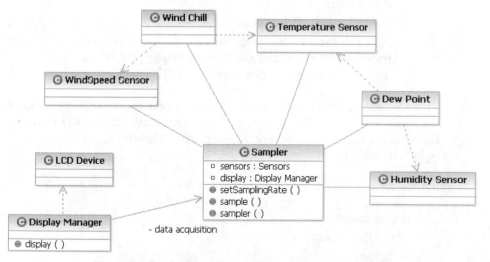

Figure 11–10 Classes for Derived Measurements

interacting with an embedded controller such as this one is still as much of an art as is designing a graphical user interface. A full treatment of how to devise such user interfaces is beyond the scope of this text, but the basic message for the software analyst is that prototyping works and indeed is fundamental in helping to mitigate the risks involved in user interface design. Furthermore, by implementing our decisions in terms of an object-oriented architecture, we make it relatively easy to change these user interface decisions without rending the fabric of our design.

Consider some possible use case scenarios of user interaction.

Use case name:
Display Max and Min Value of Measurements
Description:
This use case displays the maximum and minimum values of a selected measurement.
Basic flow:

1. The use case begins when the user presses the SELECT key.
2. The system displays SELECTING.
3. The user presses any one of the keys WIND, TEMP, PRESSURE, or HUMIDITY; any other key press (except RUN) is ignored.
4. The system flashes the corresponding label.
5. The user presses the UP or DOWN key to select display of the highest or lowest 24-hour value, respectively; any other key press (except RUN) is ignored.
6. The system displays the selected value, together with its time of occurrence.
7. Control passes back to step 3 or step 5.

   Note that the user may press the RUN key to commit or abandon the operation, at which time the flashing display, the selected value, and the SELECTING message are removed.

This scenario leads us to enhance the Display Manager class by adding both the operations flashLabel (which causes the identified label to flash or stop flashing, according to an appropriate operation argument) and displayMode (which displays a text message on the LCD device).

Setting the time and date follows a similar scenario.

Use case name:
Set Date and Time
Description:
This use case sets the date and time.

Basic flow:

1. The use case begins when the user presses the SELECT key.
2. The system displays SELECTING.
3. The user presses either of the keys TIME or DATE; any other key press (except RUN and the keys listed in step 3 of the previous scenario) is ignored.
4. The system flashes the corresponding label; the display also flashes the first field of the selected item (namely, the hours field for the time and the month field for the date).
5. The user presses the LEFT or RIGHT keys to select another field (selection wraps around); the user presses the UP or DOWN keys to raise or lower the value of the selected field.
6. Control passes back to step 3 or step 5.

   Note that the user may press the RUN key to commit or abandon the operation, at which time the flashing display and the SELECTING message are removed, and the time or date are reset.

Calibrating a particular sensor follows a related pattern of user gestures.

Use case name:

Calibrate Sensor

Description:

   This use case is used to calibrate the sensors.

Basic flow:

1. The use case begins when the user presses the CALIBRATE key.
2. The system displays CALIBRATING.
3. The user presses any one of the keys WIND, TEMP, PRESSURE, or HUMIDITY; any other key press (except RUN) is ignored.
4. The system flashes the corresponding label.
5. The user presses the UP or DOWN keys to select the high or low calibration point.
6. The display flashes the corresponding value.
7. The user presses the UP or DOWN keys to adjust the selected value.
8. Control passes back to step 3 or step 5.

   Note that the user may press the RUN key to commit or abandon the operation, at which time the flashing display and the CALIBRATING message are removed, and the calibration function is reset.

While calibrating, instances of the Sampler class must be told to not sample the selected item; otherwise, erroneous information would be displayed to the user. This scenario therefore requires that we introduce two new operations for the

`Sampler` class, namely, `inhibitSample` and `resumeSample`, both of which have a signature that specifies a particular measurement.

Our last primary scenario involving the user interface concerns setting units of measurement.

Use case name:
Set Unit of Measurement
Description:
This use case sets the unit of measurement for temperature and wind speed.
Basic flow:
1. The use case begins when the user presses the MODE key.
2. The system displays MODE.
3. The user presses either of the keys WIND or TEMP; any other key press (except RUN) is ignored.
4. The system flashes the corresponding label.
5. The user presses the UP or DOWN keys to toggle the current unit of measurement.
6. The system updates the unit of measurement for the selected item.
7. Control passes back to step 3 or step 5.
   Note that the user may press the RUN key to commit or abandon the operation, at which time the flashing display and the MODE message are removed, and the current unit of measurement for the item is set.

A study of these scenarios leads us to decide on an arrangement for buttons on the keypad (a system decision), which we illustrate in Figure 11–11.

Each of these user interface scenarios involves some form of modality or event-ordered behavior and so is well suited to expression through the use of state transition diagrams. Because these scenarios are so tightly coupled, we choose to devise a new class, `InputManager`, which is responsible for carrying out the following contractual specification.

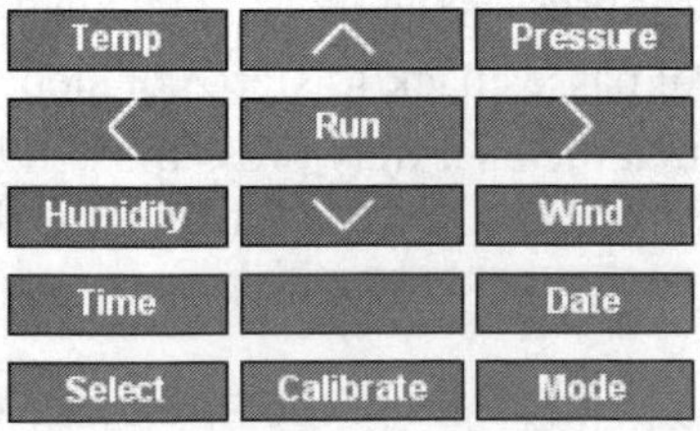

Figure 11–11 The User Keypad for the Weather Monitoring System

Class name:

   `InputManager`

Responsibility:

   Manage and dispatch user input.

Operation:

   `processKeyPress`

The sole operation, `processKeyPress`, animates the state machine that lives behind instances of this class.

As shown in Figure 11–12, the outermost state machine diagram for this class encompasses four states: `Running`, `Calibrating`, `Selecting`, and `Mode`. These states correspond directly to the earlier scenarios. We transition to the respective states based on the first key press intercepted while `Running`, and we return to the `Running` state when the last key press is again Run. Each time we enter `Running`, we clear the message on the display.

We have expanded the `Mode` state to show how we might more formally express the dynamic semantics of our scenario. As we first enter this state, our entry action is to display an appropriate message on the display. We begin in the `Waiting` state and transition out of this state if we intercept a user key press of the TEMP or WIND keys, which causes us to enter a nested state of `Processing`,

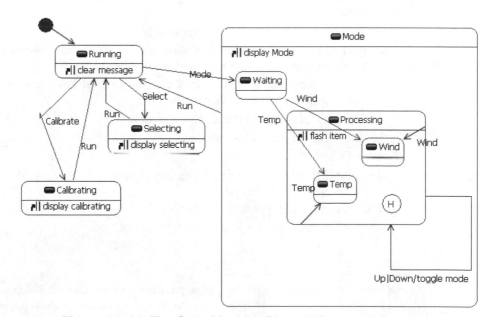

Figure 11–12 The State Machine Diagram for `InputManager`

or a user key press of RUN, which transitions us back to the outermost Running state. Each time we enter Processing, we flash the appropriate item; in subsequent entries to this state, we enter the previously entered nested state, Temp or Wind.

While in the Temp or Wind state, we may intercept one of five key presses: UP or DOWN (which toggles the corresponding mode), TEMP or WIND (which reenters the appropriate nested state), or RUN (which ejects us from the outer Mode state).

The Selecting and Calibrating states similarly expand out to reveal more nested states. We will not show their expanded state machine diagrams here because their presentation does not reveal anything particularly interesting about the problem at hand.[6]

Our final primary scenario involves powering up the system, which requires that we bring all of its objects to life in an orderly fashion, ensuring that each one starts in a stable initial state. We may write a script for our analysis of this scenario as follows.

Use case name:
    Power On
Description:
    Power up the system.
Basic flow:
1. This use case begins when power is applied.
2. Each sensor is constructed; historical sensors clear their history, and trend sensors prime their slope-calculating algorithms.
3. The user input buffer is initialized, causing garbage key presses (due to noise on power up) to be discarded.
4. The static elements of the display are drawn.
5. The sampling process is initiated.

Postconditions:
    The past high/low values of each primary measurement is set to the value and time of their first sample.
    The temperature and pressure trends are flat.
    The InputManager is in the Running state.

---

6. Of course, for a production product, a comprehensive analysis would complete the exposition of this state transition diagram. We can defer this task here because it is more tedious than not and in fact does not reveal anything we do not already know about the system under construction.

Notice the use of postconditions in our script to specify the expected state of the system after this scenario completes. As we shall see, there is no one agent in the system that carries out this scenario; rather, this behavior results from the collaboration of a number of objects, each of which is given the responsibility to bring itself to a stable initial state.

This completes our study of the Weather Monitoring System's primary scenarios. To be utterly complete, we might want to walk through the various secondary scenarios. At this point, however, we have exposed a sufficient number of the system's function points, and we want to proceed with architectural design, so that we might begin to validate our strategic decisions.

Every software system needs to have a simple yet powerful organizational philosophy (think of it as the software equivalent of a sound bite that describes the system's architecture), and the Weather Monitoring System is no exception. The next step in our development process is to articulate this architectural framework, so that we might have a stable foundation on which to evolve the system's function points.

The Architecture Framework

In data acquisition and process control domains, we might follow many possible architectural patterns, but the two most common alternatives involve either the synchronization of autonomous actors or time-frame-based processing.

In the first pattern, our architecture encompasses a number of relatively independent objects, each of which serves as a thread of control. For example, we might invent several new sensor objects that build on more primitive hardware/software abstractions, with each such object responsible for taking its own sample and reporting back to some central agent that processes these samples. This architecture has its merits; it may be the only meaningful framework if we have a distributed system in which we must collect samples from many remote locations. This architecture also allows for more local optimization of the sampling process (each sampling actor has the knowledge to adjust itself to changing conditions, perhaps by increasing or decreasing its sampling rate as conditions warrant).

However, this architectural pattern is generally not well suited to hard real-time systems, wherein we must have complete predictability over when events take place. Although the Weather Monitoring System is not hard real-time, it does require some modicum of predictable, ordered behavior. For this reason, we turn to an alternative pattern, that of time-frame-based processing.

As we illustrate in Figure 11–13, this model takes time and divides it into several (usually fixed-length) frames, which we further divide into subframes, each of

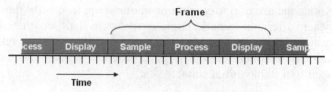

Figure 11–13 Time-Frame Processing

which encompasses some functional behavior. The activity from one frame to another may be different. For example, we might sample the wind direction every 10 frames but sample the wind speed only every 30 frames.[7] The primary merit of this architectural pattern is that we can more rigorously control the order of events.

Figure 11–14 provides a class diagram that expresses this architecture for the Weather Monitoring System. Here we find most of the classes we discovered earlier during analysis, the main difference being that we now show how all the key abstractions collaborate with one another. As is typical in class diagrams for production systems, we do not (and cannot) show every class and every relationship. For example, we have omitted the class hierarchy regarding all of the sensors.

We have invented one new class in this architecture, namely, the class `Sensors`, whose responsibility is to serve as the collection of all the physical sensors in the system. Because at least two other agents in the system (`Sampler` and `Input-Manager`) must associate with the entire collection of sensors, bundling them in one container class allows us to treat our system's sensors as a logical whole.

11.3 Construction

The central behavior of this architecture is carried out by a collaboration of the `Sampler` and `Timer` classes. We would be wise during architectural design to concretely prototype these classes so that we can validate our assumptions.

The Frame Mechanism

We begin by refining the interface of the class `Timer`, which dispatches a callback function. Figure 11–15 shows the class design.

---

7. For example, if each frame is allocated to be 1/60 second, 30 frames represents 0.5 second.

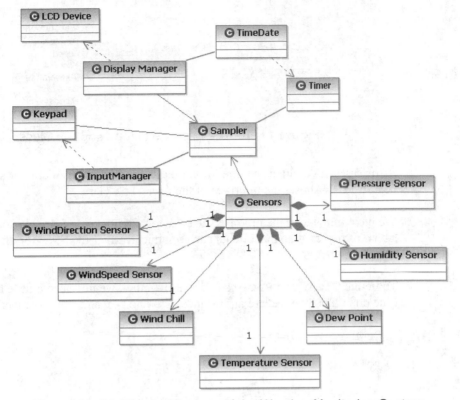

Figure 11–14 The Architecture of the Weather Monitoring System

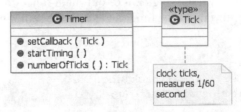

Figure 11–15 The Design of the `Timer` Class

`Timer` is an unusual class, but remember that it holds some unusual secrets. We use the first operation `setCallback` to attach a callback function to the timer. We launch the timer's behavior by invoking `startTiming`, after which time the one `Timer` entity dispatches the callback function every 1/60 of a second. Notice that we introduce an explicit starting operation because we cannot rely on any particular implementation-dependent ordering in the elaboration of declarations.

Before we turn to the `Sampler` class, we introduce a new declaration that names the various sensors in this particular system. The enumeration class

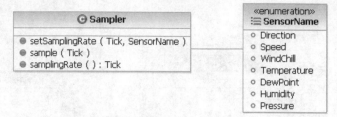

Figure 11–16 The Interface of the `Sampler` Class

`SensorName` contains enumeration literals for all the sensors in our system. Figure 11–16 shows the interface of the `Sampler` class.

We have introduced the modifier `setSamplingRate` and its selector `samplingRate` so that clients can dynamically alter the behavior of the sampling objects.

To tie the `Timer` and `Sampler` classes together, we just need a little bit of C++ glue code. First we declare an instance of `Sampler` and a nonmember function.

```
Sampler sampler;

void acquire(Tick t)
{
   sampler.sample(t);
}
```

Now we can write a fragment of our main function, which simply attaches the callback function to the timer and starts the sampling process.

```
main() {

   Timer::setCallback(acquire);
   Timer::startTiming();

   while(1) {
      ;
   }

   return 0;

}
```

This is a fairly typical main program for object-oriented systems: It is short (because the real work is delegated to key objects in the system), and it involves a dispatch loop (which in this case does nothing because we have no background processing to complete).[8]

To continue this thread of the system's architecture, we next provide an interface for the `Sensors` class (Figure 11–17). For the moment, we assume the existence of the various concrete sensor classes.

This is basically a collection type class, and for this reason we make `Sensors` a subclass of the foundation class `Collection`.[9] We make `Collection` a protected superclass because we don't want to expose most of its operations to clients of the `Sensors` class. Our declaration of `Sensors` provides only a sparse set of operations because our problem is sufficiently constrained that we know sensors are only added and never removed from the collection.

We have invented a generalized sensor collection class that can hold multiple instances of the same kind of sensor, with each instance within its class distinguished by a unique ID, numbered starting at zero.

We specify in the `Sampler` class the associations with the `Sensors` and `Display Manager` classes and revise our declaration of the one instance of the `Sampler` class (Figure 11–18).

The construction of the `Sampler` object connects this agent with the specific collection of sensors and the particular display manager used in the system.

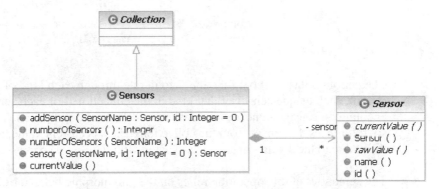

Figure 11–17 The Interface of the `Sensors` class

---

8. This is yet another common architectural pattern: Dispatch loops serve to intercept external or internal events and then dispatch them to the appropriate agents.

9. The `Collection` class is an abstract superclass that provides common operations for a collection of items supplied by language libraries.

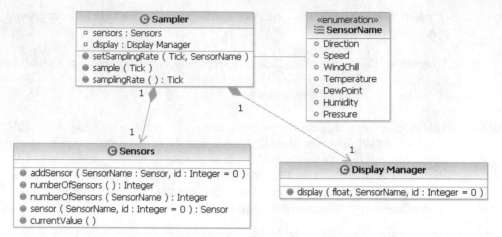

Figure 11–18 The Design of the `Sampler` Class

Now we can implement the `Sampler` class's key operation, `sample`.

```
void Sampler::sample(Tick t)
{
  for (SensorName name = Direction; name <= Pressure; name++)
    for (unsigned int id = 0; id <
          repSensors.numberOfSensors(name); id++)

      if (!(t % samplingRate(name)))

        repDisplayManager.display(repSensors.sensor(name,
            id).currentValue(), name, id);
}
```

The action of this member function is to iterate through each kind of sensor and, in turn, each unique sensor of that kind in the collection. For each sensor it encounters, `sample` checks to see whether it is time to sample its value and, if so, references the sensor from the collection, takes its current value, and delivers this value to the display manager associated with the `Sampler` instance.[10]

The semantics of this operation relies on the polymorphic behavior of the operation `currentValue` defined for the base class `Sensor`. This operation also relies on the operation `display` defined for the class `Display Manager`.

---

10. An alternate approach would be to have each sensor provide a member function that returns its sampling rate and another member function that draws the sensor on the LCD. This design would make the implementation of the `Sampler` class simpler and more extensible, although it would shift more responsibilities to the sensor classes.

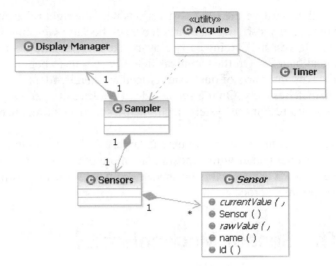

Figure 11–19 The Frame Mechanism

Now that we have refined this element of our architecture, we present a new class diagram in Figure 11–19 that highlights this frame mechanism.

Now that we have validated our architecture by walking through several scenarios, we can continue with the incremental development of the system's function points.

Release Planning

We start this process by proposing a sequence of releases, each of which builds on the previous release.

- Develop a minimal functionality release, which monitors just one sensor.
- Complete the sensor hierarchy.
- Complete the classes responsible for managing the display.
- Complete the classes responsible for managing the user interface.

We could order these releases in just about any manner, but we choose this one, which progresses from highest to lowest risk, thereby forcing our development process to directly attack the hard problems first.

Developing the minimal functionality release forces us to take a vertical slice through our architecture and implement small parts of just about every key abstraction. This activity addresses the highest risk in the project, namely, whether we have the right abstractions with the right roles and responsibilities. This activity also gives us early feedback because we can now play with an executable system. Forcing early closure like this has a number of technical and social benefits. On the technical side, it forces us to begin to bolt the hardware and software parts of our system together, thereby identifying any impedance mismatches early. On the social side, it allows us to get early feedback about the look and feel of the system, from the perspectives of real users.

Because completing this release is largely a manner of tactical implementation, we will not bother with exposing any more of its structure. We will now turn to elements of later releases because they reveal some interesting insights about the development process.

The Sensor Mechanism

In inventing the architecture for this system, we have already seen how we had to iteratively and incrementally evolve our abstraction of the sensor classes, which we began during analysis. In this evolutionary release, we expect to build on the earlier completion of a minimal functional system and finish the details of this class hierarchy.

At this point in our development cycle, the class hierarchy we first presented in Figure 11–4 remains stable, although, not surprisingly, we had to adjust the location of certain polymorphic operations in order to extract greater commonality. Specifically, in an earlier section we noted the requirement for the currentValue operation, declared in the abstract base class Sensor. We may complete our design of the Sensor class (Figure 11–20).

Notice that through the class constructor, we gave the instances of this class knowledge of their name and ID. This is essentially a kind of runtime type identification, but providing this information is unavoidable here because, per the requirements, each sensor instance must have a mapping to a particular interface. We can hide the secrets of this mapping by making this interface a function of a sensor name and ID.

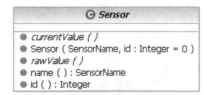

Figure 11–20 The Design of the Sensor Class

Now that we have added this new responsibility, we can go back and simplify the signature of DisplayManager::display to take only a single argument, namely, a reference to a Sensor object. We can eliminate the other arguments to this function because the Display Manager can now ask the Sensor object its name and ID.

Making this change is advisable because it simplifies certain cross-class interfaces. Indeed, if we fail to keep up with small, rippling changes such as this one, our architecture will eventually suffer as the protocols among collaborating classes become inconsistently applied.

The declaration of the immediate subclass Calibrating Sensor builds on the base class Sensor (Figure 11–21).

Calibrating Sensor introduces two new operations (setHighValue and setLowValue) and implements the previously defined function currentValue.

Next, consider the declaration of the subclass Historical Sensor, which builds on the class Calibrating Sensor (Figure 11–22).

Historical Sensor has four operations whose implementation requires collaboration with the TimeDate class for the time of the high or low values. Note that Historical Sensor is still an abstract class because we have not yet completed the definition of the abstract function rawValue, which we defer to be a concrete subclass responsibility.

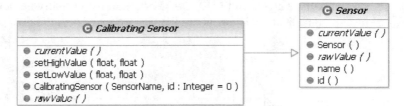

Figure 11–21 The Design of the Calibrating Sensor Class

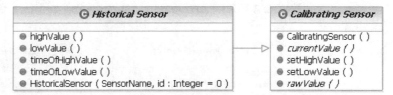

Figure 11–22 The Design of the Historical Sensor Class

The class Trend Sensor inherits from Historical Sensor and adds one new responsibility (Figure 11–23).

Trend Sensor introduces one new function. As with some of the other operations that some other intermediate classes have added, we declare trend as concrete because we do not desire that subclasses change their behavior.

Ultimately, we reach concrete subclasses such as Temperature Sensor (Figure 11–24).

Notice that the signature of this class's constructor is slightly different than its superclass's, simply because at this level of abstraction, we know the specific name of the class. Also, notice that we have introduced the operation current-Temperature, which follows from our earlier analysis. This operation is semantically the same as the polymorphic function currentValue, but we choose to include both of them because the operation currentTemperature is slightly more type-safe.

Once we have successfully completed the implementation of all classes in this hierarchy and integrated them with the previous release, we may proceed to the next level of the system's functionality.

The Display Mechanism

Implementing the next release, which completes the functionality of the classes DisplayManager and LCD Device, requires virtually no new design work, just some tactical decisions about the signature and semantics of certain func-

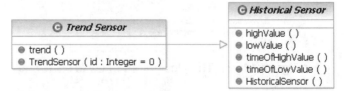

Figure 11–23 The Design of the Trend Sensor Class

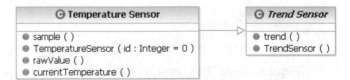

Figure 11–24 The Design of the Temperature Sensor Class

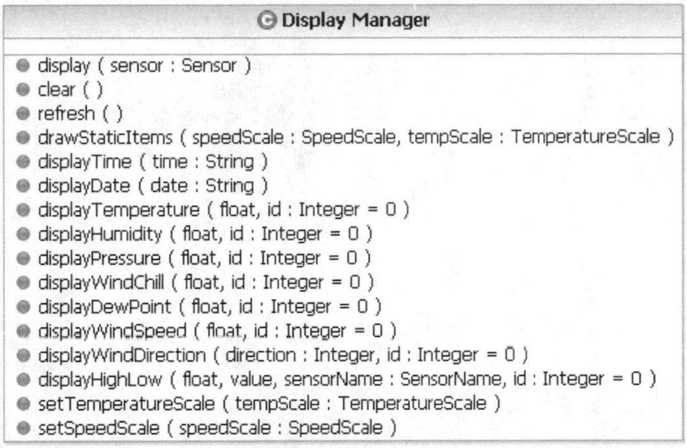

⊙ Display Manager

● display (sensor : Sensor)
● clear ( )
● refresh ( )
● drawStaticItems (speedScale : SpeedScale, tempScale : TemperatureScale)
● displayTime (time : String)
● displayDate (date : String)
● displayTemperature (float, id : Integer = 0)
● displayHumidity (float, id : Integer = 0)
● displayPressure (float, id : Integer = 0)
● displayWindChill (float, id : Integer = 0)
● displayDewPoint (float, id : Integer = 0)
● displayWindSpeed (float, id : Integer = 0)
● displayWindDirection (direction : Integer, id : Integer = 0)
● displayHighLow (float, value, sensorName : SensorName, id : Integer = 0)
● setTemperatureScale (tempScale : TemperatureScale)
● setSpeedScale (speedScale : SpeedScale)

Figure 11–25 The Design of the `Display Manager` Interface

tions. Combining the decisions we made during analysis with our first architectural prototype, wherein we made some important decisions about the protocol for displaying sensor values, we can derive the concrete interface shown in Figure 11–25.

None of these operations are abstract because we neither expect nor desire any subclasses.

Notice that this class exports several primitive operations (such as `displayTime` and `refresh`) but also exposes the composite operation `display`, whose presence greatly simplifies the action of clients that must interact with instances of `Display Manager`.

`Display Manager` ultimately uses the resources of the `LCD Device` class, which, as we described earlier, serves as a skin over the underlying hardware. In this manner, `Display Manager` raises our level of abstraction by providing a protocol that speaks more directly to the nature of the problem space.

The User Interface Mechanism

The focus of our last major release is the tactical design and implementation of the classes `Keypad` and `InputManager`. Similar to the `LCD Device` class, the `Keypad` class serves as a skin over the underlying hardware, which thereby relieves the `InputManager` of the nasty details of talking directly to the hardware. Decoupling these two abstractions also makes it far easier to replace the physical input device without destabilizing our architecture.

Figure 11–26 The Design of the Key Enumeration Class

We start with a declaration that names the physical keys in the vocabulary of our problem space. An enumeration class, Key, is defined as shown in Figure 11–26.

We use the k prefix to avoid name clashes with literals defined in SensorName.

Continuing, we may capture our abstraction of the Keypad class as shown in Figure 11–27.

The protocol of this class derives from our earlier analysis. We have added the operation inputPending so that clients can query if user input exists that has not yet been processed.

The class InputManager has a similarly sparse interface (Figure 11–28).

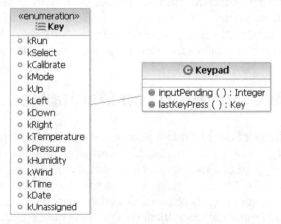

Figure 11–27 The Design of the Keypad Class

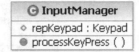

Figure 11–28 The Design of the `InputManager` Interface

As we will see, most of the interesting work of this class is carried out in the implementation of its finite state machine.

As we illustrated earlier in Figure 11–14, instances of the `Sampler`, `InputManager`, and `Keypad` classes collaborate to respond to user input. To integrate these three abstractions, we must subtly modify the interface of the `Sampler` class to include a new object, `repInputManager` (Figure 11–29).

Through this design decision, we establish an association among instances of the `Sensors`, `Display Manager`, and `InputManager` classes at the time we construct an instance of `Sampler`. This design asserts that instances of `Sampler` must always have a collection of sensors, a display manager, and an input manager.

We must also incrementally modify the implementation of the function `Sampler::sample`.

```
void Sampler::sample(Tick t)
{
  repInputManager.processKeyPress();
  for (SensorName name = Direction; name <= Pressure; name++)
    for (unsigned int id = 0; id <
        repSensors.numberOfSensors(name); id++)
      if (!(t % samplingRate(name)))
        repDisplayManager.display(repSensors.sensor(name,
        id));
}
```

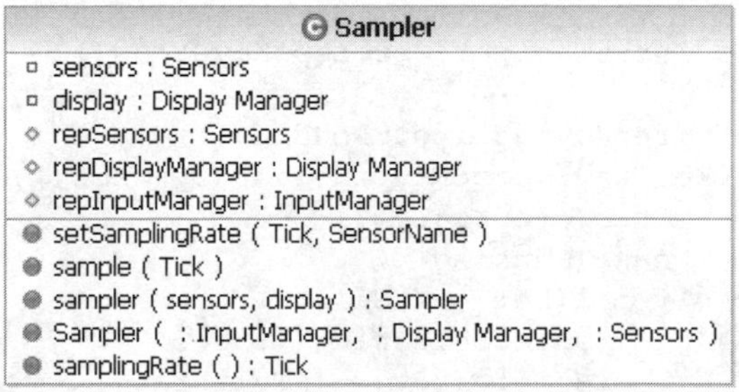

```
                          ⊙ Sampler
  ▫ sensors : Sensors
  ▫ display : Display Manager
  ◇ repSensors : Sensors
  ◇ repDisplayManager : Display Manager
  ◇ repInputManager : InputManager
  ● setSamplingRate ( Tick, SensorName )
  ● sample ( Tick )
  ● sampler ( sensors, display ) : Sampler
  ● Sampler ( : InputManager, : Display Manager, : Sensors )
  ● samplingRate ( ) : Tick
```

Figure 11–29 The Revised Design of the `Sampler` Interface

Figure 11–30 The Design of the `InputState` Enumeration Class

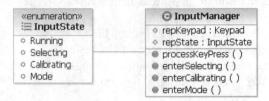

Figure 11–31 `InputManager` with the `InputState` Class Design

Here we have added an invocation to `processKeyPress` at the beginning of every time frame.

The `processKeyPress` operation is the entry point to the finite state machine that drives the instances of this class. Ultimately, there are two approaches we can take to implement this or any other finite state machine: We can explicitly represent states as objects (and thereby depend on their polymorphic behavior), or we can use enumeration literals to denote each distinct state.

For modest-sized finite state machines such as the one embodied by the `InputManager` class, it is sufficient for us to use the latter approach. Thus, we might first introduce the names of the class's outermost states (Figure 11–30).

Next, we introduce some protected helper functions (Figure 11–31).

Finally, we can begin to implement the state transitions we first introduced in Figure 11–12.

```
void InputManager::processKeyPress()
{
  if (repKeypad.inputPending()) {
    Key key = repKeypad.lastKeyPress();
    switch (repState) {
      case Running:
        if (key == kSelect)
          enterSelecting();
        else if (key == kCalibrate)
          enterCalibrating();
        else if (key == kMode)
```

```
        enterMode();
      break;
    case Selecting:
      ...
      break;
    case Calibrating:
      ...
      break;
    case Mode:
      ...
        break;
    }
  }
}
```

The implementation of this function and its associated helper functions thus parallels the state transition diagram shown in Figure 11–12.

11.4 Post-Transition

The complete implementation of this basic Weather Monitoring System is of modest size, encompassing only about 20 classes. However, for any truly useful piece of software, change is inevitable. Let's consider the impact of two enhancements to the architecture of this system.

Our system thus far provides for the monitoring of many interesting weather conditions, but we may soon discover that users want to measure rainfall as well. What is the impact of adding a rain gauge?

Happily, we do not have to radically alter our architecture; we must merely augment it. Using the architectural view of the system from Figure 11–14 as a baseline, to implement this new feature, we must do the following.

- Create a new class, RainFall Sensor, and insert it in the proper place in the sensor class hierarchy (a RainFall Sensor is a kind of Historical Sensor).
- Update the enumeration SensorName.
- Update the Display Manager so that it knows how to display values of this sensor.
- Update the InputManager so that it knows how to evaluate the newly-defined key RainFall.
- Properly add instances of this class to the system's Sensors collection.

We must deal with a few other small tactical issues needed to graft in this new abstraction, but ultimately, we need not disrupt the system's architecture or its key mechanisms.

Let's consider a totally different kind of functionality. Suppose we desire the ability to download a day's record of weather conditions to a remote computer. To implement this feature, we must make the following changes.

- Create a new class, `SerialPort`, responsible for managing a port used for serial communication.
- Invent a new class, `Report Manager`, responsible for collecting the information required for the download. Basically, this class must use the resources of the collection class `Sensors` together with its associated concrete sensors.
- Modify the implementation of `Sampler::sample` to periodically service the serial port.

It is the mark of a well-engineered object-oriented system that making this change does not rend our existing architecture but, rather, reuses and then augments its existing mechanisms.

Chapter 12

Web Application: Vacation Tracking System

For many businesses today, the independence of workers has been ever increasing. It is not uncommon for workers to divide their time across multiple projects and to report to multiple project managers. As a result, managers have fewer informal interactions with their workers and find it increasingly difficult to be aware of and manage their workers' vacation time. Thus, in the example explored in this chapter, our fictitious company has decided to develop and deploy a flexible vacation time management application for managers and employees alike to use to manage their vacation time.

The decision by a large enterprise organization to implement this and similar functionality is never made in isolation. It is unlikely that this proposed system is the first that this organization has ever created. This desired functionality must be considered in the context of any existing systems (and perhaps even with other proposed systems). As a result, many architectural decisions will already be made a priori, and in our situation, the decision to deliver this functionality as a Web application not only is well suited to the task but also will be considered an extension to the organization's existing intranet, thus providing a convenient and natural entry point for its users.

In the following sections, we discuss a summary of the architecturally significant and interesting aspects of this system. Given the space limitations of this book, we express only those aspects and content necessary to impart a general feel and understanding of the application. In the real world, an accurate and complete discussion of such a system would require significantly more content, models, and examples. However, here we cover the key or central principles of object orientation as they apply to this sort of Web application development, and we discuss several interesting issues unique to the Web application development process.

12.1 Inception

The system's requirements are presented by a summary of the vision document, key features, the use case model, key use case specifications, and architecturally significant line item requirements.

The Requirements

The vision for this project can be summarized easily.

> A Vacation Tracking System (VTS) will provide individual employees with the capability to manage their own vacation time, sick leave, and personal time off, without having to be an expert in company policy or the local facility's leave policies.

The most important goal of this system is to give individual employees the capability and responsibility to manage this particular aspect of their employment agreements with the company. The underlying motivations for this desire include the need to streamline the functions of the human resources (HR) department, to minimize noncore, business-related activities of management, and to give a sense of empowerment to the employees. These objectives will be met only if the system developed is easy to use, intuitive, and intelligent. An overriding design goal can therefore be stated simply.

> The system must be easy to use.

Anyone reading this with even the most minimal experience developing commercial software as part of a team effort will be rolling their eyes at such a vague requirement. Something so blatantly general and subjective should never be recorded as an official requirement, right? Not necessarily so. While it is clear that this simple line item is not a hard and traceable requirement, it does represent an honest feature of the desired system. It is so important that unless it at least appears to have been met by the developers and ultimately accepted by the end users alike, the delivered application will fail.

High-level and potentially vague features like this sometimes need to be part of the official requirements set, not so they can be objectively verified and tracked through testing, but rather so they can be used to support and justify other, more concrete requirements or design decisions. As an example, consider the requirements for a Web application that at some point requires the end user to submit to the system some formatted text (e.g., bold, italics, lists, paragraphs, and so on). The architects have two potential solutions. They can require the end user to incorporate special codes into the body of the text, as many popular bulletin board systems do today, or they can use a custom-built or commercially available Java applet that provides WYSIWYG formatting. The technical complexity and risk of such an applet are significant, yet the end-user advantages are also equally clear. If one of the primary system features or design goals was ease of use, the use of this applet could be justified. However, if ease of use was simply a desired rather than critical requirement, introducing the potential complexity and risk of the applet could not be justified.

The main goal of this application is to improve the internal business processes of this organization, at least with respect to the time it takes to manage vacation time requests. In the past, all vacation time had to be approved by an immediate manager and then checked by a clerk in the HR department before it was authorized. Sometimes this manual process could take days. An automated system will speed up this process and will require at most one manual approval by the immediate manager (some high-level employees may not require manager approval).

This system has the potential to save time and money mostly in the HR department, which is essentially taken out of the individual time request process and replaced by a rules-based validation system. HR personnel are still responsible for entering and updating employee vacation data in the system; however, they will no longer be a link in the chain for requesting and validating each time request.

The system will provide the following key features:

- Implements a flexible rules-based system for validating and verifying leave time requests
- Enables manager approval (optional)
- Provides access to requests for the previous calendar year, and allows requests to be made up to a year and a half in the future
- Uses e-mail notification to request manager approval and notify employees of request status changes
- Uses existing hardware and middleware
- Is implemented as an extension to the existing intranet portal system, and uses the portal's single-sign-on mechanisms for all authentication
- Keeps activity logs for all transactions
- Enables the HR and system administration personnel to override all actions restricted by rules, with logging of those overrides
- Allows managers to directly award personal leave time (with system-set limits)

- Provides a Web service interface for other internal systems to query any given employee's vacation request summary
- Interfaces with the HR department legacy systems to retrieve required employee information and changes

The Use Case Model

The top-level use case model contains four actors and eight use cases, as shown in Figure 12–1. The granularity of the use cases is reasonably coarse. For example, the use case `Manage Time` describes functionality, invoked by the `Employee`, that includes viewing, creating, and canceling vacation time requests. A use case is not a description of a single functional requirement but rather a description of something that provides significant value to the actor invoking it, in the form of scenarios. Just being able to view a vacation time request, for example, provides minimal value, but being able to manage your own vacation time does provide significant value.

An interesting observation about use cases of Web-centric systems is that they tend to be expressed very strictly in terms of stimulus and response. That is, a use case scenario is typically expressed as a list of actor actions and immediate system

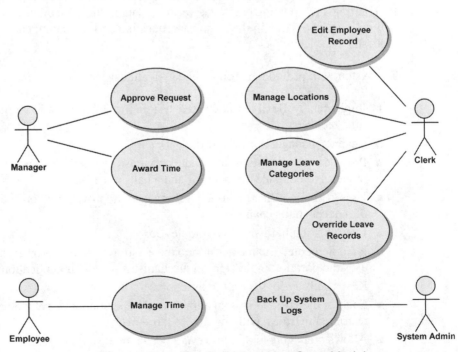

Figure 12–1 The Top-Level Use Case Model

responses. Also, there is typically a high degree of correlation of system responses to actual and individually named Web pages or screens. This is in contrast to non-Web applications, where content in the scenarios of activity focuses more on the information and use gestures being exchanged than on the identification of discrete user interface units, such as Web pages in a Web-centric system.

The system contains the following actors.

- `Employee`: The main user of this system. An employee uses this system to manage his or her vacation time.
- `Manager`: An employee who has all the abilities and goals of a regular employee, but with the added responsibility of approving vacation requests for immediate subordinates. A manager may award subordinates comp time, subject to certain limits set in the system.
- `Clerk`: A member of the HR department who has sufficient rights to view employees' personal data and is responsible for ensuring that employees' information in all HR systems is up to date and correct. An HR clerk can add or remove nearly any record in the system. In the real world, HR clerks may or may not be employees; however, if they are employees, they use two separate login IDs to manage these two different roles.
- `System Admin`: A role responsible for the smooth running of the system's technical resources (e.g., Web server, database) and for collecting and archiving all log files.

The main use cases are as follows.

- `Manage Time`: Describes how employees request and view vacation time requests.
- `Approve Request`: Describes how a manager responds to a subordinate's request for vacation time.
- `Award Time`: Describes how a manager can award a subordinate extra leave time (comp time).
- `Edit Employee Record`: Describes how an HR clerk edits an employee's information in the system. This includes setting all the leave time allowances and the maximum time that can be awarded by the manager.
- `Manage Locations`: Describes how an HR clerk manages location records and their rules.
- `Manage Leave Categories`: Describes how an HR clerk manages leave categories and their rules.
- `Override Leave Records`: Describes how an HR clerk may override any rejection of leave time requests made by the rules in the system.
- `Back Up System Logs`: Describes how the system administrator backs up the system's logs.

12.2 Elaboration

Sometimes it is not always clear when analysis starts or when requirements gathering and understanding during the Inception phase end. This is also why iterative development processes are so popular and the practicality of the waterfall process so often questioned. It is important, however, to have the most important and architecturally significant use cases described and discussed first. All the details need not be complete, but the architecturally significant ones should be addressed before a particular use case can undergo refinement.

In the ideal world, analysis of a system should be independent of an implementing architecture. The reality, however, is that prior knowledge of the implementing architecture may contribute to the shape of the analysis.

This can be especially true when the application under development is a Web application because in most cases the decision to adopt a Web-centric architecture is something that is known at Inception. In our case here, the idea that the solution will ultimately be delivered as a Web-centric application appears in the detailed requirements. For example, the statement in the main flow of the `Manage Time` use case (discussed later), "The employee should have access to a visual calendar to help select and compare selected dates," is prompted in part by the knowledge that most Web browsers do not have a common date picker or calendar widget. In the specification of a native Windows client application, this assumption of such a capability might not have been explicitly brought out since such controls are in common use on Windows-based native client applications. The use case writer in this case is explicitly identifying an area where the system needs to be user friendly. A more subtle and pervasive indication that knowledge of the architecture is known during the process of use case writing is the constant reference to "navigating to Web pages" and "submitting" information, concepts linked tightly with Web-centric architectures.

Sadly, there is no commonly agreed-upon way to quantitatively represent an arbitrary architecture. Here, we will use the 4+1 architecture view model [3], as described in Chapter 6.

The following brief descriptions of a Web application's architecture are not meant to be a complete discussion of Web-centric architectures; however, we do cover enough significant aspects here to help explain design decisions made later.

The Deployment View

A Web application, being a specialization of a client/server application, has minimally two main nodes, the server and the client browser. The server is a node that has a known address on a network and is configured to listen for HTTP requests on a specific port, typically port 80. A client browser application makes a request, at the behest of the user, for an HTML-formatted resource on the server. The server, most likely, will be concurrently running a number of services, including other Web applications, possibly a database server, an application server, and so on. In Figure 12–2, the `Client` and `Server` nodes are clearly identified.

In the Deployment View of the key components, execution environments `Tomcat` and `Cloudscape` are treated as nested nodes of the server. The `Tomcat` node is a Web application execution environment based on the Java environment. The `Tomcat` node itself is shown here deploying the artifact `VTSWeb.war`, a Web application archive file. The `Cloudscape` execution environment is a database server capable of executing SQL files and shown here deploying an artifact called `VTS.sql`.

The `Client` node in Figure 12–2 is shown deploying the `Firefox.exe` artifact, which is an executable HTML browser application. The `Client` node has a communication link to the `Server` node. This communication link may be anything from a dialup ISP to broadband or wireless. The important and logical aspect to concentrate on is that the client communicates to the nested Web and database servers via this communication link.

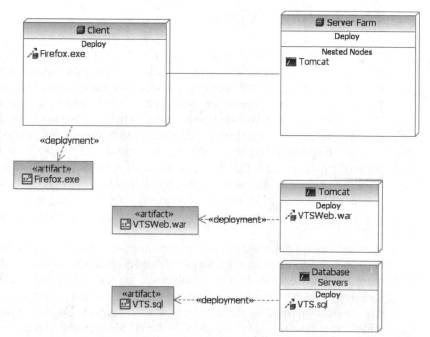

Figure 12–2 The Deployment View of the Components in a Web-Centric System

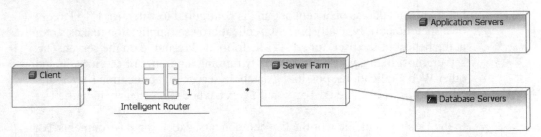

Figure 12–3 A Deployment Diagram for a Web Application Server Farm with Parallel and Redundant Processing Nodes

This representation of a Web-centric system is simplistic. In larger systems, the deployment diagrams showing the topography of all the nodes, components, servers, and communication links can be complex, resulting in the need for a good visualization and documentation system such as the UML. Figure 12–3 is an abstract deployment diagram showing how an intelligent router can be used with a Web server farm and how an entire set of applications can be run from application servers. The details of such strategies can be quite complex, but the general strategy of scaling an application by adding additional processing nodes is certainly viable in Web applications.

The Logical View

The typical Web application has at least four logical components: the browser running on the client, the Web or application container, a separate component for the application logic itself, and a database server component. In Figure 12–4, the `Firefox.exe` component is a commonly available multiplatform browser, and `Tomcat` is a popular Web container based on the Java Server Pages (JSP) specification. The `VTSWeb` component represents the business application, and `Cloudscape` is a simple portable database server. The most important logical point of this diagram is that the client browser is never in direct contact with the database or even the business application component. All access to server-side resources is mediated by the Web container. This makes the Web container an important component to consider when thinking about security requirements.

Web servers are designed to listen to certain ports, usually port 80, and respond to `GET` and `POST` requests. `GET` and `POST` are commands defined in the HTTP protocol. They are essentially two simple ways to request information from a Web server. The `POST` method is a little more extensible and used more often when data or files supplied by the user are sent to the server. The determination of which command to use is embedded in the HTML-formatted page being rendered by the browser. Usually the information returned by a browser request is an HTML-formatted document, which can be visually rendered in the browser, but

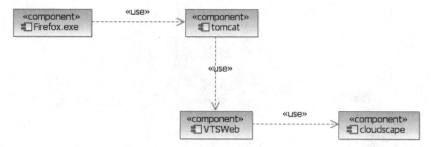

Figure 12–4 The Logical View of the Primary Components of a Web
Application

the server could return streamed data in any form, leaving the client responsible to
save or delegate the processing of the information to another locally installed
application.

Figure 12–5 shows logical classes representing elements in both the client and
server tiers of the application. On the client, a browser is responsible for requesting Web pages (or more generically, resources) with simple HTTP GET or POST
commands. These services can be provided by the operating system or may be
implemented in the browser itself (in which case the browser calls on lower-level
network APIs). The Web container is constantly listening on certain ports (e.g.,
port 80) for incoming HTTP requests. An HTTP request is packaged by the
browser and sent to the Web container. It contains a resource identifier that points
to a specific Web page or references a Web application. The request can have
accompanying it a set of key-value pairs (parameters), all represented as strings.[1]
Some HTTP requests are packaged with more complex form data that the user
supplies just before the page request is submitted.

When the Web container receives a request for a resource, it must first determine
the file or application resource to invoke. The container invokes the proper
resource, and if the resource indicates that it is dynamic and should be processed,
the Web container executes it. During processing, the HTTP request information
(parameters and form data) is examined, and the application performs the necessary business logic. Often this logic is executed in a separate application server
(e.g., an EJB container), which potentially accesses another database server.

Logically, a Web application is made up of Web pages, controllers, and entities
(the three basic stereotypes found in an analysis model). Static Web pages (no

---

1. The gory details of parameter and post data formatting can be found at the World Wide
Web Consortium Web site (www.w3.org). Fortunately, most of these details are managed
by the Web application framework on which we choose to implement the application.

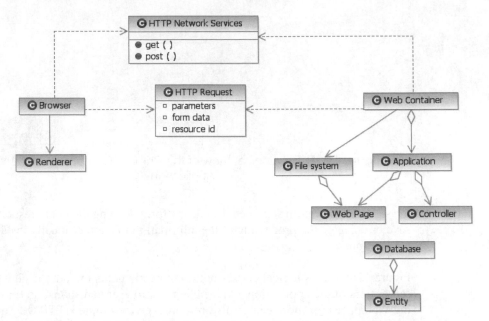

Figure 12–5 The High-Level Logical View of the Objects Involved in a Web Application

processing) may just reside in a file system, while Web pages that contain business logic processing must be loaded and executed in the context of a container. Controller objects are often embedded in components, and persistent entities are managed by databases.

The Process View

There are minimally two, but usually more, processes involved in a typical Web application. The client and server operate asynchronously, except during the handling of HTTP requests. Additional database, authentication, and messaging servers are often part of a typical Web application. They may coexist on a single server node or be distributed across multiple nodes. The process layout of a Web application has the same flexibility as any client/server architecture, with only the one requirement that client nodes must run some form of Web browser client software to initiate communication with the server-side application.

As intimated earlier, the most important thing to understand about Web application architectures is that they work in a connectionless mode. That is, the client and server are never connected longer than it takes to process the one GET or POST request. Once a server resource (i.e., HTML-formatted Web page) is requested by a browser and the server responds with that resource, the connection

Client State Management

One of the most interesting problems that Web applications face is that of managing client state on the server in a connectionless environment. Since every request and response made between client and server is completed with a new and unique connection, it is difficult for a server to keep track of the sequence of requests of any one particular client.

Managing state is important for many applications since a single use case scenario often involves navigating through a number of different Web pages. If there were no state management mechanism, you would have to continually supply all previous information entered for each new Web page. Even for the simplest applications this can get tedious. Imagine having to reenter the contents of your shopping cart from scratch every time you visit it, or entering your user name and password for every screen you visit while checking your Web-based e-mail.

The most commonly implemented solution to this problem, originally proposed by the World Wide Web Consortium (W3C), is the HTTP State Management Mechanism or, as it is more popularly known, cookies. A cookie is a piece of data that a Web server can ask a Web browser to hold on to and to return every time the browser makes a subsequent request for a HTTP resource from that server. Typically, the size of the data is small, between 100 and 1000 bytes. Web application frameworks manage client state by generating a unique identifier each time a browser first interacts with the application and places this ID in a cookie for the browser. This ID is used as a key into a map on the server that contains all the state information for that particular client.

URL redirection is an alternative approach to cookies for managing client state. In this approach, every hyperlink and form places the ID on the end of the URL submitted to the server during the next page request. The ID performs the same role as a cookie, but as a parameter of a URL it can be used with browsers that have explicitly turned off their cookie feature. The downside to this approach is that every page in a Web site must be dynamic, and the user cannot wander outside of the application in the middle of a use case scenario, lest the particular session between the client and server be broken.

The two other approaches for managing client state serialize the entire state into the URL parameters or into cookies. These are not commonly used for a number of reasons, the least of which is that they are inherently less secure since the client's state is sent over the wire back to the browser, whereas in the previous approaches the state is managed solely on the server. Also, when all state values are placed in cookies, they are limited by size (4K) and can have at most 20 cookies per domain. All state data must be encoded into simple text (no white space, semicolons, and so on). This also implies that you can't easily capture client state with higher-level objects in the session state.

between client and server is broken. Figure 12–6 shows a client making a simple GET request to the server (Tomcat). The server determines from the request which Web application and resource to invoke. A Web page inside the application is instantiated or invoked, and this represents the main trigger for the execution of business logic. Nearly all business logic in a Web application is invoked during the process of handling a GET or POST request. When the logic is finished, the application is responsible for preparing a response page (i.e., the next Web page in the scenario). It is important to realize that once the request for a Web resource is fulfilled, the application stops working for that particular client.

The implications are that it is not at all obvious how a server application can keep track of one particular client's request history and hence the relative internal state of the client. For example, without exploiting certain features of HTTP or implementing certain architectural mechanisms, a server application would have difficulty managing even a simple shopping cart or the state of a particular user walking through a multistepped wizard. Fortunately, most Web application environments provide many useful utilities and mechanisms for managing client state.

Another implication of this architecture is that the server does not know whether the user has abandoned the application in the middle of some business process. It is entirely likely that on occasion a remote user might become disconnected from the network and hence be unable to finish a particular business process that was started. In a more classic client/server application, the server might receive a notification that the client has been prematurely disconnected, but in a Web application, there are no notifications sent to the server when a user becomes disconnected or simply decides to just shut down the browser.

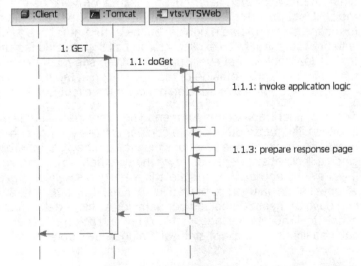

Figure 12–6 A Basic Sequence Diagram of an HTTP GET Request

Web application designs therefore must be very mindful of what resources are opened and accessed between Web page requests. For example, one cardinal rule of Web application design is to never open a transaction in one page and close it in another. The time between Web page requests from a single client is usually on the order of seconds and could at any time abruptly stop. Managing transactions and locks on this order of magnitude is surely going to bring an application server to its knees.

The Implementation View

Figure 12–7 shows an overview of the implementation model for the Vacation Tracking System and describes the system's tiers and packages. In this diagram, the main Web tier component, `VTSWeb.war`, is shown containing Web page artifacts (JSP and HTML files) as well as a set of Java classes in the `web` and `sdo` packages. This code is used to process and invoke the EJB logic in the business tier. The package `com.acme.vts` is shown, in the background, as the main namespace for all the Java components. The Deployment View would describe in more detail the deployment of the components in the tiers, and the Logical View would describe in more detail the nature and responsibility of the components.

The Use Case View

The Deployment, Logical, Process, and Implementation Views are tied together by implementing the basic stimulus/response use case. A client makes an HTTP

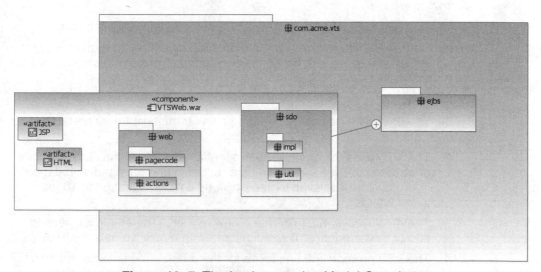

Figure 12–7 The Implementation Model Overview

request to a server for a Web page. The server examines the request and determines which application or resource needs to be loaded and executed. Some resources result in business logic processing, while others simply display static data. When the processing is complete, the application is responsible for composing a response, usually in the form of an HTML Web page that can be rendered in place of the previous Web page. This response page contains new information and options for the user to invoke or request. By assembling an entire collection of these Web pages, each specialized to display and accept information that is part of the application, an entire business process can be implemented.

In this chapter, we focus on one architecturally representative use case: Manage Time. This use case by far is the most frequently invoked and the one most viewed by all the actors of the system. As a result, it is critical to implement this use case effectively and to ensure that it meets all of the overall design goals, including the ease-of-use feature.

Many different templates can be used for use case specifications. The format used in this chapter shows more robust steps in the flows. This avoids the stimulus/response style flow that Web applications can create. Also, this style of use case specification is good for situations when there are complex or robust alternate flows. The style or format that you ultimately use is up to you and the level of formality to which your organization adheres.

The following example gives a summary of the written specification for the Manage Time use case.

Use case name: Manage Time

Actor: Employee

Goal: The employee wishes to submit a new request for vacation time.

Preconditions: The employee is authenticated by the portal framework and identified as an employee of the company with privileges to manage his or her own vacation time.

Main flow:

1. The employee begins by selecting a link from the intranet portal to the VTS.

2. The VTS uses the employee's credentials to look up the current status of all the employee's vacation time requests and outstanding balances. Information is displayed for the previous 6 months and up to 18 months in the future.

3. The employee wants to create a new request. The employee selects one of the categories of vacation time with a positive balance to use.

4. The VTS prompts the employee for the date(s) and time for which to request vacation time. The employee should have access to a visual calendar to help select and compare chosen dates.

5. The employee selects the desired dates and hours per date (e.g., four hours might indicate a half-day vacation time request). The employee enters a short title and description (no more than a paragraph in length) so that the manager will have more information with which to approve this request. When all the information is entered, the employee submits the request.

6. If the submitted information is incomplete or incorrect or does not pass validation, the Web page is redisplayed, with the errors highlighted and documented.

7. The employee has an opportunity to change the information or cancel the request.

8. If the information is complete and passes validation, the employee is returned to the main VTS home page. If the employee's vacation time requests require manager approval, an e-mail is immediately sent to the manager(s) authorized to approve the employee's requests.

9. The vacation time request is placed in a state of pending approval.

10. The manager responds to the e-mail by clicking on a link embedded in the e-mail or by explicitly logging into the intranet portal and navigating to the main VTS home page.

11. The manager may be required to supply necessary authentication credentials to gain access to the portal and VTS application.

12. The VTS home page lists the manager's own vacation time requests and outstanding balances but also has a separate section listing requests pending approval by subordinate employees. The manager selects each of these one at a time to individually approve or deny.

13. The VTS displays the details of the requested time and prompts the manager to approve or disapprove the request. If the request is disapproved, the manager is required to enter an explanation. Once the manager submits the result, the internal state of the request is changed to approved or rejected.

14. Whether a request is approved or rejected, an e-mail notification is immediately sent to the employee who made the request. The manager's screen returns to the main VTS home page, and the manager may approve other outstanding requests, make a request for him- or herself, or simply leave the VTS application.

Alternate flow: `Withdraw Request`

Goal: The employee wants to withdraw an outstanding request for vacation time.

Preconditions: An employee has made a vacation time request, and that request has yet to be approved or denied by an authorized manager. See also main flow preconditions.

1. The employee navigates to the VTS home page through the intranet portal application, which identifies and authenticates the employee with the privileges necessary for using the VTS.

2. The VTS home page contains a summary of vacation time requests, outstanding balances per category of time, and the current status of all active vacation time requests for the previous 6 months and up to 18 months in the future.

3. The employee selects a vacation time request to withdraw, one that is currently pending approval.

4. The VTS prompts the employee to confirm the request to withdraw the previously submitted vacation time request.

5. The employee confirms the desire to withdraw, and the request is removed from the manager's list of pending approvals.

6. The system sends a notification e-mail to the manager.

7. The system updates the request state to withdrawn.

Alternate flow: `Cancel Approved Request`

Goal: The employee wants to cancel an approved vacation time request.

Preconditions: The employee has a vacation time request that has been approved and is scheduled for some time in the future or the recent past (previous 5 business days). See also main flow preconditions.

1. The employee navigates to the VTS home page through the intranet portal application, which identifies and authenticates the employee with the privileges necessary for using the VTS.

2. The VTS home page contains a summary of vacation time requests, outstanding balance per category of time, and the current status of all active vacation time requests for the previous 6 months and up to 18 months in the future.

3. The employee selects a vacation time request to cancel, one that is in the future (or recent past) and has been approved.

4. If the request is in the future, the employee is prompted to confirm the cancellation. If the request is in the recent past, the employee is prompted to confirm the cancellation and provide a short explanation. If the employee approves the cancellation and provides the required information, an e-mail notification is sent to the manager, and the state of the request is changed to canceled. The time allowances used to make the request are returned to the employee. The employee can also abort the cancellation, effecting no changes to the current requests.

5. The employee is returned to the main VTS home page. The summaries are updated to reflect any changes made to the employee's outstanding vacation time requests.

Alternate flow: `Edit Pending Request`

Goal: The employee wants to edit the description or title of a pending request.

Preconditions: An employee has made a vacation time request, and that request has yet to be approved or denied by an authorized manager. See also main flow preconditions.

1. The employee navigates to the VTS home page through the intranet portal application, which identifies and authenticates the employee with the privileges necessary for using the VTS.

2. The VTS home page contains a summary of vacation time requests, outstanding balances per category of time, and the current status of all active vacation time requests for the previous 6 months and up to 18 months in the future.

3. The employee selects a request to edit, one that is pending approval.

4. The VTS displays an editable view of the request. The employee is allowed to change the title, comments, or dates. The employee can also choose to delete or withdraw this request.

5. The employee changes request information and submits the changes to the system.

6. If the employee withdraws the request, the VTS prompts for confirmation before withdrawing the request. If changes are made only to the information, the changes are accepted, and the screen returns to the main VTS home page. If there are errors or problems with the information changes, the VTS redisplays the editing page and highlights and explains all problems.

This use case description contains quite a bit of information about the proposed VTS and how it is expected to be used by a typical employee. It is for the most part a functional description of the system from the viewpoint of the Employee actor. Indeed, this is exactly what a use case is supposed to be. Unfortunately, this description is insufficient to even begin analysis with. What is needed are the nonfunctional requirements and much more information about the domain. Nonfunctional requirements typically include requirements on the environment, performance, scalability, security, and so on. Domain knowledge can be in the form of discrete requirements, for example:

- All employees work eight-hour days.
- Each employee's vacation time requests are subject to the restrictions of each employee's primary work location in addition to overall company policies and restrictions.
- Vacation time request validation rules are defined and owned by the HR department.

These types of requirements or knowledge may be found embedded in use case specifications, or they can be captured as discrete line item requirements. This type of domain knowledge may also be referenced by commonly accessible documents. For example, the detailed policies and rules for validating a vacation time request are part of a company's employee manual and most likely available through a variety of sources (e.g., intranet, forms, documents, new employee orientation presentations, and so on). A project's requirements set would simply reference these existing documents rather than try to duplicate them.

12.3 Construction

The most important task when analyzing a potential Web application, as with most types of software applications, is the identification of the system's entities and processes. The entities and processes of an application represent concepts in the business domain and are ideally independent of an architecture, but not necessarily so. In a Web application, one critical set of artifacts is the navigation map and Web page definitions. Roughly speaking, these elements correspond to the classic analysis stereotypes of entity, controller, and boundary. We'll begin with a Web-centric model: the User Experience (UX) model.

The User Experience Model

The UX model [1, 2] is one example of capturing the user interface elements of a Web application at a sufficient level of abstraction so as to express a concrete navigational map between the Web pages in the system, while ignoring the styles (fonts, sizes, colors, and so on) and other user interface specifics that are best developed later in the process. Figure 12–8 shows a high-level fragment of a UX model that describes the screens used to implement our primary use case. In this model and diagram there are two key stereotypes, «Screen» and «Form». A «Screen» stereotyped class represents a complete unit of user interface displayed to an end user or, roughly speaking, a Web page. Some screens contain HTML form elements, which are used to submit user-entered information back to the server. These stereotyped classes are always contained by a screen and when submitted result in navigation to another screen in the system. Directed association relationships indicate navigational pathways through the screens.

While Figure 12–8 is most useful for understanding the navigational flow through the screens of the system, it provides little in the way of screen content. More detailed diagrams that contain screen content are also useful at this level of abstraction. Figure 12–9 shows the content of the VTSHome screen. Attributes of a «Screen» stereotyped class indicate discrete data values, typically strings or simple types easily rendered in HTML. The employee name and current date attributes are probably used in a header or at the top of the screen. The message attribute is used to display an informative or error message after an

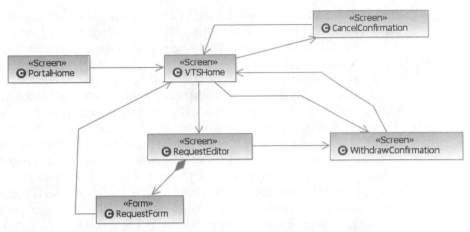

Figure 12–8 A High-Level User Experience Model

action has taken place. For example, when the employee completes a new vacation time request and returns to the home screen, the message might say something like "Your request requires the approval of your manager, who has been notified by e-mail."

Often content in a screen is multivalued and complex. To accurately represent this type of content, we define another class stereotype, «Content», that when applied to a class identifies a coherent bundle of information. Content items are often used as line items in a list. In Figure 12–9, the classes Request and PendingApproval are modeled as content items contained by the home screen. The screen potentially displays multiple instances of each. Content

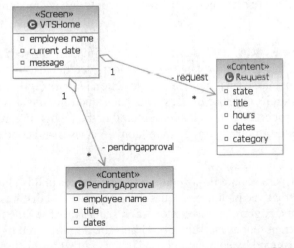

Figure 12–9 A Detailed View of the VTSHome Class

classes define attributes that are like the attributes of a screen, things that can be easily rendered in HTML. It is not important at this high level of the model to worry about actual data types. What is important is to simply define them with a name and short description.

It is interesting to note that even at this early point in user experience design, some decisions are being made that will have a significant impact on the final design. By specifying the content of the VTSHome page not only to contain the summary of current vacation requests for the employee but also to have this same page used by the manager to view pending approvals, we are implying that this screen is the home page for both employees and managers. Nowhere in the use case specifications nor the nonfunctional requirements was it stated that employees and managers should use the same home screen. Such an assumption is not without reason since managers are also employees and can do all the things (with respect to the VTS) that employees can. Decisions like this are exactly what the UX model is intended to document. Ultimately, the final design will determine the implementation; however, from the logical (and user experience) point of view, employees and managers share the same home screen.

The Analysis and Design Models

In analysis, we want to capture the entities and processes of the system. Since we know that this system will be implemented as a Web application, we are less concerned with boundaries because they are explored in the UX model. The analysis model is a first attempt at identifying the elements that will make up the solution space but using the vocabulary of the domain. This means that most of the elements of the analysis model will have names that correspond to things and activities that are described in the requirements and are recognizable by the domain and end users.

One easy way to get started is to do a simple noun-verb analysis of the use case specifications and related requirements documents. Important nouns tend to represent classes in the model, while action phrases (verbs) tend to be represented by operations on those classes. Attributes and relationships represent natural intrinsic properties of the classes captured in the model. Figure 12–10 represents an initial start, focusing on the main domain classes and concepts represented in our primary use case.

There are several important points to consider in this class diagram. First is the idea that vacation time requests are separate and distinct from vacation time grants. A grant in this context represents available time for the employee to draw on when requesting time off. Grants are administered by the HR department and determined by company policy. In the context of this use case, however, their pri-

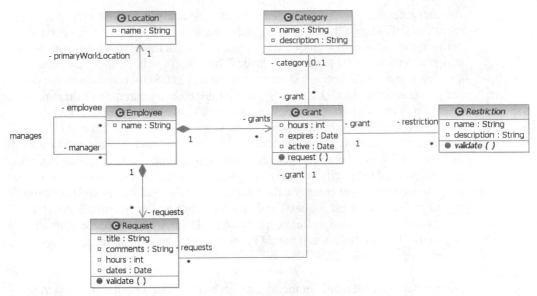

Figure 12–10 An Analysis Model Class Diagram Supporting the Primary Use Case

mary responsibility is to create new vacation time requests. Their persistent properties are the number of hours that can be requested per calendar year and when the grant expires (if at all).

Another important decision captured in this diagram is the idea that a manager *is an* employee. While it may sound obvious to everyone familiar with the popular usage of these common business terms, such assumptions cannot always be made when developing software. The class diagram goes further to say that an employee can have multiple managers. This is not meant to be a statement on the company hierarchy and organization, but rather in this context it means that an approval of an employee's request for vacation time may come from multiple sources. For example, in some companies, high-ranking executives have dedicated personal assistants. A personal assistant may be delegated to make vacation time decisions for the executive.

Other inherent properties of an employee are the name and primary work location. Note that at this level of abstraction and required usage, an employee name need only be managed with a single string data type. Other applications that manage employee information will most likely require separate values for the title and the first, last, and middle names, but in this application those distinctions are not required since the only place the employee name is used is in the display of the home screen. As a general rule, unless the problem absolutely requires a complex solution, don't propose one.

Another interesting and important aspect of most analysis models is the lack of identifier definitions. In nearly every implementation of a system with persistent entities, the concept of a unique ID is present. For example, most companies assign an employee ID to each employee. This ID uniquely defines that particular employee and is often reused if the employee leaves and then returns to the company. The need for the ID is clear given that there is no guarantee of the uniqueness of names. Yet in our model, there are no ID attributes defined. That is because in most analysis models, it can be safely assumed that IDs and other properties necessary to implement the analysis with the architecture will be added as required. Unless there is a very specific business need for information like this, there is no need to specify it during analysis. For example, suppose we had in our proposed system another actor called `Auditor`, who was responsible for browsing all the vacation time requests and checking for regulatory compliance; that actor would in fact need and expect employee IDs to cross-reference with other employee data. In this case, it would be important to explicitly specify this attribute of an employee.

Some interesting elements in the model can be elaborated with a state machine. For example, the `Request` class has a defined state machine, as shown in Figure 12–11. As far as state machines go, it is not that interesting; however, it is significant. It tells us that state is important for a `Request` and that it is well defined. In the diagram shown in Figure 12–11, we see three transitional states and four final states defined. The paths through these states are very simple and in this diagram are unlabeled.

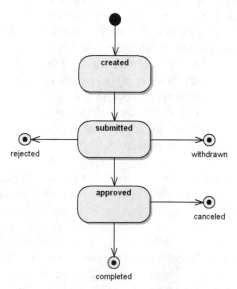

Figure 12–11 The State Machine for the `Request` Class

By far the most difficult part of the analysis was creating the elements related to ensuring that any requested vacation time passed all the rules and restrictions of the company and primary work location. Not much is stated in the use case specifications about these rules; instead, the requirements simply reference internal company documents as current examples. The requirements do state that there is to be a rules-based system managed by the HR department. This statement alone indicates that the approach must be flexible and manageable by users whose skill sets are not in computers or algorithms. This is important because one obvious and very flexible mechanism for implementing a general-purpose rules-based system is to enable the capture and interpretation of a flexible scripting language like JavaScript as a rule. Most algorithms, complex or simple, could be implemented with JavaScript and easily interact with persistent entities and objects. The principal problem with this is, of course, that the typical HR clerk, being charged with the responsibility of maintaining these aspects of the system, does not typically have JavaScript writing as a primary skill.

Long before we choose an implementation solution or even a strategy, we need to first identify the higher-level abstract elements that belong in the model. For now we can create a single class called `Restriction` and place on it all the responsibility for validating a vacation time request against the company and location-specific policies. A deeper understanding of the rules and regulations for vacation time is needed. Unfortunately, not much about the inherent structure of a rule is documented in the use case specifications, and only specific instances of the rules are captured in the company documents. Therefore, analysis leads us to study in detail and look for patterns in the current set of rules. Analysis activities like this often require interaction with domain experts.

After a careful examination of the rules implemented in company policy, and after speaking with the domain experts in the HR department, we can assemble a summary of the major rule types.

- An employee can't take more than X consecutive days of leave for Y type of grant.
- Vacation time of type X cannot be taken when directly adjacent to a company or location-specific holiday.
- Vacation time of type X is limited to Y hours per week or month.
- Vacation time may not be granted when there are only X number of employees scheduled to work from the list Y of employees.
- Vacation time may not be granted on these dates: X.
- Vacation time of this type is limited to certain days of the week: {M, T, W, Th, F, Sat, Sun}.

This more detailed understanding of potential rules for vacation time request approval will lead to some important changes to our model. It is clear that

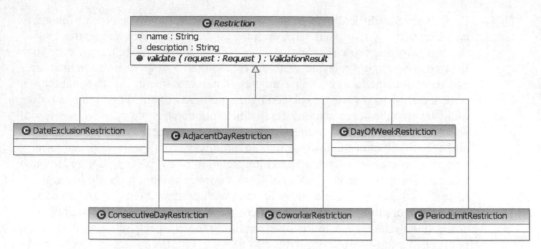

Figure 12–12 The `Restriction` Class Hierarchy

implementing restrictions is varied and requires specific, individually set information. In our attempt to formulate a solution strategy, we will create specializations of the now abstract `Restriction` class, one for each type of rule in the system, as shown in Figure 12–12.

Each specialization is required to implement the `validate()`, method which accepts a `Request` object as a parameter. From the `Request` object a `validate` algorithm can navigate to most of the information it needs (`Employee`, `Grant`, `Location`) to validate the request. Given the varied nature of restriction types, not all of the existing information is sufficient to make a validation. Therefore, each specialization will manage a set of properties or relationships to objects that cannot be derived or navigated to via the `Grant` object. For example, the `CoworkerRestriction` class will need to manage the list of coworkers as well as identify the minimum number of employees allowed to be scheduled for work (Figure 12–13). Rules like this are often associated with safety issues (e.g., there must always be at least one employee on duty who is trained in first aid).

The abstract `validate()` method initially returned just a simple Boolean indicating a pass or fail evaluation of the request. But if we look at the requirements a little closer, we see that the user needs to be notified with an explanation if he or she tries to submit an invalid vacation time request. Since the rules for validation

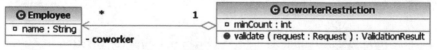

Figure 12–13 The `CoworkerRestriction` Class and Properties

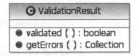

Figure 12–14 The `ValidationResult` Class

are now encapsulated in each of the `Restriction` specializations, it seems appropriate that these classes provide a mechanism to return this information to any calling process. Also, since more than one violation can occur, the results of a validation should be accessed as a collection. The result of these requirements leads us to the creation of a new class, `ValidationResult` (Figure 12–14), which is returned by the `validate()` method.

The `ValidationResult` class is actually quite simple. It defines two methods: `validated()`, which returns a simple Boolean indicating a validated request, and `getErrors()`, a method that returns a collection of string messages, each corresponding to a detected problem with the request. At the analysis level, it is sufficient to keep the class this simple. Let the activities design resolve the details of implementation. The important point here is that it must be possible for a process to validate a vacation time request, make each error result available, and provide a simple means of determining validity.

Another observation of the rules system that is evolving here is that restrictions may not be associated with a particular `Grant` or `Employee` object, but rather, are broadly applied to a `Location` or `Category` of `grants`. Thus our earlier analysis model must change (Figure 12–15). Establishing these relationships makes it easier for the HR department to apply a broad class of common rules without having to duplicate them for each employee. While it is clear this information can be navigated to during validation, the motivation for design change is

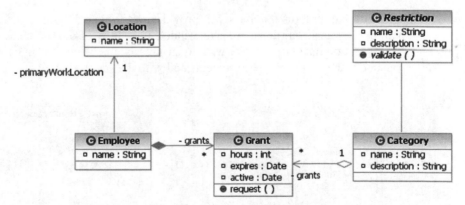

Figure 12–15 Independent and Direct Relationships among `Restriction`, `Location`, `Grant`, and `Category`

based on the overriding desire to make the system easier to use, and in this case the ease of use will be improved significantly for the HR personnel.

Now that the restrictions and rules are better defined, it may be time to revisit some of the HR use cases because now we know more information about the type and nature of information that will need to be managed by the HR department with respect to an employee's vacation time. Although beyond the scope of this simple chapter, a set of Web page screens that prompt for the unique and specific values required by each concrete type of restriction could be envisioned. In such a mechanism, it would be necessary for `Restriction` objects to publish their required parameters (i.e., the *X* and *Y* placeholders in our rules summary) so that the HR clerk could provide the values in a user interface. A helper class, `RestrictionParameterDescriptor`, is defined to encapsulate each of these values. Concrete implementations of `Restriction` are responsible for providing an array of these parameter descriptor objects. The descriptors could be used to prompt the HR clerk when defining new restrictions for an employee, location, or category. Finally, the abstract `Restriction` class should be able to accept and provide individual parameter values. This is accomplished through simple `put` and `get` parameter methods, keyed off of the parameter name. Figure 12–16 illustrates both classes.

At various points during analysis, it is useful to test the ideas being put forth in the model. However, since we are still independent of an actual concrete architecture for which we can write code, we must analyze our model a little more abstractly. We do this by executing thought experiments on the elements of our model, specifically, trying to understand in moderate detail how specific scenarios will play out given the structures and behaviors documented in the model. The area of our model dealing with restrictions is a good example of the need to verify that at least the typical and most important use cases can be implemented this way with realistic data.

A useful pair of tools that the UML provides us is object diagrams and communication diagrams. Our task here is to evaluate the ability of our model to validate a new vacation time request. We want to ensure that the behavior can be accomplished according to the requirements and with the set of defined classes and

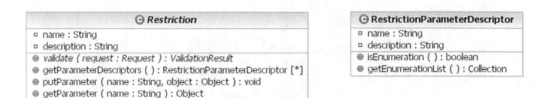

Figure 12–16 Making Restrictions Easier to Manage Programmatically and through a User Interface

objects of our model. In this thought experiment, we use these diagrams to understand how a new request for an employee named Jim who works in the North Factory might be executed.

Figure 12–17 shows the object diagram of a set of objects for our hypothetical employee, Jim, who wants to use a vacation time grant given as a bonus for completing his work on time. The figure indicates with dependencies other object instances that can be accessed or navigated to. The instances have real-life names, appropriate for the scenario, and are followed by a colon and the type or class of object they are. This diagram has been annotated with a few freeform rectangles to help emphasize and make clear the three sources of restrictions: `Grant`, `Location`, and `Category`.

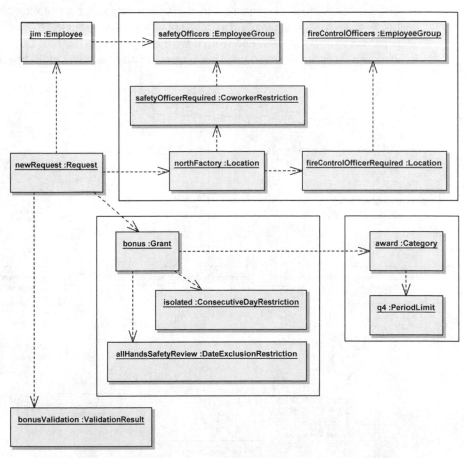

Figure 12–17 An Object Diagram Describing a Request Validation Collaboration

In Figure 12–18, we use a communication diagram to examine the communication paths for a `Request` validation. The lines represent communication paths between object instances, not structural relationships like those found in class diagrams. We examine the behavior of this collaboration by looking at the numbered messages that travel over the communication paths. The main coordinator of the behavior is the `Request` instance, which does most of the work in this scenario. The general flow is to get and validate the various restrictions for the `Location`, `Category`, and so forth by calling the `validate()` operation on each of the restrictions. If a restriction fails validation, its message is appended to the validation result instance.

One interesting flow to follow is that of the `CoworkerRestriction`. In order for a `CoworkerRestriction` to validate, it needs to know not only which `EmployeeGroup` it represents but also which `Employee` to check compliance for. A quick look at the `validate()` signature reveals that the `Request` object is passed in as parameter, and from it we can navigate to the `Employee`. However, these restrictions also need access to the vacation plans of all the other

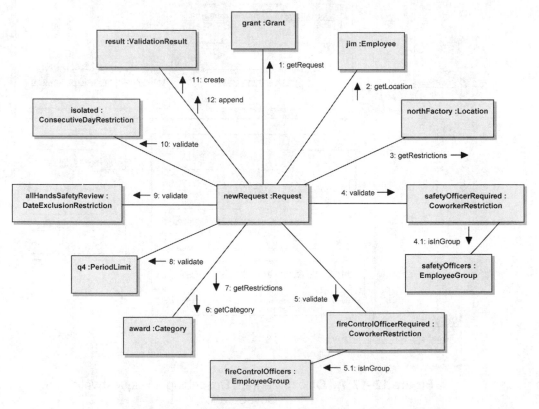

Figure 12–18 A Communication Diagram Describing a Request Validation Collaboration

employees in the group to ensure that at least one employee of the group is scheduled for the location at the request time. So far, our model has not adequately expressed how this can be accomplished. Therefore, as a result of this thought experiment, we need to revisit the model and make sure that these types of restrictions can get the information they need to validate a request.

As discussed in Chapter 6, the beginning and ending of analysis is not a milestone event. Analysis activities often take place throughout the entire development lifecycle, but for the most part they are concentrated at that time when most of the requirements are at least understood. When the analysis model has sufficiently matured, it is time to begin design. This is clearly a vague determination, but that is the reality for most project efforts. The decision to start design activities is often made on criteria that are very local, for example, the history of the project team and organization or the maturity of the architecture.

Now we convert the analysis into a design that can eventually be executed as software. Some design models are identical to executable models (or implementation models), while others are sufficiently abstract as to still require a certain amount of skill and effort during implementation. Web applications in general have a mix of these. Most business tier elements (entities and controllers) map quite closely to the resulting code in the system. Most presentation models, however, require significant effort during implementation before they are ready for the final system.

In this chapter's discussion of the VTS's design, we don't have the space to cover even a brief overview of all the interesting aspects and issues of design in Web-centric applications. Instead, we will discuss just a few of the most important design points, in particular those that are most unique to Web application architectures.

In addition to the basic architectural components of the Web, this project's architect has decided to use the following components and technologies:

- *Client tier*: Any HTML 3.2 capable browser
- *Presentation tier*: Java Server Pages (JSP), Servlets, and Java Server Faces (JSF)
- *Business tier*: Enterprise Java Beans (EJB) 2.x (specifically, Container Managed Persistence [CMP] beans for entities, and session beans for controllers), and Service Data Objects (SDO)
- *Security*: Central Authentication Service (CAS)[2]

The decision was made to use Java-based products in the overall architecture. This is not because Java-based solutions match up with the stated requirements

---

2. For more information, see www.ja-sig.org/products/cas/.

better than any other existing technology, but rather because they happen to match up better with the organization's current skill sets and tooling, in addition to being well suited to the task. This organization has built several Java-based enterprise applications with the core J2EE technologies successfully in the past. These technologies are familiar, and the tooling required to build and test these types of applications already exists on the developer's workstations. In our situation, there is no compelling reason why the architect should switch entire technology frameworks. There are only two reasons why an architect should even consider such a significant change.

1. Recent experiences demonstrated serious problems with the technology or an inability to meet the needs of the development team, maintenance team, and end users.
2. The technology itself is no longer being supported or is evolving so significantly as to make it appear like a new technology.

In the client and presentation tiers, the primary design goals are to implement an intuitive user interface that has a quick response and is easy to navigate. The interface should not have any dependencies on specific browser versions or features, or to put it more accurately, this application should behave properly on all standard HTML 3.2–capable browsers. Even though the current version of HTML at the time of this writing is version 4.01, the decision to support version 3.2 (and later) is driven not so much by the availability or popularity of browsers but by minimum required functionality. It has been determined that all of the features necessary to implement this application can be accomplished with the older version of the HTML specification. Therefore, since there is no real need to require new browsers and exclude the older versions, the application can support a broader selection of client configurations.

In addition to the core presentation technologies, JSP and Servlets, the architect has decided to use JSF components to assist in the development of the user interface. JSF is an API and custom tag library that contains a number of components for displaying forms in HTML interfaces, accepting and validating input, and assisting in page navigation. An interesting point to note here is a decision not to use the Apache Struts framework. Struts is an older model-view-controller (MVC) framework that is still very popular in JSP applications. Struts and JSF have been shown to work very well together, even if some of their functionality overlaps. While Struts does provide some of the functionality of JSF, its main strong point is its controller features. Struts is especially useful when a Web application implements long (i.e., many Web pages) business processes. It has been determined that our application's business processes are relatively short, and the value that the Struts framework would bring is not significant enough to warrant the extra layer of complexity required to implement it.

The business tier, where most if not all of the application's logic is executed, will run inside a J2EE Web and EJB container. The decision of whether or not the Web and EJB container will run on the same machine, whether they are clustered, or other such configuration information, is not a consideration of the design, except for the fact that such decisions can be made. One advantage of choosing a J2EE-based architecture is the ability to make such deployment choices late, as the system is initially deployed, or to effect these changes as a result of changing demand. The important thing to remember during the design and implementation activities is to not create or code anything that would prevent the normal ability of the J2EE container to shift or deploy components. Such development practices are often implemented in coding or design guidelines that the development team must follow.

The decision was made to use the CMP mechanism for storing all persistent data. There are many reasons to use this mechanism and many reasons why someone might not want to. Other options for persistence include the use of Plain Old Java Objects (POJOs) and a relational object persistence layer like Hibernate, Castor, or the Apache ObJectRelationalBridge (OJB). These options tend to be lighter in weight and more efficient, especially when the application is running on a single node. The decision was made to use the built-in CMP mechanism of the existing container for persistence since the performance needs of this application are not significant enough to warrant another technology or extra layer. Additionally, the use of SDO for managing the flow of data between the presentation and business tiers was adopted to make it easier to manage entity data.

One piece of this application's architecture that is not easily discarded is the use of the CAS for implementing single-sign-on. The idea of single-sign-on is that, while in the same browser, an end user need provide authentication credentials only once to access a whole range of related or unrelated Web applications. It was determined early while creating the vision that the VTS was to be an extension of the existing intranet portal system for the company, and that system currently uses CAS for authentication management. Therefore, the new VTS application will also have to use CAS to identify and authenticate end users.

Entities

The most important part of designing and implementing entities is identifying them. In any given analysis model, any objects with attributes, and even some without any defined attributes, may be designed as entities. The trick is to choose only those classes in the model that really need to be designed as persistent entities. For example, some analysis classes, even those with defined attributes, may merely be transient classes or value classes. For example, the `ValidationResult` class is used only as a return value to the `validate` method. Validations are not logged or recorded in this system, so the `ValidationResult` class does not need to be persistent. When a request is validated, an instance of this class is returned for the caller to examine the results of the validation. When finished, the results are no longer needed or referenced. Therefore, the `ValidationResult` class can remain a simple POJO.

The VTS will use CMP beans to manage all of its persistent entities. CMP has come a long way since it was first introduced. Initially there were a number of problems, specifically with relationships and in performance. However, today's newer specification and improved EJB containers have addressed many of these issues, making CMP a preferred mechanism for managing entities.

Recently, several design patterns have developed around CMP beans. It is generally recommended to use CMP beans to define only local interfaces. A local interface can be accessed only by another bean in the same container. Marshalling data across locally connected beans is much more efficient than doing so over an infrastructure that can support cross-node communication. These objects are instead accessed by a façade object that has local connections to the CMP but also publishes remote interfaces that can be accessed by other session beans and remote clients.

SDO is used to marshal data into and out of the presentation tier. These objects are created and managed by the façade objects in the business tier. SDO is the result of a recent collaboration between BEA and IBM, two big J2EE container vendors, and represents a general agreement to certain best practices when handling data in EJB applications.

Another important design pattern for CMP beans is that they should be designed with minimal, if any, business-level behavior. In fact, it is easiest to consider a CMP definition as little more than a thin wrapping around a database table. All business-level behavior is instead placed in session bean façade objects, which are responsible for orchestrating the state in the various CMP beans to accomplish a unit of business behavior. This has a direct effect on how analysis entities are designed and implemented.

We can begin understanding how all these design-level patterns and conventions get realized in code by looking at the `Category` class. This class is relatively simple because it defines only two persistent properties plus a relationship to instances of the `Grant` class. Fortunately, `Category` does not define any significant behavior at the analysis level. If it did, we would need to remove it from the entity and place it in one of the façade objects. What we are starting with here is a very simple entity.

Design entities are represented by «Entity Bean» stereotyped classes. These classes define their persistent attributes; primary key attributes are further stereotyped. The methods of an «Entity Bean» class are segregated into local and remote (although in this case Category does not define any remote methods, according to our design practices), as well as instance and class level. Each of these corresponds to the actual interface used to define them. In the Category class, we need two interfaces, CategoryLocal and CategoryLocalHome, to define the local methods that can be invoked on instances of the bean and on the home or factory object responsible for creating or finding instances. Figure 12–19 shows a UML-like diagram[3] of the Category entity bean with a relationship to the Grant entity.[4]

Working with a single model element for each entity makes it easier to understand their relationships; however, in the implementation, any given entity is in fact implemented with a number of separate and distinct classes, interfaces, or configuration files. Our Category class, for example, requires two separate interfaces (CategoryLocal and CategoryLocalHome) and one implementation class (CategoryBean), is packaged with other beans in a Java Archive (JAR) file, contributes to the EJB deployment descriptor file, and results in the definition of a table in the database (Figure 12–20). The important thing to realize is that there is typically a large fan-out of model elements as you migrate from analysis to design and implementation. One analysis element will often map to many elements in the implementation, all requiring coordination. Listing 12–1 shows a fragment

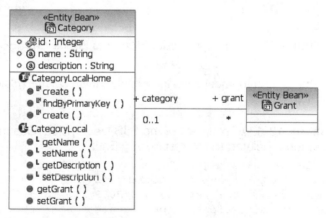

Figure 12–19 A Design Model Representation of the Category Class

---

3. This diagram is a customized view of an entity bean, which in a J2EE system includes the implementation class as well as its interfaces and some configuration information. Also, the use of getters and setters (methods that provide access to object properties) is not an object-oriented convention but rather one dictated by the use of Java and the J2EE framework.

4. Since this is a design model targeting a J2EE architecture, it is not inappropriate to use platform-specific notations.

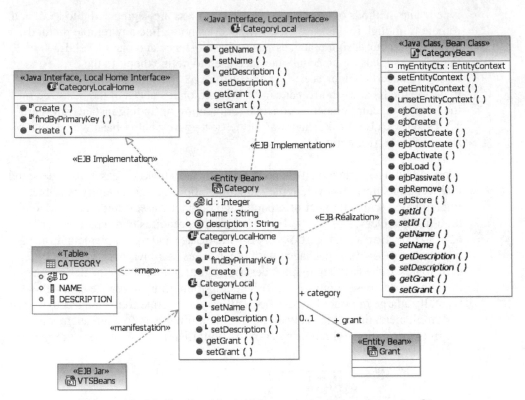

Figure 12–20 Design Model Elements for the `Category` Class

of the EJB deployment descriptor containing elements related to the `Category` entity.

Listing 12–1 A Fragment of the EJB Deployment Descriptor Containing Elements Related to the *Category* Entity

```
<ejb-jar id="ejb-jar_ID" version="2.1"
xmlns="http://java.sun.com/xml/ns/j2ee"
xmlns:xsi="http://www.w3.org/2001/XMLSchema-instance"
xsi:schemaLocation="http://java.sun.com/xml/ns/j2ee
http://java.sun.com/xml/ns/j2ee/ejb-jar_2_1.xsd">
  <display-name>VTSEJB</display-name>
  ...
    <entity id="Category">
      <ejb-name>Category</ejb-name>
      <local-home>com.acme.vts.CategoryLocalHome</local-home>
      <local>com.acme.vts.CategoryLocal</local>
      <ejb-class>com.acme.vts.CategoryBean</ejb-class>
      <persistence-type>Container</persistence-type>
      <prim-key-class>java.lang.Integer</prim-key-class>
      <reentrant>false</reentrant>
```

```
<cmp-version>2.x</cmp-version>
<abstract-schema-name>Category</abstract-schema-name>
<cmp-field id="CMPAttribute_1107874632507">
  <field-name>id</field-name>
</cmp-field>
<cmp-field id="CMPAttribute_1107874633048">
  <field-name>name</field-name>
</cmp-field>
<cmp-field id="CMPAttribute_1107874633068">
  <field-name>description</field-name>
</cmp-field>
<primkey-field>id</primkey-field>
<query>
  <description></description>
  <query-method>
    <method-name>findAll</method-name>
    <method-params/>
  </query-method>
  <ejb-ql>select object(o) from Category o</ejb-ql>
</query>
</entity>
...
</ejb-jar>
```

Following through with our design guidelines, we define a façade[5] object for the
`Category` class. The goal of a session façade is to simplify the interface to do
common tasks of a business entity. This often involves the coordination of methods in several objects. The session façade provides a simpler interface to find, create, modify, and delete entities. Fortunately for us, our development IDE provides
automation to easily create session façades for entity beans. The resulting façade
object is called `CategoryFacade` and, like the entity bean representation,
defines functionality at both the remote and local levels and the instance and factory levels. In the model, a stereotyped «facade» dependency indicates the
semantic connection between the design model–generated façade object and the
design model representation of the entity. The façade class provides a number of
utility methods for creating, finding, updating, and removing `Category` entities.
This essentially acts as a single source manager of instances of this class. Figure
12–21 illustrates such a façade object.

Service Data Objects

Another characteristic of this particular façade implementation is the use of a relatively new and emerging standard, SDO. Simply put, SDO is a mechanism for
accessing and manipulating data in a manner that is disconnected from the data

---

5. See the Session Façade pattern as described in *Core J2EE Patterns* [4].

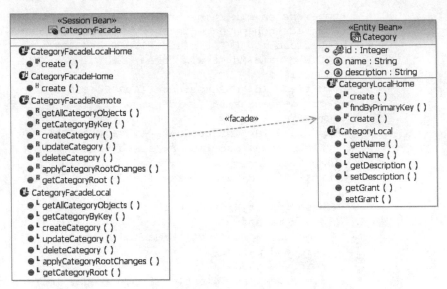

Figure 12–21 A Façade Object Governing Access to Entity Beans

source. This provides a useful means for marshalling data in a system. SDO uses disconnected data graphs and enables clients to retrieve the data graph from a source, manipulate it, and then apply the changes back to the original data source.

The use of SDO makes for a more consistent interface to bean data across the entire application. When the façade classes were generated, the corresponding set of SDO objects was also generated. Each SDO object that is created defines two interfaces: a root object (for the data graph) and an entity interface. The root object represents the conceptual root of the data graph. See Figure 12–22.

The façade object uses the SDO object as the main parameter for its create, retrieve, update, and delete (CRUD) methods. It also provides a method to update any changes made to an entire graph of SDO objects. Typical usage of this façade would be by another session bean acting as a business logic controller, perhaps fulfilling a request on behalf of a Web page. Let's take as a sample scenario the need to update and create vacation time request categories. The responsibility for this particular task falls on the HR clerk role. Such a business logic controller would need to be able to get all the existing categories (usually only a dozen or so)[6] to list on a Web page. It would then allow the user to select one for editing or

---

6. Arbitrary use of the `getAllObjects()` methods in the façade classes could lead to unexpected and serious performance issues when the system is tested in a real-life situation. Imagine the performance cost of putting into an array the collection of all the customer addresses in any medium-sized business.

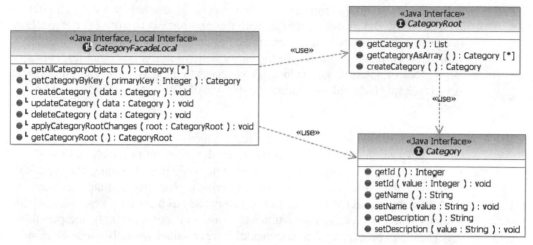

Figure 12–22 SDO Objects Used by the `CategoryFacadeLocal` Class

removal. The business logic controller can easily delete a category with a reference to the SDO or its primary key value. Changing the values of a category is similarly handled by changing the values in the SDO and then telling the façade to use its local value to update the persistent entity in the database.

Primary Key Generation

A pervasive issue in all object-relational database systems is the generation of primary keys for entity beans. The availability of natural primary key values like social security numbers or Universal Product Codes (UPCs) are highly dependent on the domain and can't always be assumed to be available. This means that the application must define and implement a strategy for creating primary keys for new entities that have no natural key attributes. In our system, the entities `Grant`, `Restriction`, and `Request` are examples of business objects that have no single attributes that could be safely used as primary key values.

In traditional database systems, a key could be manufactured as a composite of several properties and foreign key values; however, most EJB designs are more efficient with a single primary key value of a primitive type like integer or string. This means that we need to have a strategy for creating primary keys for our entities. Ideally, the same strategy and mechanism could be used for all our entity types that need generated key values.

In this application, we are have selected the Sequence Blocks strategy for primary key generation as described by Marinescu [5]. This strategy refines a very simple approach that essentially creates a new type of CMP entity responsible for managing the next available integer value that can be used as a key for a particular type of entity. The primary problem with this approach is performance, especially in a system where new entities are created often. These performance issues are addressed by managing access to the entity with a session bean that reserves a large block of potential key values. Thus access to the CMP entity holding the keys is slightly reduced, depending on the size of keys reserved by the session beans.

Incorporating this strategy in our application leads to the creation of another entity and session bean with local access by the other entity façade objects (Figure 12–23). The `SequenceEntity` bean has only two attributes: the sequence name (i.e., the name of the entity type requiring a generated primary key) and the next available integer value that can be safely used as a primary key. Because this strategy reserves blocks of key values at a time, it is entirely likely and possible that there will be gaps in the sequence of integer values actually used. Thus, no application using this strategy should make any assumptions about the order or distribution of the primary key values.

The key generator is used by the other façade objects when there is a need to create a completely new instance of an entity. This is accomplished by updating the `createCategory()` method on the façade object to check for an incoming `Category` SDO with a null `id` field. If the `id` field is null, the façade is responsible for generating a fresh key for this category. Failure to do so will result in an exception being thrown.

Getting a new primary key value is as simple as getting access to the `Sequence Session` bean and then calling the `getNextSequenceNumber()` method with the name of the entity as a parameter. The code for the `createCategory` method is shown in Listing 12–2. The `doApplyChanges()` method is an SDO

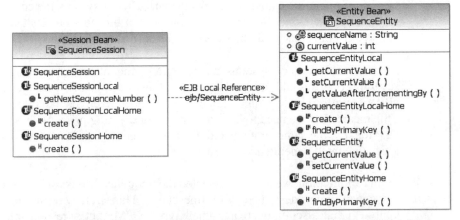

Figure 12–23 Entity and Session Beans for Primary Key Generation

framework implementation method, and generally speaking, the source code is unavailable.

Listing 12–2 Code for the *createCategory* Method

```
public void createCategory(Category data)
        throws CreateException {
  try {
    if( data.getId() == null ) {
      InitialContext ctx = new InitialContext();
      SequenceSessionLocalHome home =
          (SequenceSessionLocalHome)
          ctx.lookup("java:comp/env/ejb/SequenceSession");
      SequenceSessionLocal sequence = home.create();
      int id = sequence.getNextSequenceNumber("Category");
      data.setId( new Integer(id) );
    }
    doApplyChanges(data);
  } catch (Exception ex) {
    throw new CreateException(
        "System error while creating \"Category\".", ex);
  }
}
```

With this update to all the façade's `create` methods and the use of the `SequenceSession` and `SequenceEntity` beans, new instances of entities can be created without the worry of deriving or computing the required primary key of each instance (Figure 12–24).

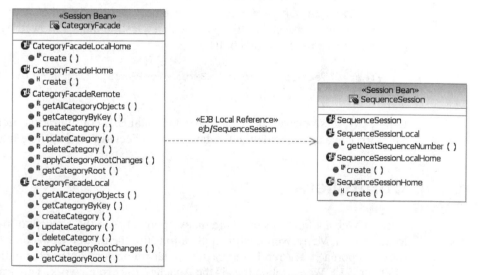

Figure 12–24 The `CategoryFacade` Session Bean Using the `SequenceSession` Bean to Create New Categories

Finders

Another important consideration in EJB entity design is the identification of finder methods. These are methods responsible for searching for specific entity instances that match a given set of criteria. The criteria can be as simple as all instances of vacation time request categories (which typically will result in a list of no more than a dozen instances). The finder may also implement a more complex search, for example, finding all employees whose requests for leaves of absence against a particular category of leave were rejected between March 1 and June 23 of the previous year. Regardless of details, the important point about finders is that the filtering of matching entities occurs on the server, ideally on the database server. Typically, this is the most efficient means of filtering large collections of entities. The only other option is to get all instances of an entity and then, after it has been potentially passed over the wire and reinstantiated in another process, iterate over all the instances and perform the matching tests. This is not the most efficient way to filter large collections.

The idea behind a finder is closely related to that of a SQL `SELECT` statement. EJB finders are expressed in a separate language, the EJB Query Language (EJB QL), which is very similar to SQL but not equivalent. For example, the following EJB QL statement will return all the `Grant` entity instances that are not associated with any restrictions.

```
select object(o) from Grant o where o.restrictions is not
empty
```

Finders can also be parameterized. In the next example, the finder query returns all `DateExclusionRestriction` instances that exclude the supplied date. Parameters are referenced in the query with a question mark followed by the parameter index in the argument list.

```
select object(o) from DateExclusionRestriction o where o.date
is ?1
```

Ultimately, these queries are captured in the main EJB configuration file `ejb-jar.xml` and associated with the Java method declared in the home interface.

Controllers

Even in Web applications there are many approaches to the concept of business logic control. Many Web-centric applications use the model-view-controller (MVC) approach. Currently the most popular framework for implementing strict MVC in J2EE Web applications is the Apache Struts framework. This framework provides a small runtime component along with a set of JSP tag libraries for implementing the user interface and for making it easier to coordinate with the control framework. The MVC design pattern is a widely used and interpreted pattern. There are countless ways to implement the basic pattern even in the context of Web-centric applications. The Struts design and implementation was perhaps the first widely accepted implementation of this pattern for Java-based Web applications.

While the idea of implementing a strict MVC paradigm in the presentation tier sounds reasonable, on closer investigation of the system-level use cases, it is unclear where such control is necessary. In the overwhelming majority of use case scenarios, the functionality required is little more than basic CRUD operations on entities. Orchestrating and coordinating complex business operations, something for which an MVC paradigm is well suited, is just not part of our simple application.

The architect of this system has decided not to use an overt MVC paradigm like that supplied by Struts but instead to rely on the inherent coordination and control supplied as part of the Web pages. For some architects, the decision to not adopt an MVC and/or Struts control framework can be surprising, as many consider MVC critical to all Web-centric applications. We, however, consider the use of middleware, components, or even strategies that are not immediately necessary to the successful release of the application, or not obviously apparent in any existing documentation or future plans for the system, not to be worth the risk.[7]

With this decision made, all of the control constructs will be either in EJB session objects in the business tier, in beans in the server tier, or embedded as tags in the Web pages.

The Web Pages and the User Interface

The design of the Web pages is really separated into two major concerns: (1) the pages themselves, their hyperlinks, and their form fields and (2) their layout. For the first concern, the system architect and information architect collaborate to determine exactly what conceptual pages are required, what should be in them, and how they can be navigated through to accomplish the business goals of the

---

7. By this same reasoning, some might wonder why the decision was made to adopt EJBs for persistence, when it can be argued that a much simpler and more efficient persistence strategy could also be employed. This decision, like many made in a real-life development project, is often based as equally on technical merit as on organization history and experience.

system. Web pages are typically implemented as JSP pages and contain a mix of presentation data and relationships to business processing beans. The second concern, however, is all about aesthetics and user understanding. The layout of a Web page defines *where* information appears in the page, not *what* information should be there. It focuses on the organization of the page so that what the page presents can be most efficiently understood and worked with by the end users. The remainder of this chapter is devoted to the first concern, as the second one is more about art and visual creativity than traditional analysis and design.

Web page design begins with the UX model. The UX model more often than not describes a very good starting candidate for Web page names, content, and links. Generally speaking, UX «screen» classes map to individual JSP pages. Pure HTML Web pages can be part of a Web application when there is no dynamic content inside the page; however, even in these situations JSP pages are preferred since some client-side state management solutions require the dynamic rewriting of all URL hyperlinks, which can be done only with dynamic pages (see the Client State Management sidebar earlier in this chapter).

Depending on the Web tooling being used, the UX model can usually be easily transformed into a site layout or design model (Figure 12–25), where «screen» elements map to JSP pages and associations map to navigation links, either simple hyperlinks or forms where the user supplies additional data.

When designing the presentation tier, there are two main considerations: how to populate the page's dynamic content and how to invoke the business logic processes during page transitions. This application's architecture is J2EE, and the architect has specified the use of JSF to help integrate page construction with these two tasks. JSF helps simplify the construction of dynamic Web pages. It defines a number of custom tags that are embedded with HTML in JSP pages that are used to invoke methods on business objects and extract data to place in HTML elements that are eventually rendered on the client screen. In addition to the JSF tags, the Java Server Pages Standard Template Library (JSTL) also provides a number of useful tags to work with data in JSP pages.

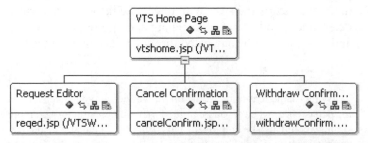

Figure 12–25 The Site Layout Represented in a Design Tool

Populating Dynamic Content

Populating a Web page with dynamic content requires a connection between a Java session bean in the presentation tier and a session bean in the business tier. This should be defined as a remote reference to enable the potential separation of tiers onto different nodes. To populate the VTS home page, we need, in addition to other information, the current employee summary of requests. This summary comes from an `Employee` CMP bean and its related `Request` CMP beans. Since access to CMP beans is governed by generated façade objects, the session bean in the presentation tier needs a remote reference to the façade object. The façade will return SDO objects to the presentation tier session bean, which in turn processes them to produce a simple Java object that can be used directly in the JSP.

In Figure 12–26, the `EmployeeSummarySession` class is a session bean that executes in the presentation tier. Its primary job is to connect to the

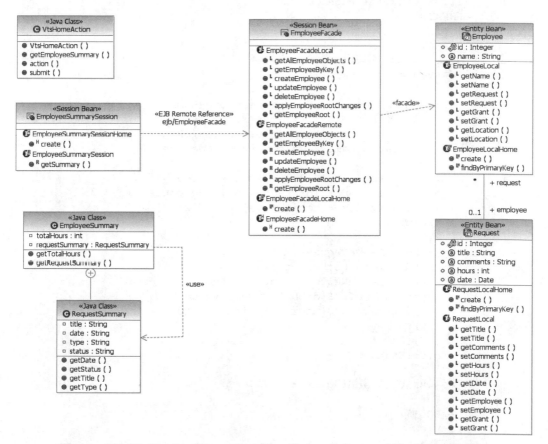

Figure 12–26 Design Elements in the Presentation and Business Tiers

EmployeeFacade and create a summary of an Employee object's requests.
This session bean will also collect and make available other employee-specific
information that will be used in the VTS home page. The EmployeeSummary
class and its public inner class RequestSummary are POJOs used directly in
the JSP pages via the JSTL and JSF tags. Part of the JSP source code for the VTS
home page is shown in Listing 12–3.

Listing 12–3 JSP Source Code for the VTS Home Page

```
<HTML>
<HEAD>
<%@ taglib uri="http://java.sun.com/jsp/jstl/core" prefix="c"%>
<%@ taglib uri="http://java.sun.com/jsf/core" prefix="f"%>
<%@ taglib uri="http://java.sun.com/jsf/html" prefix="h"%>
<%@ page language="java" contentType="text/html;
 charset=ISO-8859-1" pageEncoding="ISO-8859-1"%>
<jsp:useBean id="vtsHome" class="vtsweb.actions.VtsHomeAction"/>
...
<TITLE>VTS Home Page</TITLE>
</HEAD>
<f:view>
  <BODY>
  ...
  <P>Request Summary</P>

  <c:forEach items="${vtsHome.employeeSummary}">
    <c:url var="delUrl" value="faces/reqed">
       <c:param name="id" value="${leaveRequest.id}" />
       <c:param name="action" value="delete" />
    </c:url>
    <c:url var="edUrl" value="faces/reqed">
      <c:param name="id" value="${leaveRequest.id}" />
      <c:param name="action" value="edit" />
    </c:url>
    <tr>
      <td>${leaveRequest.date}</td>
      <td>${leaveRequest.type}</td>
      <td>${leaveRequest.status}</td>
      <td><a href="${delUrl}">delete</a></td>
      <td><a href="${edUrl}">edit</a></td>
    </tr>

  </c:forEach>

  <P><BR>Outstanding Grants</P>
  ...
  </BODY>
</f:view>
</HTML>
```

The VTS home page, like all of the JSP pages in our application, uses a number of custom tags in several different tag libraries. The three sets of tags that are used the most are the core JSF tags, the JSF HTML tags, and the JSTL tags. These are imported and associated with prefix identifiers at the beginning of the JSP source.

A JSP tag is used to bring in a reference to a presentation tier bean that is used for all access to business state and acts as a local controller for actions in the page. The bean is implemented as a POJO. It is referenced in the context of the JSP with the local reference vtsHome.

```
<jsp:useBean id="vtsHome" class=
    "vtsweb.actions.VtsHomeAction"/>
```

This bean can be used in JSF and JSTL custom tags to both extract business data and also invoke business methods. In our home page example, the JSTL forEach tag iterates over the employeeSummary collection of the bean, which contains instances of RequestSummary objects, each representing a specific vacation time request.

In general, it is a good practice to insulate JSP code and logic from the actual EJBs with a simple bean object that can be paired up with a specific page. This object is responsible for organizing and making available all the discrete values of data that can be placed in the JSP. This will also make it easier for the creative team members responsible for the final layout of the page, as they will not have to deal with the sometimes confusing technical requirements of managing EJBs.

Invoking Business Logic

Work is accomplished in Web applications primarily during page transitions. Logic is triggered by user requests to view or navigate to the next page. The next page may or may not be the actual page that the user requested. Depending on the outcome of the business logic, the desired page may get switched to a different page based on the current client's state. For example, if a user submits a request for vacation time but forgets to fill in a required field, the system will not return to the main home page as the user might expect but will return to the editing page and most likely display a warning message indicating the need for the required information.

In a JSF application, the navigation paths are defined by a configuration file called faces-config.xml. This file, among other things, defines the managed beans that can be referenced in JSP pages (e.g., VtsHomeAction). A navigation rule defines the allowed transitions from one page to another, based on an outcome value. This outcome value is computed within one of the managed beans, and when returned, the faces framework will use it to determine which page to load and construct as a response. Listing 12–4 shows the navigation rules in `faces-config.xml`.

Listing 12–4 Navigation Rules in *faces-config.xml*

```
<navigation-rule>
  <from-view-id>/reqed.jsp</from-view-id>
  <navigation-case>
    <from-outcome>failure</from-outcome>
    <to-view-id>/reqed.jsp</to-view-id>
  </navigation-case>
  <navigation-case>
    <from-outcome>success</from-outcome>
    <to-view-id>/vtshome.jsp</to-view-id>
  </navigation-case>
</navigation-rule>
```

The rule in Listing 12–4 states that when the button or hyperlink component on `reqed.jsp` is activated, the application will navigate from the `reqed.jsp` page to the `vtshome.jsp` page if the outcome referenced by the button or hyperlink component's tag is `success`. Otherwise, the application will return to `reqed.jsp`.

Hyperlinks or form buttons are placed inside the originating page with the use of the JSF HTML tags. In the following command button example, clicking on the button will cause the `submit()` method of the `vtsHomeAction` instance to be invoked because the `action` attribute references the `submit` method of the `VtsHomeAction` backing bean. The `submit()` method performs some processing and returns a logical outcome that is passed to the default navigation handler, which matches the outcome against a set of navigation rules defined in the configuration file.

```
<h:commandButton value="Submit Changes"
action="#{vtsHome.submit}"/>
```

The impact of this design is that all of the presentation tier's logic is expressed in the managed or backing beans that execute in the Web server. These beans accomplish their tasks by creating normal remote EJB references to EJBs in the business tier, which could potentially be running on a different node in the system.

12.4 Transition and Post-Transition

Web-centric architectures, especially Internet-based ones, bring with them their own special implementation and testing concerns, in addition to the usual ones of functionality and general performance. Web applications by their very nature exist in a heterogeneous environment that may be subject to change; the exact client hardware and software configuration can't be assumed. To help address these issues during design, special browser-specific technologies were purposely not used in our VTS application.

Implementing a Web application is, for the most part, the development of server-side software. Nearly all the software written in a typical Web application executes on the server side. Only when custom JavaScript is employed or specialized applets or client-side controls are developed will the developer really need to be concerned with the details of every client hardware and software configuration the application may encounter.

Even when you choose the technologies that are officially supported by the latest versions of the most popular browsers, there is no guarantee that they will perform the same way across browsers and client configurations. Such technologies and related issues include the following.

- *Java scripting*: All browsers do not implement client-side scripting in exactly the same way. Several browsers extend the scripting language with new and proprietary features. Others interpret the specifications slightly differently or have unusual side effects not governed by the official specifications.
- *Style sheets*: Style sheets and other layout-specific functionality depend on the availability of fonts and screen size. Just because you use style sheets doesn't mean that your pages will render in the same way on all client configurations.
- *Frames*: The implementation of frames has been problematic since their introduction. Scrolling, sizing, and targeting issues constantly plague the use of frames in applications. If frames are used in an application, be sure to test them completely, not only with all targeted client configurations but also in scenarios that involve more than just the use of the application being tested.
- *Bandwidth*: As our development tools become more sophisticated and it becomes easier to incorporate elaborate features into our Web pages, there is the chance that some end users will experience extremely slow page transitions due to the volume of HTML and/or the amount of scripting that must execute on the client. If the application under development is to be deployed to an anonymous user base over the Internet, special care must be taken to test and design the pages for low bandwidth and weak client configurations.

This set of issues becomes an ongoing challenge as technologies evolve over time.

Object-Oriented Programming Languages

The use of object-oriented technology is not restricted to any particular language; rather, it applies to a wide spectrum of object-based and object-oriented programming languages. As important as analysis and design are, however, we cannot ignore the details of coding, for ultimately our software architectures must be expressed in some programming language. Indeed, as Wulf has suggested, a programming language serves three purposes [1].

- It is a design tool.
- It is a vehicle for human consumption.
- It is a vehicle for instructing a computer.

This appendix is for the reader who may not be familiar with certain of the object-oriented programming languages we mention in this book. Herein we provide a summary description of a number of the more important and popular languages, together with a common example that provides a basis for comparing the syntax, semantics, and idioms of three of the most popular object-oriented programming languages, namely Smalltalk, C++, and Java.

A.1 Language Evolution

Currently, there are over 2,500 different high-order programming languages [2]. We see so many different languages because each was shaped by the particular requirements of its perceived problem domain. Furthermore, the existence of each new language enables developers to move on to more and more complex problems. With each previously unexplored application, language designers learn new lessons that change their basic assumptions about what is important in a language and what is not. This evolution of languages also has been heavily influenced by progress in the theory of computing, which has led to a formal understanding of the semantics of statements, modules, abstract data types, and processes.

As we discussed in Chapter 2, different programming languages support different abstractions: mathematic, algorithmic, data, or object-oriented. The most recent advances in programming languages have been due to the influence of the object model. As we also discussed in Chapter 2, a language is considered object-based if it directly supports data abstraction and classes. An object-oriented language is one that is object-based but also provides support for inheritance and polymorphism.

The common ancestor of almost every contemporary object-based and object-oriented programming language is Simula, developed in the 1960s by Dahl, Myrhurg, and Nygard [3]. Simula built on the ideas of ALGOL but added the concepts of encapsulation and inheritance. Perhaps even more important, Simula—as a language for describing systems and for developing simulations—introduced the discipline of writing programs that mirror the vocabulary of their problem domain.

Figure A–1 is derived from Éric Lévénez's Web site on computer language history [4] and shows the genealogy of the most influential and widely used object-based and object-oriented programming languages. The lengths of the boxes indicate development or significant usage activity for the languages in the general domain. The arrows indicate prominent influences in their development.

Determining the popularity of usage of any given programming language or even a family of languages is a daunting task, likely to raise the emotions of language zealots and the scrutiny of advanced and amateur statisticians alike. While popularity alone is no indication of the quality of a programming language, it does hint at the general usefulness and widespread availability.

The TIOBE Programming Community Index (TCP-Index) [5] is a new and novel way to determine a given programming language's popularity by examining Internet Web pages and news group searches. By using simple queries for each of the target languages, the relative percentage of pages deemed of interest are tabulated and compared with the results of previous examinations over the course of months and years. The result is an interesting indicator of the current popularity of any given language. At the time of this writing, the results shown in Table A–1 were the most recent. As you can see, the top 10 languages are dominated by object-oriented languages, with C (a procedural language) barely holding on to the top position.

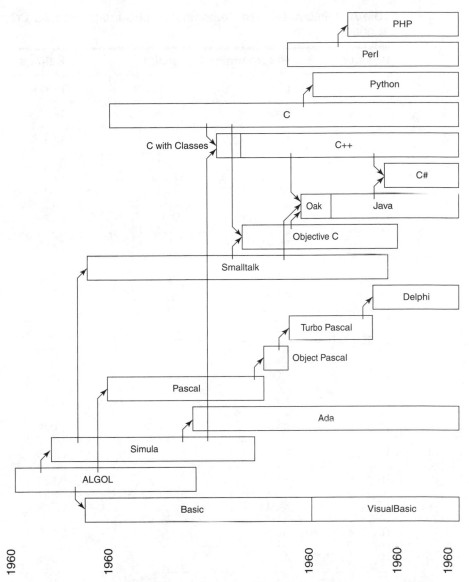

Figure A–1 The Genealogy of Influential Computer Languages

In each of the following sections, we briefly discuss a prominent object-oriented language. Examples of code are based on a simple windowing shape problem. In this problem, classes are defined to represent types of shapes that can be drawn on a display. Figure A–2 shows a generic UML model of the classes involved.

Table A–1 Internet-Based Determination of Currently Popular Programming Languages

Position	Programming Language	Ratings
1	C	19.37%
2	Java	18.57%
3	Perl	10.37%
4	C++	9.72%
5	PHP	7.97%
6	(Visual) Basic	6.78%
7	Delphi/Kylix	2.89%
8	Python	2.80%
9	C#	2.78%
10	SQL	2.65%
11	JavaScript	1.39%
12	COBOL	1.38%
13	IDL	1.23%
14	SAS	1.09%
15	Lisp	0.86%
16	Fortran	0.82%
17	MATLAB	0.78%
18	Ada	0.68%
19	Pascal	0.49%
20	AWK	0.48%

Each of the following examples attempts to demonstrate how key object-oriented features such as classes, inheritance, and polymorphism are expressed in the language. There is no attempt to optimize the stated task for the given platform.

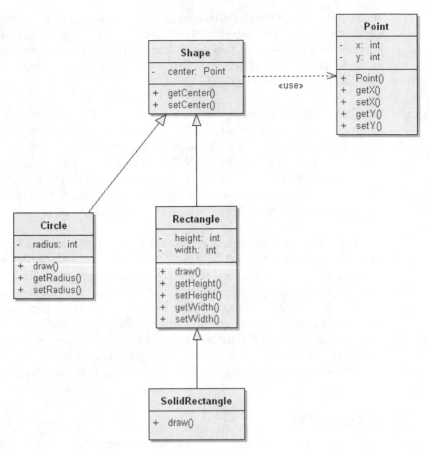

Figure A–2 A Generic UML Class Diagram Used by Each Example

A.2 Smalltalk

Smalltalk was created by the members of the Xerox Palo Alto Research Center Learning Research Group as the software element of the Dynabook, a visionary project of Alan Kay. Simula was its primary influence, although Smalltalk also took some ideas from the language FLEX and the work of Seymore Papert and Wallace Feurzeig. Smalltalk represents both a language and a software development environment. It is a pure object-oriented programming language in that everything is viewed as an object; even integers are classes. Next to Simula, Smalltalk is perhaps the most important object-oriented programming language because its concepts have influenced not only the design of almost every subsequent object-oriented programming language (even though Smalltalk itself is no longer in popular use) but also the look and feel of graphical user interfaces such as the Macintosh user interface, Windows, Motif, KDE, and Gnome, all of which are now largely taken for granted.

Smalltalk evolved over almost a decade of work and was the product of synergistic group activity. Dan Ingalls was the lead architect during most of Smalltalk's development, but there were also seminal contributions by Peter Deutsch, Glenn Krasner, and Kim McCall. In parallel, the elements of the Smalltalk environment were developed by James Althoff, Robert Flegal, Ted Kaehler, Diana Merry, and Steve Putz. Among other important roles that they played, Adele Goldberg and David Robson served as chroniclers of the Smalltalk project.

There are five identifiable early releases of Smalltalk: Smalltalk-72, -74, -76, -78, and -80. Smalltalk-72 and -74 did not provide support for inheritance, but they did lay much of the conceptual foundation of the language, including the ideas of message passing and polymorphism. Later releases of the language turned classes into first-class citizens, thus completing the view that everything in the environment could be treated as an object. Currently there are about 20 active versions of Smalltalk in existence [6], most of which are platform-specific (in terms of hardware and system) ports of Smalltalk-80. While the user interface is usually distinct, the class libraries and overall functionality are similar across these versions.

Overview

Ingalls states that "the purpose of the Smalltalk project is to support children of all ages in the world of information. The challenge is to identify and harness metaphors of sufficient simplicity and power and to allow a single person to have access to, and creative control over, information which ranges from numbers and text through sounds and images" [7]. To this end, Smalltalk is built around two simple concepts: Everything is treated as an object, and objects communicate by passing messages.

Table A–2 summarizes Smalltalk's features, relative to the seven elements of the object model. Although the table does not indicate it, multiple inheritance is possible by the redefinition of certain primitive methods [8].

Example

Consider the problem in which we have a heterogeneous list of shapes, in which each particular shape object might be a circle, a rectangle, or a solid rectangle.

Table A–2 Smalltalk Object-Oriented Feature Index

Elements of the Object Model	Feature	Included?
Abstraction	Instance variables	Yes
	Instance methods	Yes
	Class variables	Yes
	Class methods	Yes
Encapsulation	Of variables	Private
	Of methods	Public
Modularity	Kinds of modules	None
Hierarchy	Inheritance	Single
	Generic units	No
	Metaclasses	Yes
Typing	Strongly typed	No
	Polymorphism	Yes (single)
Concurrency	Multitasking	Indirectly (by classes)
Persistence	Persistent objects	No

Smalltalk has an extensive class library that already contains classes for circles and rectangles, so our solution in this language would be almost trivial; this demonstrates the importance of reuse. However, for the sake of comparison, let's assume that we have only primitive classes for drawing lines and arcs.

We begin by defining the class `AShape` as follows.

```
Object subclass: #AShape
     instanceVariableNames: 'theCenter'
     classVariableNames: ''
     poolDictionaries: ''
     category: 'Appendix'

initialize
     "Initialize the shape"

     thisCenter := Point new
```

```
setCenter: aPoint
      "Set the center of the shape"

      theCenter := aPoint

center
      "Return the center of the shape"

      ^theCenter

draw
      "Draw the shape"

      self subclassResponsibility
```

We next define the subclass ACircle.

```
AShape subclass #ACircle
      instanceVariableNames: 'theRadius'
      classVariableNames: ''
      poolDictionaries: ''
      category: 'Appendix'

setRadius: anInteger
      "Set the radius of the circle"

      theRadius := anInteger

radius
      "Return the radius of the circle"

      ^theRadius

draw
      "Draw the circle"

      | anArc index |
      anArc := Arc new.
      Index := 1.
      [index <= 4]
            whileTrue:
                  [anArc
                        center: theCenter
                        radius: theRadius
                        quadrant : index.
                        anArc display.
                        Index := index + 1]
```

Continuing, the subclass `ARectangle` may be defined as follows.

```
AShape subclass: #ARectangle
      instanceVariableNames: 'theHeight theWidth'
      classVariableNames: ''
      poolDictionaries: ''
      category: 'Appendix'

draw
      "Draw the rectangle"

      | aLine upperLeftCorner |
      aLine := Line new.
      upperLeftCorner := theCenter x - (theWidth / 2) @
(theCenter y - (theHeight / 2)).
      aLine beginPoint: upperLeftCorner
      aLine endPoint: upperLeftCorner x + theWidth @
upperLeftCorner y.
      aLine display.
      aLine beginPoint: aLine endpoint.
      aLine endpoint: upperLeftCorner x + theWidth @
(upperLeftCorner y + theHeight).
      aLine display.
      aLine beginPoint: aLine endPoint.
      aLine endPoint: upperLeftCorner x @
(upperLeftCorner y + theHeight).
      aLine display.
      aLine beginPoint: aLine endPoint.
      aLine endPoint: upperLeftCorner.
      aLine display.

setHeight: anInteger
      "Set the height of the rectangle"

      theHeight := anInteger

setWidth: anInteger
      "Set the width of the rectangle"

      theWidth := anInteger

height
      "Return the height of the rectangle"

      ^theHeight

width
      "Return the width of the rectangle"

      ^theWidth
```

Lastly, we can also define the subclass `ASolidRectangle`.

```
ARectangle subclass #ASolidRectangle
    instanceVariableNames: ''
    classVariableNames: ''
    poolDictionaries: ''
    category: 'Appendix'

draw
    "Draw the rectangle"
    | upperLeftCorner lowerRightCorner |
    super draw.
    upperLeftCorner := theCenter x - (theWidth quo: 2) + 1 @
(theCenter y - (theHeight quo: 2) + 1).
    lowerRightCorner := upperLeftCorner x + theWidth - 1 @
(upperLeftCorner y + theHeight - 1).
    Display
            fill: (upperLeftCorner corner: lowerRightCorner)
            mask: Form gray
```

References

The most current reference is the ANSI Smalltalk Standard: *Programming Language Smalltalk* [20]. Other notable references include *Smalltalk-80: The Language*, by Goldberg and Robson [9]; *Smalltalk-80: The Interactive Programming Environment*, by Goldberg [10]; and *Smalltalk-80: Bits of History, Words of Advice*, by Krasner [11]. LaLonde and Pugh [12] explore Smalltalk-80 in great depth, including both class libraries and application development.

A.3 C++

C++ was designed by Bjarne Stroustrup of AT&T Bell Laboratories. The immediate ancestor of C++ is a language called C with Classes, also developed by Stroustrup in 1980. In turn, C with Classes was heavily influenced by the languages C and Simula. C++ is largely a superset of C. However, in one sense, C++ is simply a better C, in that it provides type checking, overloaded functions, and many other improvements. Most importantly, however, C++ adds object-oriented programming features to C.

Early translator technology for C++ involved the use of a preprocessor for C, called cfront. Because this translator emitted C code as an intermediate representation, it was possible to port C++ to virtually every UNIX architecture quite quickly. Now C++ translators and native compilers are available commercially for almost every kind of instruction set architecture.

There have been several major releases of the C++ language. Version 1.0 and its minor releases added basic object-oriented programming language features to C, such as single inheritance and polymorphism, plus type checking and overloading. Version 2.0, released in 1989, improved on the previous versions in a variety of ways (such as the introduction of multiple inheritance), based on extensive experience with the language by a relatively large user community. Version 3.0, released in 1990, introduced templates (parameterized classes) and exception handling. The ANSI X3J16 C++ committee has adopted proposals for namespace control (consistent with our notion of class categories) and runtime type identification. In addition to ANSI, C++ has been standardized by the BSI (British Standards Institute), the DIN (German national standards organization), and the ISO (International Standards Organization), as well as others. The ISO standard was finalized and adopted in 1997 and ratified in August 1998. The ISO is the current maintainer of the C++ standard.

Overview

Stroustrup states that "C++ was primarily designed so that the author and his friends would not have to program in assembler, C, or various modern high order languages. Its main purpose is to make writing good programs easier and more pleasant for the individual programmer. There never was a C++ paper design; design, documentation, and implementation went on simultaneously" [13]. C++ corrects many of the deficiencies of C and adds to the language support for classes, type checking, overloading, free store management, constant types, references, inline functions, derived classes, and virtual functions [14].

We summarize the features of C++ in Table A–3, relative to the seven elements of the object model.

Table A–3 C++ Object-Oriented Feature Index

Elements of the Object Model	Feature	Included?
Abstraction	Instance variables	Yes
	Instance methods	Yes
	Class variables	Yes
	Class methods	Yes

continues

Table A–3 C++ Object-Oriented Feature Index *(Continued)*

Elements of the Object Model	Feature	Included?
Encapsulation	Of variables	Public, protected, private
	Of methods	Public, protected, private
Modularity	Kinds of modules	File
Hierarchy	Inheritance	Multiple
	Generic units	Yes
	Metaclasses	No
Typing	Strongly typed	Yes
	Polymorphism	Yes (single)
Concurrency	Multitasking	Indirectly (by classes)
Persistence	Persistent objects	No

Example

Let's reimplement the shape problem. The common style in C++ is to place the outside view of each class in header files. Thus, we may write the following.

```cpp
Struct Point {
      int x;
      int y;
};

class Shape {
public:
      Shape();
      void setCenter(Point p);
      virtual void draw() = 0;
      Point center() const;
private:
      Point theCenter;
};

class Circle : public Shape {
public:
      Circle();
      void setRadius(int r);
```

```
        virtual void draw();
        int radius() const;
private:
        int theRadius;
};

class Rectangle : public Shape {
public:
        Rectangle();
        void setHeight(int h);
        void setWidth(int w);
        virtual void Draw();
        int height() const;
        int width() const;
private:
        int theHeight;
        int theWidth;
};

class SolidRectangle : public Rectangle {
public:
        virtual void draw();
};
```

The definition of C++ does not include a class library. For our purposes, we assume
that a programmatic interface to a generic graphical display (e.g., X Windows or
Microsoft Windows) exists and that the global objects Display, Window, and
GraphicsContext exist and can be linked to. Then we may complete the
methods above in a separate file as follows.

```
Shape::Shape() {
        theCenter.x = 0;
        theCenter.y = 0;
};

void Shape::setCenter(Point p) {
        theCenter = p;
}

Point Shape::center() const {
        Return theCenter;
}

Circle::Circle() : theRadius(0) { }

void Circle::setRadius(int r) {
        theRadius = r;
}
```

```
void Circle::draw() {
      int X = (center().x - theRadius);
      int Y = (center().y - theRadius);
      XDrawArc(Display, Window, GraphicsContext,
X, Y,(theRadius * 2),
(theRadius * 2), 0, (360 * 64));
};

int Circle::radius() const {
      return theRadius;
}

Rectangle::Rectangle() : theHeight(0), theWidth(0) { }

void Rectangle::setHeight(int h) {
      theHeight = h;
}

void Rectangle::setWidth(int w) {
      theWidth = w;
}

void Rectangle::draw() {
      int X = (center().x - (theWidth / 2));
      int Y = (center().y - (theHeight / 2));
      XDrawRectangle(Display, Window, GraphicsContext,
X, Y, theWidth, theHeight);
};

int Rectangle::height() const {
      return theHeight;
};

int Rectangle::width() const {
      return theWidth;
};

void SolidRectangle::draw() {
      Rectangle::draw();
      int X = (center().x - (width() / 2));
      int Y = (center().y - (height() / 2));
      gc oldGraphicsContext - GraphicsContext;
      XSetForeground(Display, GraphicsContext, Gray);
      XDrawFilled (Display, Window, Graphics, X, Y,
width(), height());
      GraphicsContext = oldGraphicsContext;

};
```

References

The most popular reference for C++ continues to be *The Annotated C++ Reference Manual* by Ellis and Stroustrup [15], more commonly referred to as the "ARM." The most recent reference is *The C++ Standard: Incorporating Technical Corrigendum No. 1* by Stroustrup [16]. Stroustrup provides in-depth coverage of the language and its use in the context of object-oriented design in other works as well [17, 18].

A.4 Java

James Gosling and a few others in a small secluded group in Sun Microsystems created a small programming language called Oak after determining that C++ was just too difficult for what they wanted to do.

They were building advanced software for digitally controlled consumer devices such as entertainment platforms and microwave ovens. After efforts to bring this technology to the digital cable television market failed, they realized that the newly emerging commercial Internet was a perfect match for what they had. They renamed the language as Java and started to market it as a general-purpose programming language, one that could be easily marshaled throughout the Internet and executed in the context of an HTML browser.

The big break for Java came about in May 1995, when Sun Microsystems and Netscape announced Java technology was going to be incorporated into Netscape Navigator, the most commonly used browser on the Internet at the time. This effectively created an enormous market of potential users of this technology.

While early marketing efforts focused on Java's applicability for the Internet and its platform independence, it was its server-side usage that truly solidified Java as a preferred object-oriented language. While Java's graphics performance has always been criticized, most Java developers can be found today using Java on the server side (i.e., non-graphics-based components) to deliver Web pages and business tier functionality.

Even though Java has been around for only a little more than 10 years, it has seen phenomenal growth by any measure. The growth has come not only in the evolution of the language but also, more significantly, in its related technologies such as Enterprise Java Beans (EJBs), Java Server Pages (JSP), and Java 2 Micro Edition (J2ME). Java technology and standards continue to grow at a rapid yet organized pace. In 1998, Sun created the Java Community Process (JCP) to manage the development and revision of the Java technology specifications, reference implementations, and test suites. The process outlines how the community evaluates and acts on Java Specification Requests (JSRs) for new specifications or significant revisions to existing specifications. Nearly 100 specifications are currently being worked on.

Sun Microsystems continues to manage the overall development of the Java language and its related technologies.

Overview

Java is more than a programming language; like Smalltalk, it is just as much an environment and runtime as it is a language. Java technology involves the use of virtual machines and a common byte code intermediary. Also like Smalltalk, it includes a rich class library that can be extended. Java technology is such a good match for the Internet because of its portability and its rich set of standard functionality.

The language itself resembles C++ intentionally. The team at Sun started using C++ but found too many problems and decided to get around them by creating a new and more appropriate language.

> We wanted to build a system that could be programmed easily without a lot of esoteric training and which leveraged today's standard practice. Most programmers working these days use C, and most programmers doing object-oriented programming use C++. So even though we found that C++ was unsuitable, we designed Java as closely to C++ as possible in order to make the system more comprehensible. [19]

Java omits many features found in C++ such as multiple inheritance and operator overloading. One of Java's most useful features is automatic garbage collection. Java developers are not required to perform their own memory management. Instead, they can create new instances of objects and be assured that when all references to them have been removed, at some point that memory will be reclaimed. While not potentially as efficient as C++, this garbage collection does eliminate one very common source of programming errors.

Java attempts to enforce type safety wherever practical. However, because of the use of its rich class library, most notably its collection classes, strict type checking like that found in C++ is just not practical. The latest specification, Java 2 version 1.5, does include something new called Generics (JSR 14). Java Generics, also known as parameterized types, are like C++ templates and enable Java developers to create type-safe collections, among other things.

We summarize the features of Java in Table A–4, relative to the seven elements of the object model.

Table A–4 Java Object-Oriented Feature Index

Elements of the Object Model	Features	Included?
Abstraction	Instance variables	Yes
	Instance methods	Yes
	Class variables	Yes
	Class methods	Yes
Encapsulation	Of variables	Public, protected, private, package
	Of methods	Public, protected, private, package
Modularity	Kinds of modules	File
Hierarchy	Inheritance	Single
	Generic units	Yes
	Metaclasses	No
Typing	Strongly typed	No
	Polymorphism	Yes (single)
Concurrency	Multitasking	Yes
Persistence	Persistent objects	No

Example

Recreating our example for Java leads to the creation of a separate class file for each of the defined classes. First, we create the `Point` class.

```
package test;
public class Point {

        private int x = 0;
        private int y = 0;

        public Point(int x, int y) {
                this.x = x;
                this.y = y;
        }
```

```java
        public int getX() {
            return x;
        }

        public void setX(int x) {
            this.x = x;
        }

        public int getY() {
            return y;
        }

        public void setY(int y) {
            this.y = y;
        }
    }
```

Next we define the Shape class.

```java
    package test;

    public class Shape {

        private Point center;

        public Point getCenter() {
            return center;
        }

        public void setCenter(Point center) {
            this.center = center;
        }
    }
```

We follow up with the Circle class.

```java
    package test;
    import java.awt.Graphics;

    public class Circle extends Shape {
        private int radius = 0;

        public void draw(Graphics g) {
            int x = (getCenter().getX() - radius);
            int y = (getCenter().getY() - radius);
            int d = radius * 2;
            g.drawOval(x, y, d, d);
        }
```

```
        public int getRadius() {
                return radius;
        }

        public void setRadius(int radius) {
                this.radius = radius;
        }
}
```

Then we create the Rectangle class.

```
package test;
import java.awt.Graphics;

public class Rectangle extends Shape {

        private int height = 0;
        private int width = 0;

        public void draw(Graphics g) {
                int x = (getCenter().getX() - width/2);
                int y = (getCenter().getY() - height/2);
                g.drawRect(x, y, width, height);
        }

        public int getHeight() {
                return height;
        }

        public void setHeight(int height) {
                this.height = height;
        }

        public int getWidth() {
                return width;
        }

        public void setWidth(int width) {
                this.width = width;
        }
}
```

We complete our example with the SolidRectangle class.

```
package test;
import java.awt.Color;
import java.awt.Graphics;
```

```java
public class SolidRectangle extends Rectangle {

    public void draw(Graphics g) {
        super.draw(g);
        int width = getWidth()-1;
        int height = getHeight()-1;
        int x = (getCenter().getX() - width/2);
        int y = (getCenter().getY() - height/2);
        g.setColor(Color.GRAY);
        g.fillRect(x, y, width, height);
    }
}
```

References

Sun Microsystems Press (SMP) is a partnership between Sun Microsystems, Prentice Hall, and Addison-Wesley. SMP is an excellent source for very detailed books on all aspects and levels of Java technology. Since Java grew up and was propelled by the Internet, it is perhaps the best and most current source for Java information. Ken Arnold, James Gosling, and David Holmes are responsible for *The Java Programming Language, Third Edition*, a complete introduction to the Java language with insights into its basic design goals.

Further Reading

This appendix directs you to further reading for each chapter by referring to items listed in the Classified Bibliography. References here take the form [<label> <year>]. For example, Brooks [H 1975] refers to his 1975 book, *The Mythical Man-Month*, in section II (Software Engineering) of the bibliography.

Chapter 1

The challenges associated with developing complex software systems are articulately described in two classic works by Brooks [H 1975, H 1987]. Glass [H 1982], the Office of the Under Secretary of Defense for Acquisition (reporting on the Defense Science Board Task Force) [H 1987], and the U.S. Department of Defense [H 1982] provide further information on contemporary software practices. Empirical studies on the nature and causes of software failures may be found in van Genuchten [H 1991], Guindon et al. [H 1987], and Jones [H 1992].

Two of Simon's works [A 1962, A 1982] are the seminal references on the architecture of complex systems, Courtois [A 1985] applies these ideas to the domain of software. Alexander's seminal work [I 1979] provides a fresh approach to architecting physical structures. Peter [I 1986] and Petroski [I 1985] examine complexity in the context of social and physical systems, respectively. Similarly, Allen and Starr [A 1982] examine hierarchical systems in a number of domains. Flood and Carson [A 1988] offer a formal study of complexity as seen through the theory of systems science. Waldrop [A 1992] describes the emerging science of complexity and its study of complex adaptive systems, emergent behavior, and self-organization. The report by Miller [A 1956] provides empirical evidence for the fundamental limiting factors of human cognition.

There are a number of excellent references on the subject of software engineering. Ross, Goodenough, and Irvine [H 1980] and Zelkowitz [H 1978] are two of the classic papers summarizing the essential elements of software engineering. Extended works on the subject include Jensen and Tonies [H 1979], Sommerville [H 1989], Vick and Ramamoorthy [H 1984], Wegner [H 1980], Pressman [H 1992], Oman and Lewis [H 1990], Berzins and Luqi [H 1991], and Ng and Yeh [H 1990]. Other papers relevant to software engineering in general may be found in Yourdon [H 1979] and Freeman and Wasserman [H 1983]. Graham [F 1991] and Berard [H 1993] both present a broad treatment of object-oriented software engineering.

Gleick [I 1987] offers a very readable introduction to the science of chaos.

Chapter 2

The concept of the object model was first introduced by Jones [F 1979] and Williams [F 1986]. Kay's Ph.D. thesis [F 1969] established the direction for much of the work in object-oriented programming that followed.

Shaw [J 1984] provides an excellent summary regarding abstraction mechanisms in high-order programming languages. The theoretical foundation of abstraction may be found in the work of Liskov and Guttag [H 1986], Guttag [J 1980], and Hilfinger [J 1982]. Parnas [F 1979] is the seminal work on information hiding. The meaning and importance of hierarchy are discussed in the work edited by Pattee [J 1973].

Case studies of object-oriented applications may be found in Taylor [H 1990, C 1992], Berard [H 1993], Love [C 1993], and Pinson and Weiner [C 1990].

Excellent collections of papers dealing with all topics of object-oriented technology may be found in Peterson [G 1987], Schriver and Wegner [G 1987], and Khoshafian and Abnous [E 1990]. The proceedings of several yearly conferences on object-oriented technology are also excellent sources of material.

Organizations responsible for establishing standards for object technology include the Object Management Group and the ANSI X3J7 committee.

The primary reference for C++ is Ellis and Stroustrup [G 1990]. Other useful references include Stroustrup [G 2000], Lippman, LaJoie, and Moo [G 2005], and Coplien [G 1992].

A good introduction to the basics of the .NET Framework is *Introducing .NET* by Conrad et al. [G 2001].

Chapter 3

MacLennan [G 1987] discusses the distinction between values and objects. The work by Meyer [J 1987] proposes the idea of programming as contracting.

Much has been written on the topic of class hierarchies, with particular emphasis on approaches to inheritance and polymorphism. The works by Albano [G 1983], Allen and Starr [A 1982], Brachman [J 1983], Hailpern and Nguyen [G 1987], and Wegner and Zdonik [J 1988] provide an excellent theoretical foundation for all the important concepts and issues. Cook and Palsberg [J 1989] and Touretzky [G 1986] provide formal treatments of the semantics of inheritance. Wirth [J 1987] proposes a related approach for record type extensions, as used in the language Oberon. Ingalls [G 1986] provides a useful discussion on the topic of multiple polymorphism. Grogono [G 1989] studies the interplay of polymorphism and type checking, and Ponder and Buch [G 1992] warn of the dangers of unrestrained polymorphism. Practical guidance on the effective use of inheritance is offered by Meyer [G 1988] and Halbert and O'Brien [G 1988]. LaLonde and Pugh [J 1985] examine the problems of teaching the effective use of specialization and generalization.

The nature of an abstraction's roles and responsibilities are further detailed by Rubin and Goldberg [B 1992] and Wirfs-Brock, Wilkerson, and Wiener [F 1990]. Measures of goodness for class design are also considered by Coad [F 1991].

Meyer [G 1986] examines the relationships between genericity and inheritance, as viewed by the language Eiffel. Stroustrup [G 1988a] proposes a mechanism for parameterized types in C++.

An alternative to class-based hierarchies is provided by delegation, using exemplars. This approach is examined in detail by Stein [G 1987].

Chapter 4

The problem of classification is timeless. In his work titled *Statesman*, Plato introduces the classical approach to categorization, through which objects with similar properties are grouped. In *Categories*, Aristotle picks up this theme and analyzes the differences between classes and objects. Several centuries later, Aquinas, in *Summa Theologica*, and then Descartes, in *Rules for the Direction of the Mind*, ponder the philosophy of classification. Contemporary objectivist philosophers include Rand [I 1979].

Alternatives to the objectivist view of the world are discussed in Lakoff and Johnson [I 1980] and Goldstein and Alger [C 1992].

Classification is an essential human skill. Theories regarding its acquisition during early childhood development were pioneered by Piaget and are summarized by Maier [A 1969]. Lefrancois [A 1977] offers a very readable introduction to these ideas and provides an excellent discourse on children's acquisition of the object concept.

Cognitive scientists have explored the problems of classification in great detail. Newell and Simon [A 1972] provide an unmatched source of material regarding human classification skills. More general information may be found in Simon [A 1982], Hofstadter [I 1979], Siegler and Richards [A 1982], and Stillings et al. [A 1987]. Lakoff [A 1987], a linguist, offers insights into the ways different human languages have evolved to cope with the problems of classification and what this reveals about the mind. Minksy [A 1986] approaches this subject from the opposite direction, starting with a theory regarding the structure of the mind.

Conceptual clustering, an approach to knowledge representation through classification, is described in detail by Michalski and Stepp [A 1983, A 1986], Peckham and Maryanski [J 1988], and Sowa [A 1984]. Domain analysis, an approach to finding key abstractions and mechanisms by examining the vocabulary of the problem domain, is described in the comprehensive collection of papers by Prieto-Diaz and Arango [A 1991]. Iscoe [B 1988] has made several important contributions to this field. Additional information may be found in Iscoe, Browne, and Werth [B 1989], Moore and Bailin [B 1988], and Arango [B 1989].

Intelligent classification often requires looking at the world in innovative ways, and these skills can be taught (or, at least, encouraged). VonOech [I 1990] suggests some paths to creativity. Coad [A 1993] has developed a board game (the Object Game) that fosters skills in class and object identification.

Much work is being carried out in the cataloging of patterns in software systems, giving rise to a taxonomy of idioms, mechanisms, and frameworks. Interesting references include Gamma et al. [1995], Coplien [G 1992], Coad [A 1992], Johnson [A 1992], Shaw [A 1989, A 1990, A 1991], and Wirfs-Brock [C 1991]. Alexander's influential work [I 1979] applies patterns to the field of building architecture and city planning.

Mathematicians have attempted to devise empirical approaches to classification, leading to what is called measurement theory. Stevens [A 1946] and Coombs, Raiffa, and Thrall [A 1954] provide the seminal works on this topic.

The Classification Society of North America publishes a journal twice a year, containing a variety of papers on the problems of classification.

Chapter 5

The Object Management Group has produced the UML Superstructure Specification, version 2.0, which is the foundation for the books that have been written to introduce us to the use of this updated notation. It can be obtained from the UML Resource Page at www.uml.org/ [L 2004].

As we said earlier, the UML 2.0 is very rich and full featured; however, in your daily work it is likely that you will use only a fraction of the notation. If you are interested in exploring the darker corners of the UML, there are books that focus specifically on the details of the notation. We suggest Rumbaugh, Jacobson, and Booch [L 2005] and Booch, Rumbaugh, and Jacobson [L 2005] for an authoritative discussion of this topic.

Blaha and Rumbaugh [L 2005] have updated their 1991 classic text on object-oriented modeling and design with the UML 2.0 notation.

Bennett, Skelton, and Lunn [L 2005] give a practical introduction to the UML 2.0 notation, along with examples, exercises, and review questions. This is a worthwhile update to their 2001 edition and is suitable for those new to UML or UML 2.0.

Fowler [L 2003] provides a concise presentation of the typical usages of UML 2.0.

Chapter 6

An early form of the process described in this chapter was first documented by Booch [F 1982]. Berard [F 1986] later elaborated on this work. Related approaches include GOOD (General Object-Oriented Design) by Seidewitz and Stark [F 1986a, F 1986b, F 1987, F 1988], MOOD (Multiple-view Object-Oriented Design) by Kerth [F 1988], and HOOD (Hierarchical Object-Oriented Design) by CRI, CISI Ingenierie, and Matra for the European Space Station [F 1987]. An additional related work is Stroustrup [G 1991], which suggests substantially similar processes.

In addition to the works cited earlier for Chapter 2, a number of other methodologists have proposed specific object-oriented development processes, for which the bibliography provides an extensive set of references. Some of the more interesting contributions come from Kruchten [F 2003], Alabios [F 1988], Boyd [F 1987], Buhr [F 1984], Cherry [F 1987, F 1990], deChampeaux, Balzer, et al. [F 1992], deChampeaux, Lea, and Faure [F 1992], Felsinger [F 1987a, F 1987b], Firesmith [F 1986, F 1993], Hines and Unger [G 1986], Jacobson [F 1985],

Jamsa [F 1984], Kadie [F 1986], Masiero and Germano [F 1988], Nielsen [F 1988], Nies [F 1986], Rajlich and Silva [F 1987], and Shumate [F 1987].

Comparisons of various object-oriented development processes may be found in Arnold et al. [F 1991], Boehm-Davis and Ross [H 1984], deChampeaux [B 1991a, B 1991b], Cribbs, Moon, and Roe [F 1992], Fowler [F 1992], Kelly [F 1986], Mannino [F 1987], Song [F 1992], and Webster [F 1988]. Brookman [F 1991] and Fichman and Kemerer [F 1992] provide a comparison of structured and object-oriented methods.

Empirical studies of software processes may be found in Curtis, Kellner, and Over [H 1992] as well as the Software Process Workshop [H 1988]. Another interesting reference is Guindon, Krasner, and Curtis [H 1987], which studies the exploratory processes used by developers early in the development process. Rechtin [H 1992] offers pragmatic guidance to the software architect who must drive the development process.

Parnas and Clements [H 1986] is the classical reference on how to fake a mature process.

Chapter 7

van Genuchten [H 1991] and Jones [H 1992] examine common software risks. Abdel-Hamid and Madnick [H 1991] study the dynamics of development teams.

Gilb [H 1988] and Charette [H 1989] are useful references for software engineering management practices. For a realistic study of what really goes on during the development, when pragmatics chases theory out the window, see the works by Glass [H 1982], Lammers [H 1986], and Humphrey [H 1989]. DeMarco and Lister [H 1987], Yourdon [H 1989b], Rettig [H 1990], and Thomsett [H 1990] offer a number of recommendations to the development manager.

Schulmeyer and McManus [H 1992] provide an excellent general reference on software quality assurance. Chidamber and Kemerer [H 1991] and Walsh [H 1992, 1993] study quality assurance and metrics in the context of object-oriented systems. Kemerer and Darcy [H 2005] provide examples of the application of the Chidamber Kemerer (CK) metrics suite and provide observations about their practical application.

Kan [H 2002] provides a comprehensive reference for software quality engineering and metrics with specific metrics and lessons learned for object-oriented projects. Lorenz and Kidd [H 1994] and Henderson-Sellers [H 1996] provide well-regarded texts on object-oriented metrics.

Suggestions on how to transition individuals and organizations to the object model are described by Goldberg [C 1978], Goldberg and Kay [G 1977], and Kempf [G 1987].

Hantos [H 2005] provides an innovative perspective on object-oriented development risks by mapping software risk information from Boehm [H 1989, H 2002] to the object-oriented concepts from Meyer [H 1995].

Chapter 8

The Aerospace Corporation publication *GPS Primer—A Student Guide to the Global Positioning System* provides an introduction to the Global Positioning System [C 2003].

The European Commission, Directorate-General for Energy and Transportation, has a comprehensive Web site discussing Galileo, the European Satellite Navigation System [C 2006].

IEEE-Std-1471-2000 provides a framework for architectural description of software-intensive systems along with the definition of the content of the description [D 2000].

In their paper titled "ANSI/IEEE 1471 and Systems Engineering," Maier, Emery, and Hilliard [D 2004] present a rationale for using this specification during systems engineering activities to describe system architecture.

Kruchten [D 1995] introduces the 4+1 view model of architecture to describe software using five views: logical, process, physical, development, and use case.

In his paper titled "Introduction to Object-Oriented Systems Engineering," Parts 1 and 2, Krikorian [D 2003] proposes that Kruchten's 4+1 views apply to systems engineering and presents augmented 4+1 views defined for this use.

IEEE-Std-12207 consists of three parts, 12207.0, 12207.1, and 12207.2. IEEE-Std-12207.0-1996 [H 1996] provides a basis for software practices usable in both national and international business. It gives clarifications, modifications, and additions to ISO/IEC 12207: 1995. IEEE-Std-12207.1-1997 [H 1997a] gives guidance on recording lifecycle data. IEEE-Std-12207.2-1997 [H 1997b] gives guidance on the implementation of the processes of IEEE-Std-12207.0-1996.

IEEE-Std-1220-2005 [H 2005] provides an approach to applying and managing the interdisciplinary tasks of the systems engineering process while engaged in product development.

The International Council on Systems Engineering (INCOSE) has produced a comprehensive guide to the activities performed by systems engineers [I 2006].

Chapter 9

Some of the design points for the Train Traffic Management System are based on those for the Advanced Train Control System, as described by Murphy [C 1988].

Message translation and verification occur in virtually all command and control systems. Plinta, Lee, and Rissman [C 1989] provide an excellent discourse on the issues and offer the design of a mechanism for passing messages in a type-safe way across processors in a distributed system.

Chapter 10

In the context of architectural patterns, Shaw [A 1991] discusses blackboard frameworks as well as other kinds of application frameworks.

Englemore and Morgan [C 1988] furnish a comprehensive treatment of blackboard systems, including their evolution, theory, design, and application. Among other topics, there are descriptions of two object-oriented blackboard systems, BB1, from Stanford, and BLOB, developed for the British Ministry of Defense. Other useful sources of information regarding blackboard systems may be found in Hayes-Roth [J 1985] and Nii [J 1986].

Detailed discussions concerning forward- and backward-chaining in rules-based systems may be found in Barr and Feigenbaum [J 1981], Brachman and Levesque [J 1985], Hayes-Roth, Waterman, and Lenat [J 1983], and Winston and Horn [G 1989].

Meyer and Matyas [I 1982] cover the strengths and weaknesses of various kinds of ciphers, along with algorithmic approaches to breaking them.

Considerations, benefits, and drawbacks of blackboard application frameworks are discussed in Corkill [D 1991] and Hunt [D 2002].

Chapter 11

The problems of process synchronization, deadlock, livelock, and race conditions are discussed in detail in Hansen [H 1977], Ben-Ari [H 1982], and Holt et al. [H 1978]. Mellichamp [H 1983], Glass [H 1983], and Foster [H 1981] offer general references on the issues of developing real-time applications. Concurrency as viewed by the interplay of hardware and software may be found in Lorin [H 1972].

Chapter 12

Garrett [M 2002] discusses high-level user-related design issues. Constantine and Lockwood [M 1999] also discuss user-related design issues emphasizing a use case and modeling approach.

Monson-Haefel [M 2001] provides an engaging introduction to designing and programming with EJBs.

Geary and Horstmann [M 2004] address user interface design in the context of implementing reusable components for Web applications.

Cavaness [M 2004] covers the Struts framework and the model-view-controller design pattern.

Notes

Preface

Mills, H. 1985. *DPMA and Human Productivity.* Houston, TX: Data Processing Management Association.

Section I: Concepts

Wagner, J. 1986. *The Search for Signs of Intelligent Life in the Universe.* New York, NY: Harper and Row, p. 202. By permission of ICM, Inc.

Chapter 1: Complexity

[1] Brooks, F. April 1987. No Silver Bullet: Essence and Accidents of Software Engineering. *IEEE Computer* vol. 20(4), p. 12.

[2] Peters, L. 1981. *Software Design.* New York, NY: Yourdon Press, p. 22.

[3] Brooks. No Silver Bullet, p. 11.

[4] Parnas, D. July 1985. *Software Aspects of Strategic Defense Systems.* Victoria, Canada: University of Victoria, Report DCS-47-IR.

[5] Peter, L. 1986. *The Peter Pyramid.* New York, NY: William Morrow, p. 153.

[6] Waldrop, M. 1992. *Complexity: The Emerging Science at the Edge of Order and Chaos.* New York, NY: Simon and Schuster.

[7] Courtois, P. June 1985. On Time and Space Decomposition of Complex Structures. *Communications of the ACM* vol. 28(6), p. 596.

[8] Simon, H. 1982. *The Sciences of the Artificial.* Cambridge, MA: The MIT Press, p. 218.

[9]   Rechtin, E. October 1992. The Art of Systems Architecting. *IEEE Spectrum* vol. 29(10), p. 66.

[10] Simon. *Sciences*, p. 217.

[11] Ibid., p. 221.

[12] Ibid., p. 209.

[13] Gall, J. 1986. *Systemantics: How Systems Really Work and How They Fail.* Second Edition. Ann Arbor, MI: The General Systemantics Press, p. 65.

[14] Miller, G. March 1956. The Magical Number Seven, Plus or Minus Two: Some Limits on Our Capacity for Processing Information. *The Psychological Review* vol. 63(2), p. 86.

[15] Simon. *Sciences*, p. 81.

[16] Dijkstra, E. 1979. Programming Considered as a Human Activity. In *Classics in Software Engineering*. New York, NY: Yourdon Press, p. 5.

[17] Parnas, D. December 1985. Software Aspects of Strategic Defense Systems. *Communications of the ACM* vol. 28(12), p. 1328.

[18] Tsai, J., and Ridge, J. November 1988. Intelligent Support for Specifications Transformation. *IEEE Software* vol. 5(6), p. 34.

[19] Stein, J. March 1988. Object-Oriented Programming and Database Design. *Dr. Dobb's Journal of Software Tools for the Professional Programmer* no. 137, p. 18.

[20] Peters. *Software Design*.

[21] Yau, S., and Tsai, J. June 1986. A Survey of Software Design Techniques. *IEEE Transactions on Software Engineering* vol. SE-12(6).

[22] Teledyne Brown Engineering. October 1987. *Software Methodology Catalog*, Report MC87-COMM/ADP-0036. Tinton Falls, NJ.

[23] Sommerville, I. 1985. *Software Engineering*. Second Edition. Wokingham, England: Addison-Wesley, p. 68.

[24] Yourdon, E., and Constantine, L. 1979. *Structured Design*. Englewood Cliffs, NJ: Prentice-Hall.

[25] Myers, G. 1978. *Composite/Structured Design*. New York, NY: Van Nostrand Reinhold.

[26] Page-Jones, M. 1988. *The Practical Guide to Structured Systems Design*. Englewood Cliffs, NJ: Yourdon Press.

[27] Wirth, N. January 1983. Program Development by Stepwise Refinement. *Communications of the ACM* vol. 26(1).

[28] Wirth, N. 1986. *Algorithms and Data Structures*. Englewood Cliffs, NJ: Prentice-Hall.

[29] Dahl, O., Dijkstra, E., and Hoare, C. A. R. 1972. Structured Programming. London, England: Academic Press.

[30] Mills, H., Linger, R., and Hevner, A. 1986. *Principles of Information System Design and Analysis*. Orlando, FL: Academic Press.

[31] Jackson, M. 1975. *Principles of Program Design*. Orlando, FL: Academic Press.

[32] Jackson, M. 1983. *System Development*. Englewood Cliffs, NJ: Prentice-Hall.

[33] Orr, K. 1971. *Structured Systems Development*. New York, NY: Yourdon Press.

[34] Langdon, G. 1982. *Computer Design*. San Jose, CA: Computeach Press, p. 6.

[35] Miller. Magical Number, p. 95.

[36] Shaw, M. (ed.). 1981. *ALPHARD: Form and Content*. New York, NY: Springer-Verlag, p. 6.

[37] Goldberg, A. 1984. *Smalltalk-80: The Interactive Programming Environment*. Reading, MA: Addison-Wesley, p. 80.

[38] Petroski, H. 1985. *To Engineer Is Human*. New York, NY: St. Martin's Press, p. 40.

[39] Dijkstra, E. January 1993. *American Programmer* vol. 6(1).

[40] Mostow, J. Spring 1985. Toward Better Models of the Design Process. *AI Magazine* vol. 6(1), p. 44.

[41] Stroustrup, B. 1991. *The C+ Programming Language*. Second Edition. Reading, MA: Addison-Wesley, p. 366.

[42] Eastman, N. 1984. Software Engineering and Technology. *Technical Directions* vol. 10(1), p. 5.

[43] Brooks. No Silver Bullet, p. 10.

Chapter 2: The Object Model

[2] Wegner, P. June 1981. *The Ada Programming Language and Environment*. Unpublished draft.

[3] Abbott, R. August 1987. Knowledge Abstraction. *Communications of the ACM* vol. 30(8), p. 664.

[4] Ibid., p. 664.

[5] Shankar, K. 1984. Data Design: Types, Structures, and Abstractions. *Handbook of Software Engineering*. New York, NY: Van Nostrand Reinhold, p. 253.

[6] *Macintosh MacApp 1.1.1 Programmer's Reference*. 1986. Cupertino, CA: Apple Computer, p. 2.

[7] Bhaskar, K. October 1983. How Object-Oriented Is Your System? *SIGPLAN Notices* vol. 18(10), p. 8.

[8] Stefik, M., and Bobrow, D. Winter 1986. Object-Oriented Programming: Themes and Variations. *AI Magazine* vol. 6(4), p. 41.

[9] Yonezawa, A., and Tokoro, M. 1987. Object-Oriented Concurrent Programming: An Introduction. In *Object-Oriented Concurrent Programming*. Cambridge, MA: The MIT Press, p. 2.

[10] Levy, H. 1984. *Capability-Based Computer Systems*. Bedford, MA: Digital Press, p. 13.

[11] Ramamoorthy, C., and Sheu, P. Fall 1988. Object-Oriented Systems. *IEEE Expert* vol. 3(3), p. 14.

[12] Myers, G. 1982. *Advances in Computer Architecture*. Second Edition. New York, NY: John Wiley and Sons, p. 58.

[18] Dijkstra, E. May 1968. The Structure of the "THE" Multiprogramming System. *Communications of the ACM* vol. 11(5).

[19] Pashtan, A. 1982. Object-Oriented Operating Systems: An Emerging Design Methodology. *Proceedings of the ACM '82 Conference*. ACM.

[20] Parnas, D. 1979. On the Criteria to Be Used in Decomposing Systems into Modules. In *Classics in Software Engineering*. New York, NY: Yourdon Press.

[21] Liskov, B., and Zilles, S. 1977. An Introduction to Formal Specifications of Data Abstractions. In *Current Trends in Programming Methodology: Software Specification and Design* vol. 1. Englewood Cliffs, NJ: Prentice-Hall.

[22] Guttag, J. 1980. Abstract Data Types and the Development of Data Structures. In *Programming Language Design*. New York, NY: Computer Society Press.

[23] Shaw, M. October 1984. Abstraction Techniques in Modern Programming Languages. *IEEE Software* vol. 1(4), p. 10.

[24] Nygaard, K., and Dahl, O-J. 1981. The Development of the Simula Languages. In *History of Programming Languages*. New York, NY: Academic Press, p. 460.

[25] Atkinson, M., and Buneman, P. June 1987. Types and Persistence in Database Programming Languages. *ACM Computing Surveys* vol. 19(2), p. 105.

[26] Rumbaugh, J. April 1988. Relational Database Design Using an Object-Oriented Methodology. *Communications of the ACM* vol. 31(4), p. 415.

[27] Chen, P. March 1976. The Entity-Relationship Model—Toward a Unified View of Data. *ACM Transactions on Database Systems* vol. 1(1).

[28] Barr, A., and Feigenbaum, E. 1981. *The Handbook of Artificial Intelligence*. Vol. 1. Los Altos, CA: William Kaufmann, p. 216.

[29] Stillings, N., Feinstein, M., Garfield, J., Rissland, E., Rosenbaum, D., Weisler, S., and Baker-Ward, L. 1987. *Cognitive Science: An Introduction.* Cambridge, MA: The MIT Press, p. 305.

[30] Rand, Ayn. 1979. *Introduction to Objectivist Epistemology.* New York, NY: New American Library.

[31] Minsky, M. 1986. *The Society of Mind.* New York, NY: Simon and Schuster.

[32] Jones, A. 1979. The Object Model: A Conceptual Tool for Structuring Software. In *Operating Systems.* New York, NY: Springer-Verlag, p. 8.

[33] Stroustrup, B. May 1988. What Is Object-Oriented Programming? *IEEE Software* vol. 5(3), p. 10.

[34] Cardelli, L., and Wegner, P. December 1985. On Understanding Types, Data Abstraction, and Polymorphism. *ACM Computing Surveys* vol. 17(4), p. 481.

[35] DeMarco, T. 1979. *Structured Analysis and System Specification.* Englewood Cliffs, NJ: Prentice-Hall.

[36] Yourdon, E. 1989. *Modern Structured Analysis.* Englewood Cliffs, NJ: Prentice-Hall.

[37] Gane, C., and Sarson, T. 1979. *Structured Systems Analysis.* Englewood Cliffs, NJ: Prentice-Hall.

[38] Ward, P., and Mellor, S. 1985. *Structured Development for Real-Time Systems.* Englewood Cliffs, NJ: Yourdon Press.

[39] Hatley, D., and Pirbhai, I. 1988. *Strategies for Real-Time System Specification.* New York, NY: Dorset House.

[40] Jenkins, M., and Glasgow, J. January 1986. Programming Styles in Nial. *IEEE Software* vol. 3(1), p. 48.

[41] Bobrow, D., and Stefik, M. February 1986. Perspectives on Artificial Intelligence Programming. *Science* vol. 231, p. 951.

[42] Dahl, O., Dijkstra, E., and Hoare, C. A. R. 1972. *Structured Programming.* London, England: Academic Press, p. 83.

[43] Shaw. Abstraction Techniques.

[44] Berzins, V., Gray, M., and Naumann, D. May 1986. Abstraction-Based Software Development. *Communications of the ACM* vol. 29(5), p. 403.

[45] Abelson, H., and Sussman, G. 1985. *Structure and Interpretation of Computer Programs.* Cambridge, MA: The MIT Press, p. 126.

[46] Ibid., p. 132.

[47] Seidewitz, E., and Stark, M. 1986. Towards a General Object-Oriented Software Development Methodology. *Proceedings of the First International Conference on Ada Programming Language Applications*

for the NASA Space Station. NASA Lyndon B. Johnson Space Center, TX: NASA, p. D.4.6.4.

[48] Meyer, B. 1988. *Object-Oriented Software Construction.* New York, NY: Prentice Hall.

[49] Wirfs-Brock, R., and Wilkerson, B. October 1989. Object-Oriented Design: A Responsibility-Driven Approach. *SIGPLAN Notices* vol. 24(10).

[50] Ingalls, D. The Smalltalk-76 Programming System Design and Implementation. *Proceedings of the Fifth Annual ACM Symposium on Principles of Programming Languages.* ACM, p. 9.

[51] Gannon, J., Hamlet, R., and Mills, H. July 1987. Theory of Modules. *IEEE Transactions on Software Engineering* vol. SE-13(7), p. 820.

[52] Date, C. 1986. *Relational Database: Selected Writings.* Reading, MA: Addison-Wesley, p. 180.

[53] Liskov, B. May 1988. Data Abstraction and Hierarchy. *SIGPLAN Notices* vol. 23(5), p. 19.

[54] Britton, K., and Parnas, D. December 8, 1981. *A-7E Software Module Guide.* Washington, DC: Naval Research Laboratory, Report 4702, p. 24.

[56] Stroustrup, B. 1988. Private communication.

[57] Myers, G. 1978. *Composite/Structured Design.* New York, NY: Van Nostrand Reinhold, p. 21.

[58] Liskov, B. 1980. A Design Methodology for Reliable Software Systems. In *Tutorial on Software Design Techniques.* Third Edition. New York, NY: IEEE Computer Society, p. 66.

[59] Zelkowitz, M. June 1978. Perspectives on Software Engineering. *ACM Computing Surveys* vol. 10(2), p. 20.

[60] Parnas, D., Clements, P., and Weiss, D. March 1985. The Modular Structure of Complex Systems. *IEEE Transactions on Software Engineering* vol. SE-11(3), p. 260.

[61] Britton and Parnas. *A-7E Software*, p. 2.

[62] Parnas, D., Clements, P., and Weiss, D. 1983. Enhancing Reusability with Information Hiding. *Proceedings of the Workshop on Reusability in Programming,* Stratford, CT: ITT Programming, p. 241.

[63] Meyer. *Object-Oriented Software Construction*, p. 47.

[64] Cox, B. 1986. *Object-Oriented Programming: An Evolutionary Approach.* Reading, MA: Addison-Wesley, p. 69.

[65] Danforth, S., and Tomlinson, C. March 1988. Type Theories and Object-Oriented Programming. *ACM Computing Surveys* vol. 20(1), p. 34.

[66] Liskov. Data Abstraction and Hierarchy, p. 23.

[67] As quoted in Liskov. Design Methodology, p. 67.

[68] Zilles, S. 1984. Types, Algebras, and Modeling. In *On Conceptual Modeling: Perspectives from Artificial Intelligence, Databases, and Programming Languages.* New York, NY: Springer-Verlag, p. 442.

[69] Borning, A., and Ingalls, D. 1982. *A Type Declaration and Inference System for Smalltalk.* Palo Alto, CA: Xerox Palo Alto Research Center, p. 134.

[71] Stroustrup, B. 1992. Private communication.

[72] Tesler, L. August 1981. The Smalltalk Environment. *Byte* vol. 6(8), p. 142.

[73] Borning and Ingalls. *Type Declaration*, p. 133.

[74] Thomas, D. March 1989. What's in an Object? *Byte* vol. 14(3), p. 232.

[76] Lim, J., and Johnson, R. April 1989. The Heart of Object-Oriented Concurrent Programming. *SIGPLAN Notices* vol. 24(4), p. 165.

[77] Black, A., Hutchinson, N., Jul, E., Levy, H., and Cartcr, L. July 1986. *Distribution and Abstract Types in Emerald.* Report 86-02-04. Seattle, WA: University of Washington, p. 3.

[78] Proceedings of the ACM SIGPLAN Workshop on Object-Based Concurrent Programming. April 1989. *SIGPLAN Notices* vol. 24(4), p. 1.

[79] Atkinson, M., Bailey, P., Chisholm, K., Cockshott, P., and Morrison, R. 1983. An Approach to Persistent Programming. *The Computer Journal* vol. 26(4), p. 360.

[80] Khoshafian, S., and Copeland, G. November 1986. Object Identity. *SIGPLAN Notices* vol. 21(11), p. 409.

[81] *Vbase Technical Overview.* September 1987. Billerica, MA: Ontologic, p. 4.

[82] Stroustrup, B. November 1987. Possible Directions for C++. *Proceedings of the USENIX C++ Workshop.* Santa Fe, NM, p. 14.

[83] Meyer. *Object-Oriented Software Construction*, pp. 30–31.

[84] Robson, D. August 1981. Object-Oriented Software Systems. *Byte* vol. 6(8), p. 74.

[85] See www.hibernate.org for more information and downloads.

Chapter 3: Classes and Objects

[1] Lefrancois, G. 1977. *Of Children: An Introduction to Child Development.* Second Edition. Belmont, CA: Wadsworth, p. 244–246.

[2] Nygaard, K., and Dahl, O-J. 1981. The Development of the Simula Languages. In *History of Programming Languages.* New York, NY: Academic Press, p. 462.

[3] Halbert, D., and O'Brien, P. September 1988. Using Types and Inheritance in Object-Oriented Programming. *IEEE Software* vol. 4(5), p. 73.

[4]   Smith, M., and Tockey, S. 1988. *An Integrated Approach to Software Requirements Definition Using Objects*. Seattle, WA: Boeing Commercial Airplane Support Division, p. 132.

[6]   MacLennan, B. December 1982. Values and Objects in Programming Languages. *SIGPLAN Notices* vol. 17(12), p. 78.

[7]   Lippman, S. 1989. *C++ Primer*. Reading, MA: Addison-Wesley, p. 185.

[8]   Adams, S. 1993. Private communication.

[9]   Wirfs-Brock, R., Wilkerson, B., and Wiener, L. 1990. *Designing Object-Oriented Software*. Englewood Cliffs, NJ: Prentice Hall, p. 61.

[10] Rubin, K. 1993. Private communication.

[11] *Macintosh MacApp 1.1.1 Programmer's Reference*. 1986. Cupertino, CA: Apple Computer, p. 4.

[12] Khoshafian, S., and Copeland, G. November 1986. Object Identity. *SIGPLAN Notices* vol. 21(11), p. 406.

[13] Ingalls, D. 1981. Design Principles Behind Smalltalk. *Byte* vol. 6(8), p. 290.

[14] Gall, J. 1986. *Systemantics: How Systems Really Work and How They Fail*. Second Edition. Ann Arbor, MI: The General Systemantics Press, p. 158.

[16] Rumbaugh, J., Blaha, M., Premerlani, W., Eddy, F., and Lorensen, W. 1991. *Object-Oriented Modeling and Design*. Englewood Cliffs, NJ: Prentice-Hall, p. 459.

[17] *Webster's Third New International Dictionary of the English Language*, unabridged. 1986. Chicago, IL: Merriam-Webster.

[18] Stroustrup, B. 1991. *The C+ Programming Language*. Second Edition. Reading, MA: Addison-Wesley, p. 422.

[19] Meyer, B. 1987. *Programming as Contracting*. Report TR-EI-12/CO. Goleta, CA: Interactive Software Engineering.

[20] Snyder, A. November 1986. Encapsulation and Inheritance in Object-Oriented Programming Languages. *SIGPLAN Notices* vol. 21(11).

[21] LaLonde, W. April 1989. Designing Families of Data Types Using Exemplars. *ACM Transactions on Programming Languages and Systems* vol. 11(2), p. 214.

[22] Rumbaugh, J. April 1988. Relational Database Design Using an Object-Oriented Methodology. *Communications of the ACM* vol. 31(4), p. 417.

[25] Brachman, R. October 1983. What IS-A Is and Isn't: An Analysis of Taxonomic Links in Semantic Networks. *IEEE Computer* vol. 16(10), p. 30.

[29] As quoted in Harland, D., Szyplewski, M., and Wainwright, J. October 1985. An Alternative View of Polymorphism. *SIGPLAN Notices* vol. 20(10).

[30] Kaplan, S., and Johnson, R. July 21, 1986. *Designing and Implementing for Reuse*. Urbana, IL: University of Illinois, Department of Computer Science, p. 8.

[31] Deutsch, P. 1983. Efficient Implementation of the Smalltalk-80 System. In *Proceedings of the 11th Annual ACM Symposium on the Principles of Programming Languages*, p. 300.

[32] Ibid., p. 299.

[33] Duff, C. August 1986. Designing an Efficient Language. *Byte* vol. 11(8), p. 216.

[34] Stroustrup, B. 1988. Private communication.

[40] Vlissides, J., and Linton, M. 1988. Applying Object-Oriented Design to Structured Graphics. *Proceedings of USENIX C++ Conference*. Berkeley, CA: USENIX Association, p. 93.

[41] Meyer, B. 1988. *Object-Oriented Software Construction*. New York, NY: Prentice Hall, p. 274.

[44] Hendler, J. October 1986. Enhancement for Multiple Inheritance. *SIGPLAN Notices* vol. 21(10), p. 100.

[45] Object Management Group's Web site: www.omg.org/.

[51] Ingalls, D. August 1981. Design Principles Behind Smalltalk. *Byte* vol. 6(8), p. 286.

[52] Stevens, W., Myers, G., and Constantine, L. 1979. Structured Design. In *Classics in Software Engineering*. New York, NY: Yourdon Press, p. 209.

[53] Page-Jones, M. 1988. *The Practical Guide to Structured Systems Design*. Englewood Cliffs, NJ: Yourdon Press, p. 59.

[54] Meyer. *Programming as Contracting*, p. 4.

[55] Halbert, D., and O'Brien, P. September 1988. Using Types and Inheritance in Object-Oriented Programming. *IEEE Software* vol. 4(5), p. 74.

[56] Sakkinen, M. December 1988. Comments on "the Law of Demeter" and C++. *SIGPLAN Notices* vol. 23(12), p. 38.

[57] Lea, D. August 12, 1988. *User's Guide to GNU C++ Library*. Cambridge, MA: Free Software Foundation, p. 12.

[58] Ibid.

[59] Meyer. *Object-Oriented Software Construction*, p. 332.

[60] Wirth, N. 1986. *Algorithms and Data Structures*. Englewood Cliffs, NJ: Prentice-Hall, p. 37.

[61] Keene, S. 1989. *Object-Oriented Programming in Common Lisp*. Reading, MA: Addison-Wesley, p. 68.

[62] Jacobson, I., Christerson, M., Jonsson, P., and Övergaard, G. 1992. *Object-Oriented Software Engineering: A Use Case Driven Approach*. Reading, MA: Addison-Wesley, p. 186.

[63] Parnas, D., Clements, P., and Weiss, D. 1989. Enhancing Reusability with Information Hiding. In *Software Reusability*. New York, NY: ACM Press, p. 143.

Chapter 4: Classification

[2] Michalski, R., and Stepp, R. 1983. Learning from Observation: Conceptual Clustering. In *Machine Learning: An Artificial Intelligence Approach*. Palo Alto, CA: Tioga, p. 332.

[3] Alexander, C. 1979. *The Timeless Way of Building*. New York, NY: Oxford University Press, p. 203.

[4] Darwin, C. 1984. *The Origin of Species. Vol. 49 of Great Books of the Western World*. Chicago, IL: Encyclopedia Britannica, p. 207.

[5] *The New Encyclopedia Britannica*. 1985. Chicago, IL: Encyclopedia Britannica, vol. 3, p. 356.

[8] As quoted in Lewin, R. November 4, 1988. Family Relationships Are a Biological Conundrum. *Science* vol. 242, p. 671.

[9] *The New Encyclopedia Britannica* vol. 3, p. 156.

[10] Descartes, R. 1984. *Rules for the Direction of the Mind. Vol. 31 of Great Books of the Western World*. Chicago, IL: Encyclopedia Britannica, p. 32.

[11] Shaw, M. May 1989. Larger Scale Systems Require Higher-Level Abstractions. *SIGSOFT Engineering Notes* vol. 14(3), p. 143.

[12] Goldstein, T. May 1989. The Object-Oriented Programmer. *The C++ Report* vol. 1(5).

[13] Coombs, C., Raiffa, H., and Thrall, R. 1954. Some Views on Mathematical Models and Measurement Theory. *Psychological Review* vol. 61(2), p. 132.

[15] Birtwistle, G., Dahl, O-J., Myhrhaug, B., and Nygard, K. 1979. *Simula begin*. Lund, Sweden: Studentlitteratur, p. 23.

[16] Heinlein, R. 1966. *The Moon Is a Harsh Mistress*. New York, NY: The Berkeley Publishing Group, p. 11.

[17] Sowa, J. 1984. *Conceptual Structures: Information Processing in Mind and Machine*. Reading, MA: Addison-Wesley, p. 16.

[18] Lakoff, G. 1987. *Women, Fire, and Dangerous Things: What Categories Reveal About the Mind*. Chicago, IL: The University of Chicago Press, p. 161.

[19] Stepp, R., and Michalski, R. February 1986. Conceptual Clustering of Structured Objects: A Goal-Oriented Approach. *Artificial Intelligence* vol. 28(1), p. 53.

[20] Wegner, P. 1987. The Object-Oriented Classification Paradigm. In *Research Directions in Object-Oriented Programming*. Cambridge, MA: The MIT Press, p. 480.

[21] Aquinas, T. 1984. *Summa Theologica. Vol. 19 of Great Books of the Western World*. Chicago, IL: Encyclopedia Britannica, p. 71.

[22] Maier, H. 1969. *Three Theories of Child Development: The Contributions of Erik H. Erickson, Jean Piaget, and Robert R. Sears, and Their Applications*. New York, NY: Harper and Row, p. 111.

[23] Lakoff. *Women, Fire, and Dangerous Things*, p. 32.

[24] Minsky, M. 1986. *The Society of Mind*. New York, NY: Simon and Schuster, p. 199.

[25] *The Great Ideas: A Syntopicon of Great Books of the Western World*. 1984. *Vol. 1 of Great Books of the Western World*. Chicago, IL: Encyclopedia Britannica, p. 293.

[26] Kosko, B. 1992. *Neural Networks and Fuzzy Systems*. Englewood Cliffs, NJ: Prentice-Hall.

[27] Stepp and Michalski. Conceptual Clustering, p. 44.

[28] Lakoff. *Women, Fire, and Dangerous Things*, p. 7.

[29] Ibid., p. 16.

[30] Lakoff, G., and Johnson, M. 1980. *Metaphors We Live By*. Chicago, IL: The University of Chicago Press, p. 122.

[31] Meyer, B. 1988. Private communication.

[32] Shlaer, S., and Mellor, S. 1988. *Object-Oriented Systems Analysis: Modeling the World in Data*. Englewood Cliffs, NJ: Yourdon Press, p. 15.

[33] Ross, R. 1987. *Entity Modeling: Techniques and Application*. Boston, MA: Database Research Group, p. 9.

[34] Coad, P., and Yourdon, E. 1990. *Object-Oriented Analysis*. Englewood Cliffs, NJ: Prentice-Hall, p. 62.

[35] Shlaer, S., and Mellor, S. 1992. *Object Lifecycles: Modeling the World in States*. Englewood Cliffs, NJ: Yourdon Press.

[36] Wirfs-Brock, R., Wilkerson, B., and Wiener, L. 1990. *Designing Object-Oriented Software*. Englewood Cliffs, NJ: Prentice Hall, p. 61.

[37] Rubin, K., and Goldberg, A. September 1992. Object Behavior Analysis. *Communications of the ACM* vol. 35(9), p. 48.

[38] Dreger, B. 1989. *Function Point Analysis*. Englewood Cliffs, NJ: Prentice Hall, p. 4.

[39] Arango, G. May 1989. Domain Analysis: From Art Form to Engineering Discipline. *SIGSOFT Engineering Notes* vol. 14(3), p. 153.

[40] Moore, J., and Bailin, S. 1988. *Position Paper on Domain Analysis*. Laurel, MD: CTA, p. 2.

[41] Jacobson, I., Ericsson, M., and Jacobson, A. 1994. *The Object Advantage: Business Process Reengineering with Object Technology*. Wokingham, England: Addison-Wesley.

[42] Zahniseer, R. July/August 1990. Building Software in Groups. *American Programmer* vol. 3(7-8).

[44] Beck, K., and Cunningham, W. October 1989. A Laboratory for Teaching Object-Oriented Thinking. *SIGPLAN Notices* vol. 24(10).

[45] Abbott, R. November 1983. Program Design by Informal English Descriptions. *Communications of the ACM* vol. 26(11).

[47] McMenamin, S., and Palmer, J. 1984. *Essential Systems Analysis*. New York, NY: Yourdon Press, p. 267.

[48] Ward, P., and Mellor, S. 1985. *Structured Development for Real-Time Systems*. Englewood Cliffs, NJ: Yourdon Press.

[49] Seidewitz, E., and Stark, M. August 1986. *General Object-Oriented Software Development*. Report SEL-86-002. Greenbelt, MD: NASA Goddard Space Flight Center, p. 5-2.

[50] Seidewitz, E. 1990. Private communication.

[51] Goldberg, A. 1984. *Smalltalk-80: The Interactive Programming Environment*. Reading, MA: Addison-Wesley, p. 77.

[52] Thomas, D. May/June 1989. In Search of an Object-Oriented Development Process. *Journal of Object-Oriented Programming* vol. 2(1), p. 61.

[53] Stroustrup, B. 1986. *The C++ Programming Language*. Reading, MA: Addison-Wesley, p. 7.

[54] Halbert, D., and O'Brien, P. September 1988. Using Types and Inheritance in Object-Oriented Programming. *IEEE Software* vol. 4(5), p. 75.

[55] Stefik, M., and Bobrow, D. Winter 1986. Object-Oriented Programming: Themes and Variations. *AI Magazine* vol. 6(4), p. 60.

[56] Stroustrup, B. 1991. *The C+ Programming Language*. Second Edition. Reading, MA: Addison-Wesley, p. 377.

[57] Stefik and Bobrow. Object-Oriented Programming, p. 58.

[58] Lins, C. 1989. A First Look at Literate Programming. In *Structured Programming*.

[59] Gabriel, R. 1990. Private communication.

[60] Coplien, J. 1992. *Advanced C++ Programming Styles and Idioms*.
      Reading, MA: Addison-Wesley.

[61] Adams, S. July 1986. MetaMethods: The MVC Paradigm. In *HOOPLA:
      Hooray for Object-Oriented Programming Languages*. Everette, WA:
      Object-Oriented Programming for Smalltalk Applications Developers
      Association vol. 1(4), p. 6.

[63] Englemore, R., and Morgan, T. 1988. *Blackboard Systems*. Wokingham,
      England: Addison-Wesley, p. v.

[64] Coad, P. September 1992. Object-Oriented Patterns. *Communications of
      the ACM* vol. 35(9).

[65] World Resources Institute Web site. Accessed Jan. 2006. How Many
      Species Are There?. http://pubs.wri.org/pubs_content_
      text.cfm?ContentID=535.

Section II: Method

Petroski, H. 1985. *To Engineer Is Human*. New York, NY: St. Martin's
Press, p. 73.

Chapter 5: Notation

[1]   Shear, D. December 8, 1988. CASE Shows Promise, but Confusion Still
      Exists. *EDN* vol. 33(25), p. 168.

[2]   Whitehead, A. 1958. *An Introduction to Mathematics*. New York, NY:
      Oxford University Press.

[3]   Defense Science Board. September 1987. *Report of the Defense Science
      Board Task Force on Military Software*. Washington, DC: Office of the
      Undersecretary of Defense for Acquisition, p. 8.

[4]   Kleyn, M., and Gingrich, P. September 1988. GraphTrace—Understanding
      Object-Oriented Systems Using Concurrently Animated Views. *SIGPLAN
      Notices* vol. 23(11), p. 192.

[5]   Weinberg, G. 1988. *Rethinking Systems Analysis and Design*. New York,
      NY: Dorset House, p. 157.

[16] Jacobson, I., Christerson, M., Jonsson, P., and Övergaard, G. 1992. *Object-
      Oriented Software Engineering: A Use Case Driven Approach*. Reading,
      MA: Addison-Wesley.

[17] Maksimchuk, R., and Naiburg, E. 2005. *UML for Mere Mortals*. Boston,
      MA: Addison-Wesley.

[18] Blaha, M., and Rumbaugh, J. 2005. *Object-Oriented Modeling and Design
      with UML*. Second Edition. Upper Saddle River, NJ: Prentice Hall, pp.
      116–118.

[19] Rumbaugh, J., Jacobson, I., and Booch, G. 2005. *The Unified Modeling Language Reference Manual.* Second Edition. Boston, MA: Addison-Wesley, pp. 248–253.

[20] Ibid., pp. 40, 109, 171.

[21] Object Management Group. 2004. *UML 2.0 Superstructure Specification.* Needham, MA: Object Management Group, pp. 206–208.

[22] Rumbaugh, Jacobson, and Booch. *The Unified Modeling Language Reference Manual*, pp. 40, 171–172.

[23] Ibid., pp. 109, 479.

[24] Object Management Group. *UML 2.0 Superstructure Specification*, p. 222.

[25] Rumbaugh, Jacobson, and Booch. *The Unified Modeling Language Reference Manual*, p. 312.

[26] Ibid., p. 313.

[27] Object Management Group. *UML 2.0 Superstructure Specification*, p. 219.

[28] Ibid., pp. 213–214.

[29] Rumbaugh, Jacobson, and Booch. *The Unified Modeling Language Reference Manual*, pp. 187, 498.

[30] Ibid., pp. 129–133.

[31] Ibid., p. 285.

[32] Ibid., pp. 285–288.

[33] Ibid., pp. 285–287.

[34] Ibid., pp. 374–375.

[35] Ibid., p. 429.

[36] Ibid., p. 623.

[37] Object Management Group. *UML 2.0 Superstructure Specification*, p. 174.

[38] Rumbaugh, Jacobson, and Booch. *The Unified Modeling Language Reference Manual*, pp. 523–525.

[39] Object Management Group. *UML 2.0 Superstructure Specification*, pp. 189–190.

[40] Rumbaugh, Jacobson, and Booch. *The Unified Modeling Language Reference Manual*, pp. 282–283.

[41] Object Management Group. *UML 2.0 Superstructure Specification*, pp. 169, 176–181.

[42] Rumbaugh, Jacobson, and Booch. *The Unified Modeling Language Reference Manual*, pp. 42–43, 111–112, 504–507.

[43] Ibid., p. 679.

[44] Ibid., pp. 71–73, 227–231.

[45] Ibid., pp. 506–507.

[46] Object Management Group. *UML 2.0 Superstructure Specification*, pp. 169, 111–112.

[47] Ibid., pp. 111–112.

[48] Rumbaugh, Jacobson, and Booch. *The Unified Modeling Language Reference Manual*, pp. 506–507.

[49] Ibid., pp. 113, 505–506, 678–680.

[50] Object Management Group. *UML 2.0 Superstructure Specification*, pp. 109–111.

[51] Ibid., pp. 109–111.

[52] Rumbaugh, Jacobson, and Booch. *The Unified Modeling Language Reference Manual*, pp. 113, 505–506, 678–680.

[53] Ibid., pp. 112–113, 384, 505–506.

[54] Ibid., pp. 112–113, 505–506.

[55] Ibid., pp. 42, 111–112, 507.

[56] Ibid., pp. 42, 111–112, 507.

[57] Ibid., pp. 42, 111–112, 507.

[58] Ibid., pp. 42, 383–384, 505.

[59] Object Management Group. *UML 2.0 Superstructure Specification*, p. 111.

[60] Ibid., pp. 113–114.

[61] Rumbaugh, Jacobson, and Booch. *The Unified Modeling Language Reference Manual*, pp. 383–387, 505.

[62] Ibid., p. 383–387, 505.

[63] Object Management Group. *UML 2.0 Superstructure Specification*, p. 113–114.

[64] Ibid., p. 111.

[65] Rumbaugh, Jacobson, and Booch. *The Unified Modeling Language Reference Manual*, pp. 384–385, 505.

[66] Ibid., pp. 383–387, 505.

[67] Object Management Group. *UML 2.0 Superstructure Specification*, pp. 113–114.

[68] Rumbaugh, Jacobson, and Booch. *The Unified Modeling Language Reference Manual*, pp. 31, 73, 253, 255.

[69] Object Management Group. *UML 2.0 Superstructure Specification*, pp. 147, 150, 153.

[70] Ibid., p. 153.

[71] Rumbaugh, Jacobson, and Booch. *The Unified Modeling Language Reference Manual*, pp. 31, 74, 256.

[72] Ibid., pp. 74, 254, 257, 523–525.

[73] Object Management Group. *UML 2.0 Superstructure Specification*, pp. 150–151.

[74] Ibid., pp. 150–151, 154.

[75] Rumbaugh, Jacobson, and Booch. *The Unified Modeling Language Reference Manual*, pp. 31, 74, 254, 256, 416.

[76] Ibid., pp. 254, 257.

[77] Object Management Group. *UML 2.0 Superstructure Specification*, p. 162.

[78] Ibid., pp. 147, 150, 153.

[79] Rumbaugh, Jacobson, and Booch. *The Unified Modeling Language Reference Manual*, pp. 73–74, 253–254.

[80] Ibid., pp. 31–33, 257–258, 282–283.

[81] Object Management Group. *UML 2.0 Superstructure Specification*, pp. 150, 156, 160.

[82] Ibid., pp. 154–155.

[83] Rumbaugh, Jacobson, and Booch. *The Unified Modeling Language Reference Manual*, pp. 256–257, 415–417.

[84] Ibid., pp. 256–257, 418.

[85] Object Management Group. *UML 2.0 Superstructure Specification*, p. 155.

[86] Ibid., p. 155.

[87] Rumbaugh, Jacobson, and Booch. *The Unified Modeling Language Reference Manual*, pp. 256–257, 418.

[88] Object Management Group. *UML 2.0 Superstructure Specification*, pp. 155–156.

[89] Ibid., p. 150.

[90] Rumbaugh, Jacobson, and Booch. *The Unified Modeling Language Reference Manual*, p. 31.

[91] Ibid., pp. 258, 283.

[92] Object Management Group. *UML 2.0 Superstructure Specification*, pp. 160–162.

[93] Ibid., pp. 169, 176–181.

[94] Rumbaugh, Jacobson, and Booch. *The Unified Modeling Language Reference Manual*, pp. 71–73, 227–231.

[95] Ibid.

[96] Object Management Group. *UML 2.0 Superstructure Specification*, pp. 169, 176–181.

[97] Ibid.

[98] Rumbaugh, Jacobson, and Booch. *The Unified Modeling Language Reference Manual*, pp. 71–73, 227–231.

[99] Ibid.

[100] Object Management Group. *UML 2.0 Superstructure Specification*, pp. 169, 176–181.

[101] Rumbaugh, Jacobson, and Booch. *The Unified Modeling Language Reference Manual*, p. 98.

Chapter 6: Process

[1] Brooks, F. 1975. *The Mythical Man-Month*. Reading, MA: Addison-Wesley, p. 42.

[2] Stroustrup, B. 1991. *The C+ Programming Language*. Second Edition. Reading, MA: Addison-Wesley.

[6] Jones, C. September 1984. Reusability in Programming: A Survey of the State of the Art. *IEEE Transactions on Software Engineering* vol. SE-10(5).

[9] Parnas, D., and Clements, P. 1986. A Rational Design Process: How and Why to Fake It. *IEEE Transactions on Software Engineering* vol. SE-12(2).

[13] Stroustrup. *The C+ Programming Language*, p. 373.

[15] Gilb, T. 1988. *Principles of Software Engineering Management*. Reading, MA: Addison-Wesley, p. 92.

[16] Mellor, S., Hecht, A., Tryon, D., and Hywari, W. September 1988. Object-Oriented Analysis: Theory and Practice, Course Notes. In *Object-Oriented Programming Systems, Languages, and Applications*. San Diego, CA: OOPSLA'88, p. 1.3.

[24] Andert, G. 1992. Private communication.

[29] Walsh, J. *Preliminary Defect Data from the Iterative Development of a Large C++ Program*. Vancouver, Canada: OOPSLA'92.

[30] Chmura, L., Norcio, A., and Wicinski, T. July 1990. Evaluating Software Design Processes by Analyzing Change Date Over Time. *IEEE Transactions on Software Engineering* vol. 16(7).

[31] As quoted in Summerville, I. 1989. *Software Engineering*. Third Edition. Wokingham, England: Addison-Wesley, p. 546.

[32] The Zachman Institute for Framework Advancement: www.zifa.com/.

[33] Department of Defense Architecture Framework Working Group. Februrary 9, 2004. *DoD Architecture Framework, Version 1.0. Volume 1:*

Definitions and Guidelines. Accessed in January 2007 at www.dod.mil/cio-nii/docs/DoDAF_v1_Volume_I.pdf.

[34] For more information on the Federal Enterprise Architecture, visit www.whitehouse.gov/omb/egov/a-1-fea.html.

[35] Agile Alliance Web site. Accessed in January 2007 at http://agilemanifesto.org/principles.html.

[38] Boehm, B. W., and Turner, R. 2004. *Balancing Agility and Discipline: A Guide for the Perplexed*. Boston, MA: Addison-Wesley, 2004.

[39] Booch, G., Rumbaugh, J., and Jacobson, I. 1999. *The Unified Modeling Language User's Guide*. Reading, MA: Addison-Wesley, 1999.

[40] Booch, G., and Brown, A. W. October 28, 2002. *Collaborative Development Environments*. Rational Software Corporation.

[41] Eeles, P. February 15, 2006. What Is a Software Architecture? Accessed in January 2007 at www-128.ibm.com/developerworks/rational/library/feb06/eeles/.

[42] IEEE Computer Society. 2000. IEEE Recommended Practice for Architectural Description of Software Intensive Systems. IEEE Std. 1471-2000.

[43] Kruchten, P. November 1995. The 4+1 View Model of Architecture. *IEEE Software* 12(6), pp. 42–50.

[44] Kruchten, P. August 2001. Software Maintenance Cycles with the RUP. *Rational Edge*. Accessed in January 2007 at www.ibm.com/developerworks/rational/library/content/RationalEdge/aug01/SoftwareMaintenanceCycleswiththeRUPAug01.pdf.

[45] Kroll, P., and Kruchten, P. 2003. *The Rational Unified Process Made Easy*. Boston, MA: Addison-Wesley.

[46] Larman, C. 2004. *Agile and Iterative Development*. Boston, MA: Addison-Wesley.

[47] Martin, R. C. 2002. *Agile Software Development, Principles, Patterns, and Practices*. Upper Saddle River, NJ: Prentice Hall.

[48] For more information about MDA, see the Object Management Group's related Web site, www.omg.org/mda.

[51] The Rational Unified Process product produced by IBM Rational, 2006.

[52] Adams, J., Koushik, S., Vasudeva, G., and Galambos, G. 2001. *Patterns for e-Business: A Strategy for Reuse*. Double Oak, TX: IBM Press.

[53] Buschmann, F., Meunier, R., Rohnert, H., Sommerlad, P., and Stal, M. 1996. *Pattern-Oriented Software Architecture, Volume 1: A System of Patterns*. New York, NY: John Wiley & Sons.

[54] Cheesman, J., and Daniels, J. 2001. *UML Components: A Simple Process for Specifying Component-Based Software*. Boston, MA: Addison-Wesley.

[55] Gamma, E., Helm, R., Johnson, R., and Vlissides, J. 1995. *Design Patterns: Elements of Reusable Object-Oriented Software*. Reading, MA: Addison-Wesley.

[56] Herzum, P., and Sims, O. 2000. *Business Component Factory: A Comprehensive Overview of Component-Based Development for the Enterprise*. New York, NY: Wiley.

Chapter 7: Pragmatics

[1] Goldstein, H. September 2005. Who Killed the Virtual Case File? *IEEE Spectrum* vol. 42, p. 24.

[2] Miller, J. March 20, 2006. FBI Awards Lockheed $305 Million Sentinel Contract. *Government Computer News*. Accessed in January 2007 at www.gcn.com/online/vol1_no1/40145-1.html.

[3] Charette, R. September 2005. Why Software Fails. *IEEE Spectrum* vol. 42, p. 42.

[4] Hawryszkiewycz, I. 1984. *Database Analysis and Design*. Chicago, IL: Science Research Associates, p. 115.

[5] van Genuchten, M. June 1991. Why Is Software Late? An Empirical Study of Reasons for Delay in Software Development. *IEEE Transactions on Software Engineering* vol. 17(6), p. 589.

[6] Gilb, T. 1988. *Principles of Software Engineering Management*. Reading, MA: Addison-Wesley, p. 73.

[7] As quoted in Zelkowitz, M. June 1978. Perspectives on Software Engineering. *ACM Computing Surveys* vol. 10(2), p. 204.

[8] Showalter, J. 1989. Private communication.

[9] Davis, A., Bersoff, E., and Comer, E. October 1988. A Strategy for Comparing Alternative Software Development Life Cycle Models. *IEEE Transactions on Software Engineering* vol. 14(10), p. 1456.

[10] Goldberg, A. 1993. Private communication.

[11] Schulmeyer, G., and McManus, J. 1992. *Handbook of Software Quality Assurance*. Second Edition. New York, NY: Van Nostrand Reinhold, p. 7.

[12] Schulmeyer and McManus. *Handbook of Software Quality Assurance*, p. 5.

[13] Schulmeyer and McManus. *Handbook of Software Quality Assurance*, p. 184.

[14] Schulmeyer and McManus. *Handbook of Software Quality Assurance*, p. 169.

[15] Walsh, J. *Preliminary Defect Data from the Iterative Development of a Large C++ Program*. Vancouver, Canada: OOPSLA'92.

[16] Lorenz, M., and Kidd, J. 1994. *Object-Oriented Software Metrics*. Upper Saddle River, NJ: Prentice Hall.

[17] Chidamber, S., and Kemerer, C. 1993. *A Metrics Suite for Object-Oriented Design*. Cambridge, MA: MIT Sloan School of Management.

[18] Kan, S. H. 2002. *Metrics and Models in Software Quality Engineering*. Second Edition. Boston, MA: Addison-Wesley.

[19] Kemerer, C., and Darcy, D. November/December 2005. OO Metrics in Practice. *IEEE Software*, p. 17.

[20] Stix, A., and Mosley, P. H. 2002. Cognitive Complexities Confronting Software Developers Utilizing Object Technology. *The Proceedings of ISECON 2002* vol. 19, §342a.

[21] Maksimchuk, R. A., and Naiburg, E. J. 2004. *UML for Mere Mortals*. Boston, MA: Addison-Wesley, p. 208.

[22] Schmucker, K. 1986. *Object-Oriented Programming for the Macintosh*. Hasbrouk Heights, NJ: Hayden, p. 11.

[23] Taylor, D. 1992. *Object-Oriented Information Systems*. New York, NY: John Wiley and Sons.

[24] Pinson, L., and Wiener, R. 1990. *Applications of Object-Oriented Programming*. Reading, MA: Addison-Wesley.

[25] Hantos, P. February 2005. Inherent Risks in Object-Oriented Development. *CrossTalk, The Journal of Defense Software Engineering*, p. 13–16; Fig. 2. Accessed in January 2007 at www.stsc.hill.af.mil.

[26] Meyer, B. 1995. *Object Success: A Manager's Guide to Object-Oriented Technology and Its Impact on the Corporation*. Upper Saddle River, NJ: Prentice Hall.

[27] Boehm, B. 1989. *Software Risk Management (Tutorial)*. New York, NY: IEEE Computer Society Press.

[28] Boehm, B. October 2002. Software Risk Management: Overview and Recent Developments. *17th International Forum on COCOMO and Software Cost Modeling*. Los Angeles, CA: University of Southern California Center for Software Engineering.

[29] Lyons, B. 2005. Private communication.

[30] Ibid.

Section III: Applications

Minsky, M. April 1970. Form and Content in Computer Science. *Journal of the Association for Computing Machinery* vol. 17(2), p. 197.

Chapter 8: System Architecture: Satellite-Based Navigation

[1] International Council on Systems Engineering (INCOSE). June 2006. *Systems Engineering Handbook*. INCOSE-TP-2003-016-02, Version 3. Seattle, WA: INCOSE, app. 8.

[2] INCOSE. June 2004. *Systems Engineering Handbook*. INCOSE-TP-2003-016-02, Version 2a. Seattle, WA: INCOSE, p. 293.

[3] The Aerospace Corporation. 2003. *GPS Primer—A Student Guide to the Global Positioning System*, p. 2. Accessed in January 2007 at www.aero.org/education/primers/gps/GPS-Primer.pdf.

[4] Ibid., pp. 2–3.

[5] Ibid., p. 4.

[6] Ibid., p. 5.

[7] Ibid., p. 6.

[8] Rumbaugh, J., Jacobson, I., and Booch, G. 2005. *The Unified Modeling Language Reference Manual*. Second Edition. Boston, MA: Addison-Wesley, p. 37.

[9] Maier, M. W., Emery, D., and Hilliard, R. 2004. ANSI/IEEE 1471 and Systems Engineering. *Systems Engineering* vol. 7(3), p. 257.

[10] Ibid., p. 269.

[11] Krikorian, H. F. March/April 2003. Introduction to Object-Oriented Systems Engineering, Part 1. *IT Professional*, p. 40.

[12] Jacobson, I., Ericsson, M., and Jacobson, A. 1994. *The Object Advantage: Business Process Reengineering with Object Technology*. Wokingham, England: Addison-Wesley, pp. 319–337.

Chapter 9: Control System: Traffic Management

[1] Murphy, E. December 1988. All Aboard for Solid State. *IEEE Spectrum* vol. 25(13), p. 42.

[2] *Rockwell Advanced Railroad Electronic Systems*. 1989. Cedar Rapids, IA: Rockwell International.

[3] Tanenbaum, A. 1981. *Computer Networks*. Englewood Cliffs, NJ: Prentice-Hall.

Chapter 10: Artificial Intelligence: Cryptanalysis

[1] Erman, L., Lark, J., and Hayes-Roth, F. December 1988. ABE: An Environment for Engineering Intelligent Systems. *IEEE Transactions on Software Engineering* vol. 14(12), p. 1758.

[2] Shaw, M. 1991. *Heterogeneous Design Idioms for Software Architecture*. Pittsburgh, PA: Carnegie Mellon University.

[3] Meyer, C., and Matyas, S. M. 1982. *Cryptography*. New York, NY: John Wiley and Sons, p. 1.

[4] Nii, P. Summer 1986. Blackboard Systems: The Blackboard Model of Problem Solving and the Evolution of Blackboard Architectures. *AI Magazine* vol. 7(2), p. 46.

[5] Englemore, R., and Morgan, T. 1988. *Blackboard Systems*. Wokingham, England: Addison-Wesley, p. 16.

[6] Ibid., p. 19.

[7] Ibid., p. 6.

[8] Ibid., p. 12.

[9] Nii. Blackboard Systems, p. 43.

[10] Englemore and Morgan. *Blackboard Systems*, p. 11.

Chapter 12: Web Application: Vacation Tracking System

[1] Conallen, J. 2003. *Building Web Applications with UML*. Second Edition. Boston, MA: Addison-Wesley.

[2] Eeles, P., Houston, K. A., and Kozaczynski, W. 2003. *Building J2EE Applications with the Rational Unified Process*. Boston, MA: Addison-Wesley.

[3] Kruchten, P. November 1995. The 4+1 View Model of Architecture. *IEEE Software* 12(6), pp. 42–50.

[4] Alur, D., Crupi, J., and Malks, D. 2003. *Core J2EE Patterns: Best Practices and Design Strategies*. Second Edition. Upper Saddle River, NJ: Prentice Hall.

[5] Marinescu, F. 2002. *EJB Design Patterns*. New York, NY: John Wiley.

Appendix A: Object-Oriented Programming Languages

[1] Wulf, W. January 1980. Trends in the Design and Implementation of Programming Languages. *IEEE Computer* vol. 13(1), p. 15.

[2] The Language List, a compendium of programming languages, originating in the Usenet news group comp.lang.misc, currently maintained by Bill Kinnersley. http://people.ku.edu/~nkinners/LangList/Extras/langlist.htm.

[3] Birtwistle, G., Dahl, O-J., Myhrhaug, B., and Nygard, K. 1979. *Simula begin*. Lund, Sweden: Studentlitteratur.

[4] Éric Lévénez's Web site on computer language history: www.levenez.com/lang/.

[5] The TIOBE Programming Community Index: www.tiobe.com/tiobe_index/index.htm.

[6] The Smalltalk Web site: www.smalltalk.org/smalltalk/history.html.

[7] Ingalls, D. The Smalltalk-76 Programming System Design and Implementation. *Proceedings of the Fifth Annual ACM Symposium on Principals of Programming Languages*, ACM, p. 9.

[8] Borning, A., and Ingalls, D. 1982. Multiple Inheritance in Smalltalk-80. *Proceedings of the National Conference on Artificial Intelligence*. Menlo Park, CA: AAAI.

[9] Goldberg, A., and Robson, D. 1989. *Smalltalk-80: The Language*. Reading, MA: Addison-Wesley.

[10] Goldberg, A. 1984. *Smalltalk-80: The Interactive Programming Environment*. Reading, MA: Addison-Wesley.

[11] Krasner, G. 1983. *Smalltalk-80: Bits of History, Words of Advice*. Reading, MA: Addison-Wesley.

[12] LaLonde, W., and Pugh, J. 1990. *Inside Smalltalk, Volumes 1 and 2*. Englewood Cliffs, NJ: Prentice Hall.

[13] Stroustrup, B. 2000. *The C+ Programming Language*. Special Third Edition. Boston, MA: Addison-Wesley, p. 4.

[14] Gorlen, K. 1989. An Introduction to C++. In *Unix System V AT&T C++ Language System, Release 2.0 Selected Readings*. Murray Hill, NJ: AT&T Bell Laboratories, p. 2-1.

[15] Ellis, M., and Stroustrup, B. 1990. *The Annotated C++ Reference Manual*. Reading, MA: Addison-Wesley.

[16] Stroustrup, B. 2003. *The C++ Standard: Incorporating Technical Corrigendum No. 1*. Second Edition. New York, NY: John Wiley & Sons.

[17] Stroustrup, B. 1991. *The C++ Programming Language*. Second Edition. Reading, MA: Addison-Wesley.

[18] Stroustrup, B. 1994. *The Design and Evolution of C++*. Reading, MA: Addison-Wesley.

[19] The Java Language: An Overview. Accessed in January 2007 at http://java.sun.com/docs/overviews/java/java-overview-1.html.

[20] International Committee for Information Technology Standards. January 1998. *Programming Language Smalltalk*. Document Number ANSI/INCITS 319-1998.

Glossary

A

abstract class A class that has no instances. An abstract class is written with the expectation that its concrete subclasses will add to its structure and behavior, typically by implementing its abstract operations.

abstract operation An operation that is declared but not implemented by an abstract class.

abstraction The essential characteristics of an object that distinguish it from all other kinds of objects and thus provide crisply defined conceptual boundaries relative to the perspective of the viewer; the process of focusing on the essential characteristics of an object. Abstraction is one of the fundamental elements of the object model.

access control The mechanism for control of access to a model element, for example, to the contents of a package or to the structure or behavior of a class. See also *visibility*.

action node One of the three types of nodes contained by an activity. It defines the behavioral steps of an activity. UML 2 defines the available type of actions, which include those to invoke the behavior of an operation or of an activity.

active object An object that encompasses its own thread of control.

activity A specification of behavior that contains action nodes, control nodes, and object nodes.

actor An actor defines a role that an external entity plays in its interactions with a system.

aggregation A whole/part relationship where one object is composed of one or more other objects, each of which is considered a part of the whole. This relationship is a weak form of containment in that the lifetimes of the whole and its parts are independent.

algorithmic decomposition The process of breaking a system into parts, each of which represents some small step in a larger process. The application of structured design methods leads to an algorithmic decomposition, whose focus is on the flow of control within a system.

architectural mechanism A representation of a general system capability that interacts with, or supports, the basic system functionality.

architecture The logical and physical structure of a system's components and their relationships, forged by all the strategic and tactical design decisions applied during development.

association A relationship denoting a semantic connection between two classes.

attribute A part of a class whose value contributes to the state definition of a class. Collectively, the attributes of a class constitute its structure.

B

base class The most generalized class in a class structure. Most applications have many such root classes. Some languages define a primitive base class, which serves as the ultimate superclass of all classes.

behavior How an object acts and reacts, in terms of its state changes and message passing; the outwardly visible and testable activity of an object.

behavioral prototype An example that explores some element of the system, such as an aspect of an architecture, a new algorithm, a user interface model, or a database schema. Its purpose is the rapid exploration of design alternatives, so that areas of risk can be resolved early without endangering the production releases.

binding Denotes the association of a name (such as a variable declaration) with a class.

C

cardinality The number of instances that a class may have; the number of instances that participate in a class relationship.

class A set of objects that share a common structure and a common behavior. The terms *class* and *type* are usually (but not always) interchangeable; a class is a slightly different concept than a type, in that the former emphasizes the classification of structure and behavior.

class diagram Part of the notation of object-oriented design, used to show the existence of classes and their relationships in the logical design of a system. A class diagram may represent all or part of the class structure of a system.

class structure A graph whose vertices represent classes and whose arcs represent relationships among these classes. The class structure of a system is represented by a set of class diagrams.

client An object that uses the services of another object, either by operating on it or by referencing its state.

collaboration The process whereby several model elements cooperate to provide some higher-level behavior.

component A logical collection of classes that collaborate to provide a set of services offered through the component's provided interfaces. The services required by the component are requested through its required interfaces. A component may also consist of other components and may be nested to whatever level required.

composition A whole/part relationship where one object is composed of one or more other objects, each of which is considered a part of the whole. This relationship is a strong form of aggregation in that the lifetimes of the whole and its parts are dependent.

concrete class A class whose implementation is complete and thus may have instances.

concurrency The property that distinguishes an active object from one that is not active.

concurrent object An active object whose semantics are guaranteed in the presence of multiple threads of control.

constraint The expression of some semantic condition that must be preserved.

constructor An operation that creates an object and/or initializes its state.

control node One of the three types of nodes contained by an activity. It provides the starting, stopping, and action sequencing functionality of an activity.

container class A class whose instances are collections of other objects. Container classes may denote homogeneous collections (all of the objects in the collection are of the same class) or heterogeneous collections (each of the objects in the collection may be of a different class, although all must generally share a common superclass). Container classes are most often defined as parameterized classes, with some parameter designating the class of the contained objects.

CRC cards Class/Responsibilities/Collaborators; a simple tool for brainstorming about the key abstractions and mechanisms in a system.

D

data dictionary A comprehensive repository enumerating all the classes in a system.

delegation The act of one object forwarding to another object an operation to be performed on behalf of the first object.

destructor An operation that frees the state of an object and/or destroys the object itself.

device A piece of hardware that has no computational resources.

dynamic binding A binding in which the name/class association is not made until the object designated by the name is created at execution time.

E

encapsulation The process of compartmentalizing the elements of an abstraction that constitute its structure and behavior. Encapsulation separates the contractual interface of an abstraction and its implementation.

event Some occurrence that may cause the state of a system to change.

F

field A repository for part of the state of an object; collectively, the fields of an object constitute its structure. The terms *field*, *instance variable*, *member object*, and *slot* are interchangeable.

forward engineering The production of executable code from a logical or physical model.

framework A collection of classes that provide a set of services for a particular domain. A framework thus exports a number of individual classes and mechanisms that clients can use or adapt.

free subprogram A procedure or function that serves as a nonprimitive operation on an object or objects of the same or different classes. A free subprogram is any subprogram that is not a method of an object.

friend A class or operation whose implementation may reference the private parts of another class, who alone can extend the offer of friendship.

function An input/output mapping resulting from some object's behavior.

function point In the context of a requirements analysis, a single, outwardly visible and testable activity.

G

generic function An operation on an object. A generic function of a class may be redefined in subclasses; thus, for a given object, it is implemented through a set of methods declared in various classes related via their inheritance hierarchy. The terms generic function and virtual function are usually interchangeable.

guard A Boolean expression applied to an event. If true, the expression permits the event to cause the state of the system to change.

H

hierarchy A ranking or ordering of abstractions. The two most common hierarchies in a complex system include its class structure (including "is a" hierarchies) and its object structure (including "part of" hierarchies). Hierarchies may also be found in the component and deployment architectures of a complex system.

I

identity The nature of an object that distinguishes it from all other objects.

implementation The inside view of a class or object, including the secrets of its behavior.

information hiding The process of hiding all the secrets of an object that do not contribute to its essential characteristics. Typically, the structure of an object is hidden, as well as the implementation of its methods.

inheritance A relationship among classes, wherein one class shares the structure or behavior defined in one (*single inheritance*) or more (*multiple inheritance*) other classes. Inheritance defines an "is a" hierarchy among classes in which a subclass inherits from one or more generalized superclasses; a subclass typically specializes its superclasses by augmenting or redefining existing structure and behavior.

instance Something to which you can do things. An instance has state, behavior, and identity. The structure and behavior of similar instances are defined in their common class. The terms *instance* and *object* are interchangeable.

instance variable A repository for part of the state of an object. Collectively, the instance variables of an object constitute its structure. The terms *field*, *instance variable*, *member object*, and *slot* are interchangeable.

instantiation The process of filling in a template class or parameterized class to produce a class from which one can create instances.

interface The outside view of, for example, a class, object, component, or composite structure, that emphasizes its abstraction while hiding its structure and the secrets of its behavior.

invariant The Boolean expression of some condition whose truth must be preserved.

iterator An operation that permits the parts of an object to be visited.

K

key abstraction A class or object that forms part of the vocabulary of the problem domain.

L

layer The collection of components at the same level of abstraction.

level of abstraction The relative ranking of abstractions in a class structure, object structure, component architecture, or deployment architecture. In terms of the "part of" hierarchy, a given abstraction is at a higher level of abstraction than others if it builds on the others; in terms of the "is a" hierarchy, a high-level abstraction is generalized, and a low-level abstraction is specialized.

link Between two objects, one instance of an association.

M

mechanism A structure whereby objects collaborate to provide some behavior that satisfies a requirement of the problem.

member function An operation on an object, defined as part of the declaration of a class; all member functions are operations, but not all operations are member functions. The terms *member function* and *method* are usually interchangeable. In some languages, a member function stands alone and may be redefined in a subclass; in other languages, a member function may not be redefined but serves as part of the implementation of a generic function or virtual function, both of which may be redefined in a subclass.

member object A repository for part of the state of an object; collectively, the member objects of an object constitute its structure. The terms *field*, *instance variable*, *member object*, and *slot* are interchangeable.

message An operation that one object performs on another. The terms *message*, *method*, and *operation* are usually interchangeable.

metaclass The class of a class; a class whose instances are themselves classes.

method An operation on an object, defined as part of the declaration of a class. All methods are operations, but not all operations are methods. The terms *message*, *method*, and *operation* are usually interchangeable. In some languages, a method stands alone and may be redefined in a subclass; in other languages, a method may not be redefined but serves as part of the implementation of a generic function or a virtual function, both of which may be redefined in a subclass.

modularity The property of a system that has been decomposed into a set of cohesive and loosely coupled components.

monomorphism A concept in type theory, according to which a name (such as a variable declaration) may only denote objects of the same class.

O

object Something to which you can do things. An object has state, behavior, and identity; the structure and behavior of similar objects are defined in their common class. The terms *instance* and *object* are interchangeable.

object diagram Part of the notation of object-oriented design, used to show the existence of objects and their relationships in the logical design of a system. An object diagram may represent all or part of the object structure of a system and primarily illustrates the semantics of mechanisms in the logical design. A single object diagram represents a snapshot in time of an otherwise transitory event or configuration of objects.

object model The collection of principles that form the foundation of object-oriented design; a software engineering paradigm emphasizing the principles of abstraction, encapsulation, modularity, hierarchy, typing, concurrency, and persistence.

object node One of the three types of nodes contained by an activity. It defines the data that flows between the actions of an activity.

object structure A graph whose vertices represent objects and whose arcs represent relationships among those objects. The object structure of a system is represented by a set of object diagrams.

object-based programming A method of programming in which programs are organized as cooperative collections of objects, each of which represents an instance of some type, and whose types are all members of a hierarchy of types united via other than inheritance relationships. In such programs, types are generally viewed as static, whereas objects typically have a much more dynamic nature, somewhat constrained by the existence of static binding and monomorphism.

object-oriented analysis A method of analysis in which requirements are examined from the perspective of the classes and objects found in the vocabulary of the problem domain.

object-oriented decomposition The process of breaking a system into parts, each of which represents some class or object from the problem domain. The application of object-oriented design methods leads to an object-oriented decomposition, in which we view the world as a collection of objects that cooperate with one another to achieve some desired functionality.

object-oriented design A method of design encompassing the process of object-oriented decomposition and a notation for depicting both logical and physical as well as static and dynamic models of the system under design. Specifically, examples of this notation include class diagrams, object diagrams, component diagrams, and deployment diagrams.

object-oriented programming A method of implementation in which programs are organized as cooperative collections of objects, each of which represents an instance of some class, and whose classes are all members of a hierarchy of classes united via inheritance relationships. In such programs, classes are generally viewed as static, whereas objects typically have a much more dynamic nature, which is encouraged by the existence of dynamic binding and polymorphism.

operation Some work that one object performs on another in order to elicit a reaction. All of the operations on a specific object may be found in free subprograms and member functions or methods. The terms *message*, *method*, and *operation* are usually interchangeable.

P

parameterized class A class that serves as a template for other classes, in which the template may be parameterized by other classes, objects, and/or operations. A parameterized class must be instantiated (its parameters filled in) before instances can be created. Parameterized classes are typically used as container classes. The terms *template class* and *parameterized class* are interchangeable.

partition The components or subsystems that form a part of a given level of abstraction. Also, a structural division of an activity diagram that is commonly called a swimlane.

passive object An object that does not encompass its own thread of control.

persistence The property of an object by which its existence transcends time (i.e., the object continues to exist after its creator ceases to exist) and/or space (i.e., the object's location moves from the address space in which it was created).

polymorphism A concept in type theory, according to which a name (such as a variable declaration) may denote objects of many different classes that are related by some common superclass; thus, any object denoted by this name can respond to some common set of operations in different ways.

postcondition An invariant satisfied by an operation.

precondition An invariant assumed by an operation.

private A declaration that forms part of the interface of a class or object. What is declared as private is not visible to any other classes or objects.

process The activation of a single thread of control.

processor A piece of hardware that has computational resources.

protected A declaration that forms part of the interface of a class or object but is not visible to any other classes or objects except those that represent subclasses.

protocol The ways in which an object may act and react, constituting the entire static and dynamic outside view of the object. The protocol of an object defines the envelope of the object's allowable behavior.

public A declaration that forms part of the interface of a class or object and is visible to all other classes and objects that have visibility to it.

Q

qualifier An attribute whose value uniquely identifies a single target object.

R

reactive system An event-driven system. The behavior of a reactive system is not a simple input/output mapping.

real-time system A system whose essential processes must meet certain critical time deadlines. A hard-real-time system must be deterministic; missing a deadline may lead to catastrophic results.

reference architecture A predefined architectural pattern or set of patterns, possibly partially or completely instantiated, designed and proven for use in particular business and technical contexts, together with supporting artifacts to enable their use.

responsibility Some behavior for which an object is held accountable. A responsibility denotes the obligation of an object to provide a certain behavior.

reverse engineering The production of a logical or physical model from executable code.

role The purpose or capacity wherein one class or object participates in a relationship with another. The role of an object denotes the selection of a set of behaviors that are well defined at a single point in time; a role is the face an object presents to the world at a given moment.

S

scenario An outline of events that elicits some system behavior.

sequential object A passive object whose semantics are guaranteed only in the presence of a single thread of control.

server An object that never operates on other objects but is only operated on by other objects; an object that provides certain services.

service The behavior provided by a given part of a system.

signature The complete profile of an operation's formal arguments and return type.

slot A repository for part of the state of an object. Collectively, the slots of an object constitute its structure. The terms *field*, *instance variable*, *member object*, and *slot* are interchangeable.

state The cumulative results of the behavior of an object; one of the possible conditions in which an object may exist, characterized by definite quantities that are distinct from other quantities. At any given point in time, the state of an object encompasses all of the (usually static) properties of the object plus the current (usually dynamic) values of each of these properties.

state machine diagram Part of the notation of object-oriented design, used to show the state space of a given class, the events that cause a transition from one state to another, and the actions that result from a state change.

state space An enumeration of all the possible states of an object. The state space of an object encompasses an indefinite yet finite number of possible (although not always desirable or expected) states.

static binding A binding in which the name/class association is made when the name is declared (at compile time) but before the creation of the object that the name designates.

strategic design decision A design decision that has sweeping architectural implications.

strongly typed A characteristic of a programming language, according to which all expressions are guaranteed to be type-consistent.

structure The concrete representation of the state of an object. An object does not share its state with any other object, although all objects of the same class do share the same representation of their state.

structured design A method of design encompassing the process of algorithmic decomposition.

subclass A class that inherits from one or more classes (which are called its immediate *superclasses*).

subsystem A collection of components, some of which are visible to other subsystems and others of which are hidden.

superclass The class from which another class inherits (which is called its immediate *subclass*).

synchronization The concurrency semantics of an operation. An operation may be *simple* (only one thread of control is involved), *synchronous* (two processes rendezvous), *balking* (one process may rendezvous with another only if the second process is already waiting), *timeout* (one process may rendezvous with another but will wait for the second process only for a specified amount of time), or *asynchronous* (the two processes operate independently).

T

tactical design decision A design decision that has local architectural implications.

template class A class that serves as a template for other classes, in which the template may be parameterized by other classes, objects, and/or operations. A template class must be instantiated (its parameters filled in) before objects can be created. Template classes are typically used as container classes. The terms *template class* and *parameterized class* are interchangeable.

thread of control A single process. The start of a thread of control is the root from which independent dynamic action within a system occurs; a given system may have many simultaneous threads of control, some of which may dynamically come into existence and then cease to exist. Systems executing across multiple processors allow for truly concurrent threads of control, whereas systems running on a single processor can only achieve the illusion of concurrent threads of control.

transition The passing from one state to another state.

type The definition of the domain of allowable values that an object may possess and the set of operations that may be performed on the object. The terms *class* and *type* are usually (but not always) interchangeable; a type is a slightly different concept than a class, in that the former emphasizes the importance of conformance to a common protocol.

typing The enforcement of the class of an object, which prevents objects of different types from being interchanged or, at the most, allows them to be interchanged only in very restricted ways.

U

the Unified Modeling Language (UML) A language (notation) used during the conduct of object-oriented analysis and design to model aspects of a development concern.

V

virtual function An operation on an object. A virtual function may be redefined by subclasses; thus, for a given object, it is implemented through a set of methods declared in various classes related via their inheritance hierarchy. The terms *generic function* and *virtual function* are usually interchangeable.

visibility The ability of one abstraction to see another and thus reference resources in its outside view. Abstractions are visible to one another only where their scopes overlap. Export control may further restrict access to visible abstractions. Examples of visibility include *public*, *private*, *protected*, and *package*.

Classified Bibliography

This classified bibliography is divided into sections, labeled from A to M. References in Appendix B to items appearing in the bibliography take the form [<label> <year>]. For example, Brooks [H 1975] refers to his 1975 book, *The Mythical Man-Month*, in section H (Software Engineering) of the bibliography.

A. Classification

Allen, T., and Starr, T. 1982. *Hierarchy: Perspectives for Ecological Complexity.* Chicago, IL: The University of Chicago Press.

Aquinas, T. *Summa Theologica.* Vol. 19 of Great Books of the Western World. Chicago, IL: Encyclopedia Britannica.

Aristotle. *Categories.* Vol. 8 of Great Books of the Western World. Chicago, IL: Encyclopedia Britannica.

Bateson, G. 1979. *Mind and Nature: A Necessary Unity.* New York, NY: Bantam Books.

Brachman, R., McGuinness, D., Patel-Schneider, P., and Resnick, L. *Living with Classic. Principles of Semantic Networks.* San Mateo, CA: Morgan Kaufman Publishers.

Bulman, D. January 1991. Refining Candidate Objects. *Computer Language* vol. 8(1).

Cant, S., Jeffery, D., and Henderson-Sellers, B. October 1991. *A Conceptual Model of Cognitive Complexity of Elements of the Programming Process.* New South Wales, Australia: University of New South Wales.

Classification Society of North America. *Journal of Classification.* New York, NY: Springer-Verlag.

Coad, P. September 1992. Object-Oriented Patterns. *Communications of the ACM* vol. 35(9).

———. 1993. *The Object Game*. Austin, TX: Object International.

Coombs, C., Raiffa, H., and Thrall, R. 1954. Some Views on Mathematical Models and Measurement Theory. *Psychological Review* vol. 61(2).

Courtois, P. June 1985. On Time and Space Decomposition of Complex Structures. *Communications of the ACM* vol. 28(6).

Cunningham, W., and Beck, K. July/August 1989. Constructing Abstractions for Object-Oriented Abstractions. *Journal of Object-Oriented Programming* vol. 2(2).

Darwin, C. *The Origin of Species*. Vol. 49 of Great Books of the Western World. Chicago, IL: Encyclopedia Britannica.

Descartes, R. *Rules for the Direction of the Mind*. Vol. 31 of Great Books of the Western World. Chicago, IL: Encyclopedia Britannica.

Flood, R., and Carson, E. 1988. *Dealing with Complexity*. New York, NY: Plenum Press.

Gould, S. June 1992. We Are All Monkey's Uncles. *Natural History*.

Johnson, R. 1992. *Documenting Frameworks Using Patterns*. Vancouver, Canada: OOPSLA'92.

Lakoff, G. 1987. *Women, Fire, and Dangerous Things: What Categories Reveal about the Mind*. Chicago, IL: The University of Chicago Press.

Lefrancois, G. 1977. *Of Children: An Introduction to Child Development*. Second Edition. Belmont, CA: Wadsworth.

Lewin, R. November 4, 1988. Family Relationships Are a Biological Conundrum. *Science* vol. 242.

Maccoby, M. December 1991. The Innovative Mind at Work. *IEEE Spectrum* vol. 28(12).

Maier, H. 1969. *Three Theories of Child Development: The Contributions of Erik H. Erickson, Jean Piaget, and Robert R. Sears, and Their Applications*. New York, NY: Harper and Row.

May, R. September 16, 1988. How Many Species Are There on Earth? *Science* vol. 241.

Michalski, R., and Stepp, R. 1983. Learning from Observation: Conceptual Clustering. In *Machine Learning: An Artificial Intelligence Approach*, ed. R. Michalski, J. Carbonell, and T. Mitchell. Palo Alto, CA: Tioga.

Miller, G. March 1956. The Magical Number Seven, Plus or Minus Two: Some Limits on Our Capacity for Processing Information. *The Psychological Review* vol. 63(2).

Minsky, M. April 1970. Form and Content in Computer Science. *Journal of the ACM* vol. 17(2).

———. 1986. *The Society of Mind.* New York, NY: Simon and Schuster.

Moldovan, D., and Wu, C. December 1988. A Hierarchical Knowledge-Based System for Airplane Classification. *IEEE Transactions on Software Engineering* vol. 14(12).

Newell, A. 1990. *Unified Theories of Cognition.* Cambridge, MA: Harvard University Press.

Newell, A., and Simon, H. 1972. *Human Problem Solving.* Englewood Cliffs, NJ: Prentice Hall.

Papert, S. 1980. *Mindstorms: Children, Computers, and Powerful Ideas.* New York, NY: Basic Books.

Plato. *Statesman.* Vol. 7 of Great Books of the Western World. Chicago, IL: Encyclopedia Britannica.

Prieto-Diaz, R., and Arango, G. 1991. *Domain Analysis and Software Systems Modeling.* Las Alamitos, CA: Computer Society Press of the IEEE.

Shaw, M. 1989. Larger Scale Systems Require Higher-Level Abstractions. *Proceedings of the Fifth International Workshop on Software Specification and Design.* IEEE Computer Society.

———. 1990. Elements of a Design Language for Software Architecture. Pittsburgh, PA: Carnegie Mellon University.

———. 1991. *Heterogeneous Design Idioms for Software Architecture.* Pittsburgh, PA: Carnegie Mellon University.

Siegler, R., and Richards, D. 1982. The Development of Intelligence. In *Handbook of Human Intelligence*, ed. R. Sternberg. Cambridge, United Kingdom: Cambridge University Press.

Simon, H. 1962. The Architecture of Complexity. *Proceedings of the American Philosophical Society* vol. 106.

———. 1982. *The Sciences of the Artificial.* Cambridge, MA: The MIT Press.

Sowa, J. 1984. *Conceptual Structures: Information Processing in Mind and Machine.* Reading, MA: Addison-Wesley.

———. 1991. *Principles of Semantic Networks.* San Mateo, CA: Morgan Kaufman Publishers.

Stepp, R., and Michalski, R. 1986. Conceptual Clustering of Structured Objects: A Goal-Oriented Approach. *Artificial Intelligence* vol. 28(1).

Stevens, S. June 1946. On the Theory of Scales of Measurement. *Science* vol. 103(2684).

Stillings, N., Feinstein, M., Garfield, J., Rissland, E., Rosenbaum, D., Weisler, S., and Baker-Ward, L. 1987. *Cognitive Science: An Introduction*. Cambridge, MA: The MIT Press.

Waldrop, M. 1992. *Complexity: The Emerging Science at the Edge of Order and Chaos*. New York, NY: Simon and Schuster.

B. Object-Oriented Analysis

Arango, G. May 1989. Domain Analysis: From Art Form to Engineering Discipline. *SIGSOFT Engineering Notes* vol. 14(3).

Bailin, S. 1988. *Remarks on Object-Oriented Requirements Specification*. Laurel, MD: Computer Technology Associates.

Bailin, S., and Moore, J. 1987. *An Object-Oriented Specification Method for Ada*. Laurel, MD: Computer Technology Associates.

Barbier, F. May 1992. Object-Oriented Analysis of Systems through Their Dynamical Aspects. *Journal of Object-Oriented Programming* vol. 5(2).

Borgida, A., Mylogoulos, J., and Wong, H. 1984. Generalization/Specialization as a Basis for Software Specification. In *On Conceptual Modeling: Perspectives from Artificial Intelligence, Databases, and Programming Languages*, ed. M. Brodie, J. Mylopoulos, and J. Schmidt. New York, NY: Springer-Verlag.

Cernosek, G., Monterio, E., and Pribyl, W. 1987. *An Entity-Relationship Approach to Software Requirements Analysis for Object-Based Development*. Houston, TX: McDonnell Douglas Astronautics.

Coad, P. Summer 1989. OOA: Object-Oriented Analysis. *American Programmer* vol. 2(7–8).

———. April 1990. *New Advances in Object-Oriented Analysis*. Austin, TX: Object International.

Coad, P., and Yourdon, E. 1991. *Object-Oriented Analysis*. Second Edition. Englewood Cliffs, NJ: Yourdon Press.

Dahl, O-J. 1987. Object-Oriented Specifications. In *Research Directions in Object-Oriented Programming*, ed. B. Schriver and P. Wegner. Cambridge, MA: The MIT Press.

deChampeaux, D. April 1991a. *A Comparative Study of Object-Oriented Analysis Methods*. Palo Alto, CA: Hewlett-Packard Laboratories.

———. April 1991b. *Object-Oriented Analysis and Top-Down Software Development*. Palo Alto, CA: Hewlett Packard Laboratories.

DeMarco, T. 1979. *Structured Analysis and System Specification*. Englewood Cliffs, NJ: Prentice Hall.

Embley, D., Kurtz, B., and Woodfield, S. 1992. *Object-Oriented Systems Analysis: A Model-Driven Approach*. Englewood Cliffs, NJ: Yourdon Press.

EVB Software Engineering. 1989. *Object-Oriented Requirements Analysis*. Frederick, MD.

Gane, C., and Sarson, T. 1979. *Structured Systems Analysis*. Englewood Cliffs, NJ: Prentice Hall.

Hatley, D., and Pirbhai, I. 1988. *Strategies for Real-Time System Specification*. New York, NY: Dorset House.

Ho, D., and Parry, T. July 1991. *The Hewlett-Packard Method of Object-Oriented Analysis*. Palo Alto, CA: Hewlett-Packard Laboratories.

Iscoe, N. 1988. *Domain Models for Program Specification and Generation*. Austin, TX: University of Texas.

Iscoe, N., Browne, J., and Werth, J. 1989. *Modeling Domain Knowledge: An Object-Oriented Approach to Program Specification and Generation*. Austin, TX: The University of Texas.

Lang, N. January 1993. Shlaer-Mellor Object-Oriented Analysis Rules. *Software Engineering Notes* vol. 18(1).

Marca, D., and McGowan, C. 1988. *SADT™: Structured Analysis and Design Technique*. New York, NY: McGraw-Hill.

Martin, J., and Odell, J. 1992. *Object-Oriented Analysis and Design*. Englewood Cliffs, NJ: Prentice Hall.

McMenamin, S., and Palmer, J. 1984. *Essential Systems Analysis*. New York, NY: Yourdon Press.

Mellor, S., Hecht, A., Tryon, D., and Hywari, W. September 1988. *Object-Oriented Analysis: Theory and Practice, Course Notes*. San Diego, CA: OOPSLA'88.

Moore, J., and Bailin, S. 1988. *Position Paper on Domain Analysis*. Laurel, MD: Computer Technology Associates.

Page-Jones, M., and Weiss, S. Summer 1989. Synthesis: An Object-Oriented Analysis and Design Method. *American Programmer* vol. 2(7–8).

Rubin, K., and Goldberg, A. September 1992. Object Behavior Analysis. *Communications of the ACM* vol. 35(9).

Saeki, M., Horai, H., and Enomoto, H. May 1989. Software Development Process from Natural Language Specification. *Proceedings of the 11th International Conference on Software Engineering*. New York, NY: Computer Society Press of the IEEE.

Shemer, I. June 1987. Systems Analysis: A Systemic Analysis of a Conceptual Model. *Communications of the ACM* vol. 30(6).

Shlaer, S., and Mellor, S. 1988. *Object-Oriented Systems Analysis: Modeling the World in Data*. Englewood Cliffs, NJ: Yourdon Press.

———. July 1989. An Object-Oriented Approach to Domain Analysis. *Software Engineering Notes* vol. 14(5).

———. Summer 1989. Understanding Object-Oriented Analysis. *American Programmer* vol. 2(7–8).

———. 1992. *Object Lifecycles: Modeling the World in States*. Englewood Cliffs, NJ: Yourdon Press.

Stoecklin, S., Adams, E., and Smith, S. 1987. *Object-Oriented Analysis*. Tallahassee, FL: East Tennessee State University.

Sully, P. Summer 1989. Structured Analysis: Scaffolding for Object-Oriented Development. *American Programmer* vol. 2(7–8).

Tsai, J., and Ridge, J. November 1988. Intelligent Support for Specifications Transformation. *IEEE Software* vol. 5(6).

Veryard, R. 1984. *Pragmatic Data Analysis*. Oxford, England: Blackwell Scientific Publications.

Ward, P. March 1989. How to Integrate Object Orientation with Structured Analysis and Design. *IEEE Software* vol. 6(2).

Weinberg, G. 1988. *Rethinking Systems Analysis and Design*. New York, NY: Dorset House.

C. Object-Oriented Applications

Abdali, K., Cherry, G., and Soiffer, N. November 1986. A Smalltalk System for Algebraic Manipulation. *SIGPLAN Notices* vol. 21(11).

Abdel-Hamid, T., and Madnick, S. December 1989. Lessons Learned from Modeling the Dynamics of Software Development. *Communications of the ACM* vol. 32(12).

The Aerospace Corporation. 2003. *GPS Primer—A Student Guide to the Global Positioning System*. www.aero.org/education/primers/gps/GPS-Primer.pdf.

Almes, G., and Holman, C. September 1987. Edmas: An Object-Oriented, Locally Distributed Mail System. *IEEE Transactions on Software Engineering* vol. SE-13(9).

Anderson, D. November 1986. Experience with Flamingo: A Distributed, Object-Oriented User Interface System. *SIGPLAN Notices* vol. 21(11).

Archer, J., and Devlin, M. 1987. *Rational's Experience Using Ada for Very Large Systems*. Mountain View, CA: Rational.

Bagrodia, R., Chandy, M., and Misra, J. June 1987. A Message-Based Approach to Discrete-Event Simulation. *IEEE Transactions on Software Engineering* vol. SE-13(6).

Barry, B. October 1989. Prototyping a Real-Time Embedded System in Smalltalk. *SIGPLAN Notices* vol. 24(10).

Barry, B., Altoft, J., Thomas, D., and Wilson, M. October 1987. Using Objects to Design and Build Radar ESM Systems. *SIGPLAN Notices* vol. 22(12).

Basili, V., Caldiera, G., and Cantone, G. January 1992. A Reference Architecture for the Component Factory. *ACM Transactions on Software Engineering and Methodology* vol. 1(1).

Batory, D., and O'Malley, S. October 1992. The Design and Implementation of Hierarchical Software Systems with Reusable Components. *ACM Transactions on Software Engineering and Methodology* vol. 1(4).

Bezivin, J. October 1987. Some Experiments in Object-Oriented Simulation. *SIGPLAN Notices* vol. 22(12).

Bhaskar, K., and Peckol, J. November 1986. Virtual Instruments: Object-Oriented Program Synthesis. *SIGPLAN Notices* vol. 21(11).

Bihair, T., and Gopinath, P. December 1992. Object-Oriented Real-Time Systems: Concepts and Examples. *IEEE Computer* vol. 25(12).

Bjornerstedt, A., and Britts, S. September 1988. AVANCE: An Object Management System. *SIGPLAN Notices* vol. 23(11).

Bobrow, D., and Stefik, M. February 1986. Perspectives on Artificial Intelligence Programming. *Science* vol. 231.

Boltuck-Pasquier, J., Grossman, E., and Collaud, G. August 1988. Prototyping an Interactive Electronic Book System Using an Object-Oriented Approach. *Proceedings of ECOOP'88: European Conference on Object-Oriented Programming*. New York, NY: Springer-Verlag.

Bonar, J., Cunningham R., and Schultz, J. November 1986. An Object-Oriented Architecture of Intelligent Tutoring Systems. *SIGPLAN Notices* vol. 21(11).

Booch, G. 1987. *Software Components with Ada: Structures, Tools, and Subsystems*. Menlo Park, CA: Benjamin/Cummings.

Borning, A. October 1981. The Programming Language Aspects of ThingLab, a Constraint-Oriented Simulation Laboratory. *ACM Transactions on Programming Languages and Systems* vol. 3(4).

Bowman, W., and Flegal, B. August 1981. ToolBox: A Smalltalk Illustration System. *Byte* vol. 6(8).

Britcher, R., and Craig, J. May 1986. Using Modern Design Practices to Upgrade Aging Software Systems. *IEEE Software* vol. 3(3).

Britton, K., and Parnas, D. December 8, 1981. *A-7E Software Module Guide*. Report 4702. Washington, DC: Naval Research Laboratory.

Brooks, R. 1987. *A Hardware Retargetable Distributed Layered Architecture for Mobile Robot Control*. Cambridge, MA: MIT Artificial Intelligence Laboratory.

Brooks, R., and Flynn, A. June 1989. *Fast, Cheap, and Out of Control: A Robot Invasion of the Solar System*. Cambridge, MA: MIT Artificial Intelligence Laboratory.

Bruck, D. 1988. Modeling of Control Systems with C++ and PHIGS. *Proceedings of USENIX C++ Conference*. Berkeley, CA: USENIX Association.

Budd, T. January 1989. The Design of an Object-Oriented Command Interpreter. *Software—Practice and Experience* vol. 19(1).

C++ Booch Components Class Catalog. 1992. Santa Clara, CA: Rational.

Call, L., Cohrs, D., and Miller, B. October 1987. CLAM—An Open System for Graphical User Interfaces. *SIGPLAN Notices* vol. 22(12).

Campbell, R., Islam, N., and Madany, P. 1992. *The Design of an Object-Oriented Operating System: A Case Study of Choices*. Vancouver, Canada: OOPSLA'92.

Caplinger, M. October 1987. An Information System Based on Distributed Objects. *SIGPLAN Notices* vol. 22(12).

Cargill, T. November 1986. Pi: A Case Study in Object-Oriented Programming. *SIGPLAN Notices* vol. 21(11).

Carroll, M. September 1990. *Building Reusable C++ Components*. Murray Hills, NJ: AT&T Bell Laboratories.

Cmelik, R., and Genani, N. May 1988. Dimensional Analysis with C++. *IEEE Software* vol. 5(3).

Coggins, J. September 1990. *Design and Management of C+ Libraries*. Chapel Hill, NC: University of North Carolina.

Cointe, P., Briot, J., and Serpette, B. 1987. The Formes System: A Musical Application of Object-Oriented Concurrent Programming. In *Object-Oriented Concurrent Programming*, ed. Yonezawa and M. Tokoro. Cambridge, MA: The MIT Press.

Collins, D. 1990. *What Is an Object-Oriented User Interface?* Thornwood, NY: IBM Systems Research Education Center.

Comeau, G. March 1991. C++ in the Real World: Interviews with C++ Application Developers. *The C++ Report* vol. 3(3).

Coplien, J. September 1991. Experience with CRC Cards in AT&T. *The C++ Report* vol. 3(8).

Coutaz, J. September 1985. Abstractions for User Interface Design. *IEEE Computer* vol. 18(9).

Custer, H. 1993. *Inside Windows NT*. Redmond, WA: Microsoft Press.

Dasgupta, P. November 1986. A Probe-Based Monitoring Scheme for an Object-Oriented Operating System. *SIGPLAN Notices* vol. 21(11).

Davidson, C., and Moseley, R. 1987. *An Object-Oriented Real-Time Knowledge-Based System.* Albuquerque, NM: Applied Methods.

Davis, J., and Morgan, T. January 1993. Object-Oriented Development at Brooklyn Union Gas. *IEEE Software* vol. 10(1).

deChampeaux, D., Anderson, A., Lerman, D., Gasperina, M., Feldhousen, E., Glei, M., Fulton, F., Groh, C., Houston, D., Monroe, C., Raj, R., and Shultheis, D. October 1991. *Case Study of Object-Oriented Software Development.* Palo Alto, CA: Hewlett-Packard Laboratories.

Dietrich, W., Nackman, L., and Gracer, F. October 1989. Saving a Legacy with Objects. *SIGPLAN Notices* vol. 24(10).

Dijkstra, E. May 1968. The Structure of the "THE" Multiprogramming System. *Communications of the ACM* vol. 11(5).

Durand, G., Benkiran, A., Durel, C., Nga, H., and Tag, M. 1988. *Distributed Mail Service in CSE System.* Paris, France: Synergie Informatique et Development.

Englemore, R., and Morgan, T. 1988. *Blackboard Systems.* Wokingham, England: Addison-Wesley.

Epstein, D., and LaLonde, W. September 1988. A Smalltalk Window System Based on Constraints. *SIGPLAN Notices* vol. 23(11).

The European Commission, Directorate-General for Energy and Transportation. 2006. Galileo—The European Satellite Navigation System. http://ec.europa.eu/dgs/energy_transport/galileo/index_en.htm.

Ewing, J. November 1986. An Object-Oriented Operating System Interface. *SIGPLAN Notices* vol. 21(11).

Fenton, J., and Beck, K. October 1989. Playground: An Object-Oriented Simulation System with Agent Rules for Children of All Ages. *SIGPLAN Notices* vol. 24(10).

Fischer, G. 1987. *An Object-Oriented Construction and Tool Kit for Human-Computer Communication.* Boulder, CO: University of Colorado Department of Computer Science and Institute of Cognitive Science.

Foley, J., and van Dam, A. 1982. *Fundamentals of Interactive Computer Graphics.* Reading, MA: Addison-Wesley.

Frankowski, E. 1986. *Advantages of the Object Paradigm for Prototyping.* Golden Valley, MN: Honeywell.

Freburger, K. October 1987. RAPID: Prototyping Control Panel Interfaces. *SIGPLAN Notices* vol. 22(12).

Freitas, M., Moreira, A., and Guerreiro, P. July/August 1990. Object-Oriented Requirements Analysis in an Ada Project. *Ada Letters* vol. X(6).

Funk, D. 1986. Applying Ada to Beech Starship Avionics. *Proceedings of the First International Conference on Ada Programming Language*

Applications for the NASA Space Station. Houston, TX: NASA Lyndon B. Johnson Space Center.

Garrett, N., and Smith, K. November 1986. Building a Timeline Editor from Prefab Parts: The Architecture of an Object-Oriented Application. *SIGPLAN Notices* vol. 21(11).

Goldberg, A. 1978. *Smalltalk in the Classroom.* Palo Alto, CA: Xerox Palo Alto Research Center.

Goldberg, A., and Rubin, K. October 1990. Taming Object-Oriented Technology. *Computer Language* vol. 7(10).

Goldstein, N., and Alger, J. 1992. *Developing Object-Oriented Software for the Macintosh.* Reading, MA: Addison-Wesley.

Gorlen, K. December 1987. An Object-Oriented Class Library for C++ Programs. *Software—Practice and Experience* vol. 17(12).

Gray, L. 1987. *Transferring Object-Oriented Design Techniques into Use: AWIS Experience.* Fairfax, VA: TRW Federal Systems Group.

Grimshaw, A., and Liu, J. October 1987. Mentat: An Object-Oriented Macro Data Flow System. *SIGPLAN Notices* vol. 22(12).

Grossman, M., and Ege, R. October 1987. Logical Composition of Object-Oriented Interfaces. *SIGPLAN Notices* vol. 22(12).

Gutfreund, S. October 1987. ManiplIcons in ThinkerToy. *SIGPLAN Notices* vol. 22(12).

Gwinn, J. February 1992. Object-Oriented Programs in Realtime. *SIGPLAN Notices* vol. 27(2).

Harrison, W., Shilling, J., and Sweeney, P. October 1989. Good News, Bad News: Experience Building a Software Development Environment Using the Object-Oriented Paradigm. *SIGPLAN Notices* vol. 24(10).

Hekmatpour, A., Orailoglu, A., and Chau, P. April 1991. Hierarchical Modeling of the VLSI Design Process. *IEEE Expert* vol. 6(2).

Hollowell, G. November 1991. Leading the U.S. Semiconductor Manufacturing Industry Toward an Object-Oriented Technology Standard. *Hotline on Object-Oriented Technology* vol. 3(1).

Ingalls, D., Wallace, S., Chow, Y., Ludolph, F., and Doyle, K. September 1988. Fabrik: A Visual Programming Environment. *SIGPLAN Notices* vol. 23(11).

Jacky, J., and Kalet, I. November 1986. An Object-Oriented Approach to a Large Scientific Application. *SIGPLAN Notices* vol. 21(11).

Jacobson, I. January 1993. Is Object Technology Software's Industrial Platform? *IEEE Software* vol. 10(1).

Jerrell, M. October 1989. Function Minimization and Automatic Differentiation Using C++. *SIGPLAN Notices* vol. 24(10).

Johnson, R., and Foote, B. June/July 1988. Designing Reusable Classes. *Journal of Object-Oriented Programming* vol. 1(2).

Jones, M., and Rashid, R. November 1986. Mach and Matchmaker: Kernel and Language Support for Object-Oriented Distributed Systems. *SIGPLAN Notices* vol. 21(11).

Jurgen, R. May 1991. Smart Cars and Highways Go Global. *IEEE Spectrum* vol. 28(5).

Kamath, Y., and Smith, J. November/December 1992. Experiences in C++ and O-O Design. *Journal of Object-Oriented Programming* vol. 5(7).

Kay, A., and Goldberg, A. March 1977. Personal Dynamic Media. *IEEE Computer.*

Kerr, R., and Percival, D. October 1987. Use of Object-Oriented Programming in a Time Series Analysis System. *SIGPLAN Notices* vol. 22(12).

Kiyooka, G. December 1992. Object-Oriented DLLs. *Byte* vol. 17(14).

Kozaczynski, W., and Kuntzmann-Combelles, A. January 1993. What It Takes to Make O-O Work. *IEEE Software* vol. 10(1).

Krueger, C. June 1992. Software Reuse. *ACM Computing Surveys* vol. 24(2).

Kuhl, F. 1988. *Object-Oriented Design for a Workstation for Air Traffic Control.* McLean, VA: The MITRE Corporation.

LaPolla, M. 1988. *On the Classification of Object-Oriented Design: The Object-Oriented Design of the AirLand Battle Management Menu System.* Austin, TX: Lockheed Software Technology Center.

Lea, D. 1988a. *User's Guide to GNU C++ Library.* Cambridge, MA: Free Software Foundation.

———. 1988b. The GNU C++ Library. *Proceedings of USENIX C++ Conference.* Berkeley, CA: USENIX Association.

Leathers, B. July 1990. Cognos and Eiffel: A Cautionary Tale. *Hotline on Object-Oriented Technology* vol. 1(9).

Ledbetter, L., and Cox, B. June 1985. Software-ICs. *Byte* vol. 10(6).

Lee, K., and Rissman, M. February 1989. *An Object-Oriented Solution Example: A Flight Simulator Electrical System.* Pittsburgh, PA: Software Engineering Institute.

Lee, K., Rissman, M., D'Ippolito, R., Plinta, C., and Van Scoy, R. December 1987. *An OOD Paradigm for Flight Simulators.* Report CMU/SEI-87-TR-43. Pittsburgh, PA: Software Engineering Institute.

Levy, P. 1987. *Implementing Systems Software in Ada.* Mountain View, CA: Rational.

Lewis, J., Henry, S., Kafura, D., and Shulman, R. July/August 1992. On the Relationship Between the Object-Oriented Paradigm and Software Reuse:

An Empirical Investigation. *Journal of Object-Oriented Programming* vol. 5(4).

Linton, M., Vlissides, J., and Calder, P. February 1989. Composing User Interfaces with InterViews. *IEEE Computer* vol. 22(2).

Liu, L., and Horowitz, E. February 1989. Object Database Support for a Software Project Management Environment. *SIGPLAN Notices* vol. 24(2).

Locke, D., and Goodenough, J. 1988. *A Practical Application of the Ceiling Protocol in a Real-Time System.* Report CMU/SEI-88-SR-3. Pittsburgh, PA: Software Engineering Institute.

Love, T. 1993. *Object Lessons.* New York, NY: SIGS Publications.

Lu, Cary. December 1992. Objects for End Users. *Byte* vol. 17(14).

Madany, P., Leyens, D., Russo, V., and Campbell, R. 1988. A C++ Class Hierarchy for Building UNIX-like File Systems. *Proceedings of USENIX C++ Conference.* Berkeley, CA: USENIX Association.

Madduri, H., Raeuchle, T., and Silverman, J. 1987. *Object-Oriented Programming for Fault-Tolerant Distributed Systems.* Golden Valley, MN: Honeywell Computer Science Center.

Maloney, J., Borning, A., and Freeman-Benson, B. October 1989. Constraint Technology for User Interface Construction in ThingLab II. *SIGPLAN Notices* vol. 24(10).

McDonald, J. October 1989. Object-Oriented Programming for Linear Algebra. *SIGPLAN Notices* vol. 24(10).

Mentor's Lessons in the School of Hard Knocks. January 25, 1993. *Business Week.*

Meyrowitz, N. November 1986. Intermedia: The Architecture and Construction of an Object-Oriented Hypermedia System and Applications Framework. *SIGPLAN Notices* vol. 21(11).

Miller, M., Cunningham, H., Lee, C., and Vegdahl, S. November 1986. The Application Accelerator Illustration System. *SIGPLAN Notices* vol. 21(11).

Mohan, L., and Kashyap, R. May 1988. An Object-Oriented Knowledge Representation for Spatial Information. *IEEE Transactions on Software Engineering* vol. 14(5).

Morgan, T., and Davis, J. March 1991. Large-Scale Object Systems Development. *Hotline on Object-Oriented Technology* vol. 2(5).

Mraz, R. December 1986. *Performance Evaluation of Parallel Branch and Bound Search with the Intel iPSE Hypercube Computer.* Wright-Patterson Air Force Base, OH: Air Force Institute of Technology.

Muller, H., Rose, J., Kempf, J., and Stansbury, T. October 1989. The Use of Multimethods and Method Combination in a CLOS-Based Window Interface. *SIGPLAN Notices* vol. 24(10).

Murphy, E. December 1988. All Aboard for Solid State. *IEEE Spectrum* vol. 25(13).

Nerson, J. September 1992. Applying Object-Oriented Analysis and Design. *Communications of the ACM* vol. 35(9).

NeXT Embraces a New Way of Programming. November 25, 1988. *Science* vol. 242.

Orden, E. 1987. Application Talk. *HOOPLA: Hooray for Object-Oriented Programming Languages* vol. 1(1). Everette, WA: Object-Oriented Programming for Smalltalk Application Developers Association.

Orfali, R., and Harkey, D. 1992. *Client/Server Programming with OS/2*. New York, NY: Van Nostrand Reinhold.

Oshima, M., and Shirai, Y. July 1983. Object Recognition Using Three-Dimensional Information. *IEEE Transactions on Pattern Analysis and Machine Intelligence* vol. 5(4).

Page, T., Berson, S., Cheng, W., and Muntz, R. October 1989. An Object-Oriented Modeling Environment. *SIGPLAN Notices* vol. 24(10).

Pashtan, A. 1982. Object-Oriented Operating Systems: An Emerging Design Methodology. *Proceedings of the ACM '82 Conference*. New York, NY: Association of Computing Machinery.

Piersol, K. November 1986. Object-Oriented Spreadsheets: The Analytic Spreadsheet Package. *SIGPLAN Notices* vol. 21(11).

Pinson, L., and Wiener, R. 1990. *Applications of Object-Oriented Programming*. Reading, MA: Addison-Wesley.

Pittman, M. January 1993. Lessons Learned in Managing Object-Oriented Development. *IEEE Software* vol. 10(1).

Plinta, C., Lee, K., and Rissman, M. March 29, 1989. A Model Solution for C3I: Message Translation and Validation. Pittsburgh, PA: Software Engineering Institute.

Pope, S. April/May 1988. Building Smalltalk-80-Based Computer Music Tools. *Journal of Object-Oriented Programming* vol. 1(1).

Raghavan, R. 1990. *Taming Windows 3.0 and DOS Using C++*. Lake Oswego, OR: Wyatt Software.

Rockwell International. 1989. *Rockwell Advanced Railroad Electronic Systems*. Cedar Rapids, IA.

Rombach, D. March 1990. Design Measurement: Some Lessons Learned. *IEEE Software* vol. 7(2).

Rubin, K., Jones, P., Mitchell, C., and Goldstein, T. September 1988. A Smalltalk Implementation of an Intelligent Operator's Associate. *SIGPLAN Notices* vol. 23(11).

Rubin, R., Walker, J., and Golin, E. October 1990. Early Experience with the Visual Programmer's WorkBench. *IEEE Transactions on Software Engineering* vol. 16(10).

Ruspini, E., and Fraley, R. 1983. ID: An Intelligent Information Dictionary System. In *Entity-Relationship Approach to Software Engineering*, ed. C. Davis et al. Amsterdam, The Netherlands: Elsevier Science.

Russo, V., Johnston, G., and Campbell, R. September 1988. Process Management and Exception Handling in Multiprocessor Operating Systems Using Object-Oriented Design Techniques. *SIGPLAN Notices* vol. 23(11).

Sampson, J., and Womble, B. 1988. *SEND: Simulation Environment for Network Design*. Dallas, TX: Southern Methodist University.

Santori, M. August 1990. An Instrument That Isn't Really. *IEEE Spectrum* vol. 27(8).

Scaletti, C., and Johnson, R. September 1988. An Interactive Environment for Object-Oriented Music Composition and Sound Synthesis. *SIGPLAN Notices* vol. 23(11).

Schindler, J., and Joy, S. February 1992. *An Introduction to Object Technology at Liberty Mutual*. Liberty Mutual Information Systems Research and Development.

Schoen, E., Smith, R., and Buchanan, B. December 1988. Design of Knowledge-Based Systems with a Knowledge-Based Assistant. *IEEE Transactions on Software Engineering* vol. 14(12).

Schulert, A., and Erf, K. 1988. Open Dialogue: Using an Extensible Retained Object Workspace to Support a UIMS. *Proceedings of USENIX C++ Conference*. Berkeley, CA: USENIX Association.

Scott, R., Reddy, P., Edwards, R., and Campbell, D. 1988. GPIO: Extensible Objects for Electronic Design. *Proceedings of USENIX C++ Conference*. Berkeley, CA: USENIX Association.

Smith, R., Barth, P., and Young, R. 1987. A Substrate for Object-Oriented Interface Design. *Research Directions in Object-Oriented Programming*. Cambridge, MA: The MIT Press.

Smith, R., Dinitz, R., and Barth, P. November 1986. Impulse-86: A Substrate for Object-Oriented Interface Design. *SIGPLAN Notices* vol. 21(11).

Sneed, H., and Gawron, W. 1983. The Use of the Entity/Relationship Model as a Schema for Organizing the Data Processing Activities at the Bavarian Motor Works. In *Entity-Relationship Approach to Software Engineering*, ed. C. Davis et al. Amsterdam, The Netherlands: Elsevier Science.

Snodgrass, R. 1987. An Object-Oriented Command Language. In *Object-Oriented Computing: Implementations* vol. 2, ed. G. Peterson. New York, NY: Computer Society Press of the IEEE.

Software Made Simple. September 30, 1991. *Business Week*.

Sridhar, S. September 1988. Configuring Stand-Alone Smalltalk-80 Applications. *SIGPLAN Notices* vol. 23(11).

Stadel, M. January 1991. Object-Oriented Programming Techniques to Replace Software Components on the Fly in a Running Program. *SIGPLAN Notices* vol. 26(1).

Stevens, A. 1992. *C++ Database Development*. New York, NY: MIS Press.

Stokes, R. 1988. Prototyping Database Applications with a Hybrid of C++ and 4GL. *Proceedings of USENIX C++ Conference*. Berkeley, CA: USENIX Association.

Szcur, M., and Miller, P. September 1988. Transportable Applications Environment (TAE) PLUS: Experiences in Objectively Modernizing a User Interface Environment. *SIGPLAN Notices* vol. 23(11).

Szekely, P., and Myers, B. September 1988. A User Interface Toolkit Based on Graphical Objects and Constraints. *SIGPLAN Notices* vol. 23(11).

Tanner, J. April 1, 1986. *Fault Tree Analysis in an Object-Oriented Environment*. Mountain View, CA: IntelliCorp.

Taylor, D. 1992. *Object-Oriented Information Systems*. New York, NY: John Wiley and Sons.

Temte, M. November/December 1984. Object-Oriented Design and Ballistics Software. *Ada Letters* vol. 4(3).

Tripathi, A., and Aksit, M. November/December 1988. Communication, Scheduling, and Resource Management in SINA. *Journal of Object-Oriented Programming* vol. 1(4).

Tripathi, A., Ghonami, A., and Schmitz, T. 1987. Object Management in the NEXUS Distributed Operating System. *Proceedings of the Thirty-second IEEE Computer Society International Conference*. New York, NY: Computer Society Press of the IEEE.

Ursprung, P., and Zehnder, C. 1983. HIQUEL: An Interactive Query Language to Define and Use Hierarchies. In *Entity-Relationship Approach to Software Engineering*, ed. C. Davis et al. Amsterdam, The Netherlands: Elsevier Science.

van der Meulen, P. October 1987. INSIST: Interactive Simulation in Smalltalk. *SIGPLAN Notices* vol. 22(12).

Vernon, V. September/October 1989. The Forest for the Trees. *Programmer's Journal* vol. 7(5).

Vilot, M. Fall 1990. Using Object-Oriented Design and C++. *The C++ Journal* vol. 1(1).

Vines, D., and King, T. 1987. *Experiences in Building a Prototype Object-Oriented Framework in Ada*. Minneapolis, MN: Honeywell.

Vlissides, J., and Linton, M. 1988. Applying Object-Oriented Design to Structured Graphics. *Proceedings of USENIX C++ Conference*. Berkeley, CA: USENIX Association.

Volz, R., Mudge, T., and Gal, D. 1987. Using Ada as a Programming Language for Robot-Based Manufacturing Cells. In *Object-Oriented Computing: Concepts* vol. 1, ed. G. Peterson. New York, NY: Computer Society Press of the IEEE.

Walther, S., and Peskin, R. October 1989. Strategies for Scientific Prototyping in Smalltalk. *SIGPLAN Notices* vol. 24(10).

Wasserman, A., and Pircher, P. January 1991. Object-Oriented Structured Design and C++. *Computer Language* vol. 8(1).

Weinand, A., Gamma, E., and Marty, R. September 1988. ET++—An Object-Oriented Application Framework in C++. *SIGPLAN Notices* vol. 23(11).

Welch, B. July/August 1991. Securities Objects—The Complexity. *Object Magazine* vol. 1(2).

White, S. October 1986. Panel Problem: Software Controller for an Oil Hot Water Heating System. *Proceedings of COMPSAC*. New York, NY: Computer Society Press of the IEEE.

Wirfs-Brock, R. September 1988. An Integrated Color Smalltalk-80 System. *SIGPLAN Notices* vol. 23(11).

———. October 1991. Object-Oriented Frameworks. *American Programmer* vol. 4(10).

WOSA Extensions for Financial Services. December 1992. Banking Systems Vendor Council.

Wu, P. January 1992. An Object-Oriented Specification for a Compiler. *SIGPLAN Notices* vol. 27(1).

Yoshida, N., and Hino, K. September 1988. An Object-Oriented Framework of Pattern Recognition. *SIGPLAN Notices* vol. 23(11).

Yoshida, T., and Tokoro, M. March 31, 1986. *Distributed Queueing Network Simulation: An Application of a Concurrent Object-Oriented Language*. Yokohama, Japan: Keio University.

Young, R. October 1987. An Object-Oriented Framework for Interactive Data Graphics. *SIGPLAN Notices* vol. 22(12).

D. Object-Oriented Architectures

Athas, W., and Seitz, C. August 1988. Multicomputers: Message-Passing Concurrent Computers. *IEEE Computer* vol. 21(8).

Corkill, D. D. September 1991. Blackboard Systems. *AI Expert* vol. 6(9), pp. 40–47.

Dahlby, S., Henry, G., Reynolds, D., and Taylor, P. 1982. The IBM System/38: A High Level Machine. In *Computer Structures: Principles and Examples*, ed. G. Bell and A. Newell. New York, NY: McGraw-Hill.

Dally, W., and Kajiya, J. March 1985. An Object-Oriented Architecture. *SIGARCH Newsletter* vol. 13(3).

Fabry, R. 1987. Capability-Based Addressing. In *Object-Oriented Computing: Implementations* vol. 2, ed. G. Peterson. New York, NY: Computer Society Press of the IEEE.

Flynn, M. October 1980. Directions and Issues in Architecture and Language. *IEEE Computer* vol. 13(10).

Harland, D., and Beloff, B. December 1986. Microcoding an Object-Oriented Instruction Set. *Computer Architecture News* vol. 14(5).

Hillis, D. 1985. *The Connection Machine*. Cambridge, MA: The MIT Press.

Hunt, J. May 2002. Blackboard Architectures. JayDee Technology Ltd 27. www.agent.ai/doc/upload/200402/hunt02_1.pdf.

IEEE-Std-1471-2000. 2000. *IEEE Recommended Practice for Architectural Description of Software-Intensive Systems*. New York, NY: IEEE.

Iliffe, J. 1982. *Advanced Computer Design*. London, England: Prentice Hall International.

Intel. 1981. *iAPX 432 Object Primer*. Santa Clara, CA.

Ishikawa, Y., and Tokoro, M. March 1984. The Design of an Object-Oriented Architecture. *SIGARCH Newsletter* vol. 12(3).

Kavi, K., and Chen, D. 1987. Architectural Support for Object-Oriented Languages. *Proceedings of the Thirty-second IEEE Computer Society International Conference*. New York, NY: Computer Society Press of the IEEE.

Krikorian, H. F. March/April 2003. Introduction to Object-Oriented Systems Engineering, Part 1. *IT Professional*, p. 40.

Kruchten, P. 1995. The 4+1 View Model of Architecture. *IEEE Software* 12(6), pp. 42–50.

Lahtinen, P. September/October 1982. A Machine Architecture for Ada. *Ada Letters* vol. 2(2).

Lampson, B., and Pier, K. January 1981. A Processor for a High-Performance Personal Computer. In *The Dorado: A High Performance Personal Computer*. Report CSL-81-1. Palo Alto, CA: Xerox Palo Alto Research Center.

Langdon, G. 1982. *Computer Design*. San Jose, CA: Computeach Press.

Levy, H. 1984. *Capability-Based Computer Systems*. Bedford, MA: Digital Press.

Lewis, D., Galloway, D., Francis, R., and Thomson, B. November 1986. Swamp: A Fast Processor for Smalltalk-80. *SIGPLAN Notices* vol. 21(11).

Maier, M. W., Emery, D., and Hilliard, R. 2004. ANSI/IEEE 1471 and Systems Engineering. *Systems Engineering* vol. 7(3), pp. 257–270.

Mashburn, H. 1982. The C.mmp/Hydra Project: An Architectural Overview. In *Computer Structures: Principles and Examples*, ed. G. Bell and A. Newell. New York, NY: McGraw-Hill.

Myers, G. 1982. *Advances in Computer Architecture*. Second Edition. New York, NY: John Wiley and Sons.

Rattner, J. 1982. Hardware/Software Cooperation in the iAPX-432. *Proceedings of the Symposium on Architectural Support for Programming Languages and Operating Systems*. New York, NY: Association of Computing Machinery.

Rose, J. September 1988. Fast Dispatch Mechanisms for Stock Hardware. *SIGPLAN Notices* vol. 23(11).

Samples, D., Ungar, D., and Hilfinger, P. November 1986. SOAR: Smalltalk without Bytecodes. *SIGPLAN Notices* vol. 21(11).

Shaw, M., and Garlan, D. 1996. *Software Architecture, Perspectives on an Emerging Discipline*. Upper Saddle River, NJ: Prentice Hall.

Soltis, R., and Hoffman, R. 1987. Design Considerations for the IBM System/38. In *Object-Oriented Computing: Implementations* vol. 2, ed. G. Peterson. New York, NY: Computer Society Press of the IEEE.

Thacker, C., McCreight, E., Lampson, B., Sproull, R., and Boggs, D. August 1979. *Alto: A Personal Computer*, Report CSL-79-11. Palo Alto, CA: Xerox Palo Alto Research Center.

Ungar, D. 1987. *The Design and Evaluation of a High-Performance Smalltalk System*. Cambridge, MA: The MIT Press.

Ungar, D., and Patterson, D. January 1987. What Price Smalltalk? *IEEE Computer* vol. 20(1).

Ungar, D., Blau, R., Foley, P., Samples, D., and Patterson, D. March 1984. Architecture of SOAR: Smalltalk on a RISC. *SIGARCH Newsletter* vol. 12(3).

Wah, B., and Li, G. April 1986. Survey on Special Purpose Computer Architectures for AI. *SIGART Newsletter*, no. 96.

Wulf, W. January 1980. Trends in the Design and Implementation of Programming Languages. *IEEE Computer* vol. 13(1).

Wulf, W., Levin, R., and Harbison, S. 1981. *HYDRA/C.mmp: An Experimental Computer System*. New York, NY: McGraw-Hill.

E. Object-Oriented Databases

Alford, M. 1983. Derivation of Element-Relation-Attribute Database Requirements by Decomposition of System Functions. In *Entity-Relationship Approach to Software Engineering*, ed. C. Davis et al. Amsterdam, The Netherlands: Elsevier Science.

Andleigh, P., and Gretzinger, M. 1992. *Distributed Object-Oriented Data-Systems Design*. Englewood Cliffs, NJ: Prentice Hall.

Atkinson, M., Bailey, P., Chisholm, K., Cockshott, P., and Morrison, R. 1983. An Approach to Persistent Programming. *The Computer Journal* vol. 26(4).

Atkinson, M., and Buneman, P. June 1987. Types and Persistence in Database Programming Languages. *ACM Computing Surveys* vol. 19(2).

Atkinson, M., and Morrison, R. October 1985. Procedures as Persistent Data Objects. *ACM Transactions on Programming Languages and Systems* vol. 7(4).

Atwood, T. February 1991. Object-Oriented Databases. *IEEE Spectrum* vol. 28(2).

Bachman, C. 1983. The Structuring Capabilities of the Molecular Data Model. In *Entity-Relationship Approach to Software Engineering*, ed. C. Davis et al. Amsterdam, The Netherlands: Elsevier Science.

Batini, C., and Lenzerini, M. 1983. A Methodology for Data Schema Integration in the Entity-Relationship Model. In *Entity-Relationship Approach to Software Engineering*, ed. C. Davis et al. Amsterdam, The Netherlands: Elsevier Science.

Beech, D. 1987. Groundwork for an Object Database Model. In *Research Directions in Object-Oriented Programming*, ed. B. Schriver and P. Wegner. Cambridge, MA: The MIT Press.

———. September 1988. Intensional Concepts in an Object Database Model. *SIGPLAN Notices* vol. 23(11).

Bertino, E. 1983. Distributed Database Design Using the Entity-Relationship Model. In *Entity-Relationship Approach to Software Engineering*, ed. C. Davis et al. Amsterdam, The Netherlands: Elsevier Science.

Blackwell, P., Jajodia, S., and Ng, P. 1983. A View of Database Management Systems as Abstract Data Types. In *Entity-Relationship Approach to Software Engineering*, ed. C. Davis et al. Amsterdam, The Netherlands: Elsevier Science.

Bloom, T. October 1987. Issues in the Design of Object-Oriented Database Programming Languages. *SIGPLAN Notices* vol. 22(12).

Bobrow, D., Fogelsong, D., and Miller, M. 1987. Definition Groups: Making Sources into First-Class Objects. In *Research Directions in Object-Oriented Programming*, ed. B. Schriver and P. Wegner. Cambridge, MA: The MIT Press.

Brathwaite, K. 1983. An Implementation of a Data Dictionary to Support Databases Designed Using the Entity-Relationship (E-R) Approach. In *Entity-Relationship Approach to Software Engineering*, ed. C. Davis et al. Amsterdam, The Netherlands: Elsevier Science.

Breazeal, J., Blattner, M., and Burton, H. March 28, 1986. *Data Standardization Through the Use of Data Abstraction*. Livermore, CA: Lawrence Livermore National Laboratory.

Brodie, M. 1984. On the Development of Data Models. In *On Conceptual Modeling: Perspectives from Artificial Intelligence, Databases, and Programming Languages*, ed. M. Brodie, J. Mylopoulos, and J. Schmidt. New York, NY: Springer-Verlag.

Brodie, M., and Ridjanovic, D. 1984. On the Design and Specification of Database Transactions. In *On Conceptual Modeling: Perspectives from Artificial Intelligence, Databases, and Programming Languages*, ed. M. Brodie, J. Mylopoulos, and J. Schmidt. New York, NY: Springer-Verlag.

Butterworth, P., Otis, A., and Stein, J. October 1991. The GemStone Object Database Management System. *Communications of the ACM* vol. 34(10).

Carlson, C., and Arora, A. 1983. UPM: A Formal Tool for Expressing Database Update Semantics. In *Entity-Relationship Approach to Software Engineering*, ed. C. Davis et al. Amsterdam, The Netherlands: Elsevier Science.

Casanova, M. 1983. Designing Entity-Relationship Schemes for Conventional Information Systems. In *Entity-Relationship Approach to Software Engineering*, ed. C. Davis et al. Amsterdam, The Netherlands: Elsevier Science.

Cattell, R. May 1983. *Design and Implementation of a Relationship-Entity-Datum Data Model*, Report CSL-83-4. Palo Alto, CA: Xerox Palo Alto Research Center.

————. 1991. *Object Data Management*. Reading, MA: Addison-Wesley.

Chen, P. March 1976. The Entity-Relationship Model—Toward a Unified View of Data. *ACM Transactions on Database Systems* vol. 1(1).

————. 1983. ER—A Historical Perspective and Future Directions. In *Entity-Relationship Approach to Software Engineering*, ed. C. Davis et al. Amsterdam, The Netherlands: Elsevier Science.

Claybrook, B., Claybrook, A., and Williams, J. January 1985. Defining Database Views as Data Abstractions. *IEEE Transactions on Software Engineering* vol. SE-11(1).

D'Cunha, A., and Radhakrishnan, T. 1983. Applications of E-R Concepts to Data Administration. In *Entity-Relationship Approach to Software Engineering*, ed. C. Davis et al. Amsterdam, The Netherlands: Elsevier Science.

Date, C. 1981, 1983. *An Introduction to Database Systems*. Reading, MA: Addison-Wesley.

———. 1986. *Relational Database: Selected Writings*. Reading, MA: Addison-Wesley.

———. 1987. *The Guide to the SQL Standard*. Reading, MA: Addison-Wesley.

Duhl, J., and Damon, C. September 1988. A Performance Comparison of Object and Relational Databases Using the Sun Benchmark. *SIGPLAN Notices* vol. 23(11).

Harland, D., and Beloff, B. April 1987. OBJEKT—A Persistent Object Store with an Integrated Garbage Collector. *SIGPLAN Notices* vol. 22(4).

Hawryszkiewycz, I. 1984. *Database Analysis and Design*. Chicago, IL: Science Research Associates.

Higa, K., Morrison, M., Morrison, J., and Sheng, O. June 1992. An Object-Oriented Methodology for Knowledge Base/Database Coupling. *Communications of the ACM* vol. 35(6).

Hull, R., and King, R. September 1987. Semantic Database Modeling: Survey, Applications, and Research Issues. *ACM Computing Surveys* vol. 19(3).

Jajodia, S., Ng, P., and Springsteel, F. 1983. On Universal and Representative Instances for Inconsistent Databases. In *Entity-Relationship Approach to Software Engineering*, ed. C. Davis et al. Amsterdam, The Netherlands: Elsevier Science.

Ketabchi, M., and Berzins, V. January 1988. Mathematical Model of Composite Objects and Its Application for Organizing Engineering Databases. *IEEE Transactions on Software Engineering* vol. 14(1).

Ketabchi, M., and Wiens, R. 1987. Implementation of Persistent Multi-User Object-Oriented Systems. *Proceedings of the Thirty-second IEEE Computer Society International Conference*. New York, NY: Computer Society Press of the IEEE.

Khoshafian, S., and Abnous, R. 1990. *Object-Orientation: Concepts, Languages, Databases, User Interfaces*. New York, NY: John Wiley and Sons.

Kim, W., and Lochovsky, K. 1989. *Object-Oriented Concepts, Databases, and Applications*. Reading, MA: Addison-Wesley.

Kim, W., Ballou, N., Chou, H., Garze, J., Woelk, D., and Banerjee, J. September 1988. Integrating an Object-Oriented Programming System with a Database System. *SIGPLAN Notices* vol. 23(11).

Kim, W., Banerjee, J., Chou, H., Garza, J., and Woelk, D. October 1987. Composite Object Support in an Object-Oriented Database System. *SIGPLAN Notices* vol. 22(12).

Kung, C. Object Subclass Hierarchy in SQL: A Simple Approach. *Communications of the ACM* vol. 33(7).

Laenens, E., and Vermeir, D. August 1988. An Overview of OOPS+, an Object-Oriented Database Programming Language. *Proceedings of ECOOP'88: European Conference on Object-Oriented Programming*. New York, NY: Springer-Verlag.

Lamb, C., Landis, G., Orenstein, J., and Weinreb, D. October 1991. The ObjectStore Database System. *Communications of the ACM* vol. 34(10).

Larson, J., and Dwyer, P. 1983. Defining External Schemas for an Entity-Relationship Database. In *Entity-Relationship Approach to Software Engineering*, ed. C. Davis et al. Amsterdam, The Netherlands: Elsevier Science.

Maier, D., and Stein, J. 1987. Development and Implementation of an Object-Oriented DBMS. In *Research Directions in Object-Oriented Programming*, ed. B. Schriver and P. Wegner. Cambridge, MA: The MIT Press.

Margrave, G., Lusk, E., and Overbeek, R. 1983. Tools for the Creation of IMS Database Designs from Entity-Relationship Diagrams. In *Entity-Relationship Approach to Software Engineering*, ed. C. Davis et al. Amsterdam, The Netherlands: Elsevier Science.

Mark, L., and Poussopoulos, N. 1983. Integration of Data, Schema, and Meta-Schema in the Context of Self-Documenting Data Models. In *Entity-Relationship Approach to Software Engineering*, ed. C. Davis et al. Amsterdam, The Netherlands: Elsevier Science.

Markowitz, V., and Makowsky, J. August 1990. Identifying Extended Entity-Relationship Object Structures in Relational Schemas. *IEEE Transactions on Software Engineering* vol. 16(8).

Marti, R. 1983. Integrating Database and Program Descriptions Using an ER Data Dictionary. In *Entity-Relationship Approach to Software Engineering*, ed. C. Davis et al. Amsterdam, The Netherlands: Elsevier Science.

Merrow, T., and Laursen, J. October 1987. A Pragmatic System for Shared Persistent Objects. *SIGPLAN Notices* vol. 22(12).

Mitchell, J., and Wegbreit, B. 1977. Schemes: A High-Level Data Structuring Concept. In *Current Trends in Programming Methodology: Data Structuring* vol. 4, ed. R. Yeh. Englewood Cliffs, NJ: Prentice Hall.

Morrison, R., Atkinson, M., Brown, A., and Dearle, A. April 1988. Bindings in Persistent Programming Languages. *SIGPLAN Notices* vol. 23(4).

Moss, E., Herlihy, M., and Zdonik, S. September 1988. *Object-Oriented Databases, Course Notes*. San Diego, CA: OOPSLA'88.

Moss, J. August 1992. Working with Persistent Objects: To Swizzle or Not to Swizzle. *IEEE Transactions on Software Engineering* vol. 18(8).

Nastos, M. January 1988. Databases, Etc. *HOOPLA: Hooray for Object-Oriented Programming Languages* vol. 1(2). Everette, WA: Object Oriented Programming for Smalltalk Application Developers Association.

Navathe, S., and Cheng, A. 1983. A Methodology for Database Schema Mapping from Extended Entity Relationship Models into the Hierarchical Model. In *Entity-Relationship Approach to Software Engineering*, ed. C. Davis et al. Amsterdam, The Netherlands: Elsevier Science.

Ontologic. 1987. *Vbase Technical Overview*. Billerica, MA.

Oracle. 1989. *Oracle for Macintosh: References, Version 1.1*. Belmont, CA.

Penny, J., and Stein, J. October 1987. Class Modification in the GemStone Object-Oriented DBMS. *SIGPLAN Notices* vol. 22(12).

Peterson, R. 1987. Object-Oriented Database Design. In *Object-Oriented Computing: Implementations* vol. 2, ed. G. Peterson. New York, NY: Computer Society Press of the IEEE.

Premerlani, W., Blaha, M., Rumbaugh, J., and Varwig, T. November 1990. An Object-Oriented Relational Database. *Communications of the ACM* vol. 33(11).

Sakai, H. 1983. Entity-Relationship Approach to Logical Database Design. In *Entity-Relationship Approach to Software Engineering*, ed. C. Davis et al. Amsterdam, The Netherlands: Elsevier Science.

Skarra, A., and Zdonik, S. 1987. Type Evolution in an Object-Oriented Database. In *Research Directions in Object-Oriented Programming*, ed. B. Schriver and P. Wegner. Cambridge, MA: The MIT Press.

Skarra, A., and Zdonik, S. November 1986. The Management of Changing Types in an Object-Oriented Database. *SIGPLAN Notices* vol. 21(11).

Smith, D., and Smith, J. 1980. Conceptual Database Design. In *Tutorial on Software Design Techniques*, Third Edition, ed. P. Freeman and A. Wasserman. New York, NY: Computer Society Press of the IEEE.

Smith, J., and Smith, D. Database Abstractions: Aggregation and Generalization. *ACM Transactions on Database Systems* vol. 2(2).

Smith, K., and Zdonik, S. October 1987. Intermedia: A Case Study of the Differences Between Relational and Object-Oriented Database Systems. *SIGPLAN Notices* vol. 22(12).

Stein, J. March 1988. Object-Oriented Programming and Database Design. *Dr. Dobb's Journal* vol. 13(3).

Teorey, T., Yang, D., and Fry, J. June 1986. A Logical Design Methodology for Relational Databases Using the Extended Entity-Relationship Model. *ACM Computing Surveys* vol. 18(2).

Thuraisingham, M. October 1989. Mandatory Security in Object-Oriented Database Systems. *SIGPLAN Notices* vol. 24(10).

Veloso, P., and Furtado, A. 1983. View Constructs for the Specification and Design of External Schemas. In *Entity-Relationship Approach to Software Engineering*, ed. C. Davis et al. Amsterdam, The Netherlands: Elsevier Science.

Wiebe, D. November 1986. A Distributed Repository for Immutable Persistent Objects. *SIGPLAN Notices* vol. 21(11).

Wiederhold, G. December 1986. Views, Objects, and Databases. *IEEE Computer* vol. 19(12).

Wile, D., and Allard, D. May 1982. Worlds: An Organizing Structure for Object-Bases. *SIGPLAN Notices* vol. 19(5).

Zdonik, S., and Maier, D. 1990. *Readings in Object-Oriented Database Systems*. San Mateo, CA: Morgan Kaufmann.

Zhang, Z., and Mendelzon, A. 1983. A Graphical Query Language for Entity-Relationship Databases. In *Entity-Relationship Approach to Software Engineering*, ed. C. Davis et al. Amsterdam, The Netherlands: Elsevier Science.

F. Object-Oriented Design

Abbott, R. November 1983. Program Design by Informal English Descriptions. *Communications of the ACM* vol. 26(11).

———. August 1987. Knowledge Abstraction. *Communications of the ACM* vol. 30(8).

Ackroyd, M., and Daum, D. 1991. Graphical Notation for Object-Oriented Design and Programming. *Journal of Object-Oriented Programming* vol. 3(5).

Alabios, B. September 1988. Transformation of Data Flow Analysis Models to Object-Oriented Design. *SIGPLAN Notices* vol. 23(11).

Arnold, P., Bodoff, S., Coleman, D., Gilchrist, H., and Hayes, F. June 1991. *An Evaluation of Five Object-Oriented Development Methods*. Bristol, England: Hewlett-Packard Laboratories.

Bear, S., Allen, P., Coleman, D., and Hayes, F. Graphical Specification of Object-Oriented Systems. *Object-Oriented Programming Systems, Languages, and Applications*. Ottawa, Canada: OOPSLA'90.

Beck, K., and Cunningham, W. October 1989. A Laboratory for Teaching Object-Oriented Thinking. *SIGPLAN Notices* vol. 24(10).

Berard, E. 1986. *An Object-Oriented Design Handbook*. Rockville, MD: EVB Software Engineering.

Berzins, V., Gray, M., and Naumann, D. May 1986. Abstraction-Based Software Development. *Communications of the ACM* vol. 29(5).

Blaha, M. April 1988. Relational Database Design Using an Object-Oriented Methodology. *Communications of the ACM* vol. 31(4).

Booch, G. September 1981. Describing Software Design in Ada. *SIGPLAN Notices* vol. 16(9).

————. March/April 1982. Object-Oriented Design. *Ada Letters* vol. 1(3).

————. February 1986. Object-Oriented Development. *IEEE Transactions on Software Engineering* vol. 12(2).

————. 1987. *On the Concepts of Object-Oriented Design.* Denver, CO: Rational.

————. Summer 1989. What Is and What Isn't Object-Oriented Design. *American Programmer* vol. 2(7–8).

Booch, G., and Vilot, M. Object-Oriented Design. *The C++ Report.*

Booch, G., Jacobson, I., and Kerth, N. September 1988. *Specification and Design Methodologies in Support of Object-Oriented Programming, Course Notes.* San Diego, CA: OOPSLA'88.

Bowles, A. November/December 1991. Evolution vs. Revolution: Should Structured Methods Be Objectified? *Object Magazine* vol. 1(4).

Boyd, S. July/August 1987. Object-Oriented Design and PAMELA™. *Ada Letters* vol. 7(4).

Bril, R., deBunje, T., and Ouvry, A. October 1991. *Development of SCORE: Towards the Industrialization of an Object-Oriented Method Using the Formal Design Language COLD-1 as Notation.* Eindhoven, The Netherlands: Philips Research Laboratories.

Brookman, D. November/December 1991. SA/SD versus OOD. *Ada Letters* vol. XI(9).

Bruno, G., and Balsamo, A. November 1986. Petri Net-Based Object-Oriented Modeling of Distributed Systems. *SIGPLAN Notices* vol. 21(11).

Buhr, R. 1984. *System Design with Ada.* Englewood Cliffs, NJ: Prentice Hall.

————. August 22, 1988. *Machine Charts for Visual Prototyping in System Design.* SCE Report 88-2. Ottawa, Canada: Carleton University.

————. September 14, 1988. *Visual Prototyping in System Design.* SCE Report 88-14. Ottawa, Canada: Carleton University.

————. 1989. *System Design with Machine Charts: A CAD Approach with Ada Examples.* Englewood Cliffs, NJ. Prentice Hall.

Buhr, R., Karam, G., Hayes, C., and Woodside, M. March 1989. Software CAD: A Revolutionay Approach. *IEEE Transactions on Software Engineering* vol. 15(3).

Bulman, D. August 1989. An Object-Based Development Model. *Computer Language* vol. 6(8).

Cherry, G. 1987. *PAMELA 2: An Ada-Based Object-Oriented Design Method.* Reston, VA: Thought**Tools.

————. 1990. *Software Construction by Object-Oriented Pictures.* Canandaigua, NY: Thought**Tools.

Clark, R. June 1987. Designing Concurrent Objects. *Ada Letters* vol. 7(6).

Coad, P. September 1991. OOD Criteria. *Journal of Object-Oriented Programming* vol.(5).

Coleman, D., Hayes, F., and Bear, S. December 1990. *Introducing Objectcharts or How to Use Statecharts in Object-Oriented Design*. Bristol, England: Hewlett-Packard Laboratories.

Comer, E. July 1989. *Ada Box Structure Methodology Handbook*. Melbourne, FL: Software Productivity Solutions.

Constantine, L. Summer 1989. Object-Oriented and Structured Methods: Towards Integration. *American Programmer* vol. 2(7–8).

CRI, CISI Ingenierie, and Matra. June 20, 1987. *HOOD: Hierarchical Object-Oriented Design*. Paris, France.

Cribbs, J., Moon, S., and Roe, C. 1992. *An Evaluation of Object-Oriented Analysis and Design Methodologies*. Raleigh, NC: Alcatel Network Systems.

Cunningham, W., and Beck, K. November 1986. A Diagram for Object-Oriented Programs. *SIGPLAN Notices* vol. 21(11).

Davis, N., Irving, M., and Lee, J. 1988. *The Evolution of Object-Oriented Design from Concept to Method*. Surrey, United Kingdom: Logica Space and Defence Systems Limited.

Dean, H. May 1991. Object-Oriented Design Using Message Flow Decomposition. *Journal of Object-Oriented Programming* vol. 4(2).

deChampeaux, D., Balzer, B., Bulman, D., Culver-Lozo, K., Jacobson, I., and Mellor, S. 1992. *The Object-Oriented Software Development Process*. Vancouver, Canada: OOPSLA'92.

deChampeaux, D., Lea, D., and Faure, P. 1992. *The Process of Object-Oriented Design*. Vancouver, Canada: OOPSLA'92.

Edwards, J., and Henderson-Sellers, B. November 1991. *A Graphical Notation for Object-Oriented Analysis and Design*. New South Wales, Australia: University of New South Wales.

Felsinger, R. 1987a. *Integrating Object-Oriented Design, Structured Analysis/ Structured Design, and Ada for Real-Time Systems*. Mt. Pleasant, SC.

————. 1987b. *Object-Oriented Design, Course Notes*. Torrance, CA: Data Processing Management Association.

Fichman, R., and Kemerer, C. October 1992. Object-Oriented and Conventional Analysis and Design Methodologies. *IEEE Computer* vol. 25(10).

Firesmith, D. May 6, 1986. *Object-Oriented Development*. Fort Wayne, IN: Magnavox Electronic Systems Co.

————. 1993. *Object-Oriented Requirements Analysis and Logical Design*. New York, NY: John Wiley and Sons.

Fowler, M. 1992. *A Comparison of Object-Oriented Analysis and Design Methods*. Vancouver, Canada: OOPSLA'92.

Gamma, E., Helm, R., Johnson, R., and Vlissides, J. 1993. *A Catalog of Object-Oriented Design Patterns*. Cupertino, CA: Taligent.

———. 1995. *Design Patterns: Elements of Reusable Object-Oriented Software*. Reading, MA: Addison-Wesley.

Gane, C. Summer 1989. Object-Oriented Data/Process Modeling. *American Programmer* vol. 2(7–8).

Giddings, R. May 1984. Accommodating Uncertainty in Software Design. *Communications of the ACM* vol. 27(5).

Gomaa, H. September 1984. A Software Design Method for Real-Time Systems. *Communications of the ACM* vol. 27(9).

Gossain, S., and Anderson, B. *An Iterative Design Model for Reusable Objects*. Ottawa, Canada: OOPSLA'90.

Gouda, M., Han, Y., Jensen, E., Johnson, W., and Kain, R. November 1977. Towards a Methodology of Distributed Computer System Design. *Sixth Texas Conference on Computing Systems*. New York, NY: Association of Computing Machinery.

Graham, I. 1991. *Object-Oriented Methods*. Wokingham, England: Addison-Wesley.

Grosch, J. December 1983. Type Derivation Graphs—A Way to Visualize the Type Building Possibilities of Programming Languages. *SIGPLAN Notices* vol. 18(12).

Harel, D. 1987. Statecharts: A Visual Formalism for Complex Systems. *Science of Computer Programming* vol. 8.

———. May 1988. On Visual Formalisms. *Communications of the ACM* vol. 31(5).

Henderson-Sellers, B. 1992. *A Book of Object-Oriented Knowledge*. Englewood Cliffs, NJ: Prentice Hall.

Inwood, C. 1992. Analysis versus Design: Is There a Difference? *The C++ Journal* vol. 2(1).

Jackson, M. Summer 1989. Object-Oriented Software. *American Programmer* vol. 2(7–8).

Jacobson, I. August 1985. *Concepts for Modeling Large Real-Time Systems*. Academic dissertation. Stockholm, Sweden: Royal Institute of Technology, Department of Computer Science.

———. October 1987. Object-Oriented Development in an Industrial Environment. *SIGPLAN Notices* vol. 22(12).

Jacobson, I., Christerson, M., Jonsson, P., and Overgaard, G. 1992. *Object-Oriented Software Engineering*. Wokingham, England: Addison-Wesley.

Jamsa, K. January 1984. Object-Oriented Design vs. Structured Design— A Student's Perspective. *Software Engineering Notes* vol. 9(1).

Johnson, R., and Russo, V. May 1991. *Reusing Object-Oriented Designs*. Urbana, IL: University of Illinois.

Jones, A. 1979. The Object Model: A Conceptual Tool for Structuring Software. In *Operating Systems*, ed. R. Bayer et al. New York, NY: Springer-Verlag.

Kadie, C. 1986. *Refinement Through Classes: A Development Methodology for Object-Oriented Languages*. Urbana, IL: University of Illinois.

Kaplan, S., and Johnson, R. July 21, 1986. *Designing and Implementing for Reuse*. Urbana, IL: University of Illinois, Department of Computer Science.

Kay, A. August 1969. *The Reactive Engine*. Salt Lake City, UT: The University of Utah, Department of Computer Science.

Kelly, J. 1986. A Comparison of Four Design Methods for Real-Time Systems. *Proceedings of the Ninth International Conference on Software Engineering*. New York, NY: Computer Society Press of the IEEE.

Kent, W. 1983. Fact-Based Data Analysis and Design. In *Entity-Relationship Approach to Software Engineering*, ed. C. Davis et al. Amsterdam, The Netherlands: Elsevier Science.

Kerth, N. L. 1988. MOOD: A Methodology for Structured Object-Oriented Design. Tutorial presented at OOPSLA'88, San Diego, CA.

Kim, J., and Lerch, J. 1992. *Towards a Model of Cognitive Process in Logical Design: Comparing Object-Oriented and Traditional Functional Decomposition Software Methodologies*. Pittsburgh, PA: Carnegie Mellon University.

Kruchten, P. 2003. *The Rational Unified Process: An Introduction*. Third Edition. Boston, MA: Addison-Wesley.

Ladden, R. July 1988. A Survey of Issues to Be Considered in the Development of an Object-Oriented Development Methodology for Ada. *Software Engineering Notes* vol. 13(3).

Lieberherr, K., and Riel, A. October 1989. Contributions to Teaching Object-Oriented Design and Programming. *SIGPLAN Notices* vol. 24(10).

Liskov, B. 1980. A Design Methodology for Reliable Software Systems. In *Tutorial on Software Design Techniques*, Third Edition, ed. P. Freeman and A. Wasserman. New York, NY: Computer Society Press of the IEEE.

Lorenz, M. 1993. *Object-Oriented Software Development*. Englewood Cliffs, NJ: Prentice Hall.

Mannino, P. April 1987. A Presentation and Comparison of Four Information System Development Methodologies. *Software Engineering Notes* vol. 12(2).

Martin, B. 1993. *Designing Object-Oriented C++ Applications Using the Booch Method.* Englewood Cliffs, NJ: Prentice Hall.

Masiero, P., and Germano, F. July 1988. JSD as an Object-Oriented Design Method. *Software Engineering Notes* vol. 13(3).

Meyer, B. 1988. *Object-Oriented Software Construction.* Englewood Cliffs, NJ: Prentice Hall.

Meyer, B. March 1987. Reusability: The Case for Object-Oriented Design. *IEEE Software* vol. 4(2).

———. 1989. From Structured Programming to Object-Oriented Design: The Road to Eiffel. *Structured Programming* vol. 10(1).

Mills, H. June 1988. Stepwise Refinement and Verification in Box-Structured Systems. *IEEE Computer* vol. 21(6).

Mills, H., Linger, R., and Hevner, A. 1986. *Principles of Information System Design and Analysis.* Orlando, FL: Academic Press.

Minkowitz, C., and Henderson, P. March 1987. *Object-Oriented Programming of Discrete Event Simulation Using Petri Nets.* Stirling, Scotland: University of Stirling.

Monarchi, D., and Puhr, G. September 1992. A Research Typology for Object-Oriented Analysis and Design. *Communications of the ACM* vol. 35(9).

Mostow, J. Spring 1985. Toward Better Models of the Design Process. *AI Magazine* vol. 6(1).

Moulin, B. 1983. The Use of EPAS/IPSO Approach for Integrating Entity Relationship Concepts and Software Engineering Techniques. In *Entity-Relationship Approach to Software Engineering*, ed. C. Davis et al. Amsterdam, The Netherlands: Elsevier Science.

Mullin, M. 1989. *Object-Oriented Program Design with Examples in C++.* Reading, MA: Addison-Wesley.

Nielsen, K., and Shumate, K. August 1987. Designing Large Real-Time Systems with Ada. *Communications of the ACM* vol. 30(8).

Nielsen, K. March 1988. *An Object-Oriented Design Methodology for Real-Time Systems in Ada.* San Diego, CA: Hughes Aircraft Company.

Nies, S. 1986. The Ada Object-Oriented Approach. *Proceedings of the First International Conference on Ada Programming Language Applications for the NASA Space Station.* Houston, TX: NASA Lyndon B. Johnson Space Center.

Ossher, H. 1987. A Mechanism for Specifying the Structure of Large, Layered, Systems. In *Research Directions in Object-Oriented Programming*, ed. B. Schriver and P. Wegner. Cambridge, MA: The MIT Press.

Page-Jones, M., Constantine, L., and Weiss, S. October 1990. Modeling Object-Oriented Systems: The Uniform Object Notation. *Computer Language* vol. 7(10).

Parnas, D. 1979. On the Criteria to Be Used in Decomposing Systems into Modules. *Classics in Software Engineering*, ed. E. Yourdon. New York, NY: Yourdon Press.

Parnas, D., Clements, P., and Weiss, D. March 1985. The Modular Structure of Complex Systems. *IEEE Transactions on Software Engineering* vol. SE-11(3).

Pasik, A., and Schor, M. January 1984. Object-Centered Representation and Reasoning. *SIGART Newsletter* no. 87.

Rajlich, V., and Silva, J. 1987. *Two Object-Oriented Decomposition Methods*. Detroit, MI: Wayne State University.

Ramamoorthy, C., and Sheu, P. Fall 1988. Object-Oriented Systems. *IEEE Expert* vol. 3(3).

Reenskaug, T. August 1981. User-Oriented Descriptions of Smalltalk Systems. *Byte* vol. 6(8).

Reiss, S. 1987. An Object-Oriented Framework for Conceptual Programming. In *Research Directions in Object-Oriented Programming*, ed. B. Schriver and P. Wegner. Cambridge, MA: The MIT Press.

Richter, C. August 1986. An Assessment of Structured Analysis and Structured Design. *Software Engineering Notes* vol. 11(4).

Rine, D. October 1987. A Common Error in the Object Structure of Object-Oriented Methods. *Software Engineering Notes* vol. 12(4).

Rosenberg, D., and Jennett, P. July 1992. Object-Oriented Analysis and Design Methods. *Frameworks* vol. 6(4).

Ross, R. 1987. *Entity Modeling: Techniques and Application*. Boston, MA: Database Research Group.

Rosson, M., and Gold, E. October 1989. Problem-Solution Mapping in Object-Oriented Design. *SIGPLAN Notices* vol. 24(10).

Rumbaugh, J., Blaha, M., Premerlani, W., Eddy, F., and Lorensen, W. 1991. *Object-Oriented Modeling and Design*. Englewood Cliffs, NJ: Prentice Hall.

Sahraoui, A. 1987. *Towards a Design Approach Methodology Combining OOP and Petri Nets for Software Production*. Toulouse, France: Laboratoire d'Automatique et d'analyses des systemes du C.N.R.S.

Sakai, H. 1983. A Method for Entity-Relationship Behavior Modeling. In *Entity-Relationship Approach to Software Engineering*, ed. C. Davis et al. Amsterdam, The Netherlands: Elsevier Science.

Seidewitz, E. May 1985. *Object Diagrams*. Greenbelt, MD: NASA Goddard Space Flight Center.

Seidewitz, E., and Stark, M. 1986a. Towards a General Object-Oriented Software Development Methodology. *Proceedings of the First International Conference on Ada Programming Language Applications for the NASA Space Station*. Houston, TX: NASA Lyndon B. Johnson Space Center.

————. August 1986b. *General Object-Oriented Software Development*. Report SEL-86-002. Greenbelt, MD: NASA Goddard Space Flight Center.

————. July/August 1987. Towards a General Object-Oriented Design Methodology. *Ada Letters* vol. 7(4).

————. 1988. *An Introduction to General Object-Oriented Software Development*. Rockville, MD: Millennium Systems.

Shilling, J., and Sweeney, P. October 1989. Three Steps to Views: Extending the Object-Oriented Paradigm. *SIGPLAN Notices* vol. 24(10).

Shlaer, S., Mellor, S., and Hywari, W. 1990. *OODLE: A Language-Independent Notation for Object-Oriented Design*. Berkeley, CA: Project Technology, California.

Shumate, K. 1987. *Layered Virtual Machine/Object-Oriented Design*. San Diego, CA: Hughes Aircraft Company.

Smith, M., and Tockey, S. 1988. *An Integrated Approach to Software Requirements Definition Using Objects*. Seattle, WA: Boeing Commercial Airplane Support Division.

Solsi, S., and Jones, E. March/April 1991. Simple Yet Complete Heuristics for Transforming Data Flow Diagrams into Booch Style Diagrams. *Ada Letters* vol. XI(2).

Song, X. May 1992. *Comparing Software Design Methodologies Through Process Modeling*. Irvine, CA: University of California.

Stark, M. April 1986. *Abstraction Analysis: From Structured Analysis to Object-Oriented Design*. Greenbelt, MD: NASA Goddard Space Flight Center.

Strom, R. October 1986. A Comparison of the Object-Oriented and Process Paradigms. *SIGPLAN Notices* vol. 21(10).

Teledyne Brown Engineering. October 1987. *Software Methodology Catalog*, Report MC87-COMM/ADP-0036. Tinton Falls, NJ.

The Fusion Object-Oriented Analysis and Design Method. May 1992. Bristol, England: Hewlett Packard Laboratories.

Thomas, D. May/June 1989. In Search of an Object-Oriented Development Process. *Journal of Object-Oriented Programming* vol. 2(1).

Wahl, S. December 13, 1988. Introduction to Object-Oriented Software. *C++ Tutorial Program of the USENIX Conference*. Denver, CO: USENIX Association.

Walters, N. July/August 1991. An Ada Object-Based Analysis and Design Approach. *Ada Letters* vol. XI(5).

Wasserman, T., Pircher, P., and Muller, R. December 1988. *An Object-Oriented Structured Design Method for Code Generation.* San Francisco, CA: Interactive Development Environments.

————. Summer 1989. Concepts of Object-Oriented Structured Design. *American Programmer* vol. 2(7–8).

————. March 1990. The Object-Oriented Structured Design Notation for Software Design Representation. *IEEE Computer* vol. 23(3).

Webster, D. December 1988. Mapping the Design Information Representation Terrain. *IEEE Spectrum* vol. 21(12).

Williams, L. 1986. *The Object Model in Software Engineering.* Boulder, CO: Software Engineering Research.

Wirfs-Brock, R., and Wilkerson, B. October 1989. Object-Oriented Design: A Responsibility-Driven Approach. *SIGPLAN Notices* vol. 24(10).

Wirfs-Brock, R., Wilkerson, B., and Wiener, L. 1990. *Designing Object-Oriented Software.* Englewood Cliffs, NJ: Prentice Hall.

Xong, X., and Osterweil, L. June 1992. *A Detailed Objective Comparison and Integration of Two Object-Oriented Design Methodologies.* Irvine, CA: University of California.

Yau, S., and Tsai, J. June 1986. A Survey of Software Design Techniques. *IEEE Transactions on Software Engineering* vol. SE-12(6).

Zachman, J. 1987. A Framework for Information Systems Architecture. *IBM Systems Journal* vol. 26(3).

Zimmerman, R. 1983. Phases, Methods, and Tools—A Triad of System Development. In *Entity-Relationship Approach to Software Engineering*, ed. C. Davis et al. Amsterdam, The Netherlands: Elsevier Science.

G. Object-Oriented Programming

Ada and C++: Business Case Analysis. July 1991. Washington, DC: Deputy Assistant Secretary of the Air Force.

Adams, S. July 1986. MetaMethods: The MVC Paradigm. *HOOPLA: Hooray for Object-Oriented Programming Languages* vol. 1(4). Everette, WA: Object-Oriented Programming for Smalltalk Applications Developers Association.

Agha, G. October 1986. An Overview of Actor Languages. *SIGPLAN Notices* vol. 21(10).

————. 1988. *Actors: A Model of Concurrent Computation in Distributed Systems.* Cambridge, MA: The MIT Press.

Agha, G., and Hewitt, C. 1987. Actors: A Conceptual Foundation for Concurrent Object-Oriented Programming. In *Research Directions in Object-Oriented Programming*, ed. B. Schriver and P. Wegner. Cambridge, MA: The MIT Press.

Aksit, M., and Tripathi, A. September 1988. Data Abstraction Mechanisms in Sina/st. *SIGPLAN Notices* vol. 23(11).

Albano, A. June 1983. Type Hierarchies and Semantic Data Models. *SIGPLAN Notices* vol. 18(6).

Almes, G., Black, A., Lazowska, E., and Noe, J. January 1985. The Eden System: A Technical Review. *IEEE Transactions on Software Engineering* vol. SE-11(1).

Alpert, S., Woyak, S., Shrobe, H., and Arowood, L. December 1990. Object-Oriented Programming in AI. *IEEE Expert* vol. 5(6).

Althoff, J. August 1981. Building Data Structures in the Smalltalk-80 System. *Byte* vol. 6(8).

Ambler, A. 1980. Gypsy: A Language for Specification and Implementation of Verifiable Programs. In *Programming Language Design*, ed. A. Wasserman. New York, NY: Computer Society Press.

America, P. 1987. POOL-T: A Parallel Object-Oriented Language. In *Object-Oriented Concurrent Programming*, ed. Yonezawa and M. Tokoro. Cambridge, MA: The MIT Press.

Apple Computer. 1989. *MacApp: The Expandable Macintosh Application*, version 2.0B9. Cupertino, CA.

————. *Macintosh Programmer's Workshop Pascal 3.0 Reference*. Cupertino, CA.

AT&T Bell Laboratories. 1989. *UNIX System V ATT C++ Language System, Release 2.0 Library Manual*. Murray Hill, NJ.

————. *UNIX System V ATT C++ Language System, Release 2.0 Product Reference Manual*. Murray Hill, NJ.

————. *UNIX System V ATT C++ Language System, Release 2.0 Release Notes*. Murray Hill, NJ.

————. *UNIX System V ATT C++ Language System, Release 2.0 Selected Readings*. Murray Hill, NJ.

Attardi, G. 1987. Concurrent Strategy Execution in Omega. In *Object-Oriented Concurrent Programming*, ed. Yonezawa and M. Tokoro. Cambridge, MA: The MIT Press.

Bach, I. November/December 1982. On the Type Concept of Ada. *Ada Letters* vol. II(3).

Badrinath, B., and Ramamritham, K. May 1988. Synchronizing Transactions on Objects. *IEEE Transactions on Computers* vol. 37(5).

Ballard, M., Maier, D., and Wirfs-Brock, A. November 1986. QUICKTALK: A Smalltalk-80 Dialect for Defining Primitive Methods. *SIGPLAN Notices* vol. 21(11).

Beaudet, P., and Jenkins, M. June 1988. Simulating the Object-Oriented Paradigm in Nial. *SIGPLAN Notices* vol. 23(6).

Bennett, J. October 1987. The Design and Implementation of Distributed Smalltalk. *SIGPLAN Notices* vol. 22(12).

Bergin, J., and Greenfield, S. March 1988. What Does Modula-2 Need to Fully Support Object-Oriented Programming? *SIGPLAN Notices* vol. 23(3).

Bhaskar, K. October 1983. How Object-Oriented Is Your System? *SIGPLAN Notices* vol. 18(10).

Birman, K., Joseph, T., Raeuchle, T., and Abbadi, A. June 1985. Implementing Fault-Tolerant Distributed Objects. *IEEE Transactions on Software Engineering* vol. SE-11(6).

Birtwistle, G., Dahl, O-J., Myhrhaug, B., and Nygard, K. 1979. *Simula begin*. Lund, Sweden: Studentlitteratur.

Black, A., Hutchinson, N., Jul, E., and Levy, H. November 1986. Object Structure in the Emerald System. *SIGPLAN Notices* vol. 21(11).

Black, A., Hutchinson, N., Jul, E., Levy, H., and Carter, L. July 1986. *Distribution and Abstract Types in Emerald*. Report 86-02-04. Seattle, WA: University of Washington.

Blaschek, G. 1989. Implementation of Objects in Modula-2. *Structured Programming* vol. 10(3).

Blaschek, G., Pomberger, G., and Stritzinger, A. 1989. A Comparison of Object-Oriented Programming Languages. *Structured Programming* vol. 10(4).

Block, F., and Chan, N. October 1989. An Extended Frame Language. *SIGPLAN Notices* vol. 24(10).

Bobrow, D. November 1984. *If Prolog Is the Answer, What Is the Question?* Palo Alto, CA: Xerox Palo Alto Research Center.

————. 1985. An Overview of KRL, a Knowledge Representation Language. In *Readings in Knowledge Representation*, ed. R. Brachman and H. Levesque. Los Altos, CA: Morgan Kaufmann.

Bobrow, D., DeMichiel, L., Gabriel, R., Keene, S., Kiczales, G., and Moon, D. September 1988. Common Lisp Object System Specification X3J13 Document 88-002R. *SIGPLAN Notices* vol. 23.

Bobrow, D., Kahn, K., Kiczales, G., Masinter, L., Stefik, M., and Zdybel, F. August 1985. *COMMONLOOPS: Merging Common Lisp and Object-Oriented Programming*, Report ISL-85-8. Palo Alto, CA: Xerox Palo Alto Research Center, Intelligent Systems Laboratory.

Borgida, A. January 1985. Features of Languages for the Development of Information Systems at the Conceptual Level. *IEEE Software* vol. 2(1).

————. October 1986. Exceptions in Object-Oriented Languages. *SIGPLAN Notices* vol. 21(10).

Borning, A., and Ingalls, D. 1982a. A Type Declaration and Inference System for Smalltalk. Palo Alto, CA: Xerox Palo Alto Research Center.

————. 1982b. Multiple Inheritance in Smalltalk-80. *Proceedings of the National Conference on Artificial Intelligence*. Menlo Park, CA: AAAI.

Bos, J. September 1987. PCOL—A Protocol-Constrained Object Language. *SIGPLAN Notices* vol. 22(9).

Briot, J., and Cointe, P. October 1989. Programming with Explicit Metaclasses in Smalltalk. *SIGPLAN Notices* vol. 24(10).

Buzzard, G., and Mudge, T. 1987. Object-Based Computing and the Ada Programming Language. In *Object-Oriented Computing: Concepts* vol. 1, ed. G. Peterson. New York, NY: Computer Society Press of the IEEE.

Canning, P., Cook, W., Hill, W., and Olthoff, W. October 1989. Interfaces for Strongly Typed Object-Oriented Programming. *SIGPLAN Notices* vol. 24(10).

Caudill, P., and Wirfs-Brock, A. November 1986. A Third Generation Smalltalk-80 Implementation. *SIGPLAN Notices* vol. 21(11).

Chambers, C., Ungar, D., and Lee, E. October 1989. An Efficient Implementation of Self, a Dynamically Typed Object-Oriented Language Based on Prototypes. *SIGPLAN Notices* vol. 24(10).

Chang, S. 1990. *Visual Languages and Visual Programming*. New York, NY: Plenum Press.

Chin, R., and Chanson, S. March 1991. Distributed Object-Based Programming Systems. *ACM Computing Surveys* vol. 23(1).

Clark, K. December 1988. PARLOG and Its Application. *IEEE Transactions on Software Engineering* vol. 14(12).

Cleaveland, C. 1980. Programming Languages Considered as Abstract Data Types. *Communications of the ACM*.

Coad, P., and Nicola, J. 1993. *Object-Oriented Programming*. Englewood Cliffs, NJ: Yourdon Press.

Cointe, P. October 1987. Metaclasses Are First Class: The ObjVlisp Model. *SIGPLAN Notices* vol. 22(12).

Connor, R., Dearle, A., Morrison, R., and Brown, A. October 1989. An Object Addressing Mechanism for Statically Typed Languages with Multiple Inheritance. *SIGPLAN Notices* vol. 24(10).

Conrad, J., Dengler, P., Francis, B., Glynn, J., Harvey, B., Hollis, B., Ramachandran, R., Schenken, J., Short, S., and Ullman, C. 2001. *Introducing .NET*. Birmingham, United Kingdom: Wrox Press.

Conroy, T., and Pelegri-Llopart, E. 1983. An Assessment of Method-Lookup Caches for Smalltalk-80 Implementations. In *Smalltalk-80: Bits of History, Words of Advice*, ed. G. Krasner. Reading, MA: Addison-Wesley.

Coplien, J. 1992. *Advanced C++ Programming Styles and Idioms*. Reading, MA: Addison-Wesley.

Corradi, A., and Leonardi, L. December 1988. The Role of Opaque Types in Building Abstractions. *SIGPLAN Notices* vol. 23(12).

Cox, B. January 1983. The Object-Oriented Pre-compiler. *SIGPLAN Notices* vol. 18(1).

———. October/November 1983. Object-Oriented Programming in C. *Unix Review*.

———. January 1984. Message/Object Programming: An Evolutionary Change in Programming Technology. *IEEE Software* vol. 1(1).

———. February/March 1984. Object-Oriented Programming: A Power Tool for Software Craftsmen. *Unix Review*.

———. 1986. *Object-Oriented Programming: An Evolutionary Approach.* Reading, MA: Addison-Wesley.

Cox, B., and Hunt, B. August 1986. Objects, Icons, and Software-ICs. *Byte* vol. 11(8).

Cox, P., and Pietrzykowski, T. March 1989. *Prograph: A Pictorial View of Object-Oriented Programming.* Nova Scotia, Canada: Technical University of Nova Scotia.

deJong, P. October 1986. Compilation into Actors. *SIGPLAN Notices* vol. 21(10).

Deutsch, P. August 1981. Building Control Structures in the Smalltalk-80 System. *Byte* vol. 6(8).

———. 1983. Efficient Implementation of the Smalltalk-80 System. *Proceedings of the 11th Annual ACM Symposium on the Principles of Programming Languages.* New York, NY: Association of Computing Machinery.

Dewhurst, S., and Stark, K. 1989. *Programming in C++.* Englewood Cliffs, NJ: Prentice Hall.

Diederich, J., and Milton, J. May 1987. Experimental Prototyping in Smalltalk. *IEEE Software* vol. 4(3).

Dixon, R., McKee, T., Schweizer, P., and Vaughn, M. October 1989. A Fast Method Dispatcher for Compiled Languages with Multiple Inheritance. *SIGPLAN Notices* vol. 24(10).

Dony, C. August 1988. An Object-Oriented Exception Handling System for an Object-Oriented Language. *Proceedings of ECOOP'88: European Conference on Object-Oriented Programming.* New York, NY: Springer-Verlag.

Duff, C. August 1986. Designing an Efficient Language. *Byte* vol. 11(8).

Dussud, P. October 1989. TICLOS: An Implementation of CLOS for the Explorer Family. *SIGPLAN Notices* vol. 24(10).

Eccles, J. 1988. Porting from Common Lisp with Flavors to C++. *Proceedings of USENIX C++ Conference.* Berkeley, CA: USENIX Association.

Edelson, D. September 1987. How Objective Mechanisms Facilitate the Development of Large Software Systems in Three Programming Languages. *SIGPLAN Notices* vol. 22(9).

Ellis, M., and Stroustrup, B. 1990. *The Annotated C++ Reference Manual*. Reading, MA: Addison-Wesley.

Endres, T. May 1985. Clascal—An Object-Oriented Pascal. *Computer Language* vol. 2(5).

Entsminger, G. 1990. *The Tao of Objects*. Redwood City, CA: M & T Books.

Filman, R. October 1987. Retrofitting Objects. *SIGPLAN Notices* vol. 22(12).

Finzer, W., and Gould, L. June 1984. Programming by Rehearsal. *Byte* vol. 9(6).

Foote, B., and Johnson, R. October 1989. Reflective Facilities in Smalltalk-80. *SIGPLAN Notices* vol. 24(10).

Freeman-Benson, B. October 1989. A Module Mechanism for Constraints in Smalltalk. *SIGPLAN Notices* vol. 24(10).

Fukunaga, K., and Jirose, S. November 1986. An Experience with a Prolog-Based Object-Oriented Language. *SIGPLAN Notices* vol. 21(11).

Gabriel, R., White, J., and Bobrow, D. September 1991. CLOS Integrating Object-Oriented and Functional Programming. *Communications of the ACM* vol. 34(9).

Goldberg, A. August 1981. Introducing the Smalltalk-80 System. *Byte* vol. 6(8).

———. September 1988. Programmer as Reader. *IEEE Software* vol. 4(5).

Goldberg, A., and Kay, A. March 1976. *Smalltalk-72 Instruction Manual*. Palo Alto, CA: Xerox Palo Alto Research Center.

———. 1977. *Methods for Teaching the Programming Language Smalltalk*. Report SSL 77-2. Palo Alto, CA: Xerox Palo Alto Research Center.

Goldberg, A., and Pope, S. Summer 1989. Object-Oriented Programming Is Not Enough. *American Programmer* vol. 2(7–8).

Goldberg, A., and Robson, D. 1983. *Smalltalk-80: The Language and Its Implementation*. Reading, MA: Addison-Wesley.

———. 1989. *Smalltalk-80: The Language*. Reading, MA: Addison-Wesley.

Goldberg, A., and Ross, J. August 1981. Is the Smalltalk-80 System for Children? *Byte* vol. 6(8).

Goldstein, T. May 1989. The Object-Oriented Programmer. *The C++ Report* vol. 1(5).

Gonsalves, G., and Silvestri, A. December 1986. Programming in Smalltalk-80: Observations and Remarks from the Newly Initiated. *SIGPLAN Notices* vol. 21(12).

Gorlen, K. 1989. An Introduction to C++. In *UNIX System V ATT C++ Language System, Release 2.0 Selected Readings*. Murray Hill, NJ: ATT Bell Laboratories.

Gorlen, K., Orlow, S., and Plexico, P. 1990. *Data Abstraction and Object-Oriented Programming in C++*. New York, NY: John Wiley and Sons.

Gougen, J., and Meseguer, J. 1987. Unifying Functional, Object-Oriented, and Relational Programming with Logical Semantics. In *Research Directions in Object-Oriented Programming*, ed. B. Schriver and P. Wegner. Cambridge, MA: The MIT Press.

Graube, N. August 1988. Reflexive Architecture: From ObjVLisp to CLOS. *Proceedings of ECOOP'88: European Conference on Object-Oriented Programming*. New York, NY: Springer-Verlag.

Grogono, P. November 1989. Polymorphism and Type Checking in Object-Oriented Languages. *SIGPLAN Notices* vol. 24(11).

———. 1991. Issues in the Design of an Object-Oriented Programming Language. *Structured Programming* vol. 12(1).

Hagmann, R. 1983. Preferred Classes: A Proposal for Faster Smalltalk-80 Execution. In *Smalltalk-80: Bits of History, Words of Advice*, ed. G. Krasner. Reading, MA: Addison-Wesley.

Hailpern, B., and Nguyen, V. 1987. A Model for Object-Based Inheritance. In *Research Directions in Object-Oriented Programming*, ed. B. Schriver and P. Wegner. Cambridge, MA: The MIT Press.

Halbert, D., and O'Brien, P. September 1988. Using Types and Inheritance in Object-Oriented Programming. *IEEE Software* vol. 4(5).

Halstead, R. 1987. Object Management on Distributed Systems. In *Object-Oriented Computing: Implementations* vol. 2, ed. G. Peterson. New York, NY: Computer Society Press of the IEEE.

Harland, D., Szyplewski, M., and Wainwright, J. October 1985. An Alternative View of Polymorphism. *SIGPLAN Notices* vol. 20(10).

Hendler, J. October 1986. Enhancement for Multiple Inheritance. *SIGPLAN Notices* vol. 21(10).

Hines, T., and Unger, E. 1986. *Conceptual Object-Oriented Programming*. Manhattan, KS: Kansas State University.

Ingalls, D. 1978. The Smalltalk-76 Programming System Design and Implementation. *Proceedings of the Fifth Annual ACM Symposium on Principles of Programming Languages*. New York, NY: Association of Computing Machinery.

———. August 1981a. Design Principles Behind Smalltalk. *Byte* vol. 6(8).

———. August 1981b. The Smalltalk Graphics Kernel. *Byte* vol. 6(8).

———. 1983. The Evolution of the Smalltalk Virtual Machine. In *Smalltalk-80: Bits of History, Words of Advice*, ed. G. Krasner. Reading, MA: Addison-Wesley.

———. November 1986. A Simple Technique for Handling Multiple Polymorphism. *SIGPLAN Notices* vol. 21(11).

Ishikawa, Y., and Tokoro, M. 1987. Orient84/K: An Object-Oriented Concurrent Programming Language for Knowledge Representation. In *Object-Oriented Concurrent Programming*, ed. Yonezawa and M. Tokoro. Cambridge, MA: The MIT Press.

Jackson, M. May 1988. Objects and Other Subjects. *SIGPLAN Notices* vol. 23(5).

Jacky, J., and Kalet, I. September 1987. An Object-Oriented Programming Discipline for Standard Pascal. *Communications of the ACM* vol. 30(9).

Jacobson, I. November 1986. Language Support for Changeable, Large, Real-Time Systems. *SIGPLAN Notices* vol. 21(11).

Jeffery, D. February 1989. Object-Oriented Programming in ANSI C. *Computer Language*.

Jenkins, M., and Glasgow, J. January 1986. Programming Styles in Nial. *IEEE Software* vol. 3(1).

Johnson, R. November 1986. Type-Checking Smalltalk. *SIGPLAN Notices* vol. 21(11).

Johnson, R., Graver, J., and Zurawski, L. September 1988. TS: An Optimizing Compiler for Smalltalk. *SIGPLAN Notices* vol. 23(11).

Kaehler, T. November 1986. Virtual Memory on a Narrow Machine for an Object-Oriented Language. *SIGPLAN Notices* vol. 21(11).

Kaehler, T., and Patterson, D. 1986. *A Taste of Smalltalk*. New York, NY: W. W. Norton.

———. August 1986. A Small Taste of Smalltalk. *Byte* vol. 11(8).

Kahn, K., Tribble, E., Miller, M., and Bobrow, D. November 1986. Objects in Concurrent Logic Programming Languages. *SIGPLAN Notices* vol. 21(11).

———. 1987. Vulcan: Logical Concurrent Objects. In *Research Directions in Object-Oriented Programming*, ed. B. Schriver and P. Wegner. Cambridge, MA: The MIT Press.

Kaiser, G., and Garlan, D. October 1987. MELDing Data Flow and Object-Oriented Programming. *SIGPLAN Notices* vol. 22(12).

Kalme, C. March 27, 1986. *Object-Oriented Programming: A Rule-Based Perspective*. Los Angeles, CA: Inference Corporation.

Kay, A. *New Directions for Novice Programming in the 1980s*. Palo Alto, CA: Xerox Palo Alto Research Center.

Keene, S. 1989. *Object-Oriented Programming in Common Lisp*. Reading, MA: Addison-Wesley.

Kelly, K., Rischer, R., Pleasant, M., Steiner, D., McGrew, C., Rowe, J., and Rubin, M. March 30, 1986. *Textual Representations of Object-Oriented Programs for Future Programmers*. Palo Alto, CA: Xerox AI Systems.

Kempf, R. October 1987. Teaching Object-Oriented Programming with the KEE System. *SIGPLAN Notices* vol. 22(12).

Kempf, J., Harris, W., D'Souza, R., and Snyder, A. October 1987. Experience with CommonLoops. *SIGPLAN Notices* vol. 22(12).

Khoshafian, S., and Copeland, G. November 1986. Object Identity. *SIGPLAN Notices* vol. 21(11).

Kiczales, G., Rivieres, J., and Bobrow, D. 1991. *The Art of the Metaobject Protocol*. Cambridge, MA: The MIT Press.

Kilian, M. April 1987. *An Overview of the Trellis/Owl Compiler*. Hudson, MA: Digital Equipment Corporation.

Kimminau, D., and Seagren, M. 1987. *Comparison of Two Prototype Developments Using Object-Based Programming*. Naperville, IL: AT&T Bell Laboratories.

Knowledge Systems Corporation. 1987. *PluggableGauges Version 1.0 User Manual*. Cary, NC.

Knudsen, J., and Madsen, O. August 1988. Teaching Object-Oriented Programming Is More Than Teaching Object-Oriented Programming Languages. *Proceedings of ECOOP'88: European Conference on Object-Oriented Programming*. New York, NY: Springer-Verlag.

Knudsen, J. August 1988. Name Collision in Multiple Classification Hierarchies. *Proceedings of ECOOP'88: European Conference on Object-Oriented Programming*. New York, NY: Springer-Verlag.

Korson, T., and McGregor, J. September 1990. Understanding Object-Oriented: A Unifying Paradigm. *Communications of the ACM* vol. 33(9).

Koshmann, T., and Evens, M. July 1988. Bridging the Gap Between Object-Oriented and Logic Programming. *IEEE Software* vol. 5(4).

Koskimies, K., and Paakki, J. July 1987. TOOLS: A Unifying Approach to Object-Oriented Language Interpretation. *SIGPLAN Notices* vol. 22(7).

Krasner, G. August 1981. The Smalltalk-80 Virtual Machine. *Byte* vol. 6(8).

———, ed. 1983. *Smalltalk-80: Bits of History, Words of Advice*. Reading, MA: Addison-Wesley.

Krasner, G., and Pope, S. August/September 1988. A Cookbook for Using the Model-View-Controller User Interface Paradigm in Smalltalk-80. *Journal of Object-Oriented Programming* vol. 1(3).

Kristensen, B., Madsen, O., Moller-Pedersen, B., and Nygaard, K. 1987. The BETA Programming Language. In *Research Directions in Object-Oriented Programming*, ed. B. Schriver and P. Wegner. Cambridge, MA: The MIT Press.

LaLonde, W. April 1989. Designing Families of Data Types Using Exemplars. *ACM Transactions on Programming Languages and Systems* vol. 11(2).

LaLonde, W., and Pugh, J. 1990. *Inside Smalltalk* vol. 1 and 2. Englewood Cliffs, NJ: Prentice Hall.

LaLonde, W., Thomas, D., and Pugh, J. November 1986. An Examplar Based Smalltalk. *SIGPLAN Notices* vol. 21(11).

Lang, K., and Peralmutter, B. November 1986. Oaklisp: An Object-Oriented Scheme with First Class Types. *SIGPLAN Notices* vol. 21(11).

Laursen, J., and Atkinson, R. October 1987. Opus: A Smalltalk Production System. *SIGPLAN Notices* vol. 22(12).

Lieberherr, K., and Holland, I. March 1989. Formulations and Benefits of the Law of Demeter. *SIGPLAN Notices* vol. 24(3).

———. September 1989. Assuring Good Style for Object-Oriented Programs. *IEEE Software* vol. 6(5).

Lieberherr, K., Holland, I., Lee, G., and Riel, A. June 1988. An Objective Sense of Style. *IEEE Computer* vol. 21(6).

Lieberman, H. November 1986. Using Prototypical Objects to Implement Shared Behavior in Object-Oriented Systems. *SIGPLAN Notices* vol. 21(11).

———. 1987. Concurrent Object-Oriented Programming in Act 1. In *Object-Oriented Concurrent Programming*, ed. A. Yonezawa and M. Tokoro. Cambridge, MA: The MIT Press.

Lieberman, H., Stein, L., and Ungar, D. May 1988. Of Types and Prototypes: The Treaty of Orlando. *SIGPLAN Notices* vol. 23(5).

Lim, J., and Johnson, R. April 1989. The Heart of Object-Oriented Concurrent Programming. *SIGPLAN Notices* vol. 24(4).

Linowes, J. August 1988. It's an Attitude. *Byte* vol. 13(8).

Lippman, S., Lajoie, J., and Moo, B. 2005. *C++ Primer*. Fourth Edition. Boston, MA: Addison-Wesley.

Liskov, B., Atkinson, R., Bloom, T., Moss, E., Schaffert, C., Scheifler, R., and Snyder, R. 1981. *CLU Reference Manual*. New York, NY: Springer-Verlag.

Liskov, B., Snyder, A., Atkinson, R., and Schaffert, C. 1980. Abstraction Mechanisms in CLU. In *Programming Language Design*, ed. A. Wasserman. New York, NY: Computer Society Press.

Liu, C. March 1991. On the Object-Orientedness of C++. *SIGPLAN Notices* vol. 26(3).

Lujun, S., and Zhongxiu. August 1987. An Object-Oriented Programming Language for Developing Distributed Software. *SIGPLAN Notices* vol. 22(8).

MacLennan, B. 1987. Values and Objects in Programming Languages. In *Object-Oriented Computing: Concepts* vol. 1, ed. G. Peterson. New York, NY: Computer Society Press of the IEEE.

Madsen, O. 1987. Block Structure and Object-Oriented Languages. In *Research Directions in Object-Oriented Programming*, ed. B. Schriver and P. Wegner. Cambridge, MA: The MIT Press.

Madsen, O., and Moller-Pedersen, B. August 1988. What Object-Oriented Programming May Be—And What It Does Not Have to Be. *Proceedings of ECOOP'88: European Conference on Object-Oriented Programming*. New York, NY: Springer-Verlag.

———. October 1989. Virtual Classes: A Powerful Mechanism in Object-Oriented Programming. *SIGPLAN Notices* vol. 24(10).

Manci, D. 1990. *Use of Metrics to Evaluate C++*. Liberty Corner, NJ: AT&T Bell Laboratories.

Mannino, M., Choi, I., and Batory, D. November 1990. The Object-Oriented Functional Data Language. *IEEE Transactions on Software Engineering* vol. 16(11).

Marcus, R. November 1985. Generalized Inheritance. *SIGPLAN Notices* vol. 20(11).

Markowitz, V., and Raz, Y. 1983. Eroll: An Entity-Relationship, Role-Oriented Query Language. In *Entity-Relationship Approach to Software Engineering*, ed. C. Davis et al. Amsterdam, The Netherlands: Elsevier Science.

Masini, G., Napoli, A., Colnet, D., Leonard, D., and Tompre, K. 1991. *Object-Oriented Languages*. London, England: Academic Press.

Mellender, F. October 1988. An Integration of Logic and Object-Oriented Programming. *SIGPLAN Notices* vol. 23(10).

Methfessel, R. April 1987. Implementing an Access and Object-Oriented Paradigm in a Language That Supports Neither. *SIGPLAN Notices* vol. 22(4).

Meyer, B. November 1986. Genericity versus Inheritance. *SIGPLAN Notices* vol. 21(11).

———. February 1987. Eiffel: Programming for Reusability and Extendability. *SIGPLAN Notices* vol. 22(2).

———. November/December 1988. Harnessing Multiple Inheritance. *Journal of Object-Oriented Programming* vol. 1(4).

Micallef, J. April/May 1988. Encapsulation, Reusability, and Extensibility in Object-Oriented Programming Languages. *Journal of Object-Oriented Programming* vol. 1(1).

Microsoft C++ Tutorial. 1992. Redmond, WA: Microsoft Corporation.

Microsoft Windows Guide to Programming. 1992. Redmond, WA: Microsoft Corporation.

Minsky, N., and Rozenshtein, D. October 1987. A Law-Based Approach to Object-Oriented Programming. *SIGPLAN Notices* vol. 22(12).

————. October 1989. Controllable Delegation: An Exercise in Law-Governed Systems. *SIGPLAN Notices* vol. 24(10).

Miranda, E. October 1987. BrouHaHa—A Portable Smalltalk Interpreter. *SIGPLAN Notices* vol. 22(12).

Mittal, S., Bobrow, D., and Kahn, K. November 1986. Virtual Copies: At the Boundary Between Classes and Instances. *SIGPLAN Notices* vol. 21(11).

Moon, D. November 1986. Object-Oriented Programming with Flavors. *SIGPLAN Notices* vol. 21(11).

Morrison, R., Dearle, A., Connor, R., and Brown, A. July 1991. An Ad Hoc Approach to the Implementation of Polymorphism. *ACM Transactions on Programming Languages and Systems* vol. 13(3).

Mossenbock, H., and Templ, J. 1989. Object Oberon—A Modest Object-Oriented Language. *Structured Programming* vol. 10(4).

Mudge, T. March 1985. Object-Based Computing and the Ada Language. *IEEE Computer* vol. 18(3).

Murray, R. 1990. *C++ Tactics*. Liberty Corner, NJ: AT&T Bell Laboratories.

Nelson, M. October 1991. Concurrency and Object-Oriented Programming. *SIGPLAN Notices* vol. 26(10).

Nierstrasz, O. October 1987. Active Objects in Hybrid. *SIGPLAN Notices* vol. 22(12).

Novak, G. June 1983. Data Abstraction in GLISP. *SIGPLAN Notices* vol. 18(6).

————. Fall 1983. GLISP: A Lisp-Based Programming System with Data Abstraction. *AI Magazine* vol. 4(3).

Nygaard, K. October 1986. Basic Concepts in Object-Oriented Programming. *SIGPLAN Notices* vol. 21(10).

Nygaard, K., and Dahl, O-J. 1981. The Development of the Simula Languages. In *History of Programming Languages*, ed. R. Wexelblat. New York, NY: Academic Press.

O'Brien, P. November 15, 1985. *Trellis Object-Based Environment: Language Tutorial*. Hudson, MA: Digital Equipment Corporation.

O'Grady, F. July/August 1990. Is There Life After COBOL? *American Programmer* vol. 3(7–8).

Object-Oriented Programming Workshop. October 1986. *SIGPLAN Notices* vol. 21(10).

Olthoff, W. 1986. *Augmentation of Object-Oriented Programming by Concepts of Abstract Data Type Theory: The ModPascal Experience*. Kaiserslautern, West Germany: University of Kaiserslautern.

Osterbye, K. June/July 1988. Active Objects: An Access-Oriented Framework for Object-Oriented Languages. *Journal of Object-Oriented Programming* vol. 1(2).

Paepcke, A. October 1989. PCLOS: A Critical Review. *SIGPLAN Notices* vol. 24(10).

Parc Place Systems. 1988. *The Smalltalk-80 Programming System Version VI 2.3*. Palo Alto, CA.

Pascoe, G. August 1986. Elements of Object-Oriented Programming. *Byte* vol. 11(8).

————. November 1986. Encapsulators: A New Software Paradigm in Smalltalk-80. *SIGPLAN Notices* vol. 21(11).

Perez, E. September/October 1988. Simulating Inheritance with Ada. *Ada Letters* vol. 8(7).

Peterson, G., ed. 1987. *Object-Oriented Computing Concepts*. New York, NY: Computer Society Press of the IEEE.

Pinson, L., and Wiener, R. 1988. *An Introduction to Object-Oriented Programming and Smalltalk*. Reading, MA: Addison-Wesley.

Pohl, I. 1989. *C++ for C Programmers*. Redwood City, CA: Benjamin/Cummings.

Pokkunuri, B. November 1989. Object-Oriented Programming. *SIGPLAN Notices* vol. 24(11).

Ponder, C., and Bush, B. June 1992. Polymorphism Considered Harmful. *SIGPLAN Notices* vol. 27(6).

Pountain, D. August 1986. Object-Oriented FORTH. *Byte* vol. 11(8).

Proceedings of ECOOP'88: European Conference on Object-Oriented Programming. August 1988. New York, NY: Springer-Verlag.

Proceedings of OOPSLA'86: Object-Oriented Programming Systems, Languages, and Applications. November 1986. *SIGPLAN Notices* vol. 21(11).

Proceedings of OOPSLA'87: Object-Oriented Programming Systems, Languages, and Applications. October 1987. *SIGPLAN Notices* vol. 22(12).

Proceedings of OOPSLA'88: Object-Oriented Programming Systems, Languages, and Applications. September 1988. *SIGPLAN Notices* vol. 23(11).

Proceedings of OOPSLA'89: Object-Oriented Programming Systems, Languages, and Applications. October 1989. *SIGPLAN Notices* vol. 24(10).

Proceedings of OOPSLA'90. Object-Oriented Programming Systems, Languages, and Applications. October 1990. *SIGPLAN Notices* vol. 25(10).

Proceedings of OOPSLA'91. Object-Oriented Programming Systems, Languages, and Applications. November 1991. *SIGPLAN Notices* vol. 26(11).

Proceedings of OOPSLA'92. Object-Oriented Programming Systems, Languages, and Applications. October 1992. *SIGPLAN Notices* vol. 27(10).

Proceedings of the ACM SIGPLAN Workshop on Object-Based Concurrent Programming. April 1989. *SIGPLAN Notices* vol. 24(4).

Proceedings of the USENIX Association C++ Workshop. November 1987. Berkeley, CA: USENIX Association.

Proceedings of the Workshop on Data Abstraction, Databases, and Conceptual Modeling. 1980. *SIGPLAN Notices* vol. 16(1).

Pugh, J. March 1984. Actors—The Stage Is Set. *SIGPLAN Notices* vol. 19(3).

Rathke, C. 1986. *ObjTalk: Repräsentation von Wissen in einer objektorientierten Sprache.* Stuttgart, West Germany: Institut für Informatik der Universität Stuttgart.

Rentsch, T. September 1982. Object-Oriented Programming. *SIGPLAN Notices* vol. 17(12).

Rettig, M., Morgan, T., Jacobs, J., and Wimberly, D. January 1989. Object-Oriented Programming in AI. *AI Expert.*

Robson, D. August 1981. Object-Oriented Software Systems. *Byte* vol. 6(8).

Rumbaugh, J. October 1987. Relations as Semantic Constructs in an Object-Oriented Language. *SIGPLAN Notices* vol. 22(12).

Russo, V., and Kaplan, S. 1988. A C++ Interpreter for Scheme. *Proceedings of USENIX C++ Conference.* Berkeley, CA: USENIX Association.

Sakkinen, M. August 1988. On the Darker Side of C++. *Proceedings of ECOOP'88: European Conference on Object-Oriented Programming.* New York, NY: Springer-Verlag.

———. December 1988. Comments on "the Law of Demeter" and C++. *SIGPLAN Notices* vol. 23(12).

Saltzer, J. 1979. Naming and Binding of Objects. In *Operating Systems*, ed. R. Bayer et al. New York, NY: Springer-Verlag.

Sandberg, D. November 1986. An Alternative to Subclassing. *SIGPLAN Notices* vol. 21(11).

———. October 1988. Smalltalk and Exploratory Programming. *SIGPLAN Notices* vol. 23(10).

Saunders, J. March/April 1989. A Survey of Object-Oriented Programming Languages. *Journal of Object-Oriented Programming* vol. 1(6).

Schaffert, C., Cooper, T., and Wilpolt, C. November 25, 1985. *Trellis Object-Based Environment: Language Reference Manual.* Hudson, MA: Digital Equipment Corporation.

Schaffert, C., Cooper, T., Bullis, B., Kilian, M., and Wilpolt, C. November 1986. An Introduction to Trellis/Owl. *SIGPLAN Notices* vol. 21(11).

Schmucker, K. 1986a. MacApp: An Application Framework. *Byte* vol. 11(8).

———. 1986b. Object-Oriented Languages for the Macintosh. *Byte* vol. 11(8).

———. 1986c. *Object-Oriented Programming for the Macintosh*. Hasbrouk Heights, NJ: Hayden.

Schriver, B., and Wegner, P., eds. 1987. *Research Directions in Object-Oriented Programming*. Cambridge, MA: The MIT Press.

Seidewitz, E. October 1987. Object-Oriented Programming in Smalltalk and Ada. *SIGPLAN Notices* vol. 22(12).

———. March/April 1992. Object-Oriented Programming with Mixins in Ada. *Ada Letters* vol. XII(2).

Shafer, D. 1988. *Hyper Talk Programming*. Indianapolis, IN: Hayden.

Shah, A., Rumbaugh, J., Hamel, J., and Borsari, R. October 1989. DSM: An Object-Relationship Modeling Language. *SIGPLAN Notices* vol. 24(10).

Shammas, N. October 1988. Smalltalk a la C. *Byte* vol. 13(10).

Shan, Y. October 1989. An Event-Driven Model-View-Controller Framework for Smalltalk. *SIGPLAN Notices* vol. 24(10).

Shapiro, J. 1991. *A C++ Toolkit*. Englewood Cliffs, NJ: Prentice Hall.

Shaw, M. 1981. *ALPHARD: Form and Content*. New York, NY: Springer-Verlag.

Shibayama, E. September 1988. How to Invent Distributed Implementation Schemes of an Object-Based Concurrent Language—A Transformational Approach. *SIGPLAN Notices* vol. 23(11).

Shibayama, E., and Yonezawa, A. 1987. Distributed Computing in ABCL/1. In *Object-Oriented Concurrent Programming*, ed. Yonezawa and M. Tokoro. Cambridge, MA: The MIT Press.

Shopiro, J. December 13, 1988. Programming Techniques with C++. *C++ Tutorial Program of the USENIX Conference*. Denver, CO: USENIX Association.

———. December 1989. An Example of Multiple Inheritance in C++: A Model of the Iostream Library. *SIGPLAN Notices* vol. 24(12).

Simonian, R., and Crone, M. November/December 1988. InnovAda: True Object-Oriented Programming in Ada. *Journal of Object-Oriented Programming* vol. 1(4).

Snyder, A. February 1985. *Object-Oriented Programming for Common Lisp*. Report ATC-85-1. Palo Alto, CA: Hewlett-Packard.

———. November 1986. Encapsulation and Inheritance in Object-Oriented Programming Languages. *SIGPLAN Notices* vol. 21(11).

————. 1987. Inheritance and the Development of Encapsulated Software Components. In *Research Directions in Object-Oriented Programming*, ed. B. Schriver and P. Wegner. Cambridge, MA: The MIT Press.

————. January 1993. The Essence of Objects: Concepts and Terms. *IEEE Software* vol. 10(1).

Software Productivity Solutions. 1988. *Classical-Ada User Manual*. Melbourne, FL.

Stankovic, J. April 1982. Software Communication Mechanisms: Procedure Calls versus Messages. *IEEE Computer* vol. 15(4).

Stefik, M., and Bobrow, D. Winter 1986. Object-Oriented Programming: Themes and Variations. *AI Magazine* vol. 6(4).

Stefik, M., Bobrow, D., Mittal, S., and Conway, L. Fall 1983. Knowledge Programming in Loops. *AI Magazine* vol. 4(3).

Stein, L. October 1987. Delegation Is Inheritance. *SIGPLAN Notices* vol. 22(12).

Stroustrup, B. January 1982. Classes: An Abstract Data Type Facility for the C Language. *SIGPLAN Notices* vol. 17(1).

————. October 1986. An Overview of C++. *SIGPLAN Notices* vol. 21(10).

————. 1987. The Evolution of C++. *Proceedings of the USENIX C++ Workshop*. Santa Fe, NM: USENIX Association.

————. November 1987. Possible Directions for C++. *Proceedings of the USENIX C++ Workshop*. Santa Fe, NM: USENIX Association.

————. 1988a. Parameterized Types for C++. *Proceedings of USENIX C++ Conference*. Berkeley, CA: USENIX Association.

————. May 1988b. What Is Object-Oriented Programming? *IEEE Software* vol. 5(3).

————. August 1988c. A Better C? *Byte* vol. 13(8).

————. 1991. *The C+ Programming Language*. Second Edition. Reading, MA: Addison-Wesley.

————. 2000. *The C++ Programming Language*. Special Third Edition. Boston, MA: Addison-Wesley.

Suzuki, N. 1981. Inferring Types in Smalltalk. In *Proceedings of the Eighth Annual Symposium of ACM Principles of Programming Languages*. New York, NY: Association of Computing Machinery.

Suzuki, N., and Terada, M. 1983. Creating Efficient Systems for Object-Oriented Languages. *Proceedings of the 11th Annual ACM Symposium on the Principles of Programming Languages*. New York, NY: Association of Computing Machinery.

Symposium on Actor Languages. October 1980. *Creative Computing*.

Tektronix. 1988. Modular Smalltalk.

Tesler, L. August 1986. Programming Experiences. *Byte* vol. 11(8).

The Smalltalk-80 System. August 1981. *Byte* vol. 6(8).

Thomas, D. March 1989. What's in an Object? *Byte* vol. 14(3).

Tieman, M. May 1, 1988. *User's Guide to GNU C++*. Cambridge, MA: Free Software Foundation.

Tokoro, M., and Ishikawa, Y. October 1986. Concurrent Programming in Orient84/K: An Object-Oriented Knowledge Representation Language. *SIGPLAN Notices* vol. 21(10).

Touati, H. May 1987. Is Ada an Object-Oriented Programming Language? *SIGPLAN Notices* vol. 22(5).

Touretzky, D. 1986. *The Mathematics of Inheritance Systems*. Los Altos, CA: Morgan Kaufman Publishers.

Tripathi, A., and Berge, E. An Implementation of the Object-Oriented Concurrent Programming Language SINA. *Software—Practice and Experience* vol. 19(3).

U.S. Department of Defense. February 1983. *Reference Manual for the Ada Programming Language*. Washington, DC: Ada Joint Program Office.

Ungar, D. September 1988. Are Classes Obsolete? *SIGPLAN Notices* vol. 23(11).

Ungar, D., and Smith, R. October 1987. Self: The Power of Simplicity. *SIGPLAN Notices* vol. 22(12).

van den Bos, J., and Laffra, C. October 1989. PROCOL: A Parallel Object Language with Protocols. *SIGPLAN Notices* vol. 24(10).

Vaucher, J., Lapalme, G., and Malenfant, J. August 1988. SCOOP: Structured Concurrent Object-Oriented Prolog. *Proceedings of ECOOP'88: European Conference on Object-Oriented Programming*. New York, NY: Springer-Verlag.

Warren, S., and Abbe, D. May 1980. Presenting Rosetta Smalltalk. *Datamation*.

Watanabe, T., and Yonezawa, A. September 1988. Reflection in an Object-Oriented Concurrent Language. *SIGPLAN Notices* vol. 23(11).

Wegner, P. October 1987. Dimensions of Object-Based Language Design. *SIGPLAN Notices* vol. 22(12).

———. January 1988. Workshop on Object-Oriented Programming at ECOOP 1987. *SIGPLAN Notices* vol. 23(1).

———. August 1990. Concepts and Paradigms of Object-Oriented Programming. *OOPS Messenger* vol. 1(1).

———. October 1992. Dimensions of Object-Oriented Modeling. *IEEE Computer* vol. 25(10).

Wiener, R. June 1987. Object-Oriented Programming in C++—A Case Study. *SIGPLAN Notices* vol. 22(6).

Williams, G. Summer 1989. Designing the Future: The Power of Object-Oriented Programming. *American Programmer* vol. 2(7–8).

Wilson, R. November 1, 1987. Object-Oriented Languages Reorient Programming Techniques. *Computer Design* vol. 26(20).

Winblad, A., Edwards, S., and King, D. 1990. *Object-Oriented Software*. Reading, MA: Addison-Wesley.

Winston, P., and Horn, B. 1989. *Lisp*. Third Edition. Reading, MA: Addison-Wesley.

Wirfs-Brock, R., and Wilkerson, B. September 1988. An Overview of Modular Smalltalk. *SIGPLAN Notices* vol. 23(11).

Wirth, N. June 1987. Extensions of Record Types. *SIGCSE Bulletin* vol. 19(2).

———. July 1988a. From Modula to Oberon. *Software—Practice and Experience* vol. 18(7).

———. July 1988b. The Programming Language Oberon. *Software—Practice and Experience* vol. 18(7).

Wolf, W. September 1989. A Practical Comparison of Two Object-Oriented Languages. *IEEE Software* vol. 6(5).

Yokote, Y., and Tokoro, M. November 1986. The Design and Implementation of Concurrent Smalltalk. *SIGPLAN Notices* vol. 21(11).

———. October 1987. Experience and Evolution of Concurrent Smalltalk. *SIGPLAN Notices* vol. 22(12).

Yonezawa, A., and Tokoro, M., eds. 1987. *Object-Oriented Concurrent Programming*. Cambridge, MA: The MIT Press.

Yonezawa, A., Briot, J., and Shibayama, E. November 1986. Object-Oriented Concurrent Programming in ABCL/1. *SIGPLAN Notices* vol. 21(11).

Yonezawa, A., Shibayama, E., Takada, T., and Honda, Y. 1987. Modeling and Programming in an Object-Oriented Concurrent Language ABCL/1. In *Object-Oriented Concurrent Programming*, ed. Yonezawa and M. Tokoro. Cambridge, MA: The MIT Press.

Yourdon, E. February 1990. Object-Oriented COBOL. *American Programmer* vol. 3(2).

———. January 1992. Modeling Magic. *American Programmer* vol. 5(1).

Zave, P. September 1989. A Compositional Approach to Multiparadigm Programming. *IEEE Software* vol. 6(5).

H. Software Engineering

Abdel-Hamid, T., and Madnick, S. 1991. *Software Project Dynamics*. Englewood Cliffs, NJ: Prentice Hall.

Abelson, H., and Sussman, G. 1985. *Structure and Interpretation of Computer Programs*. Cambridge, MA: The MIT Press.

Andrews, D., and Leventhal, N. 1993. *FUSION: Integrating IE, CASE, and JAD: A Handbook for Reengineering the Systems Organization*. Englewood Cliffs, NJ: Yourdon Press.

Appleton, D. January 15, 1986. Very Large Projects. *Datamation*.

Aron, J. 1974a. *The Program Development Process: The Individual Programmer*. Vol. 1. Reading, MA: Addison-Wesley.

————. 1974b. *The Program Development Process: The Programming Team*. Vol. 2. Reading, MA: Addison-Wesley.

Babich, W. 1986. *Software Configuration Management*. Reading, MA: Addison-Wesley.

Ben-Ari, M. 1982. *Principles of Concurrent Programming*. Englewood Cliffs, NJ: Prentice Hall.

Berard, E. 1993. *Essays on Object-Oriented Software Engineering*. Englewood Cliffs, NJ: Prentice Hall.

Berson, A. 1992. Client/Server Architecture. New York, NY: McGraw-Hill.

Berzins, V., and Luqi. 1991. *Software Engineering with Abstractions*. Reading, MA: Addison-Wesley.

Biggerstaff, T., and Perlis, A. 1989. *Software Reusability*. New York, NY: ACM Press.

Bisant, D., and Lyle, J. October 1989. A Two-Person Inspection Method to Improve Programming Productivity. *IEEE Transactions on Software Engineering* vol. 15(10).

Bischofberger, W., and Keller, R. 1989. Enhancing the Software Life Cycle by Prototyping. *Structured Programming*.

Bloom, P. April 1993. Trends in Client-Server/Cooperative Processing Application Development Tools. *American Programmer*.

Boar, B. 1984. *Application Prototyping*. New York, NY: John Wiley and Sons.

Boehm, B. August 1986. A Spiral Model of Software Development and Enhancement. *Software Engineering Notes* vol. 11(4).

————. September 1992. Risk Control. *American Programmer* vol. 5(7).

Boehm, B. 1989. *IEEE Tutorial on Software Risk Management*. IEEE Computer Society Press.

————. October 2002. Software Risk Management: Overview and Recent Developments. *17th International Forum on COCOMO and Software Cost Modeling*. Los Angeles, CA.

Boehm, B., and Papaccio, P. 1988. Understanding and Controlling Software Costs. *IEEE Transactions on Software Engineering* vol. 4(10).

Boehm-Davis, D., and Ross, L. October 1984. *Approaches to Structuring the Software Development Process*. Report GEC/DIS/TR-84-B1V-1. Arlington, VA: General Electric.

Booch, G. 1986. *Software Engineering with Ada*. Menlo Park, CA: Benjamin/ Cummings.

Brooks, F. 1975. *The Mythical Man-Month*. Reading, MA: Addison-Wesley.

————. April 1987. No Silver Bullet: Essence and Accidents of Software Engineering. *IEEE Computer* vol. 20(4).

Charette, R. 1989. *Software Engineering Risk Analysis and Management*. New York, NY: McGraw-Hill.

Chidamber, S., and Kemerer, C. 1991. *Towards a Metrics Suite for Object-Oriented Design*. Phoenix, Arizona: OOPSLA'91.

————. 1993. *A Metrics Suite for Object-Oriented Design*. Cambridge, MA: MIT Sloan School of Management.

Chmura, L., Norcio, A., and Wicinski, T. July 1990. Evaluating Software Design Processes by Analyzing Change Date Over Time. *IEEE Transactions on Software Engineering* vol. 16(7).

Corkill, D. D. September 1991. Blackboard Systems. *AI Expert* vol. 6(9), pp. 40–47.

Cox, B. November 1990. Planning the Software Industrial Revolution. *IEEE Software* vol. 7(6).

Curtis, B. May 17, 1989. . . .*But You Have to Understand, This Isn't the Way We Develop Software at Our Company*. MCC Technical Report Number STP-203-89. Austin, TX: Microelectronics and Computer Technology Corporation.

Curtis, B., Kellner, M., and Over, J. September 1992. Process Modeling. *Communications of the ACM* vol. 35(9).

Dahl, O., Dijkstra, E., and Hoare, C. A. R. 1972. *Structured Programming*. London, England: Academic Press.

Davis, A. 1990. *Software Requirements: Analysis and Specification*. Englewood Cliffs, NJ: Prentice Hall.

Davis, A., Bersoff, E., and Comer, E. October 1988. A Strategy for Comparing Alternative Software Development Life Cycle Models. *IEEE Transactions on Software Engineering* vol. 14(10).

Davis, C., Jajodia, S., Ng, P., and Yeh, R., eds. 1983. *Entity-Relationship Approach to Software Engineering*. Amsterdam, The Netherlands: Elsevier Science.

DeMarco, T., and Lister, T. 1987. *Peopleware*. New York, NY: Dorset House.

DeRemer, F., and Kron, H. 1980. Programming-in-the-Large versus Programming-in-the-Small. In *Tutorial on Software Design Techniques*, Third Edition, ed. P. Freeman and A. Wasserman. New York, NY: Computer Society Press of the IEEE.

Dewire, D. 1992. *Client/Server Computing*. New York, NY: McGraw-Hill.

Dijkstra, E. 1979. Programming Considered as a Human Activity. In *Classics in Software Engineering*, ed. E. Yourdon. New York, NY: Yourdon Press.

———. 1982. *Selected Writings on Computing: A Personal Perspective*. New York, NY: Springer-Verlag.

Dowson, M. August 1986. The Structure of the Software Process. *Software Engineering Notes* vol. 11(4).

Dowson, M., Nejmeh, B., and Riddle, W. February 1990. *Software Engineering Practices in Europe, Japan, and the U.S.* Boulder, CO: Software Design and Analysis.

Dreger, B. 1989. *Function Point Analysis*. Englewood Cliffs, NJ: Prentice Hall.

Eastman, N. 1984. Software Engineering and Technology. *Technical Directions* vol. 10(1). Bethesda, MD: IBM Federal Systems Division.

Fagan, M. June 1976. *Design and Code Inspections and Process Control in the Development of Programs*. IBM-TR-00.73.

Foster, C. 1981. *Real-Time Programming*. Reading, MA: Addison-Wesley.

Freedman, D. February 1992. The Devil Is in the Details: Everything Important Must Be Reviewed. *American Programmer* vol. 5(2).

Freeman, P. 1975. *Software Systems Principles*. Chicago, IL: Science Research Associates.

Freeman, P., and Wasserman, A., eds. 1983. *Tutorial on Software Design Techniques*. Fourth Edition. New York, NY: Computer Society Press of the IEEE.

Gehani, N., and McGettrick, A. 1986. *Software Specification Techniques*. Reading, MA: Addison-Wesley.

Gilb, T. 1988. *Principles of Software Engineering Management*. Reading, MA: Addison-Wesley.

Glass, R. 1982. *Modern Programming Practices: A Report from Industry*. Englewood Cliffs, NJ: Prentice Hall.

———. 1983. *Real-Time Software*. Englewood Cliffs, NJ: Prentice Hall.

————. 1991. *Software Conflict*. Englewood Cliffs, NJ: Yourdon Press.

Goldberg, A., and Rubin, K. 1992. *Tutorial on Object-Oriented Project Management*. Vancouver, Canada: OOPSLA'92.

Guengerich, S. 1992. *Downsizing Information Systems*. Carmel, IN: Sams.

Guindon, R., Krasner, H., and Curtis, B. 1987. *Breakdowns and Processes During the Early Activities of Software Design by Professionals. Empirical Studies of Programmers, Second Workshop*. Norwood, NJ: Ablex Publishing Company.

Guttman, M., and Matthews, J. November/December 1992. Managing a Large Project. *Object Magazine* vol. 2(4).

Hansen, P. 1977. *The Architecture of Concurrent Programs*. Englewood Cliffs, NJ: Prentice Hall.

Hantos, P. 2005. Inherent Risks in Object-Oriented Development. U.S. Air Force Software Technology Support Center (STSC): *CrossTalk, The Journal of Defense Software Engineering*.

Henderson-Sellers, B. 1996. *Object-Oriented Metrics: Measures of Complexity*. Upper Saddle River, NJ: Prentice Hall.

Henderson-Sellers, B., and Edwards, J. September 1990. The Object-Oriented Systems Lifecycle. *Communications of the ACM* vol. 33(9).

Hoare, C. April 1984. Programming: Sorcery or Science? *IEEE Software* vol. 1(2).

Holt, R., Lazowska, E., Graham, G., and Scott, M. 1978. *Structured Concurrent Programming*. Reading, MA: Addison-Wesley.

Humphrey, W. 1988. Characterizing the Software Development Process: A Maturity Framework. *IEEE Software* vol. 5(2).

————. 1989. *Managing the Software Process*. Reading, MA: Addison-Wesley.

Hunt, J. May 2002. Blackboard Architectures. JayDee Technology Ltd 27. www.agent.ai/doc/upload/200402/hunt02_1.pdf.

IEEE-Std-1220-2005. 2005. *IEEE Standard for Application and Management of the Systems Engineering Process*. New York, NY: IEEE.

IEEE-Std-12207.0-1996. 1996. *Standard for Information Technology—Software Life Cycle Processes*. New York, NY: IEEE.

IEEE-Std-12207.1-1997. 1997a. *Standard for Information Technology—Software Life Cycle Processes—Life Cycle Data*. New York, NY: IEEE.

IEEE-Std-12207.2-1997. 1997b. *Standard for Information Technology—Software Life Cycle Processes—Implementation Considerations*. New York, NY: IEEE.

Jackson, M. 1975. *Principles of Program Design*. Orlando, FL: Academic Press.

————. 1983. *System Development*. Englewood Cliffs, NJ: Prentice Hall.

Jensen, R., and Tonies, C. 1979. *Software Engineering*. Englewood Cliffs, NJ: Prentice Hall.

Jones, C. September 1984. Reusability in Programming: A Survey of the State of the Art. *IEEE Transactions on Software Engineering* vol. SE-10(5).

————. September 1992. Risky Business: The Most Common Software Risks. *American Programmer* vol. 5(7).

Kan, S. H. 2002. *Metrics and Models in Software Quality Engineering*. Second Edition. Boston, MA: Addison-Wesley.

Karam, G., and Casselman, R. February 1993. A Cataloging Framework for Software Development Methods. *IEEE Computer*.

Kemerer, C., and Darcy, D. November/December 2005. OO Metrics in Practice. *IEEE Software* vol. 22(6), p. 17.

Kishida, K., Teramoto, M., Torri, K., and Urano, Y. September 1988. Quality Assurance Technology in Japan. *IEEE Software* vol. 4(5).

Lammers, S. 1986. *Programmers at Work*. Redmond, WA: Microsoft Press.

Laranjeira, L. May 1990. Software Size Estimation of Object-Oriented Systems. *IEEE Transactions on Software Engineering* vol. 16(5).

Ledgard, H. Summer 1985. Programmers: The Amateur vs. the Professional. *Abacus* vol. 2(4).

Lejter, M., Myers, S., and Reiss, S. December 1992. Support for Maintaining Object-Oriented Programs. *IEEE Transactions on Software Engineering* vol. 18(12).

Linger, R., and Mills, H. 1977. On the Development of Large Reliable Programs. In *Current Trends in Programming Methodology: Software Specification and Design* vol. 1, ed. R. Yeh. Englewood Cliffs, NJ: Prentice Hall.

Linger, R., Mills, H., and Witt, B. 1979. *Structured Programming: Theory and Practice*. Reading, MA: Addison-Wesley.

Liskov, B., and Guttag, J. 1986. *Abstraction and Specification in Program Development*. Cambridge, MA: The MIT Press.

Lorenz, M., and Kidd, J. 1994. *Object-Oriented Software Metrics*. Englewood Cliffs, NJ: Prentice Hall.

Lorin, H. 1972. *Parallelism in Hardware and Software*. Englewood Cliffs, NJ: Prentice Hall.

Luqi. August 1990. A Graph Model for Software Evolution. *IEEE Transactions on Software Engineering* vol. 16(8).

————. May 1990. Software Evolution Through Rapid Prototyping. *IEEE Computer* vol. 22(5).

Martin, J., and McClure, C. 1988. *Structured Techniques: The Basis for CASE*. Englewood Cliffs, NJ: Prentice Hall.

Matsubara, T. July/August 1990. Bringing Up Software Designers. *American Programmer* vol. 3(7–8).

McCabe, T., and Butler, C. December 1989. Design Complexity Measurement and Testing. *Communications of the ACM* vol. 32(12).

Mellichamp, D. 1983. *Real-Time Computing*. New York, NY: Van Nostrand Reinhold.

Meyer, B. 1995. *Object Success: A Manager's Guide to Object-Oriented Technology and Its Impact on the Corporation*. Upper Saddle River, NJ: Prentice Hall.

Mills, H. November 1986. Structured Programming: Retrospect and Prospect. *IEEE Software* vol. 3(6).

Mills, J. July 1985. A Pragmatic View of the System Architect. *Communications of the ACM* vol. 28(7).

Mimno, P. April 1993. Cilent-Server Computing. *American Programmer*.

Mullin, M. 1990. *Rapid Prototyping for Object-Oriented Systems*. Reading, MA: Addison-Wesley.

Munck, R. 1985. Toward Large Software Systems That Work. *Proceedings of the AIAA/ACM/NASA/IEEE Computers in Aerospace V Conference*. Menlo Park, CA: AIAA.

Myers, G. 1978. *Composite/Structured Design*. New York, NY: Van Nostrand Reinhold.

Newport, J. April 28, 1986. A Growing Gap in Software. *Fortune*.

Ng, P., and Yeh, R. 1990. *Modern Software Engineering*. New York, NY: Van Nostrand Reinhold.

Office of the Under Secretary of Defense for Acquisition. September 1987. *Report of the Defense Science Board Task Force on Military Software*. Washington, DC.

The Official Handbook of Mascot, Version 3.1. June 1987. London, England: Crown Copyright.

Oman, P., and Lewis, T. 1990. *Milestones in Software Evolution*. Los Alamitos, CA: Computer Society Press of the IEEE.

Orr, K. 1971. *Structured Systems Development*. New York, NY: Yourdon Press.

Page-Jones, M. 1988. *The Practical Guide to Structured Systems Design*. Englewood Cliffs, NJ: Yourdon Press.

Parnas, D. December 1985. Software Aspects of Strategic Defense Systems. *Communications of the ACM* vol. 28(12).

———. July 1985a. Why Conventional Software Development Does Not Produce Reliable Programs. *Software Aspects of Strategic Defense Systems*. Report DCS-47-IR. Victoria, Canada: University of Victoria.

————. July 1985b. Why Software Is Unreliable. *Software Aspects of Strategic Defense Systems*. Report DCS-47-IR. Victoria, Canada: University of Victoria.

Parnas, D., and Clements, P. 1986. A Rational Design Process: How and Why to Fake It. *IEEE Transactions on Software Engineering* vol. SE-12(2).

Peters, L. 1981. *Software Design*. New York, NY: Yourdon Press.

Pressman, R. 1988. *Making Software Happen*. Englewood Cliffs, NJ: Prentice Hall.

————. 1992. *Software Engineering: A Practitioner's Approach*. Third Edition. New York, NY: McGraw-Hill.

Rakos, J. 1990. *Software Project Management for Small to Medium Sized Projects*. Englewood Cliffs, NJ: Prentice Hall.

Ramamoorthy, C., Garg, V., and Prakask, A. July 1986. Programming in the Large. *IEEE Transactions on Software Engineering* vol. SE-12(7).

Rechtin, E. October 1992. The Art of Systems Architecting. *IEEE Spectrum* vol. 29(10).

Rettig, M. October 1990. Software Teams. *Communications of the ACM* vol. 33(10).

Ross, D., Goodenough, J., and Irvine, C. 1980. Software Engineering: Process, Principles, and Goals. *Tutorial on Software Design Techniques*, Third Edition, ed. P. Freeman and A. Wasserman. New York, NY: Computer Society Press of the IEEE.

Rubinstein, R., and Hersh, H. 1984. *The Human Factor*. Burlington, MA: Digital Press.

Schulmeyer, G., and McManus, J. 1992. *Handbook of Software Quality Assurance*. Second Edition. New York, NY: Van Nostrand Reinhold.

Shaw, M. November 1990. Prospects for an Engineering Discipline of Software. *IEEE Software* vol. 7(6).

Smith, M., and Robson, D. June 1992. A Framework for Testing Object-Oriented Programs. *Journal of Object-Oriented Programming* vol. 5(3).

Software Process Workshop. May 1988. *SIGSOFT Software Engineering Notes* vol. 14(4).

Sommerville, I. 1989. *Software Engineering*. Third Edition. Wokingham, England: Addison-Wesley.

Song, X., and Osterweil, L. 1993. *Executing an Iterative Design Process*. Irvine, CA: University of California.

Spector, A., and Gifford, D. April 1986. Computer Science Perspective of Bridge Design. *Communications of the ACM* vol. 29(4).

Stevens, W., Myers, G., and Constantine, L. 1979. Structured Design. In *Classics in Software Engineering*, ed. E. Yourdon. New York, NY: Yourdon Press.

Symons, C. 1988. Function Point Analysis: Difficulties and Improvements. *IEEE Transactions on Software Engineering* vol. 14(1).

Taylor, D. 1990. *Object-Oriented Technology: A Manager's Guide*. Alameda, CA: Servio Corporation.

The Software Trap: Automate—Or Else. May 9, 1988. *Business Week*.

Thomsett, R. July/August 1990. Effective Project Teams. *American Programmer* vol. 3(7–8).

———. June 1991. Managing Superlarge Projects: A Contingency Approach. *American Programmer* vol. 4(6).

U.S. Department of Defense. July 30, 1982. *Report of the DoD Joint Service Task Force on Software Problems*. Washington, DC.

van Genuchten, M. June 1991. Why Is Software Late? An Empirical Study of Reasons for Delay in Software Development. *IEEE Transactions on Software Engineering* vol. 17(6).

Vick, C., and Ramamoorthy, C. 1984. *Software Engineering*. New York, NY: Van Nostrand Reinhold.

Vonk, R. 1990. *Prototyping*. Englewood Cliffs, NJ: Prentice Hall.

Walsh, J. 1992. *Preliminary Defect Data from the Iterative Development of a Large C++ Program*. Vancouver, Canada: OOPSLA'92.

———. January 1993. *Software Quality in an Iterative Object-Oriented Development Paradigm*. Santa Clara, CA: Rational.

Ward, M. 1990. *Software That Works*. San Diego, CA: Academic Press.

Ward, P., and Mellor, S. 1985. *Structured Development for Real-Time Systems: Introduction and Tools*. Englewood Cliffs, NJ: Yourdon Press.

Wegner, P. 1980. *Research Directions in Software Technology*. Cambridge, MA: The MIT Press.

———. July 1984. Capital-Intensive Software Technology. *IEEE Software* vol. 1(3).

Weinberg, G. 1988. *Understanding the Professional Programmer*. New York, NY: Dorset House Publishing.

Weinberg, G., and Freedman, D. 1990. *Handbook of Walkthroughs, Inspections, and Technical Reviews*. New York, NY: Dorset House.

Whitten, N. 1990. *Managing Software Development Projects*. New York, NY: John Wiley and Sons.

Wilde, N., and Huitt, R. December 1992. Maintenance Support for Object-Oriented Programs. *IEEE Transactions on Software Engineering* vol. 18(12).

Wilde, N., Matthews, P., and Huitt, R. January 1993. Maintaining Object-Oriented Software. *IEEE Software* vol. 10(1).

Wirth, N. 1986. *Algorithms and Data Structures*. Englewood Cliffs, NJ: Prentice Hall.

Workshop on Software Configuration Management. November 1989. *SIGSOFT Software Engineering Notes* vol. 17(7).

Yamaura, T. January 1992. Standing Naked in the Snow. *American Programmer* vol. 5(1).

Yeh, R., ed. 1977. *Current Trends in Programming Methodology: Software Specification and Design*. Englewood Cliffs, NJ: Prentice Hall.

Yourdon, E. 1975. *Techniques of Program Structure and Design*. Englewood Cliffs, NJ: Prentice Hall.

———, ed. 1979. *Classics in Software Engineering*. New York, NY: Yourdon Press.

———. 1989a. *Modern Structured Analysis*. Englewood Cliffs, NJ: Prentice Hall.

———. 1989b. *Structured Walkthroughs*. Englewood Cliffs, NJ: Prentice Hall.

———. August 1989c. The Year of the Object. *Computer Language* vol. 6(8).

———. Summer 1989d. Object-Oriented Observations. *American Programmer* vol. 2(7–8).

Yourdon, E., and Constantine, L. 1979. *Structured Design*. Englewood Cliffs, NJ: Prentice Hall.

Zahniseer, R. July/August 1990. Building Software in Groups. *American Programmer* vol. 3(7–8).

Zave, P. February 1984. The Operational versus the Conventional Approach to Software Development. *Communications of the ACM* vol. 27(2).

Zelkowitz, M. June 1978. Perspectives on Software Engineering. *ACM Computing Surveys* vol. 10(2).

I. Special References

Alexander, C. 1979. *The Timeless Way of Building*. New York, NY: Oxford University Press.

DeGrace, P., and Stahl, L. 1990. *Wicked Problems, Righteous Solutions*. Englewood Cliffs, NJ: Yourdon Press.

Fukuyama, F. 1992. *The End of History and the Last Man*. New York, NY: The Free Press.

Gall, J. 1986. *Systemantics: How Systems Really Work and How They Fail*. Second Edition. Ann Arbor, MI: The General Systemantics Press.

Gleick, J. 1987. *Chaos*. New York, NY: Penguin Books.

Heckbert, P. 1988. Ray Tracing Jell-O Brand Gelatin. *Communications of the ACM* vol. 31(2).

Heinlein, R. 1966. *The Moon Is a Harsh Mistress*. New York, NY: The Berkeley Publishing Group.

Hofstadter, D. 1979. *Gödel, Escher, Bach: An Eternal Golden Braid*. New York, NY: Vintage Books.

International Council on Systems Engineering (INCOSE). 2006. *INCOSE Systems Engineering Handbook*. Version 3. INCOSE-TP-2003-002-03.

Inside Macintosh vol. 1–5. 1988. Reading, MA: Addison-Wesley.

Kawasaki, G. 1990. *The Macintosh Way*. Glenview, IL: Scott, Foresman and Company.

Lakoff, G., and Johnson, M. 1980. *Metaphors We Live By*. Chicago, IL: The University of Chicago Press.

Lammers, S. 1986. *Programmers at Work*. Bellevue, WA: Microsoft Press.

Meyer, C., and Matyas, S. M. 1982. *Cryptography*. New York, NY: John Wiley and Sons.

Parker, T. 1983. *Rules of Thumb*. Boston, MA: Houghton Mifflin Company.

Peter, L. 1986. *The Peter Pyramid*. New York, NY: William Morrow.

Petroski, H. 1985. *To Engineer Is Human*. New York, NY: St. Martin's Press.

Rand, Ayn. 1979. *Introduction to Objectivist Epistemology*. New York, NY: New American Library.

Reti, L. 1988. *The Unknown Leonard*. New York, NY: Abradale Press.

Sears, F., Zemansky, M., and Young., H. 1987. *University Physics*. Seventh Edition. Reading, MA: Addison-Wesley.

U.S. Department of Commerce/National Institute of Standards and Technology. October 25, 1999. *Data Encryption Standard (DES), Federal Information Processing Standards Publication 46-3*.

vonOech, R. 1990. *A Whack on the Side of the Head*. New York, NY: Warner Books.

Wagner, J. 1986. *The Search for Signs of Intelligent Life in the Universe*. New York, NY: Harper and Row.

Whitehead, A. 1958. *An Introduction to Mathematics*. New York, NY: Oxford University Press.

J. Theory

Aho, A., Hopcroft, J., and Ullman, J. 1974. *The Design and Analysis of Computer Programs*. Reading, MA: Addison-Wesley.

Almarode, J. October 1989. Rule-Based Delegation for Prototypes. *SIGPLAN Notices* vol. 24(10).

Appelbe, W., and Ravn, A. April 1984. Encapsulation Constructs in Systems Programming Languages. *ACM Transactions on Programming Languages and Systems* vol. 6(2).

Averill, E. April 1982. Theory of Design and Its Relationship to Capacity Measurement. *Proceedings of the Fourth Annual International Conference on Computer Capacity Management*. San Francisco, CA: Association of Computing Machinery.

Barr, A., and Feigenbaum, E. 1981. *The Handbook of Artificial Intelligence*. Los Altos, CA: William Kaufmann.

Bastani, F., and Iyengar, S. March 1987. The Effect of Data Structures on the Logical Complexity of Programs. *Communications of the ACM* vol. 30(3).

Bastani, F., Hilal, W., and Sitharama, S. October 1987. Efficient Abstract Data Type Components for Distributed and Parallel Systems. *IEEE Computer* vol. 20(10).

Belkhouche, B., and Urban, J. May 1986. Direct Implementation of Abstract Data Types from Abstract Specifications. *IEEE Transactions on Software Engineering* vol. SE-12(5).

Bensley, E., Brando, T., and Prelle, M. September 1988. An Execution Model for Distributed Object-Oriented Computation. *SIGPLAN Notices* vol. 23(11).

Berztiss, A. 1980. Data Abstraction, Controlled Iteration, and Communicating Processes. *Communications of the ACM*.

Bishop, J. 1986. *Data Abstraction in Programming Languages*. Wokingham, England: Addison-Wesley.

Boehm, H., Demers, A., and Donahue, J. October 1980. *An Informal Description of Russell*. Technical Report TR 80-430. Ithaca, NY: Cornell University.

Borning, A., Duisberg, R., Freeman-Benson, B., Kramer, A., and Woolf, M. October 1987. Constraint Hierarchies. *SIGPLAN Notices* vol. 22(12).

Boute, R. January 1988. Systems Semantics: Principles, Applications, and Implementation. *ACM Transactions on Programming Languages and Systems* vol. 10(1).

Brachman, R. October 1983. What Is-a Is and Isn't: An Analysis of Taxonomic Links in Semantic Networks. *IEEE Computer* vol. 16(10).

Brachman, R., and Levesque, H., eds. 1985. *Readings in Knowledge Representation*. Los Altos, CA: Morgan Kaufmann.

Brooks, R. April 1987. *Intelligence without Representation*. Cambridge, MA: MIT Artificial Intelligence Laboratory.

Bruce, K., and Wegner, P. October 1986. An Algebraic Model of Subtypes in Object-Oriented Languages. *SIGPLAN Notices* vol. 21(10).

Card, S., Moran, T., and Newell, A. 1983. *The Psychology of Human-Computer Interaction*. Hillsdale, NJ: Lawrence Erlbaum Associates.

Cardelli, L., and Wegner, P. December 1985. On Understanding Types, Data Abstraction, and Polymorphism. *ACM Computing Surveys* vol. 17(4).

Claybrook, B., and Wyckof, M. 1980. Module: An Encapsulation Mechanism for Specifying and Implementing Abstract Data Types. *Communications of the ACM*.

Cline, A., and Rich, E. December 1983. *Building and Evaluating Abstract Data Types*. Report TR-83-26. Austin, TX: University of Texas, Department of Computer Sciences.

Cohen, A. January 1984. Data Abstraction, Data Encapsulation, and Object-Oriented Programming. *SIGPLAN Notices* vol. 19(1).

Cohen, N. November/December 1985. Tasks as Abstraction Mechanisms. *Ada Letters* vol. 5(3–6).

Cohen, P., and Loiselle, C. August 1988. Beyond ISA: Structures for Plausible Inference in Semantic Nets. *Proceedings of the Seventh National Conference on Artificial Intelligence*. Saint Paul, MN: American Association for Artificial Intelligence.

Collins, W. 1992. *Data Structures: An Object-Oriented Approach*. Reading, MA: Addison-Wesley.

Cook, W., and Palsberg, J. October 1989. A Denotational Semantics of Inheritance and Its Correctness. *SIGPLAN Notices* vol. 24(10).

Courtois, P., Heymans, F., and Parnas, D. October 1971. Concurrent Control with "Readers" and "Writers." *Communications of the ACM* vol. 14(10).

Danforth, S., and Tomlinson, C. March 1988. Type Theories and Object-Oriented Programming. *ACM Computing Surveys* vol. 20(1).

Demers, A., Donahue, J., and Skinner, G. Data Types as Values: Polymorphism, Type-Checking, Encapsulation. *Proceedings of the Fifth Annual ACM Symposium on Principles of Programming Languages*. New York, NY: Association of Computing Machinery.

Dennis, J., and Van Horn, E. March 1966. Programming Semantics for Multiprogrammed Computations. *Communications of the ACM* vol. 9(3).

Donahue, J., and Demers, A. July 1985. Data Types Are Values. *ACM Transactions on Programming Languages and Systems* vol. 7(3).

Eckart, J. April 1987. Iteration and Abstract Data Types. *SIGPLAN Notices* vol. 22(4).

Embley, D., and Woodfield, S. 1988. Assessing the Quality of Abstract Data Types Written in Ada. *Proceedings of the 10th International Conference on Software Engineering*. New York, NY: Computer Society Press of the IEEE.

Ferber, J. October 1989. Computational Reflection in Class-Based Object-Oriented Languages. *SIGPLAN Notices* vol. 24(10).

Fisher, J., and Gipson, D. November 1992. In Search of Elegance. *Computer Language* vol. 9(11).

Gannon, J., Hamlet, R., and Mills, H. July 1987. Theory of Modules. *IEEE Transactions on Software Engineering* vol. SE-13(7).

Gannon, J., McMullin, P., and Hamlet, R. July 1981. Data Abstraction Implementation, Specification, and Testing. *ACM Transactions on Programming Languages and Systems* vol. 3(3).

Gardner, M. May/June 1984. When to Use Private Types. *Ada Letters* vol. 3(6).

Goguen, J., Thatcher, J., and Wagner, E. 1977. An Initial Algebra Approach to the Specification, Correctness, and Implementation of Abstract Data Types. In *Current Trends in Programming Methodology: Data Structuring* vol. 4, ed. R. Yeh. Englewood Cliffs, NJ: Prentice Hall.

Goldberg, D. 1989. *Genetic Algorithms*. Reading, MA: Addison-Wesley.

Graube, N. October 1989. Metaclass Compatibility. *SIGPLAN Notices* vol. 24(10).

Gries, D., and Prins, J. July 1985. A New Notion of Encapsulation. *SIGPLAN Notices* vol. 20(7).

Grogono, P., and Bennett, A. November 1989. Polymorphism and Type Checking in Object-Oriented Languages. *SIGPLAN Notices* vol. 24(11).

Guttag, J. 1980. Abstract Data Types and the Development of Data Structures. In *Programming Language Design*, ed. A. Wasserman. New York, NY: Computer Society Press of the IEEE.

Hammons, C., and Dobbs, P. May/June 1985. Coupling, Cohesion, and Package Unity in Ada. *Ada Letters* vol. 4(6).

Harel, D., and Kahana, C. October 1992. On Statecharts with Overlapping. *ACM Transactions on Software Engineering and Methodology* vol. 1(4).

Harel, D., Lachover, H., Naamad, A., Pnueli, A., Politi, M., Sherman, R., Shtull-Trauring, S., and Trakhtenbrot, M. April 1990. STATEMATE: A Working Environment for the Development of Complex Reactive Systems. *IEEE Transactions on Software Engineering* vol. 16(4).

Harrison, G., and Liu, D. July/August 1986. Generic Implementations Via Analogies in the Ada Programming Language. *Ada Letters* vol. 6(4).

Hayes, P. 1981. The Logic of Frames. In *Readings in Artificial Intelligence*, ed. B. Webber and N. Nilsson. Palo Alto, CA: Tioga.

Hayes-Roth, F. July 1985. A Blackboard Architecture for Control. *Artificial Intelligence* vol. 26(3).

Hayes-Roth, F., Waterman, D., and Lenat, D. 1983. *Building Expert Systems.* Reading, MA: Addison-Wesley.

Haynes, C., and Friedman, D. October 1987. Embedding Continuations in Procedural Objects. *ACM Transactions on Programming Languages and Systems* vol. 9(4).

Henderson, P. February 1986. Functional Programming, Formal Specification, and Rapid Prototyping. *IEEE Transactions on Software Engineering* vol. SE-12(2).

Herlihy, M., and Liskov, B. October 1982. A Value Transmission Method for Abstract Data Types. *ACM Transactions on Programming Languages and Systems* vol. 4(4).

Hesselink, W. January 1988. A Mathematical Approach to Nondeterminism in Data Types. *ACM Transactions on Programming Languages and Systems* vol. 10(1).

Hibbard, P., Hisgen, A., Rosenbers, J., Shaw, M., and Sherman, M. 1981. *Studies in Ada Style.* New York, NY: Springer-Verlag.

Hilfinger, P. 1982. *Abstraction Mechanisms and Language Design.* Cambridge, MA: The MIT Press.

Hoare, C. October 1974. Monitors: An Operating System Structuring Concept. *Communications of the ACM* vol. 17(10).

Hoare, C. 1985. *Communicating Sequential Processes.* Englewood Cliffs, NJ: Prentice Hall.

Hogg, J., and Weiser, S. October 1987. OTM: Applying Objects to Tasks. *SIGPLAN Notices* vol. 22(12).

Jajodia, S., and Ng. P. 1983. On Representation of Relational Structures by Entity-Relationship Diagrams. In *Entity-Relationship Approach to Software Engineering*, ed. C. Davis et al. Amsterdam, The Netherlands: Elsevier Science.

Johnson, C. 1986. Some Design Constraints Required for the Assembly of Software Components: The Incorporation of Atomic Abstract Types into Generically Structured Abstract Types. *Proceedings of the First International Conference on Ada Programming Language Applications for the NASA Space Station.* Houston, TX: NASA Lyndon B. Johnson Space Center.

Kernighan, B., and Plauger, P. 1981. *Software Tools in Pascal.* Reading, MA: Addison-Wesley.

Knight, B. 1983. A Mathematical Basis for Entity Analysis. In *Entity-Relationship Approach to Software Engineering*, ed. C. Davis et al. Amsterdam, The Netherlands: Elsevier Science.

Knuth, D. 1973. *The Art of Computer Programming* vol. 1–3. Reading, MA: Addison-Wesley.

Kosko, B. 1992. *Neural Networks and Fuzzy Systems*. Englewood Cliffs, NJ: Prentice Hall.

LaLonde, W., and Pugh, J. August 1985. Specialization, Generalization, and Inheritance: Teaching Objectives Beyond Data Structures and Data Types. *SIGPLAN Notices* vol. 20(8).

Leeson, J., and Spear, M. March 1987. Type-Independent Modules: The Preferred Approach to Generic ADTs in Modula-2. *SIGPLAN Notices* vol. 22(3).

Lenzerini, M., and Santucci, G. 1983. Cardinality Constraints in the Entity-Relationship Model. In *Entity-Relationship Approach to Software Engineering*, ed. C. Davis et al. Amsterdam, The Netherlands: Elsevier Science.

Levesque, H. July 1984. Foundations of a Functional Approach to Knowledge Representation. *Artificial Intelligence* vol. 23(2).

Lindgreen, P. 1983. Entity Sets and Their Description. In *Entity-Relationship Approach to Software Engineering*, ed. C. Davis et al. Amsterdam, The Netherlands: Elsevier Science.

Lins, C. 1989. A First Look at Literate Programming. *Structured Programming*.

Liskov, B. 1980. Programming with Abstract Data Types. In *Programming Language Design*, ed. A. Wasserman. New York, NY: Computer Society Press of the IEEE.

———. May 1988. Data Abstraction and Hierarchy. *SIGPLAN Notices* vol. 23(5).

Liskov, B., and Scheifler, R. July 1983. Guardians and Actions: Linguistic Support for Robust, Distributed Programs. *ACM Transactions on Programming Languages and Systems* vol. 5(3).

Liskov, B., and Zilles, S. 1977. An Introduction to Formal Specifications of Data Abstractions. In *Current Trends in Programming Methodology: Software Specification and Design* vol. 1, ed. R. Yeh. Englewood Cliffs, NJ: Prentice Hall.

Lowry, M., and McCartney, R.. 1991. *Automating Software Design*. Cambridge, MA: The MIT Press.

Lucco, S. October 1987. Parallel Programming in a Virtual Object Space. *SIGPLAN Notices* vol. 22(12).

Maes, P. October 1987. Concepts and Experiments in Computational Reflection. *SIGPLAN Notices* vol. 22(12).

Mark, L. 1983. What Is the Binary Relationship Approach? In *Entity-Relationship Approach to Software Engineering*, ed. C. Davis et al. Amsterdam, The Netherlands: Elsevier Science.

Markowitz, V., and Raz, Y. 1983. A Modified Relational Algebra and Its Use in an Entity-Relationship Environment. In *Entity-Relationship Approach to Software Engineering*, ed. C. Davis et al. Amsterdam, The Netherlands: Elsevier Science.

Matsuoka, S., and Kawai, S. September 1988. Using Tuple Space Communication in Distributed Object-Oriented Languages. *SIGPLAN Notices* vol. 23(11).

McAllester, D., and Zabih, F. November 1986. Boolean Classes. *SIGPLAN Notices* vol. 21(11).

McCullough, P. October 1987. Transparent Forwarding: First Steps. *SIGPLAN Notices* vol. 22(12).

Merlin, P., and Bochmann, G. January 1983. On the Construction of Submodule Specifications and Communication Protocols. *ACM Transactions on Programming Languages and Systems* vol. 5(1)

Meyer, B. 1987. *Programming as Contracting*. Report TR-EI-12/CO. Goleta, CA: Interactive Software Engineering.

———. October 1992. Applying "Design by Contract." *IEEE Computer* vol. 25(10).

Minoura, T., and Iyengar, S. January 1989. Data and Time Abstraction Techniques for Multilevel Concurrent Systems. *IEEE Transactions on Software Engineering* vol. 15(1).

Murata, T. 1984. Modeling and Analysis of Concurrent Systems. In *Software Engineering*, ed. C. Vick and C. Ramamoorthy. New York, NY: Van Nostrand Reinhold.

Mylopoulos, J., and Levesque, H. 1984. An Overview of Knowledge Representation. In *On Conceptual Modeling: Perspectives from Artificial Intelligence, Databases, and Programming Languages*, ed. M. Brodie, J. Mylopoulos, and J. Schmidt. New York, NY: Springer-Verlag.

Nakano, R. 1983. Integrity Checking in a Logic-Oriented ER Model. In *Entity-Relationship Approach to Software Engineering*, ed. C. Davis et al. Amsterdam, The Netherlands: Elsevier Science.

Newton, M., and Watkins, J. November/December 1988. The Combination of Logic and Objects for Knowledge Representation. *Journal of Object-Oriented Programming* vol. 1(4).

Nii, P. Summer 1986. Blackboard Systems: The Blackboard Model of Problem Solving and the Evolution of Blackboard Architectures. *AI Magazine* vol. 7(2).

Ohori, A., and Buneman, P. October 1989. Static Type Inference for Parametric Classes. *SIGPLAN Notices* vol. 24(10).

Pagan, F. 1981. *Formal Specification of Programming Languages*. Englewood Cliffs, NJ: Prentice Hall.

Parent, C., and Spaccapieta, S. July 1985. An Algebra for a General Entity-Relationship Model. *IEEE Transactions on Software Engineering* vol. SE-11(7).

Parnas, D. 1977. The Influence of Software Structure on Reliability. In *Current Trends in Programming Methodology: Software Specification and Design* vol. 1, ed. R. Yeh. Englewood Cliffs, NJ: Prentice Hall.

———. 1980. Designing Software for Ease of Extension and Contraction. In *Tutorial on Software Design Techniques*, Third Edition, ed. P. Freeman and A. Wasserman. New York, NY: Computer Society Press of the IEEE.

Parnas, D., Clements, P., and Weiss, D. 1983. Enhancing Reusability with Information Hiding. *Proceedings of the Workshop on Reusability in Programming*, Stratford, CT: ITT Programming.

Pattee, H. 1973. *Hierarchy Theory.* New York, NY: George Braziller.

Peckham, J., and Maryanski, F. September 1988. Semantic Data Models. *ACM Computing Surveys* vol. 20(3).

Pedersen, C. October 1989. Extending Ordinary Inheritance Schemes to Include Generalization. *SIGPLAN Notices* vol. 24(10).

Peterson, J. September 1977. Petri Nets. *Computing Surveys* vol. 9(3).

Reed, D. September 1978. Naming and Synchronization in a Decentralized Computer System. Cambridge, MA: The MIT Press.

Rich, C., and Wills, L. January 1990. Recognizing a Program's Design: A Graph-Parsing Approach. *IEEE Software* vol. 7(1).

Robinson, L., and Levitt, K. 1977. Proof Techniques for Hierarchically Structured Programs. In *Current Trends in Programming Methodology: Program Validation* vol. 2, ed. R. Yeh. Englewood Cliffs, NJ: Prentice Hall.

Ross, D. July/August 1986. Classifying Ada Packages. *Ada Letters* vol. 6(4).

Ruane, L. January 1984. Abstract Data Types in Assembly Language Programming. *SIGPLAN Notices* vol. 19(1).

Rumbaugh, J. September 1988. Controlling Propagation of Operations Using Attributes on Relations. *SIGPLAN Notices* vol. 23(11).

Sedgewick, R. 1983. *Algorithms.* Reading, MA: Addison-Wesley.

Shankar, K. 1984. Data Design: Types, Structures, and Abstractions. In *Software Engineering*, ed. C. Vick and C. Ramamoorthy. New York, NY: Van Nostrand Reinhold.

Shaw, M. 1984. The Impact of Modeling and Abstraction Concerns on Modern Programming Languages. *On Conceptual Modeling: Perspectives from Artificial Intelligence, Databases, and Programming Languages*, ed. M. Brodie, J. Mylopoulos, and J. Schmidt. New York, NY: Springer-Verlag.

———. October 1984. Abstraction Techniques in Modern Programming Languages. *IEEE Software* vol. 1(4).

————. May 1989. Larger Scale Systems Require Higher-Level Abstractions. *SIGSOFT Engineering Notes* vol. 14(3).

Shaw, M., Feldman, G., Fitzgerald, R., Hilfinger, P., Kimura, I., London, R., Rosenberg, J., and Wulf, W. 1981. Validating the Utility of Abstraction Techniques. In *ALPHARD: Form and Content*, ed. M. Shaw. New York, NY: Springer-Verlag.

Shaw, M., Wulf, W., and London, R. 1981. Abstraction and Verification in ALPHARD: Iteration and Generators. In *ALPHARD: Form and Content*, ed. M. Shaw. New York, NY: Springer-Verlag.

Sherman, M., Hisgen, A., and Rosenberg, J. 1982. A Methodology for Programming Abstract Data Types in Ada. *Proceedings of the AdaTEC Conference on Ada*. New York, NY: Association of Computing Machinery.

Siegel, J. April 1988. Twisty Little Passages. *HOOPLA: Hooray for Object-Oriented Programming Languages* vol. 1(3). Everette, WA: Object Oriented Programming for Smalltalk Application Developers Association.

Stefik, M., Bobrow, D., and Kahn, K. January 1986. Integrating Access-Oriented Programming into a Multiparadigm Environment. *IEEE Software* vol. 3(1).

Strom, R., and Yemini, S. January 1986. Typestate: A Programming Language Concept for Enhancing Software Reliability. *IEEE Transactions on Software Engineering* vol. SE-12(1).

Stubbs, D., and Webre, N. 1985. *Data Structures with Abstract Data Types and Pascal*. Monterey, CA: Brooks/Cole.

Swaine, M. June 1988. Programming Paradigms. *Dr. Dobb's Journal of Software Tools* no. 140.

Tabourier, Y. 1983. Further Development of the Occurrences Structure Concept: The EROS Approach. In *Entity-Relationship Approach to Software Engineering*, ed. C. Davis et al. Amsterdam, The Netherlands: Elsevier Science.

Tanenbaum, A. 1981. *Computer Networks*. Englewood Cliffs, NJ: Prentice Hall.

Tenenbaum, A., and Augenstein, M. 1981. *Data Structures Using Pascal*. Englewood Cliffs, NJ: Prentice Hall.

Throelli, L. October 1987. Modules and Type Checking in PL/LL. *SIGPLAN Notices* vol. 22(12).

Tomlinson, C., and Singh, V. October 1989. Inheritance and Synchronization with Enabled-sets. *SIGPLAN Notices* vol. 24(10).

Toy, W. 1984. Hardware/Software Tradeoffs. In *Software Engineering*, ed. C. Vick and C. Ramamoorthy. New York, NY: Van Nostrand Reinhold.

Vegdahl, S. November 1986. Moving Structures between Smalltalk Images. *SIGPLAN Notices* vol. 21(11).

Walters, N. October 1992. Using Harel Statecharts to Model Object-Oriented Behavior. *SIGSOFT Notices* vol. 17(4).

Wasserman, A. 1980. Introduction to Data Types. In *Programming Language Design*, ed. A. Wasserman. New York, NY: Computer Society Press of the IEEE.

Weber, H., and Ehrig, H. July 1986. Specification of Modular Systems. *IEEE Transactions on Software Engineering* vol. SE-12(7).

Wegner, P. June 6, 1981. *The Ada Programming Language and Environment*. Unpublished draft.

————. 1987a. On the Unification of Data and Program Abstraction in Ada. In *Object-Oriented Computing: Concepts* vol. 1, ed. G. Peterson. New York, NY: Computer Society Press of the IEEE.

————. 1987b. The Object-Oriented Classification Paradigm. In *Research Directions in Object-Oriented Programming*, ed. B. Schriver and P. Wegner. Cambridge, MA: The MIT Press.

Wegner, P., and Zdonik, S. August 1988. Inheritance as an Incremental Modification Mechanism or What Like Is and Isn't Like. *Proceedings of ECOOP'88: European Conference on Object-Oriented Programming*. New York, NY: Springer-Verlag.

Weihl, W., and Liskov, B. April 1985. Implementation of Resilient, Atomic Data Types. *ACM Transactions on Programming Languages and Systems* vol. 7(2)

Weinberg, G. 1971. *The Psychology of Computer Programming*. New York, NY: Van Nostrand Reinhold.

Weller, D., and York, B. May 1984. A Relational Representation of an Abstract Type System. *IEEE Transactions on Software Engineering* vol. SE-10(3).

White, J. July 1983. On the Multiple Implementation of Abstract Data Types within a Computation. *IEEE Transactions on Software Engineering* vol. SE-9(4).

Wirth, N. December 1974. On the Composition of Well-Structured Programs. *Computing Surveys* vol. 6(4).

————. January 1983. Program Development by Stepwise Refinement. *Communications of the ACM* vol. 26(1).

————. 1986. *Algorithms and Data Structures*. Second Edition. Englewood Cliffs, NJ: Prentice Hall.

————. April 1988. Type Extensions. *ACM Transactions on Programming Languages and Systems* vol. 10(2).

Wolf, A., Clarke, L., and Wileden, J. April 1988. A Model of Visibility Control. *IEEE Transactions on Software Engineering* vol. 14(4).

Woods, W. October 1983. What's Important about Knowledge Representation? *IEEE Computer* vol. 16(10).

Zilles, S. 1984. Types, Algebras, and Modeling. In *On Conceptual Modeling: Perspectives from Artificial Intelligence, Databases, and Programming Languages*, ed. M. Brodie, J. Mylopoulos, and J. Schmidt. New York, NY: Springer-Verlag.

Zippel, R. June 1983. Capsules. *SIGPLAN Notices* vol. 18(6).

K. Tools and Environments

Andrews, T., and Harris, C. 1987. *Combining Language and Database Advances in an Object-Oriented Development Environment*. Billerica, MA: Ontologic.

Corradi, A., and Leonardi, L. 1986. *An Environment Based on Parallel Objects*. Bologna, Italy: Universita di Bologna.

Deutsch, P., and Taft, E. June 1980. *Requirements for an Experimental Programming Environment*. Report CSL-80-10. Palo Alto, CA: Xerox Palo Alto Research Center.

Diederich, J., and Milton, J. October 1987. An Object-Oriented Design System Shell. *SIGPLAN Notices* vol. 22(12).

Durant, D., Carlson, G., and Yao, P. 1987. *Programmer's Guide to Windows*. Berkeley, CA: Sybex.

Erman, L., Lark, J., and Hayes-Roth, F. December 1988. ABE: An Environment for Engineering Intelligent Systems. *IEEE Transactions on Software Engineering* vol. 14(12).

Ferrel, P., and Meyer, R. October 1989. Vamp: The Aldus Application Framework. *SIGPLAN Notices* vol. 24(10).

Fischer, H., and Martin, D. 1987. *Integrating Ada Design Graphics into the Ada Software Development Process*. Encino, CA: Mark V Business Systems.

Goldberg, A. 1984a. *Smalltalk-80: The Interactive Programming Environment*. Reading, MA: Addison-Wesley.

————. 1984b. The Influence of an Object-Oriented Language on the Programming Environment. In *Interactive Programming Environments*, ed. B. Barstow. New York, NY: McGraw-Hill.

Goldstein, I., and Bobrow, D. March 1981. *An Experimental Description-Based Programming Environment*. Report CSL-81-3. Palo Alto, CA: Xerox Palo Alto Research Center.

Gorlen, K. May 1986. *Object-Oriented Program Support*. Bethesda, MD: National Institute of Health.

Hecht, A., and Simmons, A. 1986. Integrating Automated Structured Analysis and Design with Ada Programming Support Environments. *Proceedings of the First International Conference on Ada Programming Language Applications for the NASA Space Station*. Houston, TX: NASA Lyndon B. Johnson Space Center.

Hedin, G., and Magnusson B. August 1988. The Mjolner Environment: Direct Interaction with Abstractions. *Proceedings of ECOOP'88: European Conference on Object-Oriented Programming*. New York, NY: Springer-Verlag.

Hudson, S., and King, R. June 1988. The Cactic Project: Database Support for Software Environments. *IEEE Transactions on Software Engineering* vol. 14(6).

International Business Machines. April 1988. *Operating System/2 Seminar Proceedings, IBM OS/2 Standard Edition Version 1.1, IBM Operating System/2 Update, Presentation Manager*. Boca Raton, FL.

Kant, E. 1987. *Interactive Problem Solving with a Task Configuration and Control System*. Ridgefield, CT: Schlumberger-Doll Research.

Kleyn, M., and Gingrich, P. September 1988. GraphTrace—Understanding Object-Oriented Systems Using Concurrently Animated Views. *SIGPLAN Notices* vol. 23(11).

Laff, M., and Hailpern, B. July 1985. SW-2—An Object-Based Programming Environment. *SIGPLAN Notices* vol. 20(7).

MacLenna, B. July 1985. A Simple Software Environment Based on Objects and Relations. *SIGPLAN Notices* vol. 20(7).

Marques, J., and Guedes, P. October 1989. Extending the Operating System to Support an Object-Oriented Environment. *SIGPLAN Notices* vol. 24(10).

Minsky, N., and Rozenshtein, D. February 1988. A Software Development Environment for Law-Governed Systems. *SIGPLAN Notices* vol. 24(2).

Moreau, D., and Dominick, W. 1987. *Object-Oriented Graphical Information Systems: Research Plan and Evaluation Metrics*. Lafayette, LA: University of Southwestern Louisiana, Center for Advanced Computer Studies.

Nakata, S., and Yamazak, G. 1983. ISMOS: A System Based on the E-R Model and Its Application to Database-Oriented Tool Generation. In *Entity-Relationship Approach to Software Engineering*, ed. C. Davis et al. Amsterdam, The Netherlands: Elsevier Science.

Nye, A. 1989. *Xlib Programming Manual for Version 11*. Newton, MA: O'Reilly and Associates.

O'Brien, P., Halbert, D., and Kilian, M. October 1987. The Trellis Programming Environment. *SIGPLAN Notices* vol. 22(12).

Open Look Graphical User Interface Functional Specification. 1990. Reading, MA: Addison-Wesley.

OSF/Motif Style Guide, Version 1.0. 1989. Cambridge, MA: Open Software Foundation.

Penedo, M., Ploedereder, E., and Thomas, I. February 1988. Object Management Issues for Software Engineering Environments. *SIGPLAN Notices* vol. 24(2).

Reenskaug, T., and Skaar, A. October 1989. An Environment for Literate Smalltalk Programming. *SIGPLAN Notices* vol. 24(10).

Rosenplatt, W., Wileden, J., and Wolf, A. October 1989. OROS: Toward a Type Model for Software Development Environments. *SIGPLAN Notices* vol. 24(10).

Russo, V., and Campbell, R. October 1989. Virtual Memory and Backing Storage Management in Multiprocessor Operating Systems Using Object-Oriented Design Techniques. *SIGPLAN Notices* vol. 24(10).

Scheifler, R., and Gettys, J. 1986. The X Window System. *ACM Transactions on Graphics* vol. 63.

Schwan, K., and Matthews, J. July 1986. Graphical Views of Parallel Programs. *Software Engineering Notes* vol. 11(3).

Shear, D. December 8, 1988. CASE Shows Promise but Confusion Still Exists. *EDN* vol. 33(25).

Sun Microsystems. March 29, 1987. *NeWS Technical Overview.* Mountain View, CA.

Tarumi, H., Agusa, K., and Ohno, Y. 1988. A Programming Environment Supporting Reuse of Object-Oriented Software. In *Proceedings of the 10th International Conference on Software Engineering.* New York, NY: Computer Society Press of the IEEE.

Taylor, R., Belz, F., Clarke, L., Osterweil, L., Selby, R., Wileden, J., Wolf, A., and Young, M. February 1988. Foundations for the Arcadia Environment. *SIGPLAN Notices* vol. 24(2).

Tesler, L. August 1981. The Smalltalk Environment. *Byte* vol. 6(8).

Vines, D., and King, T. 1988. *Gaia: An Object-Oriented Framework for an Ada Environment.* Minneapolis, MN: Honeywell.

Weinand, A., Gamma, E., and Marty, R. 1989. Design and Implementation of ET++, a Seamless Object-Oriented Application Framework. *Structured Programming* vol. 10(2).

Wiorkowski, G., and Kull, D. 1988. *DB2 Design and Development Guide.* Reading, MA: Addison-Wesley.

L. The Unified Modeling Language

Bennett, S., Skelton, J., and Lunn, K. 2005. *Schaum's Outline of UML*. Second Edition. United Kingdom: McGraw-Hill.

Blaha, M., and Rumbaugh, J. 2005. *Object-Oriented Modeling and Design with UML*. Second Edition. Upper Saddle River, NJ: Prentice Hall.

Bock, C. 2003. UML 2 Activity and Action Models. *Journal of Object Technology* vol. 2(4), pp. 43–53. www.jot.fm/issues/issue_2003_07/column3.

———. 2003. UML 2 Activity and Action Models, Part 2: Actions. *Journal of Object Technology* vol. 2(5), pp. 41–56. www.jot.fm/issues/issue_2003_09/column4.

———. 2003. UML 2 Activity and Action Models, Part 3: Control Nodes. *Journal of Object Technology* vol. 2(6), pp. 7–23. www.jot.fm/issues/issue_2003_11/column1.

———. 2004. UML 2 Activity and Action Models, Part 4: Object Nodes. *Journal of Object Technology* vol. 3(1), pp. 27–41. www.jot.fm/issues/issue_2004_01/column3.

———. 2004. UML 2 Activity and Action Models, Part 5: Partitions. *Journal of Object Technology* vol. 3(7), pp. 37–56. www.jot.fm/issues/issue_2004_07/column4.

Booch, G., Rumbaugh, J., and Jacobson, I. 2005. *The Unified Modeling Language User Guide*. Second Edition. Boston, MA: Addison-Wesley.

Fowler, M. 2003. *UML Distilled: A Brief Guide to the Standard Object Modeling Language*. Third Edition. Boston, MA: Addison-Wesley.

Maksimchuk, R., and Naiburg, E. 2005. *UML for Mere Mortals*. Boston, MA: Addison-Wesley.

Naiburg, E., and Maksimchuk, R. 2001. *UML for Database Design*. Boston, MA: Addison-Wesley.

Rumbaugh, J., Jacobson, I., and Booch, G. 2005. *The Unified Modeling Language Reference Manual*. Second Edition. Boston, MA: Addison-Wesley.

Object Management Group. 2004. *UML Superstructure Specification, v2.0*. www.uml.org/.

M. Web-Based Modeling

Cavaness, C. 2004. *Programming Jakarta Struts*. Second Edition. Indianapolis, IN: O'Reilly.

Constantine, L. L., and Lockwood, L. A. D. 1999. *Software for Use: A Practical Guide to the Models and Methods of Usage-Centered Design*. Reading, MA: Addison-Wesley.

Garrett, J. J. 2002. *The Elements of User Experience*. Boston, MA: New Riders Press.

Geary, D., and Horstmann, C. 2004. *Core JavaServer Faces*. Upper Saddle River, NJ: Prentice Hall.

Monson-Haefel, R. 2001. *Enterprise JavaBeans*. Third Edition. Indianapolis, IN: O'Reilly.

Index

Page numbers followed by an *f* or *t* indicate figures and tables.

Get agile and master UML with these titles from the Addison-Wesley Object Technology Series

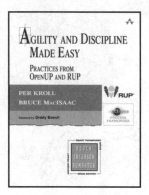

informIT

THIS BOOK IS SAFARI ENABLED

INCLUDES FREE 45-DAY ACCESS TO THE ONLINE EDITION

The Safari® Enabled icon on the cover of your favorite technology book means the book is available through Safari Bookshelf. When you buy this book, you get free access to the online edition for 45 days.

Safari Bookshelf is an electronic reference library that lets you easily search thousands of technical books, find code samples, download chapters, and access technical information whenever and wherever you need it.

TO GAIN 45-DAY SAFARI ENABLED ACCESS TO THIS BOOK:

- Go to **http://www.awprofessional.com/safarienabled**
- Complete the brief registration form
- Enter the coupon code found in the front of this book on the "Copyright" page

If you have difficulty registering on Safari Bookshelf or accessing the online edition, please e-mail customer-service@safaribooksonline.com.

Addison
Wesley